# PUBLIC SENTINEL

## NEWS MEDIA & GOVERNANCE REFORM

D1608710

# PUBLIC SENTINEL

## NEWS MEDIA & GOVERNANCE REFORM

**PIPPA NORRIS**

Editor

**THE WORLD BANK**
**Washington, DC**

Copyright © 2010
The International Bank for Reconstruction and Development / The World Bank
1818 H Street, N.W.
Washington, D.C. 20433, U.S.A.
Telephone: 202-473-1000
Internet: www.worldbank.org
E-mail: feedback@worldbank.org

1 2 3 4 13 12 11 10

ISBN: 978-0-8213-8200-4
eISBN: 978-0-8213-8201-1
DOI: 10.1596/978-0-8213-8200-4

Cover photo: North Head Lighthouse with the Pacific Ocean in the background: Harald Sund/Getty Images.

**Library of Congress Cataloging-in-Publication Data**
Public sentinel : news media & governance reform / Pippa Norris, editor.
     p. cm.
 Includes bibliographical references and index.
 ISBN 978-0-8213-8200-4 -- ISBN 978-0-8213-8201-1 (electronic)
 1. Mass media--Political aspects. 2. Journalism--Political aspects. 3. Press and politics.
 4. Democracy. 5. Representative government and representation. I. Norris, Pippa.
 II. World Bank.
 P95.8.P93 2010
 302.23--dc22
                                        2009041783

# Contents

**Figures**

**Tables**

# Foreword

Do the news media—especially if they are free, plural, and independent of government control—have an impact on the quality of governance? To many, the answer to that question is not only obvious, it is blindingly so. We all know of instances in which the news media have contributed to the improvement of governance in several countries, especially through their ability to expose corrupt deeds and speak truth to power. The problem, however, is that as the governance reform agenda evolves in the field of international development, the role of the news media is still uncertain.

There are many reasons for this uncertainty. First, traditional work in governance often still concentrates on public sector management. A focus on strengthening institutions like the news media is not yet seen as core business in many development agencies. Second, on the question of politics, often officials in donor agencies point out the sensitivity of many governments when it comes to any attempt to make the news media independent of government and better able to hold the government to account. If the issue is raised by donors, some government representatives still readily call it political interference. A minister in an international donor agency once told me that bringing up the topic of strengthening the media is the one thing that is likely to get some leaders of government angry. Third, on the question of competing agendas in international development, many priorities compete for the attention of donors, both public and private. For example, do you buy malaria bed nets or support reform of media regulation? Finally, there is this ever-present challenge: That is, how do we know for sure that the news media are a public good? What kinds of news media are good? Organized in what way?

Opportunities to strengthen the news media will always depend on the situation in each country, and will always depend on the interplay of forces within each country. In other words, the political economic realities will always determine what can be achieved. What that means is that those who want to improve media systems in their own countries must learn to build effective coalitions. That is where work is really needed. Nonetheless, it is possible to do two things. First, it is possible to bring together what we know right now about how the news media can contribute to good governance outcomes. Second, it is possible to draw the necessary policy implications. These are the two reasons CommGAP embarked upon this project. And we could not have found a better partner to lead the effort than Professor Pippa Norris of the Kennedy School of Government at Harvard. When we approached her to lead the effort, she was the director of democratic governance at the United Nations Development Programme (UNDP). She therefore brings to the task not just her outstanding academic record but also a confident mastery of the policy field. We worked with her to organize the workshop that led to this volume.

It is our hope that the book will contribute to a greater awareness of the potential contributions of independent news media to governance reform efforts around the world.

Sina Odugbemi
Program Head
Communication for Governance and Accountability Program
(CommGAP) at the World Bank

# About the Contributors

**Ibrahim Al-Marashi** is the assistant professor of communication history and policy at the IE School of Communication, IE University in Spain. He completed his DPhil at University of Oxford, with a thesis on the Iraqi invasion of Kuwait. Al-Marashi received an MA in Arab studies at Georgetown University in 1997. He has BAs in history and Near Eastern studies from the University of California Los Angeles. He is an Iraqi American who lived in Saudi Arabia, Yemen, Egypt, and Morocco. Publications include *Iraq's Armed Forces: An Analytical History* (2008). E-mail: Ibrahim.almarashi@ie.edu

**Sheila Coronel** is director of the Stabile Center for Investigative Journalism and professor of professional practice, Columbia University, New York. She began her reporting career in 1982 on the *Philippine Panorama* and later joined the *Manila Times*; she also wrote for the *Manila Chronicle*. As a stringer for the *New York Times* and the *Guardian* (London), she covered seven attempted coups d'etat against the Aquino government. In 1989, Coronel cofounded the Philippine Center for Investigative Journalism to promote investigative reporting and groundbreaking reporting on major social issues, including the military, poverty, and corruption. She is the author and editor of more than a dozen books, including *Coups, Cults & Cannibals* (1993); *Pork and Other Perks: Corruption and Governance in the Philippines* (1998); and *The Rule-makers: How the Wealthy and Well-Born Dominate Congress* (2004). She has received numerous awards for her work. She received an undergraduate degree in political science from the University of the Philippines, and a master's in political sociology from the London School of Economics. E-mail: coronel.sheila@gmail.com

**Marius Dragomir,** media researcher for the Open Society Foundation in London, has worked for almost two decades as a journalist for the Romanian and international media. He was a media critic with the *Prague Business Journal*. In 2002. Dragomir was a Senior Journalism Knight Fellow at the Washington, D.C.–based Atlantic Council of the United States, where he completed a thesis on the reform of the media in postcommunist Europe. He wrote media columns in such publications as

*Czech Business Weekly* and also conducted field training online for *Transitions*. He was the main editor of *Television Across Europe*, a major study produced by the Open Society Institute. Currently, Dragomir is a publications editor with the Open Society Foundation. E-mail: marius.dragomir@osf-eu.org

**Ronald Inglehart** is a professor of political science and program director at the Institute for Social Research at the University of Michigan. His research deals with changing belief systems and their impact on social and political change. He helped found the Eurobarometer surveys and directs the World Values Surveys, a global investigation of sociocultural and political change. Among Inglehart's more than 200 publications are *Modernization and Postmodernization: Cultural, Economic and Political Change in 43 Societies* (1997); *Human Values and Beliefs: A Cross-Cultural Sourcebook* (1998), *Rising Tide: Gender Equality and Cultural Change Around the World* (2003; with Pippa Norris); *Sacred and Secular: Religion and Politics Worldwide* (2004; with Norris); and *Modernization, Cultural Change and Democracy: The Human Development Sequence* (2005; with Christian Welzel). Inglehart has been a visiting professor or visiting scholar on several continents, and he has served as a consultant to the U.S. State Department and the European Union. He has a PhD from the University of Chicago and teaches courses on comparative politics, democratization, and social change at the University of Michigan. For more information: http://wvs.isr.umich.edu/ringlehart/index.html; E-mail: rInglehart@gmail.com

**Susan D. Moeller** is the director of the International Center for Media and the Public Agenda (ICMPA) at the University of Maryland, College Park. Moeller is also a professor of media and international affairs at the Philip Merrill College of Journalism and an affiliated faculty member of the School of Public Policy at Maryland. She is cofounder and faculty chair of the Salzburg Academy Program on Media & Global Change in Austria, an initiative of ICMPA and the Salzburg Global Seminar. She is the author of a number of books, including *Packaging Terrorism: Co-opting the News for Politics and Profit* (2009) and *Compassion Fatigue: How the Media Sell Disease, Famine, War and Death* (1999). She is the lead author and editor of a Freedom of Expression Toolkit and Model Curriculum for UNESCO's Division for Freedom of Expression, Democracy and Peace. Moeller was formerly the director of the journalism program at Brandeis University and a Fellow in the International Security Program and at the Joan Shorenstein Center for the Press, Politics and Public Policy, both at the Kennedy School of Government at Harvard University. She was twice a Fulbright Professor in international relations, in Pakistan and in Thailand, and has taught at Princeton and at Pacific Lutheran universities. Moeller received her AM and PhD from Harvard in history and the history of American civilization and her BA from Yale University, where she was selected as a Scholar of the House. Prior to her graduate work, Moeller was a journalist in Washington, D.C. In 2008, she was named a Carnegie Scholar for her work on Islam, and she was also named a Teacher of the Year by the Maryland Board of Regents.

Her commentary appears frequently in newspapers and magazines around the world, and she blogs for the HuffingtonPost, the World Bank, and *Foreign Policy* magazine. E-mail: smoeller@jmail.umd.edu

**Pippa Norris** is the McGuire Lecturer in Comparative Politics, John F. Kennedy School of Government at Harvard University. Her research compares elections and public opinion, political communications, and gender politics. She has published more than three dozen books, including related volumes for Cambridge University Press: *A Virtuous Circle: Political Communications in Postindustrial Societies* (2000), *Digital Divide: Civic Engagement, Information Poverty and the Internet Worldwide* (2001), *Democratic Phoenix: Political Activism Worldwide* (2003), *Rising Tide: Gender Equality and Cultural Change Around the Globe* (2003; with Ronald Inglehart), *Electoral Engineering: Voting Rules and Political Behavior* (2004), *Sacred and Secular: Religion and Politics Worldwide* (2004; with Inglehart), *Radical Right: Voters and Parties in the Electoral Market (2005), Driving Democracy: Do Power-Sharing Institutions Work?* (2008), and *Cultural Convergence: Cosmopolitan Communications and National Diversity* (2009; with Inglehart). She cofounded *The Harvard International Journal of Press/Politics*. Her work has been translated into more than a dozen languages. While on leave from Harvard, she recently served as the director of the Democratic Governance Practice in the United National Development Programme in New York. She has also been an expert consultant for many international official bodies, including the United Nations, UNESCO, International IDEA, the NED, the Inter-Parliamentary Union, the National Democratic Institute, the Council of Europe, the U.K. Electoral Commission, and the Afghanistan Reconstruction Project. She has been president of the Political Communication section of APSA. Prior to Harvard, she taught at Edinburgh University. She holds a master's and doctoral degree in politics from the London School of Economics. Details can be found at http://www.pippanorris.com. E-mail: pippa_norris@harvard.edu

**Sina Odugbemi** is program head of the Communication for Governance & Accountability Program (CommGAP) at the World Bank. He has more than 20 years of experience in journalism, law, and development communication. Before he joined the World Bank in 2006, he spent seven years in the U.K. development ministry, DFID. His last position was program manager and adviser in Information and Communication for Development. Odugbemi holds a bachelor's degree in English and in law from the University of Ibadan, a master's degree in legal and political philosophy (1999) from University College London, and a PhD in law (2009) from the same university on the subject *Public Opinion and Direct Accountability between Elections: A Study of the Constitutional Theories of Jeremy Bentham and A. V. Dicey*. Odugbemi's publications include a novel, *The Chief's Grand-daughter* (1986), and two coedited volumes: *With the Support of Multitudes—Using Strategic Communication to Fight Poverty through PRSPs* (2005) and *Governance Reform under Real-World Conditions: Citizens, Stakeholders, and Voice* (2008). E-mail: aodugbemi@worldbank.org

**Lawrence Pintak** is founding dean of the Edward R. Murrow College of Communication at Washington State University. Prior to that, Dr. Pintak spent four years as director of the Kamal Adham Center for Journalism Training and Research at The American University in Cairo, where he ran the only graduate journalism degree in the Arab world and a variety of training programs for professional journalists. He also created the online publication *Arab Media & Society*. A veteran of 30 years in journalism on four continents, Pintak specializes in the role of media in shaping policy and the perceptions of policy; the intersection of media, religion, and conflict; and the impact of technology, culture, and globalization on journalism. His latest book is *Reflections in a Bloodshot Lens: America, Islam & the War of Ideas* (2006). As CBS News Middle East correspondent in the 1980s, he covered the Iran-Iraq War, the Israeli invasion of Lebanon, the rise of Hezbollah, and the birth of suicide bombing. In the 1990s, he reported on the overthrow of Indonesian President Suharto for the *San Francisco Chronicle* and ABC News. His next book, *The New Arab Journalist*, will be published in early 2010. Earlier books include *Seeds of Hate: How America's Flawed Middle East Policy Ignited the Jihad* (2003) and *Beirut Outtakes: A TV Correspondent's Portrait of America's Encounter with Terror* (1988). He holds a PhD in Islamic Studies from the University of Wales, Lampeter. E-mail: lpintak@wsu.edu

**Monroe Price** is the director of the Center for Global Communication Studies at the Annenberg School, University of Pennsylvania, Philadelphia. He is also the Joseph and Sadie Danciger Professor of Law and director of the Howard M. Squadron Program in Law, Media and Society at the Cardozo School of Law. Price, who was dean of Cardozo School of Law from 1982 to 1991, graduated magna cum laude from Yale, where he was executive editor of the *Yale Law Journal*. He has been a professor at UCLA Law School and was founding director of the Program in Comparative Media Law and Policy at Wolfson College, Oxford. He has been a member of the school of social science at the Institute for Advanced Study, Princeton, and a Fellow of the Media Studies Center in spring 1998. Price is the director of the Stanhope Centre for Communications Policy Research in London and chair of the Center for Media and Communication Studies of the Central European University in Budapest. Among his many books are *Media and Sovereignty: The Global Information Revolution and Its Challenge to State Power* (2002); and *Television, The Public Sphere and National Identity* (1996). E-mail: mprice@asc.upenn.edu

**Andrew Puddephatt** is a founding director of Global Partners and Associates. He has worked to promote human rights for 20 years and has specific expertise in program development and evaluation with a focus on transparency, the role of media in society, and human rights. He was executive director of Article 19 between 1999 and 2004. He has been an expert member of both the Council of Europe and the Commonwealth Expert Working Groups on freedom of information and freedom of expression. He has led human rights organizations in the not-for-profit sector for more than a dozen years. Between 1995 and 1999 he was the director of Charter88, the leading constitutional reform organization in the United Kingdom. Between 1989 and 1995 he was general secretary of Liberty, a domestic human rights organization in the United Kingdom. He played a leading role in securing a bill of rights for the United Kingdom. In January 2003, he was made an Officer of the British Empire (OBE) for services to human rights. Puddephatt is chair of the Audit Committee for the U.K. Parliamentary Ombudsman. Recent publications include *Monitoring and Evaluation of UN-Assisted Communication for Development Programmes* (2009); *Exploring the Role of Civil Society in the Formulation and Adoption of Access to Information Laws. The Cases of Bulgaria, India, Mexico, South Africa, and the United Kingdom* (2009); *Media Development Indicators: A Framework for Assessing Media Development* (2008); and *A Guide to Measuring the Impact of Right to Information Programmes* (2006). E-mail: andrew@global-partners.co.uk

**Angela Romano** is a senior lecturer in journalism at the Queensland University of Technology, Brisbane, Australia. Romano conducts research on a wide range of issues relating to journalism and the media, including democracy and politics, corruption, gender, ethnic and cultural diversity, refugees and asylum seekers, and media education. Her major research publications include *Politics and the Press in Indonesia* (2003) and *Journalism and Democracy in Asia* (2005, coedited with Michael Bromley). She is editing a new book, *Just Journalism? Public Journalism and Other Deliberative Journalism Models from Around the World* (forthcoming 2010). Romano previously worked as a journalist in Australia and Indonesia. She engages in ongoing applied research projects in journalism, such as a series of documentary-style radio programs that won the Best Radio category of the 2005 Media Peace Awards, organized by the United Nations Association of Australia. E-mail: a.romano@qut.edu.au

**Holli A. Semetko** is vice provost for international affairs and director of the Office of International Affairs and the Claus M. Halle Institute for Global Learning, where she is also a professor of political science. Before coming to Emory University in 2003, she spent eight years at the University of Amsterdam, the Netherlands, as professor and chair of audience and public opinion research in the faculty of social and behavioral sciences, chair of the department of communication science, and founding chair of the board of the Amsterdam School for Communications Research. Major grants from the European Union and Dutch National Science Foundation supported her work on political communication and media effects in the context of European governance, referendums, and elections, and the European political and economic integration process. Recognized internationally for her research on news content, uses, and effects in a comparative context, she has received numerous grants, honors, and awards, including the Samuel H. Beer Prize for the best dissertation on British politics and the International Communication Association's Article of the Year award. She has more than 80 publications, including 5 books and more than 35 peer-reviewed journal articles. Her most recent book, with Claes de Vreese, is *Political Campaigning in Referendums* (2006). She has MSc and PhD degrees from the London School of Economics and Political Science and taught previously at Syracuse University and the University of Michigan. E-mail: holli.semetko@emory.edu

**Nicole Stremlau** is coordinator of the Programme in Comparative Media Law and Policy and a Research Fellow at the Centre for Socio-Legal Studies at the University of Oxford. She has been the director of the Africa media program at the Stanhope Centre for Communications Policy Research in London and a Research Fellow at the Centre for Global Communications Studies at the Annenberg School, University of Pennsylvania. Her primary research is on politics and media in Eastern Africa during and after successful armed insurgencies. She is coauthoring a book of oral histories of Eastern African journalists. Stremlau received her BA with honors from Wesleyan University and her MA from the School of Oriental and African Studies, University of London. Her doctoral dissertation was *The Press and Consolidation of Power in Ethiopia and Uganda*, and she received her PhD in 2008 from the London School of Economics. E-mail: nstremlau@gmail.com

**Wisdom J. Tettey** is professor and interim dean, Faculty of Communication and Culture, University of Calgary. He earned his BA and graduate diploma at the University of Ghana, his MA at the University of British Columbia, and his PhD at Queen's University, Kingston, Canada. His research interests include political economy of globalization and information technology in Africa; media, politics, and civic engagement in Africa; African higher education and the knowledge society; and transnational citizenship and the African diaspora. Tettey has published on the African mass media and their relevance for democratization processes, including *The Media, Accountability and Civic Engagement in Africa* (2002) and *African Media and the Digital Public Sphere* (2009; with O. Mudhai and F. Banda as coeditors). E-mail: tettey@ucalgary.ca

**Douglas A. Van Belle** is senior lecturer, Victoria University of Wellington, New Zealand. He has a BA, MA, and PhD from Arizona State University, and he has served as editor-in-chief of *Foreign Policy Analysis*. Van Belle is currently examining the role of press freedom in democratic politics and studying how variations in the content of news media coverage of disasters might be used to address questions of race, image, and governmental practices. Book publications include *Media, Bureaucracies, and Foreign Aid: A Comparative Analysis of the United States, the United Kingdom, Canada, France and Japan* (2004; with Rioux and Potter) and *Press Freedom and Global Politics* (2000). E-mail:douglas.vanbelle@vuw.ac.nz

**Katrin Voltmer** is a senior lecturer in political communications, University of Leeds, United Kingdom, with a PhD from the Free University in Berlin. Her research compares the role of communication in democratic life, especially the relationship between political actors and journalists; how their interests, norms, and communication strategies affect political news coverage; and citizens' responses to political messages. She is currently conducting a British Academy–funded research project, Political Communication in New Democracies: Government-Media Relationships in Transition, which covers eight countries from four continents. Her book publications include *The Media in Transitional Democracies* (editor; 2006); *Public Policy and the Media: The Interplay of Mass Communication and Political Decision Making* (coeditor, with Sigrid Koch-Baumgarten; 2009); and *Media Quality and Democracy. An Empirical Analysis of Media Performance in Election Campaigns* (1998, in German). E-mail: k.voltmer@leeds.ac.uk

**Silvio Waisbord** is associate professor in the School of Media and Public Affairs at George Washington University. He is the editor of the *International Journal of Press/Politics*. Previously, he was associate professor in the department of Journalism and Media Studies and director of the Journalism Resources Institute at Rutgers University. He has served as the senior program officer at the Academy for Educational Development and as a fellow at the Annenberg School for Communication, the Kellogg Institute for International Studies at Notre Dame University, and the Media Studies Center. His current work focuses on journalism, communication, and globalization. He is the author or coeditor of four books, including *Watchdog Journalism in South America: News, Accountability, and Democracy* (2000). His work on news, politics, globalization, and development has appeared in several academic journals and edited books. He holds an MA and PhD in sociology from the University of California at San Diego. E-mail: waisbord@gwu.edu

# Preface and Acknowledgments

This book owes a deep debt of gratitude to many friends and colleagues. The book originated with a workshop held in May 2007 at Harvard University's Kennedy School of Government, cosponsored by the Communication for Governance and Accountability Program (CommGAP) at the World Bank and the Joan Shorenstein Center on the Press, Politics and Public Policy at Harvard. The meeting was organized by Camiliakumari Wankaner, who provided an extremely efficient and well-run event. She was ably assisted in the workshop by Martin Alonso and Alagi Yorro Jallow. Further invaluable support in facilitating this event came from James Fleming, Edie Holway, Nancy Palmer, and Thomas Patterson of the Shorenstein Center.

This workshop brought together a wide range of participants. We are most grateful for the feedback and comments that were generated, especially from those who served as discussants, including Ran An (*China Newsweek*), Anne-Katrin Arnold (World Bank), Matthew Baum (Harvard University), James Baxter (*Edmonton Journal*), Charlie Beckett (London School of Economics), Jeanne Bourgault (Internews Network), Guilherme Canela (News Agency for Children's Rights), Andres Cavelier (*El Nuevo Herald*), G. Shabbir Cheema (East-West Center), Diana Chung (World Bank), William Crawley (London University), Sunday Dare (Voice of America), Richard Davis (Brigham Young University), James Deane (BBC World Service Trust), Warren Feek (Communication Initiative), Robert Gaylard (World Bank), Ronda Hauben (Columbia University), Ellen Hume (Massachusetts Institute of Technology—MIT), Komarduth Hurry (Action pour la promotion de l'éducation et dévelopment), Thomas Jacobson (Temple University), Gordana Jankovic (Open Society Institute), Danny Jara (Canadian International Development Agency), Wijayananda Jayaweera (UNESCO), Shanthi Kalathil (World Bank), Nimo Kama (Media for Development Initiative), Colleen Kaman (MIT), Karin Deutsch Karlekar (Freedom House), Sara Khan (International Islamic University), Lami Kim (Harvard University), Mark Koenig (USAID), Antonio Lambino II (World Bank), Steve Livingston (George Washington University), Johanna Martinsson (World Bank), Paul Mitchell (World Bank), Joan Mower (Broadcasting Board of Governors), Fumiko Nagano (World Bank), Mark

Nelson (World Bank Institute), Yasmin Padamsee (UNDP/Harvard's Kennedy School), Elizabeth Paluck (Harvard University), Thomas Patterson (Harvard's Kennedy School), Gowher Rizvi (Harvard University), Fernando Rodrigues (Harvard University), Holli Semetko (Emory University), Jan Servaes (University of Massachusetts at Amherst), J. H. Snider (iSalon.com), Marguerite Sullivan (National Endowment for Democracy), Caby Verzosa (World Bank), and Armorer Wason (Panos Foundation).

Finally, the report would not have been possible without the enthusiastic participation, and the willingness to meet deadlines, of all the contributors. I would like to thank all who were engaged in this project, especially the individuals in CommGAP and the Shorenstein Center, who made this possible.

Pippa Norris
Cambridge, Massachusetts

# Abbreviations

| | |
|---|---|
| AMARC | World Association of Community Radio Stations |
| AMDI | African Media Development Initiative |
| ANC | African National Congress |
| BBC | British Broadcasting Corporation |
| CIMA | Center for International Media Assistance |
| CUD | Coalition for Unity and Democracy |
| DANIDA | Danish International Development Agency |
| DEPTHnews | Development, Economic and Population Themes News Service |
| DFID | U.K. Department for International Development |
| EMMTI | Ethiopian Mass Media Training Institute |
| EPRDF | Ethiopian People's Revolutionary Democratic Front |
| IREX | International Research and Exchanges Board |
| ISAS | International Standards and Accreditation Services |
| ITU | International Telecommunication Union |
| MDI | Media for Development Initiative |
| MSF | Doctors without Borders (Médecins sans Frontières) |
| MSI | Media Sustainability Index |
| NGO | nongovernmental organization |
| RSF | Reporters without Borders (Reporters sans Frontières) |
| Sida | Swedish International Development Cooperation Agency |
| TPLF | Tigreyan People's Liberation Front |
| UNCTAD | United Nations Conference on Trade and Development |
| UNDEF | United Nations Democracy Fund |
| UNDP | United Nations Development Programme |
| UNESCO | United Nations Educational, Scientific, and Cultural Organization |
| UNICEF | United Nations Children's Fund |
| USAID | United States Agency for International Development |
| WAPOR | World Organization of Public Opinion Research |

Part I

# Introduction:
# Framing the Debate

# Evaluating Media Performance

Pippa Norris and Sina Odugbemi

Today the world faces multiple challenges in democratic governance and human development. The spread of democracy has been extraordinary; since the early 1970s, following the "third wave," more states worldwide have held multiparty elections than ever before. Today roughly two-thirds of all independent nation-states (121 out of 193) are electoral democracies.[1] Nevertheless, many indicators suggest that during the past decade, the further advance of democratic governance has stagnated or even reversed. Observers have detected signs of a democratic recession.[2] Major setbacks have been experienced in countries as diverse as Georgia, Kenya, Nigeria, Pakistan, the Russian Federation, Thailand, República Bolivariana de Venezuela, and Zimbabwe.[3] Contemporary challenges facing all democracies, old and new, include expanding opportunities for more inclusive voices in civil society. Reforms are urgently needed to improve the responsiveness, transparency, effectiveness, and accountability of governance institutions so that democracy works for the poor as well as the rich. Moreover, respect for international standards of universal human rights needs to be further strengthened in all parts of the world.

Democratic governance is important for maximizing fundamental freedoms, human choice, self-determination, and development. In 2000 the world's leaders came together at the United Nations Millennium Summit and pledged to achieve the Millennium Development Goals (MDGs). Achieving the goals would save millions of lives; empower women; eradicate the scourges of illiteracy, hunger, and malnutrition; and guarantee that children have access to education and good health. The series of specific targets highlights the urgent need for halving extreme poverty and hunger, achieving universal primary education, improving child mortality and maternal health, and promoting gender equality and women's empowerment. Many countries have made remarkable progress in lifting millions out of extreme poverty, fueled in particular by economic growth in the emerging BRIC economies (Brazil, Russia, India, and China). The United Nations' (UN) midterm assessment of progress toward the MDGs highlights that countries where the development goals are being met most successfully are those where good governance is one of the central factors, combined with resource mobilization and donor support, technical know-how, south-south cooperation, effective national and local planning, and investment in institutional and individual capacity development.[4] Despite advances in the BRIC economies, the UN reports that most low-income countries will fail to achieve their national targets. Today, past the midpoint to the target date, it is evident that the current pace of change will not be sufficient to achieve these goals by 2015.[5] Groups most at risk include the most vulnerable populations living in Sub-Saharan Africa and South Asia, which are confronting multiple developmental obstacles, and fragile states emerging from recent conflict.[6]

New problems that have arisen since the 2000 summit also threaten to derail further progress. Additional hurdles in meeting these goals include the deep recession in the global economy, the looming challenge of climate change, and the persistence of deep-rooted conflict and terrorism.[7] In particular, unless urgent steps are taken, the deepening worldwide financial crisis that started in summer 2007 will substantially shrink the pool of resources available both for investment and for aid. By fall 2008, the worsening financial environment had triggered falling world trade, plunging equity markets, a steep loss of confidence in financial institutions, growing uncertainty, and deeper aversion to risk. It is estimated that rapid growth will slow in BRIC emerging economies, while the world's poorest societies will suffer from reduced demands for their exports, loss of investment capital, and lower commodity prices. Global growth in gross domestic product (GDP) is projected to expand by only 0.9 percent in 2009, the lowest level since records began in the 1970s.[8] The urgency of the domestic economic problems afflicting rich societies at home threatens to draw attention away from concern about development challenges abroad. Nevertheless, effective solutions to alleviate the economic crisis reinforce the critical importance of building state capacity in financial regulation and management of the economy.

Within the broad context of the major issues facing the international development community, this book focuses on the performance of the news media as an institution in addressing these challenges. In particular, the book considers three related issues using normative, empirical, and strategic frameworks.

First, a normative approach asks: *what ideal roles should media systems play to strengthen democratic governance and thus bolster human development?* Although journalists and reporters can and do play multiple roles in different contexts, often they serve only as spokespersons of the state or of commercial media owners, rather than report about urgent humanitarian crises and development challenges facing the marginalized and poor, or challenging the rich and powerful. To consider how the media strengthen the democratic public sphere, this book emphasizes the institutional or collective roles of the news media as *watchdogs* over the powerful, as *agenda setters,* calling attention to natural and human-caused disasters and humanitarian crises, and as *gatekeepers,* incorporating a diverse and balanced range of political perspectives and social sectors. Each role is vital to the quality of democratic deliberation in the public sphere.

Second, the empirical approach considers independent evidence derived from cross-national comparisons and from selected case studies, asking: *under what conditions do media systems actually succeed or fail to fulfill these objectives?* This book theorizes that the capacity of media systems (and thus individual journalists embedded within these institutions) to fulfill these roles depends on the broader context determined by the profession, the market, and ultimately the state. Successive chapters in this book document the impact of these constraints upon journalists in different places, types of regimes, and global regions. The chapters examine and compare the performance of a range of media systems in places as diverse as Kenya and Mexico, Iraq and Ethiopia, Myanmar and the Democratic People's Republic of Korea, and the Arab Republic of Egypt and Qatar. Faced with the constraints of the profession, the markets, and the state, media systems' performance often falls far short of these ideals, with important consequences for the workings of the public sphere.

Third, a strategic approach asks: *what policy interventions work most effectively to close the substantial gap that exists between the democratic promise and performance of the news media as an institution?* The book identifies a menu of alternative actions. Interventions can be directed strategically at strengthening the journalistic profession, notably institutional capacity building, such as press councils, nongovernmental organizations (NGOs) that are advocates of media freedom, and organizations concerned with journalistic training and accreditation. Other reform initiatives address market failures, including developing a regulatory legal framework for media systems to ensure pluralism of ownership and diversity of content. Finally, policies also address the role of the state, including deregulation that shifts state-run broadcasting to public service broadcasting (overseen by independent broadcasting regulatory bodies) and the protection of constitutional principles of freedom of the press, speech, and expression. The most effective strategies are holistic approaches addressing all three levels, but specific initiatives need to be tailored to the specific challenges facing each country. Comprehensive media system audits and specific performance indicators should be integrated into all development projects. To consider all these issues, this chapter outlines the normative framework and the core concepts guiding the report, and then sets out the road map for the book.

## The Idea of a Democratic Public Sphere

A long tradition of liberal theorists, from Milton to Locke and Madison to John Stuart Mill, have argued that a free and independent press within each nation can play a vital role in the process of democratization by contributing toward the right of freedom of expression, thought, and conscience. To help understand these issues, this chapter turns to the concept of the *democratic public sphere,* an idea with a pedigree both ancient and impeccable. At the heart of the public sphere is the agora, the main political, civic, religious, and commercial center of the ancient Greek city. It was here that citizens traded goods, information, concepts, and ideas to better their situations and influence collective decisions, thus improving the quality of their own lives. In political philosophy, the agora has come to be known variously as the *public arena,* the *public realm,* the *public domain,* or the *public sphere.* The notion of the public sphere has appeared in a variety of writings during the 20th century, including those of Walter Lippmann, Hannah Arendt, and John Dewey, although it is probably most widely known today from the works of the theorist Jürgen Habermas.[9]

As a normative vision, and for the purposes of this discussion, the democratic public sphere represents that space between the state and the household where free and equal citizens come together to share information, to deliberate upon common concerns, and to cooperate and collaborate on solutions to social problems. For Habermas, the ideal public space (Öffentlichkeit) facilitated reasoned deliberation, critical discussion, and tolerance of alternative arguments and viewpoints. In 18th-century Europe, Habermas envisaged the public sphere as a space for critical discussion, open to all, where people came together to exchange views and share knowledge. The process of deliberation in the public sphere encouraged the development of a rational and informed consensus in public opinion, he argued, which functioned as a check on state power. The expansion of the public sphere in 18th-century Europe was aided, he theorized, by the development of new spaces for social and intellectual interaction—exemplified by the expansion of newspapers, journals, reading clubs, salons, and coffeehouses in metropolitan society. Nevertheless, Habermas was more pessimistic about contemporary society, as he believed that the public sphere eroded during the 19th and early 20th centuries. He feared that the growth of the electronic broadcast media turned the critical and active public into more passive mass audiences, while he believed that the growth of organized interest groups and political parties came to dominate parliamentary debate about public affairs.

Habermas's concept of the public sphere has been widely influential, although his vision has attracted considerable debate and criticism.[10] The theory may well have romanticized the notion of widespread public engagement in 18th-century Europe, where the moneyed elites, professional classes, and landed echelons predominated in the literary clubs, scientific societies, and journals found in Paris, London, Berlin, and Vienna. Moreover, while exaggerating the extent to which these forums were open to all the European public, Habermas may also have simultaneously underestimated the extension of the public sphere to wider social sectors in subsequent eras. In European societies, this growth was linked during the 19th century with the flowering of working men's associations, mass-branch political parties, voluntary and philanthropic groups, agricultural and economic cooperatives, professional organizations, literary and scientific societies, and trade unions. All these provided meeting places for public participation and discussion for the working class, while the gradual spread of literacy, and universal primary and secondary education, expanded the capacity of the European public for deliberative democracy.

Irrespective of the historical evidence underlying Habermas's account of the transformation of the public sphere, many of these ideas remain important. In particular, his recognition of the need for common spaces in civic society to facilitate public deliberation and critical debate about major issues of common concern, and the idea that such a process strengthens the development of an informed public opinion as an independent check on the power of the state, continue to resonate widely today.[11] As theories of social capital emphasize, informal networks, community groups, and voluntary associations are a vital part of interpersonal face-to-face communications. But the media, old and new, are the core institution facilitating mass communications in the public sphere in contemporary societies. Habermas distinguished between the early era of newspapers and pamphlets, which he regarded as a vital part of the public sphere, and the subsequent development of mass-circulation dailies and broadcast electronic media, which he denigrated. The reasons for this categorization were not clearly established theoretically, however, and this watertight distinction has become increasingly fuzzy following the growth of more decentralized electronic channels, exemplified by the role of community radio, talk radio, and local television. Indeed, since Habermas first developed his theory during the early 1960s, the growth of opportunities for social interaction and exchange through modern information and communication technologies has transformed the capacity of the electronic media to strengthen horizontal linkages as well as vertical ones. Digital communication networks— exemplified by the blogosphere; email discussion lists; political networks, such as MoveOn.org; uploaded news videos on YouTube; and feedback interactive comments and photos from readers published on news Web sites—provide the modern equivalent of 18th-century pamphlets, newspaper letters to the editor pages, journals, and periodicals.

Building loosely upon these notions, one can theorize that a modern public sphere that strengthens contemporary forms of democratic governance requires at least three minimal conditions: a constitutional and legal framework protecting civil liberties, widespread public access to multiple pluralistic sources of information and communication, and equal opportunities for inclusive participation and voice within civil society. Each can be regarded as a necessary, although not sufficient, precondition for a flourishing public sphere and thus for the development of rational and informed public opinion. Derived from these notions, figure 1.1 depicts the organizing conceptual framework for the book.

**Figure 1.1. Model of the Democratic Public Sphere**

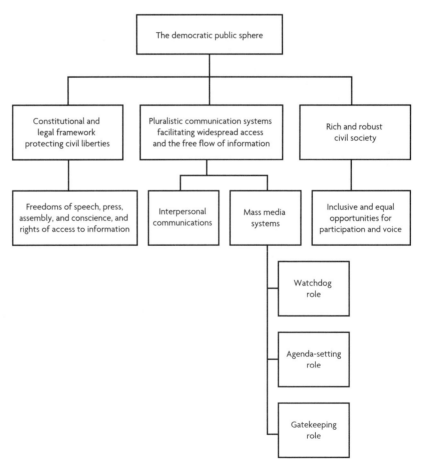

*Source:* Authors.

First, securing the democratic integrity of the public sphere requires *a constitutional and legal framework guaranteeing basic civil liberties,* including respect for the rights to free expression, argument, association, debate, and discussion, and rights of access to information. In this regard, the notion reflects the traditional concepts embodied in Article 19 of the Universal Declaration of Human Rights: "Everyone has the right to freedom of opinion and expression; this right includes freedom to hold opinions without interference and to seek, receive and impart information and ideas through any media and regardless of frontiers." More recently, this principle was reaffirmed in the United Nations Millennium Declaration (General Assembly resolution 55/2), which was unanimously adopted in September 2000 by all 189 member states of the United Nations.[12] Among other pledges, it reasserted the commitment of member states: "To ensure the freedom of the media to perform their essential role and the right of the public to have access to information." The intrinsic value of freedom of expression as a universal human right is widely recognized elsewhere, including in the European Convention on Human Rights, the American Convention on Human Rights, and the African Charter on Human and Peoples' Rights. These claims are embodied in many other national constitutions around the world, as well as in the growing body of freedom of information laws and statutes. In the United States, for example, the First Amendment of the United States Constitution prohibits Congress from passing laws that abridge freedom of the press. Freedom of expression requires an independent mass media as one of the primary channels of communication in any society, linking citizens to citizens as well as citizens and the state. Where critical discussion is muzzled or independent voices silenced through the techniques of coercion, censorship, or intimidation, this process limits fundamental freedoms.

However, formal rights are not sufficient, by themselves, to guarantee that deliberative democracy works for all. Within this context, the democratic public sphere also depends on the quality of informed discourse and thus widespread access to information derived from multiple sources of interpersonal and mediated communications. Information arises from direct interpersonal conversations among family, friends, and colleagues in their daily interactions within the local community, the workplace, and the neighborhood. With the growing diffusion of communication technologies, information today is also exchanged through person-to-person electronic networks, for example, via mobile cellular and fixed-line telephony, email, and text messaging. Much information, especially about one's own and other societies, also continues to flow from one to many through the mass media. This is transmitted via diverse channels: terrestrial, cable, and satellite broadcast television; national, regional, and community radio stations; feature films and documentaries; DVDs and video games; books; newspapers and magazines; advertising billboards and commercials; the music industry and the audiovisual arts; as well as the digital world of the Internet, Web sites, online YouTube videos, iPod players, podcasts, wikis, and blogs. This book focuses on the media systems and therefore includes traditional news outlets, such as newspapers and magazines, radio and television news, books, and pamphlets, but also includes the growing role of information and communication technologies. These are all the essential conduits for timely and accurate communications about public events and issues in modern societies. Citizens lacking widespread access to information and communication—a situation most common among social sectors such as the poor and illiterate, women, and minorities—are thereby excluded from full and equal participation in the public sphere.

Finally, the existence of information without opportunities for the communication and expression of social needs, priorities, and concerns is also not sufficient for a robust deliberative democracy. An effective public sphere depends on *opportunities for participation and interaction within civil society.* Diverse arenas and social spaces should be open to all citizens and viewpoints in any society, without excluding any sector, group, or persuasion. The notion emphasizes the role of public engagement in a variety of deliberative forums. Traditionally this process has operated through town hall and village meetings, community gatherings, local party branch assemblies, election hustings, neighborhood clubs, workshops and seminars, religious assemblies, trade unions, NGOs, and cooperative associations. The growth of mass literacy and access to mass communications also expanded opportunities for informed discourse. The process also involves modern forms of civic engagement that are evolving in contemporary societies, exemplified by participatory budgets in Brazil, social audits in India, protest politics and demonstrations in France, online networks in the United States, direct action environmental campaigns in Britain, and transnational social movements connecting local and global actors.

Out of this normative vision, the following characteristics of a democratic public sphere emerge (see figure 1.1):

- *A constitutional and legal framework protects and guarantees civil liberties and political rights,* especially the fundamental freedoms of expression, opinion, information, and assembly, as well as rights of access to information. The media are independent from state control, official censorship, and legal restrictions.
- *All people enjoy widespread access to pluralistic sources of information in the public sphere,* enabling equal opportunities for expression and participation and, especially, providing access to information for marginalized sectors within society, including women, young people, minorities, the poor, and the illiterate.
- *A rich, robust, and inclusive civil society flourishes,* with multiple organizations and diverse associations facilitating unrestricted deliberation,

cooperation, and collaboration on issues of common concern. Civil society is strengthened where diverse perspectives, social sectors, interests, parties, and political persuasions are reflected in the mass media.

Where these components function effectively, the democratic public sphere helps to promote governance that is accountable to citizens and responsive to human needs. Through this process, an independent media can strengthen the responsiveness of governments to all citizens and provide a pluralistic platform of political expression, bringing together a multiplicity of parties, groups, sectors, and interests.

The theoretical vision provided by Habermas is thus larger and richer than the simple notion of electoral democracy. The public sphere is regarded as valuable for promoting an informed citizenry and for deliberative and reasoned decision-making. But an effective public sphere also has consequences for electoral democracy, as citizens with more timely and accurate information are empowered to make better choices. Informed citizens can match their policy preferences more accurately against the political choices available in an election. Without transparency about the performance of the government and the policies offered by parties and candidates contending for elected office, the act of casting a vote becomes meaningless, and governments cannot be held to account.[13] The independent news media have often been regarded as particularly important for promoting government transparency and accountability, especially where investigative journalism highlights cases of corruption and misconduct.[14] Elected leaders also require accurate information about public concerns and social needs to be responsive to development challenges.[15] Freedom of the media is one of the key tenets of democracy that ensures government transparency and accountability.

Amartya Sen argues that the independent news media are also critical for attaining the broader goals of human development.[16] Studies suggest that information can improve the delivery of public services, forewarn against natural disasters, spread education and knowledge, and reduce preventable health risks.[17] International news helps inform the international community about severe challenges facing low-income states and urgent humanitarian crises arising from natural and human-caused disasters.[18] The flow of information across national borders is also essential for international understanding and peace. Lack of information and awareness about other communities, cultures, and viewpoints can fuel social intolerance, erode trust, and lead toward conflict.[19] Reporting conveys diplomatic signals between nations and shapes domestic perceptions about foreign countries.[20] Communication is widely regarded as the lifeblood of economic markets; it facilitates trade, transmits ideas, and diffuses innovations, and thus promotes growth. Countries with both widespread media access and an independent free press have been found to experience several beneficial consequences, including lower corruption, greater administrative efficiency, higher political stability and more effective rule of law, as well as better developmental outcomes, such as lower infant mortality rates and greater literacy.[21]

It is reasonable to acknowledge that, measured against Habermas' normative theory, no single country or place serves as a perfect example of the democratic public sphere. But this holds true for all the other outcomes in the democratic governance agenda, such as responsive and accountable public service providers and meritocratic civil service systems. The key questions tackled in this book are the following: Under what conditions do the media function in a way that most closely matches the ideals of the public sphere? Where and why do the media fail? And where there are constraints, what policy interventions strengthen the capacity of journalists to work most effectively in this regard?

## The Ideal Functions of Media Systems

Within these broad notions, this book focuses on the challenges facing the development of effective communications systems in the public sphere and, in particular, the contribution of media systems toward strengthening democratic governance and human development. In complex modern societies, the existence of the independent news media can be regarded as a necessary, although not sufficient, condition to guarantee a lively and effective public sphere. Over the years, many rival normative standards have been developed for evaluating the performance of media systems.[22] This section focuses on understanding how effectively media systems function in their roles as watchdogs, agenda setters, and gatekeepers.

To clarify the core concepts, *roles* are understood as a set of expectations governing the behavior of individuals and institutions holding a particular function in society. As a set of norms, values, and standards that defines how persons and institutions should and do work, roles have both normative and empirical dimensions. Understanding roles requires a clear vision of the idea of democratic governance and the public sphere—the ideal context within which journalists operate—providing the benchmark to evaluate their actual performance.

Roles operate at both collective and individual levels. This book focuses most attention at *collective* levels, where roles determine the institutional practices, cultural values, behavioral norms, and standard routines characteristic of the media system within any society. The book also looks at collective roles within any media sector, to compare, for example, the role of community radio with that of the local press, or in the global news arena, the role of British Broadcasting Corporation (BBC) World News with CNN International. Individual roles are embedded within this broader institutional context. The collective roles of the news media are arguably more important for the health of democratic governance and for human development than the individual role of journalists. For instance, effective democracies require a diversity of social and political viewpoints heard across all the airwaves and newspapers within any society, representing the notion of external diversity. This is arguably more vital to informed public debate than the need for impartiality, or internal diversity, established within each media outlet, by each individual reporter, or in any particular story.[23] Interventions designed to strengthen the role of the news media as an institution focus more broadly on the role of the state, markets, and the journalistic profession. Typical strategies include strengthening rights to freedom of information, expression, and publication in law; deregulating state ownership of broadcasting to facilitate a plurality of independent channels; investing in the infrastructure supporting diverse community radio stations, newspapers, and Web sites; and reforming professional journalistic training and accreditation bodies.

At the *individual* level, roles determine the norms and values, standards of behavior, and orientations shaping the jobs of individual news workers. This level includes a diverse range of occupations in the communication sector, including writers, reporters, and journalists; broadcasters and news anchors; editors and producers; analysts, experts, and commentators; press officers; public relations and market research practitioners; official spokespersons; and Internet communicators, such as Web editors and online bloggers. Journalistic roles are learned from many sources, including from personal background and experiences, professional education, apprenticeship training, observation of media routines and practices, guidance from employers and coworkers, formal guidelines and standards of professional conduct, practical job experience, organizational structures, and the incentives in the workplace.[24] Interventions designed to strengthen the individual roles of journalists commonly focus on establishing formal guidelines, expanding the institutional capacity of professional bodies and organizations (such as press councils and communication education institutes), and supporting capacity building through individual journalist training programs and workshops.

The extensive research literature seeking to understand the collective roles of the news media has usually focused on identifying and describing the perceived and actual roles of individual journalists.[25] Although the appropriate universe and the sampling frame remain difficult to identify, studies have typically gathered data derived from surveys of representative samples of individual journalists. Surveys have monitored professional routines, editorial procedures, and socialization processes, as well as expectations surrounding their work. These data are often then aggregated upward to study particular sectors, for example, to contrast the roles of print versus broadcast reporters, or to compare national journalistic cultures.[26] Such surveys have now been conducted in a wide range of countries, and this approach is currently being expanded worldwide.[27] Journalists have been examined through this method in many postindustrial societies and established democracies, including Germany, Great Britain, Italy, and the United States.[28] This approach has also been extended to low- and middle-income countries as diverse as Brazil, Indonesia, Russia, China, Egypt, Bangladesh, Nepal, and Tanzania.[29] Chapter 13 compares the results of such a survey conducted in the Arab region.

The results of this body of research suggest that news professionals perceive themselves as serving multiple functions and roles, for instance, in the priority they give to providing background analysis and interpretation of events, to facilitating public debate and expression, and to delivering timely factual coverage of events. The broadest comparison of news cultures to date, by Weaver and Wu, was based on the results of surveys of journalists conducted in 20 countries. The study concluded that the traditional ideals of objectivity and impartiality dominate many newsrooms across the globe, although important cross-cultural variations exist in role perceptions.[30] There are continuing debates about whether reporters should strive to be neutral observers of events, prioritizing principles such as objectivity, neutrality, fairness, detachment, and impartiality, or whether they should seek to be advocates, adopting a more active and committed role seeking to promote social change on behalf of the disadvantaged or a particular group, viewpoint, or political party. Roles also vary in the extent to which journalists regard themselves as adversaries to those in power, serving as the fourth estate to counterbalance the other branches of government, or the extent to which they feel they should be loyal spokespersons of the authorities. Journalists also differ in how they see themselves as servants of the public interest, providing information that helps informed citizens to govern themselves, for example, by emphasizing coverage of public affairs, economics, and foreign policy, and the degree they see themselves as providing what the audience demands, for example, by focusing on popular lifestyle, celebrity culture, and entertainment stories.

The different roles journalists actually perceive have been classified and described through the growing range of empirical studies. However, this classification has been only weakly related to, or embodied within, broader normative or prescriptive theories about the public sphere, democratic governance, and human development. Not all journalistic roles have equally positive consequences for the quality of democratic governance and human development. For example, journalists in some countries may well see their primary responsibilities as "lapdogs," acting as loyal spokespersons for state authorities, rarely questioning official information, and providing extensive coverage of ruling elites, dignitaries, and leaders. In this regard, the news media may serve as an effective propaganda machine for autocracies, reinforcing the hegemonic control of the powerful, rather than providing a countervailing force and a diversity of viewpoints. Reports reflecting the interests of the state may also fail to reflect the voice and concerns of opposition movements, reform dissidents, and politically marginalized sectors, which typically include women, rural and ethnic minorities, and the poor. Commercial pressures mean that journalists often focus on providing "soft" news about celebrities, entertainment, and sports, which drives newspaper sales, giving little sustained attention to major challenges of social development, natural disasters, international news, or dramatic failures of public policy. From a normative perspective, the notion of journalistic roles can provide a prescriptive benchmark only if it is embedded within broader theories of democratic governance and human development. Moreover, although many alternative journalistic role perceptions have been identified, this book focuses on a more limited range. This process helps to develop a clear conceptual framework, reliable and unambiguous empirical indicators and benchmarks, and consistent comparisons across countries and sectors.

Working within the wider framework of the notion of deliberative democracy and the public sphere, the book advocates that the core responsibilities of the news media should be understood to involve, at a minimum, their individual and collective roles as watchdogs, agenda setters, and gatekeepers. Through fulfilling each of these roles, as an institution the news media maximize opportunities for critical reflection and rational deliberation in the public sphere, for inclusive participation in communication processes, and, ultimately, for informed choice and human development in society.

This book advocates that as *watchdogs,* the news media have a responsibility to help guard the public interest, ensuring the accountability of powerful decision makers by highlighting cases of malfeasance, misadministration, and corruption, thereby strengthening the transparency and effectiveness of governance. As *agenda setters,* the news media have a responsibility to raise awareness of pervasive social problems, helping to turn public attention to matters of common interest, to inform governing officials about social needs, and to inform the international community about development challenges. As *gatekeepers,* the news media have a responsibility to reflect and incorporate the plurality of viewpoints and political persuasions in reporting, to maximize the diversity of perspectives and arguments heard in rational public deliberations, and to enrich the public sphere.

Many other functions can be suggested—for example, in practice, journalists may perceive their roles as educators of the public, spokespersons for authorities, active advocates for reform, or forces for strengthening collective national identities. Indeed, journalists may reject the notions offered in this book if those notions are regarded as unrealistic or impractical in many situations. Role definitions often prove to be slippery and ambiguous concepts. Nevertheless, the three roles can be regarded as the necessary, but not sufficient, collective responsibilities of the news media for the health of democratic governance and human development. Achieving these roles effectively is challenging in every society, and the media commonly fail even in established democracies. Yet the triple roles are particularly difficult in many transitional and consolidating democracies, where the structure of the news media is often in transition, and where reporters are learning new roles and adapting to changed conditions.[31] In practice, many barriers restrict the role of individual journalists, and the collective news media as an institution, from achieving these democratic ideals. The most important of those barriers arise from constraints by the state, the market, and the profession.

## Watchdogs

As *watchdogs*, it is argued, the news media should serve democracy by providing a check and balance on powerful sectors of society, including leaders within the public and private domains.[32] This represents the classic notion of the news media as the fourth estate, counterbalancing the power of the executive, legislative, and judiciary branches. According to this well-known ideal, the news media should keep a skeptical eye on the powerful, guarding the public interest and protecting it from incompetence, corruption, and misinformation. The watchdog role for reporters is sufficiently broad, fluid, and open to encompass both a more neutral function—as an evenhanded disseminator of information about public affairs that was previously hidden from public attention—and a more active role as an investigator of the behavior of decision makers or even an adversary of the powerful.[33]

The defining feature of watchdog journalism is not the political stance of the reporter, story, or media outlet, but rather the role of asking hard or probing questions of the powerful to maximize transparency and to serve the public interest. On a routine basis, timely and accurate information provided by news coverage of public affairs should help citizens evaluate the performance of political leaders and parties, for example, the government record in reducing poverty or improving economic growth. Investigative reporting commonly highlights failures in government, especially those arising from cases of bribery, corruption, and malfeasance; from abuse of power; or from incompetent management of public service delivery. Through this process, journalists should help to encourage and promote government transparency and accountability, especially by facilitating informed choice by citizens during elections. Reporters investigate claims made by public officials and scrutinize the action of corporate elites, irrespective of the party in power, economic advantage, or personal biases, to advance the broader public interest. The media can give whistleblowers a voice, spearhead the downfall of powerful politicians, and expose widespread corporate corruption. Public disclosure, though not sufficient by itself to stamp out these problems, is the sunshine that can act as a disinfectant to eradicate cases of corruption, to bring government misconduct to the attention of the electorate and the courts, and to deter others from similar behavior. The notion of reporters as watchdogs is one widely sub-scribed to by journalists in many democratic states, as confirmed by surveys of journalists in Sweden, the United States, and Britain.[34] At the same time, it is also challenged by those who believe that too much exposé journalism under-mines faith and trust in government institutions, promoting instability and undermining fragile states.

## Agenda Setters

Although conceptually distinct, watchdog journalism is related to agenda set-ting. It functions when journalists are investigating previously obscure prob-lems and thereby highlighting these issues in the news headlines. It is claimed that the news media, as an agenda setter, should function to raise awareness of social problems, especially calling attention to vital issues, such as major disas-ters, development challenges, or humanitarian crises that require urgent action. The term "agenda setting" originated with work by McCombs and Shaw during the early 1970s, and the idea has subsequently been applied to multiple issues and countries with an extensive body of literature developing over more than three decades.[35] The central normative premise of agenda-setting theory is the claim that problems covered in the news media should highlight the importance of these issues for the public and for politicians. In this regard, the theory claims that the press should operate like a burglar alarm, sounding alarm warnings and rousing people to action when major challenges and crises arise.

Coverage of these issues in the news media can inform the general public and government officials, potentially making people more responsive to social needs, humanitarian crises, and development priorities, both at home and overseas.[36] This process is thought to be particularly important for ensuring that governments react swiftly and effectively to natural and humanitarian crises. Hence, Sen made the famous claim that famines do not occur in func-tioning democracies because their leaders must be more responsive to the de-mands of the citizens or they face the risk of losing office. Coverage of local issues in the free press connects elected representatives more closely with the needs of their constituents.[37] By contrast, autocracies that strictly control the press, such as the military junta in Myanmar, lack such feedback mechanisms, as well as the need to be responsive to natural disasters in order to retain their grip on power.

In practice, however, there remains considerable dispute about the primary direction of influence in this complex dance, including who leads and who follows among the news agenda, the public agenda, and the policy agenda.[38] In the strongest version of this thesis, the news media are seen as exerting an in-dependent influence on the concerns of the public and elites. In the United States, for example, studies report that the President and Congress often re-spond to headline stories featured in the news media.[39] Alternative versions emphasize a process of mutual interaction, in which reporters are serving to link the priorities of citizens and elected officials (an important but less autonomous role). Weaker theories suggest a more passive role in which the news agenda usually simply reflects and follows preexisting public and elite priorities as well as unfolding world events. Agenda setting by reporters may arise from conscious editorial decisions in newsrooms, for example, the decision by the CBS program "60 Minutes" to break the Abu Ghraib prisoner abuse story in April 2004, or from common practices and organizational structures in media outlets. The process thereby calls attention to issues of concern among the general public and government officials. The news media are also believed to contribute to framing issues, whereby reporting triggers familiar interpretive frameworks shaping how the public thinks about social problems and their potential solutions.[40]

## Gatekeepers

Finally, as *gatekeepers,* or indeed as "gate openers," the news media can serve as the classical agora where journalists and broadcasters bring together a plurality of diverse interests, political parties, viewpoints, and social sectors to debate issues of public concern. The idea of gatekeeping was first applied to the news media by White in the early 1950s.[41] The notion has been widely used to describe the general process of selection in media work, whether the microlevel editorial decisions about the choice of headline topics, images, or specific stories, or the broader macrolevel balance of voices, parties, and interests that are represented as sources, authoritative spokespersons, or leaders in news coverage.

In this book, the focus is on the institutional role of the news media and its responsibility to provide inclusive opportunities for participation and voice. Coverage in the news media should reflect diverse perspectives, viewpoints, issues, and interests chosen from across the political and social spectrum, including from politically marginalized and poorer sectors of society. Balanced and inclusive coverage among a pluralistic range of independent news media sources is also particularly important for encouraging a vital and lively rational deliberative process, representing all political persuasions and viewpoints. This process is perhaps most critical in postconflict states and deeply divided societies, as a way of encouraging dialogue, tolerance, and interaction among diverse communities, reducing the underlying causes of conflict, and building the conditions for a lasting peace. The representation of women, the poor, and marginalized and politically excluded groups in news coverage is vital in this process, so that all voices and perspectives are heard in communication processes and within the public sphere. Balanced coverage of all political parties and issues across the news media is also particularly important during election campaigns, to provide the basis for informed choice among citizens. Where media gatekeepers consistently exclude certain voices or interests, favoring the powerful or incumbent office holders and governing parties, this condition stifles public debate and reduces the quality of democracy.

## Conditions Under Which the News Media Can Achieve These Ideals

Although not without challenge, these normative ideals are widely advocated as the minimal standards by which the news media should function to strengthen democratic governance and human development. In practice, however, numerous factors can limit the effectiveness and capacity of the news media to meet these standards, and many obstacles, discussed throughout this book, prevent them from serving the broader public interest through these roles. As subsequent chapters explore, the state, markets, and professional cultures can all severely limit the effectiveness of the watchdog, agenda setting, and gatekeeping roles of the news media. Figure 1.2 illustrates these constraints.

**Figure 1.2.  Conditions Influencing the Performance of Media Systems**

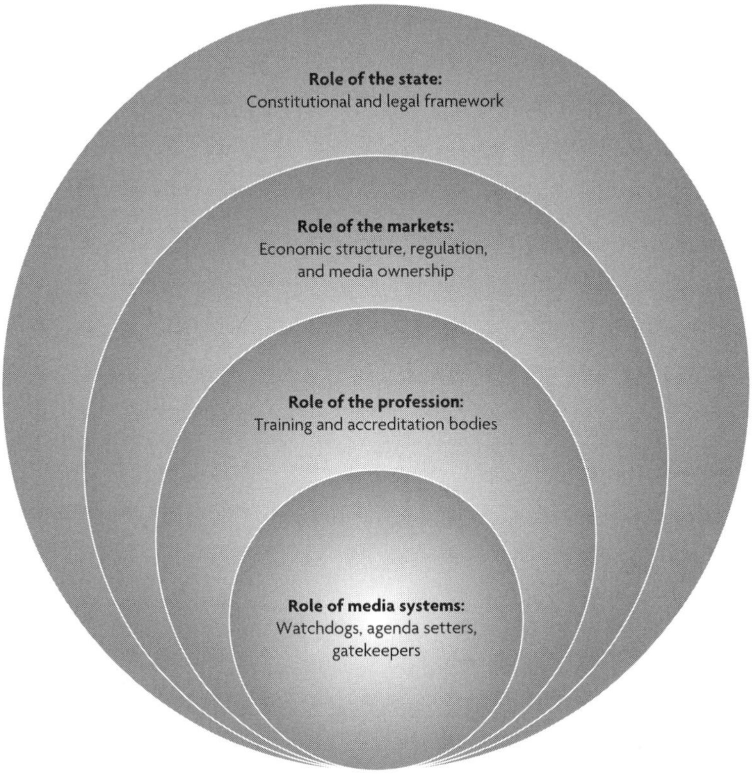

**Role of the state:**
Constitutional and legal framework

**Role of the markets:**
Economic structure, regulation,
and media ownership

**Role of the profession:**
Training and accreditation bodies

**Role of media systems:**
Watchdogs, agenda setters,
gatekeepers

*Source:* Authors.

The role of the state may be particularly important in setting the broadest context. Constitutional and legal restrictions can severely curtail freedom of expression and publication, including stringent libel laws and restrictive official secrets acts, which severely curtail how reporters can act. Human rights watch agencies and organizations concerned about protecting press freedom regularly document cases of outright violence, imprisonment, and intimidation used against journalists and broadcasters, which have been commonly been employed to shut down newspapers and to silence critical voices.[42] States also continue to use the techniques of official propaganda and censorship, and state monopolies of radio and television channels, and the policy framework regulating publication, broadcasting, and telecommunications, can limit a plurality of voices on the airwaves. Freedom of expression for investigative journalism can also be restricted by requirements for registration or licenses for journalists or newspapers; by denial of travel visas for foreign reporters or by bans on sending journalists abroad; by broadcasting regulations and laws governing broadcasting contents; and by a legal framework governing official secrecy or freedom of information, intellectual property, libel, and taxation. Where the interests of the news media are too closely aligned with the powerful or affluent, the press can fail to be sufficiently independent or critical watchdogs serving the broader public interest. Investigative reporters encounter major problems in their ability to scrutinize decisions where official information is tightly controlled or where press freedom is limited through regulation or state censorship.

Markets can also fail in societies in which competition is severely limited through heavily regulated oligopolies in commercial ownership, particularly overconcentration of ownership of the airwaves. Commercial pressures may also undermine the capacity of the news media to fulfill these functions, when concern about the market for news leads to an emphasis on soft news dominated by entertainment, celebrity culture, and trivia, rather than serious coverage of public affairs serving the broader interest. The roles of journalists can be restricted by the economic market for news, including the structure, resources, and ownership of the mass media. Important factors include the patterns of state-owned, public service, and commercial television; the availability of community radio and other local media outlets; the diversity of ownership of the print sector; levels of public access to the mass media and to newer information and communication technologies; and the role of global news flows and the permeability of cultural trade across national borders.

Roles are also shaped by the *profession,* especially by standards of training, entry, and accreditation of reporters and broadcasters; by organizational routines and the composition and social diversity of newsrooms; and by the role of professional bodies, such as journalism associations, trade unions, and press councils. These are influenced by the broader context of values and norms embedded in the national cultures of journalism.[43] Journalists may reject the legitimacy of the roles of the press as watchdogs, agenda setters, and gatekeepers if these are regarded as Western notions that fail to reflect national cultures. The news media may thereby exercise a form of self-censorship, if it is widely believed that reporters should play a role that is more loyally supportive of autocratic leaders, predominant parties, or affluent business elites.

The precise impact of each of these factors—the market, the state, and the profession—on the quality of journalism has generated an extensive debate and research literature in the field of media and development. Where there are serious problems of performance in meeting these ideal roles, a range of programmatic interventions are available, designed to strengthen both individual and institutional capacity. Understanding which programs work best and integrating these interventions into the core work of the development community are critical, both to strengthen the quality of democratic governance and to improve development outcomes. It is also necessary to understand the barriers limiting how well the news media can meet these functions, and the policy interventions that can be most effective in strengthening free, plural, and independent communication systems as a core component of democratic governance. Such a system is regarded as intrinsically valuable, as well as serving several important functions for strengthening other aspects of good governance and human development, including the transparency, accountability, and responsiveness of elected officials to the public.

New initiatives designed to strengthen the roles of the news media also require attention to a broader range of issues beyond journalism. Donors may typically think about the elements of the public sphere individually, such as building an independent media sector, strengthening civil society, or supporting freedom of information legislation. Operationally and conceptually, these are treated as separate programs; in the field, different NGOs may be responsible for the separate pieces of work. Because of this, the connective fiber among these programs remains unrealized in practice, potentially leading to lost synergies, missed opportunities, diminished impact, and even negative outcomes.

This phenomenon can be illuminated by examining it in the context of a particular arena of the governance agenda. For example, during anticorruption program design, the elements of the public sphere are treated separately; passing freedom of information legislation may be an important program component, but it is designed and carried out in isolation from other elements of the public sphere. What is missed is the interaction between that legislation and the media sector's capacity to understand and use it, as well as interaction between the legislation and the broader political culture within the country, which may or may not encourage debate and criticism of government. Investigative journalism programming may also be a separate part of the anticorruption agenda, but it is generally viewed in isolation from all of the above, not to mention from programs to address the capacity of government ombudsmen or watchdogs to effectively act upon stories of corruption that are broken in the press. Media audits provide a more comprehensive tool to assess the current state of media systems and to identify major challenges in each society. By scrutinizing the connective tissue among these discrete programs, this book can convey the importance of the public sphere as a conceptual framework for the governance agenda.

## Overview of the Book

Subsequent chapters examine how the news media function as an institution against these ideal benchmarks, using systematic cross-national empirical analysis, as well as detailed selected case studies derived from a wide range of low- and medium-income societies, as well as different types of regimes found in all regions around the globe.

To examine these issues, chapter 2 turns to the growing body of indicators and metrics available to measure how well the news media perform.[44] The chapter considers a range of important issues. What evidence and what diagnostic tools are available to compare how effectively journalists are performing in their roles as watchdogs, agenda setters, and gatekeepers in different societies? How are the core components of media freedom monitored and operationalized by alternative quantitative indexes, based on expert judgments, and are these measures valid, robust, accurate, and reliable? Do new measures and methodologies need to be developed and additional sources of data gathered? What do the available indexes suggest about the functions of the news media, including cross-national comparisons worldwide and evidence of trends over time? And can the indexes be transformed into typologies and classifications for comparing these roles?

On this basis, part II of this book examines evidence from cross-national studies and selected case studies to understand the performance of journalists and the constraints under which they operate in practice. It begins with agenda setting, particularly the extent to which the news media raise awareness of social needs and development challenges, or whether they fail to lead with these stories. Agenda setting emphasizes the importance of covering certain problems in news headlines and thereby prioritizing issues of concern. The process also involves framing, or the use of interpretive frameworks shaping how readers think about social problems and their potential solutions. Chapter 3 focuses on understanding the extent to which the news media succeed, and fail, in their agenda-setting role when covering natural crises and disasters, such as famines, floods, and pandemics. The process of agenda setting is not simply about making national governments responsive to domestic social needs; it also involves the priorities facing the international development community and donor partners. Chapter 4 considers the extent to which international news media highlight coverage of natural and human-caused humanitarian disasters and crises in developing countries overseas, and whether this process encourages the responsiveness of donor governments in sponsoring humanitarian aid and technical assistance.

Chapter 5 considers the watchdog role of investigative journalism, which holds powerful public officials and institutions responsible for their decisions and actions. Watchdog journalism is expected to prove particularly important for good governance when highlighting problems of corruption, malfeasance, cronyism, and scandal in the public sector, thereby raising standards and limiting the abuse of public office. But how active are journalists in reporting these sorts of stories in many developing countries? Does reporting that focuses too aggressively on exposing the private life of public figures contribute to public cynicism and deter future leaders from dedicating themselves to a career in public service? Extending this theme, chapter 6 discusses notions of accountability and considers evidence to see whether in practice the watchdog role of the news media contributes to more informed and engaged citizens—or to a public that is turned off by politics and more cynical about democratic institutions and processes.

Chapter 7 turns to the role and structure of the news media as gatekeepers in the public forum. The chapter focuses on campaign coverage in a series of elections in four case studies—in Kenya, Mexico, Russia, and Turkey. The study explores whether the campaign coverage provided a neutral and balanced field for parties and candidates from all political persuasions, interests, and social sectors. The issue of partisan balance and bias is particularly important in transitional autocracies and in consolidating democracies where one major party is predominant, and where the opposition parties and reform movements have difficulty getting their message out to rally popular support.

Chapter 8 builds on this to examine autocracies' capacity to strengthen popular support by silencing dissent and manipulating the news. The many ways that autocracies seek to control the media are well documented. What is less clearly established, however, is the degree to which states with restrictive media environments succeed in manipulating public opinion and strengthening their support at home. The cumulative result of years, or even decades, of tight media control in restrictive and isolated states, such as Myanmar and the Democratic People's Republic of Korea, is usually assumed to have a powerful impact on citizens. This chapter looks at evidence from the World Values Survey concerning the effects of limits on press freedom for patterns of regime support in more than 60 nations. Chapter 9 goes on to consider the role of the mass media in postconflict reconstruction, drawing upon the cases of Ethiopia and Iraq. In the early stages of any negotiated settlement, peace building, and conflict reduction, it is particularly important to have a pluralistic news media that fosters tolerance and open communication through balanced coverage of all sides involved in the conflict. However, this process often fails where the news media are highly one-sided in their coverage, especially in societies deeply divided by language or religion into separate communities. The chapter emphasizes that the roles of the media are particularly challenging in the early stages of recovery from conflict, and in building a unified nation-state, prior to the development of democracy.

Part III of the book considers how the roles of journalists as watchdogs, agenda setters, and gatekeepers in the public sphere vary across and among different world regions. Chapters 10 through 14 build upon the issues raised in earlier sections of the book and then explore them in depth using a wide range of selected case studies within Central and Eastern Europe, Sub-Saharan Africa, Latin America, the Arab States, and Asia. The comparative case studies highlight the complexity of the issues and the important challenges that exist within each region. The issues facing the newer democracies in Central and Eastern Europe, for example, emphasize the transition from state-run and -owned broadcasting to a dual public service and commercial television system. Sub-Saharan Africa has similar challenges, but there are also distinct problems in freedom of expression. By contrast, the media in Latin America have been largely organized around commercial principles for many years, and the key problems arise from the excessive power of governments and private interests. Freedom of expression has been most heavily curtailed in the Arab region, although there have been important stirrings of media reform in recent years. Asia remains highly diverse, with traditional views about journalists' roles that are often at odds with the ideals considered in this book. These chapters also emphasize the constraints on journalists fulfilling the ideal functions, especially in states governed by autocratic regimes and in consolidating democracies that continue to have weak institutions and poor quality of governance.

Finally, part IV summarizes the key findings and identifies the major policy options that are most effective for future action. Chapter 15 emphasizes prioritizing an institutional perspective by incorporating media system audits into governance diagnostics and needs analysis. Chapter 16 examines the key policy options. The menu of interventions, which provides alternatives that can be tailored to each context, includes those reforms that address the role of the state, market failures, and the journalistic profession; ensure that media systems are plural and diverse; turn state broadcasters into public service broadcasters; remove all curbs on the print media; support sustainable professional development programs; encourage links between the news media and civil society organizations; and support media literacy.

At the level of the state, one of the most important issues concerns the constitutional and legal guarantees of freedom of expression and publication, especially following peace-building initiatives and the reconstruction of fragile states. Other concerns include rights to information, official government secrecy, and the deregulation of state broadcasting following the initial transition to democracy.

To address market failures, interventions include establishing an appropriate legal framework and regulatory environment governing communication policies. These include the implementation of international treaties and agreements, as well as the establishment of effective legal structures and independent bodies regulating broadcasting licenses, concentration of media ownership, content regulation, and media competition. These policies regulate industrywide standards and determine the funding for public service and private sector broadcasting. Ensuring the most appropriate governance structure and the financial, editorial, and management independence of public service broadcasting is particularly critical.

In terms of the profession of journalism, institutional capacity building is important for sustainable solutions. This includes fostering professional journalism organizations, press councils, independent media advocacy networks and associations, and professional awards designed to strengthen standards and journalistic cultures. Professional journalism training programs and individual capacity-building efforts are also commonly employed. Although training programs remain important, it needs to be recognized that training programs often have reduced effect where individual journalists are limited from effectively fulfilling their roles as watchdogs, agenda setters, and gatekeepers by multiple structural restrictions and institutional disincentives. Therefore, the book concludes by reviewing which provisions and interventions reflect best practice in each of these areas, which institutions and agencies have been most engaged, and what can be learned from interventions about the most effective way to promote the roles of the press in the public sphere.

## Notes

1. Freedom House. 2008. "Freedom in the World 2008." Washington, DC: Freedom House. http://www.freedomhouse.org.
2. Larry Diamond. 2008. *The Spirit of Democracy: The Struggle to Build Free Societies Throughout the World.* New York: Times Books.
3. Arch Puddington. 2008. *Freedom in Retreat: Is the Tide Turning? Findings of Freedom in the World 2008.* Washington, DC: Freedom House. www.freedomhouse.org.
4. UNDP (United Nations Development Programme). 2007. *The Millennium Development Goals Report.* New York: United Nations; UN General Assembly. 2008. *Thematic Debate of the General Assembly on the Millennium Development Goals.* New York, April 1–4, 2008. http://www.un-ngls.org/docs/ga/summary_MDG_thematic_debate.pdf.
5. Ibid.
6. United Nations. 2008. *Achieving the Millennium Development Goals in Africa: Recommendations of the MDG Africa Steering Group.* New York: United Nations. http://www.mdgafrica.org.
7. World Bank. 2008. Global Monitoring Report 2008: *MDGs and the Environment: Agenda for Inclusive and Sustainable Development.* Washington, DC: World Bank.
8. World Bank. 2008. *Global Economic Prospects 2009: Commodity Markets at the Crossroads.* Washington, DC: World Bank.

9. One of the most influential reflections on the concept of the public sphere has been provided by Jürgen Habermas. 1989 (1962). *The Structural Transformation of the Public Sphere.* Cambridge: Polity Press.

10. See Calhoun, Craig, ed. 1992. *Habermas and the Public Sphere.* Cambridge, MA: MIT Press; Peter Dahlgren. 1995. Television and the Public Sphere. London: Sage; Alan McKee. 2005. The Public Sphere. New York: Cambridge University Press.

11. Alan McKee. 2005. *The Public Sphere.* New York: Cambridge University Press.

12. UN High Commissioner on Human Rights. *United Nations Millennium Declaration.* General Assembly Resolution 55/2, September 8, 2000. http://www2.ohchr.org/english/law/millennium.htm.

13. Robert Dahl. 1989. *Democracy and Its Critics.* New Haven: Yale University Press, 221.

14. Bettina Peters. 2003. "The Media's Role: Covering or Covering Up Corruption?" In *The Global Corruption Report.* Berlin: Transparency International. http://www.transparency.org/publications/gcr/download_gcr/download_gcr_2003; Silvio Waisbord. 2000. *Watchdog Journalism in South America: News, Accountability, and Democracy.* New York: Columbia University Press; S. K, Chowdhury. 2004. "The Effect of Democracy and Press Freedom on Corruption: An Empirical Test." *Economics Letters* 85 (1): 93–101; D. Fell. 2005. "Political and Media Liberalization and Political Corruption in Taiwan." *China Quarterly* (184): 875–93.

15. Timothy Besley and Roger Burgess. 2002. "The Political Economy of Government Responsiveness: Theory and Evidence from India." *Quarterly Journal of Economics* 117 (4): 1415–51.

16. Amartya Sen. 1999. *Development as Freedom.* New York: Anchor Books.

17. Roumeen Islam. Ed. 2002. *The Right to Tell: The Role of Mass Media in Economic Development.* Washington, DC: World Bank; Barry James, ed. 2006. *Media Development and Poverty Eradication.* Paris: UNESCO.

18. Douglas Van Belle, Jean-Sébastien Rioux, and David M. Potter. 2004. *Media, Bureaucracies, and Foreign Aid: A Comparative Analysis of the United States, the United Kingdom, Canada, France and Japan.* New York: Palgrave/St. Martin.

19. Gadi Wolfsfeld. 2004. *Media and Paths to Peace.* Cambridge: Cambridge University Press.

20. W. Wanta, G. Golan, and C. Lee. 2004. "Agenda Setting and International News: Media Influence on Public Perceptions of Foreign Nations." *Journalism & Mass Communication Quarterly* 81 (2): 364–77; Holli A. Semetko, J.B. Brzinski, David Weaver, and L. Willnat. 1992. "TV News and United States Public Opinion about Foreign Countries: The Impact of Exposure and Attention." *International Journal of Public Opinion Research* 4 (1): 18–36.

21. Pippa Norris. 2004. "Global Political Communication: Good Governance, Human Development and Mass Communication." In *Comparing Political Communication: Theories, Cases and Challenges,* ed. Frank Esser and Barbara Pfetsch. New York: Cambridge University Press.

22. Denis McQuail. 1992. *Media Performance: Mass Communication and the Public Interest.* London: Sage.

23. For a detailed normative discussion of objectivity and diversity see Denis McQuail. 1992. *Media Performance.*

24. For a discussion, see Pamela J. Shoemaker and Stephen D. Reese. 1996. *Mediating the Message.* New York: Longman Publishers.

25. See, for example, Daniel C. Hallin and Paolo Mancini. 2004. *Comparing Media Systems: Three Models of Media and Politics.* Cambridge and New York: Cambridge University Press; David H. Weaver and Wei Wu, eds. 1998. *The Global Journalist: News People around the World.* Cresskill, NJ: Hampton Press; Thomas E. Patterson and Wolfgang

Donsbach. 1996. "News Decisions: Journalists as Partisan Actors." *Political Communication* 13 (4): 455–68.

26. Mark Deuze. 2002. "National News Cultures: A Comparison of Dutch, German, British, Australian and U.S. Journalists." *Journalism & Mass Communication Quarterly* 79 (1): 134–49.

27. Thomas Hanitzsch. 2007. "Deconstructing Journalism Culture: Towards a Universal Theory." *Communication Theory* 17 (4): 367–85. See also the World of Journalism project, http://www.worldofjournalism.org.

28. Wolfgang Donsbach. 1983. "Journalists' Conceptions of Their Audience: Comparative Indicators for the Way British and German Journalists Define Their Relations to the Public." *Gazette* 32: 19–36; Renate Köcher. 1986. "Bloodhounds or Missionaries: Role Definitions of German and British Journalists." *European Journal of Communication* 1 (2): 43–64; Anthony Delano and John Henningham. 1995. *The News Breed: British Journalists in the 1990s.* London: School of Media, London College of Printing and Distributive Trades; John Henningham. 1996. "Australian Journalists' Professional and Ethical Values." *Journalism & Mass Communication Quarterly* 73 (2): 206–18; Thomas E. Patterson and Wolfgang Donsbach. 1996. "News Decisions: Journalists as Partisan Actors." *Political Communication* 13 (4): 455–68; Wolfgang Donsbach and Thomas E. Patterson. 2004. "Political News Journalists: Partisanship, Professionalism, and Political Roles in Five Countries." In *Comparing Political Communication: Theories, Cases, and Challenges,* 251–70, ed. Frank Esser and Barbara Pfetsch. New York: Cambridge University Press.

29. H. G. Herscovitz. 2004. "Brazilian Journalists' Perceptions of Media Roles, Ethics, and Foreign Influences on Brazilian Journalism." *Journalism Studies* 5 (1): 71–86; T. Hanitzsch. 2005. "Journalists in Indonesia: Educated but Timid Watchdogs." *Journalism Studies* 6: 493–508; J. Ramaprasad. 2001. "A Profile of Journalists in Post-Independence Tanzania." *Gazette* 63: 539–56; J. Ramaprasad and N. N. Hamdy. 2006. "Functions of Egyptian Journalists: Perceived Importance and Actual Performance." *International Communication Gazette* 68 (2): 167–85; J. Ramaprasad and J.D. Kelly. 2003. "Reporting the News from the World's Rooftop: A Survey of Nepalese Journalists." *Gazette* 65: 291–315; Wei Wu, David Weaver, and O. V. Johnson. 1996. "Professional Roles of Russian and U.S. Journalists: A Comparative Study." *Journalism & Mass Communication Quarterly* 73: 534; J. Ramaprasad and S. Rahman. 2006. "Tradition with a Twist: A Survey of Bangladeshi Journalists." *International Communication Gazette* 68 (2): 148–65; Jian-Hua Zhu, David Weaver, Ven-hwei Lo, Chongshan Chen, and Wei Wu. 1997. "Individual, Organizational, and Societal Influences on Media Role Perceptions: A Comparative Study of Journalists in China, Taiwan, and the United States." *Journalism & Mass Communication Quarterly* 74 (2): 84–96.

30. David H. Weaver and Wei Wu, eds. 1998. *The Global Journalist: News People Around the World.* Cresskill, NJ: Hampton Press.

31. Richard Gunther and Anthony Mughan. Eds. 2000. *Democracy and the Media: A Comparative Perspective.* New York: Cambridge University Press; Monroe Price, Beata Rozumilowicz, and Stefaan G. Verhulst, eds. 2001. *Media Reform: Democratizing Media, Democratizing the State.* London: Routledge; S. Pasti. 2005. "Two Generations of Contemporary Russian Journalists." *European Journal of Communication* 20 (1): 89–115; Katrin Voltmer, ed. 2006. *Mass Media and Political Communication in New Democracies.* London: Routledge.

32. See, for example, Wolfgang Donsbach. 1995. "Lapdogs, Watchdogs and Junkyard Dogs." *Media Studies Journal* 9 (4): 17–30; Bart Cammaerts and Nico Carpentier, eds. 2007. *Reclaiming the Media: Communication Rights and Democratic Media Roles.* London: Intellect Inc.

33. The Nieman Watchdog Journalism Project, part of the Nieman Foundation for Journalism at Harvard University, specified the role as follows in their mission statement: "The premise of watchdog journalism is that the press is a surrogate for the public, asking probing, penetrating questions at every level, from the town council to the state house to the White House, as well as in corporate and professional offices, in union halls, on university campuses and in religious organizations that seek to influence governmental actions. The goal of watchdog journalism is to see that people in power provide information the public should have." http://www.niemanwatchdog.org/index.cfm?fuseaction=about.Mission_Statement.

34. B. Fjaestad and P.G. Holmlov. 1976. "The Journalist's View." *Journal of Communication* 2: 108–14; J. W. L. Johnstone, E. J. Slawski, and W. W. Bowman. 1976. *The News People.* Urbana, IL: University of Illinois Press; David Weaver and C. G. Wilhoit. 1986. *The American Journalist.* Bloomington: University of Indiana Press; Renate Köcher. 1986. "Bloodhounds or Missionaries: Role Definitions of German and British Journalists." *European Journal of Communication* 1 (1): 43–64.

35. Maxwell E. McCombs and Donald L. Shaw. 1972. "The Agenda-Setting Function of the Press." *Public Opinion Quarterly* 36: 176–87; Maxwell E. McCombs and Donald L. Shaw. 1993. "The Evolution of Agenda-Setting Research: 25 Years in the Marketplace of Ideas." *Journal of Communication* 43 (2): 58–67; Maxwell E. McCombs, Donald L. Shaw, David H. Weaver, eds. 1997. *Communication and Democracy: Exploring the Intellectual Frontiers in Agenda-Setting Theory.* NJ: Lawrence Erlbaum; Maxwell E. McCombs. 1997. "Building Consensus: The News Media's Agenda-Setting Roles." *Political Communication* 14 (4): 433. For a recent longitudinal empirical study, see Yue Tan and David H. Weaver. 2007. "Agenda-Setting Effects among the Media, the Public, and Congress, 1946–2004." *Journalism and Mass Communication Quarterly* 84 (4): 729–44. For a discussion and review of the literature, see T. Takeshita. 2006. "Current Critical Problems in Agenda-Setting Research." *International Journal of Public Opinion Research* 18 (3): 275–96.

36. Douglas Van Belle, Jean-Sébastien Rioux, and David M. Potter. 2004. *Media, Bureaucracies, and Foreign Aid: A Comparative Analysis of the United States, the United Kingdom, Canada, France and Japan.* New York: Palgrave/St. Martin.

37. Amartya Sen. 1999. *Development as Freedom.* New York: Anchor Books; Timothy Besley and Roger Burgess. 2002. "The Political Economy of Government Responsiveness: Theory and Evidence from India." *Quarterly Journal of Economics* 117 (4): 1415–51.

38. Everett M. Rogers and James W. Dearing. 1988. "Agenda-Setting Research: Where Has It Been? Where Is It Going?" In *Communication Yearbook,* ed. J. A. Anderson, vol. 11, 555–94. Newbury Park, CA: Sage; Everett M. Rogers and James W. Dearing. *Agenda-setting.* Thousand Oaks, CA: Sage; Everett M. Rogers, W. B. Hart, and James W. Dearing. 1997. "A Paradigmatic History of Agenda-Setting Research." In *Do the Media Govern? Politicians, Voters, and Reporters in America,* ed. Shanto Iyengar and R. Reeves. Thousand Oaks, CA: Sage.

39. George C. Edwards. 1999. "Who Influences Whom? The President, Congress, and the Media." *American Political Science Review* 93: 327.

40. Robert M. Entman. 1993. "Framing—Toward Clarification of a Fractured Paradigm." *Journal of Communication* 43: 51.

41. D. M. White. 1950. "The Gatekeeper: A Case Study in the Selection of News." *Journalism Quarterly* 27: 383–90; M. Janowitz. 1975. "Professional Models in Journalism: Gatekeeper and Advocate." *Journalism Quarterly* 52 (4): 618.

42. See, for example, the Committee to Protect Journalists. 2007. *Attacks on the Press in 2007.* http://www.cpj.org/; Reporters without Borders. *Press Freedom Barometer, 2007.* http://www.rsf.org/article.php3?id_article=24909.

43. Mark Deuze. 2002. "National News Cultures: A Comparison of Dutch, German, British, Australian and U.S. Journalists." *Journalism & Mass Communication Quarterly* 79 (1): 134–49; Thomas Hanitzsch. 2007. "Deconstructing Journalism Culture: Towards a Universal Theory." *Communication Theory* 17 (4): 367–85. See also the World of Journalism project, http://www.worldofjournalism.org.

44. Andrew Puddephatt. 2007. *Defining Indicators of Media Development: Background Paper.* Paris: UNESCO. http://portal.unesco.org/ci/en/ev.php-URL_ID=24288&URL_DO= DO_TOPIC&URL_SECTION=201.html.

# Diagnostic Tools and Performance Indicators

Andrew Puddephatt

This chapter considers recent progress in developing diagnostic tools and performance indicators to assess how the media can contribute to democracy and development. A major concern of donor agencies is to understand where to concentrate their investment in media development—and then to assess the impact of that investment. Any attempt to answer those concerns has to start from an understanding of the actual media environment in any given country and of how that media environment supports democratic institutions and human development. Many systems exist for assessing this baseline. This chapter focuses particularly on a diagnostic tool that was recently developed for the United Nations Educational, Scientific, and Cultural Organization (UNESCO).[1] The UNESCO Media Development Indicators project reviewed existing assessment systems and generated a new, composite approach to analyzing the media's role that functions as an organizing framework rather than as a prescriptive checklist. This chapter considers how the UNESCO diagnostic tool could be used to identify focused performance indicators that can assess the impact of specific media programs.

The context for this work is the growing concern among donors regarding the general need to assess the impact of their funding. Identifying performance indicators for media development represents a major challenge. Though protection of freedom of expression has long been a precondition for much international development assistance from donors, free speech and communications have until now been at the periphery of development programs.[2] The situation changed somewhat at the advent of the 21st century, with an increasing recognition of the role that independent and healthy media play in promoting good governance and fighting corruption. In parallel, there was a growing consensus that country ownership of development programs was essential and that direct budget support was the most appropriate means of achieving this. Many believe, however, that aid delivered in this way will be effective only if public funds are used effectively and transparently by recipient governments. Democratic and inclusive media are keys to this. Post–September 11, a democratic media have been seen as a weapon in fighting extremism and terrorism. In addition, the potential for new communication and information technologies to connect poor and peripheral areas has received increased recognition.[3]

Much of the support for freedom of expression focuses on traditional press freedoms, centering on journalist training and advocacy against censorship and biased media. Donors also support programs that aim to increase access to, and use of, communication technologies, yet these tend to be framed as economic and social development projects, and they are rarely integrated with human rights and media programs.[4] Estimates put the total amount spent on media assistance programs by donors and funders outside of the United States at US$1 billion a year.[5] An additional US$142 million is spent annually by the United States.[6] There is therefore a pressing need for indicators to assess the effectiveness of this spending. Any such assessment should include a policy discussion that considers the basis for the belief that the ever-evolving media can support democracy and development, as well as include an analysis of the sociopolitical context in which the programs are being conducted, because the assumptions behind these factors are frequently not considered.

## The Link between Media, Democracy, and Development: A Brief Review of the Dominant Debates

Freedom of expression is a core aspiration of the United Nations' 1948 Universal Declaration of Human Rights and is widely seen as underpinning democratic freedoms, such as the right to form political parties, the exchange of political ideas, the questioning of public officials, and so on. Media outlets are crucial to the exercise of freedom of expression because they provide the public platform through which this right is effectively exercised. The idea of media as a platform for democratic debate embraces a wide variety of overlapping media functions.[7] This concept is explored elsewhere in this book, particularly in the introduction and in the specific regional case studies of the role of the media as watchdog, agenda setter, and gatekeeper in coverage of politics and elections. Of course, the media are widely recognized as an essential constituent of the democratic process and as one of the guarantors of free and fair elections. But beyond this, media outlets are channels through which citizens can communicate with each other, acting as a facilitator of informed debate between diverse social actors and encouraging the nonviolent resolution of disputes. The media disseminate stories, ideas, and information and act as a corrective to the "natural asymmetry of information" between governors and governed and between competing private agents.[8] The media can also function as a watchdog, promoting government transparency and public scrutiny of those with power—by exposing corruption, maladministration, and corporate wrongdoing—and thereby be a tool to enhance economic efficiency. The media can be a national voice, a means by which a society or a country can learn about itself and build a sense of community and of shared values, a vehicle for cultural expression and cultural cohesion within nation-states. Finally, it should never be forgotten that the media can function as advocates of certain issues or causes—as social actors in their own right.

The media may potentially fulfill any or all of these functions—or none of them. In some contexts, the media may reinforce the power of vested interests and exacerbate social inequalities by excluding critical or marginalized voices. In more established democracies, the role of the media has come under attack from those who believe its members are undermining democracy through the trivial, antagonistic, and personalized nature of their coverage.[9] At their most extreme, the media can also promote conflict and social divisiveness, particularly in a pluralistic society.[10] The nurturing of a media framework and practice that promote good governance and human development, rather than their opposite, is a particularly acute concern in new or restored democracies, whose media systems have been warped or shattered by totalitarianism, oppression, corruption, or the effects of war and underdevelopment.

What standards are necessary to deliver media freedom? In the past, many liberal advocates have argued for minimal state interference in the media as the necessary condition for an environment that can support democracy. This argument has particular currency in the United States, with its First Amendment statement that "Congress shall make no law … abridging freedom of speech or the press."[11] Others have argued that the construction of a modern media environment capable of supporting democracy and good governance may require a proactive role by the state—in providing infrastructure, funding a public broadcaster, and ensuring the right kind of regulatory environment. Norris and Zinnbauer argue that independent journalism, as a potential check on the abuse of power, is a necessary but not sufficient means of strengthening good governance and promoting human development. They suggest that these goals are achieved most effectively under two further conditions: first, in societies where channels of mass communications are free and independent of established interests, and second, where there is widespread access to these media.

UNESCO's approach to developing indicators took as its starting point the idea that any attempt to measure media development must embrace issues of both independence and access, as well as the absence of restrictions on the media. What matters is the extent to which all sectors of society can access the media to gain information and make their voices heard, especially those who are most disadvantaged or marginalized. Limited access to, or lack of engagement with, the media is a function of poverty and poor education. It may also be caused or exacerbated by language, gender, age, ethnicity, or the urban-rural divide. Whatever the cause, limited access to the media contributes to an environment that can undermine democratic development.

From UNESCO's perspective, the mere absence of state intervention on its own is no guarantee of a media environment that promotes freedom of expression and democracy. On the contrary, to promote a media system characterized by pluralism and diversity may require active state intervention. For example, to guarantee pluralism may require appropriate regulations of public broadcasting, commercial media, and community-based media. In an increasingly converged communications environment, the underpinning regulatory structure will be crucial in shaping private investment. If the regulatory authority does not insist upon interoperability in telecommunications providers, the ability of the data-ready mobile phone to provide widely available content (an increasing trend in Africa) will be inhibited. The state can play a crucial role by investing in human resources, specifically in building the professional capacity of media workers, both journalists and media managers, through academic and vocational training, on-the-job training, and the development of professional associations.

Infrastructure capacity is also crucial. Promoting a diverse media environment requires money to support the means of communication, including broadcast reception quality, the provision of electricity supplies, and access to telephones and the Internet. In many parts of the world there is little or no access to the means of communication—in such environments, formal freedoms mean little.

Defining the necessary media landscape in such a broad fashion is politically controversial, particularly within UNESCO. Fierce debates have been, and continue to be, conducted about whether the state has an appropriate positive role in securing a supportive media environment. Within UNESCO itself, the attempt to develop new international standards that would redefine freedom of expression in the form of a right to communicate caused a substantial split in the organization during the early 1980s. The United States and the United Kingdom, believing that a new standard would legitimize oppressive state interference in the media, left UNESCO for a period. The repercussions from that debate continue to this day, although few doubt that the state must play a role in developing infrastructure and appropriate regulation.[12]

Finally, any analysis of the media's contribution to human development must also be within the context of rapid and far-reaching changes in the platforms for communication.[13] In particular, the traditional media model of "one-to-many" is increasingly being challenged by a more interactive form of media in which conventional news commentary is supplemented and often challenged by blogs and comment of all kinds. It is noteworthy that in such countries such as Iran, where the traditional media are tightly controlled, interactive blogging has become an important tool of communication, with Farsi now one of the top 10 languages most commonly used in blogs.[14] The rapid growth of new technologies (Internet, cell phone Short Message Service [SMS], and mobile telephony) presents positive opportunities for democratization but also poses challenges in the form of fragmentation and potentially decreased opportunities for dissemination. The potential of the cellular mobile phone to emerge as the dominant platform for delivering content, particularly in the developing world, is being increasingly noticed. Assessment tools, if they are to be meaningful, must incorporate these new communications platforms, and embrace the dynamism and adaptability of the media sector itself.

## Existing Initiatives to Define Indicators of Media Development

In 2006 UNESCO commissioned an analysis of existing initiatives that seek to define indicators of media development.[15] The subsequent analysis of 26 sets of indicators by different agencies (tabulated in table 2.2) revealed a patchwork of overlapping, and at times contradictory, sets of indicators. Some were informed by different ideological values. Some prioritized different issues or sectors. Some emanated from different institutional cultures and were geared to a wide variety of purposes, including lobbying, policy guidance, and accreditation. They employed a wide variety of methodologies.

Within this variegated landscape, several types of indicators were used. Some related to any given country's national media system or to national media systems within a specific region. Others concerned specific issues (for example, violence against journalists) or particular sectors (for example, information and communication technology, or ICT), or had as their sole aim to disaggregate macro data according to particular criteria (for example, gender). Some indicators related to media development at the level of specific media assistance projects or media organizations, and others showed the correlation between media development and another key variable, such as governance.

In summary, different indicators had been designed for, and were used for, different purposes. Comparing assessment tools is rarely, if ever, comparing like things, making general conclusions difficult to draw. The danger is that policy makers select those indicator systems that fit their own preexisting hypotheses. By aggregating all of the existing indicator systems, UNESCO attempted to produce a global set that the whole donor community could draw upon.

### Existing Initiatives that Were Included in the UNESCO Mapping Exercise
A wide variety of charters, declarations of principles, and general commentaries and surveys relate to media development and freedom of the media. The

UNESCO exercise focused on those initiatives that were concerned with *measurable indicators,* whether qualitative or quantitative. The survey examined 26 different initiatives, listed in table 2.2 with identifying acronyms. Within this crowded landscape, the two most frequently cited sets of indicators were the Media Sustainability Index (MSI), published by the International Research and Exchanges Board (IREX), and the annual *Freedom of the Press* survey published by Freedom House.

### Table 2.1. Key Indicators of Media Performance

1. Freedom of expression is guaranteed in law and respected in practice.
   - National law or constitutional guarantee on freedom of expression.
   - Country has signed and ratified relevant treaty obligations, with no significant exemptions.
   - Public is aware of and exercises its right to free expression, and there are tools and bodies that guarantee the concrete application of this right.

   *Means of verification*
   - Any law or policy on the right to free expression that accords with international standards and accepted international practice.
   - Reports from credible agencies about freedom of expression.
   - Reports in national media about freedom of expression issues.
   - Legal cases concerning freedom of expression.
   - Evidence of an independent and functioning judicial system with clear rights of appeal.

2. The right to information is guaranteed in law and respected in practice.
   - National law or constitutional guarantee on the right to information.
   - Country has signed and ratified relevant treaty obligations, with no significant exemptions.
   - Public is aware of and exercises right to access official information.
   - Public bodies release information both proactively and on demand.
   - Effective and efficient appeals mechanism through an independent administrative body, for example, an information commissioner or ombudsman.
   - Any restriction on grounds of protection of personal privacy is narrowly defined so as to exclude information in which there is no legitimate public interest.

   *Means of verification*
   - Any law or policy on the right to information that accords with international standards.
   - Reports from credible agencies about right-to-information guarantees.
   - Policies of public bodies concerning release of information.
   - Evidence of state commitment to open government, for example, publication and dissemination of court decisions, parliamentary proceedings, and spending programs.
   - Statistical information about public requests for official information and their fulfillment or rejection.
   - Statistical information about appeals or complaints over information requests that have been refused.

3. Editorial independence is guaranteed in law and respected in practice.
   - Broadcasters are not required to allocate broadcasting time to, or carry specific broadcasts on behalf of, the government (aside from obligatory direct-access political broadcasts during elections).
   - Government, regulatory bodies, or commercial interests do not influence, or seek to influence, editorial content of broadcasters or press.
   - Law does not allow state actors to seize control of broadcasters in an emergency.

   *Means of verification*
   - Any law or policy on editorial independence that accords with international standards.
   - Evidence of interference in editorial decision making by state or private actors.
   - Reports by credible agencies about editorial independence issues.

**Table 2.1. Continued**

4. Journalists' right to protect their sources is guaranteed in law and respected in practice.
   - Journalists can protect confidentiality of their sources without fear of prosecution or harassment.

   *Means of verification*
   - Documented cases of journalists being forced to disclose sources.
   - Any legal guarantee concerning confidentiality of sources that accords with international standards.
   - Evidence of media organizations or professional associations actively defending right to protect sources.

5. The public and civil society organizations (CSOs) participate in shaping public policy toward the media.
   - State creates genuine opportunities for consultation with nonstate actors about legislation and public policy toward the media.

   *Means of verification*
   - Evidence of government commitment to work with civil society to develop law and policy on the media (for example, conferences, seminars, public forums, and official engagement in debates on the airwaves or in print).

*Source:* Intergovernmental Council of the International Programme for the Development of Communication (IPDC), 26th Session, "Media Development Indicators: A Framework for Assessing Media Development," UNESCO, March 26–28, 2008.

The IREX Media Sustainability Index has been incorporated into U.S. Agency for International Development evaluation schema for several countries and has been accepted as one of the World Bank's governance indicators.[16] The U.K. Department for International Development (DFID) also suggests its use in measuring the success of media systems.[17] Freedom House publishes the *Freedom of the Press* survey, and its findings are widely used by governments, international organizations, academics, and the news media in many countries. This source is adopted by Norris and Zinnbauer for their UNDP Human Development Report *Giving Voice to the Voiceless* and by the UNESCO-CPHS research project on press freedom and poverty.[18]

## Summary of Existing Indicators and Methodologies

The paper prepared for UNESCO, *Defining Indicators for Media Development,* summarizes all the initiatives concerning media development listed above, including the indicators and the methodologies used.[19] The analysis selected 15 of those initiatives (including the most prominent) and clustered the existing indicators into 25 main categories (for example, editorial independence, censorship, access to printing and distribution, and public broadcasting). These are summarized in table 2.2, which shows at a glance which categories are covered by the selected initiatives. The project demonstrated that the existing assessment tools adopt a wide range of categories, which coincide only sporadically. Most of these indicators are assessed by means of subjective processes—the aggregated opinions of groups of experts—so exact correlations are difficult to make. Nevertheless, it seems clear that common indicators can produce divergent results, depending on the methodology used.

## Table 2.2-A. Performance Indicator Agencies and Sources

| Acronym | Source of indicators |
| --- | --- |
| AMB | Media Institute of Southern Africa: African Media Barometer |
| AMDI | BBC World Service Trust: *African Media Development Initiative* |
| Bridges | bridges.org: *Comparison of E-readiness Assessment Models* |
| CPJ | Committee to Protect Journalists: *Journalists Killed Statistics* |
| DANIDA | Danish Development Agency: *Monitoring and Indicators for Communication for Development* |
| DFID | UK Department for International Development: *Monitoring and Evaluating Information and Communication for Development Programs* |
| DOI | International Telecommunication Union: *Digital Opportunity Index* |
| EFJ | European Federation of Journalists: Questionnaire on Quality in Journalism |
| FH | Freedom House: *Freedom of the Press survey* |
| GFMD | Global Forum for Media Development: *Media Matters: Perspectives on Advancing Governance and Development* |
| ISAS Press | Quality Management Systems: *Requirements for the Press* |
| ISAS RTV | Giving Voice to the Voiceless: Quality Management Systems: *Requirements for Broadcasters/Internet* |
| MMI WB Gov | Money Matters Institute: Wealth of Nations Triangle Index World Bank: *Governance Matters IV* |
| MSI | International Research and Exchanges Board: *Media Sustainability Index* |
| RSF | Reporters without Borders: *Worldwide Press Freedom Index* |
| TI | Transparency International: *National Integrity System* |
| UNESCO News | *Questionnaire on Newspaper Statistics* |
| UNESCO Pov | *Press Freedom and Poverty: An Analysis of the Correlations* |
| UNESCO RTV | *Questionnaire on Radio and Television Broadcasting Statistics* |
| UNDP | United Nations Development Programme: *Giving Voice to the Voiceless* (by Pippa Norris; Cambridge, MA: Harvard University) |
| UNDP OGC (BiH) | UNDP Oslo Governance Centre: *Supporting Public Service Broadcasting: Learning from Bosnia and Herzegovina's Experience* |
| UNDPOGC (Emp) | UNDP Oslo Governance Centre: *Communication for Empowerment: Developing Media Strategies in Support of Vulnerable Groups* |
| UNDPOGC (Info) | UNDP Oslo Governance Centre: *Guide to Measuring the Impact of Right to Information Programs* |
| WB Dev | World Bank: World Development Indicators |
| WB Gender | World Bank: *Engendering ICT Toolkit* |
| WB Gov | World Bank Institute: *Governance Matters IV* |

*Source:* Intergovernmental Council of the International Programme for the Development of Communication (IPDC), 26th Session, "Media Development Indicators: A Framework for Assessing Media Development," UNESCO, March 26–28, 2008.

**Table 2.2-B.  Dimensions of Media Performance**

| Category of indicator | MSI | ISAS RTV | ISAS Press | FH | AMDI | UNDP Info | UNDP Emp | UNESCO News | UNESCO RTV | CPJ | RSF | EFJ | TI | AMB | ITU |
|---|---|---|---|---|---|---|---|---|---|---|---|---|---|---|---|
| Freedom-of-speech guarantees | • | | • | • | | | • | | | | • | | • | • | |
| Right-to-information guarantees | • | | | • | | | | | | | • | | • | • | |
| Editorial independence guarantees | • | • | • | • | | | | | | | • | | • | • | |
| Censorship/jamming | • | | | • | | | • | | | | • | | • | • | • |
| Defamation laws, legal restrictions on media | • | | | • | | • | | | • | | | • | | | |
| Market entry, licensing, & tax structure | • | | | | | | | | | | | | | | |
| Access to printing & distribution facilities | • | | | | | | • | | | | | | | | |
| Public service broadcasting model | • | | | • | | | | | | | | | | | |
| Regulatory regime | • | | • | • | | | • | • | • | | • | | • | • | |
| Citizens' access to media unrestricted | • | | | | | | | | | | | | | • | |
| Plurality and transparency of ownership | • | | • | • | | | | | | | | | | | |
| Plurality of news sources: state, private, community balance | • | | • | • | | | • | • | • | | | | • | • | |
| Self-regulation: ethical standards, editorial guidelines, no self-censorship | • | • | • | • | | | • | | | | • | • | | | |
| Media reflect diversity of society & promote minority & social content | • | | • | | | | • | • | • | | | | | | |
| Quality of reporting: fairness, objectivity, accuracy, sourcing | • | | | | | | • | | | | | | | | |
| Quality of technical production facilities | • | | | | | | • | | | | | | | | |
| Violence/harassment against journalists | • | | | • | | | | | | • | • | | • | | |
| Access to journalism & status of profession | • | | | • | | | | | | | • | | | | |
| Commercial pressures: competitive advertising market & advertising separate from content | • | | | • | | | • | | | | • | | • | | |
| Supporting institutions: trade unions, professional associations, NGOs | • | | | | | • | • | | | | | • | | • | |
| Availability of quality journalism training (academic/vocational) | | | | | | | | | | | | • | | | |
| Trust/satisfaction in the media: audience & wider public | | • | | • | | | • | | | | | | | | |
| Media penetration: per capita coverage of various media | | | | | | • | • | • | • | | | | | | • |
| Gender indicators: access & usage of media, portrayal of women, women in the industry | | | | | | | • | • | • | | | | | • | |
| Overall integrity of media system, extent of corruption | • | | | • | | | | | | | | | | | |

*Source:* Intergovernmental Council of the International Programme for the Development of Communication (IPDC), 26th Session, "Media Development Indicators: A Framework for Assessing Media Development," UNESCO, March 26–28, 2008.

It seems sensible therefore to assess these initiatives relative to their diverse objectives. That is to say, a tool designed to generate data for lobbying purposes cannot properly be judged by the criteria of a tool aimed at providing a robust scientific measurement of media development. Any attempt to compare the different approaches set out in table 2.2 would be difficult, as like initiatives are not being compared.

## Approaches to Developing Indicators

In considering how to develop indicators, UNESCO could have taken one of three approaches. The first would have been to adopt a longitudinal analysis that compares media development over time in each country. The second would have been a comparative analysis that compares individual countries. The drawback of these first two is that genuine comparisons can often be difficult to make. How can one compare a country with limited infrastructure and weak economic development with a rich country in the Organisation for Economic Co-operation and Development with a long history of democratic freedoms and transparency? How much weight should be given to political and cultural factors, such as the different approach to public broadcasters adopted by different methodologies, or the different cultural and religious views about explicit sexuality? Low technical capacity may coexist with a positive legal and policy framework, as in Mali.[20] Elsewhere, media may evolve into a driver for greater openness even in an adverse political environment, as in Ghana. The resulting comparisons are often fiercely contested, or are inconsistent with each other and lead inevitably to the governments of evaluated states being reluctant to engage in a debate about areas of weakness that are being highlighted. This is an important consideration for international bodies, such as UNESCO, whose policies are set directly by member states.

The third approach involves a toolkit, by setting out a series of indicators but allowing the assessor to select those most appropriate to the environment. The toolkit has the advantage that it can be treated as a diagnostic tool without implying any comparison with other countries. It may therefore be easier to engage countries in a debate about identified weaknesses or gaps. Equally important, if the selection of indicators from the toolkit is not impartial, it risks giving a distorted view of media development. The process by which the toolkit is used therefore becomes vital.

For UNESCO's purposes, the most useful examination of initiatives coalesced around this toolkit approach. This is because such an approach offers an inclusive list of indicators and methods from which selections can be made according to the requirements of a particular program or intervention. The toolkit also offers guidance as to how the selection can be made, recognizing that indicators and methodologies must be customized, using local expertise, to fit the particularities of the national context. Finally, it allows for some tailoring of the indicators to the correct level of engagement within each national context (for example, the national media system, the individual media organization, or the professional group).

Examples of the toolkit approach include UNDP's *Guide to Measuring the Impact of Right to Information Programs*[21] which provides an inclusive list of potential indicators and sets out guiding principles for selecting country-specific and appropriate indicators to assess focused interventions on the right to information. In addition, UNDP's *Communication for Development: Developing Media Strategies in Support of Vulnerable Groups* offers a comprehensive range of indicators relating to how the media serve and affect poorer groups in society.[22] The Danish International Development Agency (DANIDA)[23] and the U.K. Department for International Development (DFID)[24] offer guidance on identifying and developing indicators of media development and appropriate methodologies. In its *African Media Development Initiative* (AMDI),[25] the BBC World Service Trust customized indicators within each of the 17 countries surveyed. Indicators were customized both at the regional level (across the three "hubs" of East, West, and Southern Africa) and at the country level, by local media professionals and those with a sound grasp of the methodological challenges.

## Challenges Presented by Existing Initiatives

In analyzing the existing indexes that measure media development, UNESCO considered that the indexes offered an excellent starting point for defining indicators in line with the agency's own priorities and approached a consensus among member states on which the UNESCO process could build. However, the very diversity of existing initiatives gave rise to questions about the methodologies of the various approaches. To address these questions—which could be done while updating the methodologies over time—UNESCO's own system of indicators built on five areas that needed further consideration.

### Different Value Systems

Competing approaches to measuring media development rest on different ideological assumptions, even though most approaches claim to offer universal criteria. Even established democracies do not interpret press freedom in the same way. For example, the Media Sustainability Index describes nonstate-owned media as independent, rather than commercial or privately owned. The choice of terminology reflects the fact that in the United States, the market is seen as the prime guarantor of media independence, whereas Western European countries attach greater importance to state-regulated public service broadcasting models. Yet these differences should not be overstated. For example, there is substantial agreement around the freedom-of-expression guarantees enshrined in the main international legal instruments. However, the embedded values that inform the various media assessment tools still need to be interrogated and made explicit.

## Perceived Bias

The dominant indexes of media development have been developed by U.S.–based organizations. Concerns that the underlying approach is overinfluenced by a U.S. experience of media, which is not typical in the world, have led to accusations of bias and in turn have spurred the development of alternative indexes within the developing world, such as the African Media Barometer, based on the principle of self-assessment by African nationals.

In addition, global indicators of media development drawn up in the West have been perceived as lacking the degree of customization required to reflect the local media environment in which they are being applied. For example, indicators relating to the development of community media would be expected to specify whether they relate only to licensed or also to unlicensed media; whether they include community media partly funded by the state, advertising, or private interests; and so on. It was clear in the subsequent UNESCO debate about their indicators that, although many people assumed community media were not-for-profit, the U.S. government and NGOs took a different view, which complicates the understanding of community media. Indicators would also be expected to embrace the different ways in which a community can give its mandate to a media outlet, for example, the holding of public hearings to award community radio licenses. Another obvious example is differences in the treatment of hate speech; its legal treatment in the international human rights system is quite different from that in the United States. Interpretation of acceptable restrictions on hate speech will inevitably vary depending on those drawing up the indicators.

## Imprecise Indicators and Inconsistent Results

Any attempt to measure media development requires clear and unambiguous indicators. Clarity is lost if the indicators blur the distinction between different units of analysis, fail to separate out different levels of engagement within a country, or bundle together several elements in one category. For example, the Media Sustainability Index requires that "citizens' access to domestic or international media is not restricted." A midrange score on this indicator could be interpreted as meaning that citizens have partly restricted access to both types of media, or have good access to one and severely restricted access to the other. Indexes that rank countries annually make it possible to track macrolevel changes over time. However, the comparative results they produce are sometimes inconsistent. For example, 11 of the 57 countries classified as "most free" by the Reporters without Borders (Reporters san Frontières—RSF) index are categorized as only "partly free" by Freedom House. To take another example, five Middle Eastern and North African countries categorized as "near sustainability" by the MSI are classified as "not free" by Freedom House; the Palestinian Territories are, according to the MSI, "near sustainability" yet are second to the bottom in the Freedom House scale, just above Libya.

## Lack of Data and Subjectivity

All attempts to measure media development are faced with the problem of lack of data sources. For many indicators in many countries, data either do not exist or are inaccessible, out of date, inconsistent, or a combination of all of these. By far the best data are expensive to access and are produced for commercial purposes or as a means of generating income. For newspaper readership the World Association of Newspapers produces up-to-date data, but such data are expensive to purchase. UNESCO produces free data and has released new data this year covering various broadcast and newspaper indicators. However, the data are still old, collected between 2004 and 2005 (the previous data went back to 1997). The International Telecommunication Union (ITU) provides some free data, but access to its database requires payment. The World Development Indicators, published annually by the World Bank, are a good compilation of data, including radios and televisions per 100 people, although that is only a rough estimation of broadcast penetration. Again, the downside is that payment is required. Currently the Swedish development agency Sida is commissioning work to fund the creation of useful data sources and to identify how these problems might be tackled.

The usual response has been to devise methodologies that assemble panels of media or other professionals to rate countries on the basis of qualitative assessment. An example of this approach is the African Media Barometer, developed by the Media Institute of Southern Africa to assess media development in Sub-Saharan Africa. However, this methodology carries the evident risk that even the most experienced of panels will produce results colored by their members' personal experience. For example, in the African Media Barometer, the assessment of Swaziland for the indicator "private media outlets operate as efficient and professional businesses" produces individual scores ranging from 5 ("meets all aspects of the indicator and has been doing so over time") to 1 ("does not meet the indicator"). This wide spectrum of views makes the resulting average hard to interpret definitively, however valuable the qualitative debate that underpinned the scoring.

## Absence of New Communications Platforms

Many of the media development assessment tools currently employed do not include indicators relating specifically to new communications platforms, such as the Internet, SMS, and mobile telephony. This may be a deliberate choice in some contexts. However, the mobile phone is emerging as a key platform in a world of digital convergence, either because of the phones themselves or through related wireless technologies. Least developed countries have experienced phenomenal growth rates in mobile telephony: according to the ITU, 58 percent of mobile subscribers are now based in the developing world.[26] Internet access in the developing world remains low—at just 13 percent of the world's total, according to the ITU. However, Internet penetration is growing as a result of the expansion of broadband, and mobile phones could emerge as a key platform for accessing the Internet as progress is made in the development of wireless technologies.

Initiatives to measure media development should therefore consider including indicators specifically relating to the accessibility and use of new communications platforms, especially in parts of the developing world where these technologies are gaining recognition as a driving force in social and economic development. Indicators could measure more than just the potential consumers of new communications platforms; indicators should be developed to measure the extent to which media organizations and professionals have the freedom and the capacity to use multiplatform technologies to deliver information or to engage with their audiences.

## Measuring the Correlation between Media and Development

The UNDP study by Norris and Zinnbauer (2002) found a close correlation between widespread media access and an independent free press and between systematic indicators of good governance and human development. However, Davis observes that "we are presently unable to measure and determine objectively media's influence within societies and specifically its relationship to governance and overall development, country to country."[27] Davis proposes the development of a media-governance index that directly relates to the six dimensions of governance as defined by the World Bank. Such an index would be capable of measuring negative as well as positive impacts of media activity, in areas where media behavior is working against governance or even promoting conflict. Unfortunately, no further work has proceeded along these lines, even though, as Davis notes, it could be designed as a sectoral initiative to complement and even build on existing indexes, such as the Media Sustainability Index.

## UNESCO's Approach

Having decided to develop its own system of indicators, UNESCO built upon the analysis of existing systems while aiming to avoid some of the pitfalls identified previously in this chapter.[28] Following its review of the indicators and of the relevant literature discussing the media's impact on democracy and governance, UNESCO identified five principal categories of media indicators to be developed.

## Overarching Media Indicators

The five categories of indicators used in the UNESCO project provide an organizing framework that can be adapted to the needs of media development
initiatives in any given national context, rather than a prescriptive straitjacket
that cannot adapt to circumstances. The assumption behind this approach is
that to have a media environment that is supportive of democracy and good
governance, all five categories must be positive.

*Category 1: a system of regulation and control conducive to freedom of expres-
sion, pluralism, and diversity of the media.* A legal, policy, and regulatory
framework protects and promotes freedom of expression and information,
based on international best practice standards and developed in participation
with civil society.

*Category 2: plurality and diversity of media, a level economic playing field,
and transparency of ownership.* The state actively promotes the development
of the media sector in a manner that prevents undue concentration of ownership and ensures plurality and transparency of ownership and content across
public, private, and community media.

*Category 3: media as a platform for democratic discourse.* The media, within
a prevailing climate of self-regulation and respect for the journalistic profession, reflect and represent the diversity of views and interests in society,
including those of marginalized groups. There is a high level of information
and media literacy.

*Category 4: professional capacity building and supporting institutions that
underpin freedom of expression, pluralism, and diversity.* Media workers have
access to professional training and development, both vocational and academic, at all stages of their careers, and the media sector as a whole is both
monitored and supported by professional associations and civil society
organizations.

*Category 5: infrastructural capacity that is sufficient to support independent
and pluralistic media.* The media sector is characterized by high or rising levels
of public access, including among marginalized groups, and efficient use of
technology to gather and distribute news and information appropriate to the
local context.

The UNESCO approach assumes that the five categories are taken together
to create a holistic picture of the media environment. No one category is
therefore more important than the other, and each is considered to be fundamental. Inevitably the indicators taken as a whole are an aspirational picture, but an analysis based on these categories will enable the construction of
a comprehensive map of the media environment.

The selection of categories across the existing initiatives aimed to capture
and build on the consensus about how the media can best contribute to, and
benefit from, good governance and democratic development. The proposed

framework was geared to assessing media development at the national level, not at the level of the individual media organization. Nor does it apply to the work of individual media development NGOs or organizations. Following the toolkit approach, this UNESCO methodology therefore offers an inclusive list of indicators from which selections can be made according to specific requirements. The structure can be conceptualized as a process of working down from the desired media development outcome to the specific means of verifying the extent to which this outcome is achieved in practice.

This approach is structured around the five principal categories of media development indicators, with each category subdivided into a number of issues. Researchers evaluating a media environment would begin by examining the context and main issues for each category and outlining the range of key indicators. From these headline indicators they could identify a set of subindicators to flesh out the detail of the headline indicator in concrete terms. For each subindicator, the researcher could draw on various means of verification, which are set out in the UNESCO Media Development Indicators framework. The framework also presents a guide to data sources that are available at an international level for each overall category. Though not exhaustive, this guides the evaluator toward available online and offline sources that can be supplemented by national-level data, as well as data available in local languages. As a working example, the indicators for each category are set out in table 2.1.

**Response to the Indicators**

UNESCO adopted its media development approach at a meeting of the International Program for the Development of Communication (IPDC) Committee on March 31, 2008. Subsequently UNESCO and UNDP agreed to test the usefulness of the approach by applying the indicators to up to five countries. UNESCO and UNDP are aware that the ability of the evaluators to select the most relevant categories and indicators is a critical factor in the use of this organizing framework. They have delegated the assessment to a team of local researchers; the assessment itself will also be subjected to a central process of quality control.

A number of other observations were made in the UNESCO-sponsored discussion on adoption of standards. Some UNESCO staff argued that the toolkit approach might undermine the "normative" role of UNESCO in terms of standard setting. It was suggested that UNESCO consider benchmarking countries against a minimum or optimum set of core indicators derived from the approach. At the official level, UNESCO members were lukewarm about this option, considering that it would create political difficulties in an international governmental organization. They preferred a diagnostic tool specific to an environment rather than a comparative tool dependent upon subjective judgments and inadequate data. Independent experts observed that subjective and qualitative indicators are still present in the UNESCO approach. The nature of media is such that judgments of quality are very subjective, whether it is the quality of a journalists' syndicate or the quality of journalism. In such circumstances there can be no agreed-upon objective approach. Additionally, many aspects of a media system do not lend themselves to quantitative measurement. Finally, even where data that can be measured quantitatively exists, it is very uneven across countries. These latter concerns remain, whatever system of assessment is used.

### General Remarks

The UNESCO document represents the outcome of a long period of discussion by representatives of governments within UNESCO itself as well as with independent experts. Inevitably it resembles something designed by a committee, rather than the outcome of a single coherent vision. For policy makers, this is a consequence of seeking a methodology that can find support among a range of organizations, be they bilateral or multilateral donors or implementing organizations. Evaluation systems that are used in the real world will always reflect the compromises of political imperatives (and, frequently, professional jealousies). Whether such a system achieves any kind of coherent analysis depends principally upon its implementation.

The indicators themselves range across the structure of the media, such as the system of regulation and ownership; through the content—whether the media are a platform for public discourse; to questions of capacity—the degree of professional training or ICT access available. Each of these, taken in isolation, will give no clue as to the impact of the media on society as a whole. The indicators were designed not as a specific method of analysis but to be part of a toolkit, to be drawn upon and synthesized in a way appropriate to a particular country. Some observers might prefer a more defined method, one less open to interpretation. The problem with such approaches is that they fall into the problems of data and consistency set out above—how can a system of assessment be appropriate to all types of societies in all possible circumstances? To attempt to define such a system simply invites a different set of errors.

The interest within UNESCO and UNDP is to find a set of indicators that will enable a comprehensive analysis of a current media situation, identify the main gaps to be addressed by donors, and indicate the direction reforms should take in order to foster an enabling environment for free, pluralistic, and independent media. They will be tested in a series of pilot studies to measure their effectiveness.

## From Media Indicators to Performance Indicators

The media indicators project for UNESCO has produced a diagnostic tool for examining the particular media landscape and how it supports, or fails to support, democracy. It is not designed to compare countries and can therefore be used by international agencies, which otherwise would encounter criticism if they were perceived to be engaging in politicized comparisons. UNESCO's approach can be thought of as a diagnostic tool that can identify where change to the media environment is most needed to promote democracy and, in turn, where active donor intervention is likely to have the most significant impact. It is likely to be of most value in guiding donor or implementer interventions. But the tool does not provide a methodology to assess specific media projects as a set of performance indicators would. To assess the impact of specific media programs or activities an additional stage is required.

There are two ways to approach developing performance indicators. The first is to assess the impact of donor programs themselves. Donors have invested a considerable amount of public and private money in media development over the past 15 years, although many donors are uneasy about what has been achieved with this support. There is growing interest, particularly among government donors, in looking for a means to assess the overall impact of their spending over time. This interest is made more urgent by growing concerns among domestic public opinion in donor countries about the effectiveness of aid. The second approach in considering performance indicators is at the individual project level, focusing on the performance of implementing organizations—usually NGOs, but increasingly, private companies—to see how their own assessment of their work can be made consistent with the macrolevel approach adopted by UNESCO.

## Existing Donor Activities

Despite increasing recognition of their importance, media initiatives still do not receive enough attention and resources within development programs. Approaches are too often fragmented and lack a strategy and long-term perspective. Deane suggests a number of reasons for this.[29] In a bid to increase effectiveness and country ownership of development programs, many donor organizations' decisions about funding are being decentralized to the regional and country levels, leaving programs that support democracy and freedom of expression fragmented, inconsistent, and nonstrategic. The donor trend of providing increasing amounts of aid directly to governments through budget support leaves donors unable to support the development of an independent, critical media, and governments have few direct incentives to support these programs themselves. When donors do fund media development, they are often accused by the governments of recipient countries of advancing their own policy agendas. In addition, donors too often conflate different forms of media support. In particular, three types of activities are often confused or grouped under the same media heading. One type of activity is fostering the media as an independent sphere for citizen communications that clearly supports democracy. A second activity, which should be clearly separated from the first, is public relations activity to build donor branding. Finally, there is a range of "communication for development" work that uses the media to encourage particular social practices (for example, to advance public health and combat HIV) but that sees the media as instrumental to a specific development goal.

Furthermore, media development programs often encourage competition among local organizations for funds, undermining the collaboration and cooperation needed to develop an effective and coherent agenda for a unified but diverse public sphere. Limited cooperation among donors at the country level also currently undermines strategic and coherent intervention. There is insufficient ownership of free expression programs by local NGOs and media practitioners, including a lack of participation in the formation of media support strategies. Finally, an increasing emphasis on results and evaluation has often led to the prioritization of programs that yield purely quantitative indicators of success over short periods of time. However, many aspects of media development can be captured only by qualitative means. In general, the cacophony of voices that characterizes a healthy public sphere is difficult to capture and measure using current monitoring and evaluation tools.

Rights-based approaches to development are increasingly common, following Amartya Sen's conception of "development as freedom."[30] Nevertheless, donors rarely explicitly recognize the direct links between international obligations to protect freedom of expression and efforts to promote media development and democracy in their strategies and programming. Media development work is generally seen as a tool to achieve objectives, such as good governance, but rarely as a good in itself. The fundamental role that a healthy public sphere, hosted by an independent media, plays in protecting freedom of expression and other human rights is either assumed or overlooked. Either way, coherent and coordinated programs to foster lively and inclusive public debate, in accordance with an issue agenda that is locally owned and driven, are often lacking. All of this complicates any attempt to develop a robust system for assessing the impact of donor programs, as they will have to reflect vastly different sets of political imperatives.

## Assessing the Impact of Implementing Organizations

Most donors rely on independent organizations to implement their programs. Historically, this has been considered the province of formally constituted not-for-profit organizations. More recently, many donors have taken the view that contracts can be open to any type of organization, profit-seeking or not-for-profit, which should compete against each other on price and quality. Assuming the project is implemented through a contract, it is logical for the organization issuing the contract to set the performance indicators. These terms should be written into the contract and should specify what impact the media program should have and how it should be assessed. Frequently, of course, contracts are not this specific. The donor organization has a general idea of what it wishes to achieve, and the contractor is able to suggest different project activities that aim to achieve the goal. In such cases, in which the contractor defines the activities (or is an NGO seeking a grant), it is logically the contractor's responsibility to identify how it intends to assess the impact of its work. There is often a great deal of confusion about roles and responsibilities at this interface, which does not help develop a strong system of assessment.

## Assessing Implementers

Assessing the impact of an organization's work is not possible without addressing the different levels at which an organization works. Most not-for-profit organizations have an overall goal (sometimes known as the mission or purpose), which represents the philosophical view of the organization and is the expression of its core beliefs. In the field of media development, an organization's goal will reflect its own highest-level assumptions about the role of the media in society—for example, whether it is considered a channel through which citizens can communicate with each other, or a facilitator of informed debate between diverse social actors, or is intended to encourage the nonviolent resolution of disputes, act as a watchdog, or promote government transparency and public scrutiny of those with power by exposing corruption, maladministration, and corporate wrongdoing. Different organizations focus their work on different assumptions about the role of the media. These beliefs are a given in that they constitute the reason for the organization to exist in the first place and cannot be tested at the level of specific project activities.

The impact of the organization's efforts at this level can be measured only in broad terms, over time, by perceptible shifts in the media landscape, and then only if the organization's work can be sifted out from the contributions of others and from local contingent events. For donors, however, this level of analysis is highly relevant. If donors spend millions of U.S. dollars on the media environment in a particular country, and there is no perceptible shift in that environment, they are likely to conclude that there is little value in continuing, even if the projects they support are well run and achieve the immediate deliverable goals.

The second level of performance measurement consists of the organization's specific objectives, which, though supporting the goals of the organization, are a reflection of its organizational capacity and skills. An organization whose objective is to help the media further peace and help resolve conflict is likely to have a set of objectives that promote peace journalism or even strengthen the investigative journalistic skills that enable journalists to explore the background of a conflict. By contrast, an organization that believes that the legal and regulatory structure is crucial is likely to have objectives that advocate legal reform and will have developed the requisite in-house skills. The most common objectives in the media development field are the training of journalists—justified in a number of ways and often reflecting a rather nebulous belief that creating professional capacity among journalists and business managers will, in and of itself, strengthen the media's ability to contribute to democracy or good governance. Other media organizations provide media content for local newspapers, radios, or televisions—directly or in partnership with local actors. The significant emphasis on training over the past 15 years may derive from the fact that governments prefer to fund activities that can be easily audited, even if their effectiveness is hard to measure. Although the objectives will originally determine the organizational capacity and skills of the organization, in time the objectives may become fixed, even if their relevance has diminished.

At the level of objectives, the UNESCO media development indicators help by identifying whether the particular organizational capacities are relevant to the country in which they are being applied. For example, if the overall diagnosis identifies the legal and regulatory regime as the key problem in a society (a heavily censored, state-controlled media, for example), training journalists in investigatory techniques they will never have the professional opportunity to apply is less useful than measures that promote legal and regulatory reform. This may seem an obvious point, but it is surprising how many media development programs operate without regard to this wider context. A case in point is the European government donor that invests heavily in training Arab journalists in investigative techniques, as part of its counterterrorism program, when they will have little opportunity to practice these skills in a tightly censored, state-controlled, or Saudi Arabian–owned media. By contrast, there is no training offered in online, interactive, networked journalism, which is where the genuinely independent, and usually Islamist-dominated, discourse takes place.

Other organizations may have a specific regional objective—strengthening the media in West Africa or building communications skills in Brazil—and are likely to possess particular regional expertise. In these cases, their capacity is likely to be regional knowledge and expertise. But again, the objective should still be relevant to the diagnosis that comes from applying the UNESCO methodology.

The third level that can be distinguished are the program activities of the organization—the level at which projects are formulated and implemented. An example might be a project to build the capacity of Iraqi journalists to cover the forthcoming elections, a program to establish a media center in central Asia, or a program to promote investigative journalism in China by producing an online guide in English and Mandarin. These programs may be developed as grant applications or proposals made directly to donors, or may result from tenders issued by the donor agency. These activities are the organizing blocks of work, the subjects of proposals or contracts, and the key layer where attention on assessment tends to focus.

Finally, there are the specific deliverables of each organization: the training courses, seminars, and advocacy activities that make up the program activities of the organization concerned. These are the activities that can be monitored, observed, measured, and assessed and that provide the raw material for a more developed set of performance indicators.

It is important to separate out these levels conceptually in order to assess the performance of an organization. This should be a task for the management of the organization, which in all cases should lead the process of assessing performance. The rationale of performance assessment, after all, is to improve the operation of an organization, not to catch people out. It is essential, therefore, that just as UNESCO's indicators should be used as a diagnostic tool by local stakeholders (even if quality is controlled externally), so too should the performance indicators be owned and developed by the implementing organization itself, subject to some form of external validation. These performance indicators should be divided into three components: the congruence of the different levels, internal quality checks, and external verification.

*Congruence* is an ongoing process of assessing the degree to which each level correlates and fits with the other, and how the goals shape the objectives and in turn determine activities and finally deliverables. The most common weakness in an organization is that there is either no match between the deliverables on the ground and the higher-level organizational goals or no clear internal understanding of how they connect. More specifically, the organization must understand how the deliverables relate to the program activities. Are they a practical translation of what the program seeks to achieve? If successful, will they do what is hoped for? In turn, do the activities genuinely support the organization's objectives, and are they the right fit? Is there a match between the activities and objectives and the needs of the situation, as determined by the overall diagnosis of the media environment? Finally, is there a logistical match between the deliverables and the objectives? If the organization claims to be strengthening democracy by training journalists, is it a reasonable claim to make or does it need to be more specific?

The internal quality checks should focus on the deliverables and will likely vary from project to project. When a project is designed, the implementers should assess for themselves how effective the proposed deliverables are: what is the standard they are aiming for and how will they achieve this? A high-quality training organization will have a set of service standards that define a process for determining the standard of service to be achieved, the policy required to support this service, and the accompanying evidence demonstrating that the standard has been achieved. Though service standards are common where activities are externally regulated (such as with public service provision at the national level), the field of media development has relatively few standards to draw upon. Another source for quality control is relevant international standards. One example is the International Standards and

Accreditation Services (ISAS) standards for radio and television broadcasters, the Internet, and the print media, which provide individual media organizations with a methodology to improve their contribution to social development and to make their progress measurable and transparent.[31]

Finally, the external verification should assess how effective deliverables are in reality: on the ground, do they achieve objectives? This will require a sociopolitical analysis with reference back to the UNESCO diagnostic analysis of the particular environment and may involve qualitative measures—feedback from participants, interviews on the ground with stakeholders, and quantitative measures involving data analysis and assessment. One of the significant problems in this case is the lack of reliable, up-to-date, publicly available data on media environments globally.

## Conclusions

This chapter suggests that any approach to evaluating the media's contribution to democracy should be considered in two stages. The first stage involves using the UNESCO *Media Development Indicators* framework as a diagnostic tool to audit a country's media system, identify that system's deficiencies and weaknesses, and draw up a set of improvements that need to be made. After the media environment has been audited using UNESCO's indicators, donors or implementing organizations will find it much easier to identify priorities and appropriate actions. The second stage then evaluates the programs or actions that have been implemented under stage one.

The audit stage helps identify the priorities for providing interventions and supporting all agents, whether they are donors or implementing organizations. UNESCO's indicators provide media development researchers with a comprehensive toolkit for approaching this task, with five categories of indicators that, taken together, can provide the comprehensive means to assess the media environment of any country. The UNESCO framework, as a diagnostic tool, requires an analysis of all the indicators together, as it is possible for a country to be developed in some areas and underdeveloped in others. Therefore, each country analysis will be unique. The framework does not provide a means of ranking countries against each other; rather, its purpose is to identify areas that require intervention. For example, it may be that one country has a light-touch regulatory framework but also has a heavily concentrated or politicized media. Another may lack basic communications infrastructure but may be liberal in its approach to media policy. A third may practice prior censorship of the traditional media but leave Internet communications relatively unregulated. Each of these requires a distinct policy approach, and making subjective comparisons between them will be of limited use.

The UNESCO indicators are designed to be applied by local implementers, tailoring their approach to local circumstances while working to an internationally agreed-upon template. Assigning the relevance of and weighting each of the indicators will be the task of each project team. To avoid accusations of nationalist bias, a system of external quality control, managed by UNESCO or an appropriate independent agency, will be needed to ensure that each exercise does not simply select and weight those indicators that provide the most favorable outcome for a country.

The second stage occurs after specific media programs have been implemented and involves assessing the impact of those media programs. Any evaluation of a specific project will be most effective if it is seen as an ongoing process by the implementing organization. It will be less effective if it is conducted by external evaluators rather than built into the internal management of projects. Any process of evaluation should be simple enough to operate in a busy working environment. The role of external evaluators should, in effect, be a quality control of the organization's own system for evaluating its work.

The existing approaches to evaluating the media's impact on democracy are varied and complex, and they yield results that are difficult to compare. However, pressure on public finances will make this an increasingly important issue over time. The field of media development has not reached the point at which there is an agreed-upon methodology for evaluating the effectiveness and impact of media projects, and donor objectives unique to country conditions make agreement on those methods difficult to achieve. This chapter has suggested an approach that takes into account not just specific project objectives, but the wider context of an organization's missions and its own internal systems of quality control. UNESCO's assessment framework blends different data sources, distilling the best elements of each assessment approach and enabling donors to assess the relevance of media development in relation to a country's needs. UNESCO's media development indicators framework now has the endorsement of UNESCO member states and a degree of international acceptance. The framework faces its next test—implementation—to find out how effective the framework can be.

## Notes

1. UNESCO. 2008. *Media Development Indicators: A Framework for Assessing Media Development.* http://portal.unesco.org/ci/en/files/26032/12058560693media_indicators_framework_en.pdf/media_indicators_framework_en.pdf.
2. Polis. 2007. "Development, Governance and the Media." Background paper for the "Polis Conference on Development, Governance and the Media," London, March 22. http://www.polismedia.org/dgmbackground.aspx.
3. A. Hudock. 2006. "Strategies for Media Development." In *Media Matters: Perspectives on Advancing Governance and Development from the Global Forum for Media Development,* ed. Mark Harvey. London: Internews Europe. http://www.internews.org/pubs/gfmd/mediamatters.shtm.

4. J. Karaganis and W. El-Hadidy. 2007. "Freedom of Expression at the Ford Foundation: History and Renewal." Paper for the Freedom of Expression Project. http://www .freedomofexpression.org.uk/resources/freedom+of+expression+at+the+ford +foundation+history+and+renewal.

5. L. Becker and T. Vlad. 2005. "Non-U.S. Funders of Media Assistance Projects." Miami: John S. and James L. Knight Foundation. http://www.grady.uga.edu/coxcenter/knight. htm.

6. Graves. 2007. *U.S. Public and Private Funding of Independent Media Development Abroad.* Washington, DC: Center for International Media Assistance. http://www.ned. org/cima/CIMA-US_Public_and_Private_Funding_of_Media_Development.pdf.

7. What follows is a synthesis of various reports on the media and democratic development, including Roumeen Islam. 2002. "Into the Looking Glass: What the Media Tell And Why." In *The Right to Tell: The Role of Mass Media in Economic Development.* Washington, DC: World Bank Institute. http://64.233.183.104/search?q=cache:XUOf POiFZvUJ:www.worldbank.org/wbi/RighttoTell/righttotellOverview.pdf+right+to +tell&hl=en&gl=uk&ct=clnk&cd=1; Global Forum for Media Development (2006) "Perspectives on Advancing Governance & Development from the Global Forum for Media Development;" Pippa Norris and Dieter Zinnbauer. 2002. "Giving Voice to the Voiceless: Good Governance, Human Development & Mass Communications." Occasional Paper for HDR 2002, UNDP, Human Development Report Office, New York. http://hdr.undp.org/docs/publications/background_papers/2002/Norris -Zinnbauer_2002.pdf; UNESCO Centre for Peace and Human Security. 2006. *Press Freedom and Poverty: An Analysis of the Correlations between the Freedom of the Press and Various Aspects of Human Security, Poverty and Governance,* prepared by Anne-Sophie Novel. Paris: UNESCO. http://gem.sciences-po.fr/content/publications/pdf/novel _pressfreedom_poverty__150606.pdf.

8. Roumeen Islam. 2002. "Into the Looking Glass."

9. John Lloyd. 2004. *What the Media Is Doing to Our Politics.* London: Constable.

10. Mark Thompson. 1999. *Forging War: The Media in Serbia, Croatia, Bosnia, and Herzegovina.* London: University of Luton Press.

11. United States Constitution. Bill of Rights. Cornell University Law School Web site. http://www.law.cornell.edu/constitution/constitution.billofrights.html.

12. C. Hamelink. 2003. "Draft Declaration on the Right to Communicate." Article 19, Global Campaign for Free Expression, London. Article 19. http://www.article19.org/ pdfs/analysis/hamelink-declaration-the-right-to-communicate.pdf.

13. For a useful summary see UNDP. 2006. *Communication for Empowerment: Developing Media Strategies in Support of Vulnerable Groups.* Practical Guidance Note, Bureau for Development Policy, Democratic Governance Group, UNDP, New York. http://www .undp.org/oslocentre/docs06/Communicationforempowermentfinal.pdf.

14. D. Sifry. 2007. "The State of the Live Web." Sifry's Alerts. April 5. http://www.sifry.com/ alerts/archives/000493.html.

15. Andrew Puddephatt. 2007. *Defining Indicators for Media Development, A Background Paper.* Paris: UNESCO. http://portal.unesco.org/ci/en/ev.php-URL_ID=24288&URL _DO=DO_TOPIC&URL_SECTION=201.html.

16. Mark Whitehouse. 2006. "Measuring Change in Media Systems: The Media Sustainability Index." In *Media Matters: Perspectives on Advancing Media and Development from the Global Form for Media Development,* 76–80. London: Internews Europe; Global Forum for Media Development. http://www.internews.org/pubs/gfmd/mediamatters.pdf.

17. U.K. Department for International Development (DFID). 2005. *Monitoring and Evaluating Information and Communication for Development (ICD) Programs—Guidelines.* London: DFID. http://www.dfid.gov.uk/pubs/files/icd-guidelines.pdf.

18. UNESCO Centre for Peace and Human Security. 2006. *Press Freedom and Poverty: An Analysis of the Correlations between the Freedom of the Press and Various Aspects of Human Security, Poverty and Governance,* prepared by Anne-Sophie Novel. Paris: UNESCO. http://gem.sciences-po.fr/content/publications/pdf/novel_pressfreedom _poverty__150606.pdf.

19. Andrew Puddephatt. 2007. *Defining Indicators for Media Development, A Background Paper.* Paris: UNESCO.

20. Norris and Zinnbauer. 2002. "Giving Voice to the Voiceless."

21. UNDP. 2006. *A Guide to Measuring the Impact of Right to Information Programs.* Practical Guidance Note, Bureau for Development Policy, Democratic Governance Group, New York. http://www.undp.org/oslocentre/docs06/A%20Guide%20to%20Measuring %20the%20Impact%20of%20Right%20to%20Information%20Programmes%20 -%20final%2003.08.2006.pdf.

22. UNDP. 2006. *Communication for Empowerment: Developing Media Strategies in Support of Vulnerable Groups.* Practical Guidance Note, Bureau for Development Policy, Democratic Governance Group, New York. http://www.undp.org/oslocentre/docs06/ Communicationforempowermentfinal.pdf.

23. DANIDA (Danish International Development Agency). 2005. *Monitoring and Indicators for Communication for Development.* http://webzone.k3.mah.se/projects/comdev/ _comdev_PDF_doc/Danida_ComDevt.pdf.

24. DFID (U.K. Department for International Development). 2005. *Monitoring and Evaluating Information and Communication for Development (ICD) Programs—Guidelines.* London: DFID. http://www.dfid.gov.uk/pubs/files/icd-guidelines.pdf.

25. AMDI (African Media Development Initiative). 2006. *Research Summary Report.* London: BBC World Service Trust. http://www.bbc.co.uk/worldservice/trust/specials/ 1552_trust_amdi/index.shtml.

26. International Telecommunications Union. 2006. "ICT and Telecommunications in Least Developed Countries: Midterm Review for the Decade 2001-2010." http://www .itu.int/ITU-D/ldc/pdf/ICTand%20TELinLDC-e.pdf.

27. Alan Davis. 2006. "A Road Map for Monitoring and Evaluation in the Media Development Sector." In *Media Matters: Perspectives on Advancing Media and Development from the Global Form for Media Development,* ed. Mark Harvey, 89–93. Internews Europe and the Global Forum for Media Development, 92.

28. A. Puddephatt. 2008. *Intergovernmental Council of the International Programme for the Development of Communication.* Paris: UNESCO. http://portal.unesco.org/ci/en/ev .php-URL_ID=26032&URL_DO=DO_TOPIC&URL_SECTION=201.html.

29. James Deane. 2003. "Media and Empowerment in Developing Countries." In *Communicating in the Information Society,* ed. B. Girard and S. O'Siochru. Geneva: UN Research Institute for Social Development. http://www.unrisd.org/80256B3C005BE6B5/(http-News)/BA48794733529BF6C1256DFE00470010?OpenDocument. Also see James Deane. 2007. "Democratic Advance or Retreat? Communicative Power and Current Media Developments." In *Global Civil Society Yearbook 2007/8: Communicative Power and Democracy,* ed. Martin Albrow, Helmut Anheier, Marlies Glasius, Monroe E. Price, Mary Kaldor, Centre for the Study of Global Governance, and London School of Economics. London: Sage.

30. Amartya Sen. 1999. *Development as Freedom.* Oxford: Oxford University Press.

31. Details are available from Certimedia. http://www.certimedia.org.

# Part II

# The Democratic Roles of Media Systems

# Agenda Setters: Setting Priorities

# 3

# Media Coverage of Natural Disasters and Humanitarian Crises

Susan D. Moeller

Natural disasters and crises stemming from conflict are by their very nature pivotal events. They cause tremendous disruption to the regions affected, but also often attract the world's attention to those regions—regions that may not usually be in the regular global spotlight. And while disasters are devastating to those they affect, that very devastation can generate opportunities that did not previously exist. The disasters and crises attract media coverage, and that consequent attention—as well as the real need for help—may create leverage to budge not only the new disaster-related problems but preexisting issues, such as those that underlie efforts to achieve the multilateral Millennium Development Goals (MDGs).

To find and capitalize on that potential leverage, international and bilateral development agencies—including the World Bank, U.S. Agency for International Development, and U.K. Department for International Development—can help by evaluating how both traditional and new media function and by discovering who the new stakeholders are, both in short-term disaster relief and in the longer-term MDGs. Today's world has seen an exponential growth in the number of parties who have a potential stake in alleviating the problems addressed by the MDGs, and many of those new stakeholders also see opportunities in the information and communication needs of what Paul Collier has called "the bottom billion."

## The Bottom Billion

In *The Bottom Billion: Why the Poorest Countries Are Failing and What Can Be Done About It,* Oxford economist Paul Collier analyzes the problems of 50 failing states. Collier not only lays out the "traps" that these failed countries have fallen into, but also tells his readers where they themselves have gone wrong. *The Bottom Billion* argues for new kinds of interventions, including a considered use of aid, preferential trade policies, laws against corruption, and apposite military engagement.

A large part of why poor countries are failing, Collier says, is that "our notions about the problems of the poorest countries" are shaped by "crude images … not just of noble rebels but of starving children, heartless businesses, crooked politicians. You are held prisoner by these images," he tells his readers. And "while you are held prisoner, so are our politicians, because they do what you want." So what does Collier do? "I am going to take you beyond images. Sometimes I am going to smash them. And my image smasher is statistical evidence."[1]

These images that lead all of us astray, he later clarifies, are not just photographic clichés of starving babies, they are bipolar platitudes: "Popular thinking on development is fogged by lazy images and controversies: 'Globalization will fix it' versus 'They need more protection'; 'They need more money' versus 'Aid feeds corruption'; 'They need democracy' versus 'They're locked in ethnic hatreds'; 'Go back to empire' versus 'Respect their sovereignty'; 'Support their armed struggles' versus 'Prop up our allies.'" According to Collier, "these polarizations are untenable," and he hopes that by the end of the book readers "have picked up some sense of how quantitative research on these issues challenges them."[2]

Collier's book is a short one, so he does not take the time to track where the "crude images" and "polarizations" that he cites come from. The media, in any form, are mentioned in a scant handful of references in the book. But the media are that "elephant in the room"—unexplored in his work, but the frequent source—and certain amplifier—of simplistic images and doltish truisms. The media are, in many ways, the appropriate focus for his anger. The media's role in the framing of the bottom billion is the elephant that needs to be discussed—and needs to be discussed in the same conversation that considers the problems and the solutions to all the ills that the bottom billion are heir to.

The media can be, as well, that proverbial 800-pound gorilla—the player in the room that one ignores at one's peril. There is no global issue, no political arena in which media are not leading figures in the statement of problems and the recognition of possible solutions. They can be a force that calls for accountability—witness the oft-mentioned example of the David-sized independent cable TV channel in Peru that brought down the Goliath of the

Fujimori government in September 2000 when it alone aired a video of the head of the intelligence service bribing a judge. But media can also be the voices that incite violence—witness the ethnic hate spread by SMS (short message service) messages and vernacular radio stations in the aftermath of the December 2007 Kenyan elections.

Collier argues that the power of public opinion drives the agendas of aid agencies and military interventions, but he does not articulate how that "powerful force of public opinion" is formed, changed or expressed.[3] Understanding the way in which media help set the public agenda is, however, absolutely essential for the field of development in general and specifically for the achievement of the Millennium Development Goals.[4] As George Washington University professor Silvio Waisbord has observed, "economic growth, improvement in health services, or agricultural productivity are not simply a matter of technical expertise, but, instead, are rooted in communication processes and social dynamics." However, Waisbord cautions that "just as important as injecting social thinking in fields dominated by narrow technical knowledge is to recognize that institutional mandates and bureaucratic expectations determine the place of communication in/for development."[5]

## You Can Lead, but Who Follows?

The media have never been monolithic, but the word *media* has never been more of a catchall term than it now is. Speaking of "the news media" is at once to reference such venues as international and foreign-based "mainstream" cross-platform outlets, government-owned or sponsored television, community news services, satellite radio, as well as hyperlocal vernacular radio, online blogs, podcasting, and messaging via cell phones and VoIP (voice-over Internet protocol) outlets, such as Skype. So using the word media as a shorthand way to talk about all the communication outlets that deliver news to audiences has tremendous limitations—not the least of which is that such a language habit can blind both the speaker and any listeners to the very real distinctions among various media, distinctions that dramatically affect how any given news outlet, or category of outlets, wants to and can behave.

One of those distinctions that matters relates to the presumption of many who work in the fields of development, namely, that "one of the classic roles of the news media is to raise awareness of social needs and development challenges."[6] Yet it should be asked whether media—specific types as well as cross sector—are inclined or have the capacity to play this public service, civil society role.

The media landscape has become both more dynamic and more crowded over the past two decades as a result of new technologies and liberalized environments that have lowered the financial and political costs of ownership and access. These trends have also put pressure on old business models, created new classes of commercial, advertising-dependent media and politically oriented outlets, and shifted the editorial interest of many news organizations away from public service news-you-need principles and toward entertainment-driven news-you-want standards. The same period has also seen—at the global, regional, and national levels—a growing concentration of media ownership, moving news organizations out of the hands of individuals and families and making the news side of these larger businesses more focused on the bottom line. That trend, combined with demographic changes in news consumption, has led many organizations to eviscerate their reporting staffs, especially on beats that are expensive and/or presumed to be of lesser concern to audiences of interest to advertisers, such as investigative reporting, international news, and poverty-related coverage.

Current development strategies are premised on two core ideas: that people in poverty need to have ownership of the solutions to their problems and that government and other organizations need to be accountable for their actions. Noted the World Bank: "According to the Voices of the Poor study, based on interviews with 60,000 people in 60 countries, when the poor were asked to indicate what might make the greatest difference to their lives, they responded … [that they] want NGOs and governments to be accountable to them and a development process driven by their own communities."[7] Ownership and accountability are each founded on an open exchange of information, and they presuppose an engaged media that act, at the very least, as a communication conduit, and that ideally are also themselves informed and proactive both in supporting citizen ownership of programs and in guaranteeing government and nongovernmental organization (NGO) transparency and accountability.

Yet studies looking at mainstream American and European media repeatedly find that few journalists specialize in the coverage of humanitarian crisis and relief stories; most news outlets have little interest in reporting on economic development; reporters have little specialist knowledge of specific sectors, such as health, education, and agriculture, or on the legal rights of populations being helped (all of which are critical to understand in both crisis and development reporting); and overall there is a lack of resources to finance such coverage and a lack of will to find the additional resources that would be needed.[8]

In fact, the problems are even deeper. Surveys of U.S., U.K., and European journalists who cover natural and other crises have found that few use or even know about existing humanitarian crisis-aggregating outlets, such as Reuters' AlertNet, OCHA's ReliefWeb, and ECHO's site.[9] These same surveys also identify that NGOs and governments are missing opportunities to reach media. Reporters who go to the Web sites of specific NGOs for time- and place-critical information are often frustrated by a lack of basic information on the sites (such as detailed contact information, especially for in-country staffers);

few sites offer list servers, RSS feeds, or text bulletins of value to reporters; and often search engines do not index the information, images, and video that are loaded on the site.[10] The partisan perspective on information that is on the sites—or put out via press releases—of organizations such as Oxfam, Human Rights Watch, the United Nations Development Programme, and the World Bank can also be a disincentive for certain journalists to use the information. Even when journalists share those perspectives, there can be the perception that to run with the news from such a press release is to become merely an advocate for that organization. There is therefore often little coverage, little informed coverage, and missed opportunities on the part of NGOs and other agencies to communicate with journalists on the development and humanitarian crisis beats, especially through what should be the expedited pathway of new media.

There are further problems when the parameters are expanded to take in local and national media, not just regional and international outlets. As a BBC World Service Trust policy brief on Kenya recently noted, when media liberalization laws allowed nongovernmental media to emerge, especially local language broadcast outlets, the "main incentives driving the opening of these stations were neither developmental, nor even political. It was commercial. The majority of these stations were founded as profit-making enterprises and principally as entertainment vehicles."[11] With the exception of community media (and arguably government-owned or -sponsored media), media outlets do not have a dedicated public service agenda. As occurred in Kenya, such stations can, however, become part of the chain of news and information, especially through popular talk shows, phone-in programs, and the conversations held by DJs on shows that emphasize music. Sometimes the agenda-setting role that such outlets play can be welcome—in Kenya the record turnout for the 2007 elections "can be largely be attributed to the civic awareness carried out by the media," argued the BBC brief.[12]

But because these accidental outlets for public debate are staffed by people who are not trained journalists or commentators, and certainly have "little or no training in mediating discussions in conflict situations," the media's agenda setting can also be deeply troubling. For example, the voices that could be heard on Kenyan vernacular radio following the election helped incite violence, argued L. Muthoni Wanyeki, the director of the Kenya Human Rights Commission, "in terms of prejudices spread, ethnic stereotypes made and the fear created."[13] "The ethnic hate our radio station was propagating about those from outside the community was unbelievable," admitted one of the broadcasters in a forum organized by Internews, an international NGO that fosters independent media. "The unfortunate thing is that we let these callers speak bile and laughed about it."[14] Politically motivated bulk SMS text messages sent to cell phones, and personally directed hate messages, also can have an agenda-setting effect. During the high-level mediation sessions in Nairobi, for example, several of those around the table received messages on their Black-berries saying such things as "We know who you are. We know where you are. We will get you."[15]

Such hate and prejudice gained force through being amplified via the media—such vituperation was no longer just street talk. As politics became more factionalized, so did media, and so on, in a reciprocal cycle. Politicians in Kenya learned what others elsewhere have learned: "money plays a crucial role in elections," as Mitch Odero of the Media Council of Kenya said, "and politicians have found that if you have [control or ownership of media out-lets] then you will spend less and influence more."[16] His colleague, Absalom Mutere, agreed: "The influence from boardrooms and shareholders on main-stream media has been heavy … Media have become pawns in the political game."[17] In such environments there are few incentives for calm coverage or disinterested investigative reporting—in fact, there are incentives not to look behind the headlines of events.

This is agenda setting at the most basic level, and the situation isn't con-fined to Africa. In Latin America, for example, Alfonso Gumucio Dagron, the managing director of programs for the Communication for Social Change Consortium, has bluntly stated: "Commercial mass media serves its own in-terests in Latin America as in every other region of the world … For decades, some of us in Latin America have been saying that private commer-cial media is not helping to bring about democracy and social change. They're helping only the political interests of the powerful and wealthy."[18] As the BBC report summarized: "Most media in most societies are politically biased or aligned in some way, have tendencies towards sensationalism and simplifica-tion, balance self interest—whether of profit or power—with acting in the public interest. The debate on the accountability of the media to the public is a global, not simply a Kenyan, debate."[19]

## Agenda Setting: Taking Measure of the World's Disasters and Crises

Do journalists set the agenda for foreign affairs? There has been much discus-sion over the years of a "CNN effect," or more recently of an "Al-Jazeera effect." Yet, as discussed further in the next chapter, most studies of these purported phenomena have discovered that it is less journalists than politi-cians who are the prime movers behind any "effect."[20] Governments remain the agenda setters in international affairs. The level of recognition that gov-ernments give to issues and events parallels the level of recognition that media give to them—even if, on certain occasions, the journalists criticize the gov-ernment's spin on an issue. For example, a study focused on media coverage of weapons of mass destruction identified that if the White House or Downing

Street prioritizes a story, so too does the media. If the president or prime minister ignores a story (or an angle on a story), the media is likely to do so as well.[21] The nature of much of world affairs today is such that relatively few people other than those within or close to government can speak with any authority. The statements of presidents, foreign secretaries, the heads of security services, and military officers are solicited to tell the public both the breaking news and what to think about it all.[22] When President George W. Bush said to the country that Americans are vulnerable to weapons of mass destruction in the hands of terrorists, for example, the media headlined those comments and effectively magnified the public's fears.

It is not, of course, only in the global North that governments set the agenda. As chapter 9 notes, "in many authoritarian regimes, far from serving the needs of the public, the channels of communication reinforce state control and the power of established interests." And Nadia El-Awady, president of the Arab Science Journalists Association, has noted the varied ways in which governments in the developing world are able to control the news. "In the developing world, there is a huge problem with access to information. A lot of our information must come directly from officials, and if they don't like our questions, they simply won't answer them. And documented information, if available to begin with, is more often than not misleading or plain-and-simple wrong." As a result, El-Awady writes, "To cover a story, journalists need a publication both willing to cover the costs and to publish it. A large number of local media organizations are state owned. That means either that they won't cover the 'wrong' kind of story, or that you have to work for them to publish with them. Opposition media organizations, on the other hand, often take the more sensationalistic angle in covering their stories. They want 'the juice' on the government to make it look bad. Balanced coverage frequently fails them."[23] In other words, much of the media coverage in the region either repeats the government's messages—right or wrong—or tries to attack those messages (see chapter 13). Either way, the agenda and the terms of discussion have been set by officials.

What's the lesson? It is that media validate the agenda of governments, amplify the voices of officials and help confirm their messages. This gives government tremendous power in directing the public debate and selecting certain strategic choices and opportunities, while masking others. And that does not even include those environments where governments control media in direct ways through ownership, regulation, licensing, physical intimidation, or economic strong-arming. Sasa Vucinic, director of the Media Development Loan Fund, noted: "these days economic assaults are far more common than violent attacks on journalists and media businesses—they are also certainly more difficult to trace and perhaps just as effective."[24]

From the Enlightenment forward, free and independent media have been recognized as the sina qua non of civil society. More recently, multiple observers have noted that governments are more responsive to public needs in countries with an active press—a contention famously made by the Nobel Prize–winning economist Amartya Sen. In his 1981 Coromandel lecture, Sen made his oft-referenced observation about the role that democracy and the press play in averting famine: "India has not had a famine since independence, and given the nature of Indian politics and society, it is not likely that India can have a famine even in years of great food problems. The government cannot afford to fail to take prompt action when large-scale starvation threatens. Newspapers play an important part in this in making the facts known and forcing the challenge to be faced."[25]

Yet in the past several years, others have suggested that a vibrant media presence does not necessarily prompt government's behavior to be more responsive to the needs of the poor. Twenty years after Sen's Coromandel lecture, Timothy Besley and Robin Burgess argued in their study of the role of media in Indian government policy that, whereas in democracies "elections provide an incentive for politicians to perform which can be enhanced by development of the media," there exist factors, such as voter "turnout, political competition, and the timing of elections," that can limit media's impact on crises. Who in the potential electorate is at risk is also a factor—governments are not likely to respond as enthusiastically to those who are unlikely or marginalized voters, no matter whether their plight has been well covered or not. "Overall, political effects are more pronounced for food distribution than for calamity relief. This is understandable given that the public food distribution system is a larger, more politicized operation," wrote Besley and Burgess. "In contrast, calamity relief expenditure being both limited to shock periods and benefiting a smaller fraction of the electorate are likely to attract relatively less political attention."[26] Author Alex de Waal agreed: governments act to ameliorate a disaster or crisis when they feel threatened, when influential groups (whose power is needed) are at risk, when the governments have (or believe they have) the capacity to act, and when the crisis becomes "visible." In the latter case, the crisis has to be more than just visible through media images. The crisis must be measurable. Famine fits that requirement. "Because of its particular social and economic manifestations, famine becomes a distinct, separate phenomenon from chronic poverty," noted de Waal. "Media interest should be seen as a product of famine's visibility not its cause."[27]

Although recent investigations of Sen's assertions suggest that the correlations he drew are not so direct, Besley, de Waal, and others argue that active media are essential for keeping the public informed, and that information can, when sufficiently visible to key constituencies, have a positive effect on corruption, turnover, and media capture.[28] Politicians are adept at attending to their core interests—including cleaning up their act if their own survival is at stake. It is no coincidence, therefore, that international donors have come to embrace the development strategy of supporting and building media institutions and outreach into communities. Donors want an empowered media; they want media to function as potent instruments of government and corporate accountability and as responsible information and communication conduits for the poor and dispossessed, both in times of stasis and times of crisis. The roles media played during elections in Ghana and Sierra Leone and in the peaceful democratic transition in Nepal are frequently mentioned as examples of how community media, especially, can play these roles—and to what positive ends.

And similar roles can be played following disasters. The United Nations–sponsored report on post-tsunami communications observed that "During the Nias earthquake response of March 2005, for example, the head of the UN mission gave daily interviews to the Internews radio network, updating on the finding of the assessment teams, death tolls, and the relief effort. This kept organisations and their message of neutral, humanitarian support in the public eye and also promoted transparency and accountability." Radio, local and national television, newspapers, newsletters, and even community bulletin boards are essential ingredients of outreach campaigns, as the UN report noted, and can "dramatically increase the impact of a service-based project." SMS or text messaging, the report commented, "is also a cheap, easy and popular system that offers the unique opportunity to deliver information into the hands of a number of beneficiaries instantaneously."[29] Used intelligently, with an eye not only for the news value of any information being delivered but also for its psychosocial effect, all forms of media can help donor agencies put their priorities on the local and national agenda.[30] What the effect will be, however, will depend on many conditions. As Alex de Waal observed, "Discussion has ranged far beyond Sen's linkage between civil and political liberties and effective famine prevention in India. Attention is focused on the political construction of how disasters are represented, both in the public realm and by technical measurement systems."

## International Coverage: Decisions, Decisions

International NGOs, while critically interested in the potential of indigenous media to play an internal accountability and information/communication function, are also interested in harnessing media, especially regional and international media, as advocates for particular causes and events. The focus of attention of many NGOs in times of disasters and crises—not to mention for development stories in general—is to try to secure media coverage for stories. Notes Médecins sans Frontières (MSF) USA Executive Director Nicolas de Torrenté, "We know that media coverage does not generate improvements on its own. However, it is often a precondition for increased assistance and political attention. There is perhaps nothing worse than being completely neglected and forgotten."[31]

Yet the stories that development experts believe deserve coverage are not always the ones that get attention. And even when the stories are covered, they are not always reported in ways that those experts believe is the most pertinent. For those reasons, every year for the past 10 years, MSF has publicized a list of the top 10 "most underreported humanitarian stories." According to Andrew Tyndall, eight of the countries and problems highlighted by MSF for 2007 received in total only 18 minutes of coverage on the three major U.S. television networks' nightly newscasts.[32] Three of those eight stories—Chechnya, Sri Lanka, and the Democratic Republic of Congo—were never mentioned on ABC's, CBS's, or NBC's evening news programs.

Whoever evaluates the world's disasters significantly influences what gets noticed, as well as how much attention a disaster receives. Those that garner the most attention from the American television networks, as tracked by Tyndall, are not always those ranked highest by governments, policy analysts, the NGO community, or the insurance industry.[33] Global crises are assessed by government officials often in terms of security or economic interests at stake, whereas policy analysts typically prioritize their own singular concerns (for example, China's overtaking of the United States as the world's largest producer of greenhouse gas emissions, for those occupied with climate change). The NGO sector values lives at risk, while the insurance industry considers property damage and insured loss. The U.S. mainstream media, while taking into account all of these, also assess a crisis's "gee-whiz" factor.

Exactly what American mainstream media consider to be important can be read in their coverage of the crises of 2007. The top four stories, determined by minutes of attention, according to Tyndall, were combat in Iraq, the Virginia Tech campus shooting, wildfires in California, and the stock market's gyrations. And coverage of the race for the White House was off the charts—the networks gave the presidential campaign more time in 2007 than the last four comparable years combined (1991, 1995, 1999, and 2003). Attention focused on just-breaking news, violence and dramatic pictures, Americans at risk physically and economically, and horse-race politics. Immediate actions are valued far more than process or stasis. In addition to the California wildfires, other disasters in Tyndall's top 20 stories were the blizzards and ice storms across the United States, the American tornado season, and the (continued) aftermath of Hurricane Katrina. Yet none of these American disasters made the top 20 global catastrophes in terms of victims in 2007, according to Swiss Re, the world's second largest re-insurer.[34] Swiss Re annually publishes revealing statistics on the world catastrophes, including two lists of the biggest disasters, one in terms of lives lost and a second in terms of losses for insurance companies. The two lists for 2007 were almost entirely different. Not a single U.S. disaster is in the top 20 in number of deaths—the cyclone and monsoon-generated floods in Bangladesh and India accounted for the top three catastrophes, and floods in the Democratic People's Republic of Korea and postelection rioting in Kenya are four and five on the chart. By contrast, the top five disasters in terms of insured property losses are all from Europe and the United States: storm and flood damage accounted for the top four—the first three in Europe and the United Kingdom and the fourth in the United States; and the U.S. wildfires constituted the fifth most costly disaster. A quick comparative glance at the lists from Tyndall, PEJ's NewsIndex, and Swiss Re makes clear that the number of people killed or threatened by disaster or crisis is not a good predictor of U.S. media coverage.[35] Some of the most devastating global crises are essentially absent in American mainstream media, whether conflict in Africa, flooding in Asia, or the threat of tuberculosis around the world. According to the Tyndall and PEJ measures, it is not general fatalities, but physical and economic risk to Americans that elicit coverage.

And lest it be thought that it's only American news outlets that are so inward-looking, Gareth Evans, president of the Belgian-based International Crisis Group, argued that "no one should get the impression this is only a problem of the Western media; it is universal." The Congo, Central Asia, the Caucasus—all have been passed over by the world's media, he said. For example, "the Arabic-language media have consistently ignored or underreported the underlying causes of the conflict in Darfur, Sudan, and the massive humanitarian catastrophe that has resulted."[36]

What does get a story onto the global news budgets? Name-calling can work: such as using the term "ethnic cleansing," comparing a crisis to the Holocaust, or dramatically placing blame on political leaders. In March 2005, shortly after the world had commemorated the 10th anniversary of the Rwandan genocide, Mukesh Kapila, the UN coordinator for Sudan, told Britain's Radio 4's Today program that the government of Sudan was directly responsible for "the world's greatest humanitarian crisis." Kapila was the first senior official to blame the government for the hundreds of thousands of dead—as well as to go further and compare Darfur to the Rwandan genocide. As an article by Mark Jones commented in AlertNet: "It was a calculated gamble by Kapila. Weeks earlier, the 10th anniversary of the Rwandan genocide had reopened the scars that humanitarians, politicians and journalists incurred through their failure to act faster. One question that kept coming up was: could it happen again? Frustrated by the dominance of Iraq in the media, Kapila and his media advisor, a former *Daily Mail* journalist, had concluded they were going to have to say something new." The gamble paid off. "Within hours, the message that Darfur was the new Rwanda had spread around the world. And this time, the wave of coverage persisted as politicians responded. Darfur, a previously unknown region of Sudan, was becoming a household name."[37]

Huge death tolls, sensational charges, breaking news (rather than chronic) events, innocents (preferably children) who need to be rescued, key security interests at stake, violence, scandal and/or corruption. These are what prompt media coverage. And then there is the need for still and video images. "The fact is if you haven't got a picture it won't get in the paper. It's a simple as that," asserted Anne Penketh, diplomatic editor for London's *Independent* newspaper.[38] Lindsey Hilsum, international editor of Britain's Channel 4 News, noted that with television, images are essential—and not just any images, but arresting ones. "If all the kids look fat and happy, it's hard to do a story about impending famine. That's just the nature of TV."[39]

Another tactic that can secure media attention is sending someone famous to the afflicted region—the U.S. secretary of state, the U.K. development secretary, the First Lady—or hiring a celebrity ambassador to headline the cause. Yet Nick Cater, the media director for Bob Geldorf's SportAid for Africa, warned that in addition to all the care and handling problems attendant on working with well-known faces, meaningful media coverage can still be elusive. "Celebrity-driven news not only dumbs down any issue," he observed, "but, paradoxically, can make it seem even more remote and disengaged from the lives of ordinary people." Charities might want to check whether using a celebrity actually results in a positive and quantifiable outcome. "Headlines are tools not trophies," he remarked, "what will coverage do for the hungry?"[40]

In 2002 two Danish charities examined whether media coverage actually did make a difference in funding to victims and came away with a conditional "maybe." Three factors actually seemed to matter—donor security interests, "stakeholder commitment," and media attention.[41] The most important factor the report found were the security concerns. Second were the stakeholder interests—"committed organisations being on the ground where things are taking place and being in a position to lobby and have good connections in the different headquarters of the big donor organisations." Third, was media coverage. "But never trust it!" noted Gorm Rye Olsen, the lead researcher. According to the report, media appeared to influence decision makers "only when there are no vital security issues at stake." The researchers determined this, in part, by considering humanitarian aid to Africa and the Balkans. "The widespread conviction in the aid community that the Kosovo crisis 'stole' or diverted emergency assistance from Africa to Europe (the Balkans) is difficult to substantiate," they said. "Although Kosovo received a great deal of media attention and humanitarian assistance, Angola and Sudan also received ongoing assistance, despite not featuring in the mainstream media."[42]

Beyond all these potential ways to attract coverage, there are the factors that keep stories out of the news. First there are the pedestrian-level causes, such as lack of resources and the logistical problems related to access and infrastructure—visa, travel, and information and communication technology

(ICT) problems. Ron Redmond, the head of communications at the United Nations High Commissioner for Refugees, confirmed the importance of such basics: "The inaccessibility of Darfur and Chad made them extremely difficult to cover for the media—they may as well have been the moon for many reporters and editors."[43] Then there are the stories that are dangerous to cover. And there are also the problems that arise when media outlets turn to cover the next big thing. "It's always the aftermath of a war that I find needs the most coverage when the cameras disappear," noted Janine di Giovanni, foreign correspondent for *The Times* in London. Few journalists follow up on crises they have reported on; few return to an international venue to see how those they have reported on are faring.[44]

Yet, although these are the elements that determine media coverage, there is no spreadsheet that can calculate whether any given story—even one that takes account of all these elements—will make the news on any given day, will remain in the news over a period of time, and will succeed in attracting a critical mass of coverage from multiple news outlets across multiple media platforms. There are always other factors at play. Has the White House or the Foreign Office put the story high on its agenda? Is a major event already being covered that is "closer to home": a presidential election, a shooting war, or even sensational celebrity gossip (à la Britney Spears or Carla Bruni)?

Thus, blanket recommendations of how international institutions, relief agencies, and governments should manage the message of a crisis or disaster in order to attract media interest are not infallible. Following such recommendations may lead to some exposure, but not to sustained consideration. The world's disaster victims are caught up in "a kind of humanitarian sweepstakes," argues Jan Egeland at the UN. "They are in a global lottery, really. And they play every night to seek our attention and our support. And every night 99 percent of them lose. And one percent win."[45] Fundamentally, Hilsum cautioned, the agendas of mainstream news organization and of charity organizations are different. "News is something that's happening, not something which is about to happen, or might happen. Our job is to report the news; their job is to prevent famine. Sometimes the two come together, but not always."[46]

## Natural Disasters: Not So Simple Emergencies = Not So Interesting

The perception of many observers in the aid community, as Annabel Brown of Community Aid Abroad—the Australian Oxfam—noted, is that "natural disasters capture the attention of the world, but it is the manmade crisis situations—resulting in part from the disparities and injustices in the world—that rich countries should continue to be aware of and forced to take some responsibility for."[47] And while Brown is correct in saying that natural disasters do attract the attention of the global media, that attention is typically fleeting. There are many more similarities between media's coverage of natural disasters and media's coverage of endemic humanitarian crises than are commonly believed.[48]

First, there is the problem of naming. Sweeping together very distinctive kinds of precipitating events—a tsunami and a tornado, an earthquake and a drought—into a single category called "natural disasters" grossly simplifies both the causes and the consequences of each event. The same is true of wars—all wars are manifestly not the same in either causes or consequences, yet by referencing distinctive conflicts in a single sentence or story, the emergencies are conflated and understood to be the kind of thing that happens to "those" kinds of people in "such" places. The human and political factors—even at the basic level of who is at risk—are rarely well covered. In the case of natural disasters, for example, why do so many of the victims live in the floodplain, live on land that is undergoing desertification, or live in marginal housing?

Most observers categorize natural disasters into two main types. Those clearly falling into the "act of God" category, such as hurricanes, earthquakes, and volcanic eruptions (even if abetted by the human-caused effects of climate change), are classified as "simple emergencies." Simple emergencies call for a straightforward humanitarian response: the providing of food, shelter, and medical supplies.

Distinct from that in the jargon of disaster relief is the class of "complex emergencies," disasters in which humans are self-evidently at fault: civil war, ethnic cleansing, or refugee migrations. Such emergencies demand not only humanitarian relief, but also social, political, and even military attention. Complex emergencies, even when catastrophic, do not usually have easy, event-driven "news pegs"—moments on which a front-page, top-of-the-news story can be "hung." Complex emergencies demand that the media devote significant resources of time, labor, and money, often with too little perceived return. Even a multipart story on the Congo or Colombia, for instance, is unlikely to attract readers or viewers in striking quantities. Without an enticing news event prompting a critical mass of coverage, the story of a complex emergency is a one-off, prompted more by a reporter's, editor's, or producer's belief that the public should know about the emergency rahter than propelled by a feeding frenzy of media swarming to cover the "next big thing."

Simple emergencies are much more likely to get breaking news coverage: they happen suddenly, unexpectedly, and they are often cataclysmic. To media that value what just happened, such events are irresistible—but only for a brief period of time. Even the most calamitous breaking story—a tsunami, a hurricane, an earthquake—quickly devolves into a less dramatic recovery tale of politics, patience, and stamina and so is pushed off the front pages and the top of the news by more recent, and more spectacular, stories. "We're there for the dramatic pictures, but reconstruction is a less dramatic story," admitted *Washington Post* media critic Howard Kurtz. "It doesn't have the exciting video."[49] Few reporters stay on a disaster story after the bodies have been recovered and the funerals are over. A World Health Organization (WHO) report on media coverage of the tsunami, for example, discovered the world's media grossly undercovered the psychotrauma of the disaster. By a week or so after the tsunami struck, WHO discovered, it was clear that there was a mental health "epidemic," but depression and post-traumatic stress disorder received little attention in the news.

The tsunami, Hurricane Katrina, and the earthquake in Pakistan, not to mention the cyclones in Bangladesh and Burma, have made it abundantly clear that so-called simple emergencies develop their own sets of complications. It is not enough for relief operations to bring in water tanks and to throw food parcels and tents off the back of a truck for a week or two. In today's world there is no such thing as a "simple" emergency that is truly simple and quick to solve. A spokesperson for ALNAP, the Active Learning Network for Accountability and Performance in Humanitarian Action, noted that "problems are remarkably consistent across crises that were drought-related in origin … as well as those rooted in civil strife … The recurring nature of the problems supports the contention that the challenges of complex emergencies are of a piece with those of 'natural' disasters but with an added degree of complexity."[50]

It is that observation that leads to the notion that perhaps, as far as the media are concerned, there is only a short-term difference between simple emergencies and complex ones. Although it is tempting to conclude that media cover simple emergencies relatively well, and complex emergencies poorly, the truer assessment is that media cover simple emergencies well, as long as they appear simple. Complex emergencies rarely draw significant international coverage, and neither do simple emergencies after the initial shock is passed. Once the complications of reconstruction begin, the media cover simple and complex emergencies in much the same way—which is to say that they don't cover either of them.

Case in point: In mid-April 2008 in the *New York Times* blog of columnist Nicholas Kristof, an American aid worker told of her anger and frustration with the lack of emergency assistance to Bangladesh following Cyclone Sidr, which killed 3,500 people in November 2007. A comment posted by one reader noted:

> It's incredible that this hasn't received more coverage in the international community… this reminds me of the fact that the 30,000 children dying a day in Africa of poverty-related causes rarely makes headlines, and the fact that people don't seem to rush to donate the way they do after a natural disaster. However, I'd argue that both situations qualify as "emergencies." People respond to a one-time emergency in a different way than what they perceive to be an endemic emergency like poverty. However, as natural disasters happen more frequently, they also become endemic emergencies. The response to endemic emergencies is one of helplessness, that people would rather ignore.[51]

Compassion fatigue is triggered by helplessness in the face of what seem like intractable problems. But different perspectives taken on a story—even a repeating story—can surmount such feelings. Seeking out different sources and considering other responsible actors than those villains that typically grab the headlines are ways to keep audiences as well as journalists interested in the story and its updates. That can be difficult for international media that may have a thin presence on the ground in a crisis or disaster, especially in hard-to-reach areas, but technology as well as citizen journalism can be used proactively to offset such limitations.

The trick, of course, is to encourage, develop, and implement those technical and human tools and skills before a breaking event rather than after the need becomes glaringly apparent. Classic media literacy techniques that begin with encouraging the public to read, listen, and watch multiple media outlets are already being taught in primary, secondary, and university educational settings around the world. These educational efforts are giving students critical life skills of comprehension, analysis, and evaluation, while teaching them how to identify what news matters, how to monitor media coverage, how to understand the media's role in shaping global issues, and how to be responsible contributors to media. Advanced media literacy courses can more directly highlight the connections between freedom of expression, good governance, and economic development.[52] Ultimately, citizens who are more informed about what role good media can play in civil society can help motivate media to better cover global issues and events.

## Awareness, Understanding, and Action

What does it take to get thoughtful, substantive coverage? "To what extent does the media feel that its role is to move beyond disaster reporting to examining the deeper challenges behind the bad news and the possible solutions?" asked Hilary Benn, former British secretary of state for international development. "How can we ensure … that we hear many more Southern voices talking for themselves and about what they want for the future of their country, rather than two people from the North having an argument about what we think is good for someone else?"[53]

New media offer opportunities for new players to get in the game, and media literacy tells students, educators, policy makers, and the public at large why that matters. Who controls the conversation—who is in the conversation—is, of course, an agenda-setting factor, and agenda setting of a different order. New media and the way they are used have changed users' and senders' notions about ownership and access. Journalists and the aid community have to look outside their own ranks to consider what possibilities are emerging. New media can create different dissemination patterns, can speak to different demographics, and can play different agenda-setting functions than tradition-al media of the past.

A major UN study on tsunami recovery in Aceh and Sri Lanka found that what people in the affected areas primarily wanted was "practical infor-mation that explains what aid is available, how to apply for it, why what they have received might differ from their neighbor, and what to do if they are not satisfied. They are not interested in—and can recognize—materials that sim-ply promote a particular organization. Second, they are very interested in hearing how the aid effort is going, how money is being spent, what problems are being experienced elsewhere, and what solutions are being found."[54] The survivors want to know what's happening and to be part of the conversation about what to do. To survivors of a crisis, what's needed first is just-in-time information, often through low-tech venues, such as community bulletin boards and local radio, as well as through such high-tech means as SMS mes-sages and RSS feeds. What's needed in addition is to make the crisis visible to donor agencies and governments. Here the question about how the agenda is framed becomes critical. Is it framed for the aid beneficiaries (the survivors)? For local government officials? For contractors (domestic and international)? For NGOs or donor agencies? Or is the agenda being set for the international viewing public?

Jan Chipchase, a human-behavior researcher for Nokia cell phone compa-ny, travels the world to learn about human behavior and to gather nuggets of information that might help Nokia designers better meet (and market to) the needs of the billions around the world who do not yet have cell phones or who will shortly be upgrading those they have. Chipchase is on the cutting edge of commercial entrepreneurs who are trying to discover and lead the future of mobile communications for the daily needs of those billions—as well as for their needs in times of crisis. An April 2008 article in the *New York Times Sun-day Magazine* by Sarah Corbett gave an overview of what is at stake: "Accord-ing to statistics from the market database Wireless Intelligence, it took about 20 years for the first billion mobile phones to sell worldwide. The second bil-lion sold in four years, and the third billion sold in two. Eighty percent of the world's population now lives within range of a cellular network, which is dou-ble the level in 2000. And figures from the International Telecommunications Union show that by the end of 2006, 68 percent of the world's mobile sub-scriptions were in developing countries."[55]

In 2008, the World Resources Institute, a Washington-based environmen-tal research group, published an economic study with the International Finance Corporation titled *The Next Four Billion.* The study investigated how poor people living in developing countries spend their money and found that "as a family's income grows—from $1 per day to $4, for example—their spending on ICT increases faster than spending in any other category, including health, education and housing." According to Al Hammond, the study's principal author, "What people are voting for with their pocketbooks, as soon as they have more money and even before their basic needs are met, is telecommunications." The reason for that remarkable decision, believes Chipchase, is that cell phone users, often for the first time ever, have "a fixed identity point, which, inside of populations that are constantly on the move—displaced by war, floods, drought or faltering economies—can be immensely valuable both as a means of keeping in touch with home communities and as a business tool."[56]

Chipchase confirms what the World Congress on Communication for Development affirmed in its Rome Consensus document: "Communication is essential to human, social and economic development."[57] What that assertion means for many, Chipchase argues, is that "if you wanted to take phones away from anybody in this world who has them, they'd probably say: 'You're going to have to fight me for it. Are you going to take my sewer and water away too?' And maybe you can't put communication on the same level as running water, but some people would. And I think in some contexts, it's quite viable as a fundamental right."[58]

## Traditional Media Coverage versus "New" Media: Agenda Setting Upended

On May 12, 2008, an 8.0-magnitude earthquake struck western China, killing around 70,000 and injuring more than 370,000 people. The news of the disaster broke via the micromessaging service Twitter. As the Web site VentureBeat described it:

> Before it was on CNN, before MSNBC, before the BBC, even before the United States Geological Survey (which handles earthquake data) had the information, Twitter was on it. How? Its users. While the mainstream media scrambled to put up their "'breaking news" headlines, on Twitter we had pictures, maps, videos all being sent in real-time.

Twitter first responder (and sometimes blogger), Robert Scoble, was on the news into the early hours of the morning, transferring news from the 21,185 people he follows to the 23,200 people following him. In turn, many of those folks would re-tweet (describing a message being resent) the news to their followers. Information spread like wildfire on the service.[59]

The earthquake in China was not the first news event broken by Twitter. Several smaller earthquakes in 2007 were first reported via Twitter. And there was the story of the University of California–Berkeley journalism student and his translator arrested in Egypt for photographing an antigovernment protest. The student's cameras were taken away, but on his way to the police station he managed to send out a one-word Twitter message: "Arrested." That was enough to alert his friends in Egypt and the United States and get them to rally UC–Berkeley to hire a lawyer on his behalf.[60]

Information and communication technology tools, often using SMS technology, are increasingly playing a just-in-time function, such as during the Hezbollah-Israeli war, the postelection fighting in Kenya, and the Burma cyclone, when political parties, government agencies, aid workers, and families all used the technology to pass news and information. But ICT tools are also being used for innovative news outlets—outlets that are meeting needs that traditional media are not yet filling. An example is Ushahidi.com, a site first created to track acts of violence in Kenya. Ushahidi is a "mash-up" of Google maps and citizen-provided crisis data (including deaths, looting, and rapes), the latter text messaged into the site. Similarly, Global Voices, the Hub, and AfriGadget's Grassroots Reporting Project are trying to leverage the power of a wide variety of technologies, from Weblogs (blogs), podcasts, photos, video, wikis, tags, aggregators, online chats, Twitter, and SMS to "bring quality content online ... and have more on-the-ground reporting of stories," as AfriGadget's Web site explains.[61]

These new efforts are not thinking in terms of traditional "push" media. New media, especially those that are Internet based, are nonintrusive "pull" media: their users determine and control their degree of involvement. At a basic level the users have to already be motivated to seek out information, even if there turns out to be a level of serendipity about what they find. Twitter, for example, has a search site called Summize that aggregates Twitter messages from keywords. The pickup of messages from China when the keyword "earthquake" was entered, for example, amounted to a significant eyewitness story.

The lesson here is that in times of disasters and crises, bilateral and multilateral development agencies need to think both more innovatively and more strategically about relief and alleviation. Clearly identifying the particular dynamics of a disaster or crisis, identifying what interventions and strategies will best rebuild and consolidate gains, and identifying the variety of organizations and forces that can enable those interventions and strategies are no longer pro forma exercises—if they ever were. New media, new technologies, and new stakeholders are all now in play alongside traditional media, ICT tools, and relief and development agencies.

Those in the public, in industry, even in politics, who previously felt little investment in the Millennium Development Goals can, when prompted by the immediate needs of a disaster or crisis and given their preexisting engagement with new media and/or new technologies, become fellow travelers in commitment. This is an opportunity to be seized.

## Notes

1. Paul Collier. 2007. *The Bottom Billion: Why the Poorest Countries Are Failing and What Can Be Done About It.* New York: Oxford University Press, xii.
2. Ibid., 176.
3. Ibid., 184.
4. The notion that media could be a "multiplier" for development messages has been in play since 1958 with the publication of Daniel Lerner's *The Passing of the Traditional Society.* A recent literature review of the field is Adam Rogers. 2006. "Participatory Diffusion or Semantic Confusion?" In *Media Matters: Perspectives on Advancing Governance and Development,* ed. Mark Harvey, 178–86. London: Internews Europe and the Global Forum for Media Development. http://www.internews.org/pubs/gfmd/mediamatters.shtm.
5. Silvio Waisbord. n.d. "The Irony of Communication for Social Change." MAZI Articles. http://www.communicationforsocialchange.org/mazi-articles.php?id=349.
6. The sentence is taken from the proposed outline for this specific paper written up in the "Concept Note" for this workshop on "The Role of the News Media in the Governance Agenda: Watch-Dog, Agenda-Setter, and Gate-Keepers."
7. http://www.mlge.gov.jm/nac/index2.php?option=com_content&do_pdf=1&id=221.
8. See, for example, CARMA. 2006. *The CARMA Report on Western Media Coverage of Humanitarian Disasters;* and Steven Ross. 2004. *Toward New Understandings: Journalists and Humanitarian Relief Coverage.* Fritz Institute and Reuters Foundation.
9. Steven Ross. 2004. *Toward New Understandings: Journalists and Humanitarian Relief Coverage.* Study commissioned by the Fritz Institute and Reuters Foundation. http://www.fritzinstitute.org/PDFs/InTheNews/2004/ColumbiaNews_030404.pdf.
10. For an example of what is possible, see NewsFix, offered by ITV News, which sends subscribers twice-daily notifications when its video bulletins are available for download. http://www.itv.com/News/extra1/Newsfix2/default.html.
11. James Deane and Jamal Abadi. 2008. *The Kenyan 2007 Elections and Their Aftermath: The Role of Media and Communication.* London: BBC World Service Trust.
12. Ibid.
13. Ibid.
14. Ibid.
15. On-background interview with member of the mediation team.
16. Deane and Abadi. 2008. *Elections and Their Aftermath.*
17. Ibid.
18. Alfonso Gumucio Dagron, 2006. "The Right to Communicate, Social Movements and Democratic Participation." Comments. *MAZI Articles.* http://www.communicationforsocialchange.org/mazi-articles.php?id=324.
19. Deane and Abadi. 2008. *Elections and Their Aftermath.*
20. See, for example, Nik Gowing.1994. "Real-Time Television Coverage of Armed Conflicts and Diplomatic Crises: Does It Pressure or Distort Foreign Policy Decision?" Working Paper 94-1, Joan Shorenstein Center for the Press, Politics and Public Policy, John F. Kennedy School of Government, Harvard University, Cambridge, MA.
21. Susan D. Moeller. 2004. *Media Coverage of Weapons of Mass Destruction.* College Park, MD: Center for International and Security Studies at Maryland School of Public Affairs, University of Maryland. http://www.cissm.umd.edu.
22. See, for example David Barstow. "Behind Analysts, the Pentagon's Hidden Hand." *New York Times,* April 20. http://www.nytimes.com/2008/04/20/washington/20generals.html.

23. G. Pascal Zachary. 2007. *Global Media and the Development Story: An Introduction.* Washington, DC: International Food Policy Research Institute.

24. Sasa Vacinic. 2006. "Affordable Capital: Turning Press Freedom Heroes into Entrepreneurs." In *Media Matters: Perspectives on Advancing Governance and Development,* ed. Mark Harvey, 108–13. London: Internews Europe and the Global Forum for Media Development. http://www.internews.org/pubs/gfmd/mediamatters.shtm.

25. Amartya Sen. 1981. *Poverty and Famines.* Oxford: Oxford University Press.

26. Timothy Besley and Robin Burgess. 2002. "The Political Economy of Government Responsiveness: Theory and Evidence from India." *Quarterly Journal of Economics* 117 (4): 1415–51.

27. Alex de Waal. 2006. "Towards a Comparative Political Ethnography of Disaster Prevention." *Journal of International Affairs* Spring/Summer: 129–49. In his article, de Waal takes on Sen's assertion, calling it "a hypothesis crying out for empirical examination."

28. Timothy Besley and Andrea Prat. 2005. "Handcuffs for the Grabbing Hand? Media Capture and Government Accountability." Political Economy and Public Policy Series, London School of Economics.

29. Imogen Wall. 2006. "The Right to Know: The Challenge of Public Information and Accountability in Aceh and Sri Lanka." Office of the UN Secretary General's Special Envoy for Tsunami Recovery.

30. Bart Cammaerts and Nico Carpentier. 2007. *Reclaiming the Media: Communication Rights and Democratic Media Roles,* 265–88. Bristol, U.K.: Intellect Books.

31. MSF Issues Top Ten Most Underreported Humanitarian Stories of 2006. Médecins sans Frontières. September 1, 2007. http://www.msf.org.uk/MSF_Issues_Top_Ten_Most_Underreported_Humanitarian_Stories_of_2006.news.

32. Because the MSF report is released in mid-December, both its list and the Tyndall statistics cover only the period from January through November 2007 (see note 31). The Tyndall Report. 2007 Year in Review. http://tyndallreport.com/yearinreview2007/.

33. The same observation holds for the four dozen news outlets tracked by the Pew Research Center's Project for Excellence in Journalism's News Coverage Index. http://www.journalism.org/news_index?page=1.

34. Swiss Re. 2008. New Swiss Re Sigma Study: Catastrophe Losses in 2007 Were Highest in Europe." Swiss Re, March 11. http://www.swissre.com/pws/media%20centre/news/news%20releases%202008/new%20swiss%20re%20sigma%20study%20catastrophe%20losses%20in%202007%20were%20highest%20in%20europe.html.

35. The 2007 NewsIndex dataset for the Project for Excellence in Journalism was retrieved from: http://www.journalism.org/by_the_numbers/datasets.

36. Gareth Evans. "Media Short-Sightedness Is Truly Staggering." AlertNet, March 9. http://www.alertnet.org/thefacts/reliefresources/111039372281.htm.

37. Mark Jones. "Press Forgot Tsunami's Mental Toll." AlertNet, May 6. http://www.alertnet.or/thefacts/reliefresources/111539184639.htm.

38. AlertNet. 2006. "Children, Crises and the Media." Debate. July 12. http://www.alertnet.org/thefacts/reliefresources/11527224893.htm.

39. Ruth Gridley. 2005. "Humanitarian Action Does Not Depend on Media Coverage." AlertNet, October 31. http://www.alertnet.org/thefacts/reliefresources/544251.htm.

40. Nick Cater. 2001. "Do Agencies Benefit from Celebrity Ambassadors?" AlertNet, September 14. http://www.alertnet.org/thefacts/reliefresources/115227224893.htm.

41. Gorm Rye Olsen, Nils Carstensen, and Kristian Høyen. 2003. "Humanitarian Crises: What Determines the Level of Emergency Assistance? Media Coverage, Donor Interests and the Aid Business." *Disasters* 27 (2). http://www.forgottencrises.dk/Forgotten Crises_Conference_net.pdf.

42. Ibid. Also see Ruth Gidley. 2002. "Humanitarian Action Does Not Depend on Media Coverage," AlertNet. October 31, 2002. http://www.alertnet.org/thefacts/reliefresources/ 544251.htm, and Ruth Gidley. 2005. "World's 'Forgotten' Crises Scream for Attention." AlertNet, March 9. http://www.alertnet.org/thefacts/reliefresources/111038912670.htm.

43. Mark Jones. 2005. "What Put Sudan on the Map?" AlertNet, January 19. http://www .alertnet.org/thefacts/reliefresources/11061528666.htm.

44. AlertNet. 2006. "Children, Crises and the Media." Debate. July 12.

45. ABC News. 2005. "The Sympathy Gap." *Nightline*. January 11.

46. Ruth Gidley. 2005. "It's Hard to Tell a Famine from Normality in Southern Africa." AlertNet, December 14. http://www.alertnet.org/thefacts/reliefresources/113456181375 .htm.

47. Ruth Gidley. 2005. "Congo War Tops AlertNet Poll of 'Forgotten' Crises." AlertNet, March 10. http://www.alertnet.org/thefacts/reliefresources/111038817665.htm.

48. Since September 2006, Reuters' AlertNet has captured how English-language newspapers and magazines have covered humanitarian crises across the globe. See their World Press Tracker at http://www.alertnet.org/thenews/newsdesk/FACTIVA/mediaindex .htm. Global Hand, in February 2008, posted an article that gave a useful summary of other resources that aggregate information about media coverage of humanitarian emergencies. http://www.globalhand.org/information/global-hand-news/media-and -forgotten-disasters.

49. CNN International. 2005. "Critique of Worldwide Media Coverage." *International Correspondents*, January 15.

50. ALNAP is an international, interagency humanitarian forum that includes such groups as UNHCR, UNICEF, WHO, CARE, OXFAM, Save the Children, World Vision, and the International Committee of the Red Cross. See ALNAP 2004. *Review of Humanitarian Action in 2004.* http://www.alnap.org/publications/rha.htm.

51. No Way Home. 2008. Post by Nicki Bennett on Nicholas D. Kristof blog, On the Ground, April 14. http://kristof.blogs.nytimes.com/2008/04/14/no-way-home/.

52. For several global efforts in this direction, see the work of the Salzburg Academy on Media & Global Change and UNESCO: http://www.salzburg.umd.edu.

53. Hilary Benn. 2004. "Changing the Face of the World." BBC World Service Trust/DFID conference. London, November 24.

54. Imogen Wall. 2006. "The Right to Know: The Challenge of Public Information and Accountability in Aceh and Sri Lanka." Office of the UN Secretary General's Special Envoy for Tsunami Recovery.

55. Sara Corbett. 2008. "Can the Cellphone Help End Global Poverty?" *New York Times*, April 13. All Chipchase quotes are found in the Corbett article, and background information on his work can be found in his blog: http://www.janchipchase.com/.

56. Ibid.

57. An October 2006 World Congress on Communication for Development (WCCD) held in Rome, Italy, and organized by the World Bank, the Food and Agriculture Organization (FAO) of the United Nations, and the Communication Initiative. The Congress drafted a consensus statement that was ultimately signed by the participants of the WCCD arguing the role of communication for development as a strategy for fostering sustainable social and economic processes. http://siteresources.worldbank .org/EXTDEVCOMMENG/Resources/RomeConsensus07.pdf.

58. Corbett. 2008. "Can the Cellphone Help End Global Poverty?"

59. M. G. Siegler. 2008. "Twitter is first on the scene for a major earthquake—but who cares about that, is it mainstream yet?" VentureBeat Digital Media, May 12. http:// venturebeat.com/2008/05/12/twitter-is-first-on-the-scene-for-a-major-earthquake -but-who-cares-about-that-is-it-mainstream-yet/.

60. See James Buck, "Journalism Is Not a Crime," http://www.jameskarlbuck.com/, and CNN.com. 2008. "Student 'Twitters' His Way Out of Egyptian Jail." April 25. http:// edition.cnn.com/2008/TECH/04/25/twitter.buck/index.html.

61. Global Voices, http://www.globalvoicesonline.org; The Hub, http://hub.witness.org/ en/AboutHub; and the Grassroots Reporting Project, http://www.afrigadget.com/ grassroots.

•
•

# 4

# Media Agenda Setting and Donor Aid

Douglas A. Van Belle

On December 26, 2004, the tsunami that swept across the Indian Ocean unleashed three floods. The first was quite literally a catastrophic flood—a wall of water that killed hundreds of thousands. The second was a torrent of news coverage that inundated every corner of the globe. The third was an outpouring of humanitarian assistance that was pledged and delivered on an unprecedented scale. Each of these floods was extreme to the point of being unique, and the combination of the three simply has to be considered one of those few truly exceptional events that serve as a defining moment in history. And that is the problem.

Common knowledge regarding the role of the news media in the humanitarian response to crises, and to a lesser extent the provision of development aid, is defined by events like the tsunami. All people imagine the norm in terms of the most extreme of the rarest and most unusual events. More than 14,000 disasters have been cataloged since 1965, yet the general understanding of how the media cover those disasters, and how that coverage influences the global response, is defined by four or five of the biggest and most dramatic cases.[1] A similar problem can be seen in people's understanding of media's relationship with development aid. Every year, dozens of donor countries offer development assistance to hundreds of recipient countries, and hundreds of organizations assist thousands of communities, but it is the rare instance, usually a scandal or failure of some kind, when development aid becomes prominent in the news. Because these rare cases are what the media bring to their audience's attention, the rare cases are believed to define both development aid and its relationship to the media. These extreme cases illustrate undeniable evidence of agenda setting. The flood of tsunami coverage drowned the coverage of the concurrent quake in Pakistan, and the vast majority of the assistance followed the coverage. However, these extreme cases also lead to the belief that media coverage has an overwhelming influence on aid, or that it is typical for top-level officials to be involved in the aid response, or that the aid response itself is a significant source of media coverage. In fact, these and many other things that most of the public, policy makers, and researchers think of as typical only occur in the tiniest fraction of cases.

Treating these extreme cases as the norm is more than just a problem for the general understanding of disasters, media coverage, and response. It is also prevalent in the academic research on the role of media in development assistance and disaster aid. Normative and qualitative research methodologies define a significant portion of the research—particularly in terms of disasters, media, and aid—and the vast majority of these studies examine the same huge but extremely rare events that define the popular understanding of the subject. As chapter 3 makes clear, there is significant value in such studies. Extreme events like the Indian Ocean tsunami of 2004 or Hurricane Katrina expose underlying aspects of social and political response in a way that makes these events ideal for asking questions regarding the qualities of disaster or development coverage, or how aspects of the coverage compare with ideals, or how the public, governments, or relief agencies should respond, or how the nature of a media-driven response might be inadequate, inappropriate, or inefficient. However, extracting the full value of that approach to the study of these topics requires careful analysis to establish the context of what actually is normal. The statistical empirical analyses described in this chapter are designed to identify the patterns and relationships that define that norm and help people break from the problem of treating the salient extremes as normal.

In addition to the problem of mistaking the extreme for the norm, developing a reliable explanation for how media, agenda setting, and donor responsiveness are intertwined is further complicated by the fact that the subject of study is not static. Over the past three decades, advancing communication technology and other sources of change have altered the relationship between media coverage and response. Furthermore, problematic presumptions about these changes and their effects have become part of the mythology and illusion surrounding the subject. As a result, just describing the current nature of the relationship between media and global humanitarian responses is a challenge.

Separating fact from fiction and developing the empirical and theoretical foundations needed to create a coherent explanation of the interconnections between media and aid have been an extended effort, particularly in the case of disaster or crisis aid. In 1979 a committee of policy officials and researchers gathered for a workshop not unlike the 2008 Harvard-World Bank workshop to address concerns regarding the media's role in the political and social response to disasters.[2] A great deal of research followed the 1979 workshop, but almost all of it examined local media as an instrument of policy and official response.[3]

It was not until the mid- to late-1990s that research began to examine the effects that a donor's domestic media had on the government's agenda for the provision of foreign disaster and development aid. In part, this change was due to the policy orientation of the researchers involved in much of this line of study, but it was also a consequence of the simple fact that until that time no one had any reason to believe that there might be significant agenda-setting effects acting upon foreign aid donors. The decision and implementation processes used by aid donors were almost entirely bureaucratic, and the long-standing consensus on the nature of bureaucracies was that those agencies were all but immune to most, if not all, forms of public pressure or influence.[4]

In the 1990s, two things led researchers to question that belief. First, the "humanitarian" invasion of Somalia by the United States, along with other events, unsettled the presumption that the bureaucratic fortress insulated aid from media influences. Under the commonly referred to "CNN effect," it was believed that media coverage had overwhelmed the foreign policy decision-making processes involved in aid and humanitarian response. It appeared that the media could outflank the fortifications and drive humanitarian responses. Second, the application of agency theory to the study of bureaucracy was demonstrating that the bureaucratic ramparts were far from impenetrable,[5] and it had become clear that bureaucracies were far more dynamic and far more responsive to public demand than anyone could have imagined. The research and theorizing that followed from these two factors led to a new understanding of how advances in communication technology had altered the media-aid relationship, as well as a reconceptualization of the underlying dynamics of the process in terms of agency theory. The expectation of bureaucratic responsiveness to the media, which was then developed from agency theory,[6] provided the conceptual foundation that has led to researchers' understanding of the current structure and dynamics of the media-aid relationship.

This conceptual development provides an excellent starting point for this discussion, and for the study of development aid bureaucracies, the findings are quite straightforward. Media coverage is not an overwhelming influence on the allocations made by development aid agencies, but its substantive effect on aid is roughly equal to the most influential of other factors in the process, and it is by far the most consistent influence across time and across donor agencies. *New York Times* coverage has a substantively significant influence on the levels of development aid that is roughly equal to, if not slightly greater than, the impoverishment of the recipient, and it has more influence than a recipient's alliance ties with the United States.[7] For British development aid, the substantive influence of *Times* coverage is second only to commonwealth membership, and it is greater than the poverty of the recipient. The influence of *Globe and Mail* coverage on Canadian aid is substantively greater than all other influences, including the other statistically significant factors of poverty, trade, and commonwealth membership. For French aid, *Le Monde* coverage is second in substantive influence to status as a former French colony and far more significant than poverty. *Asahi Shinbun* coverage is clearly the most substantively significant influence on Japanese development aid.

Moving to the examination of disaster aid, the story becomes far more complex. Disaster aid is made in response to events, which makes the statistical analysis of a catalog of cases far simpler, but there are some intriguing puzzles woven into the media's influence on international disaster response. Only in the past few months has enough progress been made in the examination of media's influence upon humanitarian assistance to begin to unravel the puzzles. The discussion provided below presents the first comprehensive outline of the dynamics of the relationship and what they mean for future policy and action.[8] Thus, the discussion of an agenda-setting effect on disaster aid is presented in terms of the puzzle generated by the unexpected discovery that the CNN effect is illusory. Somalia, Bosnia, and a few other high-profile events seemed to make it obvious that the 1990s marked the rise of a global political environment defined by instantaneous communication and media-driven foreign policy.[9] However, in empirical analyses of disaster assistance, it was found that starting in roughly 1990, media coverage suddenly ceased to be a statistically significant influence on the humanitarian response to natural disasters. The dynamics of the media's agenda-setting effect on disaster aid can only be described in terms of the unraveling of the apparent contradiction between the rise of the belief that media had become an overwhelming influence and the statistical studies showing that media had disappeared as an influence.

## Agency Theory

*Agency theory* provides the key conceptual foundation for understanding why aid bureaucracies, or any bureaucratic system for that matter, will respond to media coverage. Agency theory reconceptualizes bureaucracies as something roughly equivalent to a commercial service provider. Bureaucracies are thought of as agents hired to perform certain tasks on behalf of a principal, and as such, they will behave in much the same manner as agents employed in other contexts. For the study of bureaucracies, the key insight derived from this link is that constant monitoring by the principal is not necessary. Instead, principals use the threat of severe negative sanctions to force the agent to monitor its own actions and strive to provide the best possible service as efficiently as possible. Commercial agents practice this kind of quality control and constant adaptation because they fear losing the business of the principal that hired them. Bureaucratic agents monitor the political environment and constantly adjust their activity in order to avoid giving the elected officials that "hire" them a reason to pull the big stick out from behind the door[10] and threaten the tenure of senior administrators or even the very existence of the agency.

By the mid-1990s the insights from agency theory had led to a wide variety of findings detailing how government bureaucracies had responded to changes in their political environment.[11] The changes that were examined were typically big structural changes or shifts, and what had been left largely unaddressed in the application of agency theory was the means by which these bureaucratic agents monitor their environment The extensive agenda-setting literature provided the perfect suggestion—media coverage—and the cockroach theory of bureaucracy translated that into a mechanism that fit into the punishment-avoidance logic of agency theory.

## The Cockroach Theory of Bureaucracy and Aid Response

The phrase "cockroach theory of bureaucracy" began as a tongue-in-cheek reference offered in the context of a workshop for aid officials, and it turned out to be a metaphorically compelling and unfortunately memorable label.[12] Like the beloved insect, bureaucracies strive to consume as much as possible while avoiding getting stomped on. The best way for both insects and bureaucracies to accomplish this is to incorporate an avoidance of those wearing shoes into the way they operate. For bureaucracies, the wearers of shoes are usually public officials who are themselves accountable to a public constituency, such as elected officials, and in this context it is the news media that represent the light that guides the Italian loafers of doom. News media salience provides a simple and reasonably reliable means for bureaucracies to monitor what is considered politically important. Therefore bureaucracies must pay attention to what is attracting the media's attention and adjust their processes accordingly to avoid becoming the focus of negative news media attention themselves.[13]

For foreign aid bureaucracies, this translates directly into a simple and easily testable proposition. To avoid the attention of the media, aid bureaucracies want to avoid providing too little aid to recipients that the public considers important while avoiding providing too much aid to recipients that the public considers unimportant. This translates into a simple equation: more coverage means a recipient is more important, and the more important the recipient, the more aid it should receive.

Two conceptual points are significant in applying the cockroach theory to foreign aid bureaucracies. The first is that both agency theory and the media responsiveness extension of agency theory are formulated in terms of democratic bureaucracies. For nondemocratic donors, there is still reason to expect a similar correlation between media coverage and aid, but the underlying logic would be based on the expectation of a lateral communication role of the news media. The news media in nondemocracies are often used to quickly and efficiently communicate messages, such as policy priorities, across government subdivisions and agencies. Thus, it is more of a top-down mechanism, but nondemocratic bureaucracies would still follow media coverage for policy guidance, including guidance on aid priorities. Second, the simpler the structure of the aid decision and allocation process, the clearer the news media's influence appears to be. There is substantial evidence of this in the Japanese aid program.[14] Thus, when additional layers are added to the process, such as happens with multilateral aid programs, the influence should still be present in the priorities that each participant's representative brings to the process. However, the overall effect will be less clear-cut as the additional layers of decision making alter the result of the influence of the news media coverage.

## Development Assistance

Foreign development assistance has historically been analyzed in terms of a tripartite model[15] in which humanitarian, strategic, and capitalist motives all act simultaneously to influence the aid decision. The humanitarian motive is measured in terms of need, typically using some indication of the wealth of the recipient country, such as the per capita gross national product (GNP). The strategic motive is measured in terms of some sort of concrete indication of an established relationship, such as an alliance or ongoing relationship based on a colonial tie and the capitalist motive measured in terms of trade or resource exploitation. A wide variety of indicators for these motives has been used, usually applied to the study of the U.S. aid program, and most analyses find that strategic and humanitarian motives clearly influence aid in the expected way. The capitalist motive finds only occasional, marginal support, and that support is sensitive to the combination of indicators and control variables used in the analysis.[16]

This agenda-setting function was expected to work within the bounds set by other factors known to influence aid, such as need, and not to supersede or overwhelm them. From the moment that the thesis was first tested, it was clear that the media's effect on development aid was a robust and significant addition to the existing factors known to influence development aid.

Data from Van Belle, Rioux, and Potter's 2004 analysis of the U.S. development aid program are presented in table 4.1.[17] The dependent variable is the annual U.S. aid commitment to recipient countries measured in millions of inflation-adjusted U.S. dollars. *New York Times* coverage, measured as the number of stories explicitly mentioning the recipient country in the 12 months leading up to the aid commitment, is the independent variable of interest. The

**Table 4.1. Effect of *New York Times* coverage on Commitments of U.S. Development Assistance, 1985–95**

| Variable | Coefficient | Std. error | z | p > \|z\| |
|---|---|---|---|---|
| *New York Times* coverage | 0.20 | 0.04 | 4.54 | 0.00 |
| Per capita GNP (lag) | −6.71 | 1.56 | −4.30 | 0.00 |
| Trade balance (lag) | 0.00 | 0.00 | 1.95 | 0.05 |
| U.S. alliance | 16.81 | 8.13 | 2.07 | 0.04 |
| Previous year's aid | 0.53 | 0.07 | 7.70 | 0.00 |
| Constant | 17.57 | 3.30 | 5.33 | 0.00 |
| R-square | 0.42 | | | |
| Wald chi-sq (5 df) | 153.17 | | | |
| Prob > chi-square | 0.00 | | | |
| Observations | 7 | | | |

*Source:* Adapted from Van Belle, Rioux, and Potter 2004, table 3-1.
*Note:* Linear regression, panel-corrected standard errors.

independent variables used to control for other influences on the aid decision include the previous year's per capita GNP (measured in thousands of inflation-adjusted U.S. dollars), to control for the humanitarian motive; the previous year's trade balance with the United States, to address the capitalist motive; the presence of a formal alliance with the United States, to measure the strategic motive; and the previous year's aid commitment, to control for the incremental nature of foreign development aid decision making.[18]

In Van Belle, Rioux, and Potter's original analysis, extensive measures were taken to ensure that the findings presented in table 4.1 are both robust and reliable. A wide variety of additional control variables, alternative specifications of the independent variables, and alternative model specifications was tested. Most important, two complementary methods were used to make certain that aid could not be causing the media coverage. First, the media coverage measure was lagged; it measures the coverage in the 12 months leading up to the aid commitment. Second, the content of the media coverage was analyzed; development aid was almost never the subject of the *New York Times* coverage. Removing any stories that mention development assistance does not, in any way, alter the pattern of correlations reported. The results in table 4.1 are robust and representative of the influences on U.S. development aid.

To get a rough idea of the magnitude of the relationships, this analysis interprets the statistics in terms of the per-unit effects that the independent variable has in an average case. The .20 coefficient for the *New York Times* variable means that for every *New York Times* story mentioning the recipient country, the U.S. aid commitment increases by approximately US$200,000. For every $1,000 increase in per capita GNP, the aid commitment decreases by $6.7 million. A U.S. ally gets US$16.8 million more in aid, and every dollar of aid given the previous year is correlated with US$0.53 of aid in the current round. In terms of the significance of the media coverage variable, these results are also reasonably representative of what was found in all of the development aid programs analyzed by the research group that pursued the application of the cockroach theory. This includes the United States, Britain, Canada, France, and Japan.[19] Across the five donor countries, media coverage was the most robust and most consistent influence on the aid commitment. No matter what combination of independent variables was used and no matter what the form of the analysis, or what medium was used as an indicator of salience, media coverage was always statistically significant.[20] Furthermore, its substantive significance (the size of the influence the media coverage had on the aid allocation) was always roughly equal to or greater than the most influential of the other variables analyzed.

The other aspect of these analyses that is important is that they made it clear that it was salience, not content, that mattered. Consistent across all cases thus far studied is the finding that the content of the coverage does not have any kind of consistent, significant influence on the aid commitments being made.[21] The analysis of content was somewhat crude, and there were a few, rare cases where an anecdotal analysis suggested that content mattered, but it was clear from the analyses that if content mattered in any kind of comprehensive and generalizable way, its impact was nowhere near as substantial as salience. This finding fits perfectly with the conceptual foundations of agenda setting, where media coverage is either creating or indicating the importance of a subject, but not having a substantial influence on other aspects of opinion. This finding also fits with what foreign aid bureaucrats have informally said regarding the value of the content of media coverage. Most aid professionals consider the information content in news media reports to be of little or no value to them, and they always refer to professional or official resources as the only sources of substantive information that they consider to be reliable. The conclusion to be drawn is relatively simple. The media salience of a recipient country, regardless of the content of that coverage, provides a consistent and significant, but not overwhelming, boost to development aid allocations from the democratic donor countries.

## The Media, the International Environment, and Disaster Aid

Initially, examinations of U.S. foreign disaster assistance conducted by Van Belle, Rioux, and Potter and Drury, Olson, and Van Belle, were used as a robustness check to confirm that media responsiveness was applicable beyond the bounds of the development aid programs, and the results seemed to indicate just that. The basic finding also applied to the humanitarian response to natural disasters. In fact, the influence of the media was so clear and so robust and so substantial in the allocation of disaster assistance that media coverage was by far the most significant of all factors examined.[22] However, recent studies have shown that the relationship is not as simple as it first appeared,[23] and understanding the current nature of news media's influence on responses to humanitarian crises requires a historical analysis of how the current structure evolved.

Because of limitations on the temporal extent of the available data, most of what the initial studies were capturing was the relationship during what is now labeled as the baseline period, 1965 to 1980. Extending the disaster database to include the years between 1994 and 2006 led to the discovery that at or near 1990 there was a significant and unexpected change in the nature of the media's influence on disaster aid, and the discussion of the humanitarian response to disaster can be framed only in terms of that puzzle.

## The Illusion of a CNN Effect

In the early 1990s, a series of high-profile events led analysts and scholars to the conclusion that persistent media coverage could drive reluctant Western leaders into engaging with complex humanitarian emergencies they would rather avoid. This was dubbed the "CNN effect," and it quickly led to the argument that the global political environment had become defined by media-driven foreign policy.[24] This is also how most people, including policy makers and researchers, then conceptualized the media's role in the humanitarian response to disasters. However, despite what seemed to be overwhelming and undeniable anecdotal evidence, when the disaster aid database of Olsen and Drury[25] was extended to make it possible to measure the sudden change that was supposed to have occurred in roughly 1990, the results produced exactly the opposite of what was expected. Instead of an increase, the influence of the media disappeared from the disaster aid response.[26] This finding proved robust. Rigorous examinations of methods were undertaken, all the way back to the methods employed in extending the data set, and it did not appear that the disruption of the media influence was a methodological artifact or in any other way erroneous. Furthermore, a subsequent analysis identified a similar disruption in the influence of the media on the allocation of Japanese foreign disaster assistance.[27] Clearly, this presented a challenging puzzle, and sorting this out turns out to be the key to understanding the current dynamics of the relationship between media coverage and disaster aid.

## The Intellectual Fait Accompli

Even before the paradox of finding that media's influence had vanished from disaster aid rather than increasing with the rise of a belief in a CNN effect, the unusual initiation of the academic research into the CNN effect offered a clear suggestion that it might be illusory. Unlike any other theory about world politics, the CNN effect was immediately presumed to have suddenly altered the nature of global politics. As a result, instead of beginning with an idea and slowly building the evidence needed to convince skeptics and counter the arguments of critics, academic researchers were presented with the equivalent of a scientific fait accompli, and the bulk of the debate skipped right past any effort to explore the proposed relationship rigorously.

Despite this entry into the debates over foreign policy, researchers quickly realized that the CNN effect was probably overstated. Even in the cases that might be offered as the most obvious examples, the claim that leaders had lost control of policy to the whims of media coverage was immediately shown to be dubious. In the case of Somalia, Livingston and Eachus provide substantial evidence that not only were most U.S. policy actions driven by diplomatic, strategic, and bureaucratic considerations, U.S. policy actions also *preceded* spikes in coverage, with most of the coverage coming in response to those actions.[28] More generally, even when the narrowest definition of the CNN effect was employed, the degree to which news coverage actually drove Western states to intervene in complex humanitarian emergencies was unclear, and almost certainly overstated.

Though it is always dangerous to depict any research subject as homogeneous, the Livingston and Eachus study is indicative of much of the academic study of the CNN effect. Most of the past decade's worth of academic research can be depicted as the systematic reining in of the initial claims of overwhelming media influence and an ongoing effort to distill, define, refine, and consolidate the conceptual foundations of the news media's actual role in foreign policy.[29] Furthermore, most of the studies of the CNN effect were case based and ahistorical. Little or no effort was made to make systematic comparisons of large numbers of cases (large-N) to earlier periods, and that turns out to be the key.

The limited consideration of a historical perspective on the CNN effect is troubling. The initial argument was that advances in communication technology created the CNN effect by creating a technological infrastructure that enabled a truly global communication environment. But the realization of that infrastructure preceded the CNN effect by roughly a decade.[30] Remoteness as a determinant of levels of foreign coverage and the general idea of news media driving foreign policy are far older than that, with the Spanish-American war offering one of the oldest examples. This historical problem with the literature and the timing of the CNN effect produced the rather modest puzzle that led to the 2007 Van Belle study. If the two defining aspects of the CNN effect—rapid global coverage and foreign policy responsiveness to the news media—were in place for at least a decade before the live broadcast of the U.S. Marines landing on the beach near Mogadishu, why then does the idea of the CNN effect appear so suddenly in the early 1990s?

## The End of the Realist Era in Global Politics

The timing of the CNN effect wasn't much of a puzzle because an alternate explanation for the timing of the debate on the CNN effect seems obvious. Piers Robinson argued the point quite clearly.

> A frequently cited cause of the CNN effect was policy uncertainty. Many scholars (Entman; Gowing; Minear, Scott, and Weiss; Robinson; Shaw; and Strobel) agree that as policy certainty decreases, news media influence increases and that, conversely, as policy becomes more certain, the influence of news media coverage is reduced ... At the macro-level, U.S. foreign policy was characterised by a loss of direction following the end of the Cold War[31]

The argument that policy uncertainty caused by the end of the Cold War was a key element of the emergence of the CNN effect is quite logical. In fact, it seems perfectly reasonable to argue that the end of the Cold War had effects well beyond unhinging U.S. foreign policy, perhaps even to the point of altering the very nature of the international system. With a significant reduction of the influence of realist factors of power and influence that had been imposed by the Cold War conceptualization of the global context, it then seems reasonable to assert that something else, such as media, would replace those factors and provide a new conceptual and decision-making framework to define international politics.

Van Belle's 2007 study was based on the premise that this argument for the appearance of the CNN effect might be only half correct. Although the end of the Cold War removed the long-standing, bipolar realist framework for the conduct of international politics, it may not have been the case that the news media rose to fill that vacuum. Instead, removing the Cold War structure may have simply exposed the already existent, substantial influence of the news media on disaster response.[32] That and a few high-profile cases may have thrust it to the forefront of policy debates and policy analysis without really altering media's influence in any substantial way. Van Belle conducted a simple test using the update of the Olsen and Drury disaster response database.[33] Instead of distinguishing between an increase or a steady continuation of media's influence, however, the analysis exposed a profound disruption in the influence of the media at the end of the Cold War, and that did not fit with either explanation for the CNN effect.

*New York Times* coverage is measured as the number of stories that explicitly mention the specific disaster and, contrary to the expectations generated by treating the extreme events as the norm, almost none of this coverage mentions an aid response. The three variables used to measure the human impact of the event—fatalities, people affected, and people made homeless—are all defined and cataloged by the data-holding agency.

The results in table 4.2 were surprising. In the post–Cold War period, the media clearly are not the significant and substantial influence they were

Table 4.2. Global Aid Response to Lethal Natural Disasters during and after
the Cold War

|  | Variable | Cold War 1965–89 | Post–Cold War 1990–2003 |
|---|---|---|---|
| *NYT* stories | Coeff | 1,764,576.00 | 128,385.40 |
|  | SE | 173,009.00 | 875,110.00 |
|  | *p* | 0.00 | 0.88 |
| Fatalities | Coeff | 1,606.19 | 22.71 |
|  | SE | 65.57 | 1,237.50 |
|  | *p* | 0.00 | 0.98 |
| People affected | Coeff | 0.30 | 9.74 |
|  | SE | 0.13 | 0.65 |
|  | *p* | 0.02 | 0.00 |
| People made homeless | Coeff | 1.81 | −128.95 |
|  | SE | 1.17 | 15.85 |
|  | *p* | 0.12 | 0.00 |
| Constant | Coeff | 183,669.20 | 1,046,497.00 |
|  | SE | 1,157,543.00 | 5,309,881.00 |
|  | *p* | 0.87 | 0.84 |
|  | Observations | 1,741 | 3,352 |
|  | Adjusted R-sq | 0.43 | 0.06 |

*Source:* Adapted from Van Belle 2007, table 1.
*Note:* Dependant variable: U.S. aid in inflation-adjusted U.S. dollars.

during the Cold War. During the Cold War, every *New York Times* story covering the disaster led to an increase in aid of roughly US$1.76 million. In comparison to the influence of the media during the Cold War, every person killed correlated with an increase in aid of only US$1,600, but when the numbers of people killed in disaster events was considered (often in the thousands), the aid in response to fatalities can still be substantial, and these two variables account for most of the 43 percent of the aid that this regression can explain. In contrast, in the post–Cold War period, neither of these variables is statistically significant, meaning that they had no consistent influence on the aid allocation whatsoever.[34] This particular analysis is presented because of the clarity and ease of interpretation offered by a simple ordinary least squares regression model, but the choice of presenting such a simplistic analysis can also be indicative of how robust this change is.[35] Regardless of the statistical technique employed or the regression model used, or the adjustments that might be made in case selection, it is absolutely clear that there is a tremendous drop in the general, statistically identified influence of the media.

A drop from US$1.76 million in aid generated per news story to nothing is exactly the opposite of what is expected for the CNN effect, but perhaps even more interesting, and a more valuable clue to the puzzle presented by this analysis, are the more general changes that are revealed. R-squared is a measure of how much of the variation in aid spending is explained by all of the causal variables in the analysis put together, and it can be roughly interpreted as a percentage. Thus, during the Cold War, the four influences listed in the table explained roughly 43 percent of the disaster aid offered. This is more than seven times the 6 percent they explained after the end of the Cold War. This drop in the R-squared provides a significant explanatory clue. If the change that was being captured by the statistics was just the elimination of media coverage as an influence on disaster assistance, other variables should have continued to explain a fair portion of the aid allocation. Instead, the explained variance drops to nearly zero; after the Cold War it became difficult to find any consistent explanation for disaster assistance.

The drop in the influence of all the variables immediately leads to the discovery of a second explanatory clue. Comparing the standard errors attached to each of the coefficients shows a massive increase for all of the variables in the post–Cold War period. The standard error is a measure of how much randomness is attached to the variable's ability to explain what is happening. Standard errors that are much smaller than the coefficient show that the variable consistently has roughly the same effect from case to case. The larger the standard error in comparison to the coefficient, the more its influence varies from case to case, and in the post–Cold War analysis, standard errors that are several times larger than the coefficients indicate huge variations from case to case. This means that in some disasters a variable had a tremendous influence, while in others it had almost none. Though the confidence that can be attached to any interpretation of that detail is unclear, the changes shown in table 4.2 are extreme.[36] This leads to the conclusion that in the post–Cold War period, the decision-making rules used for allocating disaster aid shifted dramatically, almost randomly, from case to case. The decision making for each disaster was still a rational, considered process, but the process was not consistent from one disaster to the next.

## The Ad Hoc Period in International Politics

In their often-cited examination of models of U.S. foreign policy during and after the Cold War, Meernik, Krueger, and Poe noted a relative decline in security-driven and systemic influences on foreign policy in the beginning of the post–Cold War period.[37] Employing logic that is similar to the way that the CNN effect has been discussed, in terms of media influence replacing the influence of realist factors, Meernik, Krueger, and Poe interpreted their findings in terms of domestic ideological factors replacing strategic factors. Implicit in that interpretation, and also in the argument regarding policy uncertainty as the cause of the CNN effect, is the belief that one defining structure of world politics was replaced by another. That idea of a new structure replacing the disappearing structure includes an assumption that both of these periods are structured. Questioning the assumption of a post–Cold War structure suggests an alternative interpretation, and in that lies the explanation for the puzzle of media's disappearance as an influence on disaster aid.

Regardless of the specific technique employed, large-N statistical analyses are all designed to identify influences that are consistent across most or all cases. The goal is to separate the generalizable factors applicable to all cases from the ad hoc or stochastic (that is, random) influences that make each of the individual cases unique. In the study of international politics, statistical analyses presume that the same model of decision making, context, or process can reasonably be applied to all or most of the cases in the population being examined.

Specific to the discussion here, the statistical analyses of Cold War and post–Cold War events presume that both periods were equally explicable. The models are presumed to be different. The relative influence of specific causes is expected to vary, and perhaps different constellations of causal influences might apply to the two periods, but when statistical analyses of the two periods are conducted, researchers are assuming that both periods have an overarching structure that defines decision making. However, there is no reason to assume that there is any overarching structure in the post–Cold War period. And, in fact, the arguments regarding the effects of policy uncertainty in the explanations for the CNN effect suggest exactly the opposite.

Rather than something like media-driven foreign policy replacing the realist structure imposed by the Cold War, it is arguable that the realist structure was replaced by a complete absence of an overarching structure. The absence of an overarching structure would create an ad hoc policy environment in which the individual aspects of each case became the predominant consideration in decision making, and the stochasticity that is introduced across the whole set of cases would reduce any statistical measure of an independent variable's significance in a statistical analysis. This increase in stochasticity explains the results offered by Meernik, Krueger, and Poe as well as the explanation they offer. It also fits with the findings from many of the other analyses of a systemic change, including the findings on media and disaster assistance noted above.

The removal of a predominant structure for interaction and decision making also explains why news media suddenly appeared to become so important. The same structure that enabled certain systemic, domestic, and geostrategic variables to find consistent expression across most cases also constrained the variability of influences from case to case. The influence of any one factor was limited by the bounds defined by the Cold War environment. During the Cold War, media could influence policy only to the degree that they did not contradict the realist demands imposed by the ongoing confrontation. Removing those constraints also opens the door for any one factor to become hugely important in any one case. It was possible for media coverage to become a huge factor in the decision making on Somalia because it was no longer limited by the constraint imposed by the likely or potential Soviet reaction to U.S. action in a state that had been contested as part of the proxy conflict in the developing world. Thus, the 1990s wasn't a period of media-driven foreign policy. It was an ad hoc period in international politics, and because one of the first big events everyone noticed was Somalia, they all started thinking about it in terms of media and presumed that it represented the new structure.

The term "ad hoc" as it is being used here refers strictly to a focus on the singular as opposed to the general. Normative associations with the term need to be excluded. Of particular concern is any idea that ad hoc might refer to irrational policy. The heuristic methods used in decision making may vary radically from event to event, but they are still assumed to be coherent within the context specific to each event. In some ways, this could be argued to be better normatively than a highly structured environment, since it should re- sult in choices that are more effective because they more closely tied to the specifics of the case and would allow far more latitude for policy innovation.

## The CNN Effect as an Illusion

If the 1990s were an ad hoc period in which variation in what mattered from event to event overwhelmed any kind of consistent aid-response pattern, and this decreased the generalizable influence of most variables, including media coverage, how did it happen that this period became so closely associ- ated with the CNN effect and the idea that the world had become defined by media-driven foreign policy? Part of the explanation may simply be chance. Somalia happened to be the first prominent foreign policy event to occur after the removal of the Cold War constraints allowed something other than the U.S.-Soviet confrontation to become a significant driver of policy. It could just as easily have been the Rwanda-Burundi genocides. If that had happened, everyone might have spent a decade arguing about a laissez-faire effect char- acterized by a preference for a hands-off approach that made the avoidance of local or regional conflicts a default choice that had to be overcome by other forces.

Somalia reframed everyone's perceptions of international politics in terms of media coverage, and the unsettled context—often referred to as policy uncertainty in the CNN effect literature—made the situation ripe for the adoption of a new frame for understanding world politics. These kinds of cognitive frameworks are most easily created in new, chaotic, or empty con- ceptual spaces (not to delve too far into the social and cognitive psychology literature). People are in many ways dependent on cognitive frameworks and in an unstructured or unfamiliar context will actively seek a framework, using analogous reasoning or other mechanisms to make things fit or make sense of the incoming information.

People become wedded to cognitive frameworks, and once established, those frameworks become self-reinforcing. People use cognitive frameworks to make sense of incoming information (interpreting things to fit) and to filter incoming information (preferentially noticing and remembering what fits). Actually, the reciprocal aspect of the filtering is probably most significant, as people tend to fail to notice information that contradicts the cognitive framework being employed. As a result, displacing an existing model that people use to interpret incoming information is difficult, sustaining illusions, such as the CNN effect.

To offer an analogy as a way of blatantly using the very topic of discussion to make the point, it is like the widespread belief in lunacy. Irrespective of the bountiful evidence to the contrary, many if not most people living in a Western European–derived cultural context believe that a full moon causes insane behavior. The reason for this belief can be place squarely upon how the myth functions as a cognitive framework. Full moons are common and mildly insane behavior is common, and when a person notices them both occurring together, it is interpreted in terms of the myth of lunacy and considered to be evidence confirming the belief. However, people will fail to notice contradictory information. When the lady knitting an invisible sweater on the bus is talking to invisible Moses during the middle of the day, or when a night with a full moon passes without incident, the lunacy framework is not invoked, and that information is interpreted in terms of something else. As a result, contrary information is not considered in terms of the belief, and the belief persists.

Similarly, once the idea of a CNN effect is established as a cognitive framework, the framework is immediately recognized in the cases it fits, and information is interpreted in terms of how it fits. Even trained analysts and policy officials have difficulty noticing contradictory cases. It is also almost impossible for people to notice the absence of cases in which an explanation should have fit but did not without using scientific observation of a set of cases specifically selected to ensure that null cases are included. In the case of the full moon, unless a person specifically decides to watch for insane behavior on all nights with full moons, the nature of human cognition makes it almost impossible to notice the nights during which insanity should have occurred, but did not. Similarly, the public, policy makers, and researchers all tend to miss media coverage that does not seem to overwhelm the policy agenda. Despite the extreme efforts to avoid becoming involved in Bosnia, or the inaction in Rwanda, or the global response to the Boxing Day tsunami, all three of those events are interpreted as evidence that media coverage drives policy.

The result is the illusion of the CNN effect. The way that academic study has continually narrowed the possible scope of the CNN effect and the contradictory findings from the large-N analysis offered here suggest quite strongly that the CNN effect was illusory. And as a result, the common knowledge that everyone relies on is wrong. In the 1990s, media coverage clearly exerted influence in some disasters and humanitarian crises, occasionally a great deal of influence, but not all the time, and perhaps not even most of the time.

**Figure 4.1. Historical Developments in the Media, International Environment, and Donor Response Mechanisms**

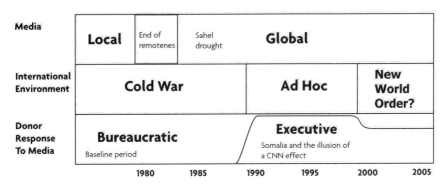

*Source:* Author.

## Remodeling of How Media's Influence Is Understood

The elements that have been discussed can all be brought together to remodel the understanding of media's influence on the humanitarian response to disasters and to provide the foundation needed for understanding both how and why media influence aid responses today.

Figure 4.1 provides a graphic representation of the three key elements for understanding how media influence aid responses: the nature of the news environment, the nature of the international environment, and the mechanism through which media coverage influences aid. Working through this as a historical narrative, from left to right in the figure, the discussion begins with the period from 1965 to roughly 1980, which might reasonably be called the baseline period.

The beginning of the baseline period, 1965 represents the establishment of a U.S. foreign aid program dedicated to disaster response, in the form of the Office of Foreign Disaster Assistance (OFDA). Though this does not by any means represent the first instance of international disaster aid, and almost certainly does not represent the start of a media influence, it does represent an analytical starting point. This was the first year that a global catalog of disasters was compiled, and it was the first year that a corresponding collection of aid response figures was reported. Analyses of these data indicate that from the very beginning, media coverage was a clear influence on the aid allocation. Measured in 1994 dollars, every *New York Times* news story correlated with an increase in aid of roughly $1.76 million.

During this period the decision mechanisms were, for all intents and purposes, entirely bureaucratic. Almost every aspect of the U.S. disaster aid response was governed by the OFDA. The international political environment also was significant during this period; there is clear evidence that the decision-making process related to aid, including the substantial influence of the media, occurred within the boundaries set by strategic aspects of the international Cold War environment. Alliances, for example, were a significant factor in selecting aid recipients.[38] Finally, it is also clear that a globalized media environment had not yet materialized during this period. The remoteness of an event still had a significant effect on coverage. Distant and hard-to-reach disasters received significantly less coverage than events that were easier to reach from the United States or Western Europe.

The first significant change to this constellation of factors was the realization of a global media system. There is no exact date on which the news media went global, but it is clear that a critical change occurred relatively quickly at the end of the 1970s that signified the shift to a global news media. Using disasters as a set of consistently newsworthy events, Livingston and Van Belle's 2005 study demonstrated that about 1980 the remoteness of an event ceased to have a negative influence on the level of coverage it received in the U.S. press. In the early 1980s the global communication infrastructure had reached the critical point at which disasters in Africa, Latin America, Europe, and Asia all received roughly the same amount of coverage.

This change in the media did not have an immediate impact on aid responses. Throughout the 1980s one news story continued to correlate with roughly $1.76 million in aid. What this change did was make it possible for remote and distant disasters to become global media events, and the first of these, the Sahel drought, is argued to have had a profound effect on decision makers.

The Sahel drought was not the first global media event. The first Apollo moon landing would certainly qualify for any reasonable definition of that category, but the moon landing and the handful of other events that might be suggested as earlier examples of global media events all share the characteristic of being closely tied to the media infrastructure of the developed world. The Sahel drought demonstrated that an event did not have to happen in the United States, Europe, or anywhere even close in order to gain massive coverage. By gaining such massive coverage, the drought signaled that the media had become truly global, but for the political leaders of the world, that lesson was secondary to what it taught them about the public response to media coverage of disasters. Regardless of the degree to which the public response to the media coverage was aided and abetted by the conspiracy of a few pop music stars, the massive public response that the media instigated was a powerful example that created a precedent that would shape future responses to the complex humanitarian emergencies of the future. It was a simple lesson: extreme levels of coverage lead to an extreme public reaction, and anything compelling enough to convince a huge portion of the voting public to voluntarily surrender their wealth without expectation of return was not the sort of thing that a democratic leader could dare to ignore. Thus, when an event gained massive coverage, presidents and prime ministers and other elected executives responded to that media coverage, directly committing funds, spurring agencies to extraordinary action, and engaging resources that are beyond the reach of aid agencies, such as military landing craft.

As the CNN effect research demonstrated, this executive mechanism for responsiveness to the media coverage of human catastrophe was more constrained than first thought. There is ample evidence of myriad political and logistical factors that limited the executive's media responsiveness, but the argument for an ad hoc period suggests that these constraints varied tremendously as the specifics of the case demanded. Thus, the relative ease of getting access to Somalia by sea gave it an advantage compared with the Sudan, and Bosnia's political and social proximity to the United States and NATO undoubtedly lowered the barriers to response in comparison to Rwanda and Burundi. But whatever the specific constraints, the appearance was that executives responded to inundations of media coverage.

These media inundations, however, were rare, and the executive mechanism was limited to the largest of the very big media events. This is a big contrast with the bureaucratic mechanism that it replaced. There is ample evidence that when the bureaucratic responsiveness mechanism did function, it was extremely sensitive to coverage. The details within the statistical analyses of the Cold War era suggest that a disaster didn't even have to gain TV news coverage to elicit a response from bureaucratic officials. It appeared that they responded to as little as a single *New York Times* story.[39] In contrast, the president or prime minister is only going to step in and personally engage a disaster that is extremely salient in the news media.

## The Reestablishment of International Structure

Robinson's argument that the CNN effect is dead is premised on the fact that 9/11 and the subsequent war on terror (re)imposed an ideological framework on the conduct of U.S. foreign policy and on international politics more generally.[40] The establishment of the counterterrorism "New World Order" framework removed the policy uncertainty that had been argued to be one of the key aspects of the international context that enabled the rise of media influence, and for all intents and purposes, according to Robinson, it extinguished the CNN effect.

Given the arguments regarding the effect the ad hoc period had on media's influence on disaster aid allocations, if some form of international structure was being reestablished, it would be directly relevant to the current media responsiveness dynamic. If a new structure leads to a set of decision rules being consistently applied across most cases, it should reduce the stochastic variation in the decision models applied, and that should lead to the return of a predictable, generalizable expectation for what factors will influence aid and how. The variables that matter and how much they matter in the "new world order," or the war on terror, or whatever the current era is eventually called, are likely to be quite different from the realist, Cold War framework. However, any kind of overarching structure should bring back a noticeable and measurable consistency.

The analysis in table 4.3 shows that some kind of new international structure has been established. This is most evident in the R-squared measure of explained variance and the return of news media as a statistically significant correlate of disaster assistance. At the end of the Cold War, standard errors jump by an order of magnitude or more, suggesting a very large increase in the variation of the influence of these factors. At the end of the ad hoc period, another massive shift in standard errors is seen, but this time they are shrinking back toward the levels seen in the Cold War. All of this fits with Robinson's argument about the end of policy uncertainty, but there are some suggestions in the data that the shift back to a structured international environment may have occurred before the attack on the World Trade Center, and this remains a point to be sorted out.

It is important to treat the findings for the new world order period as no more than a tentative indication that a consistent decision-making structure of some kind has been reestablished. The post-2003 data are not yet available for analysis, and the 2001–03 period is not just an unsettled period in world

Table 4.3. Global Aid Response to Lethal Natural Disasters during the Cold War, Ad Hoc, and War on Terror Periods

| Variable | | Cold War 1965–1989 | Ad Hoc 1990–2000 | New World Order 2001–2003 |
|---|---|---|---|---|
| NYT stories | Coeff | 1,764,576.00 | 262,268.00 | 8,528.00 |
| | SE | 173,009.00 | 1,365,012.00 | 2,829.93 |
| | p | 0.00 | 0.85 | 0.00 |
| Fatalities | Coeff | 1,606.19 | −761.05 | −19.16 |
| | SE | 65.57 | 2,273.37 | 3.61 |
| | p | 0.00 | 0.74 | 0.00 |
| People affected | Coeff | 0.30 | 15.70 | 0.00 |
| | SE | 0.13 | 1.01 | 0.00 |
| | p | 0.02 | 0.00 | 0.20 |
| People made homeless | Coeff | 1.81 | −209.11 | 6.99 |
| | SE | 1.17 | 20.94 | 0.31 |
| | p | 0.12 | 0.00 | 0.00 |
| Constant | Coeff | 183,669.20 | 2,687,645.00 | −7,285.27 |
| | SE | 1,157,543.00 | 7,941,044.00 | 17,630.32 |
| | p | 0.87 | 0.74 | 0.68 |
| Observations | | 1,741 | 2,200 | 1,152 |
| Adjusted R-squared | | 0.43 | 0.10 | 0.32 |

Source: Van Belle 2007, table 2.
Note: Dependant variable: U.S. aid in inflation-adjusted U.S. dollars.

politics; it is also too short for researchers to be confident that the random fluctuations in the occurrence of disaster events have balanced themselves out sufficiently to consider the statistical results to be definitive.

## The Current Dynamic of Agenda Setting and Disaster Response

The response to the 2004 Indian Ocean tsunami and now the Myanmar cyclone offers clear evidence that the executive response mechanism has persisted beyond the end of the ad hoc period, and when combined with the statistical significance of news coverage in the analysis of 2001–04, it seems reasonable to conclude that the current dynamic includes both a bureaucratic and an executive mechanism for response.

It is important to emphasize the caution that should be exercised in the interpretation of the results for 2001–04. With such extreme changes in the figures in comparison to the ad hoc period, it should hold up reasonably well as an indication that an overarching structure has returned, and the media coverage measure is so clearly significant that it is unlikely that future analyses will find that to be wrong. Still, the coefficient for media coverage, which represents the size of the impact each story has on aid, should be interpreted with extreme caution. Without a clear understanding of what factors are likely to be important in the current global political structure, there is no way to know what might be the right combination of factors researchers need to use to sort out just how much news coverage matters. Still, with the information currently available, it appears that the bureaucratic responsiveness mechanism is smaller than it was during the Cold War, but it is clearly there and it functions in parallel to the executive mechanism. Thus, it is probably wise to formulate policy and other actions with the expectation that every bit of news coverage in donor nations creates a small increase in aid response, and the occasional flood of coverage of a major disaster is likely to generate a massive response.

## Notes

1. The catalog was initiated with the creation of the U.S. foreign disaster aid program in 1965, and since the mid-1990s the catalog has been maintained by the Centre for Research on the Epidemiology of Disasters (Belgium).
2. Committee on Disasters and the Mass Media. 2005 *Disasters and the Mass Media: Proceedings of the Committee on Disasters and the Mass Media Workshop*. Washington, DC: National Academy of Sciences.
3. Ibid. Emphases in the research that followed from the 1979 workshop include media coverage's effect on public opinion and support for aid programs, how media professionals function in crises or emergencies, and the immediate uses of the media in a crisis situation.
4. For example, see Samuel Krislov and David H. Rosenbloom. 1981. *Representative Bureaucracy and the American Political System*. New York: Praeger.

5.  For example, see Terry M. Moe 1982. "Regulatory Performance and Presidential Administration." *American Journal of Political Science* 26: 197–224.

6.  The initial argument for bureaucratic responsiveness appears in Douglas A. Van Belle and Steven W. Hook. 2000. "Greasing the Squeaky Wheel: News Media Coverage and U.S. Foreign Aid." *International Interactions* 26 (3): 321–46. See also Douglas A. Van Belle, Jean-Sébastien Rioux, and David M. Potter. 2004. Media, Bureaucracies, and Foreign Aid: A Comparative Analysis of the United States, the United Kingdom, Canada, France and Japan. New York: Palgrave Macmillan.

7.  *Substantive significance* refers to the proportion of aid offered. Statistical significance refers to the probability that the relationship is likely.

8.  Douglas A. Van Belle and David M. Potter. 2008. "The Illusion of a CNN Effect? Using Japanese Foreign Disaster Assistance to Examine the Effect of Stochastic Policy Environments." International Studies Association Annual Meeting, San Francisco, March 26–29; Douglas A. Van Belle. 2007. "The Ad-Hoc Period in International Politics and the Illusion of a CNN Effect." International Studies Association Annual Meeting, Chicago, February 28–March 3.

9.  George F. Kennan. 1993. "If TV Drives Foreign Policy, We're in Trouble." *New York Times*, p. A14, October 24.

10. Terry M. Moe. 1982. "Regulatory Performance and Presidential Administration." *American Journal of Political Science* 26: 197–224.

11. See the discussion in B. Dan Wood and Richard W. Waterman. 1994. *Bureaucratic Dynamics: The Role of Bureaucracy in a Democracy.* Boulder: Westview Press.

12. Douglas A. Van Belle. 2001. "International Development Co-Operation in OECD Countries: Public Debate, Public Support and Public Opinion." Invited Lecturer at Informal Experts' Meeting, Dublin, Ireland, October 25–26.

13. A detailed discussion of the logic weaving media coverage into agency theory is offered in Van Belle, Rioux, and Potter. 2004. *Media, Bureaucracies, and Foreign Aid.*

14. Van Belle and Potter. 2008. "The Illusion of a CNN Effect?"

15. Steven W. Hook. 1995. *National Interest and Foreign Aid.* Boulder, CO: Lynne Rienner.

16. Van Belle, Rioux, and Potter. 2004. *Media, Bureaucracies, and Foreign Aid.*

17. Ibid.

18. The use of this control variable is the most common way to account for the fact that development aid decisions are generally made in terms of adjustments from the previous year's allocation.

19. Van Belle and Hook. 2000. "Greasing the Squeaky Wheel." Also see Van Belle, Rioux, and Potter. 2004. *Media, Bureaucracies, and Foreign Aid;* Jean-Sébastien Rioux and Douglas Van Belle. 2005. "The Influence of le Monde Coverage on French Foreign Aid Allocations." *International Studies Quarterly* 49: 481–502; Potter and Van Belle. 2004. "The Influence of News Coverage on Japanese Foreign Development Aid." *Japanese Journal of Political Science* 5: 113–35. (Reprinted in Christopher P. Hood, ed. 2008. Politics of Modern Japan: Critical Concepts in the Modern Politics of Asia. London: Routledge).

20. Douglas A. Van Belle. 2003. "Bureaucratic Responsiveness to the News Media: Comparing the Influence of *New York Times* and Network Television News Coverage on U.S. Foreign Aid Allocations." *Political Communication* 20: 263–85.

21. See note 17.

22. Douglas A. Van Belle. 1999. "Race and U.S. Foreign Disaster Aid." *International Journal of Mass Emergencies and Disasters* 17 (November): 339–65. Also see A. Cooper Drury, Richard Stuart Olson, and Douglas A. Van Belle. 2005. "The CNN Effect, Geo-strategic

Motives and the Politics of U.S. Foreign Disaster Assistance." *Journal of Politics* 67: 454–73.

23. Van Belle. 2007. "The Ad-Hoc Period in International Politics"; Van Belle and Potter. 2008. "The Illusion of a CNN Effect?"

24. Kennan. 1993. "If TV Drives Foreign Policy, We're in Trouble."

25. Richard S. Olsen and A. Cooper Drury. 1997. "Un-Therapeutic Communities: A Cross-National Analysis of Post-Disaster Political Unrest." *International Journal of Mass Emergencies and Disasters* 15: 221–38.

26. Van Belle. 2007. "The Ad-Hoc Period in International Politics."

27. Van Belle and Potter. 2008. "The Illusion of a CNN Effect?"

28. Steven Livingston and Todd Eachus. 1995. "Humanitarian Crises and U.S. Foreign Policy: Somalia and the CNN Effect Reconsidered." *Political Communication* 12: 413–29.

29. For a thorough review of the literature, see Eytan Gilboa. "The CNN Effect: The Search for a Communication Theory of International Relations." *Political Communication* 22: 27–24.

30. Steven Livingston and Douglas A. Van Belle. 2005. "The Effects of New Satellite News-gathering Technology on Newsgathering from Remote Locations." *Political Communication* 22: 45–62.

31. Piers Robinson. 2005. "The CNN Effect Revisited." *Critical Studies in Media Communication* 22: 344–49. Robinson's citations include Robert M. Entman. 2004. *Projections of Power: Framing News, Public Opinion and U.S. Foreign Policy.* Chicago: University of Chicago Press; Nik Gowing. 1994. "Real Time Television Coverage of Armed Conflicts and Diplomatic Crises: Does It Pressure or Distort Foreign Policy Decisions?" Working paper. Cambridge, MA: The Joan Shorenstein Barone Center on the Press, Politics, and Public Policy at Harvard University; Larry Minear, Colin Scott, and Thomas George Weiss. 1997. *The News Media, Civil Wars and Humanitarian Action.* Boulder, CO: Lynne Rienner; Piers Robinson. 2002. *The CNN Effect: The Myth of News, Foreign Policy and Intervention.* New York: Routledge; Martin Shaw. 1996. *Civil Society and Media in Global Crises.* London: St. Martin's Press; Warren P. Strobel. 1997. *Late Breaking Foreign Policy: The News Media's Influence on Peace Operations.* Washington, DC: U.S. Institute of Peace Press.

32. Van Belle. 1999. "Race and U.S. Foreign Disaster Aid."; Van Belle. 2003. "Bureaucratic Responsiveness to the News Media"; Drury, Olson, and Van Belle. 2005. "The CNN Effect, Geo-strategic Motives and the Politics of U.S. Foreign Disaster Assistance."

33. This analysis is from Van Belle. 2007. "The Ad-Hoc Period in International Politics." A few relevant points regarding the data and the analysis need to be noted. First, the universe of cases is defined by the cataloging agency as a disaster event. From 1965 to 1994 the cataloging agency was the U.S. Office of Disaster Assistance, and from 1994 on, cataloging and data management responsibilities were passed directly to the Center for Research on the Epidemiology of Disasters (Belgium). Patterns in this data have been noted. First, as is apparent in the numbers of disasters in the periods up to and after 1994, there is a steady increase in the number of disasters over time. Part of this increase is attributed to advances in communication technology that enable a greater sensitivity to disasters occurring in remote areas that were inaccessible in the past, but the majority of this increase is attributed to the dramatic and rapidly continuing increase in populations living in high-risk areas, such as coasts and river deltas. A significant number of these events receive no coverage and no aid response, but the proportion receiving coverage and the proportion that receive assistance have remained reasonably consistent

over time. Also, a modest proportion of cases do not receive coverage in the United States but still receive a modest amount of U.S. assistance. The inverse, however, is almost never true. It is extremely rare for an event to receive coverage and not a corresponding offer of assistance.

34. It is important to remember that this means something like "on average across the whole set of cases," and individual cases can deviate substantially from that generalization.

35. A Heckman selection model produces roughly the same results for the levels-of-aid stage and is probably a more appropriate statistical methodology to apply to the analysis of disaster aid allocations.

36. Again this is a robust finding and was tested thoroughly in Van Belle's 2007 study.

37. James Meernik, Eric Krueger, and Steven C. Poe. 1998. "Testing Models of U.S. Foreign Policy: Foreign Aid During and After the Cold War." *Journal of Politics* 60 (1): 63–85.

38. Drury, Olson, and Van Belle. 2005. "The CNN Effect, Geo-strategic Motives and the Politics of U.S. Foreign Disaster Assistance."

39. Van Belle. 2003. "Bureaucratic Responsiveness to the News Media."

40. Robinson. 2005. "The CNN Effect Revisited."

# Watchdogs:
# Guarding Governance

# 5

# Corruption and the Watchdog Role of the News Media

Sheila S. Coronel

The notion of the press as watchdog is more than 200 years old. Yet the idea of vigilant media monitoring government and exposing its excesses has gained new traction in many parts of the world. Globalization, the fall of authoritarian and socialist regimes, and the deregulation of the media worldwide have fueled a renewed interest in—as well as a surge in the efforts of various groups to support—watchdog reporting by the media.

Since the late 17th century, classical liberal theorists have argued that publicity and openness provide the best protection from the excesses of power. The idea of the press as the Fourth Estate, as an institution that exists primarily as a check on those in public office, was based on the premise that powerful states had to be prevented from overstepping their bounds. The press, working independently of government even as its freedoms were guaranteed by the state, was *supposed* to help ensure that this was so.

The 1980s and 1990s saw the revival of this centuries-old notion and its application especially to transition societies then emerging from the ruins of socialist and authoritarian regimes. It had resonance among citizens facing pervasive corruption, weak rule of law, and predatory or incompetent governments unable to deliver basic services. Today, even in countries where democracy is a fairly new experiment, or even in those like China, where democracy and a free press have yet to take root, the notion of the press as watchdogs of power is embedded in the self-definition of journalists[1] and, in varying degrees, also in public expectations of the media. It is, moreover, a particularly seductive notion to the international donor community, which, since the 1990s, began to publicly acknowledge that corrupt and inept governments were a major impediment to development efforts. As a result, donors who wanted to fund governance reforms also became interested in supporting the media in their performance of their monitoring function.

But is the press acting as watchdog always desirable? In countries where the media are hobbled by draconian state restrictions or driven largely by the imperatives of profit-obsessed markets, is such a role even possible? If so, what enabling conditions make a watchdog press effective? Finally, what impact has media monitoring had in ensuring government accountability? Is a watchdog press the key to governance reform, or is the key civil society, responsive government institutions, or an elite push for reform? Put differently, even if the press were an exemplary watchdog—rather than a lapdog or attack dog of power—can it actually make a difference, especially in societies that seem resistant to, or incapable of, change?

## The Many Faces of Watchdog Reporting

In new and old democracies, the idea of the media as the public's eyes and ears, and not merely a passive recorder of events, is today widely accepted. Indeed, the myth of the intrepid journalist doggedly pursuing the trail of wrongdoing remains very much alive, both in the media as well as popular lore. Governments, it is argued, cannot be held accountable if citizens are ill-informed about the actions of officials and institutions.

Watchdog reporting covers a wide range of different types of journalism. On a routine basis, the watchdog press monitors the day-to-day workings of government, thereby helping citizens assess the efficacy of its performance. Reporting that goes beyond what officials or their spokespersons say, to examine government performance, is also a form of watchdogging.

The genre, at least for the purposes of this chapter, covers a range of exposure journalism, regardless of where it is published or aired, and regardless of the quality, target, and initiator of the investigation. The targets of exposés range from low-level to high-level officials. They can be on small-scale wrongdoing involving petty officials like traffic policemen or clerks, but can just as well be on high-level political corruption involving millions, even billions of dollars, as in the case of dictators and kleptocracies in developing countries. The targets cut across various sectors: while many exposés are about wrongdoing in government, they can also uncover malfeasance in the private sector, such as corporations that cause damage to the public interest, as well as non-profits that take money from unsuspecting citizens. Watchdogging can involve oversight of both individuals and institutions. Almost no public person or group is immune from investigation—indeed, journalists have investigated scamming Buddhist monks (Thailand), sexual abuse in the Catholic Church (United States), and wrongdoing in venerable institutions such as the Boy Scouts (United States).

Watchdog reporting covers an array of malfeasance: from sex and personal scandals to financial wrongdoing, political corruption, enrichment in public office, and other types of wrongdoing. Investigative stories can also be classified according to who initiates the exposé: sometimes they are the results of leaks from interested parties, such as government investigators, rival businesses or politicians, or opposition political parties; others are triggered by whistleblowers inside an organization. Some are investigated first by advocacy groups and campaigners before being taken up by mainstream news organizations. The classic exposés, however, such as the Watergate investigation that resulted in the resignation of U.S. President Richard Nixon, are the product of the initiative and enterprise of journalists and, on occasion, the cooperation of government investigators. Watchdog reports are published or aired in a variety of media: from mainstream newspapers and TV programs to scandal-mongering tabloids, alternative magazines and newspapers, and muckraking Web sites. Some exposés are well researched and crafted; others publish based on rumor rather than fact. Some watchdog reporters adhere to the strictest ethical standards; others may be more compromised.

Investigative reporting, in which journalists invest time and effort to ferret out and expose wrongdoing, is perhaps watchdog journalism's most celebrated form. Investigative journalists report on how laws and regulations are violated. They compare how institutions work with how they are supposed to work. They expose how and why individuals and institutions fail. They report when things go wrong, who is responsible, how the wrongdoing was done, and its consequences. The best investigative work exposes not just individual, but also systemic, failures. Investigative reports show how individual wrongs are part of a larger pattern of negligence or abuse and the systems that make these possible. They examine what went wrong and show who suffered from the mistakes. They probe not just what is criminal or illegal, but also what may be legal and aboveboard but nonetheless harmful.

Watchdog journalism is exposure journalism. The ethical standards of the journalist or the quality of the reporting may be high or low. What distinguishes watchdogging is the exposure of wrongdoing in the public interest. Whatever motivates the journalist or the news organization that publishes a muckraking report is not the issue; what matters is that the reporting warns citizens about those who are doing them harm and empowers them with the information they need. Watchdogging can be both episodic—as in one-off exposés that may or may not have an impact—or sustained, especially where a community of journalists devotes its energies to exposing malfeasance and produces a continuous stream of reports on wrongdoing.

## Is the Watchdog Desirable?

An effective watchdog press ensures that individuals and institutions that are supposed to serve the public remain transparent and are held accountable. A vigilant press is therefore fundamental to good governance. That, at least, is the liberal democratic orthodoxy.[2] This orthodoxy is not unchallenged, however. To nonbelievers, the watchdog role should be subordinate to other, in their view more constructive, goals. Leninist views of the press, for example, which prevailed in socialist regimes, saw the press primarily as a collective propagandist and agitator, as a partner in building socialism, rather than as an entity independent—and skeptical of—government.[3] A related view, fashionable in the 1970s, was the school of development journalism, which preached that in poor countries, the media should veer away from the Western fixation on conflict and disaster and should instead promote developmental goals. From this perspective, the press blunts its critical edge and instead functions mainly as information provider and cheerleader in support of the development agenda.[4] Similarly, as discussed in chapter 14, the "Asian values" conception of the media, which had its heyday during the 1990s, stressed the importance of collective, over individual, rights and welfare. This view, premised on the uniqueness of Asian societies, cast aside Western notions of a watchdog press as inappropriate for the region, where, it is asserted, citizens are willing to sacrifice individual freedoms in exchange for economic well-being. In the Asian values school, the media's role is primarily that of helping forge social consensus for strong governments in pursuit of economic growth.[5]

Even within the liberal tradition, however, there is skepticism about whether the watchdog role of the press should take primacy. Some media scholars and critics argue that the adversarial nature of reporting erodes trust and support for government. Studies on U.S. television reporting, for example, say that TV news presents the image of government as inefficient and wasteful. These studies argue that a constant barrage of reporting on government wrongdoing may lead to the public being desensitized to actual instances of misbehavior by public officials.[6] Western scholars belonging to the "media malaise" school of media effects say that too much negative reporting undermines support for public officials, making it more difficult for them to govern effectively. They suggest that these practices also lead to rising dissatisfaction with governments and more broadly, with democratic institutions and democracy itself.[7] Elsewhere, particularly in postconflict societies, questions have been raised about whether adversarial media can endanger democratic consolidation and spark chaos.[8]

Another strain of criticism portrays media exposure of wrongdoing not as furthering their watchdog role but as morphing into their less edifying role as purveyor of scandal. Media as scandalmonger means that the end goal is to titillate and amuse citizens, rather than inform and mobilize them for reform.

The continuous stream of media exposés reinforces the "politics of permanent scandal," where there is unending controversy and frenzy on the political stage but not much substantial reform. Instead, scandals—just like elections—become an arena for political struggle among elites, rather than a venue for mobilizing the public to push for change.[9] The danger, as a Hungarian scholar writing about the Balkans put it, is that "when everyone cries wolf, the public loses all interest in accusations of corruption and normalizes it. The very high level of government corruption becomes a normal fact of life."[10]

More radical critiques of the media, on the other hand, say the opposite: that the media, far from being hypercritical, actually rarely perform their watchdog role or question the existing social order. Thus, they wonder whether the media's purpose and organizing principle ought to be based on what they do NOT do most of the time.[11] The watchdog doctrine, after all, dates back to an era when the "media" consisted largely of small-circulation and largely polemical newsletters and the state was dominated by a landed aristocracy. The argument then was that private ownership protected the press against state intervention. But private ownership has not shielded the press from market pressures, resulting in the downgrading of watchdog reporting in favor of fluff and entertainment. In other words, while a press autonomous of government should in theory act as watchdog, it cannot do so given the constraints of market-based media. The liberal orthodoxy—stuck in romantic, 18th-century notions of small papers fighting autocracy—therefore privileges the media's watchdog role with regard to the state while putting the press in the service of corporate power.[12]

## The Watchdog and Government

For sure, the way the press operates in the real world rarely corresponds with normative prescriptions of how the media ought to function. All over the world, the media are seldom immune from the pressures of either the state or the market—or, in many countries, both. In addition, the structure and ownership of the media industry, as well as professional practices, cultures, and norms, have a bearing on how well the press performs as watchdog. The relationship between the media and those in power is also a factor. Moreover, certain historical moments seem to be more conducive to watchdog reporting than others.

Without doubt, the institutional arrangements of democracy provide the most hospitable environment for watchdog reporting. The constitutional and legal protections for a free press, as well as access to government-held information, give journalists not only the right, but also the tools with which to monitor government. The checks and balances inherent in the representative system also legitimize journalistic inquiry as part of a broader framework of government accountability to citizens.

This is why watchdog reporting cannot take place in Myanmar or the Democratic People's Republic of Korea. This is also why it has emerged in new democracies, even in places like the Balkans that have no history or tradition of independent media.[13] The burst of investigative energies in the past 20 years was largely in places where repressive regimes fell apart. After years of propaganda and thought control, citizens were hungry for information, and their appetite for news and commentary was unleashed once the restraints were relaxed. New democratic leaders not only dismantled information ministries and state censorship but also liberated the media from state ownership, paving the way for entrepreneurs who took advantage of the commercial opportunities to cater to a market hungry for news. Freed from state controls, the media took on government and also made profits from their exposés. Emboldened by their freedom, their prestige, and their profits, the media in many new democracies now poke their noses into areas of public life from which they had once been barred, exposing corruption and malfeasance in both high and low places, and in areas like the military, which previously have not been subjected to press scrutiny.

What is surprising is that investigative reporting has taken root in a non-democracy like China, a one-party state where media freedoms are not guaranteed and journalists can count on few protections. There, watchdog journalism was fueled not so much by political, but by market, liberalization. Economic reforms initiated in the late 1970s led to media reforms in the 1990s, which meant decreased government subsidies for the media. This, in turn, forced media agencies to operate as commercial enterprises, as they had to depend on advertising and circulation in order to survive. Recognizing that muckraking can be profitable, journalists were encouraged to report more aggressively.[14] Soon publications and public affairs programs specializing in investigative reporting were set up, probing issues such as corruption, crime, and the environment. Although the targets of the investigations were mostly low- and midlevel officials, the new reporting represents a radical change from the past.[15]

Despite country differences, the forces that propelled investigative reporting in Latin America, Southeast Asia, and China were broadly similar: social and political upheavals that created a demand for information, journalists and media entrepreneurs who took advantage of the loosened controls and the new business opportunities to expose wrongdoing, and a restless public that was primed for muckraking reporting.[16] In earlier eras, these same factors also spurred investigative journalism elsewhere—in the United States in the early 1900s and again in the 1970s, and in the United Kingdom in the 1960s and 1970s.[17]

In all these countries, a combustible mix of social ferment, competitive media markets, and political liberalization fueled investigative energies. But the importance of journalistic agency cannot be underestimated. A community of journalists and entrepreneurs needed to seize the opportunities created by market and social forces. After all, in many developing countries investigative reporters take great risks and are poorly or modestly paid. Most of the more than 700 journalists killed worldwide since 1992 were investigating crime, politics, and corruption. More than 70 percent of those killed were specifically targeted for murder, often by contract assassins. And most of them were working for newspapers and broadcast stations in democratic countries.[18] Apart from physical attacks, investigative reporters have also been subjected to jail terms and harassment lawsuits, as well as laws that restrict information access, all of which impede their ability to expose wrongdoing.

The pathology is clear: even as democracy provides the optimum conditions for watchdog reporting, many democracies in the world are unable to provide adequate protections for journalists. And yet, neither murders nor lawsuits have succeeded in gagging the press. In democracies like the Philippines, Mexico, and Colombia, where the journalist casualty rates are among the highest in the world, the muckraking spirit remains alive. One exception is the Russian Federation, but other factors apart from killings, including the public mood and the takeover of independent media by businesspeople close to the Kremlin, may explain why Russian media have tended toward acquiescence in recent years.[19]

## The Watchdog and the Market

There is no argument that state controls are an impediment to watchdog journalism. There is far less consensus about the role of the market. On one hand, market liberalization and competition have encouraged the emergence of, and in many places, also sustained, investigative reporting. But at the same time, market pressures are a major obstacle to its continued viability. Democracies all over the world suffer from these contradictions. Most everywhere, the complaint is the same: because most of the media are organized as for-profit enterprises, the performance of democratic services is often secondary to profit making. Sometimes there is a fit: profit motives spur concern for the public welfare. But often the goals collide. There is a design flaw: Critics say that privately owned media, independent of the state but slave to the market, are at best episodic and unreliable watchdogs.[20]

This view gained currency in the United States in the 1980s with the emergence of big media conglomerates and the takeover of family-owned media enterprises by giant corporations.[21] The dumbing down of the news and the dominance of entertainment values in the media have been blamed on the rise of profit-hungry media behemoths. Even so, many big news organizations supported investigative reporting, partly because of the prestige it brought and partly because their profits could sustain it. Today, as new technologies threaten the business model that has supported journalism for the past century, the resources for watchdog reporting are being slashed. The discourse has shifted away from the shortcomings of big, commercial media to alternative ways, including nonprofit models, to sustain watchdog reporting.[22]

Elsewhere, the evidence is mixed. In Europe, a study by the Dutch-Flemish Association for Investigative Journalists (VVOJ) showed that the leading outlets for investigative reporting are national newspapers, public service broadcasters, and in some countries, weeklies and Sunday papers. Local media and commercial broadcasters rarely invested in investigations, according to the VVOJ study, which included both Eastern and Western Europe, Russia, Turkey, and Ukraine. Concerns about profitability do not seem to be the driving force. The history of the newspaper, newsroom culture, and editorial leadership are more important determinants of whether a news organization would invest in watchdog reporting.[23] Though in the past tabloids competed for scoops on political malfeasance, they were now shifting their rivalry to the coverage of celebrities. In the older democracies of Western Europe, therefore, the market does not now seem to be propelling or repressing investigative energies. Instead these energies are channeled to certain types of media.

In contrast, in China, the market has proved to be a real boon to muckraking. It could be that in countries where one party monopolizes political power and controls the media with a heavy hand, profit-oriented media provide probably the only check on power, and a competitive media market can spawn muckraking in various forms. In postauthoritarian Latin America, mainstream publications that were part of media conglomerates began investing in high-quality investigative reporting in the 1980s. With their economic power and political influence, they could risk exposing wrongdoing in government without fear of financial or political repercussions. "Profits," wrote Silvio Waisbord, "laid the groundwork for watchdog journalism, spawning a politically confident press uncompromised with government interests."[24]

In postdictatorship Southeast Asia, the emboldened media, with an eye toward profit and market share, exposed corruption and malfeasance in public life in both the prestige and tabloid press. Television, in particular, uncovered sleaze and corruption to attract viewers. "Gotcha" reporting, such as exposés of state employees receiving bribes, often dramatized with the use of hidden cameras, became part of the menu of prime-time television news, together with celebrity gossip and reports on the bizarre and the supernatural.[25] Reporting on malfeasance can indeed give a media organization competitive advantage, but it does not ensure that once the eyeballs tire of corruption, the media's gaze will not shift elsewhere. If watchdogging is primarily a marketing gimmick, it can be sustained only so long as the gimmick works. Financially viable muckraking presumes a public that is interested in the exposure of wrongdoing.

Investigative reporting is expensive and time-consuming. It requires an investment in staff and resources. It is also risky. Sometimes, however, the political and prestige rewards can offset the financial costs, as is the case in Latin America and Southern Europe, where news organizations conducted exposés in order to promote the pragmatic political or economic interests of various groups or because of petty personal rivalries.[26] In Russia, and to some extent in Latin America and Asia, journalists are sometimes used to promote a political or financial agenda through the publication of well-timed leaks. In many instances, these journalists, many of them underpaid, receive money from interested parties. The term *kompromat* in Russian refers to black public relations or the publication of dossiers prepared by the political or business rivals of the subject of the exposé. In Latin America, this is called *denuncismo*. Whatever the name, this type of compromised investigative reporting is driven neither by the market nor by journalistic initiative but by vested interests that cripple the autonomy of journalists and news organizations.

No doubt financial viability brings independence as well as the capacity to support muckraking reporting. In theory, for-profit, privately owned media can support production of exposés because of their resources and their autonomy from government. That they do not always do so is another issue. But the question that arises is what happens if privately owned media are not profitable. In some countries, state subsidies and citizen contributions, as in the case of public-service broadcasters, or philanthropic support provide an alternative source of funding for watchdog reporting.

Indeed, some of the most sophisticated and fearless watchdogging is being done by independent, nonprofit entities devoted to investigative reporting. A recent study showed that some 40 such groups have emerged since the late 1980s in such diverse places as Romania, the Philippines, Jordan, and South Africa.[27] These groups are largely funded by foundations or international donors. They fill a gap in media systems where market, ownership, or political pressures make investigative reporting by commercial or state-owned media difficult, if not impossible. These centers are involved in training and reporting and serve as models of excellence that are helping raise the standards of local journalism.

Elsewhere, start-up ventures by individual journalists are taking the lead in cutting-edge investigations. In Malaysia, the Web-based news site Malaysiakini is filling the information gap in a country where the media are in the hands of the ruling party and its business allies. The site is funded partly by foundations and partly by subscribers. In India, Tehelka, a newspaper start-up that had its origins on the Web, is doing classic muckraking involving sting operations and undercover cameras in a country where private media are immensely profitable and have a tradition of independence from government.

There may be sound economic arguments for this. An economist using game theory posits that older, bigger, and more established media companies will tend to undertake investigations only when the expected gain from exposure is large enough to justify the expenditure. On the other hand, new and emerging media entities that have little to lose are more likely to take the risk on muckraking reporting that allows them to establish a foothold, particularly in nascent media markets.[28] Unsurprisingly, a study done in the 1990s by a Swedish editor concluded that in Europe, newsrooms that were in bad shape financially tended to do more substantial investigative reporting.[29] One reason could be that they needed to compete with the market leaders. Throughout Europe, many big and profitable news organizations did not do investigative reporting at all. In contrast, many more small and financially strapped media had a tradition of exposure journalism.

In sum, watchdog reporting has been done under a variety of conditions. The type of media ownership, the size of the news organization, its financial viability, and profitability are not in themselves sufficient factors in determining whether watchdog reporting can take root and be sustained. Investigative reporting has been spawned in a variety of market conditions and has been undertaken as much to enhance profits as to further political, professional, or prestige goals. The structures that best support watchdog journalism vary over time and across countries: these could be competitive, nonstate media as in contemporary China; big and profitable private media companies in Latin America; or noncompetitive, publicly funded broadcasters in Northern Europe.

Competition appears to be a factor, which means that newsrooms are more likely to invest in exposés if these give them a competitive edge over their rivals. But competition alone is not a predictor, as media companies can compete in other areas as well; exposés do not always guarantee an audience. Moreover, the rise of nonprofits and citizen journalism Web sites engaged in watchdogging changes the equation, if only because they do not factor in profits and competitive edge in their calculations. The market is not unimportant, but it is not the rock on which the fate of watchdog journalism rests.

## The Watchdog and the Profession

It is interesting, but not surprising, that when journalists study themselves, they tend to stress agency over structure.[30] Academic studies, in contrast, tend to do the opposite, analyzing the structures that shape media development by creating the impediments as well as the opportunities to which journalists and media organizations respond. Journalists do take structural conditions seriously, but they also point to where interventions, either by individuals or news organizations, can make a difference. The VVOJ study of investigative journalism in Europe, for example, lists preconditions for watchdog reporting (press freedom, access to information, laws that facilitate rather than impede the ability of journalists to conduct investigations). But it devoted more substantial research to what conditions existed in newsrooms, what kinds of journalists tended toward muckraking, and what motivated them to do so.

"Digging" newsrooms, according to VVOJ, had more creative staff and allowed their reporters more freedom. In addition, they had stronger, more competent, and less authoritarian management. Journalists trained in investigative techniques also tended to practice these more. As elsewhere, European investigative reporters had political, personal, and professional motives for muckraking. Political motives dominate in countries where the media have political affiliations, and so news organizations work on exposés to promote partisan political goals. Personal motives take precedence where the media are no longer politically aligned but have not yet become professional. In this instance, investigations are conducted mainly by "lone wolves," that is, freelancers or staff reporters in newsrooms that do not provide much support for exposés. These highly motivated individuals driven by the watchdog ethos, initiate and catalyze interest in investigative reporting in their news organizations and in the media at large. Certainly, many of the nonprofit investigative reporting centers that have recently flourished in new democracies are driven largely by individuals of this kind. They are essentially lone wolves working at the margins of the mainstream, which is not (yet) hospitable to watchdog reporting.

Professional motives take preeminence when investigative reporting has been institutionalized in newsrooms, and the media as an industry have become professionalized (for example, journalists are academically trained, there are professional standards to which they must comply, and their news organizations take a neutral stance). The VVOJ study outlined a linear progression from partisan to professional muckraking.

There has not been a lack of academic attention on how professional norms, practices, and values affect how the media do their work. Most of the scholarly research looks at how these norms evolved as a response to larger changes in media and society. For example, the norm of journalistic objectivity is said to have emerged in the United States in the late 19th century as a response to both the elevation of science and the scientific method and the rise of newspapers that depended on advertising and circulation for their sustenance. Unlike the party presses of an earlier era, these newspapers attracted bigger audiences by promoting impartiality and factuality rather than partisanship and polemic.[31]

Professionalization in the media, some studies have argued, took place where the mass circulation press was strong and the increasingly large-scale and profitable media organizations that evolved needed professional standards and practices—as all large organizations do—in order to operate efficiently.[32] According to Hallin, all these developments were themselves a consequence of capitalist development, the rise of mass democracy, and an assertive middle class.[33]

Like VVOJ, these scholars see a progression from partisan to professional media. Certainly, this was the case in Latin America, where the ideological press monopolized watchdogging in the 1960s and 1970s. But things changed in the 1980s and 1990s, when big mainstream publications that were carriers of the ideology of professional journalism dominated the investigative scene.[34]

If this trajectory is the standard path of media development, it could be argued that it would be futile for developing countries still in the earlier phases of the development arc to aspire to the kind of professional investigative reporting done in big newsrooms in North America and Western Europe. They would need to wait for the structures to evolve to make this kind of journalism the norm. In the meantime, the flame of muckraking would be kept alive by journalists and media organizations sustained by political or personal, rather than professional or institutional, agendas.

But, yet again, the Internet puts a damper on all these calculations. The first decade of this century has seen the rise of muckraking blogs and Web sites, some of which do not adhere to 20th-century standards of professional journalism, partly because they are not part of large organizations that need to be governed by professional norms. Many of these new entities are run not by professional journalists but by savvy individuals who report and write unencumbered by the ideology of professionalism. Some of them in fact are critical of the standards and practices associated with the mainstream media. In the United States and elsewhere a range of new-media muckrakers challenge traditional professional norms. They could be foreshadowing the next step in the trajectory, a sort of post-professionalization phase brought about by the different values and norms—as well as the different news imperatives—that prevail in the online world.

In the developing world, where the media are not professionalized to the degree they are in the West, the pre- and post-professionalization phases coexist. For example, in China, where the mainstream media remain under Communist Party control, the blogosphere, despite sophisticated Internet surveillance, has provided a home for watchdogging by citizens. There were 221 million Internet users in China by 2008, making it the world's largest Internet-using population.[35] There are also tens of millions of blogs. While only a fraction of these deal with public affairs, the political bloggers take seriously their role as watchdogs of power, even if many of them remain Party supporters.[36]

China is an illustrative case of how the self-definition of journalists (and indeed, of citizens) can evolve over time. Hugo de Burgh conducted interviews with Chinese journalists and concluded in a 2003 paper that "across the generations and regardless of the medium within which they work, Chinese journalists do at present have a passion for that journalism which scrutinizes authority and delves into the failings of society."[37]

This was certainly not the case for a long time. De Burgh posited that this new ethos could be a reflection of a change in the way the Chinese see themselves and their relationship with authority. But this new watchdog role is complex, not quite what it is in the West, where investigative journalists not only expose derelictions of duty but also expand notions of duty beyond what is legally defined or normally accepted by society. Chinese journalists, said de Burgh, "are both upholders of the order and its critics, both limiting discourse to acceptable topics and extending moral boundaries."

This shows that journalists are constantly redefining their roles in response to both institutional and economic changes as well as the expectations of their audiences. Normative role definitions are adjusted to the reality in which journalists find themselves. In China, social and economic changes created an environment that required the media to be more responsive to their audience. Striving to adjust to these changes, Chinese journalists found inspiration both in Western notions of watchdog reporting and in the example of Chinese activist-journalists writing in the early part of the 20th century.[38] They were also responding to a more aware and restless citizenry angry about corruption and malfeasance. But at the same time, many of them were believers in the ambitions of China as a resurgent global power and in the idea that the media's role is as much to establish public confidence in government as it is to expose betrayals of the public trust.

The journalist as watchdog, therefore, is a role that is defined differently across countries and cultures. That definition is fluid, often contingent on the existing social, political, and economic conditions, and a reflection as much of the historical moment as it is of preexisting structures and media cultures. Journalists are inspired by liberal democratic notions of the press as watchdog, but they draw from the well of their own culture and history as well. They adjust their role definitions to the demands of their audiences, their news organizations, and the times in which they live.

Among journalists, watchdogging is not universally seen as a role that the press ought to play. This is the case even in mature democracies. David Weaver's study found that although the vast majority of British and Finnish journalists believed in the watchdog function, only 30–40 percent of German and French reporters did.[39] And certainly it is possible, as it was in China, that these perceptions will change. De Burgh and others have argued that it could well be that the preeminence of the watchdogging ethos rises and ebbs over time, depending on the appetite of consumers. Certainly in the United States, public interest in investigative reporting peaked in the early 1900s and again in the 1970s; in the intervening period, watchdogging did not capture the imagination of many journalists or the public. In the United Kingdom, the interest in exposure journalism peaked in the 1960s and again in the 1980s. Such peaks usually occur during times of social ferment, when there is widespread questioning of authority, social movements are strong, and there is great public interest in the exposure of social and political ills.

In the end, a watchdog self-definition helps channel journalistic energies to investigations in places where states and markets create enough of an opening for this kind of reporting. But it certainly helps to have audience interest and public demand for exposés. Though public interest in watchdogging may be inconstant and fleeting, the institutionalization of government monitoring and investigative reporting in journalistic practice may help ensure that the watchdog function remains alive. Journalism schools play a role in instilling the watchdog ethos and teaching investigative skills to future generations of journalists. Press associations and other professional organizations that do training in investigative skills also help. News organizations that adhere to high standards of investigative reporting help build a tradition of watchdog journalism and provide a model that others can emulate. All these efforts help sustain the notion—indeed, the myth—of watchdog reporting, even if the practice itself flags.

## The Watchdog's Impact

The proponents of watchdog journalism have high hopes for what it can do, especially in the control of corruption. By exposing wrongdoing, they say, the press prompts investigations of those involved in malfeasance and catalyzes changes in laws and regulations. It helps shape public opinion against corrupt governments and generate public hostility against those who abuse their office.[40]

In the United States, media scholars Protess et al. found that investigative reporting can produce three types of policy effects. The first type is described as "deliberative," meaning the reports result in official commitments to discuss the problems raised and the possible solutions; thus, studies may be commissioned or government bodies may initiate hearings to deliberate reform initiatives. "Individualistic" results take place when sanctions are applied against individuals or enterprises accused of wrongdoing. "Substantive" reforms happen when the investigations result in tangible changes in rules, laws, procedures, or policies or new governmental units or bodies are created or public funds are reallocated.[41]

All of these are not in the realm of possibility; they have happened. There are countless examples from all over the world of how watchdog reporting has helped cause the downfall of governments, reforms in law or policy, and the creation of new mechanisms of government accountability. But it should also be said that many well-documented investigations end up in oblivion. They may make waves, win awards, generate controversy for a couple of weeks, but the wrongdoings they expose are not acted upon. Certain institutions remain impervious to reform, while others may initiate changes only to backslide into the practices of the past.

In his study of investigative reporting in Latin America, Waisbord said that factors unrelated to the quality of journalistic work affect the impact of an exposé. These include the timing of the report's release, the prestige of the news organization, and the production values of the investigation.[42] Scandals involving well-known figures and sensational details get more public attention, as do investigations that appeal to the public's voyeuristic appetites. But, as he showed in the case of Argentina, although the "-gate" type of scandals (a reference to Watergate) generate buzz, especially in political circles, they are largely met with public indifference. Where the public is accustomed to high-level political corruption, scandal fatigue can result. In contrast, scandals on issues that affect citizens directly—such as human rights abuses in Argentina in the late 1990s—are able to engage publics not usually interested in politics.[43] In addition, the balance of political forces is an important factor. Accountability, Waisbord said, hinges on the combined actions of a network of institutions, such as the judiciary, parliament, and political parties.

The Southeast Asian experience affirms these findings. The different outcomes of journalistic investigations on official assets—one in the Philippines, and the other in Thailand, both in 2000—show that the impact of investigative reports is contingent upon the configuration of social and political forces at a particular point in time and on the ability of interested publics to mobilize against the wrongdoing that has been exposed. A great deal also depends on how the debates on the revelations of wrongdoing are framed in the public discourse.

In the Philippines, a team of investigative reporters uncovered how then-President Joseph Estrada, a former movie star who publicly paraded his four mistresses, concealed the assets of his multiple families. The reporters revealed that he was building grand houses and buying Jaguars for his paramours, acquisitions that were not reflected either in his asset disclosures or his income tax returns but that were purchased through front companies or nominees. The reporting implied that the reason for the nondisclosures was that Estrada had been accumulating wealth from illegal sources and could therefore not make a full disclosure without incriminating himself.[44]

These reports, together with the public revelation by one of the president's closest friends that he was making millions from payoffs made by illegal gamblers, were so scandalous that they let loose all the forces that had previously been held in check by the president's popularity: opposition political parties, the Catholic Church, citizens groups with a reformist agenda, and even the business community, which from the beginning had serious doubts about the president's capacity to govern.

Eventually, opposition congressmen initiated an impeachment charge against the president. The investigative reports and the revelations of the gambling whistleblower provided the initial evidence for the impeachment trial. When it seemed the trial was going to be compromised, with the refusal of the majority of senators to accept incriminating evidence against Estrada, hundreds of thousands of Filipinos massed in the center of Manila in a "people power" uprising that ousted the president in January 2001.

The debate on Estrada was framed in moral terms: his excesses were seen as transgressions of the standards on how officials should behave. The Catholic Church, which played a key role in the anti-Estrada movement, ensured that the debate would be fought on moral grounds. The key actors in the uprising were mainly middle-class reformers, professionals, students, office workers, and key sections of the Manila business community, the same constituency that took part in the 1986 revolt against Ferdinand Marcos.

At about the same time that Estrada was being subjected to a public scrutiny of his assets, a similar investigation was happening in Thailand. A Bangkok-based business biweekly revealed that Thailand's Prime Minister Thaksin Shinawatra hid US$50 million worth of shares in the names of, among others, his driver, housekeeper, security guard, and maid. Thaksin, a telecommunications and media tycoon, was among the richest businessmen in Thailand. A former police general, he had a history of using his political clout to build his business empire. The press exposé led to an investigation by the National Counter-Corruption Commission, which ruled that Thaksin had intentionally concealed his assets as part of a "dishonest scheme." The ruling was brought up to the Constitutional Court, which acquitted the prime minister in a split vote. But unlike in the Estrada case, there was no uprising on the streets of Bangkok as a result. Why the different outcomes for essentially similar cases brought to the public attention by diligent investigative reporting done in the same year?

The answer lies not so much in the failure of investigative reporting but in the success of a media-savvy prime minister in changing the parameters of the debate and in framing the discourse in different terms. The press and civil society groups in Thailand looked at the Thaksin case as part of a continuum of political reforms that had been undertaken in the country since it was hard-hit by the 1997 Asian crisis. To them, it was a simple matter of the rule of law: the prime minister lied in his statement of assets; therefore, he should be punished. Thaksin, however, "invoked popularity against the rule of law."[45] He succeeded in convincing large segments of the public that what he did—using nominees—was part of normal business practice. In the face of a critical press, he brought his case directly to the public and courted popular opinion by instituting populist measures. Riding on the phenomenal success of his telecommunications empire, Thaksin told Thais that he alone could boost the economy and get rid of poverty.

The difference between the Philippine and Thai cases was not just in the way the debate was framed, but also in the mood of politicized publics. Both Thaksin and Estrada were popular heads of state with large electoral mandates. Both also represented a departure from the past: Thaksin was a modernizing businessman, not a crusty bureaucrat; Estrada, a movie actor, not a greasy politician. Both were elected to head countries with a free press, recent histories of popular mobilization, and an influential and politically active middle class. In the Philippines, the political class—made up of a significant section of the elite, the Church, NGOs, and the middle-class—were so scandalized by the boozing, thieving, and womanizing Estrada that they wanted him out. On the other hand, in Thailand, the business community, the politicians, and the public supported Thaksin, at least in 2001, and bought into his vision of the prime minister as the country's CEO. They were willing to overlook his transgressions if he could deliver—and to some extent, he did.[46]

Certainly, one reason the Estrada investigation caught fire was that it had all the tabloid ingredients—sex and scandal, mansions, and mistresses. The issues concerning Thaksin were far more complicated and far less sexy. For the most part, the most successful investigative reports have been those that focus on individual wrongdoing, on stories with clear villains, rather than on more complex issues that have to do with social inequity, injustice, harmful public policy, or social and political structures that lack accountability. Estrada's excesses, for example, could be seen in the light of the problems inherent in the Philippines' presidential form of government, where the chief executive holds extraordinary powers unchecked by existing oversight mechanisms. The media, however, failed to frame the story in a larger context: it was primarily treated as a story of individual excess, rather than one of systemic flaws.

Structures and systems are hard to explain. Journalists throughout the world are accustomed to dealing with the current and the empirical; they are generally handicapped in handling systemic, historical, or structural questions. Even if they had this skill, however, such content would find scant space in the commercially oriented media. Stories that have a human and dramatic element sell better. It is also easier to correct wrongdoing committed by an individual rather than one that involves systemic or structural change. Investigative journalists, therefore, try to humanize and dramatize their findings by portraying individual characters and using literary and dramatic devices to highlight the wrongdoing that they expose.[47] They also try to frame their stories in a way that makes them easily understandable to, and appreciated by, the public.

For sure, the framing can be wrong, at least partially. The classic of the genre, the reporting on Watergate, has been widely regarded since the 1970s as the touchstone and archetype for investigative reporting worldwide. The Watergate investigation, more than any other in contemporary times, showed the power of the press in a democracy. But more recent critics say that Watergate's verdict, as framed by the liberal press—that "Nixon was uniquely disgraceful, his direct abuses of power and violation of the law, unprecedented"—was wrong.[48] Other presidents were guilty of equal, or even greater, betrayals of the public trust. Watergate is instructive in other respects. To begin with, Schudson noted, the press did not uncover Watergate on its own: government investigators and Congress all played a role.[49] Others go so far as to say that Watergate was driven not so much by the media or public opinion but by political insiders. The political elite drove the reporting, and this resulted in Watergate being defined as a legal issue, rather than a systemic one.[50] Certainly many media investigations in the developing world are Watergate-like in their inception and framing.

Unsurprisingly, Protess et al. were skeptical of the "mobilization model," which says that exposés, by changing public opinion and mobilizing publics, ultimately lead to policy reforms. There may be a link between press exposure and policy changes, they say, "but the link is weak and unreliable."[51] The media may change public attitudes but they don't necessarily mobilize the public to participate in political life. The press may be more influential in molding the attitude and behavior of political elites, who are much more sensitive to how the media report on them. Protess et al. examined six investigative reports and found that policy changes that result from exposés are sometimes triggered not so much by public outrage but by prepublication transactions between journalists and officials. The relationship between muckraking reporters and policy makers was not always adversarial, and it may be cooperative when press and policy agendas overlap.

All these considerations, however, do not negate the fact that, ultimately, whatever the constellation of factors that led them there, exposés of wrongdoing in public office can help make personnel and policy changes possible if the environment is ripe for reform. They can sometimes also mobilize the public, but they are often more successful in getting officials to act. Though watchdog reporting may push the wheels of change and reform, however, the media have little control of the direction these take and the obstacles they face. The impact of watchdog journalism is often diminished by the inertia of governments, the unwillingness of elites to take action, the weight of bureaucratic cultures that are resistant to change, a law-enforcement system that is incapable of punishing wrongdoing, and an apathetic and cynical public.

Despite these, Aymo Brunetti and Beatrice Weder argued that watchdog reporting is "potentially a highly effective mechanism of external control" against two particularly pernicious types of corruption.[52] The first type is extortive corruption in which a government official has the power to delay or refuse service in order to get a bribe. Brunetti and Weder posited that the press can provide a vehicle for voicing complaints about such extortions. Victims, they said, have a strong incentive to expose this type of corruption to journalists. Press reports, in turn, increase the risks of exposure of corrupt bureaucrats and, over time, act as a deterrent to official extortions. The press, however, is even more effective against collusive corruption. When there is collusion, both bureaucrats and their clients have no incentive to expose malfeasance, as in the case of extortive corruption. In a free-press system, however, journalists are motivated by competition and a professional ethos to expose wrongdoing, thus unraveling collusive arrangements and making them public.

In the long term, its proponents argue, watchdog reporting helps set off a virtuous circle of media and governance reforms. Carefully researched, high-impact investigative reports help build the media's credibility and support among the public. The press as an institution is strengthened if journalists have demonstrated that they serve the public interest by uncovering malfeasance and abuse. Not only that, a credible press is assured of popular backing if it is muzzled or otherwise constrained. Investigative reporting is also seen as contributing to journalistic freedom. By constantly digging for information, by forcing government and the private sector to release documents, and by subjecting officials and other powerful individuals to rigorous questioning, investigative journalists expand the boundaries of what is possible to print or air. At the same time, they accustom officials to an inquisitive press. In the long term, the constant give and take between journalists and officials helps develop a culture—and a tradition—of disclosure.[53] In the end, even if in the short term, exposés make little impact, they educate citizens and provide information, a process that over time enriches democratic discourse.

Such a role is particularly important during democratic transitions, when the media are still asserting their autonomy from government and helping construct the new rules of engagement with officials. Some critics say that aggressive reporting on wrongdoing by democratically elected governments may cause the withdrawal of the public's support for democracy. More recent studies of "third-wave" democracies, however, indicate that this may not be so. Citizens may, in fact, see critical reporting as an indication that the checks and balances of democracy are at work. In their study of the media in new democracies in Europe, Schmitt-Beck and Voltmer found that, despite the rise of adversarial and sensational news reporting in postauthoritarian media, on the whole, media exposure is conducive to democratic consolidation and helps build support for democracy.[54]

## The Watchdog's Dark Side

There are, however, contrarian views. Some view media exposés not as part of a virtuous circle of media and political reforms but as a component of the "politics of permanent scandal" that characterizes modern democracies.[55] In this view, a competitive media, coupled with democratic institutions and structures to scrutinize wrongdoing, create a hothouse environment for scandal politics. This type of politics becomes a permanent feature of democracies and does not necessarily result in either cleaner governments or more responsible media. Instead, scandals lead to cynicism rather than a renewed commitment to democratic values and institutions. These practices are therefore dysfunctional. They also draw public attention away from other, perhaps more crucial issues that require action. In many developing and transition societies, accusations of corruption—played out in the media—are part of the arsenal of political contestation. The charges of malfeasance, sometimes made by media organizations friendly with the accusers, have become regular media fare.

Even when the charges are true, wrote Andras Sajo, these may "distort democratic politics as the political competition centers upon the opponents' (un)cleanness" to the detriment of other issues that the public needs to address.[56] Transition societies, he added, are particularly prone to such distortion because many actors, both nationally and internationally, are interested in (and fund) the exposure of corruption in these countries: "Exposure has become professionalized."[57] To others, however, scandal and exposure can play a functional role. One argument is that scandals are "rituals of collective absolution which reaffirm the social order."[58] Through scandal, the public becomes part of a morality play, and public life is cleansed in the process. Another perspective knocks down the doomsayers despairing about the adversarial projection of politics. From this point of view, the media, despite the dominance of scandal and exposure, generate useful political information the quality and quantity of which exceed what was available to citizens of an earlier age. They keep citizens informed, although what citizens can and should do with such information is another question. But, as Brian McNair asked: "Is there, from the point of view of the efficiency and integrity of the democratic process, an optimal upper limit, as well as lower, on the quantity of information flowing in a society, and the amount of critical scrutiny exercised by the media over elites and their rhetoric?"[59]

Perhaps the most attractive perspective settles for the middle ground: scandal and exposure are contested spheres. Their outcomes therefore are uncertain. The media and politicians can profit from scandals as much as lose from them. They may lead to the renewal of a political system as much as to disaffection with it. Citizens may find scandal and exposés mere distractions, but they can equally become outraged and engaged.[60] The media's performance of its watchdog function can be seen in the same way. As shown in the examples above, the outcomes of press exposés are seldom certain. They can even end up with the press being at the losing end, if its motives and methods are challenged. No doubt, press exposure of corruption has the potential to catalyze governance reforms and to remedy some of the deficiencies that hobble the media, but it does not always succeed in doing so. At the very least, therefore, watchdog reporting offers a tool, a window for raising the level of discourse, engaging the public, and reconstructing a public sphere much diminished by the onslaught of the market and the strictures of the state. It also keeps alive the most beloved of journalistic myths: that of the press as the guardian of the public interest.[61] And that, in the end, may be the most enduring impact of watchdog journalism: it sustains the belief among both journalists and citizens that exposure and vigilance can check the abuses of power. It keeps the faith.

In sum, it should be said that at its most effective, the watchdog press can make real policy and personnel changes possible. It can raise the awareness of citizens about wrongdoing and abuse so that they demand such changes. It pushes important issues into the public sphere that would otherwise be ignored. It keeps democracy alive by forcing institutions and individuals to be accountable for what they do. Although there are limits to the media's effectiveness, the threat of media exposure helps keep both private and public institutions honest. A free and independent press is perhaps the most important accountability instrument in democracies. If it does its job well, it becomes the primary guardian of the public interest. And in the end, by exposing wrongdoing and catalyzing reforms, it renews faith in democracy and the democratic process. Citizens feel empowered if their outrage over media exposés is reflected in public policy changes. This sense of popular empowerment, in turn, contributes to a more participatory and responsive democracy as well as more effective governance.

## Policy Recommendations

By playing its watchdog role, the media help bring about reforms, and in the long term assist in creating a culture of civic discourse, transparency, and government accountability. Although the media's effectiveness and power are often overblown, the media's capacity to promote good governance is enhanced if the rights of the press are guaranteed, information is made available to the media and the public, journalists are protected, and news organizations enjoy editorial independence and abide by high ethical and professional standards. In addition, the press is most effective and less prone to capture by vested interests if there is a plurality of media entities representing diverse views and ownership patterns operating in a competitive market as well as broad public access to the media. Some specific policy interventions could include the following:

*Providing a legal and regulatory environment that allows the media to be an effective watchdog.* This entails safeguarding press independence and freedom as well as ensuring pluralism in media ownership and points of view. Such pluralism ensures that the media's ability to act as watchdog is not constrained by the interests or points of view of media proprietors. It also means the establishment of mechanisms that make the media, like government, transparent and accountable. The watchdog, after all, cannot be effective if it is not credible and accountable for what it does. This goal can involve the following specific reforms:

- Enacting firm constitutional guarantees of a free press and freedom of information
- Enacting and implementing liberal freedom of information laws

- Strengthening the courts, the police, and the justice system, and, generally, the rule of law, to provide adequate protection for journalists
- Providing legal support for watchdog journalists, including libel and liability insurance and, when possible, pro bono lawyers for financially strapped news organizations
- Enabling regulations that would lower the barriers to media ownership and reduce concentration of media ownership
- Removing restrictions that prevent the media from playing its watchdog role, such as the use of state advertising to control media content, onerous licensing requirements, laws that unduly penalize the revelation of "state secrets" and compel journalists to reveal their sources, and laws that criminalize libel and defamation
- Supporting efforts to open up governments and enable them to use the Internet and other means to provide citizens with crucial information on government spending, election contributions, the assets of officials, and other matters of public interest
- Promoting genuine public service media that will provide in-depth and informative reporting accessible to as many citizens as possible (though public service media may be subsidized by state funds, they should be run independently of government)
- Providing donor funding for nonprofit investigative reporting efforts as well as support for the long-term financial viability of investigative news organizations
- Promoting access to the media by the public, such as public terminals and reading rooms where citizens can get free access to information
- Supporting citizen, grassroots, and community media that will hold governments accountable, especially in areas not sufficiently covered by professional media
- Encouraging collaborative watchdog efforts between professional media and citizens

*Raising professional and ethical standards.* This goal involves improving the level of skills in various areas of journalism, not to mention improving working conditions and raising compensation to respectable levels. These help raise the social status of watchdog journalists and also make them less prone to corruption. It is important to build a community of journalists bound by a watchdog ethos and committed to democratic principles. Journalist unions and associations can play a role in these. So can donors that fund media development. But donors should also appreciate the limits of what journalists can do, the contingent nature of news, and the demands of the market.

Reforms in this arena can include the following:

- Training journalists in investigative reporting skills and ethical standards and providing funding for such efforts

- Teaching investigative reporting in journalism schools and including references to the watchdog role of the press in general-education curricula
- Instituting awards and other forms of recognition for excellence in watchdog reporting
- Supporting and providing more funds for investigative journalism courses, whether in universities or elsewhere
- Supporting independent press councils, citizen media-watch groups, ombudsmen, and other mechanisms to help upgrade media standards and professionalism
- Making media organizations more transparent about their ownership, their editorial decision-making process, and the pressures and restraints on reporting
- Encouraging and supporting free and independent journalist unions and associations that promote press freedom, ethical journalism, and watchdog reporting
- Providing better pay and job conditions for watchdog journalists

## Notes

1. Hugo de Burgh. 2003. "Kings without Crowns? The Re-emergence of Investigative Journalism in China." *Media, Culture & Society* 25: 801–20.
2. Fred S. Siebert, Theodore Peterson, and Wilbur Schramm. 1963. *Four Theories of the Press.* Urbana and Chicago: University of Illinois Press.
3. Ibid.
4. Christine L. Ogan. 1980. "Development Journalism/Communication: The Status of the Concept." Paper presented at the 63rd Annual Meeting of the Association for Education in Journalism, Boston, August 9–13.
5. Xu Xiaoge. 2005. *Demystifying Asian Values in Journalism.* Singapore: Cavendish, Marshall International.
6. Anthony Mughan and Richard Gunther. 2000. "The Political Impact of the Media: A Reassessment." In *Democracy and the Media: A Comparative Perspective,* ed. Anthony Mughan and Richard Gunther. New York: Cambridge University Press.
7. See the following, for example, Thomas E. Patterson. 1996. "Bad News, Bad Governance." *Annals of the American Academy of Political and Social Science* 546: 97–108; Robert D. Putnam, Susan J. Pharr, and Russel J. Dalton. 2000. "Introduction: What's Troubling the Trilateral Democracies?" In Disaffected Democracies: What's Troubling the Trilateral Countries, ed. Susan J. Pharr and Robert D. Putnam. Princeton: Princeton University Press; and David L. Swanson. 2004. "Transnational Trends in Political Communication: Conventional Views and New Realities," In Comparing Political Communication: Theories, Cases, and Challenges, ed. Frank Esser and Barbara Pfetsch. New York: Cambridge University Press.
8. Isabella Karlowicz. n.d. "The Difficult Birth of the Fourth Estate: Media Development and Democracy Assistance in the Post-Conflict Balkans." Policy Documentation Center, Central European University. http://pdc.ceu.hu/archive/00002252/. See also James Putzel and Joost van der Zwan. 2005. *Why Templates for Media Development Do Not Work in Crisis States: Defining and Understanding Media Development Strategies in Post-War and Crisis States.* London: Crisis States Research Center, London School of Economics.

9.  See Howard Tumbler and Silvio Waisbord. 2004. "Political Scandals and Media across Democracies." *American Behavioral Scientist* 47 (7); Michael Schudson. 1992. *Watergate in American Memory: How We Remember, Forget and Reconstruct the Past.* New York: Basic Books.

10. Andras Sajo. 2003. "From Corruption to Extortion: Conceptualization of Post-Communist Corruption." *Crime, Law and Social Change* 40: 180.

11. James Curran. 2005. "Mediations of Democracy." In *Mass Media and Society,* ed. James Curran and Michael Gurevitch, 4th ed. London: Hodden Arnold; Doris A. Graber. 1986. "Press Freedom and the General Welfare." *Political Science Quarterly* 101 (2): 257–75.

12. Curran. 2005. "Mediations of Democracy."

13. Isabella Karlowicz. n.d. "The Difficult Birth of the Fourth Estate: Media Development and Democracy Assistance in the Post-Conflict Balkans."

14. Sophie Beach. 2004. "In China, New Journalism and New Threats." Committee to Protect Journalists. http://www.cpj.org/Briefings/2004/China_8_04.html.

15. Hugo de Burgh. 2003. "Kings without Crowns? The Re-emergence of Investigative Journalism in China." *Media, Culture & Society* 25: 801–20.

16. On Latin America, see Silvio Waisbord 2000. *Watchdog Journalism in South America: News, Accountability, and Democracy.* New York: Columbia University Press. On Southeast Asia, see Sheila S. Coronel and Howie G. Severino. 2006. *Investigative Reporting for Television in Southeast Asia.* Manila: Philippine Center for Investigative Journalism. On China, see Hugo de Burgh. 2003. "Kings without Crowns?"

17. David Protess, Fay Lomax Cook, Jack C. Doppelt, James S. Ettema, Margaret T. Gordon, Donna R. Leff, and Peter Miller. 1991. *The Journalism of Outrage: Investigative Reporting and Agenda-Building in America.* New York: Guilford Press; Hugo de Burgh. 2000. *Investigative Journalism: Context and Practice.* London: Routledge.

18. Data from the Committee to Protect Journalists, which keeps a database of journalist killings. See http://cpj.org/deadly/index.html. Accessed April 8, 2009.

19. Masha Lipman. 2006. "Russia's Lid on the Media." *Washington Post,* A27, June 15.

20. Doris A. Graber. 1986. "Press Freedom and the General Welfare." *Political Science Quarterly* 101 (2): 257–75.

21. Ben Bagdikian. 1983. *The Media Monopoly.* Boston: Beacon Press.

22. Charles Lewis. 2007. "The Growing Importance of Nonprofit Journalism." Politics and Public Policy Working Paper Series, Joan Shorenstein Center on the Press, Harvard University. http://www.crji.org/news.php?id=128&l=2.

23. Vereniging van Onderzoeksjournalisten (VVOJ—Dutch-Flemish Association for Investigative Journalists). 2006. *Investigative Journalism in Europe.* http://www.vvoj.nl/cms/vereniging/publicaties/report-about-journalism-in-europe/.

24. Waisbord. 2000. *Watchdog Journalism in South America.*

25. Coronel and Severino. 2006. *Investigative Reporting for Television in Southeast Asia.*

26. Waisbord. 2000. *Watchdog Journalism in South America.* See also Rudiger Schmitt-Beck and Katrin Voltmer. 2007. "The Mass Media in Third-Wave Democracies: Gravediggers or Seedsmen of Democratic Consolidation?" In *Democracy, Intermediation and Voting in Four Continents,* ed. Richard Gunther, Jose Ramon Montero, and Hans-Jurgen Puhle. Oxford: Oxford University Press.

27. David Kaplan. 2007. "Global Investigative Journalism: Strategies for Support." Research Report, Center for International Media Assistance. http://cima.ned.org/tag/david-e-kaplan.

28. Samarth Vaidya. 2005. "Corruption in the Media's Gaze." *European Journal of Political Economy* 21: 667–87.

29. The study is by Torbjorn von Krog, editor of the Swedish biweekly *Pressens Tindig,* and is cited in VVOJ 2006 http://www.vvoj.nl/cms/vereniging/publicaties/report-about-journalism-in-europe/.

30. See, for example, VVOJ. 2006. *Investigative Journalism in Europe;* Lewis. 2007. "The Growing Importance of Nonprofit Journalism" and D. Kaplan. 2007. "Global Investigative Journalism."

31. Richard Kaplan. 2002. *Politics and the American Press: The Rise of Objectivity, 1865–1920.* New York: Cambridge University Press.

32. Daniel C. Hallin. 2004. *Comparing Media Systems: Three Models of Media and Politics.* New York: Cambridge University Press; John Soloski. 1989. "News Reporting and Professionalism: Some Constraints on the Reporting of News." *Media, Culture and Society* 11: 207–28.

33. Hallin. 2004. *Comparing Media Systems.*

34. Waisbord. 2000. *Watchdog Journalism in South America.*

35. "China Becomes World's Largest Internet Population." 2008. Reuters, April 24. http://www.reuters.com/article/newsOne/idUSPEK34240620080424.

36. Simon Elegant. 2006. "The Chinese Blogosphere Strikes Back." *Time,* August 31. http://www.time.com/time/world/article/0,8599,1503785,00.html.

37. de Burgh. 2003. "Kings Without Crowns?" 803.

38. Ibid.

39. David Weaver, ed. 1998. *The Global Journalist: News People around the World.* New Jersey: Hampton Press.

40. Rick Stapenhurst. 2000. *The Media's Role in Curbing Corruption.* Washington, DC: World Bank Institute in http://www.worldbank.org/wbi/governance/pdf/media.pdf.

41. Protess, Cook, Doppelt, Ettema, Gordon, Leff, and Miller. 1991. *The Journalism of Outrage.*

42. Waisbord. 2000. *Watchdog Journalism in South America.*

43. Silvio Waisbord. 2004. "Scandals, Media and Citizenship in Contemporary Argentina." *American Behavioral Scientist* 47 (8): 1072–98.

44. See Sheila S. Coronel, ed. 2000. *Investigating Estrada: Millions, Mansions and Mistresses.* Manila: Philippine Center for Investigative Journalism.

45. Pasuk Phongpaichit and Chris Baker. 2004. Thaksin: *The Business of Politics in Thailand.* Chiang Mai: Silkworm Books.

46. Ibid.

47. Protess, Cook, Doppelt, Ettema, Gordon, Leff and Miller. 1991. *The Journalism of Outrage.*

48. Schudson. 1992. *Watergate in American Memory.*

49. Ibid.

50. Gladys Lang and Kurt Lang. 1983. *The Battle for Public Opinion: The President, The Press and The Polls during Watergate.* New York: Columbia University Press.

51. Protess et al. 1991. *The Journalism of Outrage.*

52. Aymo Brunetti and Beatrice Weder. 2003. "A Free Press Is Bad News for Corruption." *Journal of Public Economics* 87 (7–8): 1801–24.

53. Sheila S. Coronel. 1999. "Recovering the Rage: Media and Public Opinion." In *No Longer Business as Usual: Fighting Bribery and Corruption.* Paris: Organisation for Economic Co-Operation and Development.

54. Rudiger Schmitt-Beck and Katrin Voltmer. 2007. "The Mass Media in Third-Wave Democracies: Gravediggers or Seedsmen of Democratic Consolidation?" In *Democracy, Intermediation and Voting in Four Continents,* ed. Richard Gunther, Jose Ramon Montero, and Hans-Jurgen Puhle. Oxford: Oxford University Press.

55. Tumbler and Waisbord. 2004. "Political Scandals and Media across Democracies."

56. Sajo. 2003. "From Corruption to Extortion," 180.

57. Sajo. 2003. "From Corruption to Extortion,"181.

58. Michael Schudson. 2004. "Notes on a Scandal and the Watergate Legacy." *American Behavioral Scientist* 47 (9): 1234.

59. Brian McNair. 1999. *Journalism and Democracy: Evaluation of the Political Public Sphere.* London: Routledge, 179.

60. Schudson. 2004. "Notes on Scandal and the Watergate Legacy."

61. See Schudson. 1992. *Watergate in American Memory.*

# 6

# The Media, Government Accountability, and Citizen Engagement

Katrin Voltmer

The past two decades or so have seen an unprecedented spread of democracy around the globe. With the fall of the Berlin wall in 1989 and the end of the Cold War, the "third wave" of democratization, which started in the early 1970s in Southern Europe and Latin America, now also encompasses countries in Asia and Africa.[1] And even in states whose governments continue to resist a more open and participatory form of governance, such as the Democratic People's Republic of Korea, Myanmar, or Zimbabwe, the idea of democracy is a powerful force that inspires people to take on a more active role in public life. However, many of the newly emerging democracies seem to fall short of some, often many, of the basic standards that define democratic rule, with irregular voting procedures, corruption, inefficiency, and autocratic styles of government being but a few of the maladies. In addition, as many of the newly emerging democracies belong to the developing world, inequality and poverty remain severe obstacles to full self-determination of the people.

The experiences of the past decades have shown that democracy is not a one-way road and that a viable democracy requires more than the implementation of the key institutions of government. Rather, an accountable and efficient government is embedded in a complex web of interdependent conditions that require considerable time and effort to develop. In the context of the apparent problems and frequent setbacks, scholars and policy makers alike have become aware of the crucial role of the media in processes of democratization and consolidation. However, like political institutions, the media in many new democracies often seem to lack the qualities that would qualify them for playing a key role in promoting accountability and inclusive politics.

They are frequently criticized for remaining too close to political power holders to be able to act as effective watchdogs; political reporting is regarded as too opinionated to provide balanced gatekeeping; and commercial pressures on news coverage often encourage an overemphasis on the trivial and popular at the expense of serious and sustained attention to international affairs and complex issues on the policy agenda.

This chapter focuses on countries that have only recently established democratic institutions. Some advanced Western democracies are also undergoing crises of public communication and political legitimacy—Italy is but one example. Yet the problems of the relationship between media and government is most pressing in transitional democracies, where the role expectations and norms that guide this relationship are still disputed among the actors involved in the public communication of politics. The study explores the notion of accountability and how it can be applied to the relationship between governments, citizens, and the media. The normative ideals are discussed in light of actual social and political processes. Particular attention is paid to the factors that limit, or strengthen, the media's ability to act as watchdogs. The chapter then analyzes whether and to what extent the media contribute to an informed and active citizenry that is able to hold governments to account. This is a critical component of an effective public sphere in civil society. Even though most theories of media's impact on democratic citizenship have been developed in Western established democracies, empirical evidence is presented that yields some conclusions about the role of the media in political life in a range of new democracies.

## Democratic Accountability: Governments, Citizens, and the Media

Although accountability is usually seen as a normative expectation that applies to political power holders, this chapter argues that democratic accountability also encompasses the citizens and the media that link governments and citizens.

### Government Accountability

Even though all governments—whether democratic or authoritarian—have to deliver a minimum of public goods in order to avoid widespread social unrest, electoral democracy provides strong institutional incentives for political officials to be accountable to their citizens. With periodic elections, citizens have a powerful instrument in their hand to reward or punish a government for its performance. Because elections are the main mechanism to allocate power in democratic systems, they link the self-interest of politicians with the requirement to act in the interest of the population. Or as the political scientist V. O. Key put it, "the fear of loss of popular support powerfully disciplines the actions of governments."[2] Yet whether or not voting can function as an effective mechanism to enforce government accountability depends on a complex set of both institutional and cultural conditions. Institutionally, the choice of electoral system, professionalism in public administration, and the independence of the judiciary are crucial factors that affect the degree to which governments respond to public demands. Culturally, the ability and willingness of the citizens to engage in political life alongside the quality of public communication play an important part in strengthening the link between those in power and the citizenry.

## Social Accountability

Building on the assumption that effective and accountable governance is unlikely to be achieved without an attentive and active citizenry, the World Bank recently introduced the concept of social, or collective, accountability.[3] From this point of view, civic engagement involves more than just voting; it also involves participation in civil society organizations and community policy making. Academic democratization research has also increasingly drawn attention to the importance of an active and supportive citizenry in the process of democratic consolidation.[4] The lack of a vibrant civil society in many new democracies has been linked to the persisting problems of corruption and ineffective governance in these countries. Especially in Eastern Europe, citizens are reluctant to join political organizations or voluntary associations, which can be put down to the constant politicization and compulsory membership under the previous communist regime. But there are also some encouraging instances of successful grassroots mobilization in Africa and Latin America.[5]

The concept of political, or civic, culture argues in a similar vein by emphasizing the link between micro- and macrolevel processes. In their seminal work, Almond and Verba (1963) pointed out that the institutional setup is not sufficient to understand why some democracies flourish and others don't. Equally important are the political orientations of individual citizens and the degree to which these microlevel orientations are congruent with the values and institutions of the democratic system. Elements of a democratic political culture include cognitive mobilization indicated by interest in public affairs and political knowledge, the willingness to participate in political life, the sense of civic competence and the belief that individuals have an impact on the course of politics, and, finally, support of democracy both as it actually exists and as a general ideal.[6] In other words, if citizens are ignorant about political issues, do not make an effort to have a say, despise their representatives, and do not believe in democratic values, the viability of that democracy might be seriously at risk—even if the institutions are perfectly designed. Almond and Verba developed the concept of political culture in the 1960s with an interest in understanding the chances of democracy taking root in "second wave" democracies that emerged after the Second World War. Not surprisingly, political culture research has seen a new renaissance over the past decade or so in response to the recent wave of democratization and the apparent problems of their consolidation.[7]

## Media Accountability

Because the media are the main source of information and a vital link between the government and citizens, the presence of the media is an indispensable precondition for both government accountability and social accountability. Without reliable information, citizens would not be able to use their power effectively at election time, nor would they be aware of the problems and issues that need active consideration beyond voting. The daily flow of news generates a running tally of government policies, political events, and the actions of political officials, on the basis of which citizens make their choices. The media are also expected to provide a forum where a broad range of voices—opposition parties, civil society actors, independent experts, and ordinary citizens—can express alternative views. Moreover, the media are widely seen as the Fourth Estate, referring to the media as an institution alongside other branches of government, which together provide a system of checks and balances to control political officials and prevent misuses of power.

Assigning these democratic roles—agenda setters, gatekeepers, and watchdogs—to the media is based on the expectation that the media act in the public interest and are accountable to the public. In his book on media accountability, McQuail discusses the historical and philosophical roots of media responsibilities and how the principle of responsibility is implemented in modern media policy.[8] However, there is an apparent tension, if not contradiction, between the notion of media accountability and the principle of freedom of the press. Surely, any obligation to produce certain goods and to adhere to certain quality standards restricts the media's degree of freedom in making their own choices. Libertarian theorists, but also many journalists, therefore deny any such obligation, arguing that it threatens the independence of the press and might even invite government interference. The influential media scholar Walter Lippman supports this view by saying: "The press is not a political institution and has no stake in organizing public opinion."[9] Other scholars contradict this view, arguing that press freedom is a right that exists for a purpose and is justified by the benefits it delivers for the society as a whole.[10] Although it cannot be denied that the notion of media accountability can be misused by those in power, the media are responsible for their behavior and its consequences. As McQuail points out, the principle of media accountability not only involves restrictions and obligations, but also calls for measures to strengthen the media's independence from government, to ensure sufficient resources, or to provide access rights to information.[11]

## Media Accountability and Journalism:
## Between Normative Ideal and Day-to-Day Practice

Up to this point the role of the media has been discussed primarily from a normative perspective, that is, how the media ought to perform. Normative ascriptions, however, reveal little about the day-to-day reality of political reporting. Research into news and journalism indicates that for various structural reasons, the media's ability to fulfill their democratic roles often does not live up to textbook ideals. One important reason is the reliance of the media on official sources. To provide their news stories with authoritative backing, journalists prefer to quote high-ranking politicians rather than, for example, civil society groups, the validity of whose claims is often difficult to establish.[12] Coverage by the U.S. media before and during the Iraq war is a recent example of the failure of the press to act as a watchdog and to question the credibility of the government's version of the events. This is not a singular case of patriotic media in the times of national threat. Rather, it illustrates a general pattern of the relationship between journalists and their sources.[13] Thus, Blumler and Gurevitch point out that watchdog journalism plays a much lesser role in political reporting than its prominence as a journalistic ideal might imply.[14] Instead, in the daily routines of news production, the interaction between journalists and politicians is characterized by a high degree of cooperation, frequently even a symbiotic relationship, where each side benefits from their respective counterpart. Journalists therefore often regard adversarialism as an unnecessary disruption of this relationship, as it can block their access to government officials and the chance of obtaining off-the-record background information.

The chances for successful watchdog journalism are even more restricted in new democracies where the functional interdependence between politicians and journalists is still overshadowed by the legacy of suppression and censorship during the old regime. Political leaders—even those who are committed to democratic values—find it hard to accept an adversarial press that demands public justification of policy decisions and political conduct. In fact, the relationship between governments and the media in most new democracies is characterized by frequent clashes—quite tellingly dubbed "media wars"—over the boundaries of government interference into the operation and structure of the media and even the content of news reporting. Meanwhile, the rules and ethics of investigative journalism are still uncertain among reporters. As a consequence, patterns of deference and even subservience persist, in particular in state-owned media, alongside instances of what can be labeled "attack dog" journalism, which takes on an extremely polemic tone and often uses rumors and fabricated accusations rather than engaging in thorough fact-checking research.

Various factors systematically affect the quality of political information produced by the media. One concerns news values, or the standards by which journalists select their stories, thereby allocating public attention and setting the agenda.[15] Some of the most important aspects that guide this selection of news are conflict, impact, deviance, negativity, proximity, high-status actors, and timeliness. Even though some of these news values might be specifically rooted in Western culture, such as the emphasis on conflict and deviance, the global flow of news and the dominance of international news agencies have brought about a fairly similar pattern of political reporting around the world.[16] Of similar importance for the quality of the public debate is the way in which the media present and frame political issues. Almost all news is essentially storytelling. Reports follow a clear narrative structure that focuses on a distinct event and a main actor—often stereotyped as hero or villain—who is depicted as being responsible for the problem or its solution. Thus, political issues are usually presented in an "episodic frame" that is person-centered and event-driven, rather than in a "thematic frame" that covers the broader social, economic, or historical context of a problem.[17]

News values and commercial news formats are designed to produce news that sells. Yet many communication scholars and media critics doubt whether they actually help citizens make intelligent choices and hold governments to account. They argue that since the news media are more concerned with drama, eye-catching headlines, and the strategic games of power, they fail to provide substantial information about policy debates. Further, long-term structural processes—such as poverty, health problems, or institution building—usually escape the attention of the media unless some dramatic development makes those topics fit to print.[18] Despite these common criticisms, recent research shows that many of the ingredients of news stories that are often regarded as detrimental for informed citizenship actually bear at least some benefits, especially for those with less-sophisticated cognitive skills. For example, the news narrative not only attracts attention, but also makes otherwise remote and abstract political issues more tangible and meaningful.[19] Even tabloids and soft news stories that are the main targets of media criticism have proved to be of some use for the acquisition of knowledge.[20]

How does the "structural bias" caused by the specific selectivity of news values affect the media's ability to promote democratization?[21] Bennett takes a pessimistic view by arguing that "it turns out that what sustains successful revolutions, whether the armed or the velvet variety, is the same thing that can discourage the subsequent formation of stable democratic institutions."[22] This suggests that the media are instrumental for regime change, but detrimental for the consolidation of new democracies. The demise of the old regime often culminates in dramatic events, such as mass demonstrations, clashes with police forces, and the resignation of the autocratic leader. Since these events perfectly match journalistic news values, they are extensively covered, by both the international media and the media of the country undergoing political change. Heavy international media coverage often triggers "demonstration effects," whereby citizens become aware of political changes elsewhere or in their own country, which further fuels mobilization against the existing authoritarian regime. For example, recent events in Myanmar show that for a dictatorship to suppress mass upheavals it is of utmost importance to cut off international communication links. However, when it comes to consolidating the newly established democratic order, news coverage that centers on single events, on conflict, and on what goes wrong might be less effective in helping citizens understand the complex process of change the country is undergoing.

Recent conceptions of journalism—in particular, civic or public journalism—have tried to overcome the limitations of political reporting set by mainstream news standards. Having originated in the United States, public journalism sees its main function as fostering public dialogue and civic participation. By engaging more closely with the audience and with local communities, it distances itself from the symbiotic relationship with political elites and gives ordinary citizens a public voice and the chance to set the agenda.[23] Not surprisingly, in Western countries, with their highly commercialized media, this model has largely remained in the world of ideals. However, similar ideas have become a significant part of journalism in the developing world, in particular in the form of community radio. A cheap, flexible, and easy-to-produce medium, radio can overcome the distance that usually exists between large, centralized media organizations and their audience. Even though it might not reach the ears of central government, community radio has been extremely instrumental in the diffusion of innovations, the empowerment of citizens, and the solution of problems at the grassroots level.[24]

Another important factor that affects the way the media report on political matters is partisanship, that is, bias. Since biased media present political issues from a particular point of view, while ignoring, or even dismissing, opposite views, partisanship is seen as an impediment for the media to fulfill their responsibilities to provide reliable information. The audience of a biased newspaper or television channel learns only half of the truth and hence might be less equipped to make informed and effective choices. However, supporting a particular cause is not only an accepted part of press freedom, but also one of several legitimate ways of representing the plurality of viewpoints in the public sphere. In fact, it is mainly in the United States that objectivity and neutrality have become the predominant journalistic norm, whereas in Europe many newspapers, including the national quality press, can easily be located within the ideological space of partisan conflict.[25] In most new democracies, in particular, postcommunist Eastern Europe and Latin America, nearly all media, whether print or audiovisual, are taking sides in favor of particular political parties, candidates, societal groups, or ideologies, whereas neutral, or balanced, news coverage is clearly an exception. Does this mean that journalism in new democracies has to be regarded as deficient because it does not adhere to the standards of objectivity?

From a normative point of view two forms of diversity—internal and external—can be distinguished.[26] Internal diversity refers to a situation in which a single media outlet comprises all relevant viewpoints without favoring a particular position. The British Broadcasting Corporation (BBC), with its commitment to balance and neutrality, is an example for this model. External diversity establishes the representation of all viewpoints through the aggregation of individual media, each promoting a particular cause or ideology. Even though internal diversity conforms most closely to the ideal of rational citizenship, the downside of balancing opposing views is that it provides little, if any, cues as to the value and validity of a position. Thus, it hardly meets the needs for orientation, which is in particularly short supply in periods of transition when the breakdown of familiar institutions and value systems can cause an acute sense of disorientation and anomie. External diversity offers this orientation. It not only constitutes trust between audiences and "their" media, but also has the potential to strengthen political alignments and encourage political participation, in short, to promote the development of civil society.[27]

Another consequence of a strong partisan press is that there is never a shortage of adversarialism. However, since the main aim of critical coverage is to damage the political opponent, it frequently takes on an aggressive and shrill tone and might even twist the truth in order to achieve its political goals. This can not only damage the credibility and effectiveness of watchdog journalism but might also trigger measures to suppress critical reporting altogether. The negative manifestations of partisan media emphasize that commitment to a particular cause, group, or ideology has to follow the standards of responsible public communication and, in spite of disagreement and conflicting interests, to show respect for the political opponent.

Since both internal and external diversity have their advantages and drawbacks, it is important to consider the political and cultural contexts when judging the implications of each of the forms of diversity for political life in the democratization process. External diversity might be a beneficial influence in contexts of high electoral volatility and weak party alignment, because of its potential for developing links between political parties and their constituencies. Advocacy is also important when significant parts of the population are excluded from the mainstream media. However, it is sometimes difficult to draw the line between a lively political contest, on the one hand, and unbridgeable hostility among adverse political camps that undermines cohesion and mutual tolerance, on the other. External diversity can be a detrimental, even dangerous, force in situations where no mechanisms have been found to moderate conflicts among antagonistic groups. This is often the case where ethnic or religious differences are the salient markers for the definition of group membership and political interests. To evaluate the political implications of external diversity, it is important to consider the distribution of views in the whole system. It is usually no problem, and often even desirable, when individual media outlets take sides for particular causes. However, external diversity can become problematic when the whole system is segmented along opposing lines and when there is no forum that provides a space to bring all these divergent voices together.[28]

## Mass Media and Democratic Citizenship: A Vicious or a Virtuous Circle?

The discrepancy between normative ideals and practices raises the question whether media that frequently fail to live up to the ideals of normative media theory can actually contribute to social accountability and the development of effective citizenship. More specifically, do the media in new democracies foster or undermine the emergence of a political culture that is conducive to the consolidation of the new democratic order? Research into the media's impact on public opinion provides a rather ambiguous picture of the power of the media in political life.

### Media Power and Its Limits

Research about media's effects on audiences is one of the key areas in the field of communications studies. The body of literature devoted to understanding the media's influence on political knowledge, political orientations, and participation is immense. Yet the empirical evidence for the media's power is ambivalent at best. Even though research on agenda setting and framing has established evidence for the media's impact on public opinion, the process that links media messages to changes in people's political orientations is extremely complex and dependent on a multitude of individual and social conditions.[29] In addition, most of the research on media effects has been carried out in established Western democracies, most notably the United States, which might be fundamentally different from the circumstances of dramatic political and economic change that characterize many emerging democracies.

Because the pervasiveness of the media in modern life is often mistaken as an indicator of their massive power over their audiences, it is useful to start with a closer look at the factors that limit the influence of the media. In their seminal work on campaign communication, carried out in the 1940s in small-town America, Lazarsfeld and his collaborators set out to establish the impact of the mass media on political orientations and voting behavior—but they could not find much evidence for this assumption.[30] According to the authors, there are three main reasons for the limited power of the media on individual political opinions. First, people try to avoid messages that contradict their own convictions, and if exposure to opposing viewpoints in the media cannot be avoided, people forget them very quickly or even misperceive them in order to adjust the message to their own beliefs. Second, voters' electoral preferences are the expression of long-standing predispositions, such as class, ethnicity, and regional identity, that bring about a distinct set of interests and values. Even if the media messages individuals are exposed to contradict these predispositions, the messages are unlikely to change the voters' electoral decisions. Third, and most important, political opinions are not simply the outcome of individual considerations but are shaped by social interactions in everyday life. As Lazarsfeld and his collaborators found, interpersonal communication with people in one's immediate social environment, for example, family members, friends, neighbors, or workmates, is more influential than the media. Most social groups are characterized by a high degree of homogeneity, that is, group members share the same beliefs, tastes, and worldviews, which is either the result of social pressure exerted on individual group members who hold deviant views or because people seek the company of like-minded others in the first place. Hence, the role of the media in public opinion building is primarily seen providing the raw material for political conversations in the form of information about recent events, but the evaluation of this information and the conclusions to be drawn from it are largely shaped by the dynamics of social interaction. As Price put it so lucidly, it is less important what a person thinks but *with whom* he or she thinks.[31]

Lazarsfeld's ideas have recently been rediscovered by academics and communication practitioners alike. Campaign advisers have realized the pitfalls of relying exclusively on the mass media. Instead, campaigns are now increasingly backed up by extensive mobilization on the ground. It is the personal encounters with the candidate and the politicization of social networks that generate enthusiasm and motivate people to turn out on election day. It is also an important mechanism to sway undecided citizens, and in some cases it might even convince disaffected partisans to vote for a different party.[32] Another area where the link between mass communication and interpersonal communication is of crucial importance is development communication. Though the media are important to disseminate information, face-to-face communication endows messages with the trustworthiness and credibility without which people would be unwilling to change their attitudes or adopt new practices.[33] Persuasion is more likely to be achieved when mediated messages are supported within the immediate social environment.

Recent scholarly research has tried to understand the relationship between interpersonal and mass communication and to assess the specific impact of each of these two forms of communication. Even though modern societies experience a much higher degree of social mobility than America in the 1940s, social networks continue to be surprisingly homogeneous, thus limiting the media's power to change political attitudes and behaviors.[34] Although this might reassure concerns about media-driven electoral volatility and the purported irrationality of public opinion, it also raises questions as to the openness of the political debate. If people remain locked up in their own milieus of political beliefs, they will be unwilling to consider contradicting arguments, even if those arguments might be better responses to the problems at hand. In extreme cases, the segmentation into homogeneous subcultures can even lead to a balkanization of the society, with the antagonisms between different groups escalating into open hostility.

News media that serve as a forum for a diversity of voices can play an important role in exposing citizens to views they do not hold and are unlikely to encounter in their own social networks. Research into the consequences of the homogeneity or heterogeneity of people's communication environments shows that those who have the opportunity to learn about opposing viewpoints through the media are more tolerant toward minority groups and show more respect for political opponents.[35] The effect is even stronger when at least some members of one's social context hold divergent views, for example, by supporting a different party. This does not necessarily mean that people change their mind when they learn about alternative opinions, but it means that people learn to recognize others they do not agree with as reasonable fellow citizens.

## The Role of the Media in Elections

Though in established democracies the impact of the media on voting is restricted by the persisting significance of long-term predispositions and the influence of primary groups, researchers still know very little about the media's role in electoral politics in new democracies. After regime change, it often takes considerable time for political parties to develop stable ties with their constituencies—and it may well be that they will never succeed.[36] Hence it can be assumed that in transitional democracies there is much more room for the media to affect people's political opinions than in contexts where the lines of the political contest have crystallized and most voters have made up their mind. The Russian Federation serves as an illustrative case study for observations of the dynamics of public communication and electoral politics, even though the specifics of the case preclude any broader generalizations. After a short honeymoon of open and investigative journalism in the early 1990s, Russian media were more and more subjected to government control and censorship. But the watershed event in the relationship between political power and the media was the presidential election in 1996, when the media voluntarily refrained from covering the campaign of the Communist candidate Zhuganov and unanimously supported the already ailing Yeltsin. Journalists justified their one-sided coverage by arguing that if the Communist Party would come back into power, it would mean the end of press freedom altogether.[37] Ever since, independent reporting has been in sharp decline; President Putin did not rest until all nationally available television networks were under the control of the Kremlin and any dissenting newspaper was closed down. As a consequence, all recent Russian elections have been criticized by international observers as being seriously flawed by the heavy pro-Kremlin bias of campaign coverage and the virtual exclusion of opposition candidates from the airwaves.

Representative surveys carried out shortly after the Duma elections in 1999 and 2003 show a close correlation between vote choice and exposure to television news. Voters who relied mainly on state television were significantly more likely to vote for Kremlin-supported United Russia than those who watched commercial television, which at that time still retained some degree of independence. Besides factors such as age and gender, exposure to television proved to be the main influence on how people voted.[38] However, the finding of massive media impact on voting decision seems to contradict observations from qualitative research. Mickiewicz conducted a series of focus groups across Russia with people from different age groups and different educational backgrounds to find out how voters respond to official news.[39] The rich material obtained in these discussions shows that Russian citizens are surprisingly sophisticated when it comes to decoding media messages. Most of them are aware of the bias in a news story, and they are able to question the purpose of the story and to reflect on who might have fabricated it. Why, then, did manipulated campaign coverage work out in virtually all recent elections in Russia?

The cognitive processes that have been found to underlie agenda-setting effects could be a plausible explanation. This theory of communication effects maintains that the media can change individual preferences not by using persuasive messages, but by selecting particular stories or aspects of a story.[40] Psychological research has demonstrated that when people make choices—whether forming an opinion on a political issue or deciding which party to vote for—they use those bits of information that can be most easily retrieved from memory. People might know alternative pieces of information, but if they have not used the information for some time, they are less likely to take them into consideration when forming an opinion on an actual issue. As a consequence, an individual will come to a different conclusion depending on which information happens to be at hand.

The role of the media in the agenda-setting process is to generate salience for some issues, or particular aspects of issues, thereby drawing public attention to a limited set of current problems. It has to be kept in mind that selectivity is an inevitable, even necessary, aspect of information processing. At any given time, an infinite number of problems are competing for public attention. That volume of detail would exceed the information-processing capacity of individuals and institutions alike if they had to deal with everything at the same time. Because for ordinary citizens, the media are the main window to the world of politics, people regard as most important those problems that have recently been given most salience in the news.[41] Thus, these problems are the basis for opinion formation and vote choices.

News values generate a particular pattern of journalists' selection of topics that might, or might not, coincide with other measures of political relevance. Partisanship can be regarded as a special case of agenda setting. Media that are aligned with a particular ideology or party will select issues that promote that cause while ignoring any aspects that have the potential to undermine its validity. In the Russian case, in which the national news media ignored oppositional candidates and parties, it would have required extraordinary cognitive effort for individuals to find alternative information. As anywhere else, the business of everyday life—work, family, queuing—usually occupies the best part of people's time and attention, and only a few would take the trouble to find information from sources other than the media to optimize the quality of their vote decision. Thus when making up their minds as to which party or which candidate to vote for, people could have questioned the credibility of the information they received, but they were stuck in the limited worldview of the official agenda.

Elisabeth Noelle-Neumann, in her theory of the "spiral of silence," develops a similar argument by demonstrating the effects of selective media coverage on the general climate of opinions.[42] As she points out, people obtain the arguments for their own beliefs and opinions primarily from the media. If the media hardly cover a particular political party, the opinions of those who support this party would be based on a limited range of reasons for that support.[43] Moreover, when talking about politics with others, they would find themselves quickly running out of arguments. If these conversations were to take place with like-minded others, mutual encouragement and mobilization would be rather superficial. If these conversations were to take place in mixed company—and this is the key argument of the theory—these people would fall silent because they would be unable to defend their views, whereas supporters of a party that was well presented in the media would feel confident enough to express their views in public. They might not initially be in the majority, but their willingness to talk—in conjunction with selective media coverage—would soon make this view the dominant one in both the public debate and interpersonal communication. It would hence be the one that has the biggest impact on the outcome of the election.

## Mass Media and Political Culture

So far the discussion has focused on voting and what is known about the media's impact on voters' decision making in the context of established and new democracies. However, as pointed out in the first section of this chapter, social accountability and citizenship go beyond elections; they also include a

whole range of democratic orientations and the general willingness to participate in public life. This issue has recently triggered a lively debate among academics and political observers alike, as growing political cynicism and
alienation are causing widespread concerns as to the viability of Western
democracies. Similarly, in new democracies, after the first enthusiasm has
faded, citizens have become rather disillusioned about democratic politics and
are increasingly withdrawing from political life. It has almost become commonplace to blame the media for these negative developments. It is argued
that the way in which the media portray politics—the general antipolitical bias
and the distrust of political officials displayed by journalists—breeds cynicism
among citizens. Furthermore, as the current styles of covering the news
emphasize strategic maneuvering of political actors over policy debates, the
media are believed to create an image of politics that has more to do with
fighting for its own sake than finding solutions to the problems that face the
country. Other authors have drawn a relationship between media consumption and the decline of civic engagement.[44]

Convincing as these arguments might sound, empirical evidence so far provides much less unequivocal results. Although some studies find negative effects, others find only positive relationships or no effects at all. In their experimental study, Cappella and Jamieson systematically varied presentation
formats of television news and found significant negative effects on individuals' political competence and on political trust. They argue that presenting
politics as a strategic game contributes to the alienation of the public from
politics. However, other authors have presented strong empirical evidence for
a more beneficial role of the media, in particular with regard to the cognitive
mobilization of citizens. In fact, never before have mass publics in Western
societies been as knowledgeable and interested in politics as today, which can
at least to some extent be attributed to the easy availability of political information through the mass media.[45] Norris reports similar results for a large
range of established European and non-European democracies. She assumes a
virtuous circle at work, theorizing that exposure to the news media contributes to knowledge and encourages civic engagement, which in turn stimulates
the appetite for more information and news use.[46]

Even though most research to date seems to support a positive role of the
media, it remains puzzling why scholars have found such contradictory results.
One reason for these inconsistent findings can be the methodology used. It
seems that experimental studies are more likely to produce results that suggest
a negative influence of the media, whereas large-scale survey research generally
comes to a more positive view. The logic of experimental research is to strictly
control the factors that are assumed to cause a certain effect while eliminating
as much as possible any other influences. Typically, participants are exposed to
a piece of news coverage that is manipulated in such a way that it emphasizes

certain elements. For example, two groups of participants are exposed to a news story that presents an event from the perspective of strategic political behavior or from a policy-centered perspective, respectively. The study then monitors responses to the different kinds of news stories immediately after exposure. In contrast, survey research is unable to control the media content that respondents are exposed to, and it is not possible to control the conditions under which the content is consumed. Hence, the results are as much affected by the processes that follow media exposure as by the content itself. As discussed previously, social experiences and interpersonal communication are important factors that can dilute, revert, or in some instances strengthen the impact of media messages. Experimental research therefore reflects the immediate reaction of audiences to news content, whereas the results of surveys encompass the complex processes of individual and collective interpretations.

Almost all research to clarify whether the media are responsible for political cynicism and disengagement has been within established democracies, and it is an open question whether the same processes are at work in new democracies. It could well be that in transitional contexts political orientations are still in a state of flux and vulnerable to negative images conveyed by the media. Politics might appear confusing and frustrating, especially when improvement of the political and economic situation is not achieved as fast as expected. A study conducted as part of the Cross National Election Project can shed some light on these questions.[47] The study analyzed representative survey data collected during the mid-1990s from six third-wave democracies—Greece, Spain, Chile, Uruguay, Bulgaria, and Hungary—in the context of national elections. These data are unique in various respects: they include a large number of variables to measure the respondents' exposure to political news, which allows the study to distinguish different levels of information quality and partisan alignment of media outlets. The surveys also include detailed measures of democratic orientations, such as political interest, political knowledge, participation (measured as involvement in various campaign-related activities), evaluation of political parties, satisfaction with democracy in one's own country, and support of democracy as a preferable form of governance. Further, the selection of countries made it possible to compare two countries from the early stage of the third wave of democratization, which can now be regarded as fully consolidated (Greece, Spain), with recent newcomers from Latin America and postcommunist Europe. In spite of the time that has elapsed since the data were collected, the results are still valid because the study is primarily interested in the relationship between variables—media exposure and democratic orientations—rather than the level of each of those variables, which might have changed in the meantime.

With these data at hand, several questions can be addressed that better illuminate the role of the media in new democracies:

- Do the media have an influence on political orientations, and if so, is this positive or negative?
- Do different types of media differ in their influence on political orientations?
- Is this influence uniform across different orientations, or does the media's influence vary depending on the specific orientation?
- Are there differences between countries?

The results of the analysis showed that the media have an effect over and above other important factors that are known from the literature to influence political orientations, in particular, age, education, gender, ideological predispositions, and socioeconomic status. About one-quarter of the variance in political orientations can be directly or indirectly attributed to exposure to the news media. Very much in line with the findings from established democracies, as reported by Norris and other scholars, media influence turns out to be largely beneficial. Citizens in new democracies—as represented by the study's set of countries—might be disaffected and disengaged, but there are no indications of a media-induced malaise. On the contrary, the empirical evidence suggests that the media facilitate democratic citizenship. However, the degree to which the media contribute to this positive result differs across media type and format. As can be expected, information-rich media have the strongest effect, with print media—quality and regional papers—being more effective than television, including the public channels that are obliged to provide more and better information than commercial television. Similar differences between print and audiovisual media have been found in established democracies, challenging the widely held assumption that it is television that is the most powerful medium in political life.[48] Apparently, the higher level of cognitive involvement that is required to take in printed information is responsible for the stronger and longer-lasting effect. The difference between the printed press and television also limits the overall positive picture of the media's role in democratic politics. The media that have the most positive effect are also those that reach only a minority of citizens. Newspapers are read by only about 40 percent of respondents, whereas the majority follow the news on television, which has fewer beneficial or no effects on democratic citizenship.

The picture becomes even more complex when distinguishing among the various dependent variables of the study. The media are clearly most powerful with regard to the cognitive mobilization of citizens; that is, exposure to the news media increases political knowledge and stimulates interest in politics. To a lesser degree, the media also promote active participation. But there are only weak media effects on support for democratic values, or none at all. Hence, the main contribution of the media to democratic politics is their ability to mobilize citizens and to enhance their cognitive competences. They are less effective in changing individuals' evaluations of politics and their general values. These are formed in more complex cognitive and socially mediated processes.

It is important to note that a single-wave survey analysis on which this study was based does not allow clear conclusions as to the direction of causality. It is equally plausible to assume that citizens who are interested in politics turn to the news media more often than those who are less interested. Also, rather than assuming that the media enhance political participation, one can argue that people who are actively involved in politics will feel a higher need for more information. From this perspective, the evidence of positive media effects can be to a certain degree audience-induced effects that are dependent on an individual's motivation to learn more about politics. In this way, a dynamic reciprocal process—a virtuous circle—is set in motion, which benefits the politically active but may eventually increase the gap between those who are competent and who have a say in politics and the ignorant and passive part of the citizenry.

Finally, the relationship between the media and democratic citizenship is not universal. Even though the direction and pattern are quite similar across countries, the strength of media influences differs markedly. Any interpretation of the differences must remain speculative, but considering the time between the regime change in each country and the conduct of the survey, it seems that citizens in countries where the political transition occurred most recently, that is, Bulgaria and Hungary, are most affected by media influences. The strength of media effects declines as a democracy becomes more established. This pattern can be explained by the increased need for orientation in times of crisis or dramatic change, which makes people more open to new information, whereas in stable and secure situations people rely on their existing knowledge and acquired interpretations.

## Conclusions

This chapter explored the relationship between government accountability, social accountability, and media accountability. The normative expectations underlying these concepts were contrasted with professional journalistic practices that generate a kind of news coverage that often falls short of these ideals. Yet it would be a mistake to assume that viewers and readers assimilate at face value the messages transmitted by the media. Therefore, the chapter went on to give a brief overview of the research that has been conducted to better understand the media's influence on citizens' politics. Overall this research suggests that the media do have an impact on their audience, but this is largely dependent on a complex set of individual and social circumstances. The chapter also presented the following conclusions about how these findings could inform policy makers who wish to strengthen the role of the media in processes of democratization.

First, when choosing media institutions, policy makers have to be clear about the first principles for regulating communications. Is press freedom regarded as an absolute value? Or is preference given to a consequentialist view that relates press freedom to its benefits for the wider public good? There is no right or wrong answer to these questions, but each view leads to different conclusions as to the best policy options. Understanding press freedom as an absolute value restricts regulative policies to a minimum that are usually designed to ensure a proper working of market forces. The assumption is that competition in the "marketplace of ideas" would eventually bring about a healthy public sphere where all relevant views are represented. And even if this were not the case, press freedom would be regarded as the overriding principle. A consequentialist approach would put the public interest first. To achieve this goal, active measures would be taken to implement structures and normative guidelines that commit the media to deliver information of a quality that fosters both government accountability and social accountability. In a given transitional situation the choice might be a pragmatic one, though. For example, in the postcommunist countries of Eastern Europe, the liberalization of the media market is an important step to distance the media from government institutions that for decades have instrumentalized the media for propaganda purposes. This option is usually less viable in poorer developing countries that are emerging from a legacy of dictatorship. Because of weak consumer markets, and hence, unsustainable advertising revenues, commercial media remain dependent on government support. The media landscape in Latin America provides yet another picture. Here a highly commercialized media industry has already flourished under the old regime and has now secured a very strong position on the global market. But the media largely fail to provide sufficient political information. In this context, the implementation of public service principles in the system would be of paramount importance.

Another basic choice relates to whether internal or external diversity is regarded as more suitable for informed citizenship. Internal diversity regards the journalistic norm of objectivity and neutrality as universal. However, external diversity and advocacy journalism can play an important role in bringing about a vibrant public sphere. Again, the choice will be largely dependent on the particular circumstances of a given transitional society. External diversity and partisanship can be an effective way of giving voice to marginalized groups and to mobilize political identities and participation. But in divided societies, external diversity can exacerbate hostilities and hatred between antagonistic groups. Media policy makers should therefore aim to introduce an open space or forum that is open to all opinions and groups. However, experience shows that the model of public service broadcasting, as most prominently represented by the BBC, is difficult to export to different cultural contexts. Even in Eastern Europe the label "public service broadcasting" is often not more than a poor disguise for state broadcasting. Innovative models are needed here that detach the function of public service media from the organizational model of public service broadcasting.

Moreover, political communicators should keep in mind that effective public communication involves more than employing professional media strategies. Although the media are very effective in disseminating knowledge, their power to change people's views and behavior is limited. Hence, to help citizens make sense of politics and actively engage in political decision making, mediated communication and social communication "on the ground" have to be merged. Recent initiatives in deliberative democracy provide examples of how information from the media can be used to initiate debate among citizens and to enhance their understanding of the political processes that are affecting their lives.[49] Practices of deliberative democracy have proved particularly effective in community decision making. Especially in new democracies, these forums can be excellent workshops for citizen empowerment and effective collective action.

## Notes

1. For the notion of waves of democratization, see Samuel Huntington. 1991. *The Third Wave: Democratization in the Late Twentieth Century.* Norman/London: University of Oklahoma Press.
2. Vernon O. Key. 1966. *The Responsible Electorate.* New York: Vintage Books, 10.
3. Carmen Malena (with Reiner Forster and Janmejay Singh). 2004. *Social Accountability: An Introduction to the Concept and Emerging Practice.* Washington, DC: World Bank.
4. Important as a vibrant civil society and broad participation might be, it should be kept in mind that voting remains the key instrument through which citizens can express their preferences and decide collectively on the allocation of power. Voting is also the form of participation that is least exclusive regarding class, education, or other sociodemographic factors. Hence, participation in voluntary organizations and community policy can only complement, but never replace, effective participation in elections.
5. See Larry Diamond. 1999. *Developing Democracy. Toward Consolidation.* Baltimore/London: Johns Hopkins University Press; Jean Grugel. 2002. *Democratization. A Critical Introduction.* Basingstoke: Palgrave; Marc Morje Howard. 2003. *The Weakness of Civil Society in Post-Communist Europe.* Cambridge: Cambridge University Press.
6. Gabriel A. Almond and Sidney Verba. 1963. *The Civic Culture. Political Attitudes and Democracy in Five Nations.* Princeton, NJ: Princeton University Press. For recent critical review of the concept see William M. Reisinger. 1995. "The Renaissance of a Rubric: Political Culture as Concept and Theory." *International Journal of Public Opinion Research* 7 (4):328–52; Richard W. Wilson. 2000. "The Many Voices of Political Culture. Assessing Different Approaches." *World Politics* 52: 246–73.
7. Larry Diamond, ed. 1993. *Political Culture and Democracy in Developing Countries.* Boulder/London: Lynne Rienner; Fritz Plasser and Andreas Pribersky, eds. 1996. *Political Culture in East Central Europe.* Aldershot: Avebury.
8. Denis McQuail. 2003. *Media Accountability and Freedom of Publication.* Oxford: Oxford University Press.

9. Walter Lippman. 1922/1997. *Public Opinion.* New York: Free Press.

10. Eric Barendt. 1985. *Freedom of Speech.* Oxford: Clarendon Press; Judith Lichtenberg, ed. 1990. *Democracy and the Mass Media.* Cambridge: Cambridge University Press.

11. McQuail. 2003. *Media Accountability and Freedom of Publication,* 171.

12. Gaye Tuchman. 1972. "Objectivity as Strategic Ritual. An Examination of Newsmen's Notion of Objectivity." *American Journal of Sociology* 77: 660–79.

13. W. Lance Bennett and Regina G. Lawrence. 2008. "Press Freedom and Democratic Accountability in a Time of War, Commercialism, and the Internet." In *The Politics of News. The News of Politics,* ed. Doris A. Graber, Denis McQuail, and Pippa Norris. Washington, DC: Congressional Quarterly Press; Shanto Iyengar and Richard Reeves, eds. 1997. *Do the Media Govern? Politicians, Voters, and Reporters in America.* London: Sage.

14. Jay G. Blumler and Michael Gurevitch. 1995. *The Crisis of Public Communication.* London: Routledge.

15. See W. Lance Bennett. 1997. "Cracking the News Code. Some Rules Journalists Live By." In *Do the Media Govern?* ed. Shanto Iyengar and Richard Reeves. London: Sage; Joachim F. Staab. 1990. "The Role of News Factors in News Selection. A Theoretical Reconsideration." *European Journal of Communication* 5: 423–43.

16. See Terhi Rantanen. 2004. *The Media and Globalization.* London: Sage.

17. Shanto Iyengar. 1991. *Is Anyone Responsible? How Television Frames Political Issues.* Chicago: University of Chicago Press.

18. The famous motto of the *New York Times,* "All the news that's fit to print," indirectly implies that there is other news out there that is not fit to print and therefore not covered.

19. Marcel Machill, Sebastian Koehler, and Markus Waldhauser. 2007. "The Use of Narrative Structures in Television News. An Experiment in Innovative Forms of Journalistic Presentation." *European Journal of Communication* 22 (2): 185–205.

20. A. Matthew Baum. 2002. "Sex, Lies, and War. How Soft News Brings Foreign Policy to the Inattentive Public." *American Political Science Review* 96: 91–110; Kees Brants. 1998. "Who's Afraid of Infotainment?" *European Journal of Communication* 13 (3): 315–35.

21. Ranney distinguishes between structural bias and political bias. The former refers to distortions caused by journalistic news values, organizational routines, and technological constraints, the latter to distortions caused by ideological preferences and partisanship. Structural biases are often mistaken to be ideologically motivated, but, for example, the antigovernment sentiments of the media in the United States are directed against any government, notwithstanding which political party is in power. See Austin Ranney. 1983. *Channels of Power. The Impact of Television on American Politics.* New York: Basic Books.

22. W. Lance Bennett. 1998. "The Media and Democratic Development. The Social Basis of Political Communication." In *Communicating Democracy. The Media and Political Transitions,* ed. Patrick H. O'Neil, 201. Boulder: Lynne Rienner.

23. McQuail. 2003. *Media Accountability,* 60.

24. See Marcelo Solervicens. 2006. "Community Radio: Perspectives on Media Reach and Audience Access." In *Media Matters. Perspectives on Advancing Governance and Development,* ed. Mark Harvey. London: Internews Europe/Global Forum for Media Development. Also, Myers describes a case study from one of the world's poorest countries. See Mary Myers. 1998. "The Promotion of Democracy at the Grass-roots: The Example of Radio in Mali." *Democratization* 5 (2): 200–16.

25. Jean K. Chalaby. 1998. *The Invention of Journalism.* London: Macmillan.

26. For a detailed normative discussion of objectivity and diversity, see Denis McQuail. 1992. *Media Performance: Mass Communication and the Public Interest.* London: Sage.

27. Silvio Waisbord. 2006. "In Journalism We Trust? Credibility and Fragmented Journalism in Latin America." In *Mass Media and Political Communication in New Democracies,* ed. Katrin Voltmer. London: Routledge; Russell J. Dalton, Paul A. Beck, and Robert Huckfeldt. 1998. "Partisan Cues and the Media: Information Flows in the 1992 Presidential Election." *American Political Science Review* 92: 111–26.

28. Many European countries have designed their public service broadcasting as forum media to counterbalance a highly partisan press. Examples are the British BBC or the German ARD and ZDF. Other countries have chosen to structure public service broadcasting along existing societal divisions, as the Netherlands has done; by political parties, as in Italy; or by linguistic groups, as in Switzerland; see Peter J. Humphreys. 1996. *Mass Media and Media Policy in Western Europe.* Manchester: Manchester University Press.

29. For an overview see Sonia Livingstone. 1996. "On the Continuing Problem of Media Effects." In *Mass Media and Society,* ed. James Curran and Michael Gurevitch, 2nd ed. London/New York: Arnold.

30. Paul F. Lazarsfeld, Bernard Berelson, and Hazel Gaudet. 1948/1968. *The People's Choice. How the Voter Makes Up His Mind in a Presidential Campaign.* New York: Columbia University Press. The study is based on a panel survey that interviewed the same people over a period of several months in the run-up to the 1942 presidential election. *The People's Choice* is regarded as the cornerstone of both empirical election studies and communication research. The ideas of this initial study were then further explored in Elihu Katz and Paul F. Lazarsfeld. 1955. *Personal Influence. The Part Played by People in the Flow of Mass Communication.* New York: Free Press.

31. Vincent Price. 1992. *Public Opinion.* London: Sage.

32. Rüdiger Schmitt-Beck. 2003. "Mass Communication, Personal Communication and Vote Choice: The Filter Hypothesis of Media Influence in Comparative Perspective." *British Journal of Political Science* 33: 233–59; Steven E. Finkel. 1993. "Reexamining the "Minimal Effects" Model in Recent Presidential Campaigns." *Journal of Politics* 55 (1): 1–21.

33. Sven Windahl and Benno Signitzer (with Jean T. Olson). 1992. *Using Communication Theory: An Introduction to Planned Communication.* London: Sage.

34. In particular, Huckfeldt's work is based on the tradition laid down by Lazarsfeld; see Robert Huckfeldt and John Sprague. 1995. *Citizens, Politics, and Social Communication. Information and Influence in an Election Campaign.* Cambridge: Cambridge University Press. See also Jack M. McLeod, Dietram A. Scheufele, and Patricia Moy. 1999. "Community, Communication, and Participation. The Role of Mass Media and Interpersonal Discussion in Local Political Participation." *Political Communication* 16 (3): 315–36.

35. Robert Huckfeldt, Paul E. Johnson, and John Sprague. 2004. *Political Disagreement. The Survival of Diverse Opinions Within Communication Networks.* Cambridge: Cambridge University Press; Diana C. Mutz and Paul S. Martin. 2001. "Facilitating Communication across Lines of Political Difference: The Role of the Mass Media." *American Political Science Review* 95 (1): 97–114; Diana C. Mutz. 2006. *Hearing the Other Side. Deliberative versus Participatory Democracy.* Cambridge: Cambridge University Press; Katrin Voltmer and Mansur Lalljee. 2007. "Agree to Disagree. Communication and Respect for Political Opponents." In *British Social Attitudes. The 23rd Report,* ed. Alison Park et al. London: Sage.

36. When comparing electoral politics in established and emerging democracies, one must keep in mind that the former are also undergoing fundamental changes with a marked erosion of party affiliation and, as a consequence, a growing number of undecided voters; see Russell J. Dalton and Martin P. Wattenberg, eds. 2002. *Parties Without Partisans. Political Change in Advanced Industrial Democracies.* Oxford: Oxford University Press.

37. Hedwig de Smaele. 2006. "In the Name of Democracy: The Paradox of Democracy and Press Freedom in Post-Communist Russia." In *Mass Media and Political Communication in New Democracies*, ed. Katrin Voltmer. London: Routledge; Katrin Voltmer. 2000. "Constructing Political Reality in Russia. Izvestiya—between Old and New Journalistic Practices." *European Journal of Communication* 14 (4): 469–500.

38. See Stephen White, Ian McAllister, and Sarah Oates. 2002. "Was It Russian Public Television that Won It?" *International Journal of Press/Politics* 7 (2): 17–33.

39. Ellen Mickiewicz. 2008. *Television, Power, and the Public in Russia.* Cambridge: Cambridge University Press.

40. Shanto Iyengar and Donald R. Kinder. 1987. *News That Matters: Television and American Opinion.* Chicago: University of Chicago Press; Shanto Iyengar. 1990. "The Accessibility Bias in Politics: Television News and Public Opinion." *International Journal of Public Opinion Research* 2: 1–15; Daniel Kahneman and Amos Tversky. 1984. "Choices, Values, and Frames." *American Psychologist* 39: 341–350; Maxwell McCombs et al., eds. 1997. *Communication and Democracy: Exploring the Intellectual Frontiers of Agenda-Setting Theory.* Mahwah, NJ/London: Erlbaum. For a concise overview see James W. Dearing and Everett M. Rogers. 1996. *Agenda Setting.* London: Sage.

41. There are some exceptions with regard to so-called obtrusive issues that can be directly experienced in everyday life. Examples of obtrusive issues are inflation and unemployment, which are usually only poorly covered by the media but are high on people's agenda; see Iyengar and Kinder. 1987. *News That Matters.*

42. Elisabeth Noelle-Neumann. 1993. *The Spiral of Silence. Public Opinion—Our Social Skin.* Chicago: University of Chicago Press.

43. Noelle-Neumann's study focuses on election campaign communication, both mediated and personal. The large body of literature that is based on the ideas of her theory shows that similar dynamics are at work with any other public issues; see W. J. Gonzenbach and R.L. Stevenson. 1994. "Children with AIDS Attending Public School: An Analysis of the Spiral of Silence." *Political Communication* 11: 3–18; Patricia Moy, David Domke, and Keith Stamm. 2001. "Children with AIDS Attending Public School: An Analysis of the Spiral of Silence." *Political Communication* 11: 3–18; J. Shamir. 1995. "Information Cues and Indicators of the Climate of Opinion. The Spiral of Silence Theory in the Intifada." *Communication Research* 22: 23–53.

44. Kathleen H. Jamieson. 1992. *Dirty Politics. Deception, Distraction, and Democracy.* Oxford: Oxford University Press; Thomas E. Patterson. 1993. *Out of Order.* New York: Knopf; Robert D. Putnam. 2000. *Bowling Alone. The Collapse and Revival of American Community.* New York: Simon & Schuster.

45. Russell J. Dalton. 1996. *Citizen Politics. Public Opinion and Political Parties in Advanced Industrial Democracies.* 2nd ed. Chatham: Chatham House; Kenneth Newton. 1999. "Mass Media Effects: Mobilization or Media Malaise?" *British Journal of Political Science* 29: 577–99.

46. Pippa Norris. 2000. *A Virtuous Circle. Political Communications in Postindustrial Societies.* Cambridge: Cambridge University Press.

47. Rüdiger Schmitt-Beck and Katrin Voltmer. 2007. "The Mass Media in Third-Wave Democracies: Gravediggers or Seedsmen of Democratic Consolidation?" In *Democracy, Intermediation, and Voting on Four Continents,* ed. Richard Gunther, Jose Ramon Montero, and Hans-Jürgen Puhle. Oxford: Oxford University Press. The study is part of the Cross National Election Project (CNEP2).

48. William P. Eveland and Dietram Scheufele. 2000. "'Connecting News Media Use with Gaps in Knowledge and Participation." *Political Communication* 17 (3): 215–237; Michael X. Delli Carpini and Scott Keeter. 1996. *What Americans Know about Politics and Why It Matters.* New Haven: Yale University Press.

49. James Fishkin. 1991. *Democracy and Deliberation. New Directions of Democratic Reforms.* New Haven, CT: Yale University Press; John Gastil and Peter Levine, eds. 2005. *The Deliberative Democracy Handbook. Strategies for Effective Civic Engagement in the 21st Century.* San Francisco: Jossey Bass.

# Gatekeepers:
# Inclusive Voices

# 7

# Election Campaigns, Partisan Balance, and the News Media

Holli A. Semetko

The mass media are the most common source for information about election campaigns in democracies and societies in transition around the world. In terms of the sheer volume of information available to citizens via the media on issues, political parties, and leaders, election campaigns often represent a high point for political communications. Concerns about political bias in the mass media are at the heart of debates about the roles and responsibilities of the media at election time. Behind these concerns is the assumption that the media's actions may have an effect, intended or unintended, on public opinion and political behavior and, ultimately, electoral outcomes.

In every election campaign, citizens must decide not only what party or candidate they wish to support; they also must decide whether they will vote at all. In democracies that do not mandate compulsory voting, most political observers would agree that turnout in an election is a measure of success, with the higher the turnout, the better. In most cases, parties and candidates use all means to stimulate turnout and motivate supporters to go to the polls. In some cases, however, parties and political camps aim to repress turnout to accomplish their goals. It is the larger context of political party strategies and tactics, and the structure of the mass media environment, that researchers also need to consider when addressing questions about balance during election campaigns.

## The Normative Concepts of Balance and Bias

What does the normative concept of balance imply for the news? Although balance is problematic to define, it remains an assumption behind allegations of political bias in the news, especially at election time. Political parties monitor media coverage closely and sometimes complain loudly when they perceive themselves to be given less time, less prominence, or less favorable coverage in comparison with their leading contenders.

In established democracies, broadcast journalists, whose medium is often mandated to provide impartial reporting of politics at election time, are confronted with the problem of balance when reporting election campaigns.[1] Research on television news has shown that the principle of balance, though used during election campaigns in a number of established democracies, has been applied quite differently. If the principle of balance in reporting on contending parties and candidates is strictly adhered to, it conflicts with the journalistic principle of objectivity, which drives story selection. News values provide objective criteria by which editors determine what stories end up in the news. If television news is responsible for presenting a range of political voices at election time, normal news values will need to be suspended to accomplish these objectives.

Allegations of political bias in the media may be aimed at the system level or at the program and individual level. An example of the former is the allegation by Edward Herman and Noam Chomsky that there is an ideological bias in U.S. news reporting on Central and Latin America that supports U.S. government foreign policy.[2] An example of allegations of political bias at the program/individual level are those that emerged in the early part of the fall 2008 U.S. presidential election campaign about political talk shows and news programs on MSNBC and Fox networks.

Some of the earliest research on media and elections in the United States stemmed from a concern about media bias having an impact on electoral outcomes. Paul Lazarsfeld and his colleagues compared radio and press reporting on the presidential candidates in the 1940 U.S. election. They found that Roosevelt had a visibility advantage in the news by a margin of 3 to 2 in quantitative terms, but the tone of the news actually favored Wilkie by a margin of 2 to 1, illustrating the independence of measures of degree and of direction of attention.[3] This early research illustrates two important dimensions to assessing balance in the news: namely, visibility and valence.

In established democracies, the concepts of visibility and valence have been applied to the main political parties in assessing balance and bias in the news in election campaigns.[4] The visibility of party spokespersons and party leaders, and the tone of coverage toward these political actors, may be a component of the analysis. Though the notions of balance and bias in the news at election time are often about political parties, they might also be extended to include interest groups and regions. In the context of a postconflict election, and in societies in transition with little in the way of established political parties, it may be more difficult to apply these concepts to assessing the news coverage during an election campaign. Another question is whether internal diversity or external diversity is most important. The former refers to reporting that takes into account the full range of parties and viewpoints within a news program, and the latter refers to the balance of coverage across all different news outlets. In comparing a number of established democracies on these questions, the answers are by no means identical.

## Four Case Studies

This issue of partisan balance in election campaigns is particularly important in transnational autocracies and consolidating democracies when one party is dominant, and where opposition parties and reform movements have difficulty in getting their message out to mobilize voters. Based on the experience with recent elections and the extent to which media reporting was seen to be an issue, and the national trajectories on the paths of democracy and development, this study examines four countries: Kenya, Mexico, the Russian Federation, and Turkey.

These are diverse cases, drawn from different world regions and cultures. Some of these countries have more resources available to study election campaigns and changes in partisan balance in the media over time. Mexico and Turkey, for example, each have teams of researchers working on national election studies based on survey and panel data, as well as media content analysis of campaign news. Russia also has been the subject of much research with respect to media and politics, public opinion, and elections. Kenya has had media monitoring and public opinion polls, but no systematic data collection that enables linking the two to address questions about influence. Although access to television in Kenya is far less widespread than in the other three countries, in which 9 out of 10 households have television, television news reporting was perceived as imbalanced in the 2007 elections, and this has been connected to the election's violent aftermath. In the sections that follow, the discussion of each case draws on available scholarship and reports from recent elections.

Table 7.1 presents a matrix with key features of political and media system characteristics in the four countries. On the basis of the latest available Freedom House rating, these countries represent different levels of democracy, ranging from free (Mexico) to not free (Russia), with Turkey and Kenya in between described as partly free. Press freedom is less variable, with Russia described as not free and the other countries as partly free, based on Freedom House ratings. The number of journalists killed in the country is another indicator of press freedom, and the common unfortunate degree of experience in Mexico and Russia on this indicator sets them apart from Kenya and Turkey over the past five years. All countries have mixed broadcasting systems with

**Table 7.1. Political and Media System Characteristics**

| | Kenya | Mexico | Russian Federation | Turkey |
|---|---|---|---|---|
| Freedom 2008, Freedom House | partly free (7) | free (5) | not free (11) | partly free (6) |
| Press Freedom 2008, Freedom House | partly free (59) | partly free (48) | not free (75) | partly free (49) |
| GDP per capita, purchasing power parity (PPP) (US$) | 1,240 | 10,751 | 10,845 | 8,407 |
| Human Development Index | .521 (148th) | .829 (52nd) | .802 (67th) | .775 (84th) |
| **Journalists killed** | | | | |
| 2006–08 | 0 | 9 | 5 | 2 |
| 2003–05 | 0 | 6 | 8 | 0 |
| **Type of broadcasting system** | | | | |
| Number of terrestrial public and private nationwide channels | 7 | 4 | 6 | 8 (about 300 private) |
| **Type of newspaper market** | | | | |
| Number of national daily titles | 5 | 300 | 250 | 588 |
| Daily circulation per 1,000 | | 92.76 | 91.78 | |
| **Level of literacy** | 73.6 | 91.6 | 99.4 | 87.4 |
| **Access** | | | | |
| Internet users per 1,000 | 32.43 | 180.64 | 152.33 | 222.02 |
| Radios per 1,000 | 104 | 325 | 418 | 180 |
| Household with television (%) | 16.83 | 92.37 | 97.77 | 96.29 |
| **Political context** | | | | |
| Type of executive | Presidential | Presidential | Mixed executive | Mixed executive |
| Share of votes/seats of the largest party (year of election) | 56.1 (2002) 125 out of 210 | 34.6 (2006) 206 out of 500 | 64.3 (2007) 315 out of 450 | 46.7 (2008) 341 out of 550 |

*Sources:* Journalists killed (International Press Institute, http://www.freemedia.at/cms/ipi/deathwatch.html); newspaper data (World Bank, World Development Indicators); access and type of executive data (http://www.pippanorris.com Democracy Cross-National Data); share of votes (Psephos, http://psephos.adam-carr.net/).

public service (government funded) and private or commercial channels that operate nationwide, in addition to a number of regional and local channels. The countries vary in terms of the number of national newspapers, reflecting to some extent the variance in the reported level of literacy. Mexico, Russia, and Turkey stand apart from Kenya in terms of literacy, Internet use, and access to television and radio. Though television is a very accessible medium in Mexico, Russia, and Turkey, reaching more than 90 percent of households in those countries, less than 18 percent of households in Kenya have access to television, and radio use is more widespread. The political systems vary from presidential in Kenya and Mexico to a mixed executive in Russia and Turkey, and the share of votes received by the largest party in the last election suggests the least amount of electoral competition in Russia.

## Kenya

Kenya became independent from British rule in 1963. Kenya's constitution guarantees freedom of the press, free speech, and freedom of assembly. The public service broadcasting ethos, with the duty to "inform, educate, and entertain," predominates. Journalists are known for independent and objective reporting.[5] Broadcasting in Kenya was originally modeled on the British Broadcasting Corporation (BBC), following the introduction of radio in 1927 under British colonial rule. Television stations include the government-owned Kenya Broadcasting Corporation (KBC), Kenya Television Network (KTN), among others, as well as international channels. Newspapers in Kenya are privately owned, and they have played a Fourth Estate role when criticizing the government, policies, and political leaders.

In recent decades, until the fateful elections of December 2007, Kenya was viewed as one of Africa's most stable democratic countries, with a thriving tourism industry and growing economy due to political stability, a developed financial sector, communications networks, and liberal economic policies. The nation shares borders with Ethiopia, Somalia, Sudan, Tanzania, and Uganda.

The December, 27, 2007, presidential election had nine candidates on the national ballot, representing nine parties. Turnout was 69 percent. Incumbent President Mwai Kibaki (Party of National Unity, PNU) took 46.4 percent of the votes compared with Raila Odinga (Orange Democratic Movement, ODM), who took 44.1 percent. Kalonzo Musyoka (Orange Democratic movement–Kenya, ODM-K) came in a distant third with 8.9 percent, and all other candidates received less than 1 percent. Although the 2007 election is most remembered for its violent aftermath, which was reported in some detail in news media around the world, in fact, there were also a considerable number of violent incidents during the election campaign that received attention in Kenya's news media. The campaign violence reported in the Kenyan media appears to have been described in terms of who the victims supported and who the perpetrators supported.

In the run-up to the 2007 general election, the United Nations Development Programme (UNDP) contracted Strategic Public Relations and Research Ltd. to conduct monitoring from September through December 2007, with the goal of informing journalists, the public, and politicians to ensure "enhanced fair and accurate media reporting on electoral issues."[6] Balance, accuracy, impartiality, and fairness were the goals of the exercise, with a focus on equitable access to media by political parties. Media monitoring reports were issued regularly, with quantitative and qualitative assessments of political news in six newspapers and on four television channels, six English-Swahili radio stations, and 10 vernacular radio stations.[7]

The media monitoring operation specifically aimed to influence journalists, editors, and media owners to provide accurate, impartial, and fair reporting, and to encourage adherence to professional standards by journalists. By publicizing results periodically during the months preceding the election, the monitoring operation aimed to alert citizens to question their sources of information and to encourage parties and candidates to refrain from negative campaigning. The UNDP project also sought to advocate for new legislation to protect freedom of the press, the right to information, and the right of expression.

Kenya's four leading television channels are owned by different media groups. Citizen TV is owned by Royal Media, a Kenyan multimedia house; Nation TV (NTV) is owned by Nation Media group, a Kenyan media company. KBC, which is the equivalent to Britain's BBC, is owned by the government. And KTN is owned by the Standard Group, a regional media company.

Kenya's code of conduct and practice of journalism provide guidelines on a number of issues to ensure free, fair, and accurate coverage of election campaigns, including accuracy and fairness; right of reply; letter to the editor; unnamed sources confidentiality; misrepresentation; obscenity, taste, and tone in reporting; pay for news; plagiarism; discrimination; reporting on ethnic, religious, and sectarian conflict; recording of interviews and conversations; privacy; intrusion into grief and shock; sex discrimination; financial journalism; protection of children; victims of sex crimes; use of pictures and names; innocent relatives and friends; acts of violence; editor's responsibilities; and advertisements. There are also guidelines for election coverage that have been developed by news practitioners and media owners, with the goal of facilitating free, fair, and democratic elections. Subjects of the guidelines include accuracy and fairness, sources of information, favors and special treatment, role of media owners, opinion polls, hate speech and incitement, minorities, state media, private media separation of fact and opinion, advertorials, identification, attacks and threats, journalists and assignments, electoral processes and malpractice, informing and educating of voters, human rights, and political activity.[8]

The first report, at the end of September 2007, pointed out the political highlights of that month, including the launch of the PNU, which was a coalition including parties that supported the reelection of President Mwai Kibaki. An opinion poll showed the ODM party leader and presidential candidate Raila Odinga ahead of President Kibaki, and a third candidate, Kalonzo Musyoka, as the most popular presidential candidate. A political rally in Kisii became violent, with ODM leaders injured in the chaos. Kenya's Electoral Commission refuted allegations that it was to blame for the Kisii violence and pointed to police for acting as bystanders. The third political group was the ODM-K, which ranked third in visibility, far below the other two. Print media in general gave more coverage to PNU and its affiliate parties than to other competing parties. The pattern is also evident in the coverage of parties on mainstream radio, with PNU first, receiving the most coverage, ODM second, and ODM-K a distant third. Vernacular radio stations provided more opportunity for ODM than PNU in three out of five stations. Incumbent Kibaki received the most coverage in all types of media, followed by Raila Odinga, and Kalonzo Musyoka, coming in a distant third. The first media monitoring report concluded that there was a general bias favoring the incumbent president in both state-owned and private media, in terms of more time and space in all major media, with largely favorable coverage. ODM's Odinga was second in all major media, and despite some negative coverage, "the media largely reported it factually." The third candidate was far less visible, and the reporting was labeled accurate and fair. The tone of reporting on television was described as positive or neutral, and none of the programs on television critically engaged the parties or candidates. The first report pointed up a tendency for television to avoid reporting a story rather than present a negative story. Hate speech was a focus of the first monitoring study because mainstream media have attempted to censor speeches that may cause violence and chaos. But, the report pointed out, there were cases in which editors did not have the time to edit out inflammatory statements, such as live broadcasts, and the PNU launch was one such occasion.

Gender was also a focus of the monitoring study, and the first month's report concluded that women candidates received minimal coverage compared with their male counterparts, with only 6 percent of the total coverage of candidates on television given to women. This cannot be explained away by the lower number of women candidates, as channel comparisons found that, in many cases, political activities by women candidates often went unreported in the news. One newspaper story by Maxwell Masava reported on a poll that asked voters the likelihood they would support a female candidate to be Member of Parliament: 54 percent said slightly or very unlikely, compared with 46 percent who said slightly or very likely. The article pictured three women candidates under the headline "Number of women MPs set to rise after poll," and key subheadlines in the article revealed the gist of the story: "Jealousy was cited as the main reason why women were not voted in as leaders," and "Men seen by voters as more courageous and less jealous."[9]

The conclusion of the first monitoring report recognized the visibility bonus given to the incumbent president and the PNU, but judged the situation overall to be a "significant improvement in the coverage of the competing political parties and candidates." Biases in favor of the incumbent president and his party, sitting MPs, and male candidates were highlighted. The study urged media to provide more news on underrepresented groups such as women and the disabled.

The second monitoring report one month later, at the end of October 2007, concluded that there was "extensive, preferential coverage … given to the incumbent presidential candidate and the ruling party and little coverage or resources were assigned to opposition parties."[10] The Electoral Law was criticized for being vague so that the allocation of airtime on broadcast media was very selective, as "all broadcast media monitored failed to comply with the basic obligations of balance and equitable coverage of parties and candidates." The press was deemed to be less biased than broadcasting, though it was also described as clearly leaning toward the ruling party in its reporting.

The report made several recommendations:

- The free airtime granted to candidates should be made available during prime time, as this can be the only time that candidates have access to media.
- Paid political advertising should be regulated and clearly labeled, accompanied by financial transparency to ensure equality among contestants.
- Publicly funded broadcasting organizations and print media should serve the public and not the political forces, and therefore be guaranteed editorial and financial independence.
- There should be a clear separation between election programs and other programs that are not about the campaign, and the latter should not be used to promote political parties and candidates.

These recommendations suggest that although the British model of public service broadcasting was introduced in Kenya, it did not result in the extensive efforts to balance campaign reporting that have been found in flagship news programs in the United Kingdom, namely, on BBC and ITN.[11] The free provision of airtime to political parties also follows the British PSB model, but the allocation of this time to the parties was obviously highly contested in Kenya's 2007 campaign, and the placement of these party broadcasts outside of prime time failed to reach many potential voters. There was also a clear tension in Kenya's PSB and state-funded media, with less of a tendency to take a critical stance in reporting on the parties and top candidates. The report also condemned the use of entertainment programming to promote political parties and leaders, so the spillover into a variety of formats that is so common across media at election time in Western democracies was clearly seen as problematic in the Kenyan context.

The third monitoring report covered October 29–November 25, 2007, and during this period the party manifestos were launched and the presidential candidates were nominated. At these routine campaign events, the British PSB model would have given the same amount of airtime to each main party, but this was not the case in Kenya. Each of the four television channels displayed noticeable differences in amounts of airtime given to the manifesto launches of each party, and in three of the four cases, ODM-K received the most, with PNU a close second, and ODM a distant third. On KTN, for example, ODM received just slightly over half the amount of airtime given to ODM-K's launch, and PNU came in with just a few minutes less than ODM-K. By contrast, on the coverage of the presidential nominations on these four channels, the ODM-K candidate Kalonzo came in a distant third on three out of four channels. On KTN, Raila was almost twice as far ahead of Kibaki in terms of the coverage given to his nomination, and the gap between the two was much less on KBC, with Kibaki in the lead, and almost no gap between the two on NTV. CTV gave almost a third more airtime to the nomination of Kibaki than ODM's Raila, who was closely followed by ODM-K's Kalonzo.

The third report finds that across all television channels, PNU, the incumbent's party, had the most coverage, followed by ODM, and channels NTV and KTN appeared to aim for some parity across the three main parties, while channels KBC and CTV gave significantly more airtime to PNU than the other two parties. With respect to reporting on the presidential candidates, KBC and KTN gave more coverage to the PNU incumbent Kibaki than the others, NTV gave the most balanced coverage to all the candidates, and CTV gave the most negative coverage to Raila. Newspapers were deemed to have provided comparatively fair reporting on the top three parties and candidates, with PNU coming first in the papers *Nation*, *People*, and *Kenya Times*, and ODM first in the *Standard* and *Nairobi Star*. Across all newspapers monitored, Kibaki and PNU received the most positive coverage.

Violence became a part of the nomination process, and the report states that supporters of candidates who lost resorted to violence and demonstrations to protest the outcomes of the party primaries. ODM was the focus of more postnomination coverage than other parties, all of which portrayed the party negatively. The report blames the media for releasing preliminary results in an attempt to beat each other on forecasting outcomes, which precipitated violence. The report also criticized the media for overemphasizing violence, citing the example that CTV covered a demonstration against ODM in Moyale for about a half hour.

The third report also offered a number of conclusions about women and elections: women were not given any special treatment in the media; there were commentaries in the media on the difficulties women face running for office; all media treated women candidates as equal to their male counterparts; and women who complained of unfair treatment were given a fair audience by the media. These conclusions were presented without any data to substantiate them.

A fourth report, November 27–December 10, focused exclusively on election violence. The report concluded that violence had been an important issue in the elections, and the government and the Electoral Commission were left to handle the situation after news about violence was transmitted by the media to the public.

The fifth report, dated December 13, 2007, drew attention to the fact that reporting on opinion polls in the media had improved over the course of the campaign. For example, media called attention to the sponsors of the surveys, sample size and allocation, margins of error and confidence levels, survey instruments and their administration, and data analysis procedures. The report also pointed out that there were fewer cases in which politicians alleged bias or misrepresentation by the media, which the report indicated suggests greater fairness and accuracy in reporting.

The final report, covering December 11–20, 2007, found that PNU and ODM led in terms of the amount of radio coverage during prime time. But the sections of the report regarding television and the press did not offer general conclusions about the visibility bias or tone of coverage toward each of the main candidates and parties, and instead only showed a number of charts, presumably to leave conclusions to the reader. Those charts suggest that, for television, the incumbent Kibaki maintained his visibility lead over the other candidates, with Raila only even or almost even with him on KTN and NTV, and Kibaki was always the more likely lead news story on all four channels. The PNU (Kibaki's party) also maintained this visibility bonus on all channels apart from KTN. Kibaki also received the most favorable coverage of all the candidates on all four television channels, exceeding Raila's percentage of favorable coverage by some 10 percentage points on KTN and KBC, with less of a gap between the two on NTV and CTV. The press was more balanced than television with respect to the top two presidential candidates' visibility and the visibility of the two leading parties PNU and ODM. The report offered no charts or qualitative judgment of the tone of the coverage in the press, however.

The report concluded that there have been improvements in coverage with respect to fairness and accuracy:

> Even though sections of the media have provided inordinate coverage to certain parties and candidates, the media has generally attempted a fair balance and has largely reported accurately … Cases of misrepresentation have greatly reduced … The coverage of delicate issues such as ethnic, religious, and other sectarian

differences has been well handled with none of the mainstream media overtly taking stands in such cases.[12]

This official monitoring exercise attributed some blame for the violence during the campaign to both media reporting and the ineffective response of the Electoral Commission and the civil authorities. What was not addressed is what specifically was provoking the violence during the campaign in various parts of the country. The monitoring also did not discuss the issues that were reported on in connection with the coverage of the main parties and leading presidential candidates, and it is important to know how and whether certain issues played favorably for one or another candidate and party. The absence of issue reporting is also an important finding; these monitoring reports give no indication of the importance of issues in the news during this historic campaign.

There is a need for a stronger regulatory framework governing elections in Kenya that can also exert some influence over access to television and radio. There also appears to be little in the way of expert research on the consequences of election reporting on political behavior and electoral outcomes. Although two publications discussed below highlight the role of the media in the campaign and offer valuable policy suggestions, there remains a lack of systematic data collection on media content, public opinion, and voting behavior in Kenyan elections.

A 16-page policy briefing by the BBC World Trust Service was published in January 2008 on the role of the media in the postelection violence in Kenya. The following are 12 specific policy-relevant conclusions that pertain to the media in the 2007 Kenyan election campaign:

- The media ... play a central role in shaping Kenya's democracy. The recent record of the media, according to many within it, is that media has undermined as well as invigorated that democracy ... [The briefing urges] development actors to be better engaged and more supportive of media in the future.
- The problem facing Kenya's media is not an excess of media freedom [but rather] a lack of it ... Journalists and broadcasters face immense commercial and political constraints which are constraining their journalistic independence and integrity.
- Some local language radio stations have incited fear and hatred ... Talk shows have provided the greatest opportunities for hate speech and ... [hosts] are not trained in conflict reporting or moderation ... [T]his [training] was [felt to be] a priority.
- [L]ocal language stations appear to have been playing an important role in calming tension and promoting dialogue. A strengthening of such a role ... will form a critical contribution.

- Training ... remains a major priority, [particularly] training talk show hosts and others engaged in facilitating public debate. Training [journalists] on conflict reporting [is] now consider[ed] ... an urgent need.
- [A] debate [on media policy and regulatory environment] should be encouraged, and particular attention could usefully be focused on a public interest approach to broadcasting and media.
- Media monitoring by civil society and research organizations has done a good deal to discourage the broadcast of hate speech by media organizations. Such monitoring is currently haphazard and could be more systematic and better supported.
- Community media has ... emerged with great credit [in calming the violence] and arguably provides a model for the future. It requires better, more strategic engagement and support in Kenya and elsewhere. This support is partly a question of policy engagement, partly one of financial, funding and sustainability models.
- The poor remuneration, status and safety of journalists is hampering a free and plural media. Substantial progress in strengthening the media will not be possible unless the working conditions of journalists are improved.
- There is no independent public service broadcaster in Kenya. If there is a debate and a move in the country to transform [a station] ... into one, it could usefully be intensively supported.
- Kenya faces the most important public debate in its history. The media will be central to its character, [its] conduct and its outcome. An inclusive and balanced debate may need financial support.
- Coordination, information sharing and long-term strategic planning of media support within Kenya could be substantially improved, including in ensuring that external media support is both demand led and strategically coherent. Much capacity building of media over recent years has been donor led (focused, for example, on specific health or other issues) rather than addressing the core challenges facing media in Kenya.

The policy briefing was based on a number of interviews by the authors Jamal Abdi Ismail and James Deane with national and international figures in the Kenyan media and supporting organizations.[13]

The *Journal of Eastern African Studies* devoted a special issue in July 2008 to the 2007 Kenyan elections, with more than a dozen articles on the background and context, the campaign, the vote, the violence, and the future.[14] The deeply contested official results are the subject of one article in the special issues, whose author, Toni Weis notes, "Even if these figures are questionable, their effects are quite real: however flawed the numbers are, they profoundly shape the political reality Kenya will have to live with in the years to come."[15]

## Mexico

For most of the 20th century, media in Mexico were inextricably entwined with the country's single-party system. But in the past two decades, Mexico has made a remarkable transition from a government-controlled media system to a market-driven competitive system. This transformation in Mexico's media system furthered democratization in the country. Competition encouraged new forms of reporting to appeal to audiences and, according to Chappell Lawson, these "changes in media coverage themselves exerted a powerful influence on politics and political transition," including "increased scrutiny of government actions and decisions [and] … greater coverage of opposition parties during election campaigns."[16] The shift to a market-driven media system did not occur simultaneously in the broadcast and print media; it started earlier in the press and took place over a longer period, whereas a culture of independence developed more slowly among owners and journalists in broadcast media.

With respect to newspapers, which have a very limited readership in Mexico, below 10,000 copies per day in the mid-1990s, there was the important recognition among journalists that greater independence comes from financial autonomy. Lawson described the remarkable transition to a Fourth Estate print media in these terms:

> In the 1970s, 1980s, and 1990s, journalists with a different vision of their profession founded a series of independent publications: *Proceso, El Financiero, La Jornada, Reforma, Siglo21*, and others. Because these publications were more popular than their traditional counterparts, they were able to attain some measure of financial autonomy. Financial autonomy, in turn, enabled these publications to better resist official pressures and encouraged other papers to follow suit. Ultimately, independent journalism spread to virtually all major media markets. By the late 1990s, Mexico's Fourth Estate was firmly established in the print media.[17]

While entrepreneurial newspaper journalists were responsible for building the Fourth Estate in the press over several decades, Televisa was the single company that dominated Mexican television from the 1970s to the mid-1990s. It took an earthquake in 1985, registering 8.1 on the Richter scale in Mexico City, for Televisa to recognize extreme public dissatisfaction with the government and to demonstrate to media owners that the Mexican public demanded accurate information. Radio forged ahead with timely and accurate assessments of damage, while Televisia "continued to transmit mild reports of the damage—up until its own tower collapsed and it was forced off the air."[18] A large number of the channel's employees were killed. By the 1990s, Televisa's coverage of earthquakes and other natural disasters had become "extensive and graphic." The 1988 presidential election coverage was influenced by the earthquake, with radio offering a more even-handed approach to reporting the Institutional Revolutionary Party's (PRI) electoral challengers, though television coverage continued to provide a "profoundly biased" view of the race, to the point that it became an issue in the election campaign itself.

With the economic liberalization program of President Carlos Salinas, the broadcast media landscape was forever altered following the privatization of government-owned television channels. TV Azteca brought competition into the television landscape and, financed by banks in Texas and Mexico and by the U.S. network NBC, the new network specifically challenged Televisa as an alternative national broadcaster. It took several years, however, for the new private television channel to become more assertive in the delivery of political news, with ratings rivaling Televisa's by 1997.

With legislation in 1996 to guarantee the autonomy of the Federal Election Institute (IFE), there was a deliberate attempt to ensure balance in broadcast news coverage during the 1997 and 2000 elections, despite the fact that IFE had no authority to sanction networks. IFE provided public funds to political parties after 1996 to pay for TV advertising and television networks competed for their business. Broadcast journalists insist that the opening of television occurred from the bottom up and that despite the changes made by the Salinas administration, the president actually had a negative influence on the process of opening the broadcast media.

The 1997 Mexico City mayoral elections brought PRI opponent Cuauhté- moc Cárdenas, a candidate of the Party of the Democratic Revolution (PRD), into power, and some observers claim that Mexico's transition to democracy was solidified when PRI President Ernesto Zedillo officially recognized the victory of Cárdenas in this mayoral race. Others point to the presidential elec- tion of 2000 as the watershed election that guaranteed the transition to de- mocracy in Mexico.

The election of Vicente Fox, of the National Action Party (PAN), in 2000 altered the political landscape; Fox was the first opposition party leader to ascend to power peacefully, and many therefore say he was responsible for bringing democracy to Mexico.[19] As president, he brought major changes in the news media and in the laws and practices governing free expression and freedom-of-information legislation, which opened most areas of government to external scrutiny. The establishment of the Federal Institute for Access to Public Information, which processes requests for government documents and files, and the release of tens of thousands of secret files by the government, for example, brought about an unprecedented openness in the country. In 2001, President Fox launched "e-Mexico" to have the Internet provide more access to government information.

With the result of the 2000 election, and a newly elected President Fox, the many print media found themselves in a difficult position, as they had supported the incumbent PRI candidate Francisco Labastida Ochoa, and had been subsidized by the state or the party for years. Television and broadcast media had also worked closely with the incumbent PRI. The election of Fox and the end of the accommodating relationship between the state and the media brought about a new era, one in which there was no longer room for conscious avoidance of criticism of the government and the president. A new, critical, Fourth Estate role was evidenced by a number of exchanges Fox himself had with the media.

Televisa continues to be Mexico's leading broadcasting company and is also among the world's leading syndicators. Televisa controls a number of Mexico's national broadcast channels that are among the favorite channels of television viewers, and the company also has interests in radio, cable, magazines, sports, film, and TV production studios. TV Azteca, the main competitor to Televisa, was launched in the mid-1990s under the administration of President Carlos Salinas through the sale of state-owned networks in an effort to privatize and democratize. The fact later emerged that the networks that became TV Azteca were bought by a businessman whose opportunity to purchase was facilitated through payments to the president's brother, Raul Salinas, and TV Azteca came to support PRI and the government just as Televisa had.

Research on Mexico's 2000 presidential campaign found that privately owned television stations were generally more balanced than public broadcasters, which continued to follow propagandistic models of reporting. Yet private ownership also often involved special arrangements between broadcasters and politicians based on the prospect of future business, which Hughes and Lawson describe as "crony capitalism."[20] Changes in ownership therefore do not appear to be eradicating partisan bias in the news.

Content analysis of the coverage of the 2000 election campaign on the country's two leading television channels found that the tone of the news reporting on PAN candidate Vicente Fox on Televisa shifted considerably over the course of the campaign, with a marked change against him after it became evident that he might actually defeat the PRI nominee.[21] Many political observers viewed the change in Televisa's reporting on Fox as a consequence of government pressure on the network.

A panel survey conducted during and surrounding Mexico's watershed presidential elections in 2000 found that exposure to television news had significant effects on both attitudes and vote choices.[22] By 2000, public disenchantment with the government's handling of the economy, and with corruption, was widespread, and this was an important influence on voters. News coverage was also a key factor in influencing voter attitudes and behavior in 2000. There were differences in the tone of coverage on the main candidates, which indeed shaped citizens' comparative assessments of those candidates. In cases in which reporting was balanced, the effects of exposure to television news were not important, but key differences in the tone of coverage to which citizens were exposed did emerge in public opinion. With respect to voter choice, the study shows that President Fox benefitted from the fact that those who were exposed to network news on TV Azteca displayed declining support for the PRI's Labastida over the course of the campaign, whereas only modest effects emerged among Televisa audiences.

Mexico held simultaneous presidential and national legislative elections on July 2, 2006. The result of the presidential race was very close between the PAN and PRD candidates, with turnout at 59 percent. Felipe de Jesus Calderon Hinojose (PAN) took 36.7 percent of the vote compared with 36.1 percent for Andres Manuel Lopez Obrador (PRD). Roberto Madrazo Pintado (PRI) was a distant third, with 22.7 percent of the vote. In the Senate, which has 128 seats, PAN took 52 seats, PRD took 36 seats, and PRI took 38 seats. In the Chamber of Deputies, which has 500 seats, the results for the three largest parties were 206 seats for PAN, 160 for PRD, and 121 for PRI. The 2000 election therefore paved the way for PAN to succeed in 2006, winning across the board. Alejandro Moreno shows how economic voting was activated in the 2006 presidential campaign.[23]

Content analysis of campaign news on television found that during the first part of the 2006 race, TV Azteca leaned toward Lopez Obrador (PRD), in part because the channel wanted his advertising money and in part because "it was betting on him to win."[24] The channel's coverage tilted against Obrador after the race began to narrow and the new law regulating television—nicknamed Ley Televisa—was passed. In analysis of the period from January 19 through July 2, 2006, on the two main television channels, Televisa and Tevision Azetca, TV news was slightly more negative toward the PRD/Left (5.6 percent) compared with the PRI (2.7 percent) and PAN (2.5 percent), while the vast bulk of television news was coded as neutral in its depiction of the 2006 federal elections. Positive coverage of the parties was 1 percent or less on television. There was a greater difference among the parties in terms of visibility on TV news, however. The PRI received the most television news time, with 1,118,701 seconds, followed by PRD with 903,175 seconds, and PAN with 864,723 seconds. Radio news was more negative: PRD/Left with 14.3 percent, PRI with 9.9 percent, and PAN with 6.8 percent. Radio also ranked the parties differently on airtime: PRD/Left with 4,682,634 seconds, PAN with 3,830,639 seconds, and PRI with 3,604,812 seconds. All of these data come from Mexico's Federal Election Institute.[25] The visuals of candidates on television have been almost always favorable or neutral, with net positive ratings for all of the three main presidential candidates receiving about 30 percent in both 2000 and 2006 campaigns.[26]

In terms of political advertising, parties traditionally invest heavily in television relative to other media outlets; in 2006 this spending was a ratio of 3:1 television to radio, and a ratio of 6:1 television to nonbroadcast media. The legislation introduced in 2007 curbed the level of public funds provided to the parties, but they remain well funded, with about US$100 million annually in nonelection years for activities, up to about $130 million in years with midterm elections, and $150 million in presidential election years. Parties will not be permitted to purchase time on television or radio with these funds, but they will receive substantial free advertising time during campaigns. Television is therefore expected to continue to be the main medium for party campaigning and for voter information during election campaigns. Central party organizations with state funding are expected to continue to dominate campaigning.

The 2006 elections occurred before the implementation of Article 79-A of the Ley Televisa, so the next election will be the basis for understanding how this new regulatory environment affects balance and access in campaigns. At present, Mexico's electoral authorities are in the process of translating the broad legal mandates into specific regulations. The Federal Election Institute was affected by the 2007 reforms. The president of the IFE will serve for six years with the possibility of reelection for one additional six-year term, and other members are to serve single terms of nine years. Current IFE members were selected in 2003, and their replacement will be staggered to prevent influence of party politics. The IFE oversees a large number of civil servants and political appointees who train polling station workers and supervise the campaign, as well as negotiate with political parties, which are required to report campaign expenditures to the IFE. The 2007 reforms put the IFE in charge of allocating free airtime to the parties during the campaign, and no other group is allowed to purchase airtime, thus preventing "swift-boating" by outside interest groups, as occurred in the U.S. 2004 presidential election campaign. The IFE will also have the power to stop broadcasts that it considers to be in violation of the provisions and to ban spots based on accuracy and tone. In 2005 the IFE issued bans on 29 separate spots "deemed deceptive, defamatory or excessively nasty."[27] Mexican law does not give the IFE the right to sanction channels for the tone and content of news coverage, however, and it has been suggested that this leaves "room for bias stemming from collusive relationships between broadcasters and the political leaders."[28] The regulatory changes continue to be in development, however. By the summer of 2007, Mexico's Supreme Court in effect nullified a number of key provisions of the Ley Televisa with several rulings, which, alongside the contested outcome of the 2006 election, presented an opportunity for the Congress to produce legislation on electoral reform that "further ensures the integrity and authority of Mexican electoral institutions."[29]

In sum, Mexico has all the pieces in place to guarantee an opportunity for media access to the main political parties and presidential candidates during election campaigns. Mexican elections are also the focus of research among a vibrant and growing community of scholars and polling experts. Their research on Mexican election campaigns is guaranteed to unveil any perceived biases in the news media and their potential consequences for electoral outcomes and may, in fact, have implications for future regulatory policy.

## Russian Federation

Russians went to the polls in national legislative elections on December 2, 2007, and then again on March 2, 2008, to vote in the presidential election. In both cases, one party, United Russia (ER), took the majority of votes. In the legislative election, ER took 64.3 percent of the vote, followed by the Communist Party of the Russian Federation (KPRF), with 11.6 percent of the vote, and turnout of 63.7 percent. In the presidential election, Dmitrii Medvedev received 70.3 percent of the vote, well ahead of the Communist Party candidate Gennadii Zyuganov with 17.7 percent, on a turnout of 69.7 percent. Since the presidential election, Vladimir Putin has been appointed prime minister by President Medvedev. This overwhelming support for one party by the public mirrored the overwhelming consensus in the Russian media.

The Soviet Union retained the system of censorship that existed in czarist Russia, in which self-censorship by journalists themselves was the key. The purpose of news organizations was to extend to the public the Party's view and stimulate national support for the regime. News was drab, official, and unchallenging. Despite this, the Soviet press was widely read, and television news was widely viewed. When Mikhail Gorbachev took office in 1985, his introduction of glasnost was welcomed by media in the form of questioning government policy, yet most of the revelations were "carefully orchestrated and leaked by Gorbachev's few close supporters," or by himself, so that it was essentially "free speech from the top down."[30]

The 1991 Russian Law on the Mass Media predated the 1993 constitution. While censorship was barred and freedom of information guaranteed, there was no law guaranteeing journalists the right of access to government information. Journalists could also be required by the courts to disclose their sources. Media were liable for defamation and left the news organization with the burden of proof, which led to many lawsuits, especially in the provinces, by government officials, individuals, and businesses. Two government agencies were created: the State Committee on the Press, which registered print media and distributed state subsidies, and the Federal Service of Television and Radio Broadcasting, which issued and revoked broadcasting licenses.

All media were hard hit by the economic crises in Russia in the 1990s, and many saw advertising revenues fall appreciably. Economic pressures on the news organizations and their poorly paid or unpaid employees made fertile soil for the growth of a culture of corruption in journalism, which already had a precedent in the Soviet era. Some journalists and editors took payments for publishing certain stories. Focus groups with journalists conducted for the United States Information Agency (USIA) in 1998 pointed out that bribes were common during the 1996 election campaign. One analyst at the respected Moscow business newspaper Kommersant-daily said: "There was no objectivity at all in election coverage. Every person stood up for his own specific interests. I, for instance, bought myself an apartment."[31]

A content analysis of television reporting on Russian elections in 1995 and 1996 concluded:

> The results of coding television news during the campaign periods for the 1995 Duma campaign and the 1996 presidential race show that these channels generally failed to contribute fully to the legitimization of the electoral process. During the parliamentary campaign, state-controlled Russian Public Television (ORT) focused on pro-government parties and neglected coverage of the competition. Although the election coverage on the private NTV station was more balanced, the elections were relatively ignored in favor of aggressive coverage of the war in Chechnya. By the 1996 presidential election, the two stations both abandoned the pretense of neutrality to promote the incumbent presidential candidate, Boris Yeltsin. What emerges from this study is evidence of a missed opportunity to consolidate the growth of an independent media in Russia—and the failure of voters to obtain disinterested information from primary television outlets in a fragile democracy.[32]

There is a considerable literature on Russian voting and public opinion since the early 1990s.[33] The European Institute for the Media shows that Russian journalists view themselves as political players more than watchdogs or challengers to the status quo. Although citizens are aware of the biases in television news on state-run Channel 1, it continues to be one of the most trusted institutions in Russia. In 34 focus groups in 2000 and 2004, run by Sarah Oates with support from the British Economic and Social Research Council, citizens in Russia commented that they rely on state-run television especially for news, and they supported the role of television as a political player.[34]

There were five national television organizations in Russia in 2000: RTR, which was owned by the government and controlled by the Kremlin; ORT, which had the largest news audience, and in which the government held 51 percent ownership (though it was known that media oligarch Berezovsky exercised control on ORT news programs); TV Center, which was private but in practice controlled by the government of the mayor of Moscow, which began in 1997; NTV, a wholly private operation, founded in 1993, controlled by Gusinsky's conglomerate Media-Most until the 2001 takeover by Gazprom administrators supportive of the Kremlin; and TV-6, which was largely entertainment television founded as a joint venture with Turner Broadcasting, which later withdrew (Berezovsky also had a large stake in the company). There continued to be many newspapers in Russia in 2000. The Moscow dailies and weeklies continued to set the national media agenda when investigative pieces prompted official responses or were picked up by television. In May 2001, a Noviye Izvestia correspondent said that there was no room for independent investigative reporting because "every article in the newspaper is bought and paid for."[35]

The USIA focus groups among educated elites in Moscow and three provincial cities in late 1998 revealed a consensus that the Russian media became much less diverse and free with the start of the 1996 election campaign. The 1996 presidential campaign led to the perception that manipulation of public opinion was one of the main functions of the Russian media. The reporting appears to have been less biased in the 2000 presidential campaign, in part because one of the main private broadcast networks, NTV, opposed Putin and the other two, ORT and RTR, supported him.

Once Putin came into office, his government quickly took steps to diminish the power of media barons who were perceived to be a challenge to the Kremlin. Gusinsky (owner of NTV) was the first target. His conglomerate, Media-Most, owed an estimated US$1.5 billion to Gazprom. He fled to Spain, and by April 2001 Gazprom officials took over Media-Most and the conglomerate's daily newspapers and radio station. Berezovsky was next. He owned 49 percent of ORT but effectively controlled the channel because he paid the salaries of the news division staff. He exiled himself from Russia, and there were reports in July 2001 that he had sold his share of ORT to Roman Abramovich, oil baron and governor of Chukotka who was supportive of the Kremlin. After these takeovers, Russian national television became more muted in reporting news and opinion that might offend the Kremlin, but it was not entirely silenced, and alternative perspectives were still present in print and local broadcast media.

Putin also signed the new law on Duma elections on December 20, 2002, which has some good intentions with respect to objectivity and balance in the informational materials carried by the mass media and disseminated by the political parties. But the overly specific restrictions accompanying the law make it unworkable, and the law has little to do with Russian media reality. Much of the news is positive to progovernment parties and candidates, often in the form of a visibility advantage in the news.[36]

The democratic intentions in the design of the electoral system, the media, and campaign practices since 1993 were no guarantee of democratic government. Oates explained in an interview what came out of these good intentions:

> Manipulation of the media and the party system constrained the development of functional political parties. As a result, "broadcast parties" that are little more than a marketing exercise manipulated by the power and money of elites replaced grassroots parties. As such, elections increasingly became an exercise in propaganda and image, with more legitimate parties such as the Communist Party of the Russian Federation and Yabloko marginalized and finally excluded from real power. The link between party identification or judgment of a party by prospective/retrospective evaluation doesn't function in Russia; hence, the media coverage is not particularly relevant in the classic sense. But it is important in terms of the image exercise![37]

## Turkey

Established in 1923, the Republic of Turkey has at times experienced a critical press in a Fourth Estate role and at other times a censored press subject to closure and legislation designed to limit the media's role in reporting. From the launch of the press during the Ottoman Empire, legislation in 1858 restricted the press from criticizing government officials, and violation resulted in fines or sometimes even closure.[38] The publication of photos and humor deemed to be not in good taste were also an offense. Legislation in 1864 required government permission to publish, although this is no longer the case. In short, the history of the press in Turkey has been one of government influence or control to guarantee no serious criticism of the government.

The media industry in general in contemporary Turkey is characterized by high levels of concentration of ownership. The Dogan Group owns nearly half of the total newspaper circulation in the country, two very important television stations (Kanal D and CNN-Turk), dozens of magazines, and three radio stations. The Sabah Group is the second largest owner of media, with five newspapers, including one of the largest in circulation (*Sabah*). Three additional groups own the remainder of the country's media.

Media concentration of ownership has been criticized for resulting in less diversity in news and information as well as conflicts of interest in displaying a lack of critical reporting on the nonmedia institutions and organizations owned by media groups. Government subsidies in recent years intended to expand newspapers have also been said to have diminished both critical reporting on corruption and press credibility.

Circulation measures do not adequately capture the reach of newspapers, as many are also read in public places, such as coffee houses and in the workplace. At least 13 daily newspapers are circulated to more than 100,000 people each, and 7 sell more than half a million copies each day. The tabloid-style sensationalized coverage of crime and partially dressed women, on the order of some of the British press, is matched by a sober and serious quality daily press that has a long history. *Cumhuriyet* (Republic), for example, is one of the country's oldest daily newspapers, launched in 1924 with the mission of explaining to the people the principles of Ataturk. According to the BBC, major newspapers include two mass circulation dailies, *Hürriyet* and *Milliyet*; one left-wing daily, *Cumhuriyet*; and several English-language newspapers: *Sabah*, Today's *Zaman* (the English version of a Turkish daily), *The New Anatolian*, and *Turkish Daily News*.

Turkey, like most of Europe, had a public broadcasting monopoly until the late 1980s. The summer of 1990 brought privately owned radio and television stations from Europe via satellite dishes, without permission from the government. Turkey's 1982 constitution authorized the state only to establish broadcasting stations. By 1993 Parliament legalized private broadcasting with a constitutional amendment known as Article 133, which noted: "Radio and television channels may be freely established and managed within the stipulations to be regulated by law. The independence and the impartiality of the only radio and television institution established by the state as a public corporate body and news agencies aided as public corporate bodies are essential." Today there are some 300 local television channels owned privately, and more than a dozen nationally broadcast private channels, with more than 1,000 private radio stations, competing with the state broadcaster TNT, which operates four national networks. Although the majority of private channels are commercial and feature entertainment, sports, and news as in the United States, religious groups in Turkey own or control some channels and include programming on Islamic practice and topics. The growth of the Internet in Turkey has been substantial over the past decade. Online news media launched by journalists who lost their jobs in the financial crisis, which hit the country and particularly the journalism industry hard in 2001, are finding a large and active audience.

Turkey's major television channels include TRT, which is the state broadcaster; Star TV, private and the first to break the state's TV monopoly; and Show TV and Kanal D, both private, high-ratings networks. Less-watched private networks are ATV, TGRT, NTV, and CNN-Turk. TRT is also the country's leading radio station, with cultural and educational programming on TRT 1, popular music on TRT 3, and folk and classical music on TRT 4. Show radio and Capital radio are commercial radio stations with wide reach, and Radio Foreks is a news station with wide reach.

The Supreme Council of Radio and Television is appointed by the government to monitor and regulate broadcast media and apply sanctions when it observes a violation of the law. It is a crime to spread separatist (read Kurdish) propaganda, and it is also an offense to provoke enmity or hatred by displaying hatred or regionalism. Many reporters and news organizations have been charged with breaking these laws over the past two decades. One of the sanctions imposed by the Supreme Council included a one-day ban on broadcasting by CNN-Turk, which is a joint venture between CNN and the Dogan Group. The ban resulted when the host of a talk show raised a question about whether Abdullah Ocalan, the Kurdish revolutionary leader, who is otherwise known as a terrorist, could ever acquire the stature of Nelson Mandela.

The BBC describes the difficult environment in which journalists in Turkey are working. Journalists may face arrest and criminal prosecution when dealing with highly sensitive subjects, such as the military, Kurds, and political Islam. Broadcasts by radio and TV stations are commonly suspended for containing sensitive material. In its efforts to meet entry requirements to the European Union, Turkey has lifted the most repressive sanctions against journalists. But the BBC described a 2006 report by Reporters without Borders that said journalists were "'still at the mercy of arbitrary court decisions.' An article in the penal code [that] makes it a crime to insult Turkish national identity

… has been used to prosecute journalists and publishers. Kurdish-language broadcasts, banned for many years, were introduced by the state broadcaster in June 2004 as a part of reforms intended to meet EU criteria on minorities. Some overseas-based Kurdish TV channels broadcast via satellite."[39]

In November 2002, Turkish politics was transformed with the general election results that brought a new political party to power with nearly two-thirds of the seats in the parliament. The Justice and Development Party (AKP) came out of a tradition of Islamic-oriented political parties, which have challenged the state's practices on religious policy.[40] In the past, Islamic parties had been banned from running in elections, but over time this resulted in a reframing of the message in order to work with the constraints of the system.[41]

To the dismay of many in Turkey's secular establishment, Recep Tayyip Erdogan was first named prime minister in 2003 as leader of the Justice and Development Party (AKP). The AKP had become the country's largest party in Parliament and claimed to be secular, but the party is criticized for having a hidden Islamic agenda to bring about sharia law and for openly supporting pro-Islamic reforms to Turkish law, such as lifting the ban on the turban in universities and government institutions. In the 1990s Erdogan was a member of what was a precursor to the AKP, then called the Welfare Party, which was an openly Islamist party whose members also included his close ally, Abdullah Gul.

By 2006, Prime Minister Erdogan was expressing possible interest in being a candidate himself for the position of president, which would have made him the first president from the AKP and the first president whose wife wears a turban. It is important to understand the meaning of the turban in the Turkish context, which is not the traditional Islamic headscarf or veil often seen worn by Muslim women in western European countries: "The turban is not a traditional Islamic head-cover which has no political connotation and is not at all problematized within the system. That is our grandmother's attire. The turban on the other hand is politicized and is a very modern attire of urban conservative circles. Not much of a rural base exists in the rural segments of the society for turban."[42]

Many Turks were alarmed by the thought of a first lady in a turban appearing at official functions and expressed that it would roll back 80 years of progress and the secular state. The press was also fascinated with this story, but at the same time concerned about what a powerful leader might do to harm its interest if the widely popular Erdogan became president and another AKP member became prime minister. The president is not elected directly by the public but by a majority in the Parliament.

As it became clear from public opinion through the press that this was a very hot issue, Erdogan decided that he himself should not be considered a possible candidate. Instead, he claimed he would consult various groups in society before deciding whom he would endorse for the position of president.

A cartoon showed Erdogan saying that he will ask for the opinion of group a, group b, group c, group d, and finally he would even ask the press, which shows the journalist running away in shock and possibly also fear.

Based on the timing of the 2002 election, the due date for the next election was in November 2007. In May 2007, however, the Turkish Grand National Assembly, controlled by the AKP, failed to elect the 11th president of the Republic. This came after a long and very polarizing debate over the candidates, the procedures, and the implications of the election for the Republican regime. This legal and political debacle forced the AKP to call for elections about three and a half months earlier than their due date.

On July 22, 2007, Turkish voters went to the polls for the 15th time since the first contested elections of 1950. Of the six main parties contesting 550 seats, the AKP took 46.7 percent of the vote, which represented a 12.4 percent increase on its share of the vote since 2002, and the Republican People's Party (CHP) took 20.8 percent, which represented only a 1.4 percent increase since 2002. Despite these increases in share of vote, the AKP lost 22 seats and the CHP lost 68 seats in 2007 because the Nationalist Movement Party (MHP) took 14.3 percent of the vote, which represented an increase of 6 percent and 70 seats since 2002. Turnout was 84.4 percent. The independents, who were Kurdish nationalists who ran as independents to circumvent the 10 percent threshold for parties to win seats, took 5.2 percent and 28 seats. The 2007 election was the second parliamentary election in which citizens opted for a "progressive" Islamic party over a "conservative" secular party.

In 2007, the AKP, led by Erdogan, won an unprecedented percentage of the national vote, which was viewed as a landslide by many observers. Shortly thereafter, Erdogan endorsed his close friend and political ally and AKP member Abudllah Gul for the office of president. Parliament elected him with an even bigger majority than before, and Gul took office. President Gul's wife also wears a turban but rarely appears at official functions.

The larger questions are now being asked by scholars of electoral behavior as they analyze the data from the 2007 Turkish national election study: How far has the AKP been able to transform itself from a marginal ideological movement into a party of the center of Turkish society?[43] To what extent does the AKP's heightened electoral self-confidence coincide with continued commitment to democratic reform? Çarkoglu posed the question: is Turkey moving to a one-party system similar to India, Japan, and Italy prior to the 1990s?[44] He noted that the AKP is the only party with pro-Islamist roots to have increased its vote share in competitive elections after nearly five years in office. The AKP's second general election victory is significant since it seems the success of the incumbent government was primarily due to evaluations of its performance rather than to ideological cleavages. Another critical factor was the AKP's successful transformation, in less than five years, of its traditionally euroskeptic constituency into the only party constituency that is predominantly pro-EU. As a result, the AKP remains the sole political engine behind Turkey's efforts to become a member of the EU. Consequently, the AKP's conservative pro-Islamist ideological roots and constituency characteristics offer a continued identity challenge for the EU, as the membership negotiations continue to unfold.[45]

Research under way on the 2007 election campaign includes a study of the reporting on the campaign in major news media over the 10 weeks prior to the election, May 7 through June 22, 2007.[46] Preliminary findings are just out from content analysis of four national daily newspapers: *Hürriyet*, *Zaman*, *Posta*, and *Cumhuriyet*. *Hürriyet* and *Zaman* are broadsheets, the former is a mainstream quality newspaper, and the latter is a quality conservative newspaper with an Islamist leaning. *Posta* is the tabloid with the highest readership in Turkey. *Cumhuriyet* is an intellectual, quality broadsheet and has the lowest circulation of these four newspapers. The front page of each newspaper was analyzed for each day, as was a randomly selected inside page for which each story was coded. The news story is the unit of analysis, and each was coded for such characteristics as length and placement, a primary and secondary topic, and whether the election was mentioned. Up to 10 actors (party leaders and candidates) were coded in each story. AKP politicians and spokespersons were the most visible actors in the press, far above other party spokespersons, as the election drew closer. MHP and CHP were the next most visible parties in the press, but well below the AKP. High visibility did not mean positive coverage, however. With respect to tone toward main party actors in the news, most of the stories in all newspapers were negative, and there was very little in the way of positive coverage with the exception of CHP and DP (Democratic Party) in *Cumhuriyet*. Future research will focus on completing the coding of the television news programs that were collected during the campaign.

## Conclusion

Elections are high points for political communication in the lives of democracies and societies in transition. In most societies, television continues to be the medium of choice for information about the election campaign, the parties, leaders, and policy issues. In the four case studies presented here—Kenya, Mexico, Russia, and Turkey—television has been the focus of much attention during recent election campaigns, and it is perceived as an influential player in the electoral process. Citizens' responses ranged from resigned acceptance in Russia, to ethnic violence in Kenya, and protest in Turkey and Mexico. Legislative action and regulatory change emerged in Mexico, and the new regulatory environment governing television in election campaigns will be in place in the next national election.

The case studies show four countries at very different points with respect to addressing questions about balance in the mass media during election campaigns. By almost all accounts, Russia is a "failed state" in these terms, yet the public votes and the citizens appear to trust state-controlled television news in large numbers, despite evidence of overwhelming bias in the news at election time. By contrast, Mexico and Turkey, in the most recent elections, appear to have all the mechanisms in place to study and assess the contents, uses, and impacts of the mass media in election campaigns. Research is still under way on the most recent elections in these countries on the content of the news coverage and the possible consequences for electoral behavior. Of the four countries studied here, Kenya is unique in having a journalistic culture that espouses a Fourth Estate role. That said, the little evidence available from the most recent election campaign suggests that media helped to facilitate the problem of ethnic violence in the election's aftermath, and unbalanced coverage in television news during the campaign may have contributed to what at the time was perceived as random acts of violence during the campaign.

Free and fair elections are a core principle for democratic development. As campaigns mark high points for political reporting in national and international news media, the consequences of a problematic campaign and unclear electoral outcome may reverberate in the national economy and the national consciousness for some time. Even in an established democracy like the Netherlands, many international business investors pulled out after the highly charged and rhetorically intense 2002 election, when a right-wing leader was gunned down just days before the vote and his leaderless new political party, LPF, went on to win an unprecedented number of seats. The contested election outcome in Kenya in 2007 and the violent aftermath of the campaign shut down tourism in the country for some time and diminished international investment considerably.

The four cases studied here are at different points along the path of putting systems into place that recognize the importance of the media in elections and enable experts to assess its role and impact. Important goals are (1) *to enhance media literacy* among citizens before, during, and after election campaigns; (2) *to monitor and measure media coverage* in a systematic fashion that enables comparisons across media in real time during campaigns; and (3) *to establish and strengthen existing national election studies* to provide the independent collection of valid and reliable survey data before, during, and after election campaigns. Technical assistance can build capacity in each of these areas.

*Media literacy* refers to the ability of audience members to ask questions about the information they are receiving rather than accept it immediately without question. Although much has been done to educate young people to become media literate, these efforts have been concentrated in media-saturated societies. In 1982, the United Nations Educational, Scientific, and Cultural Organization (UNESCO) founded the Grünwald Declaration of 1982 to "emphasize the need for political and educational systems to promote citizens' critical understanding of the phenomena of communication."[47] In June 2008, UNESCO brought together experts from around the world to share methods for introducing media literacy into teacher training worldwide. Election campaigns are ideal territory for testing the critical thinking skills necessary for media literacy.

Best practices in media coverage of elections can contribute to a larger media literacy education campaign, to enhance citizens' awareness and abilities to reflect critically upon the information before them. Such a project would bring together media professionals and expert researchers on media in elections to identify international standards for election news reporting and best examples to be shared.

Real-time monitoring of election news is done in a number of countries, and this information is used by campaigners, interest groups, and citizens. Best practices in coding and storing these real-time data should be the focus of one component of the project, to enable the use of a standard number of variables and formats for coding information so that it can be leveraged by those studying the effects of the media on citizens' political attitudes and electoral behavior.

The United Nations Democracy Fund (UNDEF) was established in 2005 to support democratization throughout the world and to finance projects that build and strengthen democratic institutions, promote human rights, and ensure the participation of all groups in democratic processes. UNDEF complements ongoing UN efforts to strengthen democracy and expand it around the world. The ACE (administration and costs for elections) Electoral Knowledge Network provides online information on elections, promotes interaction among election professionals around the world, and enhances capacity development for electoral management. The ACE Electoral Knowledge Network helps electoral commissions in a number of countries to identify what role the commissions play in election campaign reporting, in the context of the best practices project.[48]

Technical assistance in surveying the public to assess the influence of the election campaign and the media coverage of the campaign on political attitudes and behavior can draw on a variety of experts. Many are active in international survey organizations such as the World Organization of Public Opinion Research (WAPOR), and they also include researchers in universities that serve on national election studies and international comparative research projects. One of the goals in this part of the best practices project is to ensure that the surveys ask key questions about the news media and communication sources. The World Values Survey, for example, in its most recent wave included a series of questions on media use that enables scholars to address important questions about how media influence cultural convergence on a global scale.[49] In the context of election campaigns, researchers working on national election studies, as well as those in the field of comparative electoral and survey research, can help to build capacity for survey fieldwork and research in various contexts, to determine the most effective methods for capturing public perceptions of the campaign and campaign effects on electoral outcomes.

## Notes

1. Holli A. Semetko. 1996. "Political Balance on Television: Campaigns in the US, Britain and Germany." *Harvard International Journal of Press/Politics* 1 (1): 51–71.
2. Edward Herman and Noam Chomsky. 2002. *Manufacturing Consent: The Political Economy of the Mass Media,* 2nd ed. New York: Pantheon.
3. Denis McQuail. 1992. *Media Performance: Mass Communication and the Public Interest.* London/Newbury Park, CA: Sage, 225.
4. See, for example, Holli A. Semetko, Jay G. Blumler, Michael Gurevitch, and David H. Weaver. 1991. *The Formation of Campaign Agendas: A Comparative Analysis of Party and Media Roles in Recent American and British Elections.* Hillsdale, NJ: Lawrence Erlbaum.
5. Nicholas K. Boas. 2003. "Status of Media in East Africa." *Encyclopedia of International Media and Communications.* Vol. 6: 461–68. San Diego, CA: Elsevier Science.
6. The link to the contractor's report was not working at the time of this printing. See UNDP (United Nations Development Programme). Media and Elections in Kenya. http://www.ke.undp.org/mediaandelections.htm. Accessed April 28, 2009.
7. Newspapers: *East African, Kenya Times, Nairobi Star, Nation, People,* and *Standard.* Television: Citizen, KBC, KTN, and NTV. English-Swahili radio: Capital FM, Classic, Easy FM, KBC, Kiss, and Simba. Vernacular radio: Coro, Egessa, Iqra, Inooro, Kameme, Kass, Mulembe, Musyi, Ramogi, Sayare.
8. UNDP. 2007. *Kenya Monthly Media Monitoring for 2007 Elections Report.* September 10–30, 2007, prepared by Strategic Public Relations and Research Ltd. Link to reports may be found at UNDP Media and Elections in Kenya. http://www.ke.undp.org/media-aandelections.htm.
9. Ibid.
10. Ibid.
11. See, for example, Semetko et al. 1991. *The Formation of Campaign Agendas.*
12. UNDP. 2007. *Kenya Monthly Media Monitoring for 2007 Elections Report.* September 10–30, 2007, prepared by Strategic Public Relations and Research Ltd. Link to reports may be found at UNDP Media and Elections in Kenya. http://www.ke.undp.org/media-aandelections.htm.
13. BBC World Service Trust. 2008. "Policy Briefing #1. The Kenyan 2007 Elections and Their Aftermath: The Role of Media and Communication." British Broadcasting Corporation, London. The 12 conclusions are online at the Democracy and Governance Web site: http://www.comminit.com/en/node/269468/348.
14. See "Election Fever: Kenya's Crisis." 2008. Special issue, *Journal of Eastern African Studies* 2 (2).
15. Toni Weis. 2008. "The Results of the 2007 Kenyan General Election." *Journal of Eastern African Studies* 2 (2): 1–41, 1.
16. Chappell H. Lawson. 2002. *Building the Fourth Estate: Democratization and the Rise of a Free Press in Mexico.* Berkeley and London: University of California Press, 5.
17. Ibid., 91.

18. Ibid., 100.

19. Alejandro Moreno. 2003. "Campaign Effects in Mexico: Evidence from the 2000–2002 National Panel Study and the 2003 Election." Paper presented at the annual meetings of the American Political Science Association, Philadelphia, PA, August 28–31.

20. Sallie Hughes and Chappell Lawson. 2004. "Propaganda and Crony Capitalism: Partisan Bias in Mexican Television News." *Latin American Research Review* 39 (3): 81–105, 81. See also Sallie Hughes and Chappell Lawson. 2005. "The Barriers to Media Opening in Latin America." *Political Communication* 22: 9–25.

21. Chappell Lawson. 2004. "Television Coverage, Vote Choice, and the 2000 Campaign." In *Mexico's Pivotal Democratic Election: Candidates, Voters and the Presidential Campaign of 2000,* ed. J. I. Dominguez and C. Lawson, 187–209. Stanford, CA: Stanford University Press/San Diego: The Center for U.S.–Mexican Studies, University of California.

22. Chappell Lawson and James A. McCann. 2004. "Television News, Mexico's 2000 Elections and Media Effects in Emerging Democracies." *British Journal of Political Science* 34: 1–30. See also Alejandro Moreno. 2003. "The Effects of Negative Campaigns on Mexican Voters." In *Mexico's Pivotal Democratic Election: Campaigns, Voting Behavior, and the 2000 Presidential Race,* ed. Jorge I. Domínguez and Chappell Lawson. Stanford, CA: Stanford University Press; Alejandro Moreno. 2007. "The 2006 Mexican Presidential Election: The Economy, Oil Revenues, and Ideology." *PS: Political Science and Politics* 40 (1): 15–19.

23. Alejandro Moreno. Forthcoming. "'It's the Economy, Stupid!' The Activation of Economic Voting in the 2006 Mexican Presidential Election Campaign" In *Consolidating Democracy in Mexico: The 2006 Presidential Campaign in Comparative Perspective,* ed. Jorge Domínguez, Chappell Lawson, and Alejandro Moreno. Baltimore: Johns Hopkins University Press.

24. Chappell Lawson. 2008. "Election Coverage in Mexico: Regulation Meets Crony Capitalism." In *The Handbook of Election News Coverage Around the World,* ed. Jesper Stromback and Lynda Lee Kaid, 368–83. New York: Taylor and Francis, 378.

25. These findings are presented in table 23.1 of Chappell Lawson. 2008. "Election Coverage in Mexico.

26. Chappell Lawson. 2004. "Television Coverage, Vote Choice, and the 2000 Campaign;" Chappell Lawson, James McCann, and M. Flores. 2007. Content analysis of news coverage of the 2006 Mexican campaign. Data set.

27. Lawson. 2008. "Election Coverage in Mexico: Regulation Meets Crony Capitalism," 379.

28. Ibid, 380.

29. Ibid, 380.

30. Michael J. Berlin. 2003. "Status of the Media in Russia." *Encyclopedia of International Media and Communications.* Vol. 4: 103–113. San Diego, CA: Elsevier Science, 105. Much of this section on the historical development of the Russian media system draws on Berlin 2003.

31. Ibid, 113.

32. Sarah Oates and Laura Roselle. 2000. "Russian Elections and TV News: Comparison of Campaign News on State-Controlled and Commercial Television Channels." Abstract. *Harvard International Journal of Press/Politics* 5 (2): 30.

33. Since the launch of the Russian Federation in January 1992, the Centre for the Study of Public Policy (CSPP) at the University of Aberdeen, Scotland, has been conducting barometer surveys monitoring mass response to transformation across

Central and Eastern Europe and the former Soviet Union. http://www.russiavotes.org/ president/presidency_vote_preferences.php?S776173303132=63924c6f1c2ac7d04fc6 b7b8edb49e54. Also see Steven White, Richard Rose, and Ian McAllister. 1997. *How Russia Votes.* Washington, DC: Congressional Quarterly Press; Richard Rose and Neil Munro. 2002. *Elections without Order: Russia's Challenge to Vladimir Putin.* New York and/Cambridge: Cambridge University Press; Sarah Oates. 2006. *Television, Democracy and Elections in Russia.* London: Routledge Curzon.

34. Sarah Oates. 2008. "Election Coverage in the Russian Federation." In *The Handbook of Election News Coverage Around the World*, ed. Jesper Stromback and Lynda Lee Kaid, 355–67. New York: Taylor and Francis.

35. Berlin. 2003. "Status of the Media in Russia," 113.

36. Oates. 2008. "Election Coverage in the Russian Federation," 360.

37. Interview with Oates, May 15, 2008.

38. This discussion of the development of the Turkish media system draws extensively upon Christine Ogan. 2003. "Status of the Media in Turkey." *Encyclopedia of International Media and Communications.* Vol. 4: 511–17. San Diego, CA: Elsevier Science.

39. BBC News. Country Profile: Turkey. http://news.bbc.co.uk/go/pr/fr/-/1/hi/world/ europe/country_profiles/1022222.stm. Page last updated March 5, 2009.

40. Ali Çarkoglu. 2003. "The Rise of the New Generation Pro-Islamists in Turkey: The Justice and Development Party Phenomenon in the November 2002 Elections in Turkey." *South European Society and Politics* 7 (3): 123–56.

41. R. Quinn Mecham. 2004. "From the Ashes of Virtue, a Promise of Light: The Transformation of Political Islam in Turkey." *Third World Quarterly* 25 (2): 339–58.

42. Interview with a Turkish political scientist, May 12, 2008.

43. See Ali Çarkoglu and Ersin Kalaycıo lu. 2007. *Turkish Democracy Today: Elections, Protest and Stability in an Islamic Society.* London and New York: I. B. Tauris.

44. Ali Carkoglu, 2007. "A New Electoral Victory for the 'Pro-Islamists' or the 'New Centre-Right'? The Justice and Development Party Phenomenon in the July 2007 Parliamentary Elections in Turkey." *South European Society and Politics* 12 (4): 501–19.

45. Ibid.

46. Canan Balkir, Susan Banducci, Didem Soyaltin & Huriye Toker. 2008. "Expecting the Unforeseeable: The 2007 Turkish Elections in the Media." *Turkish Studies.* 9 (2): 199–214.

47. See United Nations Educational, Scientific and Cultural Organization (UNESCO). Media Literacy. http://portal.unesco.org/ci/en/ev.php-URL_ID=27056&URL_DO=DO _TOPIC&URL_SECTION=201.html.

48. United Nations Democracy Fund. "News from the Field: The ACE Electoral Knowledge Network Launches New Regional Centers," October 19, 2007. http://www.un.org/ democracyfund/XNewsACEElectoralKnowledge.htm.

49. See Pippa Norris and Ronald Inglehart. 2009. *Cultural Convergence? Cosmopolitan Communications and National Diversity.* New York/London: Cambridge University Press.

8

.
.

# Limits on Press Freedom and Regime Support

Pippa Norris and Ronald Inglehart

In late September 2007, thousands of monks and civilians took to the streets of Yangon in a weeklong uprising against the Myanmar government. In response, the military junta shut down the Internet, arrested or intimidated Myanmar journalists, and severed mobile and landline phone links to the outside world. A Japanese video journalist from Agence France-Presse news was shot dead. Cameras and video cell phones were confiscated by soldiers. The official Division for Press Scrutiny and Registration pressured local editors to publish stories claiming that the unrest was organized by saboteurs. In the immediate aftermath of these events, thousands of monks were said to have been arrested, but after the media clampdown, no images of these events were published in the domestic and international news.[1] Even in less turbulent times, critical coverage of the Myanmar junta is restricted in domestic news media, silencing negative stories about the military leadership. Citizens are punished for listening to overseas radio broadcasts. These are not isolated instances of state control of the airwaves, as discussed in chapter 14 (other examples include Chinese suppression of news about Tibetan protests in March 2008). Although Myanmar is an extreme case, regularly ranking near the bottom of worldwide annual assessments of press freedom (produced by Reporters without Borders and Freedom House), human rights observers report that many other states routinely deploy techniques designed to suppress independent journalism, manipulate and slant news selectively in their favor, and limit critical coverage of the regime.

The fact that autocracies seek to control the main channels of mass communications is well documented. What is not clear is whether states with restrictive media environments succeed in manipulating public opinion and thereby strengthen the regime's domestic support. The cumulative result of years, or even decades, of tight media control in restrictive and isolated societies, such as Myanmar and the Democratic People's Republic of Korea, is usually assumed to have a powerful impact on citizens, especially the effect of state propaganda during wartime.[2] But the regime's efforts to influence public opinion may fail, if people learn to mistrust news coverage so that they discount the information that the media disseminate. These issues have been debated ever since the earliest work by Lasswell (1927), the rise of mass advertising, the development of scientific notions of public opinion, and the experimental studies monitoring the effects of propaganda by the allies during and after the Second World War.[3]

Section one of this chapter reviews the literature in this debate, develops a theoretical framework, and outlines the core propositions to be investigated. The second section develops a comparative framework to examine the empirical evidence for testing these propositions. The next section analyzes cross-national survey evidence, comparing regime support at the macrolevel in restrictive and nonrestrictive societies and then at the microlevel among the news audience living within each type of media environment. Empirical evidence is derived from a unique database, the fifth wave of the World Values Survey (WVS-5), with fieldwork conducted in more than 40 nations in 2005 and 2006.[4] Regime support is understood as a multidimensional concept that is measured at three levels: (1) confidence in core regime institutions, such as the government, civil service, political parties, and courts; (2) more diffuse nationalistic attitudes; and (3) ideological attitudes toward democracy and military rule. The analysis works on the hypothesis that in authoritarian societies, restrictions on the media are designed to produce greater support for authoritarian rule and less support for democratization.

The results of the comparison at macrolevel presented in the analysis reveals that *confidence in government was indeed higher in societies with restricted media environments,* such as China, the Islamic Republic of Iran, and Vietnam, than in such countries as France and Sweden. This pattern certainly suggests that state control of the media has strong effects, but it cannot be viewed as conclusive proof, since various other factors could conceivably be generating this pattern. The results of the microlevel analysis give additional support to this interpretation, however. The analysis found that in states with restricted media environments, people who are most often exposed to the news media show significantly stronger confidence in government and support for authoritarian rule than those who do not regularly use television or radio news, newspapers, or the Internet for information. These patterns proved robust in multivariate models examining a range of measures of regime support, even with a battery of prior social controls. The television and radio audience were also more negative toward democratic values than nonusers in restricted media environments. By contrast, in pluralistic media environments, news consumers were more positive toward democratic values than nonusers. These findings led to the conclusion that state restrictions over news broadcasting can often achieve their intended effects, as many commentators have long feared. The final section interprets these results, counters some potential criticisms, and reflects on the broader implications of the findings.

## Theoretical Framework

The study starts from the premise that autocracies with restrictive media environments aim to suppress dissent and to provide positive messages about the regime, rallying support for the authorities as well as generating more diffuse feelings of patriotism and spreading ideological values favorable to the regime. If state control succeeds in its objectives, regular exposure to the news media in this environment would be expected to generate confidence in the authorities, to encourage negative attitudes toward democratic values, and to reinforce nationalism. The direct effects of this process should be strongest among regular consumers of radio and television news—the sector of the mass media where the state usually exercises the greatest control. Similar effects would not be expected in pluralistic media environments, where competition among different media outlets and sources provides mixed messages about the regime. And these effects would likely be weaker or absent in media such sectors as newspapers and Internet, where the state generally has less direct control over ownership and content.

The idea that states use restrictions on the free press to suppress dissent and to mobilize support is widely accepted. Liberal philosophers and human rights advocates have traditionally mounted a strong defense of an unfettered and independent press, as embodied in the fundamental freedoms of expression, information, thought, speech, and conscience. These principles are widely recognized as human rights in all major conventions endorsed by political leaders, including the 1948 United Nations Universal Declaration of Human Rights, the European Convention on Human Rights, the American Convention on Human Rights, and the African Charter on Human and Peoples' Rights. Article 19 of the 1948 Universal Declaration of Human Rights states: "Everyone has the right to freedom of opinion and expression; this right includes freedom to hold opinions without interference and to seek, receive and impart information and ideas through any media and regardless of frontiers." Rights to freedom of the press are widely recognized as essential in procedural definitions of representative democracy. For example, Dahl emphasized that citizens cannot make meaningful choices in contested elections without access to alternative sources of information.[5] The prevention of corruption and abuse of power by public officials also requires transparency, so that the public can evaluate the outcome of government actions and hold elected representatives to account.[6]

## Techniques of Suppression

Despite the acknowledged importance of these universal rights, a substantial literature has documented how states regularly subvert freedom of expression and seek to control the independent media.[7] The use of techniques to repress and manipulate information has also been documented by human rights observers, including regular reports issued by Amnesty International, Human Rights Watch, the Committee to Protect Journalists, the World Press Freedom Committee, and Reporters without Borders (RSF). In the most extreme cases, methods used by autocratic states include overt official censorship; state monopoly of radio and television channels, or severely limited competition through oligopolies in commercial ownership; legal restrictions on freedom of expression and publication (such as stringent libel laws and restrictive official secrets acts); the use of outright violence, imprisonment, and intimidation against journalists and broadcasters; and the techniques of propaganda to spread state ideologies. Freedom of expression can also be restricted by less draconian factors, including requirements for registration or licenses for journalists or newspapers; broadcasting regulations as well as laws governing broadcasting content; concentration of ownership; and a legal framework governing official secrecy or freedom of information, intellectual property, libel, and taxation.

In the Democratic People's Republic of Korea, for example, one of the most rigid state-controlled and inaccessible societies, television and radio news broadcasts are dominated by flattering reports of the activities of the leader, Kim Jong-Il, along with patriotic stories emphasizing national unity.[8] Citizens caught listening to foreign radio broadcasts face serious punishment, foreign broadcasts are blocked, and individual radios are sealed so that they can only receive official stations. In Malaysia, as a less extreme example, human rights observers report that the state has manipulated the media to stifle internal dissent and forced journalists employed by the international press to modify or suppress news stories unflattering to the regime.[9] Elsewhere, governments in Uzbekistan, Sri Lanka, and Saudi Arabia, among others, place serious restrictions on media's freedom to criticize government rulers through official regulations, legal restrictions, and state censorship.[10] It remains more difficult for governments to censor online communications, but nevertheless, in China and Cuba, state-controlled monopolies provide the only Internet service and thereby filter both access and content.[11] Media freedom and human rights organizations have documented numerous cases of media professionals who are killed or injured in the course of their work each year. In the Arab Republic of Egypt, Colombia, Liberia, Sierra Leone, and Zimbabwe, for example, the

International Federation of Journalists reports that many journalists, broadcasters, and editors have experienced intimidation or harassment, while journalists in many parts of the world face the daily threat of personal danger from wars or imprisonment by the security services.[12] Mickiewicz has demonstrated the degree of progovernment bias and the lack of partisan balance in patterns of news broadcasts in the Russian Federation during presidential and Duma elections.[13] Others have documented the impact of official state censorship and propaganda on what different media outlets in China cover and the impact of deregulation and liberalization of the newspaper market.[14] The impact of state control may be particularly strong in culturally isolated autocracies with state broadcasting monopolies and the least permeable national borders, such as China, the Democratic People's Republic of Korea, and Myanmar, with more limited effects in societies where the public has access to alternative broadcasts, as in the communist German Democratic Republic.[15]

## The Impact on Processes of Democratization

Many scholars have also described the positive contribution of media liberalization and independent journalism in the transition and consolidation of democracy. Research has examined this process in postcommunist Europe, as well as in Africa.[16] These studies suggest that the initial transition from autocracy liberalizes ownership and control of the media, loosens the dead hand of official censorship, and weakens state control of information. The public is thereby exposed to a wider variety of cultural products and ideas through access to multiple alternative newspapers, radio, and television channels, as well as new communication technologies, such as the Internet and mobile telephones. Once media liberalization has commenced, this process is widely believed to reinforce processes of democratic consolidation and good governance; watchdog journalism can highlight government corruption and malfeasance, alternative news outlets can provide a forum for multiple voices in public debate, and reporters can encourage officials to be more responsive toward social needs and concerns.[17]

## The Impact of Restrictive Practices on Mass Attitudes

In short, practices and techniques that restrict the independent media and limit freedom of expression are well documented, as is the way that a free press contributes toward the process of democratization. Yet far less systematic cross-national research has examined the impact of restrictions of press freedom on public opinion, especially comparing the effects of different types of media environments on mass attitudes. State control of information aims to suppress potential support for opposition movements, and to bolster the popularity of the regime, trust and confidence in political institutions, and feelings of national pride and identity, as well as shape broader ideological beliefs. Despite the importance of this issue, the effects of such practices on citizens' attitudes and values have not been clearly and systematically demonstrated. One reason is the difficulty of conducting reliable survey research in autocracies that regularly impose serious limits on freedom of speech, particularly in getting access to, and asking questions about, politically sensitive issues, such as confidence in government or trust in the authorities. This context may also encourage a climate of self-censorship; survey respondents may believe that it would be dangerous to provide critical evaluations of those in power, raising difficulties in how researchers can best interpret their replies (an issue that returns in the conclusion). Meanwhile, even when these difficulties are overcome, cross-national surveys need to gauge both regime support and systematic patterns of media use.

The case studies that are available also warn that the effects of the media environment may not be as straightforward as often assumed by overly simple stimulus-response models of state hegemonic control over the gullible public, and considerable caution is needed when extrapolating directly from the type of coverage presented in the news media to the distribution of public opinion and attitudes. For example, a 10-nation comparison by Gunther and Mughan concluded that the ability of autocracies to shape political attitudes and values remains limited.[18] The authors highlight detailed cases of strong state control of the media, for example, in Chile under Pinochet and in Spain under Franco. Yet in both cases, surveys conducted shortly after these regimes ended suggested widespread public support for democracy and a rejection of the authoritarian past. The study cautions that, rather than a direct impact, the effect of state control of the media on the public is often complex and contingent upon many factors, such as the presence of media technologies, the nature of political institutions, and the characteristics of citizens.

States also seek to disseminate more positive images and messages through propaganda, especially in wartime, but early studies also emphasized the limits of these techniques. Classic experimental studies conducted during World War II found that U.S. military training films, such as Why We Fight, were relatively ineffective in altering soldiers' attitudes and behavior.[19] The research conducted in that era generated a consensus that attempts at using radio and films alone for political persuasion tended not to convert attitudes or to change behavior, at least in the short term. Indeed, a wide range of literature during the height of the Cold War era emphasized the limited direct effects of the mass media for short-term persuasion in contrast to the primacy of primary ties and face-to-face communication.[20] In this perspective, autocracies seek to strengthen regime support through positive images presented in state propaganda, but such techniques are likely to fail. Moreover, the early direct effects model of the role of media propaganda has come under sustained challenge from cognitive theories in education and social psychology, derived originally from the work of Jean Piaget, which emphasize constructivist accounts of learning.[21] When applied to the role of the mass media, in this perspective, recipients of media messages play an active role when processing information and extracting meaning from information; for example, state propaganda may prove highly ineffective if citizens suspect the reliability of the source and thereby discount progovernment messages. People may learn to discount media messages in a restrictive media environment if they are aware of censorship or partisan bias in the news and they do not trust the source.

In addition, the news media represent only one factor shaping confidence in authorities, and it may not be the most important driver. Ever since Easton, a range of explanations for the underlying causes of system support have been offered in the literature.[22] Theories of socialization usually emphasize the influence of the family, school, and local community as the key agencies that shape children and adolescents during their formative years, more than the role of the mass media in adult life. Moreover, modernization theories focus on a glacial erosion of support for many traditional sources of political authority, including representative government, and established, hierarchical institutions, such as the army, police, and church, leading toward more elite-challenging behavior among the young and well-educated in postindustrial societies.[23] Instrumental accounts deriving from the political economy focus on the performance of the government, especially pocketbook evaluations of the competence of leaders in managing the economy and delivering basic public services.[24] By contrast, institutional explanations focus on the role of intermediary structures linking citizens and the state, such as parties and voluntary associations, as well as the way election outcomes shape attitudes toward political authorities.[25] The assumption that state control of the news media has a simple and direct effect on confidence in government is challenged by a range of alternative sociological, developmental, economic, and institutional accounts in the literature.

For all these reasons, the impact of state control of the news media on patterns of regime support deserves to be carefully reexamined in the light of empirical evidence. To reiterate the core propositions, if state control of the media achieves its intended effects, this study predicts that certain patterns of regime support will be evident among the general public. In particular, if state control works, the study predicts the following:

Hypothesis 1: *The publics of countries with a restricted media environment will prove more supportive of their society's regime than the publics of societies with a pluralistic media environment.*

Many factors could conceivably cause this macrolevel pattern. To provide additional supporting evidence that exposure to the state-controlled news media per se contributed to these effects, the study carried out six additional tests of this hypothesis within given countries. Comparison of users and nonusers of the news media within each type of media environment, with prior controls, provides a critical test. Because regime support is understood as a multidimensional concept, it needs to be disaggregated. Accordingly, the study predicts that, within countries having restrictive media environments:

H1.1  *News users will display greater confidence in regime institutions than nonusers.*

H1.2  *News users will express more negative attitudes toward democratic values than nonusers.*

H1.3  *News users will have stronger feelings of nationalism than nonusers.*

Any direct effects from this process are also expected to vary by media sector, depending on the degree of state control. In particular, the study predicts that the effects of exposure to the broadcast media will be strongest since this is the sector where the state has the greatest potential control over ownership and content. The effects of newspapers are likely to be weaker since it is generally more difficult for officials to limit information flows, owing to the relatively large number of printed outlets and to the diversity of information contained in these sources. Finally, techniques of censorship can also be applied to new digital technologies.[26] Nevertheless, the Internet tends to be the channel through which autocracies are least able to control the content from beyond their borders, so it may provide dissidents and opposition movements with the easiest access to alternative information. Accordingly, the study predicts the following within restricted environments:

H2.1  *The effects of exposure on regime support will be stronger among regular consumers of radio and television news than among nonusers.*

H2.2  *The effects of exposure on regime support will be weaker among regular users of newspapers and the Internet than among nonusers.*

H2.3  *The effects of exposure on regime support will be negative among regular users of the Internet as compared with nonusers.*

For each of these hypotheses, as an additional control, similar models can be compared in pluralistic media environments, although the theoretical framework outlined above does not make any clear predictions about the strength or direction of any media effects in this context. If the media malaise thesis holds, exposure to the news media (especially television news) will generate more negative regime support. If, however, the alternative virtuous circle thesis holds, exposure to the news media will generate more positive orientations toward the regime.[27]

## Classification of Macrolevel Media Environments

### Monitoring Regime Support

Evidence of attitudes and values in many different societies is available in the fifth wave of the World Values Survey (WVS-5), which covers a wide range of countries from all major cultural regions, as well as democratic and autocratic regimes that vary in their levels of press freedom, with China, Vietnam, and Russia having the most restrictive policies. The World Values Survey is a global investigation of sociocultural and political change. This project has carried out representative national surveys of the basic values and beliefs of the publics in more than 90 independent countries, containing more than 88 percent of the world's population and covering all six inhabited continents. It builds on the European Values Surveys, first carried out in 22 countries in 1981. A second wave of surveys, in 41 countries, was completed during 1990–91. The third wave was carried out in 55 nations over 1995–96. The fourth wave, with 59 nation-states, took place during 1999–2001. The fifth wave is now being completed during 2005–07.[28]

The WVS survey includes some of the most affluent market economies in the world, such as Japan, Switzerland, and the United States, with per capita annual incomes as high as US$40,000, together with middle-level industrializing economies, including Brazil; Taiwan, China; and Turkey, as well as poorer agrarian societies, exemplified by Nigeria, Uganda, and Vietnam, with per capita annual incomes of US$300 or less. Some smaller nations have populations below 1 million, such as Iceland, Luxembourg, and Malta, while at the other extreme almost 1 billion people live in India and more than 1 billion live in China. The survey contains older democracies, such as Australia, India, and the Netherlands; newer democracies, including El Salvador, Estonia, and Taiwan, China; and autocracies, such as China, Egypt, Pakistan, and Zimbabwe. The transition process also varies markedly: some nations have experienced a rapid consolidation of democracy during the 1990s; today Argentina, the Czech Republic, and Latvia currently rank as high as Belgium, the Netherlands, and the United States on political rights and civil liberties, though these countries have a long tradition of democracy.[29] The survey also includes some of the first systematic data on public opinion in many Muslim states, including Arab countries, such as Egypt, the Islamic Republic of Iran, Jordan, and Morocco, as well as in Bangladesh, Indonesia, Pakistan, and Turkey. The most comprehensive coverage comes from Western Europe, North America, and Scandinavia, where public opinion surveys have the longest tradition, but countries are included from all world regions, including Sub-Saharan Africa. Since the battery of items monitoring media use was only included in the fifth wave, this study draws primarily on the latest survey, covering more than 40 societies, although other items, such as confidence in governing institutions were included in earlier waves and can be compared across a wider range of states.

### Classifying Media Environments

As a first step toward examining the empirical evidence, it is necessary to classify and compare how the media environment, and thus the degree of state intervention and control of the news media, can be classified and compared across diverse societies and types of regimes. The media environment is understood in this study to cover all the major features determining the relationship between the state and the news media in any society. This includes issues of ownership, regulation, and control; the legal framework governing freedom of expression and information (such as penalties for press offenses); patterns of intimidation and violations of press freedom affecting journalists and the mass media (such as cases of imprisonment and harassment of reporters); and the nature of state intervention in the media (such as state monopolies of broadcasting or the use of official censorship).

Both categorical typologies and continuous measures of media freedom can be employed to compare media environments. The standard theoretical typology of macrolevel media systems was established in the mid-20th century by Siebert, Peterson, and Schramm's classic *Four Theories of the Press*.[30] Following their work, two ideal types of media system have commonly been identified and compared in advanced industrial societies: the more market-oriented commercial broadcasting industry, which developed in the United States and throughout much of Latin America, is often contrasted with the public service model of broadcasting traditionally dominating contemporary Western Europe and Scandinavia. A growing number of countries have evolved toward a mixed system, such as that used in Great Britain, which combines both forms of broadcasting.[31] Moreover, the simple distinction between market-oriented and state-oriented media systems, as well as between commercial and public service broadcasting, hides important differences within each category.

Following in the footsteps of Siebert et al., recent cross-national research by Hallin and Mancini proposed a revised classification of the structure of media systems found in advanced industrialized societies.[32] The authors distinguished the extent to which countries differ in the development of media markets (especially for newspapers), the strength of linkages between parties and the media, the degree of journalistic professionalism, and the nature of state intervention in the media system. On the basis of these criteria, among Western countries, the typology identified an Anglo-American (liberal) model (found, for example, in Canada, Great Britain, and the United States), a Mediterranean (polarized pluralism) model (for example, in France, Italy, and Spain), and a democratic-pluralist model (for example, Austria, the Netherlands, and Norway).

These classifications have been challenged. For example, in many regards the British dual commercial-public service media system may have more in common with the North European model than with the American television market. Moreover, as numerous observers have noted, the traditional distinction between commercial and public service television has been diluted, with convergence caused by the deregulation, commercialization, and proliferation of channels now available in European societies, as well as the spread of global media conglomerates, which have also affected the American market.[33] A broader comparison that goes beyond postindustrial societies is necessary to understand the issues at the heart of this study. This comparison also needs to include the remaining state-controlled media systems within contemporary autocracies, such as China and Vietnam, as well as examine whether journalists play a distinctive function in newer democracies and in developing societies.[34] Typologies are important tools, but unfortunately there is no consensus in political communications about the most appropriate conceptualization and categorization of contemporary media systems. It is difficult to develop clear-cut rules from the Hallin and Mancini typology that could be used to classify types of media environments worldwide with any degree of reliability and consistency.

An alternative approach to comparison has classified rights to freedom of expression contained in written constitutions, or whether countries have passed freedom of information laws.[35] These measures are an important step toward an open society, but they were not used in this study because what determines the actual degree of press freedom is the *implementation* of such rights or legislation. Colombia, the Kyrgyz Republic, and Russia have freedom of information laws, for example, and Uzbekistan's constitution nominally guarantees freedom of speech and the press, but this does not mean that journalists are safe in these countries or that such regulations have proved effective in promoting partisan balance in the news, freedom of expression, or transparency in government. Moreover, freedom of information is only one aspect of the media environment, and, though often closely related to freedom of speech and freedom of the press, these are not equivalent concepts.

Given these reflections, this study used indexes of press freedom derived from expert judgments. It classified countries based on the Worldwide Press Freedom Index, which is produced annually by Reporters without Borders (RSF).[36] The index is constructed to reflect the degree of freedom journalists and news organizations enjoy in each country, and the efforts made by the state to ensure respect for this freedom. The organization compiles a questionnaire with 52 criteria used for assessing the state of press freedom in each country every year. It includes every kind of violation directly affecting journalists (such as murders, imprisonment, physical attacks, and threats) and news media (censorship, confiscation of publications, searches, and harassment). It registers the degree of impunity enjoyed by those responsible for such violations. It also takes account of the legal situation affecting the news media (such as penalties for press offenses, the existence of a state monopoly in certain areas, and the existence of a regulatory body), the behavior of the authorities toward the state-owned news media and the foreign press, and the main obstacles to the free flow of information on the Internet. The Worldwide Press Freedom Index reflects not only abuses attributable to the state, but also those by armed militias, clandestine organizations, or pressure groups that can pose a real threat to press freedom. The survey questionnaire was sent to RSF partner organizations, including 14 freedom of expression groups in five continents and to RSF's 130 correspondents around the world, as well as to journalists, researchers, jurists, and human rights activists. A 100-point country score was estimated for each country under comparison. Using the 2005 score, the study compared and ranked the 168 countries in the press freedom index. The scale was standardized around the mean (Z-scores) and the ranking reversed for ease of interpretation, so that a higher ranking represents an estimate of greater press freedom.

To check whether the index was reliable and unbiased, the Worldwide Press Freedom Index was compared with the results of Freedom House's annual index of press freedom.[37] The latter measured how much diversity of news content was influenced by the structure of the news industry and by legal and administrative decisions, the degree of political influence or control, the economic influences exerted by the government or private entrepreneurs, and actual incidents violating press autonomy, including censorship, harassment, and physical threats to journalists. The assessment of press freedom by Freedom House distinguishes between the broadcast and print media, and the resulting ratings are expressed as a 100-point scale for each country under comparison. As with the RSF press freedom index, the Freedom House index was also reversed and standardized around the mean.

To test for reliability, both indexes were compared in the 44 nation-states under comparison in the fifth wave of the World Values Survey. The results, illustrated in the scatter plot presented in figure 8.1, show a strong correlation across both these measures (R = .869, sig .001, cubic $R^2$ = .77, sig .001). There are a few outliers, such as Mexico and Taiwan, China, where the estimates produced by the two organizations differ slightly. Although the two indexes differ in their construction, data sources, and conceptualization, they produce similar estimates, which increase this study's confidence in their reliability.[38] Many countries scoring high on press freedom by both these indicators are highly developed nations, such as the Netherlands and Sweden, which is consistent with the well-established links between wealth and democracy. But other countries that score high on high press freedom are less affluent, such as Mali and Trinidad and Tobago, Ghana, and Poland, as well as Burkina Faso; Taiwan, China; and Uruguay. The countries ranked as having the most restrictive media environments by both organizations include China, Vietnam, and Iraq, with Ethiopia, Colombia, and Russia classified as less extreme outliers. The countries included in the WVS-5 are skewed toward the more plural-

**Figure 8.1.  Indicators of Press Freedom, 2005**

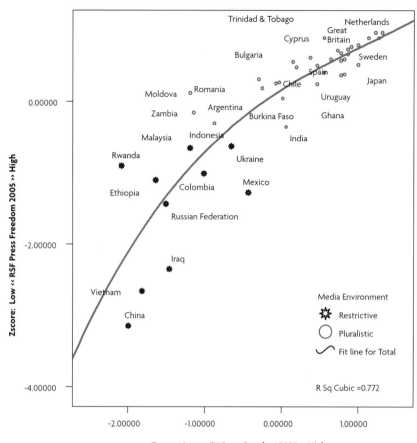

*Sources:* Freedom House 2006; RSF 2005.
*Note:* The ratings of press freedom for 2005 are provided by Freedom House (FH) and Reporters without Borders for the 44 countries included in the fifth wave of the World Values Survey, 2005–06. The 100-point survey scores were reversed and standardized around the mean (Z-scores).

istic media environments, but there are enough restrictive cases to permit comparative analysis, giving special attention to the outliers.

The Worldwide Press Freedom Index was used to gauge the degree of press freedom in the nation-states contained in the fifth wave of the World Values Survey. For ease of analysis, the index was dichotomized to facilitate comparison of attitudes and values found among the publics living in two types of societies: *pluralistic media environments*, which are characterized by relatively high levels of press freedom, versus *restricted media environments*, with relatively low levels of press freedom. The cases clustered around the cutoff points are ones where judgment has to be exercised and alternative divisions at a higher or lower point could alter the classification, for example, for India, Indonesia, and Zambia. Using this dichotomy allows public opinion to be compared when the survey data are aggregated in both types of media environments, reducing any "noise" caused by minor differences in the estimates of press freedom, for example, between Uruguay and Bulgaria or between Russia and Colombia. The 10 most restrictive media environments are cases in which both indexes were in broad agreement.

## The Impact of Media Environments on Regime Support

The classification of societies allows comparison of public opinion within each type of media environment. If states with restrictive media environments are effective in shaping attitudes and values, the publics living in these societies are expected to prove more positive toward the regime. One of the standard ways to evaluate this issue concerns trust and confidence in political institutions. Studies have compared attitudes toward the government, parliament, courts, police, state bureaucracies, political parties, and armed forces, as well as confidence in the press and television.[39] Such studies measure generalized support for given institutions—that is, approval of the performance of the presidency rather than support for the president, and support for parties rather than particular party leaders—although in practice, people do not always distinguish clearly between the office and incumbents. Using this approach, the World Values Survey measured confidence in government as follows: "I am going to name a number of organizations. For each one, could you tell me how much confidence you have in them: is it a great deal of confidence, quite a lot of confidence, not very much confidence or none at all? ...The government in your nation's capital." The attitudes can be compared among all the countries included in the fourth and fifth waves of the WVS (1999–2000 and 2005–06).

The results of the macrolevel comparisons illustrated in figure 8.2 confirm that confidence in government was indeed higher among the publics living under restricted media environments, compared with those living in pluralistic media environments, as predicted by the first hypothesis. This striking pattern was most evident with the public expressing the greatest confidence in government in China and Vietnam, both one-party communist states where the techniques of censorship and propaganda are stringently enforced, and in the Islamic Republic of Iran, which practices widespread censorship by the Ministry of Culture and Islamic Guidance. Relatively high levels of confidence in government were even expressed in Zimbabwe and Bangladesh, which can be classified as dysfunctional states. Indeed, in 2005–06 it is striking that confidence in government was far higher in Iraq—despite all the problems Iraq has experienced in providing basic public services and utilities, reducing violence, and maintaining order—than in Sweden, which by most standards has

Figure 8.2.  Press Freedom and Confidence in Government

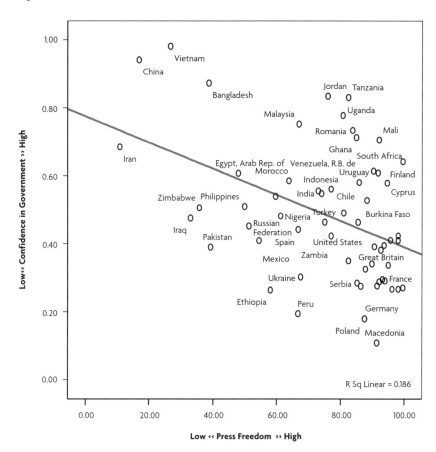

*Sources:* World Values Survey waves 4 and 5 combined. Press Freedom measured by Freedom House http://www.
freedomhouse.org.
*Note:* Proportion in each country expressing "a great deal" or "quite a lot" of confidence in their country's
government, in World Values Survey waves 4 and 5 combined.

one of the world's best-functioning societies. This is not an isolated case; less
confidence in government was expressed by publics living in many advanced
industrialized societies and stable democracies, such as France, Great Britain,
and Germany, than in many autocracies. This pattern is also consistent with
other studies that have documented the phenomenon of "critical citizens" and
with the erosion of confidence in government found in many affluent postindustrial societies.[40]

This initial finding certainly suggests that restrictive media environments
that limit negative news about the regime, can sometimes manipulate public
opinion and generate popular support for those in authority, as predicted.
At the same time, the results should be interpreted carefully. The simple correlations found at macrolevel do not provide conclusive proof that restricted

media environments boost popular support for the regime. One can readily think of alternative explanations. For example, performance-based accounts in a political economy could emphasize surging levels of prosperity, such as those that are transforming urban China and Vietnam. Developmental explanations might focus on long-term processes of cultural value change and rising levels of education that are making the younger generation of citizens within postindustrial societies more critical of those in authority.

To test the impact of state control of the media more conclusively, the study carried out microlevel analyses within each society. In particular, it examined the impact of exposure to given sources of news information within each country, comparing the attitudes of those who are regularly exposed to certain types of media with the attitudes of those who are not. The strongest effects were expected to be linked with exposure to television and radio news since that is the sector that is most open to state control. The public's access to radio and television news, newspapers, and the Internet varies substantially in countries around the world.[41] The media environment determines the extent to which citizens in developing societies have easy access to the news media, and the extent of information gaps, which vary by income, education, literacy, age, and gender.[42] To assess news consumption patterns, the 2005–06 World Values Survey asked the following question: "People use different sources to learn what is going on in their country and the world. For each of the following sources, please indicate whether you used it last week or did not use it last week to obtain information." The news media sources included daily newspaper, news broadcast on radio or television, and the Internet/email. These news media sources can be combined to examine the proportion of respondents in each country who reported no regular use of any of the news media (television or radio news, daily newspapers, or the Internet). Other sources that were monitored in the World Values Survey included books, printed magazines, and in-depth reports on radio or television, but these were not analyzed because only small numbers of respondents reported that they used them regularly.

The results shown in figure 8.3 demonstrate the striking contrasts in media exposure in the societies under comparison: more than one-third of the population had no access to the news media in some of the poorest developing societies, such as Burkina Faso, India, and Rwanda, while about one-quarter reported having no access in China, Mali, and Zambia. By contrast, in most postindustrial societies, news access was virtually ubiquitous; thus, in Australia, Japan, and Sweden almost everyone reported regularly accessing information from at least one of these news media. The attitudes and values of the groups who report regular exposure to television and radio news can be compared with those who are not so exposed. Although news might also have a diffuse effect through interpersonal communications, when people discuss events and stories that they saw on television, heard on the radio, or read

**Figure 8.3. Access to the News Media**

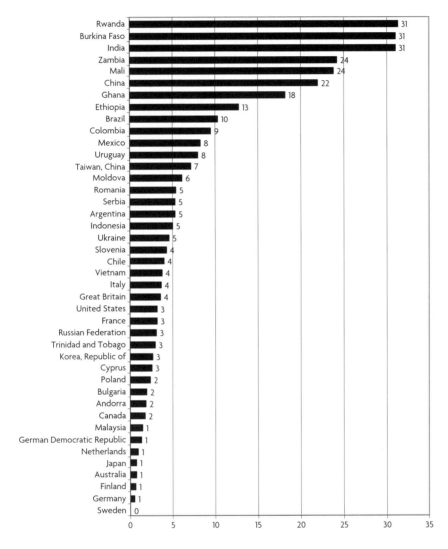

**Proportion of the population with no regular use of any news media**

*Sources:* World Values Survey 2005–06.
*Note:* The figure illustrates the proportion of respondents reporting use of a media source-a daily newspaper, news broadcasts on radio or television, or the Internet/email-for information in the past week.

in newspapers with friends and family (the so-called water cooler effect), the groups who regularly use the news media are more likely to be directly influenced by the media.

As Easton argued, political support reflects several different dimensions.[43] *Regime support* is understood here as a multidimensional concept that can be measured at three distinct levels: (1) confidence and trust in the government and in core regime institutions, such as the civil service, political parties, and courts; (2) more general ideological attitudes toward the principles of democracy and military rule; and (3) more diffuse attitudes of national pride and identity. This study used factor analysis to examine the dimensions of regime support, and the results in table 8.1 confirmed three separate components representing support for regime institutions, regime principles, and national community. These items were summed to create scales as the three dependent variables for analysis. The multivariate models also need to control for the standard social and demographic variables that could influence both patterns of access to the news media and attitudes toward the regime. Hence, the models in this study include controls for gender and age (as men and the older population are often more regular consumers of news), as well as for education and household income (which are closely associated with literacy in developing societies and which have the strongest effects on use of newspapers and the Internet). The models also monitored the effects of political interest since this could also plausibly shape news media habits and also levels of regime support. The annex to this chapter lists all variables and coding procedures.

The ordinary least squares regression models in tables 8.2–8.4 show the outcome of the analysis, and the main findings are summarized in table 8.5. The results indicate that the television and radio news audience living in

Table 8.1. Factor Analysis of Regime Support

| | Confidence in regime institutions | Support for democratic principles | Support for nationalism |
|---|---|---|---|
| Confidence in government | .809 | | |
| Confidence in parties | .795 | | |
| Confidence in the civil service | .783 | | |
| Confidence in the courts | .777 | | |
| Against having a strong leader who does not bother with parliament and elections | | .760 | |
| Against having the army rule | | .738 | |
| Favor having a democratic political system | | .631 | |
| Strong feeling of national pride | | | .921 |
| Confidence in the armed forces | .471 | | .504 |
| % variance | 32.7 | 17.1 | 11.1 |

Source: World Values Survey 2005–06.
Note: The table represents the results of principal component factor analysis using varimax rotation with kaiser normalization, excluding all coefficients below .40. See the annex for details of all variables.

Table 8.2.  Confidence in Regime Institutions

| | Restricted media environment | | | | Pluralistic media environment | | | |
|---|---|---|---|---|---|---|---|---|
| | B | Std. error | Beta | Sig. | B | Std. error | Beta | Sig. |
| *Information sources* | | | | | | | | |
| Use TV/radio | .992 | .122 | .085 | *** | .066 | .057 | .007 | |
| Use daily newspaper | .217 | .075 | .032 | ** | .011 | .036 | .002 | |
| Use Internet/email | -.222 | .094 | -.027 | ** | -.109 | .037 | -.020 | ** |
| *Controls* | | | | | | | | |
| Income | .243 | .016 | .176 | *** | .086 | .008 | .074 | *** |
| Education | -.435 | .060 | -.088 | *** | -.233 | .026 | -.064 | *** |
| Age | .142 | .025 | .059 | *** | -.038 | .011 | -.023 | *** |
| Gender | .001 | .069 | .000 | -.083 | .032 | -.016 | *** | |
| Interest | .740 | .039 | .195 | *** | .598 | .017 | .218 | *** |
| Constant | 6.26 | | | | 8.03 | | | |
| Adjusted R$^2$ | .083 | | | | .053 | | | |
| N respondents | 8,696 | | | | 24,632 | | | |
| N nation-states | 10 | | | | 34 | | | |

*Source:* World Values Survey 2005–06.
*Note:* The table presents the results of OLS linear regression models where the dependent variable, confidence in regime institutions, was measured on a 16-point scale. See the annex for the items used to construct each variable. The figures represent the unstandardized beta coefficient (B), the standard error, the standardized beta, and the significance of the coefficient (sig. *p* \*.05 \*\*.01 \*\*\*.001). All models were checked to be free of any problems of multicollinearity.

Table 8.3. Support for Democratic Principles

| | Restricted media environment | | | | Pluralistic media environment | | | |
|---|---|---|---|---|---|---|---|---|
| | B | Std. error | Beta | Sig. | B | Std. error | Beta | Sig. |
| *Information sources* | | | | | | | | |
| Use TV/radio | -.256 | .073 | -.036 | *** | .325 | .041 | .051 | *** |
| Use daily newspaper | -.114 | .045 | -.028 | ** | .107 | .026 | .028 | *** |
| Use Internet/email | -.665 | .057 | -.131 | *** | .332 | .027 | .087 | *** |
| *Controls* | | | | | | | | |
| Income | .130 | .010 | .155 | *** | .042 | .005 | .050 | *** |
| Education | .653 | .036 | .217 | *** | .235 | .019 | .090 | *** |
| Age | .020 | .015 | .013 | | .137 | .008 | .117 | *** |
| Gender | -.058 | .042 | -.014 | | .016 | .023 | .004 | |
| Interest | .272 | .024 | .117 | *** | .139 | .012 | .071 | *** |
| Constant | 6.09 | | | | | | | |
| Adjusted R$^2$ | .102 | | | | .052 | | | |
| N respondents | 8,696 | | | | | | | |
| N nation-states | 10 | | | | 34 | | | |

*Source:* World Values Survey 2005–06.
*Note:* The table presents the results of OLS linear regression models where the dependent variable, support for democratic principles, was measured on a 12-point scale. See the annex for the items used to construct each variable. The figures represent the unstandardized beta coefficient (B), the standard error, the standardized beta, and the significance of the coefficient (sig. *p* \*.05 \*\*.01 \*\*\*.001). All models were checked to be free of any problems of multicollinearity.

restricted media environments expressed significantly more regime support than nonusers, even after applying prior controls for the social characteristics of the audience. Moreover, this holds true for a broad range of indicators; similar patterns are found for confidence in regime institutions, attitudes toward democratic values and principles, and support for the national community.

As table 8.2 demonstrates, within restricted media environments, confidence in regime institutions is significantly higher among users of television and radio news, even after controlling for a variety of other variables that might plausibly shape confidence in the regime. Use of daily newspapers is also significantly related to greater confidence in the regime, although with weaker effects than broadcasting. By contrast, use of the Internet is significantly linked with less confidence in regime institutions. In pluralistic media environments, use of television or radio news and newspapers was not significantly related to institutional confidence, and use of the Internet was also negatively associated with confidence.

If political propaganda achieves its objectives, in restricted media environments the news media could also be expected to shape broader attitudes and values toward the core principles and ideologies underpinning each type of regime. These values were summarized in a 12-point scale measuring negative attitudes toward "strong leadership without the need for elections," expert rule, military rule, and positive approval of democracy as an ideal political system. The results in table 8.3 show that use of all types of news media

**Table 8.4. Support for National Community**

| | Restricted media environment | | | | Pluralistic media environment | | | |
|---|---|---|---|---|---|---|---|---|
| | B | Std. error | Beta | Sig. | B | Std. error | Beta | Sig. |
| *Information sources* | | | | | | | | |
| Use TV/radio | .668 | .045 | .157 | *** | .122 | .029 | .027 | *** |
| Use daily newspaper | -.013 | .028 | -.005 | .017 | .018 | .006 | | |
| Use Internet/email | -.017 | .035 | -.006 | -.158 | .019 | -.059 | *** | |
| *Controls* | | | | | | | | |
| Income | .039 | .006 | .078 | *** | .028 | .004 | .024 | *** |
| Education | -.189 | .022 | -.105 | *** | -.155 | .013 | -.085 | *** |
| Age | .046 | .009 | .052 | *** | .037 | .005 | .045 | *** |
| Gender | .133 | .026 | .055 | *** | .063 | .016 | .024 | *** |
| Interest | .142 | .015 | .102 | *** | .147 | .009 | .108 | *** |
| Constant | 5.54 | | | | 5.78 | | | |
| Adjusted $R^2$ | .052 | | | | .028 | .028 | | |
| N respondents | 8,696 | | | | 24,632 | | | |
| N nation-states | 10 | | | | 34 | | | |

*Source:* World Values Survey 2005–06.
*Note:* The table presents the results of OLS linear regression models where the dependent variable, support for national community, was measured on an 8-point scale. See the annex for the items used to construct each variable. The figures represent the unstandardized beta coefficient (B), the standard error, the standardized beta, and the significance of the coefficient (sig. $p$ *.05 **.01 ***.001). All models were checked to be free of any problems of multicollinearity.

**Table 8.5.  Summary of Results**

| | Restricted media environment | | | Pluralistic media environment | | |
|---|---|---|---|---|---|---|
| | TV/Radio | Newspapers | Internet | TV/Radio | Newspapers | Internet |
| Confidence in regime institutions | + | + | – | N/s | N/s | – |
| Support for democratic principles | – | – | – | + | + | + |
| Support for national community | + | N/s | N/s | **+** | N/s | – |

*Source:* Author.

*Note:* See tables 8.2–8.5 for details. The symbols summarize the direction of any significant coefficients established in the previous regression models. The symbols highlighted in bold have the polarity that is consistent with the core hypotheses.

consistently showed a negative link with support for democratic principles in restricted media environments. In sharp contrast, in pluralistic media environments, media use was associated with *positive* support for democracy.

Finally, national pride and identification with the national community represent the most diffuse form of system support. Nationalistic feelings were measured here by a scale combining national pride with confidence in the armed forces, which emerged as a distinct dimension of regime support. Here exposure to television and radio news was a strong and significant predictor of nationalism in restricted media environments, although similar findings were also evident in pluralistic media environments.

## Conclusion and Implications

How should these findings be interpreted? In the United States, classic debates about the impact of foreign propaganda during wartime were concerned that it posed a major threat to America by altering attitudes and behavior among the gullible public.[44] Lasswell also thought that propaganda has a positive value, if employed to reinforce democratic values.[45] Contrary to these beliefs about strong media effects, the earliest experimental evidence from studying the impact of allied film propaganda on soldiers concluded that there were only minimal short-term changes in attitudes and behavior arising from this process.[46] These conclusions fueled the "minimal effects" thesis, emphasizing the limited power of the mass media to convert, compared with the stronger influence of interpersonal communication in small groups.[47] This claim remained the conventional wisdom during most of the Cold War era. But the short-term impact of official propaganda is only one way that states can try to use the news media to shape public support and ideological values. Assessing the long-term way that attitudes and values may be shaped by living in restrictive media environments requires alternative methods of investigation and different research designs.

This study started with the hypothesis that in autocracies where the state consistently restricts media freedom and controls broadcasting, regular exposure to the domestic news media would generate more positive orientations toward the regime. These direct effects were predicted to be strongest among regular consumers of radio and television news, the sector of the mass media where the state usually exercises the greatest control over the ownership and content. Equivalent results were not expected to be found in pluralistic media environments, where audiences receive both multiple positive and negative messages about the regime, nor were they expected to be evident in sectors where the state exercises less direct control over the contents. The empirical findings that emerged from the analysis largely confirmed these propositions.

To summarize the key results, the study examined how regime support varied under restrictive and pluralistic media environments. The macrolevel comparisons confirmed, as expected, that confidence in government was significantly higher in societies with restrictive rather than pluralistic media environments. This cannot be regarded as conclusive proof that state control of the media directly causes public support for the regime, though it points in that direction.

Multivariate regression models examined the microlevel effects of exposure to various types of news media within restrictive or pluralistic media environments. These analyses included controls for common social and demographic background variables, such as education, income, age, and gender, as well as political interest, which could plausibly affect both media access and attitudes toward the regime. Analysis of the microlevel data revealed that in societies with limited media freedom, regime support was significantly higher among the regular audience for television and radio news, whether measured by confidence in regime institutions, attitudes toward democratic principles, or nationalistic feelings. Similar models run at national level, not reported in detail here, show that this relationship was particularly strong in China, Colombia, Ethiopia, Mexico, Serbia, and Zambia, all societies with limited independent journalism, while at the same time no equivalent effect was found in poorer democracies with more pluralistic media systems, such as Ghana and India.

In interpreting these results, certain important issues need to be considered, namely whether survey data monitoring support for the government tap real attitudes in societies that suppress free speech. Conceivably, the respondents may be expressing the politically correct response, rather than expressing their true feelings. It is not possible to test this proposition with the available survey evidence; if there is self-censorship on any sensitive issue, all surveys can do is report what respondents say. Nevertheless, if respondents are offering what they believe is the politically correct response, it is striking that the media effects documented in this study are most clearly evident for the broadcasting sector, where the state can exercise the greatest control, but those effects are not consistently found among those who use the Internet. There is no obvious reason why any self-censorship response effect should vary across users of different media sectors. Moreover, even if the analysis accepts the claim that in restricted media environments respondents are masking their true evaluations of the government, this in itself is important for the social construction of reality and for what is perceived as socially acceptable in these countries.

The evidence presented here tends to support the proposition that state control of the broadcast media and limits on press freedom do achieve their intended effect, by strengthening regime support among the news audience in these societies. Contrary to conventional notions of limited media effects, derived from the classic Hovland experiments and the long tradition established by Lazarsfeld, state control of the airwaves matters.[48] What still needs to be determined in further research is which techniques prove most important in this process, in particular, whether confidence in government is the result of official propaganda disseminating positive images and messages about the leadership and authorities, or whether state censorship of independent journalism restricts alternative viewpoints and perspectives. To do so will require closer examination of the content of the news and what messages are most persuasive; it is suspected that some combination of propaganda and censorship allows autocracies to reinforce their popular support. These findings emphasize the importance of liberalizing the media in such societies as the Democratic People's Republic of Korea, Myanmar, and Zimbabwe, strengthening freedom of expression, publication, and information. Media liberalization not only would improve human rights in these states, but also generate conditions most conducive to the transition from autocracy and the consolidation of democratic governance.

## Annex

### Table 8.A1. Technical Annex

| Variable | Question | Coded |
|---|---|---|
| Household income | V.253 "On a card is a scale of incomes on which 1 indicates the 'lowest income decile' and 10 'the highest income decile' in your country. We would like to know in what group your income falls, counting all wages, salaries, pensions, and other incomes that come in." | Coded 1 (low) to 10 (high) |
| Gender | V235. | 1 = Male, 0 = Female |
| Education | V238. "What is the highest educational level that you have attained?" | 8 categories, from "No formal education" (1) to "University degree" (8) |
| Age | V237. Age in years | Recoded into 6 age groups from 18 to 85. |
| Interest | V7. "For each of the following, indicate how important it is in your life....Politics." | Very important (4), rather important (3), not very important (2), not at all important (1) |
| Use radio/TV | "People use different sources to learn what is going on in their country and the world. For each of the following sources, please indicate whether you used it last week or did not use it last week to obtain information. Radio/TV" | Used last week (1), Not (0) |
| Use daily newspaper | "People use different sources to learn what is going on in their country and the world. For each of the following sources, please indicate whether you used it last week or did not use it last week to obtain information. Daily newspaper" | Used last week (1), Not (0) |
| Use Internet/ email | "People use different sources to learn what is going on in their country and the world. For each of the following sources, please indicate whether you used it last week or did not use it last week to obtain information. Internet/email." | Used last week (1), Not (0) |

| Variable | Question | Coded |
|---|---|---|
| Media environment | Classified from the RSF Worldwide Press Freedom Index | 0 = Restrictive (China, Colombia, Ethiopia, Iraq, Malaysia, Mexico, Russian Federation, Rwanda, Vietnam, Ukraine), 1 = Pluralistic (all the remainder) |
| Institutional confidence | V131–147. "I am going to name a number of organizations. For each one, could you tell me how much confidence you have in them? | 4 = A great deal of confidence, 3 = quite a lot of confidence, 2 = not very much confidence, 1 = none at all |
| | Government in [your nation's capital], political parties, the civil service, the courts." | Summed for a 16-point scale (confidence in government + political parties + civil service + the courts) |
| Support for the national community | V132. Confidence in the armed forces (item coded as above) | 4 = very proud, 3 = quite proud, 2 = not very proud, 1 = not at all proud. |
| | V209. "How proud are you to be [nationality]?" | Summed to an 8-point scale. |
| Support for democratic principles | "I am going to describe various types of political systems and ask what you think about each as a way of governing this country. For each one, would you say it is a very good, fairly good, fairly bad, or very bad way of governing this country? | The three items were recoded in a consistent prodemocratic direction and then summed to form a 12-point scale. |
| | V148. Having a strong leader who does not have to bother with parliament and elections? | |
| | V150. Having the army rule? | |
| | V151. Having a democratic political system?" | |

*Source:* Author.

# Notes

1. Reporters without Borders. 2007. "At Least Five Journalists Arrested in Rangoon, Including Japanese Daily's Correspondent." September 30, 2007. http://www.rsf.org/article.php3?id_article=23837.
2. Brett Gary. 1999. *The Nervous Liberals: Propaganda Anxieties from World War I to the Cold War.* New York: Columbia University Press.
3. Edward S. Herman and Noam Chomsky. 1988. *Manufacturing Consent: The Political Economy of the Mass Media.* New York: Pantheon Books; Garth S. Jowett and Victoria O'Donnell. 2006. *Propaganda and Persuasion.* 4th ed. Thousand Oaks, CA: Sage.
4. For more technical details of the World Values Survey methodology and fieldwork, see http://www.worldvaluessurvey.org/.
5. Robert Dahl. 1971. *Polyarchy: Participation and Opposition.* New Haven: Yale University Press.

6.  Roumeen Islam, ed. 2002. *The Right to Tell: The Role of Mass Media in Economic Development.* Washington, DC: World Bank; Roumeen Islam. 2003. *Do More Transparent Governments Govern Better?* Washington, DC: World Bank.

7.  Louis Edward Inglehart. 1998. *Press and Speech Freedoms in the World, from Antiquity until 1998: A Chronology.* Westport, CT: Greenwood Press; Leonard R. Sussman. 2001. *Press Freedom in Our Genes.* Reston, VA: World Press Freedom Committee; Alasdair Roberts. 2006. *Blacked Out: Government Secrecy in the Information Age.* New York: Cambridge University Press.

8.  Reporters without Borders. 2007. *North Korea Annual Report 2007.* http://www.rsf.org/country-50.php3?id_mot=260&Valider=OK.

9.  See, for example, the International Federation of Journalists, http://www.ifj.org/, and Human Rights Watch, http://www.hrw.org/.

10. See for example cases documented by the Index on Censorship, http://www.index-oncensorship.org/, the World Press Freedom Council, http://www.wpfc.org, and the International Press Institute, http://www.freemedia.at.

11. Leonard R. Sussman. 2000. "Censor Dot Gov: The Internet and Press Freedom." *Press Freedom Survey 2000.* Washington, DC: Freedom House. http://www.freedomhouse.com; Shanthi Kalathil and Taylor C. Boas. 2001. *The Internet and State Control in Authoritarian Regimes: China, Cuba and the Counterrevolution.* Global Policy Program No. 21. Washington, DC: Carnegie Endowment for International Peace.

12. See for example the International Federation of Journalists. http://www.ifj.org/, and Human Rights Watch, http://www.hrw.org/.

13. Ellen Mickiewicz. 1999. *Changing Channels: Television and the Struggle for Power in Russia.* Durham, NC: Duke University Press; J. Becker. 2004. "Lessons from Russia: A Neo-Authoritarian Media System." *European Journal of Communication* 19 (2): 139–63.

14. L.L. Chu. 1994. "Continuity and Change in China Media Reform." *Journal of Communication* 44 (3): 4–21; Richard Cullen and Hua Ling Fu. 1998. "Seeking Theory from Experience: Media Regulation in China." *Democratization* 5: 155–78.

15. Richard Gunther and Anthony Mughan, eds. 2000. *Democracy and the Media: A Comparative Perspective.* New York: Cambridge University Press.

16. Colin Sparks and A. Reading. 1994. "Understanding Media Change in East-Central-Europe." *Media Culture & Society* 16 (2): 243–70; Matthew Taylor. 2000. "Media Relations in Bosnia: A Role for Public Relations in Building Civil Society." *Public Relations Review* 26 (1): 1–14; J. Becker. 2004. "Lessons from Russia: A Neo-Authoritarian Media System." *European Journal of Communication* 19 (2): 139–63; Anna Amelina. 2007. "Evolution of the Media and Media Control in Post-Soviet Russia." *Soziale Welt-Zeitschrift Fur Sozialwissenschaftliche Forschung Und Praxis* 58 (2): 163; D. Anable. 2006. "The Role of Georgia's Media—and Western Aid—in the Rose Revolution." *Harvard International Journal of Press/Politics* 11 (3): 7–43; Michael McFaul. 2005. "Transitions from Post-Communism." *Journal of Democracy* 16 (3): 5–19.

17. Barry James, ed. 2006. *Media development and poverty eradication.* Paris: UNESCO.

18. Gunther and Mughan, eds. 2000. *Democracy and the Media.*

19. C. I. Hovland, A. Lumsdaine, and F. Sheffield. 1949. *Experiments on Mass Communication.* Princeton, NJ: Princeton University Press.

20. Elihu Katz and Paul F. Lazarsfeld. 1955. *Personal Influence: The Part Played by People in the Flow of Mass Communications.* Glencoe, IL: Free Press.

21. W. Russell Neuman, Marion R. Just, and Ann N. Crigler. 1992. *Common Knowledge: News and the Construction of Political Meaning.* Chicago: University Of Chicago Press.

22. David Easton. 1965. *A Systems Analysis of Political Life*. New York: Wiley; David Easton. 1975. "A Reassessment of the Concept of Political Support." *British Journal of Political Science* 5: 435–57; Pippa Norris. 1999. *Critical Citizens: Global Support for Democratic Governance*. Oxford: Oxford University Press.

23. Ronald Inglehart. 1997. *Modernization and Postmodernization: Cultural, Economic and Political Change in 43 Societies*. Princeton: Princeton University Press; Ronald Inglehart and Christian Welzel. 2005. *Modernization, Cultural Change and Democracy*. New York and Cambridge: Cambridge University Press.

24. Arthur H. Miller. 1974. "Political Issues and Trust in Government, 1964–1970." *American Political Science Review* 68: 951–72; Ian McAllister. 1999. "The Economic Performance of Governments." In *Critical Citizens: Global Support for Democratic Governance*, ed. Pippa Norris. Oxford: Oxford University Press.

25. Russell J. Dalton. 1999. "Political Support in Advanced Industrialized Democracies." In *Critical Citizens: Global Support for Democratic Governance*, ed. Pippa Norris. Oxford: Oxford University Press; Russell J. Dalton. 2004. *Democratic Challenges, Democratic Choices*. Oxford: Oxford University Press.

26. Ronald Deibert, John Palfrey, Rafal Rohozinski and Jonathan Zittrain. 2008. *Access Denied: The Practice and Policy of Global Internet Filtering*. Cambridge, MA: MIT Press.

27. Pippa Norris. 2000. *A Virtuous Circle: Political Communications in Post-industrial Societies*. New York: Cambridge University Press.

28. Full methodological details about the World Values Surveys, including the questionnaires, sampling procedures, fieldwork procedures, principal investigators, and organization can be found at http://wvs.isr.umich.edu/wvs-samp.html.

29. These countries are ranked as equally "free" according to the 2007 Freedom House assessments of political rights and civil liberties. Freedom House. 2007. *Freedom in the World 2000–2001*. http://www.freedomhouse.org.

30. Friedrich S. Siebert, Theodore Peterson, and Wilbur Schramm. 1956. *Four Theories of the Press*. Champaign: University of Illinois Press.

31. Norris. 2000. *A Virtuous Circle*; Richard Gunther and Anthony Mughan, eds. 2000. *Democracy and the Media: A Comparative Perspective*. New York: Cambridge University Press.

32. Daniel C. Hallin and Paolo Mancini. 2004. *Comparing Media Systems: Three Models of Media and Politics*. Cambridge and New York: Cambridge University Press.

33. Mary Kelly, Gianpietro Mazzoleni, and Denis McQuail, eds. 2004. *The Media in Europe*. London: Sage; Frank Esser and Barbara Pfetsch, eds. 2004. *Comparing Political Communication: Theories, Cases, and Challenges*. Cambridge and New York: Cambridge University Press.

34. Goran Hyden, Michael Leslie, and Folu F. Ogundimu, eds. 2002. *Media and Democracy in Africa*. Uppsala: Nordiska Afrikainstitutet; Katrin Voltmer, ed. 2006. *Mass Media and Political Communication in New Democracies*. London: Routledge.

35. David Banisar. 2006. *Freedom of Information Around the World 2006: A Global Survey of Access to Government Records Laws*. http://www.freedominfo.org.

36. For details on the methodology and annual rankings, see Reporters without Borders. 2006. *Annual Worldwide Press Freedom Index*. http://www.rsf.org.

37. For more methodological details and results, see Freedom House 2007. *Global Press Freedom* 2007. http://www.freedomhouse.org. The International Research and Exchanges Board (IREX) Media Sustainability Index provides another set of indicators (http://www.irex.org/resources/index.asp). IREX benchmarks the conditions for independent

media in a more limited range of countries across Europe, Eurasia, the Middle East, and North Africa. Unfortunately, the IREX index does not contain sufficient cases of countries included in the WVS-5 to be useful as a cross-check for this study.

38. Further analysis found that replication of the core regression models in this study using the Freedom House classification suggests that the results remain robust and consistent irrespective of which particular measure of press freedom is used, which is hardly surprising given the strong intercorrelation of both measures.

39. Ola Listhaug and Matti Wiberg. 1995. "Confidence in Political and Private Institutions." In *Citizens and the State*, ed. Hans-Dieter Klingemann and Dieter Fuchs. Oxford: Oxford University Press.

40. Pippa Norris. 1999. *Critical Citizens: Global Support for Democratic Governance*. Oxford: Oxford University Press.

41. See UNESCO. *Annual Yearbooks*. Paris: UNESCO.

42. Pippa Norris. 2000. *A Virtuous Circle: Political Communications in Post-industrial Societies*. New York: Cambridge University Press; Pippa Norris. 2001. Digital Divide. New York: Cambridge University Press.

43. David Easton. 1975. "A Reassessment of the Concept of Political Support." *British Journal of Political Science* 5: 435–57; Norris. 1999. Critical Citizens.

44. Brett Gary. 1999. *The Nervous Liberals: Propaganda Anxieties from World War I to the Cold War*. New York: Columbia University Press.

45. Harold W. Lasswell. 1971/1927. *Propaganda Techniques in World War I*. Cambridge, MA: MIT Press.

46. C. I. Hovland, A. Lumsdaine, and F. Sheffield. 1949. *Experiments on Mass Communication*. Princeton, NJ: Princeton University Press.

47. Elihu Katz and Paul F. Lazarsfeld. 1955. *Personal Influence: The Part Played by People in the Flow of Mass Communications*. Glencoe, IL: Free Press.

48. Ibid.

•
•

# 9

# Media in the Peace-Building Process: Ethiopia and Iraq

Monroe E. Price, Ibrahim Al-Marashi, and
Nicole A. Stremlau

The idea that one can consider a governance reform agenda in a postconflict society assumes that there is governance and, in particular, governance that has about it a structure, preferably a rational one. This study could be said to be about outliers: conditions or contexts during, after, or before conflict, in which the governance agenda is merely a hope. The optimist views the democratic role of the news media, in as many contexts as possible, as that of a watchdog, agenda setter, and gatekeeper. This chapter points to variables that influence how realistic the optimistic agenda may be, principally by looking at patterns of evolution in political structure.

There is little that is static about the peace-building process. The postconflict period can extend for many years, particularly if fundamental issues have yet to be resolved. The complex state and nation-building processes cannot be seen simply as short transitional periods but may continue for decades. Even if the postconflict period could be bounded, opportunities during this stage are, to a great extent, shaped by media approaches both before and during the conflict. This study focuses on two cases—Ethiopia and Iraq—that represent very different instances and stages of peace building.

Both countries have experienced significant violent conflict and have liberalized their media systems to some degree. Ethiopia and Iraq are, however, at different points in the nation- and state-building process. In Ethiopia, after a decades-long civil war that ended in the early 1990s, pockets of conflict continue. Fifteen years later, there are fundamental disagreements, particularly among elites, about the constitution and the nature of the state. There has been no effective process of reconciliation and the media have been deeply polarized, reflecting some of the divisions. In Iraq, the government's project to bring peace has been similarly complex. Despite recent progress, Iraq is still largely a country in conflict, where the central government struggles to set the national agenda and maintain peace.

This chapter does not set out to directly compare Ethiopia and Iraq, but rather to ask similar questions in the two contexts, in an effort to draw out some issues as to why a liberalized press after violent conflict might not contribute to the governance agenda. The bias of this study is empirical, responding to the need to ask what role the media should play normatively in these societies, and how the media-political relationship is actually shaped in practice. On the political side, the question could be how the state and other actors have sought to shape the media space, and with what discourse or methods. More broadly, how has the process of reconciliation progressed? How has the government incorporated (or failed to incorporate) different perspectives, how has it sought to engage with those that represent different viewpoints, and what is the government's approach to dialogue?

Because the media in such environments often do not necessarily perform the watchdog, agenda setting, or gatekeeping functions specifically assigned in the ideal, a diagnostic mode is needed for thinking of these contexts. The study posits four questions: (1) Do the media foster a process of dialogue between government and insurgents or between opposition groups or political parties, or a process of power sharing? (2) Do the media help define the question "what is the nation"? (3) Does their functioning contribute to a viable state capable of governing? And (4), reflected in the above three, at a minimum are the media restrained from encouraging violent outcomes?

*If power sharing and dialogue* are keys to conflict resolution—as they seem to be in some, though not all, contexts—then one question might be, what media arrangements make dialogue more effective, including dialogue leading to power sharing? And what media arrangements then maintain the power-sharing agreement that was put in place (by agreement or by imposition)?

In terms of *framing the state, or nation*, Nancy Fraser recently discussed some of these issues.[1] Originally, Fraser considered that it was important to look at the shift in thinking about justice from redistribution to representation. But she has recently revised this to think about what she calls the "who" factor, namely, the frame in which issues of redistribution and representation are contained. In thinking about conflict zones and structure of the media, this issue of the frame—in this instance the nature of the entity that is to emerge or about which an architecture should be decided—is obviously both the understood objective and the overriding complexity. In many (though not all) conflict zones, the very definition of the frame is fundamental to determining the approach to understanding the nature of the media. The frame influences what would be considered pluralist and what remedy there is for intense partisanship. The media both participate in and reflect the negotiation of the frame itself. The media have a central role in providing this space and negotiating and articulating divergent perspectives—for example, by reflecting reconciliation and building consensus on historical events—but the involvement of the state in negotiation and dialogue is key.

In terms of *media enabling government to govern*, in 2006, the Crisis States Programme at the London School of Economics (LSE) issued a report called "Why Templates for Media Development Do Not Work in Crisis States." This was a somewhat controversial report, partly because it sought to part from orthodox approaches to the functioning of the media (both press and broadcast) in conflict zones. Almost by definition, the situation of *governance* in a fragile state is itself in the balance. The process of elite coalition formation is central to obtaining a context in which an entity can and does govern, and the role of the media in this project is an important, often overlooked role. In a recent paper, James Putzel, one of the authors of the LSE report, argues that in the Democratic Republic of Congo, "Standard templates of 'good governance' involving the devolution of power and the promotion of private and non-governmental agents of development may be, not only inadequate to the challenge of state-building, but positively counter-productive if not accompanied by singular efforts to support elite coalition formation and significantly increase capacity at the level of the central state."[2]

This process of elite coalition formation is closely linked to the idea of power sharing. Florian Bieber, who has studied postconflict states in the former Yugoslavia, locates the systematic failures of power sharing in "the lack of consensus among the political elites from the different communities over the state and the institutional set-up."[3] Bieber seeks to determine "the broader significance for our understanding of accommodating diversity in post-conflict societies." Power sharing can be imposed externally or reached by compromise (or a combination of various methods), with different results.

As to *avoiding violence and preventing civil war*, Donald Ellis[4] and Robin Williams[5] provide detailed studies of how ethnic divisions in the former Yugoslavia and Rwanda were mobilized through the use of media to activate ethnic identities for the gains of political elites, though they give only a partial insight into the factors that motivate conflict media. An International Media Support (IMS) report outlines several factors that encouraged the emergence of a conflict media in Rwanda: a strong ideology, control over a mass media, psychological preparation to hate, and a call to violence.[6] A strong ideology is propagated by prominent academics, journalists, or politicians who develop theories of their ethnic or sectarian group. Such theories in the media portray their group as a "stronger race" and "a race with a glorious past," or as victims who have to unite in order to deal with a threat posed by other groups so that they will not be eliminated from the political process or annihilated from within the state altogether. In the final case, violence conducted by one community against the other is portrayed as a matter of self-defense. Without sufficiently considering the political and historical context, or the role of the state, these frameworks risk characterizing conflicts as tribal and the expression of deep-seated hatreds—a simplistic presentation often employed by the media. Nevertheless, these factors are useful in beginning to identify the emergence of conflict media.

This chapter turns first to Ethiopia and then to Iraq as part of an ongoing study of how the media structure relates to the four factors set out above, and how media development reflects or influences power structures. In both cases, questions about who is participating in the nation-building project are asked, including whose definitions and historical visions are being reconciled, and who is competing for power. The media not only are active participants but also reflect these processes.

In Ethiopia, the focus is on the printed press, and in the case of Iraq, the focus is on broadcasting. Radio stations have strongly affected the media landscape across much of Africa in interesting and important ways, but Ethiopia has been excluded from this trend. Newspapers, however, set the media agenda in the early 1990s, when many African governments were changing, and have retained their importance across much of the continent. In Iraq, on the other hand, there has been a burgeoning of both broadcast and print media in the postwar period, with radio and television having a strong impact.

## Ethiopia

After seizing power in 1991, the Tigrayan People's Liberation Front's (TPLF) guerrilla commander, Meles Zenawi, sought to differentiate himself from his predecessors and generate domestic and international support for the new regime. One way he did this was through some liberalization of the media space. A free press was compatible with the TPLF's political ideology, revolutionary democracy, and was also a response to domestic and international pressures calling for a competitive political space. Tolerating media freedoms helped the image of Meles as one of Africa's "new leaders" presiding over a democratically inclined developmental state. There was a widespread hope that he, along with others in the region, including Yoweri Museveni from Uganda, Isais Afeworki from Eritrea, and Paul Kagame from Rwanda, would bring about a broader African renaissance. None of these leaders, however, has relinquished control, and each still presides over a highly centralized autocratic regime.

Until the aftermath of contentious elections in 2005, Ethiopia's press was vibrant but deeply polarized. It served as a principal forum for expressing perspectives that diverged from the ruling party on issues that have been dividing Ethiopian society for decades, such as the rights of ethnic groups, land ownership, and a federalist constitution. The postelection period exposed critical failings in the nation- and state-building project. In widespread violence, more than 100 people were killed, mostly by government forces, and tens of thousands were arrested. Dozens of journalists were jailed, as was a substantial part of the leadership of the opposition Coalition for Unity and Democracy (CUD) party. The private press has largely been silenced and is no longer able to serve as the forum for alternative visions of nation building, as it once did. In an effort to understand the role of the media in postwar Ethiopia, this chapter visits each of the four questions proposed for the media in postconflict environments, reflecting on the critical decisions that were made in the early 1990s, as well as on the factors the led up to the 2005 elections, in which the media suffered dramatic closures.

## Do the Media Facilitate a Process of Dialogue?

Despite the attempts by some in the media to negotiate different visions of Ethiopia, the government, a crucial partner in any postwar dialogue, has refused to participate in dialogue. The TPLF saw little need to directly engage those whom it defeated, particularly those that were aligned with the communist Derg regime that the TPLF overthrew.

Because the TPLF's power base was located in Tigray, a region in northern Ethiopia with less than 10 percent of the country's population, the group had little choice but to form a multiethnic coalition. The Ethiopian People's Revolutionary Democratic Front (EPRDF) was formed by the TPLF several years before it successfully defeated the Derg regime and came to Addis. In theory, the EPRDF was to be an umbrella organization holding together different political parties representative of the complex Ethiopian landscape. But not all opposition groups were eager to join the EPRDF, and many groups that did join became quickly disenchanted during the transitional period. Despite repeated calls from those in the previous government and others who felt excluded from the transitional government, the TPLF pursued its own agenda with little compromise. The TPLF also believed that tangible development rather than persuasion or dialogue would convince the rest of the country of the merit of its policies and leadership. This strategy emerged from the TPLF's experience of convincing the peasantry to join the struggle during the war.

The unilateral process of constitution making has polarized the press and continues to be a deeply divisive and unresolved issue. Central to the TPLF's struggle was the idea that Ethiopia's ethnic diversity would be best served by a federal arrangement that would have at its core the right of secession. The TPLF also made it clear that it planned to continue to control the executive committee and entrenched its power ethnically within the military, as at least 50 percent of the fighters were drawn from Tigray. One of the first (and most contested) actions the EPRDF took when it first came to power was to allow Eritrea to secede.[7] The move angered many and was seen as a unilateral and inadequately consultative decision. Many of the early press commentaries called for a dialogue and national discussion on federalism, which to some Ethiopians was seen as destroying the Ethiopian nation-state. For example, in the early 1990s, in an effort to draw attention to their desire to participate in the political discussions, as well as to express concern, if not outrage, at the federalist arrangement, many political groups came together for the Conference on Peace and Reconciliation. The government refused to engage, claiming there was no need for a peace conference in a country that was already at peace, and labeling the participants as antipeace. Many of the newspapers were behind this conference and actively supporting it. But the government was not willing to recognize the conference or the recommendations and dismissed it as a demand by a limited number of intellectuals. Since those early days, the press has continued calling for reconciliation, power sharing, and more dialogue. In some cases journalists represented the agenda of political parties that were critical of the EPRDF, and in other cases their motives were more personal and ethnically based.

Rather than negotiating with or co-opting opponents, the EPRDF simply ignored them or in some cases tried to isolate them. This strategy further exacerbated an already tense period. As one of former president Mengistu Haile Mariam's former colleagues describes:

> When the TPLF first came they didn't know who was who. They locked us all up. A new order was unfolding. It was not a new government but a new order, a new era. Everything of the other regime was gotten rid of ... Sensitive places were taken over ... [they] didn't want any interference or to coexist with anyone. That was the aspiration of communism and Lenin's [theory of] political cleansing—getting rid of the Tsarists. The EPRDF wanted to get rid of these people so they couldn't have any feelings of the past ... Many of them lost their jobs in the state media. The government sent others to retirement. So people thought it's not a new government, but a new ethnic group.[8]

Many of the journalists who lost their jobs went on to start private publications that were deeply critical of the government.

*Tobiya*, one of the first newspapers that appeared after the EPRDF seized power, became one of the most dynamic, experienced, and influential publications in the immediate postconflict period. The paper began in 1992 with 15 former journalists who had worked for the Ministry of Information during the Derg, as well as some who were outside the Ministry. The founders included Mulugeta Lule, former editor of the Derg party's magazine, and Goshu Mogus, who ran the censorship office for the Derg. Mairegu Bezibeh, another journalist for *Tobiya*, spent a year and a half in jail on charges of genocide for having executed more than 300 people under the Derg, but the EPRDF government could not prove the case.[9]

The background of many of these journalists is fundamental to understanding the role a substantial portion of the press has played in Ethiopia, why the government has been reluctant to engage, and why the press has been so polarized. First, the conflict between some journalists and EPRDF leaders dates back decades to the student movement in the early 1970s. During this period, contentious debates over Marxist-Leninist ideology took place, and rifts between student groups (which included precursors to the TPLF and the Derg) over issues such as the role of ethnic identities were evident. Second, after a long guerrilla struggle, the EPRDF, when it came to power, felt little need to negotiate or include those that it defeated or those that were also fighting the Derg at the same time, since the TPLF "carried the others on its shoulders."[10] Because the EPRDF did not consider it necessary to explain its actions or policies domestically, Meles would seldom speak with or even acknowledge private journalists. Not only were journalists of private papers unable to write balanced reports, but the exclusion also contributed to a deep level of frustration. By failing to engage with the private press, or the arguments themselves, the government has done little to create a political mainstream or to facilitate a dialogue.

## Do the Media Help Define the Question of "What Is a Nation"?

In Ethiopia, a consensus on "what is a nation" has yet to be entirely established, partly because the above-mentioned dialogue between elite constituencies—including the press and those in power—failed to occur.

The government press has been strongly propagandistic and has not even acknowledged alternative positions on key policies. But since its establishment in the early 1990s, the independent press, including *Tobiya*, has been presenting contrasting visions of the Ethiopian state. This segment of the press has come to reflect the political divisions of the disenfranchised ethnic groups, particularly the Amhara, who dominate the intellectual class and were the major force in Ethiopian politics for generations. For the many private journalists who see national identity as a single Ethiopia of "one people" that was built by the imperial regimes, the EPRDF's deconstruction of this idea has been deeply disturbing and something that the media continue to address.

The editorial policy of *Tobiya* on this issue was clear. According to Derbew Temesgen, a founding journalist, "the editorial policy was against ethnic politics and against the separation of Eritrea. Ethnic politics is not good for the unity of the country."[11] The papers and magazines consistently argued against the right to secession and often accused the Ethiopian government of allowing Eritreans to intervene in, if not overtly control, local affairs.[12] The paper would also argue for reconciliation or a new spirit of forgiveness,[13] as well as suggest that the current government should be held accountable for current violations of human rights, as it was aspiring to do for former leaders of the Derg.[14] Indeed, early editorials and articles emphasize this line. The following example illustrates the arguments that were common in the early months of publication:

The attempt by the fascist Italians to divide the people and the country was not successful, but now it is getting rooted thanks to the current regime. The people

of the country are being divided along ethnic lines … The 1991 Charter follows
and adheres to the secessionist ideology of a few Eritreans … The attempt to
view unity as a marriage is very simplistic and incorrect. The people of Ethiopia
are connected by history, nature, culture, and psychological make-up … We
also think that no group should be allowed to disintegrate the country. In the
new Ethiopia, the unique and terrifying term is "unity." The charter is not in
favor of unity … The regime supports the division and disintegration of the
country and we think this is the first national government to do such a thing in
the world.[15]

While the private press has been effective in discussing issues of national
identity, the system as a whole has been too polarized to set or define a national agenda. Much of the failure lies with the government for refusing to
engage in these serious discussions or to respond to the arguments presented
in the private press. Until the 2005 elections, the government thought such
criticism was relatively restricted to the literate elites in Addis Ababa. After
the elections the government has felt so threatened by these competing ideas
that any possibility for such discussion is severely limited. Existing papers are
allowed to be critical of the government but only on the implementation, not
the fundamentals, of policies (such as ethnic federalism). This is related to the
third point of this analysis, which looks at the contribution of the media in
state building, and particularly emphasizes the role of the government.

### Do the Media Help Contribute to Establishing a Viable State Capable of Governing?

The private press has not been able to contribute to the goal that there be
a viable state capable of governing. This is primarily for two reasons. First,
the government's unwillingness to include the press in a national project or
engage in any sort of dialogue has limited the press's potential role in state
building. Second, government press and propaganda efforts have failed to encourage trust and reconciliation, instead increasing tensions and polarization.
Successive Ethiopian governments have regularly modeled their development
strategies on the experiences of other countries.[16] Ethiopia's present vision of
a developmental state draws on the experiences of the Republic of Korea and
Taiwan, where criticism and opposition parties are tolerated, as long as they
do not present a serious distraction to the ruling party's leadership and, particularly, the state's economic development.

Meles's arguments on defining fundamental policies clearly establish a
precedent that the debates within the media are to center around issues of
development, rather than political questions, such as the constitution or issues
of secession, federalism, or land. In the school of journalism,[17] lecturers argue
that journalists should follow the developmental role of the media in China.
Similarly, journalists and the editors at the government media outlets emphasize their role in the economic development of the country.

The EPRDF's overall strategy for managing information flows is to control the message from the center to the periphery. Information and communication technologies (ICTs), for example, have become a major tool for centralizing EPRDF control and ensuring that cadres across the country are conveying the same message. This communication, though employing an interactive mechanism, is largely one-way. Meles or another party leader disseminates a message through videoconferencing or through local officials who are trained in party ideology. Since 2005, there have been some efforts to use ICT, through a project called WoredaNet, for two-way communication, with local officials offering reports to regional heads about the situation within their area, but this has not been the government's focus.

Overall, the EPRDF's basic information strategy targets the peasantry. This has received a greater push in the aftermath of the 2005 elections. There are parallels between the current strategy as well as the pre-2005 strategy and the strategy used during the guerrilla war. The EPRDF is currently focusing on what Bereket Simon, the political adviser to the EPRDF, calls "the advanced elements of the rural community" or those farmers who are more receptive to party ideals. These people are then organized into small groups that receive training and serve as a source of information but, most important, serve as conduits for developmental messages. At the grassroots level, information is not theoretical; the "advanced elements of the rural community" are encouraged to get rich and then help others to get rich. In this context, radio is used for disseminating best practices of development—particularly agriculture.

However, the focus on the peasantry has come at the expense of other groups, including intellectuals and members of the previous government. As the EPRDF appears to have little desire or strategy to engage such critics, the failure of negotiation of power and voice has exposed dangerous rifts in the state-building process, as most recently demonstrated after the 2005 elections.

### Are the Media Restrained from Encouraging Violence?

In the worst case, the difficulties that the Ethiopian government has had, both in making its own propaganda successful and in effectively managing nongovernmental flows of information, lead to violent outcomes. In the aftermath of the 2005 elections, the media were so deeply polarized that both the private and the government media exacerbated an already delicate situation and had a strong role in provoking the violence.

Though the private press was not overtly calling for violence, the choice of words and discourse on both sides amplified the tensions. The government propaganda is primarily aimed at people in the rural areas whom it views as its real constituencies. But in the postelection period, the government was overwhelmed by the success of the opposition's electoral gains and fearful of what the future held for the ruling EPRDF. Thus, because the government lacked an effective communication strategy and felt exceptionally insecure, it turned to blatant progovernment propaganda. This quickly became counterproductive, particularly among the private press and the opposition supporters, whose messages it was trying to counter.[18] The Cambridge-based scholar Christopher Clapham accurately summed this up in his "Comments on the Aftermath of the Ethiopian Crisis" when he noted:

> It is difficult to exaggerate the enormous amount of damage that has been done to the EPRDF government by Bereket Simon, the former Minister of Information and now information adviser to the Prime Minister, who has become the principal spokesman for the government. His neurotic and consistently inflammatory pronouncements, extending even to threats of an equivalent to the Rwanda genocide, have conveyed a very clear impression, both to the opposition and to the outside world, that the EPRDF is entirely unwilling to engage in any normal or reasonable political process.[19]

The issue of polarization and ethnic divisiveness in the press during the elections has been complex. While it is true that many of the private papers referred to the EPRDF as a minority-led regime and expressed grievances with its ethnic basis, the government also sought to manipulate the ethnicity issue.[20] In many respects it appears, as Clapham suggests, that it has been the government itself that has been exploiting and driving this issue. Although ethnic violence could be a potential problem, it is far from the government-sponsored genocide in Rwanda. As an editorial in *Lisane Hezeb* noted, in the debates, "EPRDF's labeling of CUD [the Coalition for Unity and Democracy] as the Interhamwe of Rwanda is irresponsible."[21]

Similarly, a journalist at the government's Ethiopian News Agency (ENA) anonymously corroborated this when he recognized that:

> At the ENA we have been compiling our reports from the election. The reporting is biased and you can visibly see the difference between pre- and post-election reporting ... The adjectives for the CUD [Coalition for Unity and Democracy—the opposition party] came after polling day. For the city riots there was an established phrase "the street violence that was instigated by the CUD"—everything started with this phrase. It has not yet been investigated yet we accuse them.[22]

Over the past year or so, the government has begun to recognize that it must communicate more effectively if it wishes to remain in power but also reduce the possibility of political violence. This strategy is part of its developmental agenda (and a renewed emphasis on communicating development projects rather than politics) but is also evident in the continued closure of political space. In 2008 the government proposed new civil society legislation that will close many of the local nongovernmental organizations, and virtually all of the international ones, that work in the human rights and governance fields. In addition, the government continues to restrict the flow of competing ideas, whether in the newspapers, on the radios, or in blogs. With this continued censorship the propensity for violence in the short term may be hindered, but in the long term the situation that provoked the violence in 2005 remains unresolved. Because the Ethiopian nation- and state-building project remains precarious, it is likely that in the future the media may reemerge as a force that will lead to even greater violence.

## Iraq

Iraq presents an enormous contrast to Ethiopia. Among the many political variables that appear, Iraq is an instance of "occupation," as compared with radical domestic change in Ethiopia; there are large-scale shifts in the technology of media delivery in Iraq compared with milder technological change in Ethiopia; and perhaps most important, the powers in Ethiopia have the capacity to seek to impose information hegemony, even while harboring some pluralism, as opposed to the absence of authoritarian control over media in postconflict Iraq. Iraq became a theater for competition among many influences (using satellites, for example), while in Ethiopia the media players were fewer though intense.

The availability of media in Iraq changed drastically with the 2003 war. Prior to 2003, media options were limited: newspapers, and radio and television stations, were owned by the state, and satellite TV and Internet could be accessed only by Ba'ath Party elites. Following the war, more than a hundred newspapers emerged, reflecting political parties espousing everything from communist to Kurdish nationalist to Islamist ideologies. Iraqi citizens can now access the Internet, freely own satellite dishes, and access hundreds of terrestrial and satellite radio and TV stations broadcasting from within Iraq and from the region.

In Iraq, the idea of a balanced and pluralistic media was established as a goal, first in the Athens Conference that was held shortly after the U.S. invasion, but, more important, in the key Coalition Provisional Authority Orders 65 and 66, issued March 20, 2004, which articulated the generally accepted objectives for an idealized postconflict media. Order 65 created a National Communications and Media Commission (NCMC) designed, in part, to "encourage pluralism and diverse political debate"; Order 66 established the equivalent of a public service broadcaster (from the shell of state television). In 2004, the NCMC issued an Interim Broadcasting Programme Code of Practice that provided standards to avoid violence. For example, the code provided that "Programmes shall meet with generally accepted standards of civility and respect for ethnic, cultural and religious diversity of Iraq."[23] Despite the efforts to establish an ideal media system, the postwar development of Iraq's media indicates the difficulties encountered in implementation in the context of a continuing conflict, in particular in relation to issues of dialogue, the framing of the state, governance, and the promotion of violence.

As Iraq pursued democratization after 2003, the postwar chaos led to fractured identities based on ethnic, sectarian, and tribal divisions. The nation's Shia, Sunnis, Kurds, Turkmens, and Christians found themselves in a security vacuum within a fragile political system dominated by exiled and opposition organizations, for the most part formed along ethnosectarian lines. Facing weak state institutions, Islamist parties in the government, as well as the opposition, augmented their power with calls for nationalism. Political elites, opposition leaders, and nonstate actors, employing methods of patronage-based politics that have characterized the Iraqi state since its formation in the 1920s, mobilized ethnosectarian communities, enshrining the insecurity and warlordism based on primordial identities.

The embattled government has been unable to effectively enforce media legislation or regulate media outlets and media content, and unlicensed radio and TV stations have proliferated. When the NCMC was established, and when its licensing mandate was implemented, little attention was paid to the relationship between license applicants and power distribution within the society. The model for issuing licenses was basically first-come, first-served, as long as applicants met prescribed standards. Groups not meeting these standards also obtained media outlets to assist their cause through various mechanisms, including self-help, operation in an unlicensed manner, and satellite broadcasting without a license.

The result has been the positive, though accidental, emergence of a pluralistic media sector. As in other contexts, in the wake of conflict and the recent establishment of an independent media, since the 2003 Iraq War, ideal internal media pluralism is hardly present.[24] Most of the stations in Iraq are now independently owned, but they operate as extensions of ethnosectarian political institutions. The dominant Arab media are owned by Islamist parties, and various political factions, deeming it necessary to have a TV channel to convey political propaganda and to inspire their constituents, have media outlets at their disposal. The largest Shia, Arab Sunni, and Kurdish parties own satellite channels—Al-Furat TV, Al-Baghdad TV, and Kurdsat, respectively—that are viewed in Iraq and abroad.

During times of political stability among the factions, Iraq's polarized pluralistic media ownership reflects that stability. During times of discord and disintegration, however, media polarization further undermines the capacity of the weak state to govern, and the political parties have the capability of reinforcing the country's sectarian divisions. In late 2007, Iraqi Sunni Islamist factions and tribes began to oppose the strict religious parastate created by

Al-Qa'ida, eventually realigning themselves against the terrorists. The tribes coalesced into the Reawakening Councils known as Al-Sahwa' and managed to bring relative stability to their areas, forcing Al-Qa'ida elements to disperse and seek refuge in other parts of Iraq. Once this conflict de-escalated, so did the "war of the airwaves." As of 2008, no Iraqi channels have directly incited one party to violence, but nevertheless there are a multitude of channels that form an ethnosectarian media landscape, reflecting the political structure that emerged in Iraq as of 2003.

Studies conducted by the United States Institute of Peace on media in conflict states warn of the capability of media becoming tools of warlords as a result of rushed and hastily conceived media plans.[25] Izabella Karlowicz, in her work on media development in postconflict Balkans, warns that "unregulated media may be dangerous and can encourage, rather than calm, nationalistic tendencies." Karlowicz highlights "the dangers of poorly planned assistance to the development of the Fourth Estate in post-conflict areas, which may cause an outburst of ethnic conflict rather than fostering peaceful cohabitation."[26] Just such an "outburst of ethnic conflict," in Karlowicz's words, or in the Iraqi case, "ethnosectarian conflict," has become a reality.

The literature on ethnic conflict stresses that ethnic cleavages in deeply divided societies are not precursors in and of themselves for intrastate violence. Rather, it is the mobilization techniques used by political elites that engage communal groups and gear them up for an identity conflict.[27] Jenkins and Gottlieb define identity conflict as "any rivalry between two or more groups that define themselves in mutually exclusive terms that use a collective 'we/they' definition."[28] Political Islamist elites make other communities scapegoats as a strategy to legitimize their rule. In the Middle East, elites often blame the "others" for problems, diverting attention from their own shortcomings. Such elites, it is argued, "present themselves as loyal protectors of group heritage. By propagating ethnic ideologies that dehumanize or devalue other groups, these ethnic entrepreneurs incite hatred and mobilize attacks."[29] This theoretical approach is valuable when bearing in mind that numerous ethnic groups in deeply divided societies do not engage in organized political actions based on a collective identity basis. Williams argues that a first requirement for a group to take part in a conflict is some sort of mobilization based on a real or imagined grievance shared among the identity based-group: "Without some sense of grievance, people do not mobilize."[30] In fact, over centuries, Iraq's Shia have followed a tradition of political quietism, enduring or acquiescing to their lack of power during the Ottoman era and the formation of the Republic of Iraq. It was only after 2003, when the Shia became full participants in the political process, with access to political parties and the agencies of the state, that Shia political elites emerged to move this group to action.

This study posed the following questions about the role of the media in postconflict environments to understand how mobilization and patronage have affected media developments in Iraq.

## Do the Media Facilitate a Process of Dialogue?

Iraq's ethnosectarian media were established to represent positions to polarized sectors, not necessarily as instruments of dialogue, yet the pluralistic media environment that emerged in the chaos of the postwar period has allowed more dialogue to occur than would otherwise.

The political movements that took part in the January and December 2005 elections mobilized as Kurdish, Shia, and Sunni Islamist parties that maintained their own militias. These parties, as in most nearly every conflict in a deeply divided society, were the first to organize and did well in postconflict elections. The ethnosectarian factions, some radical, rallied support among the populace on a platform of promising to protect each community's identity-based interests. One could characterize the dynamic as "mediated patronage." The parties demonstrated that they could provide security for their own media, highlighting the successes of their security forces against the insurgents. In this fray of mediated patronage, political parties and movements based on nonsectarian platforms did not have time to develop before the elections were held and thus could not provide this protection for their constituencies; voters thus chose parties along the ethnosectarian divide.

Thus, rather than seeking to promote or foster dialogue, the party and militia that owned each channel promised protection from the inimical other and dominance in the political process. The parties sought to employ agenda-setting tactics to further their view on the role of Islam in the state, the nature of federalism, and how to maintain security, all of which are intimately related with issues of power sharing. Federalism would augment the Kurdish and Shia parties' power, at the expense of Sunni and Turkmen parties, while an Islamist state would augment the power of the Shia Islamist parties and threaten the power of secular Kurdish parties. Thus, dialogue on these channels was hardly encouraged, and contradicting viewpoints were neglected. The channels owned by political factions also failed to foster dialogue by excluding guests from other communities on their political, social, or religious programs. For example, religious programming on Sunni channels tended to host only Arab Sunni clerics, and a political talk show on a Shia channel would primarily feature Arab Shia politicians.

Pluralism also allowed an Iraqi media with no political affiliation and agenda to emerge; these media are trying to provide an alternative to the Islamist media owned by ethnic Kurdish and Turkmen or sectarian Shia and Sunni political parties. The Al-Baghdadiyya TV channel (not to be confused with the Al-Baghdad station) has ensured that guests on its program include Arab Shia and Sunni, Kurds, and Christians.

## Do the Media Help Define the Question of "What Is a Nation?"

The post-2003 Iraq conflict emerged as an identity-based struggle that failed to form a cohesive Iraqi nation. The notion of an Iraqi nation is contested and still in flux. Arab Sunni parties tend to favor the status quo; they declare loyalty to a centralized Iraqi nation that is part of the greater Arab world and oppose plans for a future federated Iraq as a "foreign scheme" to divide the nation and leave them in a landlocked state. The Shia and Kurdish parties tend to favor a binational federation that distances itself from the political conflicts in the region; the Kurdish parties' vision seeks a Kurdish regional government administering the multiethnic, oil-rich city of Kirkuk.

The state-owned Iraqi Media Network constructed by the U.S. Coalition Provisional Authority (CPA) under Order 66 had the aim of reinforcing a national identity, but the ability to accomplish that goal was mired in banal contracting and confused goals during the critical period of the channel's formation. The IMN, and its flagship station, Al-Iraqiyya, stands, though weakly, for a unified country, but its alliance with the ruling party has called into question its ability to broker among candidates and parties. According to its critics, the station, reflecting its relationship with the current government (dominated by an alliance of Shia Islamist groups, known as the United Iraqi Alliance, and an alliance of ethnic Kurdish groups, known as the Kurdish Coalition), has an inherent Shia-Kurdish bias. However, the station has tried to encourage dialogue by allowing more of its content to be devoted to Arab Sunni and Turkmen guests, who use the channel to express their grievances, if not criticize the government directly. Furthermore the station has attempted to minimize the differences between Iraq's Sunni and Shia by broadcasting live coverage of Friday sermons in which religious leaders from both communities preach against the nation's sectarian divide and stress "Iraqi unity." It also holds televised meetings between Shia and Sunni leaders as a means of intersectarian dialogue.

The capacity to maintain an information hegemony with respect to defining the state was strongly affected by the existence of the abundant private media. In postwar Iraq, some private media seek to stress the unity of Islam in Iraq and forge a concept of a unified Iraqi nation. While the Shia Al-Furat channel has a distinct Shia leaning, it does not focus on issues of ethnicity. Songs between programs support peace and unity among Iraq's various ethnic and sectarian communities, and the station avoids direct references to the Shia as a distinct religious group, emphasizing Iraqi unity based on an inclusive Iraqi Muslim identity. The news program rarely refers to Iraq as part of the "Arab world" as do other Arab Sunni or independent Iraqi satellite channels. The Al-Sumariyya channel produces its own announcements that call for peace among Iraq's communities. The station also features on-the-street interviews with the Iraqi public and interviews with program guests, who stress unity among Sunni and Shia. Al-Baghdadiyya stresses that it seeks to promote

Iraqi culture and to urge Iraqis "to unite" through various advertisements and music clips.

Alongside these calls for unity, private Iraqi media with ownership in the hands of competing political Islamist and ethnic factions reflect these conflicting ethnosectarian agendas. While no party seeks to break up the Iraqi nation, each party argues that it is best suited to be at the helm of power, and knows what is best for Iraq. Paradoxically, while each party stresses its commitment to Iraqi unity, the ethnosectarian media have exhibited the potential to widen the gap between Iraq's communities and weaken any kind of national belonging. Though none of Iraq's ethnosectarian parties sought the state's partition during the most intense periods of the sectarian conflict, their media ultimately served the goal of enhancing the power of the parties that owned them. The result that emerged was not a national media sphere, but ethnosectarian media "spherecules," further developing identities along sectarian lines and setting the country on a course of partition in terms of identity. Iraqis who watch only Shia, Sunni, or Kurdish channels may have communal loyalties to begin with, or these channels can further the formation of communal identities. Regardless, these channels do provide the visual imagery and rhetoric to make subnational identities more concrete.

### Do the Media Help Contribute to Establishing a Viable State Capable of Governing?

As a public service broadcaster, Al-Iraqiyya is inclined to portray the vision that there is a viable state capable of governing. As a result, the channel's programming features mostly progovernment programs that stress optimism in the progress being made in reconstruction and security. In its depictions of violence, the station's progovernment line is represented with features on the operations of the Iraqi security forces that give viewers the impression that they are taking an active role in quelling insurgent and sectarian violence. The channel also seeks to frame state violence as legitimate by featuring public service announcements calling upon the Iraqi public to volunteer information on the "terrorists."

At the same time, the channel provides a space for Iraq's citizens to interact and communicate with politicians and the government, providing an alternative for the acts of violence that are in themselves protests against the Iraqi state. Shows include live call-in segments to which viewers can direct questions about political affairs to government officials and political leaders. Programs also allow representatives of the state to discuss elections, military operations, and the agendas of various Iraqi political parties, with studio audience participation.

Private channels not affiliated with political parties also offer the Iraqi citizen a civic forum to address constructive criticisms to the Iraqi government through studio or on-the-street interviews or viewer call-ins. For example,

Al-Sumariyya's "Who Is Responsible?" interviews Iraqi citizens on the hardships they face, and then allows the invited guest, usually a government official, on the show to discuss how they are dealing with these problems.

Because the Shia party that owns the Furat channel is dominant in the government, Furat's programs tends to frame violence in Iraq with a progovernment stance, just as Al-Iraqiyya does. Programs on the Kurdish-owned stations stress the progress of the Kurdish north, the ability of the parties to provide security, and support for Kurdish members of the government.

On the far end of the spectrum, the case of the Al-Zawra satellite channel, owned by Mishan Al-Jaburi, a renegade member of the Iraqi government, illustrates how unregulated, free media can pose a danger to a postconflict state. Following Mishan's expulsion from the National Assembly, the channel evolved into a platform for insurgents, airing insurgent-produced videos with footage of attacks against multinational forces. When former Iraqi president Saddam Hussein's death sentence was announced on November 5, 2006, Al-Zawra featured videos and songs supportive of the outlawed Ba'ath party, as well as exhortations for Iraqis to join groups fighting the U.S. "occupation forces" and the Iraqi government and its "sectarian gangs."

### Are the Media Restrained from Encouraging Violence?

After 2003, most Iraqi Islamist parties used their media to stress unity among Iraq's communities. However, from 2004 to 2007, and particularly following the February 2006 bombing of the revered Shia Al-'Askariyya shrine in the city of Samarra—when intercommunal violence between Shia and Sunni was at its highest—the various sectarian and ethnic factions used their media outlets to legitimize the violence and portray their respective groups as victims, encouraging both Shia and Sunni to defend themselves in the ensuing sectarian conflict.

Shia TV channels sought to inflame tensions by blaming Sunni Muslims for targeting their communities. (This discourse does not target Iraq's Sunni population per se, but rather attacks the foreign Arab fighters who came to Iraq who subscribe to the Wahhabi or Salafist ideologies, and those Iraqis who cooperate with them.) The Shia channels provided a visual discourse that stressed notions of a past marred by "victimization," and of a community "oppressed" since the Ottoman Empire and the creation of the Iraqi state. Such suffering culminated under Saddam Hussein's rule. Victimization was also expressed after suicide attacks on the Shia religious Ashura processions and after attacks on Shia shrines. Shia channels have called on the Shia to have faith in the security forces (most of whom are Shia) to restore stability. Furthermore, the Shia media have expressed a sense of abandonment by the predominantly Sunni Arab world. Al-Furat TV, owned by the largest Shia party, covers intersectarian violence against Iraq's Shia Muslims, although the station does not advocate revenge but rather patience and obedience to those Shia leaders who have called for restraint. Another example is the TV show "Deported in the Homeland," which profiles internally displaced families (most of whom are Shia, as evidenced by the last names of those interviewed and the phrases used) who have relocated because of sectarian violence.

On the other side, the Arab Sunni discourse focuses on notions of "disempowerment" and "victimization" at the hands of U.S. "occupying forces," and the "militias," a euphemism for Shia death squads that operate privately or within the Iraqi security forces. For example, Sunni Islamist channels highlighted, if not glorified, insurgent attacks against U.S. forces (this practice ended after the parties entered into an alliance with the Iraqi government). A dominant frame on Al-Baghdad is "resistance" to the U.S military forces, referred to as "occupation forces." This view of violence in Iraq mirrors the Arab Sunni Accord Front's. Unlike Al-Iraqiyya or Al-Furat, this station refers to insurgents as "armed men" rather than "terrorists." Al-Baghdad did not incite violence, but did legitimize nonstate violence.

Although channels like Al-Zawra directly incited violence, and provided a channel for insurgents to air their broadcasts, channels with no political affiliation have refused to air any material that incites ethnic or sectarian divisions. For example, Al-Sumariyya, which claims no affiliation with any sectarian, ethnic, or political party, does not carry live statements or press conferences of any Iraqi politicians, indicating the station's effort to maintain its neutrality. Al-Diyar rarely shows live footage of the aftermath of insurgent attacks; its news programs usually focus on domestic news, with an emphasis on social affairs rather than violence.

Following the violence that ensued after the 2006 bombing of the Al-'Askariyya shrine, the various sectarian and ethnic media outlets eventually called for restraint among Iraq's communities, and tensions further de-escalated by 2007 with the closure of Al-Zawra.

## Conclusions

This has been a study in contrasts in terms of control of information, stability, nation building, and maturation of political institutions. What is clear from the study, however, is that a reformulated grid of press functions needs to be defined in postconflict contexts. It is not enough to say that the media should serve the roles established in the ideal of watchdog, agenda setter, and gatekeeper. In order to understand these adjusted or altered roles, one must examine the players affecting the media market and their goals. Ethiopia and Iraq present two very different examples of the role the media can have in the nature of postconflict governance, with the media in each case either reflecting or exacerbating the divisions and coalitions of elites or other groups.

By looking at select examples of these cases through the framework presented in this chapter, it becomes evident that capacity to govern, stability, and the nation-building project can be anterior or even superior to the media's role in promoting democracy or good governance. Understanding the media's potential for encouraging the development of a stable state is a key part of promoting peace. And although the media reflect the political processes—including that of reconciliation and the development of a government (either coalition or minority led)—they also have a role in these processes. Although it can be useful to suggest, as the normative governance agenda does, that journalists should be watchdogs of the government, focusing on that role leaves little room for understanding the complex ways in which journalists see their work. Journalists often have nuanced roles in the nation- and state-building exercise, which cannot be easily divorced from the political realities.

In both Ethiopia and Iraq, it is evident how quickly after a conflict the media can both reflect and negotiate the process of dialogue and power sharing. For a free media system to be an effective part of the nation-building project, government involvement is required. The leadership has a responsibility to participate in this "elite sphere" by responding to criticisms and debates. If it fails to do so, as has been the case in Ethiopia, the media can contribute little to reconciliation and only exacerbate polarization. This chapter does not argue that polarization is necessarily part of the postconflict period, but circumstances frequently mean that it will be, and any theory of postconflict environments must accommodate that likelihood.

This chapter has dealt with states that deploy language of democratic aspirations but are not comfortably categorized as democratic, nor at peace. Both Ethiopia and Iraq are engaged in a continued nation-building process. Each is a messy, nonlinear project. If Ethiopia offers any indication, the process of conflict and conflict resolution in Iraq will continue for years; evidence of a free press is only a sign, and not necessarily a convincing one, for those wishing the nation to be on a democratic trajectory. The examples from this chapter do provide some indications of how to mitigate the chances that a polarized media system exacerbates the potential for instability and violence. In each case the structure of the media must be seen in relationship to the political process—the consolidation of power; reconciliation; power sharing; and the relationship between present, future, and past regimes and their efforts at building a state and extending power.

All this must be kept in mind when considering what, if any, relationship might exist between the media and a governance agenda. The nature of the crisis and the complexity of the factors at play indicate why polarized media or government control are often the outcome in these contexts, as well as why prevention of violence, the framing of the state, and the contribution to dialogue and conflict resolution are so significant in describing the way the media function.

Policies should also recognize this reality and work to understand the polarization in the broader processes of nation building, what opportunities can be taken from the situation, and how all actors should best engage in the circumstances. The emerging state can have a strong role in defining the frame of the nation, but polarization and segmentation may make that problematic. This chapter emphasized the continuum that characterizes preconflict, conflict, and postconflict resolution. One way of increasing the opportunities that may be available to engage with the polarized media is to deepen an understanding of how the government and parties are approaching the information sphere based on their prior experiences of communication, persuasion, and political ideologies. It is usually only the normative governance agenda that assumes a break and a fresh start postconflict; the reality for the actors on the ground is typically more complex and bears the burden of continuity.

External goals are to achieve governments that can govern fairly, and with legitimacy; progress toward democratic values; and an agenda that leads to just outcomes in economic and social progress. This chapter hopes to contribute to understanding this process, starting by understanding contexts where the goals, to varying degrees, seem remote.

## Notes

1. Nancy Fraser. 2008. "Shifting Landscapes of Political Claims Making." Presented at a workshop on "1989 and Beyond: The Future of Democracy," New School, New York, April.
2. James Putzel, Stefan Lindemann, and Claire Schouten. 2008. "Drivers of Change in the Democratic Republic of Congo: The Rise and Decline of the State and Challenges for Reconstruction, A Literature Review." Working paper 26, Development as State-Making series, Crisis States Research Centre, London School of Economics, 2.
3. Florian Bieber. 2008. "Balkans: Promotion of Power-Sharing by Outsiders." Paper presented at Sawyer Seminar, University of Pennsylvania, April 15.
4. Donald G. Ellis. 2006. *Transforming Conflict: Communication and Ethnopolitical Conflict.* New York and Oxford: Rowman and Littlefield, 66–7.
5. Robin M. Williams, Jr. 2003. *The Wars Within: Peoples and States in Conflict.* Ithaca and London: Cornell University Press, 151.
6. Monique Alexis and Ines Mpambara. 2003. "IMS Assessment Mission: The Rwanda Media Experience from the Genocide." International Media Support, Copenhagen.
7. The TPLF fought against Mengistu with the Eritrean People's Liberation Front (EPLF).
8. Interview with a former colleague of Mengistu, 2005.
9. During Mairegu's time as editor-in-chief of *Tobiya,* he was also charged with murder, but the charge was downgraded to incitement. This experience encouraged him to take time off from the paper and work as an information officer at the European Union. He later began teaching in the Department of Journalism at Unity College and remained involved with the newspaper, helping to start and write for *Lisane Hezeb.*
10. Interview with Ahmed Hassan, 2008.
11. Interview with Derbew Temesgen, 2006.
12. Editorial, *Tobiya,* January 13, 1994, quoted in *Press Digest,* January 20, 1994, 4.
13. For example, an article from *Tobiya* on July 21, 1994, argued "there is a need for a spirit of forgiveness which is a prime requirement for reconciliation and reconstruction. In Ethiopia, the government is actively advancing enmity between the peoples of

Ethiopia through the media and has also been living in the past in the last three-and-a-half years. Such dishonest and politically dangerous ways are pursued in order to monopolize power. This country's future rests not on any one dominant group but on every Ethiopian" (quoted July 25, 1994, in *Seven Days Update*, p. 6).

14. In an article, a reporter from *Tobiya* argued "the crimes of the past are to be exposed soon and the criminals to be sentenced in public. Yet, there is no proof that the very same crimes are not being repeated today. Human rights organizations repeatedly lament the growing violation of democratic and human rights, indicating that the country is moving from one era of darkness to another (quoted in *Seven Days Update*, November 28, 1994, p. 6).

15. "A Serious Threat Faces the Country More Than Ever." 1994. Editorial, *Tobiya*, February 24, 2.

16. Christopher Clapham. 2006. "Ethiopian Development: The Politics of Emulation." *Commonwealth and Comparative Politics* (1): 137 – 50.

17. The Ethiopian Mass Media Training Institute (EMMTI), which was established in 1996 under the Ministry of Information, has been the central institution for training journalists but has consistently restricted its students to members of the government media.

18. An editorial in *Lisane Hezeb* (August 13, 2003) noted that "the programmes are actually reinforcing people's hatred towards this media."

19. Christopher Clapham. 2005. "Comments on the Political Crisis in Ethiopia." *Ethiomedia.com*, November 14. http://www.ethiomedia.com/fastpress/clapham_on_ethiopian_crisis.html.

20. For a general discussion on ethnic federalism in Ethiopia see David Turton, ed. 2006. *Ethnic Federalism: The Ethiopian Experience in Comparative Perspective.* Oxford: James Currey.

21. *Lisane Hezeb*. Editorial, April 14, 2005. Former U.S. President Jimmy Carter also noted in his election trip report that "The EPRDF's likening the opposition to Rwanda's interhamwe is as, or more, regrettable as are some opposition slurs against the Tigrayans in the ruling party." "Ethiopia Elections: Jimmy Carter Trip Report Postelection Statement," May 19, 2005. http://www.cartercenter.org/news/documents/doc2097.html.

22. Interview with a journalist at the government's Ethiopian News Agency, 2006.

23. Stanhope Centre. n.d. "NCMC Code and Discussion." *Iraq Media Developments Newsletter* 26, http://www.stanhopecentre.org/research/26.shtml#1. Also see the original CPA documents at http://www.cpa-iraq.org/regulations/20040320_CPAORD65.pdf and http://www.cpa-iraq.org/regulations/20040320_CPAORD66.pdf.

24. An important study in this subject in the Balkans is in Izabella Karlowicz. 2003. "The Difficult Birth of the Fourth Estate: Media Development and Democracy Assistance in Post-Conflict Balkans." In *Reinventing Media: Media Policy Reform in East-Central Europe*, ed. Miklos Sukosd and Peter Bajomi-Lazar. Budapest: Central European University Center for Policy Studies.

25. Mark Frohardt and Jonathan Temin. 2003. *Use and Abuse of Media in Vulnerable Societies*. Washington, DC: United States Institute of Peace; Yll Bajraktari and Emily Hsu. 2007. *Developing Media in Stabilization and Reconstruction Operations*. Washington, DC: United States Institute of Peace.

26. Karlowicz. 2003. "The Difficult Birth of the Fourth Estate," 127.

27. J. Craig Jenkins and Esther E. Gottlieb. 2007. *Identity Conflicts: Can Violence Be Regulated?* New Brunswick and London: Transaction, 1; James M. Jasper and Jeff Goodwin. 1999. "Trouble in Paradigms." *Sociological Forum* 14 (1): 107–25, 117.

28. Jenkins and Gottlieb. 2007. *Identity Conflicts*, 1.

29. Ibid., 11.

30. Williams. 2003. *The Wars Within*, 149.

# Part III
# Regional Case-Studies of Media Roles

●
●
●

# 10

# Central and Eastern Europe

Marius Dragomir

European broadcasting has come under fierce criticism in recent years for failing to provide a balanced public forum for all political and cultural perspectives and viewpoints. There are notable examples in Western Europe where public service broadcasters fulfill their mission to provide diversity and pluralism in their programming. In the young democracies in Central and Eastern Europe, however, public service broadcasting is still heavily politicized; every change in political power triggers immediate changes in the management and governing structures of public service broadcasters. Commercial broadcasting in this region often promotes the interests of the broadcasters' owners, which commonly coalesce with those of the political elites. In this environment, examples of objective news coverage and solid investigative reporting are marginal, and public service broadcasting can fail to provide balanced information.

This chapter focuses on Central and Eastern European television in comparison with the experience of Western Europe.[1] This study describes the general historical evolution of European broadcasting, as radio and television in Central and Eastern Europe shifted from the old state-controlled model found under communist regimes to dual systems. The chapter contrasts the public broadcasting and commercial sectors in terms of their regulatory and legal framework, organizational and management structure, audience share, and funding. The chapter also considers the main challenges from digitalization and technological convergence. Given this background, the chapter then analyzes how far television in the region functions in its gatekeeping role as a balanced public forum, considering evidence for evaluating the objectivity of news reporting on television in both public service and commercial broadcasting. Finally, it also describes the watchdog role of television news in ensuring government transparency and efforts to stamp out corruption. Overall, the chapter concludes that serious limits on media systems remain despite considerable reform, and, far from being a balanced public forum or independent watchdog of the powerful, television in the region (especially public broadcasting) continues to favor state interests.

## European Broadcasting at a Glance

This section offers a historical review of the development of European broadcasting, followed by an analysis of audiences and programming available and the main regulatory frameworks for broadcasting that are in place.

### A Historical Outline

The television business in Europe has seen similar, although not simultaneous, development in Western, Central, and Eastern Europe. The sector remained largely controlled by the state for more than half a century. Unlike other systems, such as in the United States, European broadcasting developed over the past three decades on the dual public-private pattern, combining public service broadcasting (increasingly competing with the commercial sector and often becoming the weaker side) and commercial broadcasting (controlled by private owners).

Television in Western Europe was originally envisaged as a national enterprise in charge of promoting culture and education and the dissemination of controlled political information. The Reithian motto "to inform, to educate and to entertain" became, in the early days of broadcasting, the cornerstone of broadcasting, not only in the United Kingdom, but also in other Western European nations. The first phase in the development of broadcasting in Europe was the development of state or public service radio and television. The second phase, which started in 1955 when ITV network kicked off in the United Kingdom, was characterized by the development of the dual system, combining public service broadcasting with private television. The development of the dual system occurred during the 1980s in the rest of Western Europe. In France, for example, the state monopoly on broadcasting saw its final days in 1982, when private players were permitted on the market; however, the state has continued to play an important role in the regulation of broadcasting.

In Central and Eastern Europe, broadcasting remained a state propaganda machine until the fall of the Berlin Wall in 1990. The postcommunist countries in Europe saw a similar, however delayed, pattern of development. Soon after 1990, postcommunist governments in Central and Eastern Europe began the reforms of their national broadcasting systems, which were conducted on two fronts: first, the transformation of state broadcasters into public service broadcasters, and second, the buildup of a private sector in broadcasting with the opening of the frequency spectrum to private players. For example, by 1991 Slovak Television (STV) formally became a public service broadcaster, and in the early 1990s, six private TV operators were licensed. In some countries, the state would-be public service broadcaster maintained its hegemony in broadcasting until the late 1990s. In Hungary, the first private TV operators landed in the country in 1997. The 1990s were marked by a series of turbulent events, including media wars waged by emerging political elites against journalists who were trying to build an independent media sector. At the same time, the process of broadcasting reform was marred by confusion stemming from the lack of clear policies or legal frameworks, which led in many places to an explosion of unlicensed broadcasting outlets. In Poland, for example, by early 1993, 57 illegal television broadcasters were operating; not until 2007 was the licensing of the major nationwide TV broadcasters completed.

Some experts talk about a generic European model that was employed in the course of the media reform in postcommunist nations. The model is based on two components: a private media sector complying with domestic legislation and rules imposed by national regulators, and a public service broadcasting sector, which should be independent from the state. The reform of the broadcasting sector in Central and Eastern Europe was therefore part of a larger process of Europeanization, which encompassed instituting political liberties and building media structures. This process varied widely from country to country and each country has developed its specific broadcasting legislation.[2] Farther east, in some states that gained their independence from the former Soviet Union in the 1990s, such as Uzbekistan or Belarus, one can still see some unreconstructed holdouts of state-controlled broadcasting systems.

## Audiences and Programming

Television markets in Europe are experiencing increasing fragmentation of audiences because of the entrance of more players on the market and the expansion of the distribution networks. However, the bulk of the nationwide audience is still concentrated in many markets on the three largest channels. Croatia, the Czech Republic, and France were among the most concentrated markets in 2006 (see table 10.1). In contrast, the German and Romanian markets were the least concentrated. Worth noting is that the Italian market does not appear as concentrated in various measurements of the number of channels. In reality, in a measure of the influence of the two main broadcasting groups in the country, public service RAI with its three channels, and the private Mediaset group with three channels, Italy is the most concentrated broadcast market in Europe. Mediaset is owned by the Milan entrepreneur Silvio Berlusconi, who returned to power as prime minister, for the third time, in April 2008. As he also controls much of RAI, the Italian public service

**Table 10.1.  Channel Fragmentation Index, 2006**

| Country | Channel fragmentation |
|---|---|
| Czech Republic | 2,706 |
| Croatia | 2,394 |
| France | 1,832 |
| Slovak Republic | 1,773 |
| Poland | 1,585 |
| Slovenia | 1,570 |
| Spain | 1,566 |
| Serbia | 1,490 |
| Hungary | 1,481 |
| Lithuania | 1,451 |
| Italy | 1,428 |
| Estonia | 1,294 |
| United Kingdom | 1,221 |
| Latvia | 1,016 |
| Macedonia, FYR | 927 |
| Bulgaria | 896 |
| Romania | 893 |
| Germany | 792 |

*Sources:* Thomas Kirsch. 2007. *Television 2007. International Key Facts*, October 2007. IP International Marketing Committee (CMI).

*Note:* Fragmentation is measured by the Herfindahl-Hirschman Index: Calculations based on the market shares of channels.

broadcaster, it is safe to say that 90 percent of the Italian media was for almost a decade (except for the period 2006–08, when Berlusconi lost power) in the hands of a single entrepreneur.

In general, in Western European countries, public service television usually commands the largest audience on news programs. In Central and Eastern Europe, however, private TV stations' newscasts tend to dominate (see table 10.2). In 2003, for example, only the public service broadcasters in Bosnia and Herzegovina, Croatia, Italy, Poland, Romania, and the United Kingdom managed to command higher audience shares than their private competitors, and since then, public service broadcasters in Croatia, Poland, and Romania have seen their audiences diminish.

## Regulation

Broadcasting regulation in Europe is part of the broader political process. The main rationale behind the creation of a regulatory framework in the early days of broadcasting was the limited number of frequencies. This "scarcity rationale" called for public service broadcasters to provide generalist channels and to ensure universal coverage, with due care for programming for minorities.[3] Since the beginning, broadcast regulators were under the influence of political institutions and their representatives, who were seen as legitimate representatives of the public. However, the history of broadcasting, mainly in the post-communist countries, was a series of political pressures and interference with

Table 10.2. Most-Watched Newscasts, 2006

| Country | Channel | Type of channel |
|---|---|---|
| Bulgaria | BTV | Private |
| Croatia | HTV1 | Public |
| Czech Republic | TV Nova | Private |
| Estonia | ETV | Public |
| France | TF1 | Private |
| Germany | ARD | Public |
| Hungary | TV2 | Private |
| Italy | Canale 5 | Private |
| Latvia | LNT | Private |
| Lithuania | LTV | Public |
| Macedonia, FYR | A1 | Private |
| Poland | TVP1 | Public |
| Romania | Pro TV | Private |
| Serbia | RTS1 | Public |
| Slovak Republic | TV Markíza | Private |
| Slovenia | Pop TV | Private |
| Spain | TVE1 | Public |
| Switzerland | SF1 | Public |
| Ukraine | Inter | Private |

*Source:* Marius Dragomir and Mark Thompson, eds. 2008. *Television across Europe: Follow-up Reports 2008.* Budapest: Open Society Institute. http://www.mediapolicy.org.

the work of the regulators, aimed at pursuing economic and political interests. The main tasks of the broadcast regulators include the following:

- Licensing of broadcasting activities (including sometimes setting programming criteria and public service obligations in the license contracts)
- Monitoring of how broadcasters fulfill the requirements hammered out in legislation and license contracts
- Enforcement of legal provisions and sanctioning (ranging from warnings to fines and revocation of the broadcast license)

In some countries, the broadcast regulators also have some specific tasks, such as appointing management bodies of the public service broadcasters and developing media policy and proposing laws. Nationwide broadcast regulators regulate all terrestrial broadcasters (nationwide, regional, and local) and broadcasters airing via cable and satellite. In some countries, the state is directly involved in regulating the broadcasting. In Estonia, for example, licensing of private broadcasters and monitoring of their work is carried out by the Ministry of Culture. In the former Yugoslav Republic of Macedonia, until three years ago, the government was licensing broadcasters, albeit in cooperation with the Broadcasting Council. With the change in legislation in 2005, the Macedonian Broadcasting Council took over this task from the government.

The regulatory frameworks in Europe also consist of a technical component, represented by a manager of the frequency spectrum. The influence of technical regulators in broadcasting varies from country to country. Usually their involvement in broadcast regulation is minimal, their task being to inform the broadcast regulator about available frequencies and to confirm to those companies licensed by broadcast regulators the right to use a certain frequency. With the rise of new technologies and convergence of technological platforms, there is a tendency to merge the two regulators. Such models have been established, mostly in Western Europe.[4]

The independence of the regulators is central to the health of the broadcasting sector because the regulators, through their decisions, shape the market. Legislation almost everywhere guarantees freedom of expression and sets obligations on broadcasters to present unbiased and objective information. But how this legislation is implemented depends to a large extent on the regulators who are there to monitor any breaches of legal provisions. However, in this process, regulators are still faced with harsh pressures, most commonly coming from political and business circles.

The appointment procedures still leave room for political interference. The Czech Council for Radio and Television Broadcasting (RRTV) has its members officially appointed by the prime minister. In practice, however, the whole process is in the hands of the Chamber of Deputies, the lower house of Parliament. Their right to appoint and remove these members makes the regulator a heavily politicized institution, which mirrors the political parties in the Chamber of Deputies. The prime minister's final approval is a mere formality.

The involvement of the civil society organizations in the appointment procedures of the regulators was seen by some media observers and critics as a positive step in diluting the political control over these bodies. In Lithuania, a majority of the regulator's members come from professional associations. Nine of the 13 members are appointed by professional organizations or groups, such as painters, cinematographers, writers, and journalists. That process significantly reduced the opportunity for the government or parliament to meddle in the regulator's internal affairs. However, civil society involvement can be easily hijacked by political power and businesses. In some countries, such as the Czech Republic, where civil society organizations can nominate members for the regulatory body, political parties have started to recruit these candidates to serve their interests.

Besides political circles, lobbying of commercial TV stations is also directly threatening the independence of the regulators. There have been numerous cases of corruption involving the broadcasting regulators in Central and Eastern Europe. One of the most notorious of such scandals was the "Rywingate" in Poland, where the National Broadcasting Council was involved in illegally changing legal provisions to satisfy the interests of private media interested in purchasing more outlets.[5] Legislation generally sets provisions on conflict of interest for the regulator's members, barring members of political parties or of government structures and people linked with broadcasting and broadcasting-related companies from being appointed on these bodies. Despite such provisions, in most of the cases, appointees are affiliated with various political circles. Rarely are members of the broadcasting councils appointed based on their professional qualifications.

## Public Service Broadcasting

Public service television has enjoyed a special place in the European broadcasting landscape, being envisaged as a vital contributor to democracy and as a constitutive part of the European cultural heritage. Its mission was also to offer an alternative to, and even to raise the standards of, commercial television.[6] In the past decade, however, public service broadcasting has come under fierce criticism. The European Commission, for example, has demanded more transparency and accountability in the finances of public service broadcasting. The World Trade Organization (WTO) criticized the privileged position that public service broadcasting has been enjoying in terms of funding, which in many cases comes from license fees imposed on households, or state budget money.[7]

During the mid-1990s, the monopoly of the former state broadcasters in Central and Eastern Europe was dismantled. Following the entrance of private broadcasters in these markets, public service broadcasters have seen a continual, and in many cases steep, decline in their audiences. Despite the deteriorating environment for public service broadcasting, the concept still gathers support. "The argument for public service broadcasting remains compelling. Public service broadcasting is not only a bulwark against commercial trends that, left unchecked, would be likely to drive standards further down, reducing the less lucrative strands towards invisibility. It also provides essential leverage for raising standards in all program genres."[8]

### Governing Structures

Although legally, and in theory, public service broadcasting operators are public organizations independent from the state, in Central and Eastern Europe they have always experienced harsh politicization. They have shown acute deficiencies in their governance structures, easy manipulability of the sources of funding, and slow reform of their programming, to be distinguished from commercial broadcasters. It is common for the governing bodies of the public service broadcasters to be filled with people close to the local political elite. It has become a norm that each change in administration triggers immediate changes in the boards and management of the public service broadcasters, which has shown that these stations continue to be treated as the fiefdom of the politicians in power.

The obligations imposed on public service broadcasters are based on three main principles: programming tailored to public service broadcasting, impartial and accurate information, and universal access. The public service broadcasting programming obligations include the following:

- Airing independent, accurate, impartial, balanced, and objective news and information
- Ensuring diversity of programming and viewpoints
- Broadcasting a certain proportion of news, cultural, artistic, educational, minority, religious, children's, and entertainment programming
- Promoting local culture and values
- Producing and broadcasting programs relevant for all the regions in the country
- Providing free-of-charge airtime for public interest announcements, such as health care, road safety, and urgent messages of state authorities

A number of countries impose a set of common obligations on both public and commercial television stations, but they vary significantly. Public service broadcasters are required to produce and air cultural and educational programming, programs for minorities, and regional news. Public service broadcasters are expected to play a much wider societal role than the commercial stations, including promotion of local culture, traditions, and values.

Public service broadcasters are governed by two main structures. They have, on the one hand, a council of governors that enforces the station's general policy and oversees the station's budget and, activities, and on the other hand, a management board responsible for carrying out the daily management of the broadcaster. The management body is led by a general director, who sometimes has significant powers, making the position in itself a third layer of governing power. There are variations from this model. Czech Television, for example, also has in place a commission that supervises the activity of the council and management and carries out a financial audit of the station. Estonian public service broadcaster ETV is governed by an external council, which is in charge of appointing the station's management and monitoring their activities. The performance of the governing structures is essential in securing the independence of the public service broadcasters and the quality of their programs. The appointment procedures of these structures has much in common with those in place for the national broadcasting regulators. Their members are generally pushed through by parliaments. As a result, public service broadcasting governing structures change according to the changes in the political power. In various Central and Eastern European countries, the general director plays a crucial role in the governing equation. In some countries, such as Romania, the director is chosen by parliament, and that has obvious negative influence on the station's independence. Romania is also sporting an oddly dangerous system, according to which the station's general director is at the same time the chair of the Council of Administration, the structure in charge of supervising the station's management. In other words, the station's director is at the same time the *controller* and the *controlled*.

### Who Pays the Bill?

The system of funding public service broadcasting is also of major importance for the independence of these stations, which are generally large enterprises with bloated staff. The funding of the public service broadcasting is often a hybrid model, combining revenues from various sources. The most common are the license fees paid by TV households, state subsidies, and commercial income from advertising and broadcasting rights. Some public service broadcasters also generate cash from donations and from renting their technical equipment and other assets.

The financing of public service broadcasters from the state budget is seen as the most hazardous model, as it automatically creates dependence of the broadcaster on the state structures. The license fee, paid by all owners of TV sets, was considered for years as the most appropriate model of financing public service broadcasting because it does not come directly from the state budget, ensuring more financial independence (see table 10.3). At the same time, simply imposing a public service television license fee on taxpayers is not sufficient to secure the financial independence of the public service broadcaster if the fee is not linked with economic indicators that allow its fluctuation according to the economic outlook. In many countries, parliament or the government decides when to increase the fee, using this as an

Table 10.3. Television License Fee Cost Per Year, 2006

| Country | Annual fee (euros) |
| --- | --- |
| Denmark | 294 |
| Norway | 248 |
| Sweden | 221 |
| Germany | 204 |
| United Kingdom | 196 |
| Slovenia | 132 |
| France | 117 |
| Croatia | 108 |
| Italy | 104 |
| Macedonia, FYR | 64 |
| Poland | 49 |
| Czech Republic | 44 |
| Slovak Republic | 35 |
| Romania | 14 |
| Bulgaria | None |
| Lithuania | None |
| Albania | 4 |

*Sources:* Thomas Kirsch/IP International Marketing Committee (CMI). *Television 2005. International Key Facts; Television 2006. International Key Facts; Television 2007. International Key Facts.*

instrument of pressure on broadcasters.[9] With the exception of France, where the license fee decreased by 0.1 percent between 2003 and 2007, and Switzerland, where it did not change over the period, in all other European countries the licensing fee increased by between 0.8 percent in Denmark to 12.5 percent in the Czech Republic.

However, many countries show a decline in payment of the license fee due to a combination of factors, including deficient systems of collection, widespread poverty, and the refusal of householders to pay the fee because they do not see any value for it. In recent years, public service broadcasters in Central and Eastern Europe have experienced serious economic hardships, and some of them, such as Macedonian MRT, are on the verge of collapse (the Macedonian state had to inject cash in the country's public service broadcaster in 2007 to save it from extinction). Financial and management independence are crucial for the editorial independence of the public service broadcasters. They need sound financing to be able to carry out investigative and news reporting and also management structures that are guaranteed immunity against external pressures. Public funding is the basic financing model for public service broadcasting for cultural and political reasons. Yet the political and social acceptance of the license fee may decline where new digital receiver equipment makes this model of collection (based on the possession of a radio or TV receiver) problematic. In Poland, the government wants to abolish the license fee, while in the Slovak Republic, various economists have called for a referendum to see whether citizens still want to pay the license fee.

Another problem that public service broadcasters will face in terms of financing is the fact that the revenue from license fees, despite being the most stable and predictable source of financing, remains a static source. It has grown generally, but still does not have a potential to meet the needs of the public service broadcaster in the digital market. That makes even more imperative the need to establish a model of automatic indexing of the fee according to the rate of inflation and other economic indicators. In the Netherlands, for example, the license fee was replaced by a government contribution to public service broadcasting. This money is raised by imposing a supplement to income tax. "Realizing the developments in the market (multi-media, and the change in the media value chain) public broadcasters cannot, in the long run, avoid co-operation with commercial companies performing gate-keeping functions. Thus, it may be more and more difficult to separate public broadcasting from the wholly commercial market and its sources of financing, and to draw a clear line between commercial and non-commercial activities."[10] Nissen speaks about three solutions in solving the public service broadcasting financing conundrum. They are (1) to expand the basis for collecting the fee to all types of devices able to receive and display public service media, (2) to abandon the fee completely and find a new source of financing, or (3) to change the fee regime to a compulsory "excise duty" collected from all households and citizens.[11]

## Commercial Television

Commercial television in Europe has undergone a process of consolidation and concentration of ownership. Legal ceilings on concentration of ownership have prompted media owners in many countries to resort to various ways of hiding the traces of their ownership in order to escape legal requirements on their ownership. In Central and Eastern European countries, broadcasting stations were used by their owners more as a tool for pursuing the political or business interests of their owner or their owner's cronies. Lack of transparency on the media ownership is a direct threat to the editorial independence of these media outlets.

In general, commercial television broadcasters in Europe are sacrificing quality in their desperate search for ever-larger audiences, which are the engines of advertising spending. Commercial television stations in Western Europe are usually under some general obligations to serve the public interest, but the same cannot be said about the young democracies in Central and Eastern Europe, where strict public service obligations are not imposed on commercial broadcasters. In general, both public service and commercial broadcasters are bound to a legal set of general content obligations, such as protection of minors, a ban on incitement to ethnic or religious hatred, and so forth.[12] In some countries, commercial broadcasters are subject to a set of additional programming obligations stipulated in the license agreement. But otherwise, commercial broadcasters are not subject to distinct public service obligations.

In general, commercial television broadcasters are not standard setters for investigative journalism and quality news programs. Their main yardstick of success is the size of their audience. Therefore, in their effort to beef up their ratings, these stations increasingly promote lowbrow entertainment and sensationalist newscasts. In many Central and Eastern European countries, commercial TV stations rarely employ self-regulatory mechanisms, and their journalists are often targets of direct or indirect pressures.

The most negative development in the commercial television sector, with serious repercussions mostly on their news coverage, has been the steady concentration of ownership, which translates into concentration of influence that can be used for political, personal, ideological, or commercial gains.[13] Following the opening of the Central and Eastern European markets in the 1990s, several Western groups built large TV networks in the region. The largest panregional television operators in Central and Eastern Europe include the U.S. company Central European Media Enterprises (CME), the German RTL

Group, part of the Bertelsmann media conglomerate, the Swedish Modern Times Group (MTG), News Corporation, and German ProSiebenSat.1 Media, which bought SBS Broadcasting in 2007. With the exception of a few countries, legislation commonly forbids cross-ownership between two broadcasters with similar footprints and between print media and broadcasting media. However, in the past decade, media owners have used sophisticated ownership structures to hide their ownership. One preferred way to do this was registering media companies in offshore countries, such as Cyprus, or in states, such as Switzerland, where confidentiality of ownership is guaranteed. For years, the real ownership of Romanian and Bulgarian broadcasters remained a mystery. Lack of transparency of media ownership hides conflicts of interests and owners' interference with the stations' programming.[14]

## Changing Times and New Technologies

The fast development of new technologies, with digitalization of broadcasting and technological convergence, is fundamentally changing the media environment. The past several years have seen major archeological shifts in the media. Some analysts in the 2000s have dwarfed the importance of digitalization and the potential of the Internet in the media business. But it has become clear that digitalization does not mean merely replacing analog production and distribution technology with digital equipment. Digitalization is already altering the workflow in the process of program production and prompts the retraining of staff to respond to the new challenges. At the same time, it opens a whole range of new media services to the public. The main driver in the dynamics of the broadcast media is the technological convergence of voice, data, and video into a single platform—and the linking of computing and other information technologies, media content, and communication networks—which triggers unprecedented changes in the market, regulatory framework, and user behavior.

### The Market

The main trend in today's media market is its internationalization, with the main actors on the media scene becoming international corporations that go beyond national frontiers. They have no territorial links or cultural obligations. The internationalization of the media market is accompanied by a sustained process of concentration in the value chains of different parts of the media industry. Distribution via the old analog terrestrial networks was a neutral technical function fulfilled usually by telecom companies that used to be public corporations. However, digitalization is creating "a more differentiated value chain" comprising a new important function, that of gatekeeper (Nissen 2006).

"[The gatekeepers] are the ones who control customer access to content and those who make and package channels." They control various key functions such as the Subscription Management System, or SMS, which monitors payments from viewers for decoding and accessing content that is encrypted, compressed, and packed in bundles (*multiplexes*), and the Electronic Program Guides (EPGs), which are comparable to the search engines on the Internet. "Those who are in control of these functions also control to a large extent the whole value chain."[15]

## Challenges on Regulatory Frameworks

In Europe, regulation is tightly linked with the state. The behavior of governments and parliaments in shaping new models of regulation is crucial in the new context. Expansion of satellite distribution covering cross-national territories, the increase in the number of large transnational media corporations, and the boom in the distribution of content via the Internet have created an international market of content, which is already outside the regulation.

One result of these trends has been more freedom of choice for the viewers and listeners. But it is still questionable whether having the new media means, in reality, free choice and more diversity. TV programs have become commodities traded by commercial companies in a growing market, which is in search of completely new business and economic models. "It is self-evident that such a market will tend to become homogenous, leaving little room either for content of an experimental character or for programs catering for small language groups, national and regional cultures, all of which characterize the European scene."[16]

The traditional pattern of consuming television was based on access to scheduled programs. The digital revolution is already changing this pattern. With the use of digital personal video recorders (PVRs) becoming increasingly popular, consumers of broadcasting are in the position of better controlling their choices. In other words, the viewers are now in a position to watch "what-when-and-how" they want. This change in the pattern of media consumption has led in a very short time to a marked fragmenting and individualization of the audiences.

## Where Public Service Broadcasting is Going

The arguments in favor of the public service media used to be in the analog media environment of a technical and economic nature. The rationale behind the privileged position of public service broadcasting had to do first with the scarcity of the frequency spectrum. This argument was also the rationale behind the regulation of broadcasting since the inception of commercial broadcasting. At the same time, with a limited number of frequencies up for grabs, the argument for creating and maintaining a space for a public service broadcaster that would cater to the general public, parts of which could not find their programs on commercial broadcasters, was compelling. But such arguments are becoming obsolete, because with digitalization the frequency spectrum is enlarging extraordinarily. Therefore, the arguments for public service media turn now to be more value based and rooted more in cultural policies (Nissen).

In this new environment, public service broadcasting has to reinvent itself. One of the most important quantitative criteria for its success should be universal reach. Public service broadcasting stations have to reach the entire population with a wide range of content. Until now, most public service broadcasting stations based their programming philosophy on the "flow paradigm" whereby popular, more commercial programs worked as the lead-in to distinctive programs, such as news, current affairs, and culture. With an increasing number of interactive, on-demand, and multichannel platforms for airing broadcast content, public service broadcasters will have to create schedules that are more distinctive and that slash commercial programming.

Second, practitioners argue that public service broadcasters should refocus on the quality of content and its price. The governance structures of the public service broadcasting system must also be fundamentally redesigned. In many countries, especially in Central and Eastern Europe, public service broadcasting organizations are usually linked with the government. With a few exceptions, public service broadcasting is coming under increased politicization in many European countries. In explaining this trend, Nissen (2006) speaks about a change in the culture and the nature of political communication. In the past century, print media lost many of their affiliations with political parties, becoming "omnibus newspapers" targeting mass audiences in a competitive, commercial market. That change was seen by political parties and governments as a loss to their system of communication with their constituencies. The political codes and behaviors have also seen major changes. "The strategic, long-term perspectives based on political ideology and formulated in party programs have been toned down and replaced by a more tactical way of operation in day-to-day politics. In such a scenario, the communicative aspects of political initiatives, both the message itself and its timing, often have just as much importance as their material substance."[17] With segmentation and individualization, public service media have to adapt to a completely new model, moving away from collective broadcasting to a model based on providing tailor-made content and services.

## The Fate of News

In this fast-changing environment remodeled by the new technologies, two trends dominate the production and distribution of news. First, the number of news sources is expanding at a fast pace, making access to information much easier than in the analog world. Secondly, the growth of news distributors is accompanied by an unprecedented loss of the authority that the media had in the analog world.

How much these trends affect the overall quality of news is at the heart of the debate. One school of thought argues that the new media are killing journalism. Andrew Keen, the leading contemporary critic of the Internet, argued that the online world transformed journalists into bloggers. He calls the blogosphere a "rebellion against the authority of professional journalists" and bitterly criticizes the cult of the amateur that the Internet has promoted.[18] In such an environment, the sources of news are "personalized networks of friends" that are increasingly pushing traditional media out of the game. The tradition of balanced reporting, proponents of this critical school say, is going to be lost with the unregulated broadcasting via the Internet.

The opposite opinion is that the Internet and new technologies only help journalism. The second generation of web development, Web 2.0, is a viable platform for the journalism of the future.[19] Moreover, according to defenders of this viewpoint, trends like blogging and user-generated content should not be seen as dangers to balanced, impartial, objective journalism but rather as a conscience keeping an eye on journalism. The expansion of news production is also a response to the weaknesses and biases of the journalism profession, which on numerous occasions has performed dishearteningly.

Between the two opposing opinions, other voices argue that the digital era is in fact a redefinition of the economy of the media. Journalism's monopoly has been shaken, and a more networked type of journalism has been born. A clear distinction must be made between journalism, which is and will remain a profession, and general communication, which has been made easier and more convenient by the Internet. In this environment, the key is finding viable economic models because those employed in the traditional media market are no longer working. In other words, media have to adapt to the new environment shaped by the Internet. Those media companies that anticipated the upcoming shifts in the media landscape have already established a strong presence on the new platforms.

## Media Gatekeepers and the Concept of a Balanced Public Forum

What has changed in the functions and roles of the news media? The idea of a balanced public forum, in which journalists as gatekeepers include all sectors and viewpoints, has long been central to the discussion about the objectivity of news. The concept implies that the news media should reflect all perspectives and points of view in any major controversy, as well as include the voices of a diverse range of actors, groups, and interests. In particular, in election campaigns, balanced coverage emphasizes the inclusion and fair treatment of all parties and candidates so that citizens can make informed choices at the ballot box. Partisan balance of reporting during election campaigns is only one aspect of this broader phenomenon, but it is particularly important for democratic governance. If the major news agencies are heavily skewed in favor of the incumbent power holders, citizens will lack access to a wide range of independent sources of information to evaluate the performance of the government and to assess the policy proposals of opposition parties and candidates.

Two notions can describe how this process should operate.[20] *Internal* diversity emphasizes that any specific media outlet should contain a rich plurality of perspectives and viewpoints, exemplified by including both liberal and conservative commentators in the editorial pages of major newspapers, or by devoting equal time in the main TV news bulletin to the speeches of spokespersons on either side of a dispute. Alternatively, *external* diversity emphasizes the need for a plurality of perspectives to be evident across media markets and a wide range of outlets, without major restrictions or censorship limiting freedom of expression. External diversity can be achieved, for example, by the publication of a wide range of highly partisan newspapers and magazines—reflecting all points of view across the political spectrum, from anarchist, communist, liberal, conservative, to the radical right—available through bookstands (bookstores) and news agents, as well as through the Internet. Each partisan publication can preach to a particular sector, but pluralism is still preserved through the unrestricted choice of media outlets. The issue of media pluralism is often analyzed exclusively in regard to its aspect of external pluralism, related to the effects of the concentration of ownership on editorial policies and standards. Internal pluralism is equally important, and in this respect, the public service broadcasting in Europe was meant to be, among other things, a corrective for market failure. Therefore, where public service broadcasting fails to provide a balanced public forum in many Central and Eastern European countries, despite strict obligations through legislation to play precisely this role, this failure has had negative repercussions for public opinion formation.

In evaluating the degree of internal or external balance in the news on television, content analysis methodologies have examined television news both quantitatively and qualitatively. The quantitative approach measures "stopwatch" balance by weighing the amount of time devoted to reporting about each party, candidate, interest group, issue, or spokesperson.[21] In particular, the stopwatch concept is applied most strictly during election campaigns by measuring the time devoted to particular political parties or candidates in any television news program, or measuring the amount of coverage aggregated across a particular TV station or channel. More exposure, it is assumed, provides political actors with a greater advantage during election campaigns. Stopwatch balance can also be applied to assess the proportion of time that other actors are presented in newscasts, such as the balance between the coverage of the business sector and trade unions in an industrial dispute, or the gender and minority balance in news reports. In politics, the set of topics tackled in newscasts is analyzed in connection with the issues attached to various political parties. For example, disproportionate coverage of international security issues in the election campaign in the United Kingdom in 1987 was seen as favoring Prime Minister Thatcher's government.[22]

The notion of equal time is relatively easily measured and hence widely used by monitoring agencies. To be more meaningful, however, this simple indicator needs to be supplemented by a more qualitative examination of the news contents.[23] After all, extensive coverage can be devoted to a party or political leader, but this can all be heavily critical. A more comprehensive assessment needs to include directional balance, measured by the tone of the reporting, including whether the news coverage is regarded as negative, neutral, or positive.[24] In theory, news can be categorized as impartial if stories include all relevant sides in a report; by contrast, it is considered biased if the news is inadequately critical or if it is overtly partisan. In practice, however, making such judgments is often difficult and controversial.

More broadly still, the notion of balance can also be applied to many other aspects of news coverage, such as how much soft versus hard news is aired by TV newscasts. "Hard" news encompasses business and economy, consumer affairs, education, environment, health, home security and crime, international affairs, political party affairs, political affairs, public services, and social issues. "Soft" news, by contrast, encompasses arts and culture, celebrity, entertainment, human interest, lifestyle, religion, science, sports, and women's issues.[25]

## Television News as a Balanced Public Forum

In general, TV stations in Europe have been scrambling over the past decade to find innovative, dynamic, and frequently sensationalist program formats. There is a tendency to hybridize television formats, mixing news and political debates with light entertainment. This is part of the larger trend of building newscasts on a markedly tabloid structure from which hard investigative reporting is being removed. In the Central and Eastern European countries, news production is under pressure equally from the market and from political agents and owners. All-news TV channels have unfolded at a fast pace in the region, gaining healthy popularity. With the appetite for news reaching new heights, news has become the favorite genre on television. However, that is not translated in most of cases into solid reporting and high-quality news production, which are often rare commodities.

### Moving Away from the State

Public service broadcasters in the Central and Eastern European countries have been continually criticized for failing to play their public service role. Their transformation from state-run to public service broadcasters, much influenced by Western models and practices, has been difficult, with the state and politicians unwilling to lose their control over these stations. However, over the past two decades, public service broadcasters in Central and Eastern Europe have generally managed to move away from authorities and stopped being the mere mouthpieces of the incumbent governments. At the same time, commercial broadcasters have come closer to the ordinary citizens.[26] Most public service television broadcasters in the region have thus managed to produce more impartial programs with an evident distance.

In general, public service broadcasters tend to devote more time to domestic political life and international affairs than commercial TV stations (see tables 10.4 and 10.5). In several Central and Eastern European countries, at least half of the content in prime-time newscasts on public service television is devoted to domestic political affairs and international news. In Hungary, for example, in 2007 the largest commercial station covered national and international political life in only 9 percent of its newscasts, less than the average coverage on all the commercial TV stations, which accounted for almost 40 percent. There are exceptions, such as Serbia, where the widely acclaimed private station B92 devotes more than 50 percent of the prime-time newscast's time to such issues, or Bosnia and Herzegovina, where private NTV Hayat covers these topics in more than 66 percent of the prime-time newscast's time.

At the same time, broadcasters have made some progress in producing and airing unbiased news (see tables 10.6 and 10.7). Content analyses have shown that both public service and commercial broadcasters in a number of countries surveyed in the region take a neutral attitude in the majority of their reports.[27] Some negative examples are the leading commercial broadcasters in Montenegro and FYR Macedonia, where 34 percent and 58 percent, respectively, of their news reports have been cataloged as positively or negatively biased. Among public service broadcasters, the worst balance was found in Moldova, where the country's public service broadcaster was positively biased toward the state and other authorities in half of its total prime-time news programming.

## Public Service Broadcasters

Although public service broadcasters in the transition countries in Central and Eastern Europe have managed to move away from the state authorities, they are still far from fulfilling their public service role in creating a balanced public forum. In this region, the tradition of the communist state's control over broadcasting has left a heavy legacy on the region's media. Regimes have continued to use these broadcasters to strengthen their power and in the war-battered former Yugoslavia, television was a tool of propaganda and source of instigation of ethnic hatred. Today, despite reforms of the state broadcasting behemoths, the old practice of acting as an institution biased in favor of the state and political power still survive, preventing real progress for fully fledged public service broadcasters. Hardly a public service broadcaster

**Table 10.4. Coverage of Topics on Public Service Television**
*percentage*

| Country (station) | Domestic political life | World affairs | Country's international politics | Economy and business | Culture, art, education, ecology, religion | Sports | Crime | Social protection and health care | Other |
|---|---|---|---|---|---|---|---|---|---|
| Albania (TVSH) | 24 | 13 | 11 | 16 | 18 | 3 | 3 | 7 | 5 |
| Bosnia & Herzegovina (BHT) | 24 | 11 | 20b | 11 | 14 | 0 | 10 | 3 | 7 |
| Bulgaria (BNT) | 21 | 19a | 7 | 4 | 19 | 3 | 1 | 5 | 21 |
| Croatia (HTV) | 23 | 23 | 6 | 8 | 12 | 4 | 0 | 1 | 23 |
| Hungary (MTV) | 19 | 4 | 2 | 8 | 12 | 2 | 0 | 15 | 38 |
| Macedonia, FYR (MTV) | 25 | 17 | 14 | 17 | 11 | 0 | 0 | 5 | 11 |
| Moldova (Moldova 1) | 14 | 12 | 5 | 21 | 21 | 0 | 0 | 19 | 8 |
| Montenegro (TVCG) | 25 | 12 | 17 | 15 | 10 | 9 | 0 | 2 | 10 |
| Romania (TVRI) | 29 | 16 | 0 | 9 | 8 | 8 | 12c | 5 | 12 |
| Serbia (RTS) | 8 | 19 | 30 | 8 | 13 | 0 | 0 | 5 | 17 |

*Source:* Compiled using data from Radenko Udovicic, ed. 2007. *TV Prime Time Domestic News—Monitoring and Analysis of TV News Programs in 10 SEENPM Countries—Indicator of Public Interest.* Sarajevo: Media Plan Institute.

*Note:* Percentage based on total programming hours.

a. Includes reports on war crimes and terrorism.

b. Includes reports on war crimes.

c. Includes reports on justice and internal affairs.

**Table 10.5. Coverage of Topics on Commercial Television**

percentage

| Country (station) | Domestic political life | World affairs | Country's international politics | Economy and business | Culture, art, education, ecology, religion | Sports | Crime | Social protection and health care | Other |
|---|---|---|---|---|---|---|---|---|---|
| Albania (Top Channel) | 15 | 10 | 2 | 17 | 6 | 5 | 5 | 9 | 31 |
| Bosnia & Herzegovina (NTV Hayat) | 25 | 21 | 18a | 9 | 7 | 4 | 1 | 1 | 10 |
| Bulgaria (bTV) | 17 | 16b | 7 | 4 | 24 | 5 | 2 | 5 | 20 |
| Croatia (Nova TV) | 24 | 17 | 5 | 6 | 9 | 4 | 0 | 1 | 34 |
| Hungary | 7 | 2 | 0 | 3 | 12 | 3 | 0 | 9 | 64 |
| Macedonia, FYR (A1) | 21 | 11 | 4 | 37 | 7 | 1 | 0 | 4 | 15 |
| Moldova (TV7) | 25 | 3 | 1 | 15 | 15 | 14 | 0 | 20 | 7 |
| Montenegro (TV IN) | 16 | 19 | 9 | 20 | 10 | 6 | 0 | 4 | 16 |
| Romania (Antena 1) | 17 | 6 | 1 | 9 | 13 | 6 | 6c | 7 | 35 |
| Serbia (B92) | 19 | 17 | 16 | 7 | 10 | 1 | 0 | 7 | 23 |
| Serbia (RUV) | 16 | 2 | 14 | 25 | 11 | 0 | 0 | 2 | 30 |

*Source:* Compiled using data from Radenko Udovicic. 2007. *TV Prime Time Domestic News* (see table 10.4).

*Note:* Percentage of total programming hours.

a. Includes reports on war crimes.

b. Includes reports on war crimes and terrorism.

c. Includes justice and internal affairs.

**Table 10.6. Directional Balance on Public Service Television**
*percentage*

| Country (station) | Positive attitude | Neutral attitude | Negative attitude |
|---|---|---|---|
| Albania (TVSH) | 11 | 88 | 1 |
| Bosnia & Herzegovina (BHT) | 7 | 91 | 2 |
| Bulgaria (BNT) | 0 | 100 | 0 |
| Croatia (HTV) | 28 | 60 | 12 |
| Hungary (MTV) | 5 | 93 | 2 |
| Macedonia, FYR (MTV) | 31 | 61 | 8 |
| Moldova (Moldova 1) | 50 | 45 | 5 |
| Montenegro (TVCG) | 46 | 38 | 16 |
| Romania (TVR1) | 2 | 89 | 9 |
| Serbia (RTS) | 24 | 65 | 11 |

*Source:* Compiled using data from Radenko Udovicic. 2007. TV Prime Time Domestic News (see table 10.4).
*Note:* Percentage of total programming hours.

**Table 10.7. Directional Balance on Commercial Television**
*percentage*

| Country (station) | Positive attitude | Neutral attitude | Negative attitude |
|---|---|---|---|
| Albania (Top Channel) | 0 | 83 | 17 |
| Bosnia and Herzegovina (NTV Hayat) | 5 | 93 | 2 |
| Bulgaria (bTV) | 0 | 100 | 0 |
| Croatia (Nova TV) | 7 | 83 | 10 |
| Hungary (RTL Klub) | 9 | 78 | 13 |
| Macedonia, FYR (A1) | 11 | 66 | 23 |
| Moldova (TV7) | 17 | 75 | 8 |
| Montenegro (TV IN) | 41 | 42 | 17 |
| Romania (Antena 1) | 7 | 80 | 13 |
| Serbia (B92) | 9 | 71 | 20 |

*Source:* Compiled using data from Radenko Udovicic. 2007. *TV Prime Time Domestic News* (see table 10.4).
*Note:* Percentage is of total programming hours.

is to be found in the region that has managed to fully articulate its program structure to fit the public interest. "The traditional difference in news between public and commercial media appears to be fading," wrote Radenko Udovicic based on a content analysis study that covered news in 10 southeastern European countries.[28] "It should come as no surprise that the market is gaining increasing control over the media and that the media field has been the most attractive field for public relations for quite some time. Media are controlled by a combination of private ownership, advertising strongmen, elite sources, State pressure and cultural dominance."[29]

The frailties of the news coverage by the public service broadcasters have their roots in the days of monopolistic state television during communism. Critical stances on the news on communist state television would never target the government or state bodies. In the 1990s, Hungarian public service television MTV was visibly favorable to the government. Only recently did the station make more progress toward impartiality and independence. In general, smaller TV stations in Hungary tend to be more biased than large ones.[30]

The newscast on RTS1, the first channel of the public service broadcaster in Serbia, has traditionally attracted the largest audience, beating sometimes even popular soap operas or quiz shows aired by commercial stations. The program has equally stirred fierce criticism for failing to be a public forum and being more a supporter of the government and the ruling party. After 2000, RTS1 managed to achieve greater editorial autonomy, making more efforts to promote pluralism of opinions in its news programming.[31]

RTS1 is seen as a promoter of state policies rather than an independent outlet that would serve first as a public forum where a wide variety of opinions would find a place. RTS1's prime-time newscast is usually comprehensive and free of attacks on anyone. However, it still proved to have a lack of professionalism in various instances. For example, when covering Kosovo, the Albanian majority-populated new independent state that used to be part of Serbia, the news is dominated by the preponderant public opinion and prejudices. News reports covering Kosovo include statements by local and international officials and experts. However, the station has repeatedly failed to make room in its news reports for the viewpoint of the Albanian side.[32]

One of the most extreme examples of a public service broadcaster blatantly favoring the authorities is Moldova. Public television here is devoting the bulk of its news coverage to the authorities, mostly the president of the country. News reports about irrelevant appearances and acts of the president, such as opening a tractor station in a village or addressing Parliament on his economic initiatives, can go as long as six minutes. At the same time, the station is continually avoiding covering topics that can put the government in a negative light. Some of the commercial stations regularly report on such sensitive issues.[33] In Moldova, commercial broadcasters are closer to offering an open forum for debate and pluralism of opinions. The station's first channel, Moldova1, is notorious for interviewing only officials. There is almost no report including opinions of common people. During electoral campaigns, commercial stations always polled ordinary people and candidates for the mayor's office in the capital of Chisinau, but Moldova1 has never run a single poll. Moreover, the opinions of officials aired by the public service broadcaster usually go on unchecked and unquestioned. Moldova1 has never included in its reports the opinion of any independent experts or representatives of nongovernmental organizations.

A similar situation was found in Serbia, where private television rather than the public service broadcaster sometimes better fulfills the role of a balanced public forum. Commercial television B92 often promotes civil society activism in its newscasts, something that public service does not do regularly.

In most countries in Central and Eastern Europe, public service broadcasters have a completely different approach in their news coverage from their commercial peers. Commercial TV station Nova TV in Croatia makes its news simpler and easier to understand, while the public service station HTV has become known for a more serious approach in presenting the news, which is more conservative and treats more weighty topics. That is, in the opinion of some media experts, a guarantee of credibility. In Croatia, when it comes to diversity of topics and actors presented in the news, the differences between the public service broadcaster and the commercial stations are minor. Croatian public service TV puts more emphasis on the economic and business news, political affairs, and public service topics. Because the public service broadcaster pulls in some 80 percent of the national audience in news and current affairs programs, they give their viewers what they want (and those viewers don't want official sources or celebrities).[34]

In Western Europe, both public and private broadcasters fulfill their role of a balanced public forum better than in Central and Eastern Europe. The largest single group presented on the news is the general public, followed by political parties. In Italy, celebrities are popular on TV newscasts, whereas experts are more often present on news in the United Kingdom. Although a broad range of stakeholders are given access to news sources, TV stations in Western Europe have the tendency to rely on political institutions and the general public, marginalizing civil society organizations and interest groups. More worrisome is the gender imbalance in some Western European countries. In a 2006 study, the most frequently shown faces on newscasts in three Western European countries (Italy, Norway, and the United Kingdom) were men, with women representing only one-fifth of the interviewees in news bulletins.[35]

## Media Watchdogs or Lapdogs?

When studying how television newscasts contribute to the creation of a balanced public forum, it is important to also look at how they manage to play their watchdog role. By blatantly avoiding certain topics or presenting some issues in a biased manner in response to outside pressures from interest groups or powerful political actors, television prevents certain voices from having access to the screen.

Serbian station B92 is an example of a private broadcaster that is a tireless watchdog over powerful interests. The station follows a strict editorial policy focused on serving the public by creating a space for a wide array of opinions and on covering issues that other stations do not cover. B92 is known for its solid investigative reporting on sensitive issues, such as corruption and crime. Founded in 1989 as a youth radio broadcaster in Belgrade, B92 expanded into a multimedia house that today runs a regional radio station, a nationwide TV station, a Web site, and a cultural center. It was highly praised internationally for its brave coverage and promotion of human rights. Since TV B92 launched its broadcasting in 2000, it has gained high popularity, becoming the fastest developing broadcaster in the country.[36]

Such examples are rare in Central and Eastern Europe, however. In FYR Macedonia, the commercial TV station A1, the largest in the country, was in several instances promoting the interests of its owners rather than sticking to principles of impartiality and objectivity. The station became known for promoting events organized by the "Ramkovski foundation," an organization founded by the station's owner.[37] The same could be said about the commercial NTV Hayat in Bosnia and Herzegovina, which runs numerous positive reports about various companies. That was seen by media observers as concealed advertising. However, any connections with these companies are not always easy to prove.

Newscasts are increasingly turned into tabloid formats, more markedly on private TV stations. On the one hand, this is triggered by the public's appetite for trivial and frivolous topics, which brings hefty ratings to the TV stations; on the other hand, many television stations choose to focus on frivolous topics such as cases of domestic violence, petty thefts, or celebrity affairs to avoid reporting on sensitive issues. Their coverage is becoming increasingly *apolitical* instead of being politically neutral.

In Romania, especially until 2004, some of the largest TV stations—indebted to the state budget after they failed to pay back taxes—turned their newscasts into tabloid news programs to avoid relevant but controversial issues that could have triggered controls and harassment from the state tax offices or other administrative bodies. Romanian commercial TV station Antena 1 constantly skips relevant political, economic, and social issues, and instead reports in prime-time newscasts about such topics as a several-month-old baby in the United States who received a recruitment letter from the army or about a cat that traveled 800 kilometers to find its masters.[38] Such news reports are less common on the Romanian public service channel, which leads its newscasts mostly with hard news on politics and foreign affairs, and only at the end of the newscast devotes time to trivia.

Public service broadcasters have moved somewhat away from the state. However, old habits remain in place, and it is on public service television that one sees more positive bias in the coverage of the state structures, partly triggered by the pressures exerted by political power. In contrast, on private television, there is a more marked slant in favor of allies and businesses related to the owners of the private TV stations.

In some countries all stations are the same when it comes to news coverage. In Montenegro, public service and commercial TV stations report similarly in prime-time newscasts on sessions of parliament and press conferences. Differences are related mostly to how they define their priorities and how they package the reports. What is common for both commercial and public service broadcasters in this country is the disheartening lack of criticism in their reporting. News reports look like promotional reports. The public service television, TVCG, is also known for its laudatory tone in covering Montenegro's state policies.[39]

The watchdog function of the media continues to be jeopardized when journalists are often subjected to criminal prosecution based on secrecy or defamation laws. Such practices have been found in 20 European countries despite campaigns by international organizations for decriminalization of such laws.[40] Even in such Western European countries as Germany and the Netherlands, governments misuse the law to protect themselves from incriminatory evidence proving their incompetence. In Ireland, the editor and a reporter of the *Irish Times* have been sued for refusing the orders of the courts to disclose the source of information published in an investigative report on corruption surrounding the country's serving prime minister.[41] Recent years have witnessed renewed efforts by politicians to control the media. "As the impact of the media, especially television, has grown, political leaders have not only grown more sophisticated, hiring 'spin doctors' and trying to win the media over with blandishments or privileges. They have also grown more intolerant of criticism. The Czech Prime Minister, Mirek Topolanek, accused the media of bias against him and threatened to enact a new law to curb press freedom. In [the Slovak Republic] Prime Minister Robert Fico branded the media as 'the political opposition.'"[42]

In Romania, setbacks in the country's anticorruption campaign were linked to bitter infighting within the media for and against the reformist President Traian Basescu. The saga of a corruption case in Romania and the manner in which it was handled by the political power show the weakness of the public service broadcaster in defending its independence. On October 10, 2007, Romanian public service broadcaster TVR aired in its prime-time newscast a video featuring the minister of agriculture, Decebal Traian Remes, allegedly receiving a bribe from a former minister of agriculture, in exchange for favoring a businessman in a public tender. The secretly filmed video showed Remes accepting 15,000 euros, 20 kilos of sausages, and 100 liters of plum brandy through a middleman. Following the ruckus provoked by the video, Remes resigned. He refused to make any comments. Instead of criticizing his colleague for what he did, the country's prime minister threw a tantrum against TVR for what he called Remes's "public execution."

The filming stirred a heated debate, with the director of the station himself saying publicly that the video was illegal and incorrect because it breached the presumption of innocence. Media organizations and the broadcast regulator said that it was legitimate to air the video because it served the public interest.[43] The story was followed by politicians' intense attacks against the station. TVR's board reorganized the station's news department into two divisions, one dealing with news and sports and the other working on research for the news programs. One of the most critical journalists in the station, Rodica Culcer, was generously given the task to supervise the two departments. In reality, the move was aimed at denting the scope of Culcer's decision making. Such reorganization inside state institutions has been a typical practice through which ruling parties in Romania managed to reduce the decisional power of nonloyal people. They preferred such strategies to other moves, which would have attracted criticism and accusations of censorship. More independent journalists were then removed from the prime-time newscast to unattractive afternoon or night news slots.[44]

The interference of owners in the programming of their TV stations badly hurt news coverage. The private Top Channel in Albania was particularly biased, as its owner also has a majority stake in the digital TV platform DigitAlb. Top Channel's coverage sometimes went too far in promoting the interests of its owners. It ran, for example, a report about a family with three sons who were all paralyzed by a genetically inherited disease. The report did not refrain from saying that despite the poverty of the family, the only entertainment for the sick children was the programming aired by DigitAlb, which made their parents buy a DigitAlb subscription card every month.[45]

In examining how television news ensures a balanced public forum, it is important to look at how the concentration of ownership leads sometimes to narrowing the number and diversity of major media owners. Opinions differ on how concentration of media ownership affects pluralism of content. Some researchers argue that concentration hinders the free formation of public opinion, a basic principle of the foundation of democratic societies. Others argue that, on the contrary, concentration of ownership does not have a negative impact on pluralism and diversity in the news because larger media conglomerates are able to invest in solid newsrooms and investigative reporting. Without money, media outlets will only resort to reproducing or rewriting wire and TV reports, without being able to do in-depth reporting.

Yet, the larger media holdings become, the more they cut costs and struggle to maximize their bottom line. A trend that has characterized the television market over the past years was the focus on cost reductions, which badly hit the capacity of these stations to produce investigative reporting. Solid news coverage and investigative reporting are also affected by the interests of the owners to maintain a healthy flow of advertising money. Owners are afraid that programs that are controversial or too specialized for a large audience can dent their sales or audience. The news coverage and editorial lines of these broadcasters further suffer in transnational media companies because of the lack of transparency on the ownership of these outlets. "The traditional link between the owner of the media and the audience served created transparency (the audience knew who the owner was) and responsibility (the owner lived 'among' the audience, and could also be approached personally). This link does not exist in the transnational media, or only to a very limited extent. The traditional responsibility to serve the audience and enlighten or educate the public, especially in relation to democratic processes, has suffered accordingly. The focus on profits and the corresponding focus on the audience not as the public but as consumers have direct consequences on the programming schedules."[46]

Then there is the group of broadcasting owners interested in promoting various political or ideological views. The cases abound in both Eastern and Western European countries. It has been shown, however, that direct intervention of owners in the work of journalists is rare. More worrying is the self-censorship professed at a large scale by editors and journalists who avoid raising issues that are in conflict with the owner's views and economic interests. Other studies have shown, however, that there is no direct link between media concentration and content diversity and pluralism in quantitative terms. The diversity of content is influenced by another group of factors, such as the resources of the media outlet, the size of the market where certain media operate, and the set of regulatory obligations imposed on them. "Where commercial broadcasters have minimum or no positive regulatory obligations there is a distinct lack of programming of high social value and an absence of domestic investment in programming with a heavy reliance on imported programs."[47]

In a content analysis covering Croatia, Italy, Norway, and the United Kingdom, Ward identifies the establishment of three tiers of broadcasters: broadcasters that have programming of high social value, established commercial broadcasters with some high social value programming, and commercial broadcasters whose schedules are essentially entertainment and import-based programs. Although the first tier is mainly represented by public service broadcasters, it is not exclusively the playing field of public media. The newscasts on public service broadcasters are largely dominated by hard news,[48] with the U.K. channels boasting the greatest percentage of international news coverage, unlike their Italian peer, RAI, whose first channel tends to focus on nationally based topics. The preferred topics tackled by newscasts are issues related to home security and crime. Only U.K. channels give more prominence to political affairs. Foreign affairs, political affairs, and social issues are also included in news bulletins on both public service and commercial broadcasters.[49]

## Conclusion

Television, which has remained the most influential medium and source of information for decades, has failed to play a major role in building a balanced public forum in Central and Eastern Europe. Started as a state enterprise back in the first half of the 20th century, television broadcasting in Europe has developed into a dual model. The state released its control over broadcasting in

Western Europe in the 1980s to let private broadcasting compete in the market. The same occurred in the 1990s in Central and Eastern Europe.

On a positive note, over the past decade, public service broadcasting has made visible progress toward more independence and balanced coverage in the news in Central and Eastern Europe. Linked not long ago with the state structures, for which they acted as a mere mouthpiece, public service broadcasters have managed to move away from state authorities to a certain extent. Another encouraging development in the region over in the past 10 years was a certain professionalization of the broadcast media, with TV stations taking a more neutral stance in their news reporting. Public service broadcasters have managed to preserve a certain distinctiveness in news coverage. They air more serious content, covering political affairs and foreign news more extensively, while commercial TV stations are usually recognized for their trivial and sensationalist approach in the selection of topics and the manner of coverage.

On a more negative note, however, television is still far from building a balanced public forum in Central and Eastern Europe. Public service broadcasters are still prone to favor state institutions or politicians in power. They are confronted with political pressures on their boards, which are still elected and controlled by the political power. These realities, more difficult to uncover and analyze scientifically, have been proved through investigative research in the field. Far from being concerned about its role in the society, and obsessed by ratings, audience, and advertising sales, commercial broadcasting has come closer to the ordinary citizen and is sometimes excelling in covering social issues. However, in most of the cases, the news coverage on commercial broadcasting is either aiming at scoring high ratings through tabloid programming or has become a mere tool for pursuing the personal, economic, and ideological interests and ambitions of the stations' owners. Despite a fragmentation of TV audiences, television news still attracts massive interest, being watched and accessed on a larger number of platforms. Television news still plays an important role in shaping public opinion. In this context, much is expected from public service broadcasting. Bolstering public service values in broadcasting through regulation, financial support of the media that promotes objective and balanced news coverage, and continual efforts aimed at professionalization of journalists are essential for improving the balance in news coverage.

## Notes

1. The focus of this paper is represented by what the authors generically call Central and Eastern Europe, a cluster of countries that have been studied extensively in the past five years, although it does not cover the countries of the former Soviet Union, except for Moldova, where content analysis studies have been carried out recently. The study also discusses some Western European broadcast markets for comparison.

2. Marius Dragomir, Dušan Reljic, and Mark Thompson, eds. 2005. *Television across Europe: Regulation, Policy and Independence.* Vol. 1. Budapest: Open Society Institute.

3. Digital Strategy Group of the European Broadcasting Union. 2002. *Media with a Purpose. Public Service Broadcasting in the Digital Era.* Geneva: European Broadcasting Union.

4. France's High Council for Broadcasting (CSA), Italy's Communications Guarantee Authority (AGCOM), and the United Kingdom's Office of Communications are some examples of such a regulation pattern.

5. Marius Dragomir, Dušan Reljic, and Mark Thompson, eds. 2005. *Television across Europe: Regulation, Policy and Independence,* Vol. 2, "Poland," 1097–98. Budapest: Open Society Institute.

6. Marius Dragomir, Dušan Reljic, Mark Thompson, eds. 2005. *Television across Europe: Regulation, Policy and Independence.* Vol. 1. Budapest: Open Society Institute, 25.

7. Ibid., 22.

8. Ibid., 23.

9. Ibid., 62.

10. Digital Strategy Group of the European Broadcasting Union. 2002. *Media with a Purpose. Public Service Broadcasting in the Digital Era.* Geneva: European Broadcasting Union, 50.

11. Christian S. Nissen. 2006. "Public Service Media in the Information Society." Report prepared for the Group of Specialists on Public Service Broadcasting in the Information Society (MC-S-PSB), Media Division, Directorate General of Human Rights, Council of Europe, Strasbourg.

12. Dragomir, Reljic, Thompson, eds. 2005. *Television across Europe: Regulation, Policy and Independence,* 66.

13. Ibid., 67.

14. Ibid., 69.

15. Nissen. 2006. "Public Service Media in the Information Society," 10.

16. Ibid., 12.

17. Ibid., 36.

18. "New Media Is Killing Journalism." 2008. World Press Freedom Day Debate, Frontline Club, London, May 2. 2008.

19. Web 2.0 allows communication, secure information sharing, collaboration, and interoperability on the World Wide Web, and it has made possible the evolution of Web-based communities, hosted services, and such applications as social networking sites, wikis, blogs, and video-sharing sites.

20. For a detailed normative discussion of objectivity and diversity see Denis McQuail. 1992. *Media Performance: Mass Communication and the Public Interest.* London: Sage.

21. Pippa Norris and David Sanders. 1998. "Does Balance Matter? Experiments in TV News." Paper prepared for Panel 38-12, "The ABC of Media Effects in British Elections: Agenda, Balance and Change," at the Annual Meeting of the American Political Science Association, Boston, September 3–6.

22. William L. Miller, Neil Sonntag, and David Broughton. 1989. "Television in the 1987 British Election Campaign: Its Content and Influence." *Political Studies* 37 (4): 630–50.

23. McQuail. 1992. *Media Performance.*

24. Norris and Sanders. 1998. "'Does Balance Matter?"

25. David Ward. 2006. "Final Report: The Assessment of Content Diversity in Newspapers and Television in the Context of Increasing Trends Towards Concentration of Media Markets." Report prepared for the Group of Specialists on Media Diversity (MC-S-MD), Media Division, Directorate General of Human Rights, Council of Europe, Strasbourg.

26. Radenko Udovicic, ed. 2007. *TV Prime Time Domestic News—Monitoring and Analysis of TV News Programs in 10 SEENPM Countries—Indicator of Public Interest.* Sarajevo: Media Plan Institute.

27. Analyzing bias in the news carries a certain degree of subjectivity. Researching the directional balance includes analysis of the journalists' attitudes and the stances they take in covering the report and at the same time analysis of the tone of the report.

28. Udovicic. 2007. "Introduction," 14.

29. Adam *Briggs and Paul Cobley. 2005. Uvod u studije medija (The Media: An Introduction).* Belgrade: Clio, 141.

30. Péter Bajomi-Lázár & Áron Monori. 2007. "Hungary." In *TV Prime Time Domestic News—Monitoring and Analysis of TV News Programs in 10 SEENPM Countries—Indicator of Public Interest,* ed. Radenko Udovicic, 109–26. Sarajevo: Media Plan Institute.

31. Dragomir, Reljic, Thompson. 2005. *Television across Europe: Regulation, Policy and Independence.*

32. Dubravka Valic Nedeljkovic and Višnja Bacanovic. 2007. "Serbia" In *TV Prime Time Domestic News—Monitoring and Analysis of TV News Programs in 10 SEENPM Countries—Indicator of Public Interest,* ed. Radenko Udovicic, 197–230. Sarajevo: Media Plan Institute.

33. IJC Research Center. 2007. "Moldova" In *TV Prime Time Domestic News—Monitoring and Analysis of TV News Programs in 10 SEENPM Countries—Indicator of Public Interest,* ed. Radenko Udovicic, 145–60. Sarajevo: Media Plan Institute.

34. Zrinjka Peruško and Helena Popovic. 2006. "Content Diversity vs. Ownership Concentration in a New Media Market: The Case of Croatia." Paper presented at the International *Conference* on Cultural Policy Research (ICCPR), Vienna, July 12–16.

35. Ward. 2006. "Final Report: The Assessment of Content Diversity in Newspapers and Television."

36. Dubravka Valic Nedeljkovic and Višnja Bacanovic. 2007. "Serbia" In *TV Prime Time Domestic News.*

37. Vesna Šopar. 2008. "Republic of Macedonia." In *Television across Europe: Follow-up Reports 2008,* ed. Marius Dragomir and Mark Thompson. Budapest: Open Society Institute. http://www.mediapolicy.org.

38. Manuela Preoteasa. 2007. "Romania." In *TV Prime Time Domestic News—Monitoring and Analysis of TV News Programs in 10 SEENPM Countries—Indicator of Public Interest,* ed. Radenko Udovicic, 175–95. Sarajevo: Media Plan Institute.

39. Association of Young Journalists. 2007. "Montenegro." In *TV Prime Time Domestic News—Monitoring and Analysis of TV News Programs in 10 SEENPM Countries—Indicator of Public Interest,* ed. Radenko Udovicic, 161–74. Sarajevo: Media Plan Institute.

40. William Horsley, ed. 2007. "Goodbye to Freedom? A Survey of Media Freedom across Europe." Association of European Journalists, Brussels.

41. Ibid.

42. Ibid., 5.

43. Manuela Preoteasa. 2008. "Romania." In *Television across Europe: Follow-up Reports 2008,* ed. Marius Dragomir and Mark Thompson. Budapest: Open Society Institute. http://www.mediapolicy.org.

44. Preoteasa. 2008. "Romania."

45. Udovicic. 2007. "Introduction."

46. "Transnational Media Concentrations in Europe." 2004. Advisory Panel to the CDMM on Media Concentrations, Pluralism and Diversity Questions (AP-MD), Media Division, Directorate General of Human Rights, Council of Europe, Strasbourg..

47. Ward. 2006. "Final Report: The Assessment of Content Diversity in Newspapers and Television."

48. Ward distinguishes between hard news, consisting of business and economy, consumer affairs, education, environment, health, home security and crime, international affairs, party political affairs, political affairs, public services, social issues, and soft news, consisting of arts and culture, celebrity, entertainment, human interest, lifestyle, religion, science, sports, women's issues.

49. Ward. 2006. "Final Report: The Assessment of Content Diversity in Newspapers and Television."

# 11

# Sub-Saharan Africa

Wisdom J. Tettey

A major fillip to the process of democratization and citizen engagement in Africa has been the changes in media ownership and pluralism over the past two decades or so. There is no question about the fact that the media landscape in Africa over this period has shown significant shifts, with tremendous expansion in the number of media outlets, as democratic transformations make inroads into what used to be largely dictatorial political environments.[1] Even countries with regimes that are not receptive to democratic ideals have not escaped these developments and have seen spaces open for mediated politics.

Various analysts contend that there is a positive relationship between expanded access to information, political pluralism, and demands for more accountable government. As Jacob points out: "It is widely agreed that the health of democracy in the 20th and 21st century is linked to the health of systems of communication, though of course democracy cannot be reduced to issues of the media."[2] Yet pessimists argue that the benefits expected to flow from media privatization do not necessarily yield the expected dividends but rather reinforce the influence, and protect the interests, of powerful elements in society.

This chapter investigates the extent to which the African media are a critical factor in the development and consolidation of democratic governance through their gatekeeping, agenda-setting, and watchdog roles. It contends that the media's ability to make positive contributions is dependent on a contingent configuration of conditions, including a commitment to an ethos of democratic engagement and expression by governments and citizens. Also critical are progressive, professional, and responsible media personnel and organizations that demonstrate critical independence, democratic constructiveness, and commercial viability.[3] The chapter argues, further, that the success of the media in accomplishing their roles will depend, to a significant degree, on the efficacy of institutions of vertical and horizontal accountability in ensuring that democratic principles are adhered to by all actors.

The chapter establishes the basis for this argument through comparative analysis of different media systems in Africa and their relationship to democratic governance. The framework is anchored in themes that proceed from the contingent variables mentioned above. It thus allows the examination of the contributions the media have made to democratic accountability, political education, and an informed citizenry. The framework also enables a critical interrogation of the challenges that confront the media as they strive to accomplish their normative gatekeeping, agenda-setting, and watchdog roles. In sum, the framework facilitates an analysis of triggers that enhance the media's ability to influence the public sphere, as a progressive force, and contribute to accountability on the part of various actors in society, while at the same time engaging with the constraints on those triggers. The ensuing sections are built around these dimensions of the analytical framework.

The framework, though based on such concepts as the gatekeeping, agenda-setting, and watchdog role of the media, does not see them as discrete categories but rather as mutually reinforcing and fluid. The ensuing analyses, therefore, reflect the intersection of these concepts in understanding the major themes around which this discussion of the media, accountability, and good governance nexus takes place. The objective of this chapter is not to dichotomize "good" or "bad" countries, but to interrogate and provide an overview of what are good or bad practices and enabling or disabling conditions in various countries. Such an approach not only credits, and encourages learning from, the efforts of media practitioners and citizens in countries that score poorly on indicators of media freedom, but also cautions against omnibus adulation and complacency in jurisdictions that rank high on the barometer of democracy watchers, such as Freedom House or the Afrobarometer.

## Gatekeeping and Fostering of Civic Competence

As noted in earlier parts of this book, gatekeeping is a vital process that determines the silencing or expression of various voices. Those who control the conduits for expression have the power to filter what kind of information, or whose, gets into the public realm and hence gets attention or shapes the public discourse. The media have a significant influence on the public sphere, through the exercise of this control. Depending on how they exercise this control, the media can help shape civic competence among citizens. *Civic competence* is the citizens' ability to understand, engage with, and make appropriate demands on the state while meeting their responsibilities and obligations as citizens, for example, through voting and public service. The following sections explore how the media in Africa are helping to generate civic competence through their gatekeeping roles.

### Gatekeepers, Information Flow, and Informed Citizenship

It is no secret that governments everywhere are not enamored with coverage that will put them in a bad light. However, an informed and engaged citizenry is not cultivated by foisting on them only the politically palatable. The media in various African countries have demonstrated that they are willing to defy the wrath of their governments to bring information to the public that will enable them to assess their political leaders accurately and to hold them accountable.

In his analysis of South African media, Jacobs contends that "media are not merely conduits for the government, political parties or citizens in post-apartheid South Africa, but have emerged as autonomous power centers in competition with other power centers."[4] This is vividly illustrated by the significant influence that the media have had in relation to civic education, election monitoring, and results tallying. The extent to which a vibrant media environment affects citizens' engagement with their political system, particularly in relation to elections, has been extensively established by several studies. Kuenzi and Lambright, for example, conclude, based on a study of countries that have had two consecutive multiparty elections since the early 1990s, that a significant positive relationship exists between media exposure and voter turnout in Africa's multiparty democratic elections.[5]

In their analysis of the impact of private media growth in Madagascar, Andriantsoa et al. note that "over 90 private radio stations and 15 private television stations have begun operation over the last decade. The resulting profusion of private media has played a key role in improving governance, most recently in the hotly contested presidential election of 2001."[6] Private media not only became sources for a diverse array of perspectives and political platforms, but also provided the conduit for civic action in support of particular causes, as they were used to galvanize and mobilize supporters of opposition parties for rallies against the incumbent regime, a scenario that was inconceivable when only state-controlled media existed. In the Democratic Republic of Congo, community radio stations were credited with playing a critical role in getting information about the country's political transition and elections to the public, particularly in areas isolated by the long, drawn-out conflict.

The extensive opacity of government transactions in Africa is inimical to good governance because it makes it difficult for citizens to know the whys and hows of processes and decisions that affect their lives and, therefore, their ability to hold their public officials to account. It is therefore refreshing when the media bring transparency to those transactions and interactions and help citizens understand the basis for certain occurrences and consequences and actions that will otherwise not be known to them. This was the case in Uganda, when President Museveni sent a letter to his prime minister and members of Parliament on May 4, 2008, expressing concern about the inflation of road construction costs and corruption in the award of road contracts. In order to situate the president's concerns within a context, the *Daily Monitor* managed to get access to the brief on the basis of which the president wrote his letter. It then provided the public with information that showed the extent of impropriety within the Road Agency and Formation Unit (RAFU) of the Ministry of Works. According to the *Daily Monitor*'s report:

> The brief to the President noted that the contract award figures differed sharply with estimates of external consulting engineers hired by the ministry and noted that the government in the worst case scenario could have saved US$20 million for the three projects, if the tendering process had been transparent. For example, while consultants—PKS Group of South Africa—estimated the Kabale-Kisoro Road construction to cost US$36 million (approx. Shs 65 billion [Ugandan shillings]), RAFU later contracted it out at a cost of US$80 million (approx. Shs 147 billion). This means that the government is paying Shs 82 billion more than the consultant's estimates. The accompanying analysis for the brief handed over to the President also notes that another consultant, Gauff Engineering Ltd., had estimated the cost of Soroti-Dokolo-Lira Road at US$47 million (approx. Shs 85 billion) but RAFU handed over the tender to China Road and Bridge at US$88 million (approx. Shs 160 billion).[7]

In a country where the road network is falling apart, it is useful for the public to fully understand the machinations behind escalating construction costs and shoddy work in order to counter other narratives explaining why they have to contend with crumbling infrastructure.

The same desire to contextualize developments that affect the public explains why, despite efforts by the Nigerien regime of Mamadou Tandja to clamp down on coverage of the Tuareg question by jailing several journalists who write about the matter, the persistence of those journalists has succeeded in bringing it to the attention of the international community. Drawing Nigeriens', as well as worldwide, attention to the conflict between the rebels and the government is important. It helps to unravel the real reasons behind the conflict, to expose its nature, and to critically assess the role of the various actors in order to foster solutions that go beyond those based on the government's claim that the rebels are just drug traffickers or bandits. In the words of Callahan, "Journalism is a profession with unique privileges and obligations. Journalists can claim their goal is to seek and communicate truths about the world on behalf of the common good."[8]

In view of the relationship between an informed citizenry and a sophisticated voter, it is obvious that the more people are able to access information, and engage with the public discourses around them, the more likely they are to hold politicians accountable, make the political choices that benefit them, reward or sanction governments through those choices, and hence increase the chances of getting a responsive state. As Schaffner writes: "The extent to which elections are useful instruments of accountability is closely related to the ability of citizens to acquire and utilize information about candidates and elected officials running in those contests. If citizens are not presented with a sufficient amount of information about competing candidates, then they may be less able to evaluate these candidates and to make reasonable choices between them."[9]

### Gatekeepers, Inclusive Citizenship, and Progressive Media Activism

It is fair to acknowledge that much of the mediated public sphere in Africa is captured by elite discourses, raising concerns about whose interests are served by the spaces opened up by processes of democratization. Although this issue of a constricted public sphere will be taken up later, it is important to note the efforts being made by sections of the media to champion the interests of the marginalized and vulnerable in society and to ensure that their situations are given visibility on the national agenda. This was the case with a group of Sudanese journalists who were arrested in August 2006 while investigating the negative impact of a dam on dislocated residents of Marawi and the displacement of people in Algazera province as a result of the authorities giving their lands to a foreign businessman. Efforts such as these allow the public to raise questions about government actions and their impacts, and to hold their officials accountable, even if there is no immediate respite for the victims. The work of Uganda Media Women's Association in educating women, particularly in rural areas, about their rights; providing them with avenues to articulate their concerns; and inserting those voices into deliberations in the public sphere is another laudable achievement by the media on behalf of the marginalized. These acts constitute what Carroll and Hacket call progressive media activism.[10]

A fundamental responsibility of the media in support of democratic governance is their serving as a means for the expression of varied views. A sign of the development of democratic discourse in Africa is that, even in a country such as Sudan, where the authorities were obdurately intolerant of dissent a decade ago, editorials, such as the pro-South *Khartoum Monitor*'s of March 18, 2007, excoriated China and Russia for fueling the Darfur conflict by pursuing activities in Sudan that put pecuniary gain above human rights. The editorial argues that "it is not solely the government of Sudan that kills its own people, but it does so in collaboration with whoever helps it reach these heinous levels of human rights violation." On the same day, the *Citizen* slammed the Sudanese government's links to the Janjeweed militia, denouncing it as "a racist regime that is in many respects worse than the Apartheid regime in South Africa, which at least had the dignity not to employ rape as a tactic of suppression." The foregoing provides the context for the following comment from Adil Elbaz, editor of the private paper *Al-Sahafa*: "The Sudanese press is not really free, ... but we are making progress."[11]

The need for the media to use their control over access to the public sphere to enhance inclusive citizenship and free democratic expression is exemplified by the principled position taken by the editor-in-chief of Ghana's *Statesman* newspaper, Gabby Otchere Darko, who came out in support of what is considered a taboo by arguing for the rights of gays, lesbians, bisexuals, and transgendered people to inclusive citizenship. He made this contribution in the wake of extensive public outrage against the gay lifestyle, following some media reports about a purported gay conference in the country in late 2006. The bold position adopted by such a high-profile journalist is highly commendable in view of the fact that his position was significantly out of tune with that of an overwhelming majority of citizens, public officials, journalists and media outlets, religious leaders, and the statutory body tasked with protecting human rights in the country, the Commission on Human Rights and Administrative Justice. The chairman of the commission stated unequivocally that the commission will not advocate gay rights. What the journalist did was to educate the public on the need to protect minority rights in a democracy and to provoke a discourse that pushed for a critical assessment of the basis for public revulsion toward homosexuality and the laws that criminalize that lifestyle. His intervention helped to fulfill a vital role for media practitioners in support of democracy, which is to educate the public to understand and appreciate the value of substantive citizenship for all members of society and the importance of protecting it.

In African countries, where political differences and their attendant tensions can create highly volatile political situations, the media have a significant role in curbing those potentials, by ensuring a critical balance between diversity of voices and responsible journalism. This critical balance was demonstrated by some media practitioners during the postelection violence that engulfed Kenya between late 2007 and early 2008. Although the media were not able to prevent the eruption, spread, and continuation of violence, some made a conscious effort not to exacerbate the situation. They did this by bringing to the fore perspectives that aimed at calming tempers and promoting reconciliation among the various factions. In fact, a number of traditional rivals in the media rose above the fray and came together to forge a common purpose of galvanizing support for peace and defusing the political tension. On January 3, 2007, the *Nation* and the *Standard* published a common editorial, headlined "Save Our Nation." That caption was echoed by television stations, as they streamed the words across television screens, and radio stations carried the editorials.

As noted in a report by Reporters without Borders, "the press very quickly agreed on appealing for calm and collective prayers, running joint editorials in Nairobi's main newspapers and avoiding sensationalism and comments likely to aggravate ethnic divisions. The line was "peace above all."[12]

Many African journalists are living with, and haunted by, the aftermath of indelible images imprinted on their consciousness partly as a result of some Rwandese media's complicity in the genocide of 1994. Consequently, they are careful not to fan sentiments that could degenerate into chaos, discrimination, and targeted reprisals. Indeed, Kenya had seen the markings of such tendencies when, during the 2005 constitutional referendum, some media organizations were accused of fomenting violence and division between those groups that supported the Constitution and those that did not—divisions that broke down largely along ethnic lines. *Kass FM*, a private radio station that broadcast in Kalenjin, was, for example, suspended as a result of these accusations.

## Watchdog Journalism, Agenda Setting, and Democratic Accountability

The watchdog role of the media entails exercising some oversight over the public realm in ways that ensure that various actors and agents are kept in check and held to the requirements of their roles in the polity. The watchdog function is closely related to democratic accountability, which is

> based on the understanding that the only way that the various freedoms, civil liberties, and other constitutional provisions, and indeed democracy itself, can be protected and sustained is when those who occupy positions of responsibility in the state are made to respect those provisions and freedoms. That is to say, they must imbibe, protect, and practice the tenets of the rule of law, thereby eschewing any inclination toward arbitrariness and abuse. Accountability also flows from the notion of good governance, which is premised on the expectation that office holders will manifest behaviors, attitudes, and actions that are in conformity with the principles of transparency, efficiency, and integrity. These political actors are also expected to be open to monitoring by citizens, civil society organizations, and other institutions of the state.[13]

The concept of agenda setting, for its part, is based on the premise that the media have the ability to shape the nature and focus of public discourse because of their control over the means of information dissemination. What is considered important in a country depends, to a significant extent, on the visibility and salience that the media put on it. "Watchdogging," agenda setting, and democratic accountability are interrelated. What the media choose to monitor and report on shape the public agenda and elicit answerability from relevant actors and the imposition of appropriate sanctions by citizens or state institutions. The extent to which the African media play these intersecting roles is the focus of the following discussion.

## Demanding State Action and Accountability

One of the areas where these intersecting roles have been remarkably demonstrated by the African media has to do with respect for human rights. The
leadership role taken by some of Africa's media to advocate respect for human
rights, in spite of the dangers entailed in such advocacy, is vividly illustrated
by two cases. The first involves a report in early May 2008 by Uganda's *Independent*, which documented alleged abuse and torture of civilian detainees by
operatives of the state's paramilitary institutions, thereby drawing attention
to the plight of the alleged victims and raising questions about the appropri-
ateness of the state's tactics in dealing with civilian detainees. In that case the
detainees were accused of having links to rebel groups, such as the People's
Redemption Army; associating with the opposition Allied Democratic Forces
(ADF); or leaking classified government information.[14] As Jones admonishes:
"Truth telling speaks to the responsibility of journalism to cover those people
who normally may not have access to the media and to cover those issues that
need light shone upon them. Investigative journalism, in particular, should
not be a witless apologist for dominant values— ... stories can expand, even
if only a little, the community's understanding of its values, along with its
willingness to apply them more justly—or it may reveal that the community
no longer cares."[15]

The second case involves *Joyfm*, a private radio station in Ghana, which
went beyond reporting to mobilize financial support for the medical expenses
of a seven-year-old victim of sexual abuse at the hands of her 67-year-old
grandfather.[16] Not only did the station raise thousands of dollars for the treatment of the victim, whose health was severely damaged by the abuse and who
is now HIV-positive, it also kept the issue of pedophilia on the national consciousness in a very palpable but sensitive way, leading to the prosecution of
the grandfather and demonstrations expressing outrage at the increasing spate
of child rape in the country. Indeed, there is growing realization among media
practitioners that they are not just there to report facts, but have a responsibility to put those facts in context, tease out the reasons behind them as
well as their implications, and elevate them as the focus of public engagement
and state action. As noted by several media practitioners in Ghana's Northern
Region, following training programs by Journalists for Human Rights (JHR),
journalists' perceptions about human rights have changed. "We just reported
incidents like, 'A man in Saboba has raped a school girl,' but we wouldn't
investigate it further. We wouldn't go into the societal problems underlying
it." *Radio Justice* now has a weekly human rights program and regularly covers human rights issues in its daily news updates. At Radio Justice, Ramadan
Abdul Razak, an investigative reporter, said, "We always looked at human
interest, not human rights. We would just get the facts. We never followed up
to make a change. Now we push to change things. We now realize there are
human rights issues in every story."[17]

Various media organizations and practitioners have played a significant role in holding public officials and institutions to account by exposing acts of commission and omission that undermine good governance. One such major case involves the "Oilgate Scandal" in South Africa, which was exposed in 2005 by investigative journalists from the *Mail & Guardian (M&G)*. The gist of the scandal, which is worth quoting directly from the newspaper, is as follows:

> A *Mail & Guardian* investigation into covert party funding has revealed how R 11-million of public money was diverted to African National Congress coffers ahead of the 2004 elections. In what may be the biggest political funding scandal since 1994, the *M&G* has established that South Africa's state oil company, Pet-roSA, irregularly paid R 15-million to Imvume Management—a company closely tied to the ANC—at a time when the party was desperate for funds to fight elections. The *M&G* possesses bank statements and has seen other forensic evidence proving that Imvume transferred the lion's share of this to the ANC within days. PetroSA this week said it was unaware of this. The ANC denied impropriety and said it was not obliged to discuss its funders. The scheme unfolded in two stages. First, PetroSA management bent over backwards to pay Imvume the money as an advance for the procurement of oil condensate. Then, when Imvume diverted the funds to the ANC instead of paying its own foreign suppliers, PetroSA had to cover the shortfall by paying the same amount again. A multimillion-rand hole remains in the parastatal's books. PetroSA has gone through the motions to recover the debt by suing Imvume—but most of it remains outstanding. The effect of the entire transaction was that PetroSA, and ultimately the taxpayer, subsidised the ruling party's election campaign: a blatant abuse of public resources.[18]

The revelations from this story led to an investigation by the Public Protector, a statutory position under the South African Constitution, whose responsibility it is to hold public officials accountable. The Public Protector subsequently issued a report that was seen by many observers as unsatisfactory. In the context of this reaction, it is revealing of the commitment of the South African media to their watchdog and agenda-setting roles that the *Mail & Guardian* did not rest on its laurels after revealing the alleged connivance among the African National Congress (ANC), Imvume, and PetroSA. For two years, since the report's release in 2005, it vigorously pursued another line of action that focused the lens on the public prosecutor and the quality of the investigations; it sought recourse to the courts for the report to be reviewed, under the Promotion of Administrative Justice Act. This was to ensure that certain dimensions of the initial allegations that were not taken up by the Public Protector, or for which the parties involved were exonerated, were explored further. The newspaper's efforts paid off when, in November 2007, a court started hearing its case. It is worth noting that the allegations of campaign contributions from Imvume were confirmed when the ANC's former treasurer disclosed at the Party's Congress in December 2007 that the party did receive the R 11 million donation, but "immediately returned the entire donation to the donor in two instalments of R 6-million on the 31st May 2005 and R 5-million on the 20th June 2005."[19] In spite of the assertion from the ANC that the issue was resolved by repaying the donation, the newspaper continues to keep the matter on the national agenda by raising certain unresolved questions, and the opposition parties have taken up the issue as well. Similar work by other South African media outlets have helped to expose the nefarious activities of public officials, such as the links between former police chief Jackie Selebi and associates of slain shadowy businessman Brett Kebble. In Ghana, investigations by the *Inquirer* led to credible recorded allegations, by a chairman of the New Patriotic Party of President Kufuor, that his government was receiving kickbacks from contractors working on government projects.[20]

The valuable role of the media in agenda setting is borne out by the fact that initial investigative work by various journalists has provided the basis from which relevant state institutions have taken up and pursued lapses in performance, malfeasance, corruption in government, and so forth, and consequently brought those concerned to book. For example, the *Beeld*'s Adriaan Basson and Carien du Plessis were responsible for revelations of impropriety on the part of former prisons commissioner Linda Mti in the awarding of contracts, an exposure that eventually led to the "early departure" of the commissioner and the Department of Correctional Services' chief financial officer from their posts. "Despite being threatened with court action, the two journalists established a link between Mti and a company that won a dubious, multimillion-rand tender, and then proved that the tender document had been written by the company which won it."[21]

A critical role of government is the exercise of due diligence. Unfortunately, many governments on the continent have shirked these responsibilities, with significant repercussions for the national purse and the provision of quality stewardship to their citizens. Fortunately, the media are stepping in to fill this gap by scrutinizing legislative and executive decisions, for example, to ensure that they are credible, feasible, and in the national interest. The work of some Ghanaian media helps to illustrate this contribution. In 2002 the Kufour government sought parliamentary approval of a loan agreement with International Finance Consortium (IFC) for an amount totaling about US$1 billion. Investigations by the *Ghana Palavar*, an opposition newspaper, revealed that the company was bogus and was using an acronym similar to that of the International Finance Corporation of the World Bank to gain credibility for its dubious operations.[22]

The revelations led to pressure on the government by opposition parties, other media organizations, and the public to defend its decision to enter into the agreement or to save the country from a hoax of tremendous proportions by pulling out.[23] The latter option eventually prevailed. The fact that the same government got caught up in another sham loan agreement with Chinese New Techniques Construction Investments Limited (CNTCI) is troubling and shows that in the absence of an active public sphere, where such agreements are subject to public scrutiny, the country can be taken for ransom. In the latter case, the leading opposition party, the National Democratic Congress, raised significant questions about the trustworthiness of the agreement, after it was passed by Parliament. Follow-up investigations by *Ghana Palavar* and *Radio Gold* confirmed the fraud when they revealed that the address of CNTCI, indicated on the agreement, was occupied by a hairdressing salon.[24]

## Holding Nonstate Actors Accountable

There is a tendency among analysts who look at the media's watchdog role, in the context of democracies and transitional polities, to focus on state officials and government institutions to the neglect of other actors and centers of activity whose actions have significant implications for good governance, democratic accountability, and the sustainability of democratic institutions and practices. This dimension of the media's watchdog and agenda-setting roles is manifested by the efforts of journalists in Guinea-Bissau to bring visibility to the activities of drug traffickers in their country and to seek action on the part of state institutions to stem the trade and expose officials who are aiding and abetting the barons. The work of Allen Yéro Emballo and Agnello Regala in this respect is noteworthy, even though it has led to exile for the former and continued threats and intimidation of the latter by highly placed military officials suspected of being accomplices. The media's work in keeping an eye on this burgeoning transnational drug business is as critical to building and sustaining good governance as the traditional focus on state-media relations. This is because these activities tend to undermine and corrupt state institutions, cow journalists, and sow seeds of fear among the populace in ways that take away the public's ability to confront the perpetrators and protect the rule of law.

The media are also extending their scrutiny of the public realm to encompass private companies whose activities undermine the integrity of the polity and undercuts the ability of the public to get what it deserves. In South Africa, *Independent Newspapers'* Bruce Cameron investigated a pension-fund scandal, unearthing the fact that companies administering the retirement fund were making, and stashing away, huge profits to the detriment of beneficiaries. The significance of this story is captured in the following citation by a panel of judges, explaining the basis for declaring Cameron the winner of the *Sanlam Financial Journalist of the Year Award* for 2006: "Cameron's tenacity in exposing undesired practices in the financial services industry, and generally promoting consumer education, has set new standards for personal finance and investigative journalism in the country. In his entries, he exposed how Alexander Forbes skimmed off millions of 'secret profits' at the expense of retirement funds and their members—arguably the most telling financial story break of 2006 with wide-ranging consequences for the financial services industry. The exposé resulted, amongst other things, in an industry-wide [Financial Services Board] investigation, proposed legislative amendments, and a repayment of some R 500 million to retirement funds."[25]

There have been numerous stories across the continent outlining the impact of private extractive industries on the lives of marginalized communities whose voice has been drowned by the exigencies and dictates of a neoliberal economic agenda being pursued by governments and corporations.[26] By focusing on such development news, the media not only reveal the immediate detrimental impacts that come with the operations of these industries, but also engage the public in a larger debate about the benefits and beneficiaries of state and private company policies, including the socioeconomic dislocation of communities, the impact on the environment, and sustainable livelihoods. A May 19, 2008, editorial by the *Citizen*, of Tanzania, explores these issues as it analyzes the plight of

> about 200 families in Geita District [who] are living as refugees in their own country after their houses were demolished to pave the way for large-scale mining.... It is cause for concern that conflicts over land pitting big business against ordinary Tanzanians are now an all too familiar occurrence in the country. Apart from the Geita tug-of-war, there are similar disputes in Dar es Salaam, Arusha, and Mara regions, some of which are the subjects of long drawn-out court cases. Some of these conflicts have turned bloody as locals resist eviction from land which some have occupied for years.[27]

## Postnational Constellations, the Virtual Public Sphere, and Civic Discourse[28]

An important consequence of the opportunities provided by the Internet is the extent to which the state's hold on its citizens has been ruptured, if not completely eliminated. Under the media configurations of the past, characterized by centralized control of mass-mediated information production and dissemination in African countries, the ability of citizens to produce content and share their views was constrained by the gatekeeping role of state agents. The transformations in media ownership, control, and information dissemination made possible by the Internet means that counter-discourses that challenge the hegemonic viewpoint of the state are being vigorously articulated within the virtual architecture of this reconfigured public sphere.[29]

These opportunities are particularly available to Africans located outside the territorial boundaries of their states of origin. The location of Africans in the diaspora gives them the opportunity to access and assess information in ways that most of their compatriots may not be able to. They are, consequently, better able to authenticate or debunk various narratives that may be put out by state actors in their countries of origin. Their observations are then posted to support or challenge those dominant discourses. Discussion forums and chat rooms thus provide a plethora of deliberative politics, as burning issues are brought up, opinions are expressed, and analyses are provided. This process is illustrated by Bernal's (2006) study of Eritrean Internet networks,[30] which provide a veritable public sphere in which ideas that cannot be expressed in the context of the oppressive controls of the state are articulated, disseminated, and debated among interactants who may not be familiar with each other in physical space but engage one another in cyberspace. It is obvious that the poster quoted below will not have the temerity to say the following words in the real world of Nigerian politics without fear of physically harmful retribution: "No incorrigible president has a case, moral or otherwise, against an incorrigible deputy. You keep writing like OBJ has some moral ground to stand on here, he doesn't. *OBJ and Atiku are murderers and thieves* [emphasis in the original]. They were both disbursing money from government accounts to buy cars for girlfriends while Nigerian children were dying from treatable diseases like malaria. Why not ask how Atiku should have dealt with the issue? In the fight between two rogues, he is doing what he should be doing exactly. Otherwise, he would have ended up like the Audu Ogbehs and Theophilus Danjumas who stole with OBJ, then got their hands chopped off while OBJ kept eating."[31]

One of the conduits for exercising voice is the blogosphere. In 2007 Wael Abbas, an Egyptian blogger who had been showcasing alleged police abuses inside prisons and against protestors on his site, went worldwide. "A video posting he made on YouTube, of a bus driver being sodomized with a stick at the hands of Egyptian police, forced an international spotlight on Egypt's security forces and their tactics. Two policemen from that incident were later sentenced to jail time, and Egypt is taking action over other incidents. Still, Abbas, who briefly had his YouTube account suspended some weeks ago, wants more—to inspire the Egyptian people to demand change. And as the first blogger to win the prestigious Knight International Journalism Award by the International Center for Journalists in early 2008, Abbas intends to keep up the fight online and keep his check on the Egyptian government."[32]

The ability of the Internet to allow for subjective narratives of history is significant enough; but its capacity to bring alive images that are ubiquitous and accessible to myriad people, (re)generate passions, contest particular versions of history, and mobilize transnational constituencies for the purpose of holding governments and various actors accountable for their actions make it a very powerful tool for democratic expression. In the African context, such imagery is exemplified by a Web site that was set up by some citizens of Anlo, in the Volta region of Ghana, to publish images of victims of what they considered to be government-supported police brutality during a confrontation among factions in a chieftaincy dispute. The caption accompanying the images states: "This Website (prototype) is being created to Honor of [sic] the Heroes and those who Paid the Ultimate Sacrifice to protect The Heritage and

Culture of the Anlo's [sic] on November 1 2007 in the Volta Region of Ghana. May Their Souls Rest in Peace!"[33]

## Challenges to Media as Facilitators of Accountability in Africa

The ability of the media to serve the interest of democratic governance in Africa is constrained by various obstacles. A significant part of these limitations derives from states that are unresponsive to democratic principles. It must be acknowledged, though, that the efficacious exercise of the media's influence is, to some extent, hampered by the actions of media personnel and organizations as well. The challenges posed by factors within these two arenas are the subject of the next two subsections.

### Obstacles to the Media-Democracy Nexus: The Role of the State

The African peer review mechanism has so far not been used as a credible tool to uphold and promote freedom of expression and independent media in several African states. In fact, many African governments use covert and overt means to deny access to information or to intimidate media houses and personnel. Among the most notorious of regimes in this respect are Eritrea, Zimbabwe, and Ethiopia. In spite of gains made over the past several years, "freedom of the press in Africa was badly damaged in 2007. On at least 12 occasions during the year, men received orders to kill journalists. Police received orders on almost 150 occasions to make an arrest, not of a corrupt minister or a notorious killer but of a journalist. Even governments of countries in which Reporters without Borders had invested some hope in previous years have brought instruments of repression to bear against the press."[34]

On a continent where access to information, through state institutions, is a huge challenge, the media have to depend on ordinary citizens to provide relevant insights upon which the press may pursue its responsibilities of informing deliberations and galvanizing action in the public sphere. Unfortunately, the fear of reprisals by targets of media scrutiny dissuades some citizens from taking up the role of informer. Such fears are not unfounded, as demonstrated in a case involving the head teacher of a primary school in Ghana who is believed, by most observers, to have been demoted and transferred as a result of granting journalists an interview in which she lamented low enrollments in the school, thereby critiquing the effectiveness of the government's education reform program.[35] In 2006, the Rwandese interior minister directed police to hold, in custody, any journalist who publishes an official document until he or she identifies the source of the leak. Such a fate stared Max Hamata, the editor of Namibia's *Informante*, in the face when he was threatened with imprisonment in February 2008 if he refused to reveal the source of information that formed the basis for a story the paper wrote about the mayor of Windhoek. These types of orders and threats are not comforting to prospective sources of information for journalists. In the light of these facts, President Kibaki has to be commended for refusing to sign the Media Bill of 2007, which included a provision that would have compelled journalists to reveal their sources. According to Kibaki, such a provision constitutes a threat to freedom of expression and undermines the country's democratic achievements.

Although states with a sanguine attitude toward the media have created an environment for journalists and media organizations to build or enhance their capacity as active voices and vessels for democratic discourse in the public sphere, their brutal, intolerant, and dictatorial counterparts have succeeded in eroding the capacity of media practitioners to champion democratic causes. This erosion occurs because the most accomplished journalists, who are unwilling to compromise professionalism and commitment to vocation, are being lost through jail sentences, death, or exile. These developments take a heavy toll on the ability of the profession to regenerate itself in ways that allow members to contribute meaningfully to the emergence, growth, and sustainability of a pluralistic democratic polity.

As the Internet becomes a powerful nexus for information dissemination, civic engagement, and contestations of state action and propaganda, a number of governments are beginning to monitor it and to curb expression in this virtual public sphere. Since 2006, the Ethiopian government has blocked access to Web sites and blogs that it considers critical of the regime, with the Ethiopian Telecommunications Agency instructing cybercafes to record names and addresses of customers so that they could be punished, including being imprisoned, for any untoward behavior. Similar requirements prevail in Tunisia. Zimbabwe has secured Chinese technology to enable it to implement the provisions of the Interception of Communication Act, which authorizes state agencies to monitor telephone, fax, and email messages. The Egyptian government, for its part, has increased online censorship, coming down very hard on bloggers who express critical views. In fact, in the summer of 2006, the government passed a law on Internet regulation that facilitates such clamping down under the pretext of protecting national security. Several bloggers were arrested and incarcerated for varying lengths of time, in 2007, for expressing their opinions.[36] State monitoring of the Internet for dissenting views is what led to the arrest, in March 2007, of Fatou Jaw Manneh, a U.S.-based Gambian journalist, when she arrived in the country. She had published several articles on Web sites, including AllGambain.net, and was prosecuted for an article, in October 2005, in which she accused President Yahya Jammeh of "tearing our beloved country to shreds" and described the head of state as a "bundle of terror." She was charged with "intention to commit sedition," "publication of seditious words," and "publication of false news intended to create public fear and alarm," and faces three years in prison.[37]

The use of legislation and executive fiat is a tried, tested, and effective weapon in the hands of governments that want to hide behind self-serving legality to circumscribe deliberations in the mediated public sphere and beyond. In Sudan, for example, Article 130 of the Code of Criminal Procedure is used to gag reportage on significant events that the government does not want exposed. This provision was invoked to indefinitely suspend *Al-Sudani* in 2007 for making reference to the murder of Mohammed Taha, editor of *Al-Waifaq*. *Al-Sudani*'s action was in defiance of a government directive imposing a news blackout on the case, ostensibly to avert any trouble. In August 2006, Rwanda's highest court upheld the "public offence" conviction of Charles Kaonero, editor of *Umuseso*, a weekly private newspaper. He was given a one-year suspended prison sentence and fined one million Rwandan francs (1,450 euros) for articles that appeared in the newspaper criticizing the conduct of government business and raising questions about the political influence of the country's deputy speaker who was alleged to have rented offices in his private building to various state institutions.

The reintroduction of an advanced censorship committee in Chad, under state-of-emergency legislation, has been the bane of newspapers, as has the banning, on radio and television, of issues considered inimical to national security. The media's ability to inform, raise questions, and critically engage with issues confronting the citizenry, at a time of national turmoil and desperation, has been severely eroded. Apart from one pro-government private newspaper, *Le Progrès*, all publications in Njamena come to the newsstands with substantial parts blacked out. Ostensibly to protect the national interest, a journalist of a community radio station, Radio Brakoss, was arrested by state security forces and jailed in 2007 for publishing a story accusing the local police chief of extorting money from local residents. His crime?—"ruthless handling of sensitive news which could harm national cohesion"![38]

Laws that punish media practitioners for "insulting the president" continue to be preponderant. These laws restrict the use of the media for legitimate critique of government policies and officials. The laws are able to do this because of the nebulous definition given to such violations. Any views against the stance of the president could be characterized as an insult for which the persons expressing them could be arrested and incarcerated. It is a sad commentary on the state of democracy on the continent that even countries, such as Kenya, which are considered to be beacons of democracy, have retrogressive laws that punish journalists, ostensibly for the "publication of false news." For example, a story in the February 25, 2007, edition of the *Standard*, indicating that a meeting had taken place between the president and a former cabinet minister (who had left the government several months earlier because of his opposition to the government's draft constitution) evoked the government's anger. This led to the arrests of the paper's managing editor, editor, and a reporter. They were charged with publishing false rumors with the aim of causing public panic. This was followed, days later, with a raid on the premises of the paper's printer by police, who seized and burned copies of the March 2 edition. Instead of punishing journalists who may have made genuine errors in their reportage, it is more useful to see these mistakes as an indictment on governments that are reluctant to grant access to relevant information, thereby compelling journalists to scramble through other means to gather news and to inform the public. The above incidents in Kenya illustrate why it is important that analyses of the media-democracy nexus in Africa not lose sight of the fact that a vibrant and diverse media system is not necessarily coterminous with civil liberties for journalists.[39] This is also exemplified by Nigeria, probably the most animated media setting on the continent, where attacks, intimidation, and arrests of journalists are commonplace. The notorious State Security Service (SSS) continues to wage a constant assault on media freedom.[40]

In some instances, aggrieved public officials take it upon themselves to settle scores with the media for subjecting their government to public scrutiny and for providing a forum for perspectives that contradict or are critical of those espoused by state officials. A most ignominious example of this occurred in Ghana in April 2008 when a government minister angrily interrupted a live discussion program on *Metro TV*, broadcasting on location at a facility where a United Nations Conference on Trade and Development (UNCTAD) meeting was taking place, and ordered it closed. He said later that his goal was to protest the views of one guest, presumably for being partisan in violation of UNCTAD rules that the conference premises should not be used for political purposes. A more credible reason seems to be the fact that this guest, who is a regular critic of the government's economic policies and a leading member of an opposition party, was voicing unpleasant views in the presence of international media and conference participants.

The targets of the state actions referred to above are not just local journalists, but extend to foreign journalists whose portrayals of events are considered contrary to the interest of the governments in power. Thus, many foreign journalists who seek to cover the atrocities in Darfur, for example, are characterized as spies, refused visas, or denied permits to go to that region because they are seen as reflecting perspectives that do not put the government in a positive light in the global community. As noted by Reporters without Borders, blacklisting of foreign journalists stems from the perception that "many media have proved to be insulting towards the Sudanese government." In other words, it is portrayed as a legitimate self-defense by the government in reaction to criticism in the U.S. and European press since the start of the civil war in Darfur and, before that, during the 21 years of fighting between government troops and the southern rebels, especially John Garang's Sudan People's Liberation Army.[41]

Restrictions on the movement of journalists are not limited to the Sudan. Prior to the last presidential elections in Uganda, the Media Center, a recently created government-controlled media surveillance entity, summoned foreign correspondents to its offices and instructed them not to travel more than 100 kilometers outside of Kampala without its authorization. The BBC's Will Ross had his accreditation slashed from one year to four months soon after he filed a report about the death of seven civilians in a refugee camp in the north of the country. In the face of such obstacles, it is not surprising that some journalists are compelled to use unconventional, and sometimes illegal, means to get their stories, including unsanctioned entry into the country or certain areas. In Eritrea, foreign journalists function at the behest of the information minister, who has no qualms about revoking their permits if their coverage is deemed unfavorable to the government, such as reporting on violations of civil and political rights. However, in some instances, foreign media personnel have given governments cause to react negatively to them, owing to their lack of understanding of local realities, a fact that is betrayed by their reportage.

Governments and state officials employ not just the crude and brazen tactics referred to above to prevent the media from pursuing their roles of holding those officials accountable for their stewardship; they also deploy subtle means to intimidate media personnel and their organizations or to deprive the public of access to diverse political views. One such tactic is to starve media organizations that are critical of the government of advertising revenues, a very damaging tactic, since such revenues constitute a significant part of operating funds for private print and electronic media. The use of this tactic is exemplified by the Kenyan government's advice to public sector institutions, in April 2007, not to advertise in the *Standard* newspaper and Kenyan Television Network, both of which belong to the Standard Group. The government's email message instructed the institutions to send their ads to media organizations that were favorably disposed to the government's policies. The relationship between the government and the Standard Group had been frosty since a publication by the *Standard*, about a year earlier, suggesting that a minister had had discussions with a group of Armenian hit men to eliminate the son of former president Arap Moi.

Another tactic employed by some governments to block the public's access to opposing viewpoints is jamming broadcast signals. In fact, in February 2007, Zimbabwe's Deputy Minister of Information and Publicity, Bright Mutongo, acknowledged before Parliament that the government was jamming signals from Studio 7, a Washington, DC, station that broadcasts programs by Zimbabwean journalists in the United States that can be received in Zimbabwe on short- and medium-wave frequencies. In Cameroon, the government of Paul Biya simply limited access to the airwaves by not implementing a 1990 law allowing private broadcasting, waiting until 2000 to pass legislation to outline its implementation, and only granting licenses to the first four private broadcasters in 2007. Criminal or civil libel suits continue to be a strategy of choice to compel the media to acquiesce, self-censor, or fold up under the weight of fines or imprisonment.

Although the media landscape generally reveals significant challenges that still need to be addressed, the obstacles that confront the media are particularly dire in conflict areas. Here, the emotional proximity of journalists to atrocious realities that affect their very lives, and the difficulty of being dispassionate with regard to the different interests and claims behind the conflicts, affect journalists' objectivity. The consequent mistrust toward journalists held by various protagonists complicates journalistic practice and the role of the media in fostering compromises, consensus, national unity, or peace. In Darfur, for example, a human rights activist acknowledges that "displaced persons 'mistrust Sudanese journalists and, more generally, those from the Arab world' unless they are accompanied by trusted people"[42] In addition to the above challenges in conflict areas is the constant threat of physical violence. Somalia continues to be the most dangerous location for journalists. "The heavy toll for the Somali press reads as follows: Eight dead, four injured, some 50 journalists in exile, and others holed up at home after abandoning their work in fear. To this toll must be added 53 journalists arrested while doing their jobs, either in southern Somalia, where the capital Mogadishu is, in semiautonomous Puntland in the north, or in the self-proclaimed state of Somaliland in the northwest."[43]

## Watching the Watchdogs, Agenda Setters, and Gatekeepers

As this chapter explores the relationship between the media and democratic governance, the focus must include pointing a critical lens at the media as well. This is to ensure that the positive contributions discussed previously are not undermined by the lack of credibility as a result of the unprofessional conduct on the part of some journalists and media organizations.[44] As noted by Reporters without Borders: "Across the continent, chiefly in the French-speaking part, there are numerous scandal sheets, which feed on ordinary corruption, chasing spectacular headlines and 'little envelopes.' But the politicians, from Madagascar to Mauritania, from Guinea to Cameroon, via Côte d'Ivoire and the Central African Republic, are the main beneficiaries, making use of badly or unpaid journalists to settle their scores with opponents through bogus 'revelations.'"[45]

The erosion of solidarity among media practitioners in upholding the fundamental right to free expression can be the single most damaging threat to the media's role as a forum for the exercise of democratic citizenship and a catalyst for sustaining democratic institutions and practices. It is in this context that recent developments within Rwanda's inky fraternity are troubling. The Rwanda Media Ethics Commission, together with some media owners and journalists, issued a statement on March 19, 2008, indicating their resolve to sue the privately owned *Umoco* newspaper for publishing slanderous and defamatory articles against President Kegame in its March 12–27 editions.[46]

They accused the paper of tarnishing the reputation of the president by likening him to Adolf Hitler and criticized it for offering outrageous options for the president to consider in light of the indictments brought against 40 Rwandese defense forces officers by a Spanish court. The group suggested that, through the article, the paper was denying the 1994 genocide in Rwanda and that the story had caused panic among the populace. It therefore called on the High Council of the Press to withdraw the paper's accreditation and to ask the line ministry to ban it for a year.

The right of this group to caution against and condemn incendiary comments from journalists that could create sociopolitical chaos is appreciated and respected. What is disturbing is the fact that a group of media practitioners deems itself fit to arrogate to themselves the right to be the president's unsolicited legal team, to pursue criminal charges against the editor, and to urge the authorities to ban the publication. Not only are they encouraging a government that has a record of clamping down on opposition to continue its hostility toward dissenting voices, but they also are undermining the principles of free expression that are the best protection the media have against state harassment.

As alluded to earlier, there are concerns about the extent to which the mass-mediated public sphere in Africa has largely been constricted to the advantage of particular segments of society. These concerns, which echo what has been expressed in other places, challenge the Harbermasian ideal of equally situated citizens engaging in deliberative politics.[47] Jacobs notes, in relation to mediated politics in South Africa, that "the new deliberation processes are restricted to policy professional and already empowered (meanly largely 'white' and neo-liberal) non-governmental, business, professional lobby groups as well as think tanks … 'the irony is that the levels of involvement in political and civic issues were higher under the repressive machinery than under the new democratic dispensation.'"[48]

Elite capture of the mass-mediated public sphere might be portentous for democratic governance in a number of ways. First, it could mean a multiplicity of voices that produce different versions of the class interests of the most powerful groups. The "have nots" might not have a place in the discourses that shape the direction of their countries and, therefore, might be unable to have their interests served in the new democratic dispensations that are taking hold on the continent. The signs of such exclusion are evident in the nature and language of the preponderant discourses in the media landscape, the locations of major media outlets, and the distributional contours for media output. The majority of the continent's media are located in urban areas, use European languages, and have a reach that does not extend far beyond their areas of production. Rural dwellers constitute the majority of the population in many countries but do not attract the media because they do not have the economic power on which these media depend. By extension, their voices do not get articulated in the mediated public sphere. Though the commitment of various media practitioners to democratic consolidation is not in doubt, the reality is that, for many media organizations, the economic imperatives behind their operations tend to trump their public service role.[49] As Kivikuru points out in the assessment of community radio in South Africa and Namibia, "It is easy to talk about community and grassroots orientation, but to implement such policies is difficult, especially when the basic task is to promote democracy and citizenship").[50]

A second concern regarding elite capture is that if these media outlets become means for spewing the views of their backers and owners, without providing the opportunity for contending perspectives to challenge those views and thereby cross-fertilizing them, Africans might end up with a cacophony of media silos and voices that do not produce a useful synthesis of well-distilled ideas that can move society forward. This situation veers very closely to corroborating Gerstl-Pepin's skepticism about the mediated public sphere, in which she argues that "although the media can function as a form of the public sphere ... they essentially operate as a 'thin' public sphere ... in the sense that genuine dialogue about governance issues does not take place in most forms of media coverage. Instead, the media operate more as a billboard of opposing viewpoints rather than a forum for debates and analysis of issues."[51]

Another concern about elite capture stems from trends that show that the media may become tools for limiting democratic expression to the wealthy, who might use them for their own parochial political interests rather than as true catalysts of a vibrant, accessible, and open public sphere. For example, "some danger signs have emerged in Madagascar's media transition. Money matters much more in politics now than it did before. Wealthy candidates, who can afford to purchase their own media outlets, become more competitive most quickly. Private media ownership appears to have reduced incentives for direct candidate debates, as candidates prefer to run propaganda wars from their own media outlets."[52]

The results of such propaganda wars can be catastrophic if they are not controlled and conducted with circumspection. A case in point is the mayhem in the Democratic Republic of Congo that resulted from a statement by Jean-Pierre Bemba on one of his radio stations, after he lost the presidential election in 2006. He claimed that the top echelon of the army was "embezzling 500 million Congolese francs a month from the army payroll. Over the next two days, bloody clashes erupted in the streets of Kinshasa, pitting the DR Congo Armed Forces (FARDC) against the personal guard of Senator Bemba ... Repeated death threats forced numbers of staff on Jean-Pierre Bemba-owned media into hiding."[53]

In view of the foregoing concerns about elite and commercial capture, it is necessary that alternative media that champion the cause of the marginalized and provide disinterested and diverse perspectives on national and local issues be supported. In Madagascar, for example, "highly respected religious publications and broadcasts offer a valuable counterweight to the purely commercial private press. Unlike purely commercial stations, the religious media are actively striving to serve rural communities more fully. The national print media, though private, have likewise contributed to political debate, some with strongly partisan rhetoric, others counterbalancing the purely political press by contrasting candidate positions and providing content-focused political analysis."[54]

One of the challenges with which the media have had to contend is finding a balance between the public's right to know and the need for political stability and national security. The dilemma imposed by the dialectics of responsible journalism and self-censorship is manifested in several cases in which journalists and media organizations have had to decide whether to toe the government's line with respect to what the public needs to know or to pursue the media's right to free expression. It is important to take into account the context in which these journalists operate when assessing whether or not they are pandering to the government of the day. It is thus understandable that in the midst of Kenya's 2007–08 postelection violence, media outlets were willing to follow instructions from the Ministry of Information to broadcast news items with a delay.

It is important, though, that these mechanisms not be used to deny the public access to relevant information because that information might not carve a positive image for the one group or the other. Self-censorship has dire consequences for democratic accountability. In the context of Kenya's postelection violence, for example, some analysts of the media scene have criticized journalists for not pursuing issues intensively and extensively enough because of the gnawing fear that they might undermine national security. Consequently, the truth about the reality that people were living was not adequately unraveled, thereby making it difficult to determine who the real winner of the presidential elections was and what the nature and extent of malfeasance was. These insights are necessary in order to (1) assess the veracity of claims and counterclaims regarding the conduct of the elections, (2) hold people accountable, (3) protect the vulnerable, and (4) ensure that there is no future replication of the triggers of the violence. According to Reporters without Borders, one of the country's most senior journalists acknowledged that: "The media failed … It did not properly investigate what happened after the voting, and he said that the failure has haunted him ever since. Journalists had not pushed to find out the truth after it was clear the results were rigged. [However], so much was at stake that not seeking the truth was impermissible."[55]

The failure of the media to verify, authenticate, or challenge state officials' rendition of reality might rob the public of the critical conversation needed to develop appropriate policy interventions and to correct erroneous impressions that can have dangerous consequences. Danso and McDonald provide evidence of such failure and its consequences in South Africa, when they assert that the print media was partly responsible for some of the worst examples of xenophobic rhetoric in the country by failing to check the veracity of government statements on immigration, arguing thus: "There is a self-reinforcing mechanism at play, with the Department of Home Affairs (as well as the police and defence forces) issuing anti-immigrant statements and statistics and the media uncritically reproducing them. This creates a feedback loop back to bureaucrats and policy makers as to the legitimacy and "correctness" of what they are saying. When combined with the highly xenophobic attitudes of the population at large, this self-reinforcing mechanism serves to foreclose more progressive policy options and acts to stifle (and even shut down) more informed public debates about the issues."[56] The significance of this assessment was eerily brought home by attacks on, and killing of, immigrants in various parts of the country in May 2008.

## Conclusions: Conditions Facilitating the Media's Normative Roles

The foregoing analysis shows that many media outlets and journalists in Africa are fulfilling their watchdog, agenda-setting, and gatekeeping roles commendably under trying circumstances. They are making tremendous contributions toward the building of democratic practices and institutions. It is also clear that the traditional media are being complemented significantly by the opportunities made possible by the Internet. As Tettey notes, "cyberspace has encouraged the development of a civic culture and an active citizenry that integrates the local and the global and compels the state to be responsive to a public sphere that is external to it and over which it does not exercise complete, if any, sovereign control. This is not to suggest that domestic politics is driven by virtual politics, but just that [the former] is inflected by [the latter] in some instances."[57]

These achievements notwithstanding, the evidence also shows that the development of an active, diverse, and critical mediated public sphere faces tremendous obstacles that need to be removed if the continent is to make strides in creating an environment that is conducive to democratic expression and accountability that facilitate good governance. One of the ways that African media can be supported to perform their critical function as facilitators of critical discourse in the public sphere is through solidarity among various stakeholders in civil society; that is, working together to demonstrate their commitment to a multivocal public sphere and standing up to support diversity in the media whenever that comes under attack. Such solidarity sends a message to even the most unyielding dictators that media practitioners are not just a fringe group of troublemakers whose views are not shared by society at large and that they cannot continue to pursue hostile policies toward the media without eroding their own political security. Mobilization in support of media freedom, through protests by journalists and media organizations, was effective in getting the Sudanese government to revoke the suspension of *Al-Sudani*, referred to above, after 48 hours. Such acts demonstrate, in the words of Dahlgren, not just "civic agency" but also "civic competence," which means that "for democracy to work, we must look beyond its institutionalized structures and dynamics. While these are essential, if they are not filled by real flesh-and-blood people with relevant values, virtues and competencies, democracy will become merely a hollow formalism."[58] Engaged citizens, or civic curiosity, triggers and sustains media scrutiny.

The media are a crucial ingredient for democratic governance and its consolidation. However, they will not be able to play this role without support from other key institutions of the state. These include the legislature, which should ensure that the media are not hamstrung by laws that are inimical to a vibrant and pluralistic public sphere and that degrade media's ability to hold various actors accountable to the citizenry. Laws that support the cultivation and sustenance of such an environment are necessary. The judiciary also needs to interpret laws in ways that are not dictated by loyalty to persons in government but to the cause of democracy, civil liberties, and political freedoms.

In spite of the difficulty of getting African governments to pass freedom of information and whistleblower legislation, civil society organizations, journalists, and the general public should continue advocating and lobbying for these. It is only through the opportunities presented by these laws that the media, and citizens in general, can accomplish their role of holding governments accountable and providing the public with information it deserves to know, without the onerous obstacles and threats to their lives and freedoms that they currently have to endure. A number of countries, such as Nigeria, Ghana, and Kenya, have come close to passing such laws, and further pressure is needed to get their governments to make them a reality.[59] It is in the interest of governments to pass these laws because the transparency that comes with unfettered access to government information and the protections that comes with a whistleblower act help to build trust in government, which in turn helps to elicit the support of the citizenry for decisions and actions of state institutions. As Fard et al. point out, "public trust has a tremendous effect on the quality of public administration. Trust is one of the most valuable social capitals, and its decline will impose heavy expenditure on the political system."[60]

The media themselves have a role in sustaining their place as vessels for democratic expression, accountability, and democratic consolidation. Based on the discussion above, it is appropriate that the enthusiasm surrounding the numerical pluralization of the media landscape in Africa be balanced with what Karppinen refers to as the "ethos of pluralization," which requires "an understanding of the media structures and the public sphere in which the point is not to celebrate all multiplicity and heterogeneity but rather an effort to question the inclusiveness of current pluralist discourses and their understanding of economic and political power."[61]

The watchdog role of the media has been enhanced not only by developments in ICTs, but also by migration and the attendant creation of diasporas that serve as expansive sources of information for media outlets located in their countries of origin. This fact, together with the time-space compression made possible by ICTs, means that local media can receive information relevant to their countries from compatriots located in other parts of the world. This connection is strengthened by the intense interest that many Africans domiciled abroad have in the politics of their home countries and their willingness to inject themselves into the deterritorialized public spheres of those countries.

## Notes

1. Kwame Karikari. 2004. "Press Freedom in Africa." *New Economy* 11 (3): 184–86.
2. Sean Jacobs. 2002. "How Good Is the South African Media for Democracy?" *African and Asian Studies* 1 (4): 279–302, 280.
3. Andrew Kuper and Jocelyn Kuper. 2001. "Serving a New Democracy: Must the Media 'Speak Softly'? Learning from South Africa." *International Journal of Public Opinion Research* 13 (4): 355–76.
4. Sean Jacobs. 2002. "How Good Is the South African Media for Democracy?" 152.
5. M. Kuenzi and G. Lambright. 2007. "Voter Turnout in Africa's Multiparty Regimes." *Comparative Political Studies* 40 (6): 665–90.
6. P. Andriantsoa, N. Andriasendrarivony, S. Haggblade, B. Minten, M. Rakotojaona, F. Rakotovoavy. 2005. "Media Proliferation and Democratic Transition in Africa: The Case of Madagascar." *World Development* 33 (11): 1939–57, 1939.
7. *Monitor Online.* 2008. "How Museveni Learnt of Roads Corruption." May 14. http://www.monitor.co.ug/artman/publish/news/How_Museveni_learnt_of_roads_corruption_printer.shtml.
8. Sidney Callahan. 2003. "New Challenges of Globalization for Journalism." *Journal of Mass Media Ethics* 18 (1): 3–15, 3.
9. Brian Schaffner. 2006. "The Political Geography of Campaign Advertising in U.S. House Elections." *Political Geography* 25 (7): 775–88, 776.
10. William Carroll and Robert Hackett. 2006. "Democratic Media Activism through the Lens of Social Movement Theory." *Media, Culture and Society* 28 (1): 83–104.
11. Reporters without Borders. 2007. *Darfur: An Investigation into a Tragedy's Forgotten Actors.* Paris: RSF, 7–8.
12. Reporters without Borders. 2008. *How Far to Go? Kenya's Media Caught in the Turmoil of a Failed Election.* http://www.rsf.org/IMG/pdf/Kenya_RSF-IMS-A19_ENG.pdf.
13. Wisdom J. Tettey. 2002. *The Media, Accountability and Civic Engagement in Africa.* Background paper for HDR 2002, UNDP, New York, 5.
14. *Independent.* 2008. "Tortured in a Safe House." http://www.independent.co.ug/index.php?option=com_content&task=view&id=469&Itemid=2475. (accessed May 15, 2008). Also see Wendy Glauser. 2008. "Evidence Points to Routine Use of Torture by Ugandan Government." *World Politics Review,* May 16. http://www.worldpoliticsreview.com/article.aspx?id=2132; and Human Rights Watch. 2009. "Open Secret," April 8. http://www.hrw.org/de/node/82072/section/8.

15. Nicola Jones. 2005. "News Values, Ethics and Violence in KwaZulu-Natal: Has Media Coverage Reformed?" *Critical Arts: A South-North Journal of Cultural & Media Studies* 19 (1/2): 150–66, 164.

16. Joy Online. 2006. "Grandpa Rapes 7-Year-Old Granddaughter." January 18. http://www.ghanaweb.com/GhanaHomePage/NewsArchive/artikel.php?ID=97772.

17. J. Llewelin, N. Whaites, and A. Filipowich. 2007. *Human Rights Reporting through Radio in Northern Ghana: Innovations in Media Governance and Democracy Case Study.* Toronto: Journalists for Human Rights, 3. http://www.jhr.ca/en/aboutjhr/downloads/publications/Human%20Rights%20Reporting%20Through%20Radio%20in%20Northern%20Ghana.%20Innovations%20in%20Media%20Governance%20Case%20Study.%20Journalists%20for%20Human%20Rights%20(2007).pdf).

18. *Mail & Guardian Online.* 2005. "The ANC's Oilgate," May 3. http://www.mg.co.za/article/2005-05-03-the-ancs-oilgate.

19. *Mail & Guardian.* 2007. "ANC Purse Raises Questions," December 21. http://www.mg.co.za/article/2007-12-21-anc-purse-raises-questions.

20. *Enquirer.* 2005. "Castle Hijacks Kickbacks," November 22. http://www.ghanaweb.com/GhanaHomePage/rumor/artikel.php?ID=94785.

21. *Mail & Guardian Online.* 2007. "Beeld Scoops Prize for Investigative Journalism," March 26. http://www.mg.co.za/printformat/single/2007-04-26-beeld-scoops-prize-for-investigative-journalism.

22. Palavar. 2002. "NPP in $1billion '419' Scam." July 5. http://www.ghanaweb.com/GhanaHomePage/NewsArchive/printnews.php?ID=25386.

23. *Ghana Home Page.* 2005. "Minister Blames Media for Sabotaging Fake Loans," January 27. http://www.ghanaweb.com/GhanaHomePage/NewsArchive/artikel.php?ID=74211.

24. *Ghana Palaver.* 2004. "$300 Million Loan from Hairdressing Salon? Govt Heads for Another IFC Like Embarrassment," May 11. http://www.ghanaweb.com/GhanaHomePage/NewsArchive/artikel.php?ID=57552.

25. Wits Journalism. 2007. "Cameron Wins Sanlam Award." http://www.journalism.co.za/news/index.php?option=com_content&task=view&id=761&Itemid=5.

26. See Mahmood Monshipouri, Claude Welch Jr., and Evan Kennedy. 2003. "Multinational Corporations and the Ethics of Global Responsibility: Problems and Possibilities." *Human Rights Quarterly* 25: 965–89.

27. *Citizen.* 2008. "Tanzania: Act on the Plight of Geita Evictees." Editorial. May 19. http://allafrica.com/stories/printable/200805190605.html.

28. This section draws from Wisdom J. Tettey. 2009. "Transnationalism, the African Diaspora, and the Deterritorialized Politics of the Internet." In *African Media and the Digital Public Sphere,* ed. Okoth Fred Mudhai, Wisdom J. Tettey, and Fackson Banda, 143–63. New York: Palgrave Macmillan.

29. Brenda Chan. 2005. "Imagining the Homeland: The Internet and Diasporic Discourse of Nationalism." *Journal of Communication Inquiry* 29 (4): 336–68; Ananda Mitra. 2001. "Diasporic Voices in Cyberspace." *New Media and Society* 3 (1): 29–48; Jo Bardoel and Leen d'Haenens. 2004. "Media Meet the Citizen: Beyond Market Mechanisms and Government Regulations." *European Journal of Communication* 19 (2): 172.

30. Victoria Bernal. 2006. "Diaspora, Cyberspace and Political Imagination: The Eritrean Diaspora Online." *Global Networks* 6 (2): 161–79.

31. Oladipo. 2007. Posted on Nigeriaworld: Mon Apr 16, 2007, 2:13 pm. http://www.nigeriaworld.com/board/viewtopic.php?t=3650&highlight=oladipo.

32. CNN. 2007. "Inside the Middle East's 'People of the Year'—Your Votes." Inside the Middle East Blog, December 31. http://edition.cnn.com/CNNI/Programs/middle.east/blog/2007/12/inside-middle-easts-people-of-year-your.html.

33. Anloland. 2007. "Brutalities." http://www.anloland.org; also see Tettey. 2009. "Transnationalism, the African Diaspora, and the Deterritorialized Politics of the Internet," 158.

34. Reporters without Borders. 2008. *2008 Annual Report—Africa.* Paris: RSF, 7.

35. Ghana News Agency. 2007. "NAPTA Condemns Demotion of Head Teacher." October 10. http://www.ghanaweb.com/GhanaHomePage/NewsArchive/artikel.php?ID=132169.

36. See also Naomi Sakr. 2003. "Freedom of Expression, Accountability and Development in the Arab Region." *Journal of Human Development* 4 (1): 29–46.

37. Reporters without Borders. 2008. *2008 Annual Report—Africa.* Paris: RSF, 17.

38. Ibid., 8.

39. Okoth Mudhai. 2007. "Light at the End of the tunnel? Pushing the Boundaries in Africa." *Journalism* 8 (5): 536–44.

40. Reporters without Borders. 2008. *Nigeria—Annual Report 2008.* Paris: RSF. http://www.rsf.org/print.php3?id_article=25399.

41. Reporters without Borders. 2007. *Darfur: An Investigation into a Tragedy's Forgotten Actors.* Paris: RSF, 2–3.

42. Ibid., 12.

43. Reporters without Borders. 2008. 2008 *Annual Report—Africa.* Paris: RSF, 26.

44. Wisdom Tettey. 2006. "The Politics of Media Accountability in Africa: An Examinatin of Mechanisms and Institutions." *International Communication Gazette* 68 (3): 229–48; Okoth Mudhai. 2007. "Light at the End of the tunnel? Pushing the Boundaries in Africa." *Journalism* 8 (5): 536–44, 538.

45. Reporters without Borders. 2008. *2008 Annual Report—Africa.* Paris: RSF, 7.

46. Munyaneza, James. 2008. "Rwanda: Journalists Want Umuco Newspaper Suspended." *New Times,* March 20. http://allafrica.com/stories/200803200153.html.

47. Axel Bruns. 2008. "Life Beyond the Public Sphere: Towards a Networked Model of Political Deliberation." *Information Polity* 13 (1/2): 71–85; Doug Walton. 2007. "Revitalizing the Public Sphere: The Current System of Discourse and the Need for the Participative Design of Social Action." *Systemic Practice and Action Research* 20 (5): 369–86.

48. Sean Jacobs. 2002. "How Good Is the South African Media for Democracy?" *African and Asian Studies* 1 (4): 279–302, 298.

49. See P. Green. 2004. "Transforming Journalism as Democracy Emerges." *Nieman Reports* 58 (3): 41–43; Wisdom Tettey. 2004. "The Politics of Radio and Radio Politics in Ghana: A Critical Appraisal of Broadcasting Reform." In *African Media Cultures: Transdisciplinary Perspectives,* ed. Rose Marie Beck and Frank Wittmann, 215–39. Köln: Rüdiger Köppe Verlag; Wisdom Tettey. 2001. "The Media and Democratization in Africa: Contributions, Constraints and Concerns of the Private Press." *Media, Culture and Society* 23 (1): 5–31.

50. Ullamaija Kivikuru. 2006. "Top-Down or Bottom-Up?: Radio in the Service of Democracy: Experiences from South Africa and Namibia." *International Communication Gazette* 68 (1): 5.

51. Cynthia Gerstl-Pepin. 2007. "Introduction to the Special Issue on the Media, Democracy, and the Politics of Education." *Peabody Journal of Education* 82 (1): 4.

52. P. Andriantsoa, N. Andriasendrarivony, S. Haggblade, B. Minten, M. Rakotojaona, and F. Rakotovoavy. 2005. "Media Proliferation and Democratic Transition in Africa: The Case of Madagascar." *World Development* 33 (11): 1955.

53. Reporters without Borders. 2008. *2008 Annual Report—Africa.* Paris: RSF, 10.

54. P. Andriantsoa, N. Andriasendrarivony, S. Haggblade, B. Minten, M. Rakotojaona, F. Rakotovoavy. 2005. "Media Proliferation and Democratic Transition in Africa: The Case of Madagascar." *World Development* 33 (11): 1939–57, 1955.

55. Reporters without Borders. 2008. *2008 Annual Report—Africa*. Paris: RSF, 5.

56. Ransford Danso and David McDonald. 2001. "Writing Xenophobia: Immigration and the Print Media in Post-Apartheid South Africa." *Africa Today* 48 (3): 115–37, 132.

57. Tettey. 2009. "Transnationalism, the African Diaspora, and the Deterritorialized Politics of the Internet," 150–51.

58. Peter Dahlgren. 2006. "Doing Citizenship: The Cultural Origins of Civic Agency in the Public Sphere." *European Journal of Cultural Studies* 9 (3): 267–86, 272.

59. See Juliet Gill and Sallie Hughes. 2005. "Bureaucratic Compliance with Mexico's New Access to Information Law." *Critical Studies in Media Communication* 22 (2): 121–37, 134.

60. Hassan Fard, Ali Asghar, and Anvary Rostamy. 2007. "Promoting Public Trust in Public Organizations: Explaining the Role of Public Accountability." *Public Organization Review* 7 (4): 331–44, 332.

61. Kari Karppinen. 2007. "Against Naïve Pluralism in Media Politics: On the Implications of the Radical Pluralist Approach to the Public Sphere." *Media, Culture and Society* 29 (3): 495–508, 496.

•
•
•

# 12

# Latin America

Silvio Waisbord

The press contributes to democratic governance by monitoring and holding the powerful accountable (watchdog), covering issues of public significance that require the attention of citizens and policy makers (agenda setting), and facilitating the expression of myriad perspectives (gatekeeping). This study reviews the conditions that affect the performance of the press as watchdog, agenda setter, and gatekeeper in Latin America, and discusses courses of action to strengthen the quality of press reporting on a wide range of issues and views.[1]

By performing watchdog, agenda-setting, and gatekeeping functions, the press promotes criticism, deliberation, and diversity of opinion. These are key principles of the democratic public sphere, the communicative space for the formation of public opinion and the promotion of civic interests. As analyzed by Jürgen Habermas, the notion of the public sphere remains useful to assess the state of the press in contemporary democracies.[2] Surely, as several authors have perceptively observed, Habermas's original analysis presents some limitations, namely an idealized reconstruction of the conditions for public discourse in European bourgeois democracies, and an excessively pessimistic view about the decline of the quality of democratic speech in late-modernity.[3] Despite its shortcomings, the notion of the public sphere remains relevant, both as a conceptual construct and as a normative ideal to assess the performance of the press. It rightly points out problems for civic expression created by encroaching state and market power. It holds public deliberation and critical information as central to the democratic process through which citizens scrutinize governments and other powerful actors, identify public demands, and shape policy. It draws attention to the role of institutions, including the press, in fostering reflexive and critical publics. Although Habermas's theory of communication action turned to locating democratic speech in intersubjective, unmediated situations (rather than institutions, as he did previously), his recognition of the need for formal forums to nurture deliberation and criticism still grounds the notion that the press is a preeminent institution in the public sphere.[4]

From this perspective, the press should offer platforms for public dialogue, stimulate conversations on a wide range of public issues, and turn the attention of policy makers and citizens to matters of relevant public interest. Press theories have identified several conditions for the press to perform its democratic obligations. Liberal positions have stressed the need for constitutional prerogatives to shelter the press from government intrusion. Radical and communitarian arguments have emphasized the need for dispersed ownership to avoid monopolistic information markets and ensure a diversity of perspectives. Social responsibility positions have raised the issue of fair access and public ethics as crucial for the democratic press.[5] In contemporary democracies, all these conditions are necessary to facilitate the wide availability of information that monitors state actions and business practices, highlights issues of public interest, and brings out multiple perspectives.

Although the ideal of the public sphere still offers a compelling framework to assess the state of the media in democracy, it does not offer concrete guidelines about press policies and journalistic practices. Classic analyses of the public sphere, notably the work of Habermas and Hannah Arendt, focused on small-group settings and restricted polities. Thus, the ideals of deliberation and criticism need to be rethought in the contexts of large-scale and mediated democracies.[6] How can those ideals inform large media systems and journalistic practices in contemporary democracies? How can they be made effective in today's press, an institution vastly different and more complex than the print media in colonial America or in British and French bourgeois democracies? How can Habermas's vision of unmediated discourse as "ideal speech" be reconciled with the fact that journalism's defining task is to mediate the flow of information? These questions are central to understanding the conditions that strengthen the contribution of the press to democratic governance.

This chapter's interest is to place in the foreground the idea of media diversity as the fundamental principle for the press to promote deliberation and criticism in Latin America. Although media diversity is a contested notion, it provides a blueprint for media democracy that is characterized by the heterogeneity of content and structures.[7] For Denis McQuail, media diversity contributes to democracy by reflecting differences in society, giving equal access to various points of view, and offering wide choices.[8] The focus here is on *structural* diversity, an institutional feature of press systems as a whole related to ownership and regulation, and *performance* diversity, which refers to the practices and content produced by news organizations. Both are important to promote media democracy; both continue to have severe problems in the region. The existence of news organizations anchored in different principles as well as the production of diverse content are both equally necessary to expand the range of perspectives in the media.

From a public sphere perspective, media diversity is crucial to preserving communicative spaces that limit the influence of governments and large business. In Latin America, it requires overcoming persistent obstacles that have historically undermined democratic journalism and opportunities for civic expression in the press. Specifically, media diversity demands regulating the influence of states and markets, promoting dispersed ownership, and leveling citizens' access to newsmaking.

Media pluralism offers a point of reference to assess whether press systems effectively expand the range of issues and perspectives in the public sphere. A plural media system offers a stronger basis for the press to represent a diversity of interests. It is anchored in institutional pluralism, that is, a hybrid and balanced order integrated by organizations that function according to a mix of civic, political, and commercial principles.[9] Institutional pluralism is necessary to preserve and renew deliberation and criticism as core principles of the public sphere in contemporary democracies.

Despite recent advances in democratic expression, media pluralism remains weak in Latin American democracies. The succession of civilian administrations in the past 25 years has ushered in better conditions for the press and public expression.[10] Only sporadically, however, the press offers a wide set of perspectives on issues of public interest, and scrutinizes official secrecy and wrongdoing. The persistent weakness of media diversity coupled with the primacy of official news undercut potential opportunities for the press to make a stronger contribution to democratic expression.

The end of military dictatorships improved the conditions for journalistic practice and civic participation. An extensive literature has documented significant actions toward participation and emancipation in past decades.[11] The existence of robust and vibrant public spheres is a remarkable characteristic of contemporary Latin American democracies. The mobilization of human rights and indigenous, women's, youth, and environmental movements; the emergence of novel forms of citizens' participation and journalism; the rise and consolidation of various protest groups; experiments in participatory administration and budgeting; and the mushrooming of nongovernmental organizations and civic advocacy organizations demonstrate the vitality of civic expression. These forms of civic participation, however, should not be considered uncritically. Public spheres brimming with mobilized groups are not inevitably synonymous with democratic deliberation and institutionalized governance. Although some groups are expressions of critical debate and progressive participation, other groups contribute to political polarization. While some groups are authentic expressions of grassroots mobilization, others are closely linked to state interests and clientelistic networks.[12]

The consolidation of liberal democracies and the affirmation of a vibrant civil society have not been sufficient conditions to institutionalize media pluralism. A participative and lively public sphere, in principle, offers a rich reservoir for the affirmation of plural press systems and democratic journalism. It does not necessarily improve the performance of the press, however. The tenuous institutional linkages between the press and the public sphere undermine the potential of the press to strengthen democratic governance. This chapter explores why the connective tissues between the press and the public sphere remain weak in Latin America, and it concludes by offering actions to strengthen those ties.

## The Legacy of Weak Media Pluralism

Contemporary Latin American democracies inherited a weak legacy of media pluralism. Although the region has a rich tradition of civic initiatives to democratize information and expression, the prospects for pluralistic media systems have been compromised by authoritarianism, turbulent politics, and collusion between the state and business. Unregulated influence of governments and markets coupled with the close proximity between official and business interests have historically undermined media democracy.[13]

These dynamics took different shapes in authoritarian and democratic periods. Authoritarian regimes bulldozed democratic expression through censorship and repression. While they persecuted oppositional media, they sought to ensure positive news by favoring owners with business deals. During democratic periods, governments did not engage in formal censorship and repression, but they were not inclined to change fundamental structures to promote civic interests. The result was the consolidation of press systems dominated by a mix of state and market interests. Although print and broadcast media largely followed a commercial logic, they assiduously courted governments to reap political and economic benefits. Under these conditions, truly independent journalism was exceptional. Keeping a healthy autonomy from the state was not sound business for news organizations that pursued commercial goals.

Throughout the region, the oldest and most influential newspapers were born as projects of partisan factions and powerful families during the post-independence period. Many of today's leading newspapers (for example, Peru's *El Comercio*, Brazil's *Estado de São Paulo*, Chile's *El Mercurio*, and Argentina's *La Nación*) were founded during the oligarchic republics of the 19th century. In the context of restricted democracies, in which a small percentage of the population held political rights, newspapers expressed the economic and political ambitions of elite factions and political parties. Likewise, the press was partisan in countries under prolonged dictatorial regimes. They were conceived as political endeavors, often funded by personal funds, rather than market-driven enterprises to ensure means for public expression. Partisan journalism remained dominant during the gradual expansion of democracy in the first decades of the 20th century. Partisanism was central to newspapers that expressed the interests of urban middle classes and the working classes that fought for the expansion of political and social rights. Mass-market tabloids avoided being closely identified with political parties, but they still maintained close links to governments and political leaders.

Despite the long tradition of proximity between political parties and the press, a partisan press did not become dominant during the 20th century. Continuous political instability undermined the continuity of political parties and, thus, the long-term survival of partisan newspapers. Colombia was the only exception; the stability of its bipartisan democracy allowed the traditional liberal and conservative parties to hold moderate influence over newspapers.[14] In most countries, however, the continuous cycles of civil and military regimes and decades-long dictatorships undermined the lifespan of the partisan press as well as newspapers that expressed the views of civic groups (for example, trade unions and religious groups). The partisan press could not survive censorship and persecution, social upheaval, and economic turmoil. The weakness of the partisan press paved the way for the consolidation of a market-based press. National press systems typically featured elite newspapers that represented the interests of dominant economic and political groups, and broadsheets and tabloids that catered to middle classes and the working class. The "market" logic prevailed over the "partisan" logic.

The fact that the press has been largely organized around commercial principles, however, did not result in the complete separation of the press from the state. In fact, the mainstream press and the state have consistently been close. This relationship was based on economic and political linkages and mutual advantages. Government officials needed the news media to advance their political goals, and the business prospects of media companies were pinned to maintaining good relations with the state. Officials were able to influence newspapers through discretionary control of public finances, such as government advertising, control over newsprint production and/or importation, and arbitrary control of "special" funds. In some cases, coronelismo electrônico (electronic clientelism), as it is called in Brazil, was dominant, particularly in rural areas, where vast numbers of media properties have been in the hands of government officials.[15]

So, the problem was not state ownership of the press, but rather the excessive power of governments and private interests. Despite the overall growth of market-based media, government advertising continued to be a significant source of media revenue, particularly in countries and regions with small economies and advertising budgets.[16] Though officials found it beneficial to court newspapers to ensure favorable coverage, newspapers with close connections to governing powers reaped economic benefits, such as advertising, tax breaks, importation permits, and broadcasting licenses. More than long-standing, organic mouthpieces for political parties, newspapers offered short-term support for specific administrations.

Although these dynamics have prevailed, at times the relations between the press and national governments were conflictive. Whereas press dissent during military dictatorships was rare and mostly confined to alternative, left-wing publications, mainstream newspapers clashed with governments during democratic periods. Ideological differences typically caused conflicts between governments and the press. For example, conservative dailies not only opposed populist governments, such as Juan Perón's in Argentina and Getúlio Vargas's in Brazil between the 1930s and 1950s, and the socialist administration of Salvador Allende in Chile in the early 1970s; they also actively supported military interventions. Leftist and liberal newspapers opposed conservative governments and military dictatorships. Press-government tensions escalated during times of political polarization. Presidents and cabinet members admonished critical newspapers, and sought to punish them by ordering investigations into newspaper finances and temporary closures and by passing draconian legislation.[17]

Similar dynamics also affected broadcasting policies. Private interests dominated radio and television since their beginnings. Neither public broadcasting nor mixed systems were strong alternatives to the private model. Public stations have been chronically underfunded and remained controlled by governments. Private broadcasting, however, was not completely distant from the state. Like newspaper owners, radio and television station proprietors were also interested in maintaining close links with governments to keep licenses and expand business. Governments controlled official advertising, which, particularly for stations in small towns and economically depressed areas, remained a vital financial source. In some cases, such as Brazil and Mexico, tight-knit linkages between state and private interests were crucial for the consolidation of behemoth broadcasting companies, such as Globo and Televisa, respectively.[18]

In summary, the legacy of press and democracy has been plagued simultaneously by "market capture" and "state capture." Both authoritarian and populist regimes used state resources to control media markets and suppress deliberation and criticism. Powerful businesses, in turn, influenced government policies to expand and consolidate power. The basis for media pluralism was weak by the time the region shifted from authoritarianism to democracy in the 1980s.

## Media Pluralism, a Forgotten Priority

The consolidation of democratic rule has not significantly altered the historical structural relations among media, state, and markets. Unquestionably, today's conditions are significantly better than during the military dictatorships. The absence of state-sponsored efforts to suppress freedom of expression and persecute dissidents, the abolition of formal censorship, and the moderate enforcement of constitutional rights have contributed to the improvement of the conditions for democratic expression in the region.

Overall, conditions are troubling, however. Table 12.1 shows the consolidation of clear patterns during the past years.

Annual surveys conducted by Freedom House and Reporters without Borders (Reporters sans Frontières—RSF) have identified three groups of countries in terms of the conditions for press democracy and public expression. The first is a small group of countries (Chile, Costa Rica, and Uruguay) where conditions have been consistently better than in the rest of the region. This is not surprising, considering that the overall quality of democracy in these countries has also been praised by scholars and international agencies.[19] The second group consists of two countries (Cuba and República Bolivariana de Venezuela) where conditions have been extremely difficult for the press because of the political characteristics of the ruling governments. It would

**Table 12.1. Press Freedom in Latin America, 2002–07**

| Country | Year | | | | | |
|---|---|---|---|---|---|---|
|  | 2002 | 2003 | 2004 | 2005 | 2006 | 2007 |
| Argentina | PF | PF | PF | PF | PF | PF |
| Bolivia | F | F | PF | PF | PF | PF |
| Brazil | PF | PF | PF | PF | PF | PF |
| Chile | F | F | F | F | F | F |
| Colombia | NF | NF | NF | NF | NF | PF |
| Costa Rica | F | F | F | F | F | F |
| Cuba | NF | NF | NF | NF | NF | NF |
| Dominican Republic | PF | PF | PF | PF | PF | PF |
| Ecuador | PF | PF | PF | PF | PF | PF |
| El Salvador | PF | PF | PF | PF | PF | PF |
| Guatemala | PF | PF | NF | PF | PF | PF |
| Haiti | PF | PF | PF | PF | PF | PF |
| Mexico | PF | PF | PF | PF | PF | PF |
| Nicaragua | PF | PF | PF | PF | PF | PF |
| Panama | PF | PF | PF | PF | PF | PF |
| Paraguay | PF | PF | PF | PF | PF | PF |
| Peru | F | PF | PF | PF | PF | PF |
| Uruguay | F | F | F | F | F | F |
| Venezuela, R. B. de | NF | NF | NF | NF | NF | NF |

Source: Freedom House. *Freedom of the Press: A Global Survey of Media Independence.* http://www.freedomhouse.org; annual reports, 2002–07.
Note: F = free, PF = partly free, NF = not free.

be shortsighted to equate conditions in both countries, given the differences between Cuba's decades-old communist rule and Chavez's socialist-populist regime. Despite the latter's attempt to suppress criticism, forms of dissenting journalism in both print and broadcasting persist amidst political polarization in Venezuela. The situation in Colombia, a country that was included in this group until recently, seems to be changing. Against a historical context of prolonged internal conflict and extensive antipress violence, the ongoing process of pacification has gained renewed force and has benefited media democracy, too. Third, the conditions in the majority of countries fit Freedom House's "partly free" category. After the initial process of liberalization during the transition to democratic rule in the 1980s and 1990s, media democratization has languished in most countries. Media pluralism hasn't showed significant improvements, but there hasn't been a major reversal toward authoritarian policies.

The main challenges for media pluralism in the region include violence against the press, private media concentration, the lack of media legislation on community and public media, and preferential allocation of official advertising (see table 12.2). The common problem among these challenges is that old structural obstacles remain in place. There have not been major policy initiatives to reform press systems in order to promote diversity and strengthen countervailing forces to state and market powers. The vast majority of elected administrations have been equivocally committed to democratic communication. Regardless of whether they embraced neoconservative or populist policies, governments have generally aimed to preserve the status quo. At best, some administrations have tolerated dissent without persecuting critics. At worst, others have tried to cajole the media through various means. In neither case has media pluralism been a main policy priority.[20]

Press organizations have recorded numerous cases of local and national governments that have continued to run roughshod over the media. The governments have resorted to various means.

First, governments have continued to manipulate public resources to reward complacent news organizations and punish critical journalism. The allocation of official advertising, tax breaks, and favorable loans on state-owned banks to news companies is still plagued with secrecy and favoritism.[21] Some governments have blatantly bribed publishers and poured astronomical funds into newspapers and broadcasting stations.[22] "Public broadcasting" has been prone to cronyism and propaganda. Officials have arbitrarily granted and renewed television and station licenses, and in many countries have personally benefitted from the privatization of radio and television stations.

Second, although governments have used legislation to advance short-term political goals and business interests, they have been reluctant to support legal changes to facilitate media diversity and public scrutiny. On the one hand, some administrations have relaxed cross-media ownership laws to further

Table 12.2. Threats to Media Pluralism

| Country | Violence against the press[1] | Private media concentration[2] | Media legislation on community and public media[3] | Preferential allocation of official advertising[4] |
|---|---|---|---|---|
| Argentina | | + | | + |
| Bolivia | | + | + | + |
| Brazil | + | + | + | + |
| Chile | | + | | + |
| Colombia | + | + | + | + |
| Costa Rica | | | | + |
| Cuba | | | | |
| Dominican Republic | | + | | |
| Ecuador | | + | | |
| El Salvador | | + | | |
| Guatemala | | + | | |
| Haiti | | + | | |
| Honduras | | + | | |
| Mexico | + | + | + | |
| Nicaragua | | + | | |
| Panama | | + | | |
| Paraguay | | + | | |
| Peru | | + | + | |
| Uruguay | | + | + | |
| Venezuela, R. B. de | | + | | |

*Source:* Committee to Protect Journalists.
*Note:* Types of threats to media pluralism are as follows:
1. Ten or more deaths of journalists occurred between 1992 and 2008.
2. A handful of companies control substantial holdings in one media industry (newspaper, magazine, radio, over-the-air television, cable television, satellite television).
3. Press and broadcasting laws passed during authoritarian regimes are still in force.
4. Cases of preferential assignation of official advertising have been recorded between 2000 and 2008.

promote the ambitions of media corporations. Critics have dubbed new legislation the "Clarin law" and the "Televisa law," in Argentina and Mexico, respectively, as they were ostensibly intended to benefit the most powerful media corporations in each country.[23] In Peru, the 2004 broadcasting law lacks mechanisms to control executive decisions, promote civic participation, increase transparency of media operations, and defend audience interests. New laws and government inaction have facilitated concentration of media ownership.[24] A handful of large corporations control the leading newspapers in many countries, including Argentina, Bolivia, Chile, Guatemala, and Venezuela.[25] Likewise, most television markets have become consolidated in "imperfect duopolies," such as in Brazil and Mexico, in which two corporations control the main over-the-air stations and cable systems.

On the other hand, civilian governments have been largely uninterested in promoting a legal environment that encourages critical journalism. Tellingly, many press laws passed during authoritarian regimes have not been overturned yet. Libel and slander laws provide officials with a range of legal weapons to browbeat the press. The majority of countries lack legal mechanisms to require the recording of all official communication and proceedings, and to facilitate public access to government information. Doubtless, the passing of freedom of information laws in recent years in Argentina, Mexico, and Peru is auspicious. Mobilized coalitions of civic groups should be credited for raising awareness and conducting advocacy with legislators to pass adequate legislation. Unfortunately, various problems weaken the effective enforcement of the laws and, ultimately, their contributions to accountability and transparency.[26]

Third, antipress violence has continued. Human rights and press freedom organizations have recorded scores of cases of official coercion of the press. Methods include verbal attacks on news organizations, pressure on journalists and media owners to suppress critical stories or cancel news programs, and the ordering of tax inquiries and police raids of newsrooms. One issue of particular concern is that official tirades against the press legitimize antipress violence in such countries as Colombia, where journalists are frequently the target of attacks by the police, the military, and extralegal groups. Furthermore, government inaction perpetuates impunity and undermines press democracy. The failure of governments to conduct thorough investigations and prosecute offenders exacerbates the lack of accountability.

In summary, opacity and arbitrariness characterize government decisions affecting the press. Governments have been effective at passing legislation to benefit officials and business allies and preserving laws that shelter officials from public scrutiny. Regrettably, they have showed little interest in supporting policies to promote media pluralism. This would have required reinforcing government accountability, rolling back legislation that discourages critical reporting, enforcing "sunshine" laws, diversifying patterns of media ownership, and soliciting and ensuring broad participation from civic society.

With a few exceptions, none of these steps were taken. There have been limited efforts to democratize access to public broadcasting.[27] The case of community radio is an example. Although leading stations in metropolitan areas have increasingly been incorporated into cross-media corporations, myriad public, private, mixed, and community groups own and manage radio stations scattered throughout the region. Radio ownership in the region is more dispersed than in other countries, largely owing to the significant increase in the number of stations and lower barriers to entry. A more disaggregated market structure partially explains why radio, in principle, offers better opportunities for public expression than newspapers and television.[28] However, the majority of community radio stations are in legal limbo. Governments have been reluctant to pass legislation to provide a legal framework to support their operations.

Although the collusion between government and large media corporations has remained dominant, relations have not always been peaceful. The ascendancy of populism in the past decade has ushered in clashes between governments and right-wing proprietors. They have battled over communication policies and official criticism of the press. Frequently, presidents used a strong nationalistic and class-based rhetoric to castigate owners. In response, associations representing large media owners have excoriated governments. These conflicts have taken place against a backdrop of increased political polarization in the region.

Doubtless, the lead case has been the conflictive relations between the Chavez administration and traditional media owners in República Bolivariana de Venezuela. Since coming to power in 1999, Chavez has passed laws that were fiercely opposed by media owners.[29] The government accused conservative proprietors of supporting the failed 2002 coup. The controversial decision not to renew the license of Radio Television Caracas, one of the oldest television stations in the country and owned by an anti-Chavez business group, was the flashpoint in a decade of tense relations.

In other countries, populist administrations and large media groups also engaged in fierce, mostly rhetorical, battles. Although confrontations did not reach a showdown as they did in República Bolivariana de Venezuela, conflicts between government and media corporations have occurred in Argentina, Bolivia, Ecuador, and Nicaragua.[30] Presidents have frequently criticized media owners for defending "anti-popular interests" and offering biased reporting of government policies. Despite high-profile verbal sparring, populist governments have not faced undivided opposition from media proprietors. In fact, they have enjoyed amicable relations with owners who have not criticized government policies.

Besides the unregulated influence of governments and business, "statelessness" is another major obstacle for democratic journalism, particularly in the interior of many countries. *Statelessness* refers to situations in which governments fail to meet key obligations, such as the control over the legitimate means of violence and the guarantee of civic rights. In such situations, extralegal actors (for example, paramilitary and parapolice organizations, drug traffickers, or other mafia-like operations) exert absolute and autonomous power through violence. Governments are ineffective in controlling violence and enforcing laws. Certainly, such situations not only negatively affect the press, but they also erode political and economic stability that is essential for the public sphere. However, journalists and civic organizations, particularly those who reveal corruption and call for accountability, are the main targets of violence.

The lack of serious investigation and prosecution of perpetrators further deepens statelessness. Colombia and Mexico, which global press organizations have considered some of the world's most dangerous places for journalists in the past decade, are examples of this situation. Areas such as Colombia's Magdalena Medio or Mexico's northern border with the United States are notorious no-state zones. Community radio stations and print journalists who have challenged paramilitary forces and drug traffickers and exposed complicity between government officials and illegal actors, have suffered the brunt of the attacks. In these circumstances, any form of critical journalism is impossible. Peace and security, two minimal conditions for the existence of the press and the public sphere, are missing. Reasoned, moderate, and critical public discourse is anathema to the exercise of naked violence and absentee government.

The combination of quid pro quo practices between the state and media corporations, the persistent lack of media pluralism, and the condition of state-lessness undermine the prospects for a democratic press in Latin America.

## The Tensions of Watchdog Journalism

The conditions described in the previous section provide the backdrop to ana-lyze the performance of the press as watchdog, agenda setter, and gatekeeper. The argument in this chapter is that, although the mainstream press occasion-ally scrutinizes wrongdoing and brings out a plurality of civic voices, efforts to promote wide deliberation and criticism are often drowned out in press systems that prioritize the interests of governments and large corporations.

Several studies have analyzed the state of watchdog journalism in the past decades.[31] Throughout the region, press exposés have had significant politi-cal repercussions, including judicial and congressional investigations and the resignation of public officials. The series of exposés and scandals in the region suggested auspicious innovations and the contributions of news organizations to social accountability.[32] Although these have been unprecedented develop-ments in the region, they should not be mistaken for the consolidation of adversarial, public-minded journalism. The press has not radically changed from lapdog to watchdog journalism. Watchdog journalism has evolved along a seesaw path, as its fortunes changed according to political circumstances.

Some analysts have recently suggested that watchdog journalism has lost much of its vigor.[33] News organizations have sporadically revealed public and private wrongdoing. Hard-hitting, investigative reporting has remained mar-ginal. Leading news organizations have dismantled investigative units. Numer-ous reporters and editors, who produced exposés and headed investigations in the 1990s, left daily journalism. Newspapers that symbolized watchdog jour-nalism have seemingly abandoned critical reporting, changed ownership, or closed down because of economic difficulties (which were, in some cases, the result of advertising boycotts from advertisers and governments).

Structural arrangements and dynamics between the state and the market account for the uneven presence of watchdog journalism. Several country-wide surveys show that reporters blame editorial timidity and government influence for limited opportunities for critical stories.[34] Although it is hard to produce concrete evidence of behind-the-scenes maneuvers and decisions, opinion columns and newsroom grapevines are filled with speculation about government and business pressures on news organizations to refrain from publishing critical reports. Practicing watchdog journalism has often brought negative consequences for news organizations, such as tightened advertising revenues, restrictions to official events and press conferences, verbal threats, physical attacks, assassinations, and bombings.

Three issues should be considered to assess the contributions of watchdog journalism to deliberation and criticism: the thematic agenda of exposés, editorial bias, and the quality of coverage.

The portfolio of watchdog stories has focused on a range of crucial subjects. Revelations on human rights abuses and criminal activities by military and police officers have demonstrated persistent violations of civil rights and corruption. Investigations into drug trafficking have laid bare complex linkages between government officials and illegal trade. Stories on kickbacks for government contracts and cash-for-votes schemes in congresses revealed wrongdoing at the core of democratic institutions. Exposés of fraudulent practices by small business and crimes by low-level officials (mayors, council members, and police officers) have shed light on widespread corruption. Revelations about cases of pedophilia in the Catholic Church shed light on an institution that has historically wielded significant power in the region. Stories scrutinizing corporate wrongdoing, however, have been few and far between. Even when stories have put the spotlight on cases of corruption showing complicity between governments and businesses, the coverage has disproportionately focused on the responsibility of public officials. The scarcity of investigations about corporate malfeasance reflects political-institutional factors that shape news production, namely, editorial politics combined with the power of official sources and journalistic values and practices.

The rise of watchdog journalism needs to be understood against the backdrop of new political communication dynamics. The press has moved to center stage, as public officials and mobilized publics have chosen to wage political battles against the media. Given their status as newsmakers and "legitimate" sources, political elites hold unmatched advantage to influence news. Scores of press investigations have originated in the efforts of elites to influence the press. For reporters, government infighting has often provided copious and sensitive information. Power battles among government officials have been the breeding ground for exposés. Cabinet members, congressional committees and judges, and disgruntled military and police officers have often piqued newsroom attention and provided evidence of government wrongdoing.[35]

Whereas officials' leaks have prodded reporters and editors to pursue stories, the organizational culture of journalism and the political economy of the press have influenced the evolution of stories. On the one hand, the centrality and prestige of official news skews journalism toward covering official wrongdoing. Just like presidential declarations and congressional hearings, exposés are another form of official news. Newsroom practices that prioritize official news also stimulate interest in official corruption. Official news regularly becomes lead stories and receives prime space in the news. Cadres of reporters maintain regular contact with official sources. Domestic politics remains the most prestigious news beat in the professional culture of journalism.[36] Thus, explosive information from official sources is more likely to turn into "what-a-story" denunciations. On the other hand, ownership patterns in press economies limit the thematic agenda of watchdog journalism. It is hard to imagine that watchdog journalism would sniff out corporate corruption given that the largest news companies in such countries as Colombia, the Dominican Republic, and Ecuador, just to mention three examples, are part of business groups with extensive holdings in key industries, for example, banking, big agribusiness, tourism, mining, energy, food, and telecommunications). The lack of media diversity does not exclude watchdog journalism, but it narrows down the range of potential issues for investigation.

Press ownership is tied to a second important aspect of watchdog journalism: the role of editorial partisanism. Editorial sympathies have motivated news organizations to reveal different cases of wrongdoing. As mentioned earlier, although the majority of news organizations do not maintain organic linkages with political parties, they are identified with specific ideologies and political-economic interests. Most Latin American countries lack solid party systems to support partisan journalism. Instead, news organizations have supported administrations and officials for various reasons, including common ideology and business pragmatism.[37]

Not surprisingly, then, editorial interest in different cases of wrongdoing has fallen along ideological and political divisions. Left-leaning and liberal news organizations have exposed human rights abuses and wrongdoing in conservative administrations. Conservative news media, instead, have scrutinized wrongdoing during leftist and populist administrations. News organizations with ideologically diffused editorial politics have covered a wide range of cases of corruption. Political polarization has sharpened such divisions. In times when conflicts between administrations and news organizations escalated, such as during the recent skirmishes between populist governments and right-wing proprietors, watchdog journalism has been tainted by political and ideological rifts. The scrutiny of government power has often been motivated by political antagonism rather than some post-political professional goal to serve the public interest. Current political conditions make it difficult to conceive any form of watchdog journalism that stays above the political fray. Political polarization forces the press to take sides, and, in turn, the press sharpens political polarization.

Two reactions are possible with regard to the chronic weakness of professional journalism in Latin America and its impact on the performance of watchdog journalism. From a position that embraces the ideals of professional journalism, one could lament this situation on the grounds that partisanism inevitably compromises quality and fairness. From a perspective that is skeptical about the prospects of postpolitical journalism in the region, one could suggest that competitive politics are the main reservoir for the press to foster democratic deliberation and criticism in the public sphere. The presence of competitive elites and organized publics, rather than journalistic commitment to professional values, sets the basis for press criticism.

These positions carry normative and empirical implications: What kind of watchdog journalism is better for the democratic public sphere? The kind that scrutinizes power animated by wanting to serve the public interest? Or watchdog journalism inspired by partisan ideology? What kind is feasible in Latin America, given political polarization, lack of government transparency, and concentrated media markets? A persuasive answer to these questions is lacking. The prescriptive and pragmatic ramifications of possible answers need to be carefully considered, particularly to assess the appropriate courses of action to strengthen watchdog journalism.

A third issue is the quality of press denunciations. Watchdog journalism has rarely been truly investigative. In the print media, it has often been absorbed by news events that are relatively easy and cheap to cover. On television news, watchdog reporting has typically resorted to hidden cameras and other ethically dubious news-gathering techniques to produce ratings-friendly stories. Consequently, exposés have been focused on individuals, episodic events, and "what-a-story" news, rather than on structural causes and dynamics of corruption. Events are rarely used to produce in-depth coverage of structural factors underlying wrongdoing. For example, news broadcasts about the devastating consequences of hurricanes and earthquakes are rarely used to report on policies to mitigate disasters, social patterns of residential distribution, and land and property issues. Thematic coverage requires editors to remove reporters from the pressures of daily deadlines and provide financial support to conduct investigations. In addition to obstacles to accessing official information, inadequate working conditions make reporters too dependent on official leaks and news from other interested parties for their information gathering. Frequently, the results are stories with flimsy evidence, undocumented conclusions, and bird's-eye views of deep-seated problems and complex webs of corruption.

In summary, the tensions of watchdog journalism are found in the linkages between news organizations with markets and governments, newsroom routines, and professional criteria for determining news. Although structural connections between the press and the state reduce the chances for scrutinizing official actions, conflicts between governments and news organizations increase opportunities for adversarial journalism. Though concentrated media ownership discourages journalism from investigating corporate wrongdoing, it does not exclude the possibility that news organizations may probe corruption in other areas. Although professional criteria push reporters to cover big stories about official wrongdoing, organizational routines drive reporters to cover event-centered news about corruption. Structural and organizational constraints do not completely push out watchdog journalism, but they narrow the potential topics and undermine the quality of reporting that holds power accountable.

## The Press as Agenda Setter and Gatekeeper

Structural dynamics and professional biases also constrain the agenda-setting and gatekeeping roles of the press. As agenda setter, the press should report on a variety of significant public problems that need attention from citizens and policy makers. As gatekeepers, journalists should facilitate dialogue among multiple perspectives by bringing out a range of views from individuals and organized groups. The press in Latin America is ill-equipped to give adequate and balanced attention to issues and opinions. It is predisposed to report on issues that are important to official sources and other individuals and institutions with fluid media access. It is biased, covering issues that are primarily the concerns of well-off media audiences. It is unwilling to focus on issues that may antagonize powerful officials and major advertisers.

The press focuses on issues that are relevant to powerful newsmakers, conventional news sources, and urban and wealthier audiences.[38] It tends to ignore issues affecting citizens without media and political clout. For example, the press fails to pay attention to health issues that mainly affect the young, the old, the poor, ethnic minorities, and rural populations.[39] Environmental issues that affect urban populations are likely to get more press attention than issues affecting rural areas.[40] Crime in wealthier neighborhoods draws more coverage and often feeds "media panics" and "crime waves" that do not match actual incidence or social distribution.[41]

The press not only presents a narrow range of issues, but it also fails to give balanced space to different perspectives. Several studies have concluded that political elites remain primary definers of the news, and that the news media neglect to provide adequate coverage of issues affecting disempowered citizens. In Chile, poor citizens are less frequently present in news coverage. When they get media attention, they are often portrayed as hapless victims or crime perpetrators.[42] In Colombia, coverage of the prolonged internal armed conflict has been dominated by official sources, mainly politicians and military officers. Voices proposing peaceful solutions have received substantially less attention. Poor and rural citizens, who disproportionately make the swelling numbers of people displaced by the conflict, are rarely given opportunities to present their views.[43] Although Brazilian journalism has increasingly offered more coverage on environmental issues, it tends to focus on official opinions and concerns rather than civic voices and local actions to address problems.

The institutional conditions of news production account for bias in agenda setting and gatekeeping. Prevalent journalistic values and work conditions favor reporting on specific kinds of issues and perspectives. Reporting practices and rules reinforce the agenda-setting status of official sources and other powerful newsmakers. The reluctance of news organizations to assign adequate resources puts pressures on reporters to produce fast and low-cost news, instead of time-consuming news gathering. Rushed to deliver content under tight deadlines, reporters typically resort to conventional sources who, expectedly, prioritize specific issues and perspectives. Consequently, a combination of shoddy reporting and editorial constraints produces superficial, inchoate, and incomplete coverage.

Because they lack political influence and news-making prestige, civic voices are at a disadvantage to influence news and public agendas. Admittedly, the rise of civic advocacy journalism in recent years suggests promising changes to enrich the range of issues and perspectives that are presented.[44] A growing number of civic associations and nongovernmental organizations in the region have engaged in news production. From the Brazil-based network *Agencia Nacional de Direitos da Infancia* to Argentina's *Red de Periodismo Social,* a range of civic groups has aimed to change news coverage of myriad social issues in the mainstream press. Hoping to improve the quality of news coverage on social issues, they have used a variety of "sourcing" strategies, such as establishing specialized news services, cultivating relations with reporters, staging news events, and producing stories for mass distribution.

The limitations of the press as agenda setter and gatekeeper raise questions about suitable interventions to improve coverage of issues that are central to democratic governance. It is not obvious whether civic actors can effectively influence institutional practices that influence news content. Civic voices not only are notoriously underrepresented in media ownership, but they also are consistently sidelined by journalistic routines that favor top-down official news. In societies with appalling social disparities and governance problems, the press remains hamstrung by narrow political and private interests.

These problems reflect the thinness of the connective tissues between the press and civic society. As long as the press prioritizes relations with the state and the market, it is hard to envision how news organizations would consistently offer critical and balanced information on issues that affect substantial segments of the population, particularly those who are already socially marginalized.

Latin America offers an interesting case of uneven advances in civic expression. Conditions for freedom of expression are considerably more open than in any other period in the modern political history of the region. Deliberation and criticism are hardly absent in the public sphere. There is no shortage of mobilized publics around a diverse set of issues. The effervescence of multiple forms of civic expression suggests dynamic national public spheres. The press, however, has failed to tap into civic society in ways that it could better serve a diversity of public interests. It has often cautiously followed, reacted, and/or simply ignored emerging demands as well as new political and social movements. Opportunities to scrutinize power and cover a wider set of public issues and perspectives are subordinated to covering political elites and not offending major economic interests.

## Obstacles and Options

To enhance the quality of press performance, it is necessary to promote media pluralism, increase accountability of government decisions affecting the press, and strengthen coverage of civic issues and opinions. The goal should be to reinforce the connective tissues between the press and the public sphere. Such changes would not happen without a perspective that prioritizes institution strengthening and is backed by substantive political will. Although some reforms could be accommodated within prevalent structures, achieving media pluralism and accountability are unimaginable without wrestling influence from government and private interests. Interventions need to be guided by assessments of obstacles for democratic journalism and lessons from past experiences of media reform in the region.

An institutionalist perspective should take precedence over views that reduce media pluralism to the impact of globalization and new technologies. Recently, globalization and technological innovations have animated hopeful views about the prospects for press and democracy. Although global movements for civic expression and technology-based forms of citizen journalism (for example, blogs, cell phones and SMS, and electronic social networks) provide new opportunities for civic expression, it would be a mistake to automatically consider them the bellwether of press democracy. One should not exaggerate their ability to chip away at calcified structures and practices in the Latin American press. Although cross-border civic movements contribute to raising attention about press issues, governments maintain considerable discretion over the dissemination of information and media policies. The use of new technologies remains highly unequal across social strata. While the Internet offers information that is not available in the old media, television and radio still attract the largest audiences. Different forms of citizen journalism remain peripheral in press systems dominated by state and commercial interests. What needs to be asked is whether globalization and new technologies effectively redress major institutional obstacles at the core of press systems.

As a conclusion, this section discusses three approaches to advance the contributions of the press to democratic governance in Latin America. It proposes a combination of interventions to transform media structures, government accountability, and journalistic practices.

One set of interventions needs to support the *diversification of media ownership* and actions for media reform. Some illustrative ideas include, one, supporting advocacy among key actors (government, business, and civic society) to spearhead changes in legislation to reduce the influence of large corporations in press systems; and two, raising the visibility of media pluralism in global and regional forums, and discuss alternatives for media reform with governments and other relevant parties. For example, Peru's Veeduría Ciudadana (Citizens' Watchdog) and Uruguay's chapter of the World Association of Community Radio Stations (AMARC) played key roles in advocating for policy changes and conducting consultative meetings. Although the specifics of the 2004 broadcasting law were far from what the Veeduria had proposed, the group successfully mobilized public and private sectors and generated widespread debate about media policies. In Uruguay, AMARC had a protagonist role during the public debates and congressional process that resulted in the passing of the community broadcasting law in 2007.

A third way to contribute to the diversification of media ownership is through strengthening the financial viability of small print, broadcasting, and Web-based media that are not affiliated with governments or corporations, particularly in areas with weak economies and government manipulation of public funds. The Swiss Foundation Avina, for example, gives grants to community radio stations to develop media management skills (among other goals) to increase the prospects for their future sustainability. Multilateral and bilateral donors can support programs that offer economic incentives (for example, microloans, grants, or subsidies) and opportunities for strengthening media management competencies.[45] These programs, especially if governments are the recipients of funds and co-implementers, require transparency and civic participation to avoid favoritism and corruption.

A second set of actions should aim to *reduce discretionary control of the executive on decisions that affect press performance.* More transparency and public participation in the use of public resources may help to redress centralized power and media patronage. Some areas of intervention include management of official advertising, structure and control of public broadcasting, and decision making around issues such as taxation, importation permits, and newsprint production. Organizations such as Argentina's Asociación por los Derechos Civiles have done a pioneering task through monitoring and publicizing the preferential allocation of public advertising by governments, the use of freedom of information laws, and other vital issues for democratic governance. It is also important to foster the sense that government information is a public resource rather than a private good. Shifting such a mind-set is tantamount to a major revolution. It demands ensuring the collection and preservation of public records, strengthening the capacity of government offices to respond to requests from citizens and journalists, and informing the population about the existence of laws. By the same token, the revocation of punitive legislation against journalists and the passing and enforcement of "access to information" laws are critical, too. Here the work of Mexico's Group Oaxaca stands out, for it led the process that resulted in the approval of the federal Freedom of Information law in 2001.

A third area of intervention is *journalistic practice*. Two complementary strategies are recommended. One is to work with news organizations and journalistic associations. Certainly, there is no shortage of training programs that aim to promote a democratic press in Latin America. An impressive number of associations, universities, and donors regularly offer workshops that cover a range of reporting skills. Standard training programs, however, are incomplete and fail to institutionalize civic voices in the press. Curricula that focus on teaching tools and competencies often miss the fact that training alone does not change journalistic practices. Without the interest of news organizations to modify the current system of incentives and expectations, capacity-strengthening programs are unlikely to achieve substantial changes. Although they might be of interest to reporters, new skills are unlikely to bring significant differences as long as routines and cultures that affect performance remain unchanged. To put it differently, capacity strengthening is not about simply transmitting and acquiring skills. It is about reinforcing democratic institutions and distributive competencies across the public sphere to promote the use of journalistic competencies that favor civic perspectives.

Continuous support for professional associations is also important. Many associations (Peru's Instituto de Prensa y Sociedad, Argentina's Foro de Periodismo Argentino, Brazil's Observatorio da Imprensa) have played a key role in advocating freedom of information laws, raising concerns about antipress violence, and offering spaces for reporters to discuss issues of common interest. A second strategy should aim to facilitate communication between journalists and civic groups. In Latin America, growing numbers of civic groups regularly produce and collect information and have expertise on a wide range of issues. Linking them to newsrooms may help to raise the visibility of civic interests and address newsroom obstacles to produce quality, indepth reporting. Simultaneously, it is important to strengthen the capacity of civic organizations to produce and distribute news through their own media and mainstream newsrooms. The Agência Nacional de Direitos da Infancia (National Agency for Children's Rights) and the organizations that are part of its regional network, and Mexico's Comunicación e Información de la Mujer (Women's Communication and Information), for example, have successfully promoted linkages between mainstream civic society and journalism by acting as regular sources, providing information, holding specialized training, monitoring coverage on specific issues, and advocating socially responsible reporting.

The implementation of different interventions confronts varying levels of difficulty. Changing power relations in favor of media pluralism, in principle, is likely to face more severe obstacles than offering training workshops. Also, opportunities may be different across countries and regions. From the commitment of government officials to media reform to the structure of press markets, various factors affect the opportunities and impact of interventions. Just as current structures and dynamics shape conditions for public expression, they, too, affect the prospects for local and global actions to catalyze changes.

Certainly, many suggested actions have already been implemented in Latin America. For decades, international donors and civic associations have supported countless initiatives in support of the press and democracy. Efforts, however, have often worked in isolation. They lacked a common vision of media reform that maximizes contributions from different institutions and programs. The challenge is to bring together dispersed initiatives and institutions around basic objectives and actions. Only then would it be possible to nurture and consolidate local social movements for media reform at both country and regional levels. Profound and long-lasting changes in the press require sustainable civic actions.

Bringing the press closer to mobilized publics will contribute to transferring a wide spectrum of civic demands into the policy-making arena. Throughout the region, the public sphere has an impressive stock of citizens' initiatives and democratic practices that are insufficiently presented and represented in the press. For the press to enhance democratic governance, it should tap into those experiences and widen opportunities for deliberation and criticism. A more democratic public sphere is unthinkable as long as sharp disparities in access to the press persist.

## Notes

1. See Pippa Norris. 2005. "Global Political Communication: Good Governance, Human Developments and Mass Communication." In *Comparing Political Communication: Theories, Cases, and Challenges,* ed. Frank Esser and Barbara Pfetsch. New York: Cambridge University Press.
2. Jurgen Habermas. 1989. *The Structural Transformation of the Public Sphere.* Cambridge, MA: MIT Press.
3. Craig J. Calhoun. 1992. *Habermas and the Public Sphere.* Cambridge, MA: MIT Press.
4. Habermas developed this point largely in response to his critics, particularly Nancy Fraser's argument about the need to distinguish between "weak" and "strong" publics in the public sphere. See her contribution in Calhoun. 1992. *Habermas and the Public Sphere.* Cambridge, MA: MIT Press.
5. On the liberal model, the locus classicus is Fredrick S. Siebert, Theodore Peterson, and Wilbur Schramm. 1956. *Four Theories of the Press.* Champaign: University of Illinois Press. For a critique, see John Nerone. 1995. *Last Rights: Revisiting Four Theories of the Press.* Champaign: University of Illinois Press. A comprehensive discussion on press models is found in Dennis McQuail. 2000. *Mass Communication Theory.* London: Sage.
6. For discussions on media policies and journalistic practices along the lines of public sphere principles, see Peter Dahlgren and Colin Sparks, eds. 1991. *Communication and*

*Citizenship: Journalism and the Public Sphere in the New Media Age.* London: Sage; James Curran and Jean Seaton. 2003. *Power Without Responsibility: The Press, Broadcasting, and New Media in Britain.* London: Routledge; Tanni Haas and Linda Steiner. 2001. "Public Journalism as a Journalism of Publics: Implications of the Habermas-Fraser Debate for Public Journalism." *Journalism* 2 (2): 123–47; Jim McGuigan and Stuart Allan. 2006. "Mediating Politics: Jurgen Habermas and the Public Sphere." In *Radical Mass Media Criticism: A Cultural Genealogy,* ed. David Berry and John Theobald. Montreal: Black Rose Books; Nico Carpentier. 2007. "Coping with the Agoraphobia Media Professional: A Typology of Journalistic Practices Reinforcing Democracy and Participation." In *Reclaiming the Media,* ed. Bart Cammaerts and Nico Carpentier. Bristol, UK: Intellect.

7. Among others, see Kari Karpinnen. 2006. "Media Diversity and the Politics of Criteria." *Nordicom Review* 2: 53–68; Jan van Cuilenberg. 1999. "On Competition, Access, and Diversity in Media, Old and New." *New Media and Society* 1 (2): 183–207.

8. Denis McQuail. 1992. *Media Performance: Mass Communication and the Public Interest.* London: Sage.

9. See James Curran and Michael Gurevitch, eds. 2001. *Mass Media and Society.* 3rd ed. London: Arnold; John Keane. 1991. *The Media and Democracy.* Cambridge: Polity Press.

10. Among others, see Chappell Lawson and Sallie Hughes. 2005. "Latin America's Post-authoritarian Media." In *(Un)civil Societies: Human Rights and Democratic Transitions in Eastern Europe and Latin America,* ed. Rachel May and Andrew Milton. Lanham: Lexington Books; Chappell Lawson. 2002. *Building the Fourth Estate: Democratization and the Rise of a Free Press in Mexico.* Berkeley: University of California Press; and Sallie Hughes. 2006. *Newsrooms in Conflict: Journalism and the Democratization of Mexico.* Pittsburgh, PA: University of Pittsburgh Press.

11. For a thorough discussion of this subject, see Leonardo Avritzer. 2002. *Democracy and the Public Space in Latin America.* Princeton, NJ: Princeton University Press.

12. See Richard Feinberg, Carlos H. Waisman, and León Zamosc, eds. 2006. Civil Society and Democracy in Latin America. New York: Palgrave Macmillan.

13. See Silvio Waisbord. 2000. "Media in South America: Between the Rock of the State and the Hard Place of the Market." In *De-Westernizing Media Studies,* ed. James Curran and M. Park. London: Arnold.

14. Maria Teresa Herran and Javier Restrepo. 1995. *Etica para Periodistas.* Bogota: Tercer Mundo.

15. A 2001 study estimated that almost a quarter of broadcasting companies in Brazil are owned by politicians. Politicians were granted almost 78 percent of new licenses between 1999 and 2001. This reinforces existing patterns by which political families have a stronghold on both print and broadcast in the majority of Brazilian states. See Rogerio Christofoletti. 2003. "Dez impasses para uma efetiva critica de midia no Brasil." Paper presented at the meeting of INTERCOM, Belo Horizonte, September 2003.

16. A substantial literature in the region has analyzed this issue. On Brazil, see Alcira Abreu. 2002. *A Modernização da Imprensa, 1970–2000.* Rio de Janeiro: Jorge Zahar.

17. Elizabeth Fox, ed. 1988. *The Struggle for Democracy.* London: Sage.

18. John Sinclair. 2002. "The Aging Dynasties." In *Latin Politics, Global Media,* ed. Elizabeth Fox and Silvio Waisbord. Austin: University of Texas Press.

19. UNDP (United Nations Development Programme). 2004. *Democracy in Latin America: Towards a Citizens' Democracy.* Buenos Aires: Aguilar, Altea, Taurus, Alfaguara.

20. See Fox and Waisbord, eds. 2002. *Latin Politics, Global Media;* Guillermo Mastrini, ed. 2005. *Mucho Ruido y Pocas Leyes.* Buenos Aires: La Crujía.

21. For example, see Carlos Monsiváis and Julio Scherer. 2003. *Tiempo de saber. Prensa y poder en México*. Mexico City: Editorial Nuevo Siglo; Kris Kodrich. 2008. "The Role of State Advertising in Latin American Newspapers: Was the Demise of Nicaragua's Barricada Newspaper Political Sabotage?" *Bulletin of Latin American Research* 27 (1): 61–82; Maria O'Donnell. 2007. *Propaganda K: Una Maquinaria de Promoción con Dinero del Estado*. Buenos Aires: Planeta.

22. In a region with plenty of examples of government manipulation of the press, the Fujimori administration in Peru stands out for its blatant use of public funds and blackmailing to build a propaganda arsenal. See Catherine Conaghan. 2005. *Fujimori's Peru: Deception in the Public Sphere*. Pittsburgh, PA: University of Pittsburgh Press; John McMillan and Pablo Zoido. 2004. "How to Subvert Democracy: Montesinos in Peru." *Journal of Economic Perspectives* 18 (4): 69–92.

23. See Raul Trejo Delabre. 2006. "Después de la Ley Televisa." http://raultrejo.tripod.com/Mediosensayos/RTDLeyTelevisaZocaloabril06.htm.

24. See Fox and Waisbord, eds. 2002. *Latin Politics, Global Media;* Guillermo Sunkel and Esteban Geoffroy, eds. 2001. *Concentración económica de los medios de comunicación*. Santiago: Lom; Guillermo Mastrini and Martín Becerra, eds. 2006. *Periodistas y Magnates: Estructura y concentración de las industrias culturales en América Latina*. Buenos Aires: Prometeo Libros.

25. Rosalind Bresnahan. 2003. "The Media and the Neoliberal Transition in Chile," *Latin American Perspectives* 30 (6): 39–68.

26. Ernesto Villanueva. 2003. *Derecho de acceso a la información pública en Latinoamérica*. Mexico City: Universidad Nacional Autónoma de México; Juliet Gill and Sallie Hughes. 2005. "Bureaucratic Compliance with Mexico's New Access to Information Law." *Critical Studies in Mass Communication* 22 (2): 121–37.

27. Valerio Fuenzalida. 2000. *La televisión pública en América Latina. Reforma o privatización*. Santiago de Chile: Fondo de Cultura Económica.

28. Rosalía Winocur. 2003. "Media and Participative Strategies: The Inclusion of Private Necessities in the Public Sphere." *Television & New Media* 4 (1): 25–42.

29. Certainly, many civic groups have also opposed Chavez's changes in press and media laws. See Marcelino Bisbal. 2006. "Redescubrir el valor del periodismo en la Venezuela del presente." Contratexto 14:51–78; Andres Cañizales and C. Correa. 2003. *Venezuela: Situación del derecho a la libertad de expresión e información*. Caracas. Espacio Público; Eleazar Diaz Rangel and others. 2003. *Chávez y los medios de comunicación social*. Caracas: Alfadil Editores.

30. Ronald Grebe. 2007. "Evo morales y los medios." *Chasqui* 98. http://chasqui.comunica.org/content/view/552/142/.

31. See Rosental Alves. 2005. "From Lapdog to Watchdog: The Role of the Press in Latin America's Democratization." In *Making Journalists*, ed. Hugo de Burgh, 181–204. London: Routledge; and Silvio Waisbord. 2000. *Watchdog Journalism in South America*. New York: Columbia University Press. The discussion below largely draws from my book.

32. Enrique Peruzzotti and Catalina Smulovitz, eds. 2006. *Enforcing the Rule of Law: Social Accountability in the New Latin American Democracies*. Pittsburgh, PA: University of Pittsburgh Press.

33. Juliet Gill. 2006. "Muzzling the Watchdog: Changing Media Performance in Democratic Argentina." PhD diss., University of Miami, FL; J. Brito. 2003. "El león fuera de su jaula: la 'primavera fiscalizadora' del periodismo chileno." *Información Pública*, 1 (2): 309–36.

34. See Foro de Periodismo Argentino. 2005. *Sobre los periodistas y la profesión.* Buenos Aires: FOPEA; Observatorio de Medios. 2003. *Informe sobre el estado actual de la libertad de prensa en Colombia.* Chia: Universidad de la Sabana.

35. For examples, see Waisbord. 2000. *Watchdog Journalism in South America.*

36. See Fundación Konrad Adenauer y el Instituto Prensa y Sociedad. 2005. *Hábitos de trabajo del periodista Latinoamericano.* Lima: Fundación Konrad Adenauer y el Instituto Prensa y Sociedad.

37. See discussion in Silvio Waisbord. 2006. "In Journalism We Trust?" In *Mass Media and New Democracies,* ed. Katrin Voltmer. London: Routledge.

38. An overview is offered in Santiago Pedraglio. 2005. "Agendas distantes: Los medios de comunicación y los partidos políticos en la Región Andina." Institute for Democracy and Electoral Assistance, *Democracia en la Región Andina, los telones de fondo.* Lima: IDEA and Transparencia Peru.

39. Rina Alcalay and Carmen T. Mendoza. 2000. "Proyecto COMSALUD: Un estudio comparativo de mensajes relacionados con salud en los medios masivos Latinoamericanos." Washington, DC: Pan American Health Organization. Aurea M. da Rocha, ed. 1995. *Saude & comunicação: Visibilidades e silêncios.* São Paulo: Hucitec/Abrasco.

40. J. C. González. 2007. "El papel de la prensa en la construcción de las representaciones sobre la problemática ambiental." *Convergencia* 14: 39–71; Diane Jukofsky. 2000. "El periodismo ambiental: Una especia en extinción." *Chasqui* 70. http://www.comunica. org/chasqui/jukofsky70.htm.

41. A summary is found in Jorge Bonilla Velez and Camilo Gómez. 2006. "Medios de comunicación y violencias en America Latina." *Controversia* 187. http://www.cinep.org .co/revistas/controversia/controversia187/art06_mediosdecomunicacion.pdf.

42. Soledad Larrain and Andrea Valenzuela. 2004. *Televisión y ciudadanía.* Santiago: Fucatel.

43. There is an extensive literature in Spanish on this subject. See Liliana Gutiérrez. 2007. "La prensa como creadora de estereotipos sobre los reinsertados y el proceso de paz en Colombia." *Palabra Clave* 10: 2. Wendy Arenas and others. 2003. *El conflicto armado en las páginas de El Tiempo.* Bogota: El Tiempo.

44. For an overview, see Silvio Waisbord. 2009. "Advocacy Journalism in a Global Context: The 'Journalist' and the 'Civic' Model." In *Handbook of Journalism Studies,* ed. Karin Wahl-Jorgensen and Thomas Hanitzsch. London: Routledge.

45. Center for International Media Assistance and National Endowment for Democracy. 2007. "Toward Economic Sustainability of the Media in Developing Countries." Washington, DC: Center for International Media Assistance.

13

•
•
•

# Arab States

Lawrence Pintak

The Arab Republic of Egypt is a place where torture is institutionalized. Human Rights Watch calls the abuse of prisoners in Egypt "epidemic,"[1] Amnesty International says it is "common and systematic,"[2] and the U.S. State Department's 2007 Country Report on Egypt concluded that "police, security personnel, and prison guards routinely tortured and abused prisoners and detainees."[3] The country is one of several to which the Central Intelligence Agency (CIA), under the now-infamous rendition program, sent prisoners to be interrogated using techniques too harsh for the agency's own operatives to administer.[4]

So when two Egyptian policemen were convicted of torture in late 2007 and sent to prison, it was a landmark victory for human rights activists. It was also a seminal moment for the media.[5] The case, in which Cairo police used a nightstick to sodomize a cab driver in their custody, came to light only when Egyptian blogger Wael Abbas posted cell phone video of the assault on You-Tube, sparking a media feeding frenzy that ultimately forced the government to prosecute the kind of conduct that has long been condoned.

## The Mouthpiece Tradition

In the Arab world, the media have traditionally been gatekeepers favoring those in power. Until the past decade, all television stations in the region were owned by governments—"television journalism" was an oxymoron—and most print media were tightly controlled. The extent of that control was evidenced in the fact that when Saddam Hussein's armies invaded Kuwait in 1990, media in neighboring Saudi Arabia waited more than 48 hours before telling the Saudi public, giving the panicked government time to formulate its response.[6] It was the equivalent of the French media ignoring a German occupation of Belgium.

Before the advent of Arab satellite television, the idea that media might drive public opinion in a direction other than that dictated by government was essentially unthinkable, much less that media would have an agenda-setting effect independent from that of those in power. The theory of agenda setting as applied to the Arab media thus attracted little scholarly interest, even though the Arab-Israeli conflict served as an important case study for agenda setting in the Western[7] and Israeli media.[8] It was not until 2007, for example, that the historical role of the Palestinian media in shaping public attitudes toward the British occupation and the early Zionists was documented.[9] The few other examples of research in the field quickly became dated. A study of Saudi Arabian media found that whereas Saudi news organizations were very effective at influencing the international agenda among Saudi civil servants, they had little impact on domestic issues; but that research was completed in 1992, well before the advent of Arab satellite television.[10] Another major study concluded that the print press in the region was far more important than the electronic media, a notion even the casual observer of the Arab world knows has been turned on its head since government broadcasters lost their television monopoly.[11]

Much of the credit for that turnabout goes to the emir of Qatar. In 1996, he invested US$120 million and hired much of the team from an ill-fated BBC-Saudi television venture to start Al-Jazeera, with a mandate to shake up the media landscape. Make no mistake: Al-Jazeera is owned by, and answerable to, the Qatari government. But the channel was given a very long leash and soon brought to the region's television screens a diversity of voices and a kind of questioning journalism never before seen in the Arab world. Its *raison d'être* was political and social change, which is precisely why, over the past decade, at one time or another its reporters have been thrown out of virtually every Arab country and, as of this writing, remain banned from Saudi Arabia.

The Qatari ruler did not create Al-Jazeera because he saw himself as the patron saint of media freedom—Qatar's domestic media remain firmly under heel—but rather to give himself a powerful weapon in the struggle for regional influence with his neighbor and erstwhile rival, the House of Saud (it was the same reason he agreed to host the U.S. Central Command when Washington decided to shift most of its forces out of Saudi Arabia). But the effect was still the same. Arab journalism would never be the same.

Arab reporters who had spent their entire careers as little more than a mouthpiece for their respective governments were now exposed to a new way of practicing their profession. Many of them aspired to emulate their

Al-Jazeera colleagues. This desire to break new ground was particularly evident in the newsrooms of the handful of semi-independent newspapers that began appearing in the region, such as *Al-Masri al-Youm* in Egypt and Jordan's *Al-Ghad*. "We started *Al-Masri* to bring a new, more professional kind of journalism to Egypt," founder Hisham Kassem said. The impact of this more aggressive form of journalism quickly became evident. A 2004 study of Egypt's main government daily, *Al-Ahram*, and *Al-Wafd*, the official organ of the opposition party by the same name, found a high correlation between the agenda of the opposition paper and its readers and low correlations between that of *Al-Ahram* and its readers.[12] But even those working on government-controlled newspapers and television stations began pushing the envelope. "We want change too," the editor of a key government-owned newspaper said during a closed-door session of Egyptian editors and journalism educators. "We just have to go about it a little differently."[13]

Meanwhile, there was an explosion of new Arab satellite channels. More than 300 free-to-air Arab satellite broadcasters now crowd the spectrum, representing every political and social viewpoint, from royalists to revolutionaries to religious extremists. Among them are several direct competitors to Al-Jazeera, which means that few major regional events take place beyond the glare of the television lens. And that is a reality governments are slowly learning they cannot ignore.

## Agenda Setting and (Incremental) Change

The intrinsic link between the arrival of pan-Arab satellite television and shifting public attitudes toward the now-faltering democracy agenda across the region—the so-called Al-Jazeera effect—is well documented.[14] One of the more interesting studies traces a direct connection between the proreform agenda of Al-Jazeera, that of its more conservative Saudi-controlled rival, Al-Arabiya, and the relative attitudes of their audiences toward questions of political and social change.[15]

But media-fueled aspirations for change and real change are two very different things. More than a decade after Al-Jazeera revolutionized the very nature of Arab political dialogue with its mantra of "The opinion—and the other opinion," not a single Arab ruler has lost his job through popular pressure. Political control remains a family affair. In three of the four countries where change came through natural causes—Jordan, Morocco, and the Syrian Arab Republic—the sons have risen to fill the void. In Saudi Arabia, power shifted to the late king's brother, while in Egypt, Mubarak's son Gamal waits in the wings for his own coronation. The so-called Arab Spring of 2005 has given way to a renewed cold snap as the Bush administration's "forward strategy of freedom" has faltered, leaving the region's reformers "increasingly scornful of a democracy agenda that seems selectively applied to suit narrow U.S. interests."[16]

But while media has yet to create broad political change, its impact on policy is beginning to become evident—even if still nascent enough that one can easily cite most instances when it has been apparent.

The Lebanon conflict in the summer of 2006 was one of the most vivid examples of media driving Arab government policy. At the beginning of the conflict, Saudi Arabia and other Sunni-majority Gulf states criticized the Shiite militia Hezbollah for provoking the Israeli assault on Lebanon. In the early days of the war, Al-Jazeera's main competitor, Saudi-owned Al-Arabiya, downplayed the conflict. But it was not long before it joined Al-Jazeera, the privately owned Lebanon Broadcasting Corporation, and Hezbollah's own channel, Al-Manar, in providing wall-to-wall 24/7 coverage of the war. The Arab world was transfixed. Public opinion from Morocco to the Republic of Yemen united firmly behind Hezbollah's defense of the Lebanese homeland. Tensions between Sunni and Shia, and political differences between Arab nationalists and Islamists, were—for the moment—largely set aside. Crowds in Cairo held high, side-by-side pictures of the late Arab nationalist leader Gamal Abdul Nasser and Hezbollah chief Hassan Nasrallah, an unheard-of juxtaposition. As the conflict dragged on, LBC producer Marwan Matni, a Christian, later said, "I felt myself changing. Lebanon was under attack. We were all Lebanese. By the end, I, too, felt myself to be Hezbollah."[17] The sentiment was shared by Arabs across the region to a degree governments could not ignore. Soon after hostilities ended, Nasrallah was welcomed in the Gulf as a conquering hero. "The Lebanese people and their resistance have achieved the first Arab victory, something we had longed for," said Qatar's emir, Hamad bin Khalifa al-Thani.[18] In a matter of a few weeks, Gulf policy had changed 180 degrees.

Lebanon also served as the backdrop for another, even more dramatic, confluence of media and policy. Since the country was carved off from Greater Syria by the colonial powers after World War I, the government in Damascus has considered Lebanon its natural fief. For 29 years, since their initial intervention during the civil war, Syrian troops had kept a permanent presence in Lebanon, fighting at one point or another on the side of virtually all of the confessional groups. Though various factions tried, no militia had the power to force the Syrians to go home. But with the 2005 assassination of former Lebanese Prime Minister Rafiq Hariri, whose death was widely assumed to be the work of the Damascus regime, the political landscape changed. Tens of thousands of Lebanese took to the streets to demand a Syrian withdrawal in what was quickly dubbed the "Cedar Revolution."[19] The movement featured a made-for-TV color scheme reminiscent of the Ukraine's Orange Revolution and produced 24/7 coverage by all of the main Arab satellite channels. As during the conflict with Israel a year later, Arab audiences were riveted to their television screens. Here, on live TV, was a revolution against one of the most brutal Arab regimes.

At one point, Syrian President Bashar Assad forlornly called on the cameras to "zoom out" to show that the crowds weren't as large as they appeared on the TV screen, but it was not long before he gave in to the new media reality. The powerful army of Syria was ordered home. It would be misleading to say that television alone forced Assad's hand. The Bush administration had been increasing its pressure on Damascus even before the Hariri assassination, and with the murder of the former prime minister, who was related by marriage to the Saudi royal family, Riyadh also began turning the diplomatic and economic screws. But a credible argument can be made that without the unblinking lens of Arab television, which in turn drove anti-Syrian sentiment across the region, Assad might easily have resorted to the kind of brutal tactics that led his father to wipe one of his own cities off the map to put down an Islamist revolt in the 1980s, back in the days when punishment could be applied well out of frame.

The impact of media is also being seen on what were once purely internal issues, long ignored or hidden by the tame domestic media. A case in point is that of an 18-year-old Saudi girl who was gang raped by seven men when they discovered her sitting in a car with a male schoolmate, who was also gang raped. Under Saudi law, it is illegal for an unrelated man and woman to be alone. When the woman, who was about to get married, reported the assault, she was arrested and eventually sentenced to six months in prison and 90 lashes for violating the separation of sexes law. But when she went public to protest the sentence, a rare move in that controlled society, the court increased the punishment to 200 lashes because of "her attempt to aggravate and influence the judiciary through the media." Her plight set off a bitter debate in the Saudi media, which dubbed her "Qatif girl," for the town where the attack occurred. "Qatif girl's dream of redeeming any of her self-respect through the judicial system was crushed in front of her own eyes," the *Saudi Gazette* reported.[20]

The story was quickly picked up by pan-Arab satellite channels, with talk show hosts like LBC's Shatha Omar pitting government officials, the girl's lawyer, and her husband in live debates. The Ministry of Justice reacted to the media fracas by, as one Saudi blogger put it, "slandering the girl and portray[ing] her like a slut who deserved to be raped."[21] Adding fuel to the fire, an appeals court judge told the Saudi daily *Okaz* that the controversy was all a conspiracy on the part of the foreign media and said everyone involved in the incident—including the girl—should receive the death penalty.[22] By that point, the story was making headlines around the world and the Saudi government was firmly on the defensive, with the White House calling the situation "outrageous" and Canada decrying the sentence as "barbaric."[23] Saudi commentators on both ends of the political spectrum expressed concern about the damage to the country's reputation. In the face of the domestic and international uproar, King Abdullah finally stepped in and overruled the court with a pardon read live on Saudi television by the justice minister. The crime, said the King, was "brutal," and a pardon was justified because "the woman and the man who was with her were subject to torture and stubbornness that is considered in itself sufficient in disciplining both of them and to learn from the lesson."[24] It was a ruling designed to placate both the critics and those on the right who felt the girl deserved punishment, but it also represented an undeniable, and unprecedented, response to media-driven pressure by a man labeled by Reporters without Borders (RSF) as one of the Arab world's "predators of press freedom."[25]

Along with violence against women in places like Saudi Arabia and Jordan, many other once-forbidden issues are now being reported in the Arab media. In 2005, the United Nations Children's Fund (UNICEF) noted a sharp spike in the number of inquiries from journalists on topics such as HIV-AIDS and female genital mutilation.[26] One reason is that the rise of Arab satellite television has brought a growing acceptance of discussion about human sexuality. That has filtered down to national print media as well. Front-page reporting of the deaths of two young Egyptian girls who died after botched circumcisions sparked an unprecedented debate that led to a national campaign against the practice, led by Suzanne Mubarak, wife of Egypt's president. Much the same was happening with other sensitive topics. Governments like those of Egypt, Saudi Arabia, and the United Arab Emirates were still jailing on homosexuality charges men who were diagnosed as HIV-positive, but fact-based stories on the disease, its methods of transmission and treatment, were beginning to appear in media across the region.

The United Nations Educational, Scientific, and Cultural Organization (UNESCO) also noted a dramatic increase in media interest in Darfur, a story Arab journalists had struggled with for years. The fighting turned on its head the narrative of Arab as victim—as in coverage of Palestine and Iraq. In Darfur, Arab tribes were responsible for the killing. It was an Arab *Jihad on Horseback*, as Al-Arabiya titled a documentary on the conflict. That program, produced in 2005, never aired. It was killed after a phone call from Sudan's president to the then-Saudi crown prince, who in turn called the owner of Al-Arabiya, who also happened to be King Fahd's brother-in-law. But by that point, other Arab journalists were breaking out of the old model in which they parroted the pronouncements of Sudan's Arab government; they were skipping the government-run guided tours and slipping into Darfur on their own to take an uncensored view. Suddenly, a new version of the story was being reported: Muslim victims of Arab Muslim fighters.

## Watchdogs and Lapdogs

One of the criticisms of the pan-Arab media is that while they focus on the big regional stories like Lebanon, Palestine, Iraq, and, more recently, Darfur, they ignore local issues—like water, sanitation, and roads—that are far less sexy. They also avoid soiling their own nests. In Al-Jazeera's case, that involves largely ignoring domestic Qatari issues; for Al-Arabiya, the "red lines" of self-censorship involve Saudi politics, religion, and domestic terrorism.[27]

The contrast between regional and local media was vividly played out during the April 2008 bread riots in Egypt, centered on a textile mill in the Delta town of Mahalla. There, thousands of protesters clashed with government troops in violence that left several dead, including a 15-year-old bystander, and hundreds injured and resulted in scores of arrests. Al-Jazeera and other pan-Arab channels featured graphic footage of the violence; and still photos of protestors stomping on posters of Egyptian President Hosni Mubarak; and bleeding victims of the violence appeared on the Web sites of Egyptian bloggers and foreign news organizations, until the government banned journalists from the area. But such images were harder to find in the domestic media. Even pan-Arab broadcasters such as Orbit, Dream, and Al-Mehwar, which are based in Egypt's so-called free zone Media City, largely avoided showing the more dramatic scenes. News managers at those channels stated privately that they had been warned by the Mubarak regime to tone down their coverage and to make sure their talk shows included a heavy representation of the government's viewpoint. The implicit "or else" did not need to be stated: just days before, Egypt pulled the plug on a London-based channel highly critical of the regime that had been distributed on the Egyptian-owned satellite.

The move was facilitated by the adoption of an Arab League Satellite Charter, authored by the Egyptians and Saudis, who control the two main satellites in the region, Nilesat and Arabsat. The charter contained vague language warning against jeopardizing "social peace, national unity, public order and general propriety" and ordering that channels must protect "the supreme interests of the Arab countries."[28] Other sections warned against offending "moral, social and cultural values"[29] and "threatening national unity, spreading propaganda and harming the overarching interests of the country."[30] Similar catch-all phrases had long been used to shut down newspapers, block Internet sites, and jail journalists.

Charter supporters insisted the document was aimed at hard-line Islamist channels that were allegedly radicalizing the youth;[31] but the silencing of Al-Hiwar, a secular antiregime channel, just weeks after the charter was adopted appeared to put the lie to that claim. So, too, did subsequent raids in Cairo to confiscate satellite transmission equipment used by Al-Jazeera and other international broadcasters, the closure of the Cairo offices of several foreign satellite channels, a campaign against satellite channels in the state-run Egyptian media, and the introduction of a draft law in the Egyptian parliament that would prohibit journalists from undermining social peace, national unity, pubic order, and public values.[32]

As the Mahalla riots dragged on, dozens of activists were arrested in security sweeps in Cairo. Bloggers were among the targets, including "Facebook

Girl," a 27-year-old woman who created a group on the social networking site that became the focal point for a one-day national strike in support of the Mahalla workers.[33] The government's attitude was summed up by Prime Minister Ahmed Nazif when, during a speech at Cairo University, he told a student in the audience who defended Facebook Girl, "There is a thin line between expressing your opinion and encouraging destruction, striking and rioting."[34] The fact that the student was arrested a few days later and briefly detained underlines just how thin that line really is.

Amid the riots and roundups, which coincided with local elections widely condemned as rigged by the regime, the reporting in government-owned *Al-Ahram* seemed to hark back to an earlier era. As the paper framed it, the government's response to the riots was magnanimous: "President Hosni Mubarak agreed yesterday to give a one-month bonus to the workers in the Mahalla textile factory, in addition to a 15-day bonus granted to textile workers throughout the republic in appreciation of their noble positions."

*Al-Ahram*'s coverage was an example of the lapdog function of the government-controlled press in much of the Arab world. But even those semi-independent and opposition papers that aspire to be watchdogs often lack teeth. Criminal libel laws in many countries mean that journalists who try to root out corruption and uncover malfeasance often find themselves being sent to jail as a result of lawsuits filed by the subjects of their stories. And truth is no defense. A reporter and editor for a newspaper in Alexandria, Egypt, for example, were given prison sentences after being convicted of libel, even though their corruption story was factually correct. Similar examples could be found across the region. As the Committee to Protect Journalists reported in 2007, "scores of journalists who challenged the political order were threatened by government agents, hauled before the courts, thrown in prison, or censored in media crackdowns that stretched from Algeria to Yemen."[35]

Many Arab governments talk about freedom of the press, but it is often code for precisely the opposite. The Freedom House map of press freedom in the Arab world is monochromatic; most of the region is colored dark blue for "not free." In the 2008 edition, just three countries qualified as "partly free" (see table 13.1). But that is very much a relative term; Arab countries occupy the bottom third of the global rankings. One of those "partly free" countries is Lebanon, where several high-profile journalists have been assassinated or maimed in assassination attempts. Another is Kuwait, where laws were recently adopted making it a crime to criticize the constitution, the emir, or Islam, or to incite acts that "offend public morality, religious sensibilities, or the basic convictions of the nation."[36] And the third is Egypt, which was moved from the "not free" category as a result of the appearance of several new semi-independent media outlets and despite the increased government campaign against the media.

Table 13.1.  Press Freedom in the Arab Region, 2008

| Global rank (of 195) | Country | Rating | Status |
| --- | --- | --- | --- |
| 114 | Kuwait | 54 | Partly free |
| 117 | Lebanon | 55 | Partly free |
| 124 | Egypt, Arab Rep. of | 59 | Partly free |
| 134 | Algeria | 62 | Not free |
| 135 | Jordan | 63 | Not free |
| 138 (tie) | Morocco | 64 | Not free |
| 138 (tie) | Qatar | 64 | Not free |
| 151 | United Arab Emirates | 68 | Not free |
| 153 | Iraq | 69 | Not free |
| 157 (tie) | Bahrain | 71 | Not free |
| 157 (tie) | Oman | 71 | Not free |
| 160 | Djibouti | 72 | Not free |
| 161 | Chad | 74 | Not free |
| 170 (tie) | Yemen, Republic of | 78 | Not free |
| 170 (tie) | Sudan | 78 | Not free |
| 175 (tie) | Saudi Arabia | 81 | Not free |
| 175 (tie) | Tunisia | 81 | Not free |
| 179 | Syrian Arab Rep. | 83 | Not free |
| 181 (tie) | Palestinian Territories | 84 | Not free |
| 181 (tie) | Somalia | 84 | Not free |
| 190 | Libya | 94 | Not free |

*Source:* Freedom House. 2008. *Freedom of the Press 2008,* http://www.Freedomhouse.org.

But even in places where there seems to be a commitment to media reform, the contradictions between words and actions abound. At a gathering of American and Arab reporters at the Dead Sea in the spring of 2008, Princess Rym Ali, sister-in-law of Jordan's King Abdullah, made an impassioned speech in support of press freedom. There was no doubt of her sincerity. The former Rym Brahimi is herself a former CNN correspondent. Also present was Osama al-Sharif, former editor of Jordan's *Al-Dustour* newspaper, who, just days before, had been sentenced to three months in prison on charges of contempt of the judiciary for reporting—correctly—that a Jordanian had filed a lawsuit against a court that stripped him of his citizenship.[37] The disconnect between commitment to media reform in Jordan and its implementation, al-Sharif and other Jordanian journalists say, lies in the gulf between the desires of the palace and the agenda of the bureaucracy that implements the laws. In other places, they are completely in sync, but not in a positive sense.

Nowhere does the national agenda take a back seat to media reform. Even the facade of freedom in Dubai's much-vaunted Media City, where news organizations are supposedly guaranteed the right to operate without interference, proved hollow when Pakistan declared martial law in November 2007. After two private Pakistani channels based in Media City, GEO TV and Ary One, refused a demand from the Musharraf government to sign a new "code of conduct," Emirati authorities gave them two hours to stop broadcasting.

Officials left little doubt the principles of press freedom on which Media City was supposedly based had taken a back seat to Emirati foreign policy. "As an entity within the UAE, Dubai Media City would also observe the broadcast principals of the country's foreign policy and prevent the telecast of news and material that would undermine those principles," said Amina Al Rustamani, executive director of Dubai Media City.[38]

The incident underlined the schizophrenic approach to media in the Arab world. Media is power, nowhere more so than in the Middle East. By controlling the messenger while fostering some perception of media independence, Arab governments can at least attempt to control the nature and pace of change. At a major Saudi-financed conference on the media in Dubai in the fall of 2005, the president of the Arab Thought Foundation, Prince Bandar bin Khaled al Faisal, was asked why a nation—that was, after all, a feudal monarchy with no pretensions to representational democracy—would finance a gathering on media freedom, itself a historic precursor to democracy. "Journalism is a part of change," said Bandar, the owner of Saudi Arabia's *Al-Watan* newspaper. "And this conference is an effort to say, 'OK, maybe we should expedite the process a little bit because we really do have a lot to lose.'"

On one level, national leaders want the power and prestige of high-profile media outlets; the Saudis, Qataris, and Emiratis, in particular, are in a cycle of media one-upmanship. They point to their supposedly independent media as evidence of political and social reform. But the facade is often far prettier than what is going on behind the scenes. No project is more emblematic of this contradiction than the *National*, an English-language daily with a staff of almost 200, including high-priced reporters and editors from the *New York Times*, the *Daily Telegraph*, the *Wall Street Journal*, and a variety of other Western news organizations.

Hyped by its British editor as "the last great newspaper launch in history,"[39] the inaugural issue of the *National* was modern and flashy in design but its content was vacuous; in all, the new paper was strikingly similar to that of Singapore's well-designed but toothless government-owned *Straights-Times*. The *National's* front-page in its first week highlighted cheerleading stories about UAE government reform, "five-star food" in the country's prisons, and the first Emirati kidney transplant. It was not exactly crusading journalism, but not surprising for a newspaper owned by the government and backed by Abu Dhabi's $850 billion investment fund. Within days, foreign reporters on the paper were grumbling about a "go easy" mandate from the top and a virtual ban on controversial stories, such as the plight of foreign laborers in the emirates. A media executive who had considered taking a post at the paper said the approach was described to him this way: "It's not Arab censorship; it's Arab sensitivity."

But the paper's deputy editor, former *New York Times* correspondent Hassan Fattah, says that if they are going to help set the agenda, Arab media cannot afford to emulate the attack-dog approach of some of their Western counterparts. "We're not screaming. We're trying to influence and convince," he said in a phone interview one week after the first issue hit the street. The lead story that day was a much-hyped investigation into the private trade in rare animals, which was actually based on the work of a government agency, not the paper's own reporters. "We are part of a broader reform initiative. By definition, we will push boundaries and try to make change, but in the Arab world change does come slowly."[40]

Meanwhile, Al-Jazeera's effort to address criticisms of its failure to focus on more local issues by launching a daily broadcast from Rabat about the Maghreb ended abruptly when the Moroccan government pulled the plug after some local reporting that cut a little too close to home.

Despite their fascination with media, some Arab leaders clearly are still struggling to understand—or refusing to accept—the implications of the new media landscape. On one level, they are hungry for the instant access to information made possible by the media revolution. In the first days of the U.S. invasion of Iraq, a media monitoring command center was established at the Emirates Center for Strategic Studies and Research in Abu Dhabi. In a small villa in a residential area of the city, a special team sat in front of a wall of television monitors 24 hours a day, while in the next room video decks recorded every minute of coverage on every channel. The smallest development was instantly sent by SMS to all of the rulers in the Gulf, and major breaking news required an immediate telephone call to their aides-de-camp.

Yet, in stark contrast, when in the summer of 2007 the media began to report rumors that Egyptian President Hosni Mubarak was seriously ill, or perhaps even dead, the government failed to respond for more than a week: no statement, no photo op with the president, nothing—which naturally meant the rumors spread like wildfire. Eventually, the government had the first lady give an interview in which she said her husband was healthy, expecting that would be taken as gospel. It was not, and only then did the president appear in public. It was a textbook example of a government locked in the old media paradigm, underscored by the fact that the regime followed up by arresting the editors who published the rumors and eventually sentenced them to prison.

The catch-22 of press freedom is that the media help drive political reform, but, without some modicum of political openness, the very media struggle for a foothold. As the final communiqué of the 2005 conference "Media and Good Governance" put it, "The role of the media in supporting good governance is conditional on the freedom and the independence of the media as well as its professionalism," and "the lip service pledges made by the governments through various official declarations have not been translated into serious and effective acts … An arsenal of laws and regulations have remained that block any attempts for accountability and transparency, both in the areas of access to receive and impart information … which make the attempts of the press to question corruption and abuse of power next to impossible."[41] In the West, the idea of media as watchdog is grudgingly accepted by political leaders as part of the checks and balances of government. In the Arab world, the watchdog is treated as if he or she is a rabid stray. "Arab rulers, regardless of their differences, agree on one thing—all of them consider the Arab press to be their sworn enemy," according to Jamal Amer, editor-in-chief of *Al-Wasat* in the Republic of Yemen,[42] where RSF said a "climate of violence" exists.[43] Some reporters—and news organizations—don't even make a pretense of being a watchdog. When asked during a chat about the attacks on Lebanese journalists, "What kind of pressures do you face?" the editor of one Gulf paper replied, "None. We don't report about political issues."[44] Complained another senior Gulf editor: "Our press is infected with the self-censorship virus."[45]

## Centurions at the Gate

Self-censorship is as real on the satellite spectrum as it is in the local newsrooms. "Red lines," as they are known in the Arab world, surround many issues. As noted above, for Al-Arabiya, those involve issues of Saudi domestic politics, domestic terrorism, and many areas of religious debate. The constraints at Al-Jazeera are less restrictive, but just as real. Al-Jazeera was created to break the lock on Saudi media hegemony in the region. It was one piece in the regional power struggle between Qatar and Saudi Arabia. On Al-Jazeera's airwaves, Saudi Arabia was fair game. Few stories were off limits. But in the face of the rising threat from Shiite Iran in late 2007, Sunni Arab governments began to close ranks. In Doha, the palace sent word to the Al-Jazeera newsroom: Back off on the Saudis. The channel's coverage wasn't the only victim. Plans for an Al-Jazeera newspaper to challenge Saudi Arabia's stranglehold on the pan-Arab print media were put on hold. "We were sacrificed on the altar of regional politics," stated one senior journalist involved in the project.

The incident is emblematic not only of the degree to which governments still set the media agenda, rather than the other way around, but also of the fact that, all too often, Arab media are protagonists to the region's conflicts. The traditional media gatekeeper role, as discussed in the introduction to this chapter, involves "encouraging dialogue, tolerance, and interaction among diverse communities." Instead, Arab journalists commonly help fan the flames of conflict and intolerance, whether in the case of the regional Cold War that arose in 2007 between the Sunni-led Arab states and Iran—and, by default, Sunnis and Shia in the region—or within individual countries. In Egypt, much of the media alternate between being dismissive of the religious element of Muslim attacks on Coptic Christians and fanning the flames of sectarian strife. The fact that Iraq is the most dangerous place in the world to be a journalist has much to do with the partisan nature of media outlets, which are virtually all owned by one faction or another. The same is true in Lebanon, where what has been termed a "refeudalization" of the media landscape meant that when Hezbollah and its allies briefly took over West Beirut in the spring of 2008, they immediately stormed the newsrooms of a television and newspaper company owned by their main political rival.

Gatekeepers are also supposed to provide balanced coverage of groups across the political spectrum. Suffice to say, that doesn't happen in Iraq or Lebanon, but in places where journalists do strive to achieve that goal, roadblocks are often thrown in their path. Egyptian media were encouraged to give (relatively) equal time to opposition candidates in the 2005 parliamentary elections, but it was all part of a carefully stage-managed effort to allow President Hosni Mubarak to present the facade of democracy after he had successfully crushed the secular opposition, leaving only the bogeyman of the outlawed Muslim Brotherhood. But by the 2007 local elections, the media had been driven back into its corral through a campaign of intimidation, which a lawyer for the Press Syndicate estimated included more than 1,000 summonses and 500 court cases.[46]

A study of media coverage of the 2006 Bahraini elections by a human rights group concluded that despite "the relative margin of liberty in Bahrain … the media played a role in hindering democracy instead of supporting it" through self-censorship, favoritism, and one-sided access. The report concluded: "When radio and TV channels lack independence and refuse to take a campaigning role, and when the *national* newspapers lack impartiality and professionalism, and when candidates lack effective means to reach voters, that all reflects negatively on participation, the voter's right to access to information, and their ability to make the right choice, which would put under question the credibility of the entire democratic process."[47]

The report was issued by the Bahrain Center for Human Rights, whose own Internet site was blocked by the government prior to the election, one of several dozen Web sites shut down by the authorities in the tiny island nation. Subsequently, the government would detain dozens of journalists and ban publication of a controversial report that claimed the Sunni Muslim royal family had financed an effort to undermine the majority Shia during the elections, through tactics that included handing out Bahraini citizenship to Sunnis from other countries. Elections in the Republic of Yemen that same year saw broadcast outlets relegate opposition candidates to the late-night hours and newspapers simply reprint identical accounts of President Ali Abdullah Saleh's rallies written by the official national news agency. Numerous Web sites were blocked, and in the run-up to the election, five new newspapers appeared on the street, reporting positively about the president and attacking journalists who took a less laudatory approach.[48] Syria's government-controlled media took a somewhat modestly professional approach to that country's 2007 elections, yet journalists, bloggers, and human rights activists regularly found themselves being questioned or behind bars.

Although the pan-Arab media are certainly helping to write the region's broad narrative, the gatekeeper role in most domestic media—like that of agenda setter and watchdog—remains limited, for all the same reasons. Those "alternate voices" that the theory says journalistic gatekeepers are supposed to empower remain marginalized in the mainstream media across the region. Civil society, the foundation of representative democracy, is given short shrift; human rights groups are often ignored. Indeed, even on the more outspoken domestic media outlets, many journalists harbor high levels of suspicion and resentment toward activists in the nongovernmental organizations (NGOs), whom they frequently accuse of being mercenaries doing the bidding of foreign aid agencies and governments. That was epitomized by the muted reaction to conviction in absentia of Egyptian civil society activist and one-time presidential candidate Saad Eddine Ibrahim in the summer of 2008.

Along with being subject to the obvious tactics of arrests and intimidation, news organizations that try to give voice to the voiceless often find themselves silenced by an array of other weapons wielded by the centurions of the government security services who man the proverbial gate. In most Arab countries, the government-run press controls the printing and distribution infrastructure and is thus able to freeze individual issues with which the government takes umbrage. They can also wield an economic stick. Just as a boycott by Saudi Arabia, which dominates the advertising industry in the region, means Al-Jazeera has few commercials despite its huge audience, independent publications on the local level can also find themselves frozen out of the market.

Tunisia's *Al Mawqif* is one of the few newspapers in that tightly controlled country to report on civil society organizations. As a result, most newsstands refuse to carry it and revenues are sparse. "We do not even have access to private advertising because companies know that buying ad space in our paper can lead to problems," says editor-in-chief Rachid Khechana. "Companies even remove their ads from newspapers if they write about sensitive issues." As a result, he says, the paper's reporters and editors practice self-censorship when it comes to issues like corruption and coverage of the president, which frees them to continue to focus on civil society. "We have to choose between carrying a part of the message or present ourselves as victims of repression. We have decided to pass the message," Khechana says. But, as in many Arab countries, the "red lines" of self-censorship are continually moving. "Even sunny weather can be censored if it is bad news for agriculture. Taboo topics are updated by the government on a daily basis," says Sihem Bensedrine, the editor of the online newspaper *Kalima*, who was herself barred from leaving the country and roughed up by security police at Tunis airport in late summer 2008.[49]

## Change Agents

The good news is that, despite the challenges, Arab journalists continue to push the envelope. The results of one survey of 601 journalists from 14 Arab countries painted a portrait of a press corps determined to drive political and social change.[50] "Encourage political reform" was ranked as the most significant job of an Arab journalist by 75 percent of those surveyed. The next six choices—to educate the public, use news for the social good, serve as a voice for the poor, encourage civil engagement, drive regional and national development, and analyze issues—all supported that change-agent mission (figure 13.1). Likewise, a total of 96 percent said Arab society must be reformed (figure 13.2). But the majority of journalists surveyed agreed with Hassan Fattah's observation about the pace of change in the Arab world, with 64 percent indicating that "Arab society must be gradually reformed," and one-third indicating that reform must be "radical." That sense of caution was also seen in the fact that the traditional watchdog role of investigating government claims, which U.S. journalists rank as their top priority, did not make the top 10 job functions cited by the Arab journalists.

The Arab journalists surveyed also cited political reform as the most important issue facing the region, followed closely by human rights, poverty, and education (figure 13.3), while "lack of political change" virtually tied with U.S. policy as the greatest threat facing the region, when the ever-present issue of Israel was put aside (figure 13.4).

Almost half the journalists surveyed described themselves politically as supporters of democratic change, as opposed to self-identifying as Arab

**Figure 13.1. Journalists' Perceptions of Their Roles**

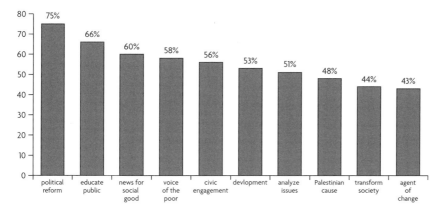

Source: Lawrence Pintak and Jeremy Ginges. 2008. "The Mission of Arab Journalism: Creating Change in a Time of Turmoil." *International Journal of Press/Politics* 13: 3(3).
Note: "Complete the following sentence, 'It is the job of a journalist to … '" Participants were given a list of 21 choices; totals reflect percentage answering "most important." Survey of Arab Journalists. *N* = 601.

**Figure 13.2.  Journalistic Attitudes toward Reform of Arab Society**

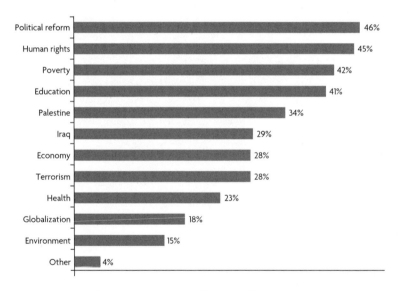

*Source:* Lawrence Pintak and Jeremy Ginges. 2008. "The Mission of Arab Journalism: Creating Change in a Time of Turmoil." *International Journal of Press/Politics* 13: 3(3).
*Note:* "Please choose the one which best describes your own opinion: 'Arab society … '" Survey of Arab Journalists. *N* = 601.

**Figure 13.3.  Journalistic Perceptions of the Most Important Issues Facing the Arab World**

| Issue | Percent |
|---|---|
| Political reform | 46% |
| Human rights | 45% |
| Poverty | 42% |
| Education | 41% |
| Palestine | 34% |
| Iraq | 29% |
| Economy | 28% |
| Terrorism | 28% |
| Health | 23% |
| Globalization | 18% |
| Environment | 15% |
| Other | 4% |

*Source:* Lawrence Pintak and Jeremy Ginges. 2008. "The Mission of Arab Journalism: Creating Change in a Time of Turmoil." *International Journal of Press/Politics* 13: 3(3).
*Note:* "Rate the importance of the following issues in the Arab world today." Participants were given a list of 12 choices; totals reflect the percentage answering "most important." Survey of Arab Journalists. *N* = 601.

nationalists, Islamists, or nationalists (figure 13.5), and "government control" essentially tied with the lack of professionalism as the most significant challenge to Arab journalism (figure 13.6).

Significantly, journalists working for domestic media (78 percent) were even more supportive of the reform agenda than those working for pan-Arab news organizations (58 percent). The overall results in the Pintak and

Figure 13.4. Journalistic Perceptions of the Greatest Threats Facing the Arab Region

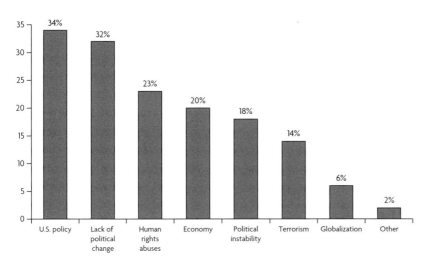

*Source:* Lawrence Pintak and Jeremy Ginges. 2008. "The Mission of Arab Journalism: Creating Change in a Time of Turmoil." *International Journal of Press/Politics* 13: 3(3).
*Note:* "Please indicate how significant you think the following challenges are to the Arab region." Totals reflect percentage answering "most significant." Survey of Arab Journalists. *N* = 601.

Figure 13.5. Political Identity of Arab Journalists

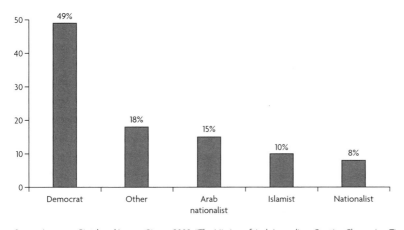

*Source:* Lawrence Pintak and Jeremy Ginges. 2008. "The Mission of Arab Journalism: Creating Change in a Time of Turmoil." *International Journal of Press/Politics* 13: 3(3).
*Note:* "Politically, which philosophy best describes you?" Survey of Arab Journalists. *n* = 578.

Ginges survey demonstrate that the majority of Arab journalists fall within the "change agent" typology, a set of priorities unique to the Arab media, in which setting an agenda based on political and social change is the top priority. This self-perceived role puts Arab journalists firmly at odds with the ruling powers of the region.

Figure 13.6. Journalistic Perceptions of the Most Significant Challenges to Arab Journalism

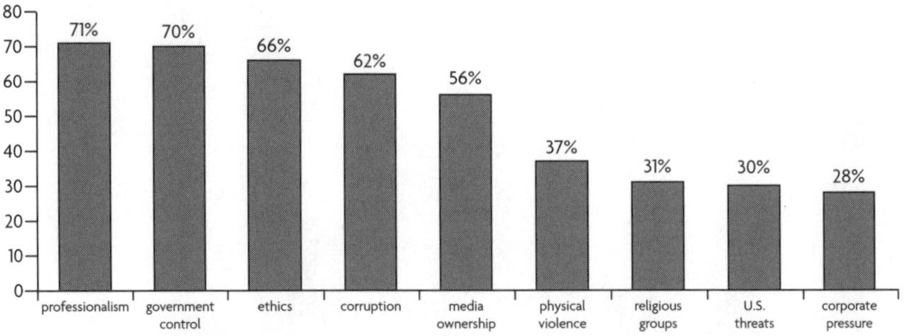

*Source:* Lawrence Pintak and Jeremy Ginges. 2008. "The Mission of Arab Journalism: Creating Change in a Time of Turmoil." *International Journal of Press/Politics* 13: 3(3).
*Note:* "Please indicate how significant you think the following challenges are to Arab journalism." Participants were provided with nine choices; totals reflect percentage answering "most significant." N = 601.

## Conclusions and Recommendations

It is clear that media in the Arab world are beginning to have an impact on policy in the region. It is also clear that the Arab media are on a collision course with the entrenched regimes of the Gulf, the Levant (Jordan, Lebanon, Palestine, and Syria), and North Africa. The confrontation is, and will continue to be, painful for both sides and fraught with contradiction. If Arab journalism is going to continue to evolve as a catalyst for change and, eventually, an independent and responsible partner in governance, much support is needed. As a recent National Endowment for Democracy report observed, media assistance is a fundamental building block in the government reform process that can "help countries make democratic transitions, spur economic growth, improve government accountability, conduct public health campaigns, increase education and literacy levels, and empower women and minorities."[51]

Concrete steps can be taken by international agencies, governments, and private donors. The targets for such reforms include changes affecting the role of the state, the market, and the profession. Policy interventions directed at each of these reforms include regulatory and legal changes, alternative media, journalism training, media education, and media literacy.

*Reform of the regulatory environment and the legal framework of civil liberties.* Arab media will never be free until governments decide to allow such freedom. Nor, in this age of satellite television and the Internet, will governments ever again truly be able to control the media. To date, most media reform efforts have focused on convincing governments they must adopt a Western model. Little effort has been expended on helping them understand how the process has evolved in non-Western countries. International agencies should explore

initiatives that bring Arab government officials together with their counterparts in countries that have already experienced media reform, such as Eastern
Europe, South Asia, and Indonesia, in order to expose them to concepts and
approaches that might better suit their cultural and political environments. In
the meantime, international agencies and foreign governments must use their
influence to support journalists being targeted by government pressures, and
government-to-government encouragement of media reform must continue.

*Development of alternative media.* The growth of online media should be
encouraged. It is particularly important to foster the evolution of Arab online
journalism, as opposed to pure activism, to make it harder for governments
to crack down on Internet sites using the excuse that they are irresponsible
and vitriolic. Private funders should also provide financial support to online
ventures that break new ground. Examples include Ammanet, a private radio
station in Jordan that covers the kind of grassroots local news ignored by the
mainstream media and that began as a purely online venture funded by foreign agencies; and Mogtamana.org, created by the Adham Center for Journalism at the American University in Cairo with U.S. Agency for International
Development (USAID) funding to serve as an information portal by and for
Egyptian civil society. Coupled with an extensive training program in civil
society coverage, the project has produced a notable increase in reporting on
the sector within the mainstream media and opened new lines of communication between the media and NGOs.

*Journalism training.* Substantial funds are being put into professional training for Arab journalists by various international organizations, notable among
them USAID, the British Council, and the governments of Canada, Germany,
the Netherlands, and Sweden, along with a variety of private donors, such
as the Open Society Institute, Carnegie Corporation of New York, and others. However, there is a significant hit-or-miss aspect to this training, with
virtually no coordination among the donors. The result is a plethora of short,
one-off workshops and a lack of strategic vision. Donors should consider creating a mechanism for, at a minimum, exchanging notes on training projects
or, more ambitiously, pooling efforts to support a series of regional training
facilities. Such facilities could create comprehensive training programs that
provide ongoing support and professional development focused on an array
of basic journalistic tools, specialized reporting skills, and the kind of management expertise needed to foster an economically sustainable media sector.
Most journalism training in the Arab world is also carried out by Western
journalists and trainers. Yet vibrant forms of journalism are being practiced in
Eastern Europe, South and Southeast Asia, Latin America, and parts of Africa.
Arab journalists have much to learn from how their profession has evolved
and is practiced in non-Western parts of the world. Training projects that
draw on the talent in these regions should be encouraged.

*Media education.* There are just a handful of academic journalism programs in the Arab world. Most universities teach a more theoretical approach to "mass media," with little application in the newsroom. But reform is beginning. Projects are under way to build serious Arabic-language undergraduate and graduate journalism programs in such places as Jordan and Dubai, whereas mass communication programs in Saudi Arabia, Qatar, and North Africa are beginning the process of curriculum reform to introduce practical journalism programs. These programs need advice, expertise, and, in some cases, financial support.

*Media literacy.* "You can't believe everything you read in the newspaper." That adage is accepted wisdom in the developed world, but the degree to which it rings true elsewhere in the world varies dramatically. As the Arab world rapidly transitions from a controlled media model to one in which there are numerous competing voices, including a cacophony of bloggers, Arab publics must learn to distinguish truth—or near-truth—from carefully manufactured fiction. Media literacy programs at the region's universities provide a venue that deserves support; so, too, do literacy projects run from regional NGOs to reach the grassroots.

There is no panacea for media reform in the Arab world, no magic wand that can be waved to create overnight a journalistic corps of agenda setters, watchdogs, and gatekeepers. It is also possible that Arab journalists will never easily fall into those democratic roles. Arab media are in the midst of a revolution; so, too, is the relationship between journalists and governments. International agencies can support, defend, nurture, and encourage, but they cannot dictate. It is for the Arabs themselves to decide the precise model of media-government relations that will emerge.

## Notes

1. Human Rights Watch. 2004. "Egypt's Torture Epidemic." In *Briefing Papers,* New York: Human Rights Watch.
2. Amnesty International. 2007. *Amnesty International Report 2007—Egypt.* London: Amnesty International.
3. Arabic Network for Human Rights Information (HRInfo). 2008. "Freedom of Opinion and Expression in Egypt 2007." Arabic Network for Human Rights Information, Cairo. http://www.openarab.net/en/node/273.
4. Douglas Jehl and David Johnston. 2005. "Rule Change Lets C.I.A. Freely Send Suspects Abroad to Jails." *New York Times,* March 6.
5. Human Rights Watch. 2007. "Egypt: Police Officers Get Three Years for Beating, Raping Detainee," November 6. http://hrw.org/english/docs/2007/11/07/egypt17263.htm.
6. Lawrence Pintak. 2006. *Reflections in a Bloodshot Lens: America, Islam and the War of Ideas.* London and Ann Arbor, MI: Pluto.
7. George C. Edwards and B. Dan Wood. 1999. "Who Influences Whom? The President, the Media, and the Public Agenda." *American Political Science Review* 93: 327–44; B. Dan Wood and Jeffrey S. Peake. 1998. "The Dynamics of Foreign Policy Agenda Setting." *American Political Science Review* 92: 173–84.

8. Anat First. 1997. "Television in the Construction of Reality: An Israeli Case Study." In *Communication and Democracy: Exploring the Intellectual Frontiers in Agenda-Setting Theory,* ed. Maxwell E. McCombs, Donald Lewis Shaw, and David H. Weaver. Mahwah, NJ: Lawrence Erlbaum; Chanen Naveh. 2001. "The Role of the Media in Shaping Israeli Public Opinion: Israel after Rabin." In *Peacemaking in a Divided Society,* ed. Sasson Sofer. London: Frank Cass.

9. Mustafa Kabha. 2007. *The Palestinian Press as Shaper of Public Opinion, 1929–1931: Writing Up a Storm.* Edgeware, UK, and Portland, OR: Vallentine Mitchell.

10. Abdallah S. Al-Haweel, and Srinivas R. Melkote. 1995. "International Agenda-Setting Effects of Saudi Arabian Media: A Case Study." *Gazette* 55: 17–37.

11. To be clear, satellite television did exist when the study was conducted. But the only channel offering news was the Middle East Broadcasting Centre, a Saudi-owned station that largely toed the official line.

12. Hamza Mohamed. 2006. Agenda-Setting in a Quasi-Democratic Country: A Case Study of Egypt." Paper prepared for the "7th International Agenda-Setting Conference," Bonn, Germany, October 11–13. http://www.agendasetting.com/2006/case_studies/new_paper.pdf.

13. Author's contemporaneous notes.

14. M. I. Ayish. 2002. "Political Communication on Arab World Television: Evolving Patterns." *Political Communication* 19 (2): 137–54; Marc Lynch. 2006. *Voices of the New Arab Public: Iraq, Al-Jazeera, and Middle East Politics Today.* New York: Columbia University Press; Lawrence Pintak. 2006. *Reflections in a Bloodshot Lens: America, Islam and the War of ideas. London and Ann Arbor, MI: Pluto;* Naomi Sakr. 2001. *Satellite Realms: Transnational Television, Globalization and the Middle East.* London: I. B. Tauris; Philip Seib. 2008. *The Al Jazeera Effect: How the New Global Media Are Reshaping World Politics.* Washington, DC: Potomac Books.

15. Erik C. Nisbet, Matthew C. Nisbet, Dietram A. Scheufele and James E. Shanahan. 2003. "Public Diplomacy, Television News, and Muslim Opinion." *Harvard Journal of Press/Politics* 9 (2): 11–37.

16. Radwan Masmoudi and Joseph Loconte. 2008. "A Faltering Freedom Agenda: The Disillusion of Muslim Reformers." *The Weekly Standard* (Washington, DC), April 23.

17. Marwan Matni, in conversation with the author. Monte Carlo, October 21, 2006.

18. *The Peninsula.* 2006. "Qatar Emir Hails First Arab Victory." Aug 22. http://www.gulfinthemedia.com/index.php?m=search&id=237173&lang=en.

19. Paula Dobriansky, undersecretary of state for global affairs, told reporters, "As the president noted in Bratislava just last week, there was a rose revolution in Georgia, an orange revolution in Ukraine, and, most recently, a purple revolution in Iraq. In Lebanon, we see growing momentum for a cedar revolution." See U.S. Dept. of State. 2005. *On-the-Record Briefing on the Release of the 2004 Annual Report on Human Rights,* vol. 2007. Washington, DC: U.S. Department of State.

20. Suzan Zawawi. 2007. "The Agony of the 'Qatif Girl.'" *Saudi Gazette,* November 20.

21. Ahmed Al-Omran. 2007. 'The Qatif Girl Again." In Saudi Jeans (blog). Riyadh. Nov. 27, 2007.

22. Abdullah El Areefg. 2007. "The Judge in El Riyad: Ulterior Motives of How the Foreign Media Dealt with the Kotaif Girl Incident." *Okaz* (Riyadh), November 26.

23. Andrew Hammond. 2007. "Saudi Gang-Rape Victim Pardoned after Outcry." The *Independent* (London), December 18.

24. Ebtihal Mubarak. 2007. "'Qatif Girl' Subjected to Brutal Crime: King." *Arab News* (Jeddah), December 19.

25. Reporters without Borders. 2007. "Predators of Press Freedom," May 6. http://www.rsf.org/article.php3?id_article=21963.

26. M. Anis Salem. 2008. "Development Communication: Advocacy, Programming and Participation." Cairo: American University in Cairo.

27. Private conversations with executives of Al-Jazeera and Al-Arabiya.

28. The Arab League. 2008. "Arab League Satellite Broadcasting Charter." *Arab Media & Society.* Online journal. Kamal Adham Center for Journalism, Training and Research, Cairo. http://www.arabmediasociety.org/?article=684.

29. Amy Glass. 2008. "Du CEO Plays Down Net Censorship." Arabianbusiness.com, April 14. http://www.arabianbusiness.com/516483-du-exec-plays-down-restriction-fears.

30. International Freedom of Expression Exchange (IFEX). 2008. "Government Cancels License of Independent Weekly." *Alert,* April 7. http://www.ifex.org/en/content/view/full/92396/.

31. Hussein Amin. 2008. "The Arab States Charter for Satellite Television: A quest for regulation." *Arab Media & Society.* Cairo: Kamal Adham Center for Journalism Training and Research. http://www.arabmediasociety.com/?article=649.

32. Alaa al-Ghatrifi. 2008. "Al-Masry Al-Youm Exclusively Publishes the Draft Law of Audio-Visual Transmission and Monitoring the Internet." *Al-Masry Al-Youm* (Cairo), July 9. http://www.almasry-alyoum.com/default.aspx?l=en&IssueID=1096.

33. Yasime Saleh. 2008. "Lawyer Expects 'Facebook Girl' to become Mahalla Scapegoat, Receive Prison Sentence." *Egypt Daily News,* April 12–13. It later turned out that she was acting at the behest of her boss, a political activist and blogger, who was them himself arrested and, according to his account, stripped, hung by his arms, and tortured.

34. Safaa Abdoun. 2008. "Nazif's Heckler at Cairo University Says He Was Provoked by PM's Speech." *Egypt Daily News* (Cairo), April 22.

35. Joel Campagna. 2007. *Attacks on the Press 2007: Middle East and North Africa.* New York: Committee to Protect Journalists.

36. Freedom House. 2007. *Freedom of the Press 2007.* New York: Freedom House.

37. International Freedom of Expression Exchange (IFEX). 2008. "Five Journalists Given Three-Month Prison Sentences over Critical Articles." AAI/IFEX, Amman, March 18. http://www.ifex.org/en/content/view/full/91766/.

38. Emirates News Agency (WAM). 2007. "National Media Council Clarifies Closure of GEO, ARY TV stations." WAM, Dubai, November 17. http://www.wam.org.ae/servlet/Satellite?c=WamLocEnews&cid=1193028279857&pagename=WAM%2FWamLocEnews%2FW-T-LEN-FullNews.

39. Sonia Verma. 2008. "New Abu Dhabi Newspaper Aims to Create Fully Free Press." *Globe and Mail* (Toronto), April 19.

40. Telephone interview with the author. Abu Dhabi and Cairo. April, 23, 2008.

41. CDFJ (Center for Defending the Freedom of Journalists). 2005. "The Role of Media in Activating Good Governance. Final Report." 2005 conference on "Media and Good Governance," Amman, Jordan, February 14–16, 1–2.

42. World Association of Newspapers. 2006. "Beirut Forum Examines Widespread Press Freedom Abuses," Press release, December 11. http://www.wan-press.org/article12653.html.

43. Reporters without Borders. 2007. "Letter to President Saleh about Threats to Press Freedom." Paris: Reporters sans Frontières. Published letter. September 4. http://www.rsf.org/article.php3?id_article=23524.

44. Conversation with an anonymous editor, Beirut, September 18, 2006.

45. Abdul Hamid Ahmad. 2006. "Self-Censorship Virus Plagues Media." *Gulf News,* May 5.

46. Arabic Network for Human Rights Information (HRInfo). 2008. *Freedom of Opinion and Expression in Egypt 2007*. Annual Report. Cairo: HRInfo. http://www.openarab.net/en/node/273.

47. Bahrain Center for Human Rights. 2008. "On World Press Freedom Day: A Report by a Regional Group Calls for Reforming the Media in Bahrain." Press release, May 6. http://www.bahrainrights.org/en/freespeech?page=10.

48. Egyptian Organization for Human Rights. 2006. "Despite Progress, Media Performance Flawed During Presidential Elections, says EOHR," November 7. http://www.eohr.org.

49. Arab Press Network. 2006. "Newspapers Punished and Information Controlled in Tunisia." Newsletter No. 18/2006 Edition. Cairo: Arab Press Network. For details on the airport encounter, see Observatory for Freedom of the Press, Publishing and Creation in Tunisia (OLPEC). "Journalist Attacked at Tunis Carthage Airport, Barred from Leaving Country," August 20, 2008.

50. Lawrence Pintak and Jeremy Ginges. 2008. "The Mission of Arab Journalism: Creating Change in a Time of Turmoil." *International Journal of Press/Politics* 13: 3 (3). The survey subjects included a small group based in the United States and Europe but working for media outlets in the Arab world.

51. David E. Kaplan. 2008. "Empowering Independent Media: U.S. Efforts to Foster Free and Independent News around the World." Washington, DC: National Endowment for Democracy.

# 14

•
•
•

# Asia

Angela Romano

Reporters without Borders (RSF) has repeatedly declared Asia to be the most demanding continent for journalists and their news organizations to operate within, and in some countries even simply to survive. The many reports issued by RSF and other global agencies—such as the World Association of Newspapers, Freedom House, and Committee to Protect Journalists—regularly show Asia to be the region with the highest number of murders of journalists per year, a pattern that persists even when Asian-Arabic states and Central Asia are not included in the definition of Asia. The reports describe numerous physical, legal, and economic threats, as well as serious political repression and restrictions that journalists face as they attempt to function as watchdogs, agenda setters, and gatekeepers for their societies. The statistics and examples provided within these reports, however, do not provide the full picture. Most Asian nations also host vibrant media cultures in which journalists play an important role in supporting social and democratic processes and activities.

An exploration of the roles, operating conditions, and challenges of Asian journalists is significant not just for their impact upon governance and democracy within Asia. Issues in the region have broader implications for global journalism and democracy, especially given the great and exponentially increasing geopolitical consequence of China and India. Furthermore, an understanding of such issues is critical to ensuring that initiatives by aid agencies to develop the mass media are tailored to work effectively in the cultural, economic, and political conditions specific to Asia. International aid agencies spend hundreds of millions of dollars each year on training, equipment, and other forms of aid to help build the capacity of Asian journalism, but sometimes these programs provide little substantive identifiable improvement in the overall quality of journalism in the countries concerned.

This chapter describes some of the overarching issues that affect the journalists' contributions to governance and democracy in the world's most populous continent, while also recognizing the diversity of cultural, religious, economic, political, and media systems between and within Asian nations. This vast continent covers almost one-third of the world's land area and is home to more than 60 percent of the human population. The chapter discusses issues that affect the 33 countries in South, East, Southeast, and Central Asia.[1]

## Political and Economic Influences on Asian Journalism

The full range of political and economic systems exists within Asia. This range includes both Hong Kong, China, and Singapore, two fully developed, liberal economies that are rated as the top two societies in the world on the conservative Cato Institute's Economic Freedom Index.[2] Asia contains the world's largest single-party communist and socialist republics, including China, the Democratic People's Republic of Korea, Vietnam, and the Lao People's Democratic Republic, as well as former communist nations, such as Mongolia and Cambodia. Post-Soviet nations are represented by Kazakhstan, Kyrgyzstan, Tajikistan, Turkmenistan, and Uzbekistan. It also includes the Islamic Republics of Afghanistan, Iran, and Pakistan; absolute monarchies headed by Islamic sultans, such as Brunei; the military junta of Myanmar; and nations that have alternated between military junta leadership and parliamentary democracy, such as Thailand.

Regardless of their differences, Asian nations share a common history in that all have undergone enormous political, economic, and/or social evolution or restructuring since World War II. The majority are still relatively new states that were created or substantially reconfigured after throwing off colonial or occupying forces after World War II, or, in the case of the Central Asian nations, when they seceded from the former Soviet Union. In new nations and transitional societies, such as those in Asia, journalism plays a particularly important role in creating what Benedict Anderson calls "imagined communities."[3] The news media helps geographically bound populations to form, extend, and reshape their understanding of themselves as citizens of a national community who have joint interests and common values.

Asian nations that attained independence after World War II are also made up of many disparate communities that initially had little in common with each other apart from their shared history of "belonging" to the same colonial power. For example, the government of the Republic of Indonesia, formed in August 1945, faces the challenge of creating cohesion and shared identity among a population of 300 distinct ethnic groups dispersed across approximately 6,000 islands, 742 different languages and dialects, and 6 main religions. Not surprisingly, Indonesia's national motto has become Bhinneka tunggal ika (Unity in diversity).

Given this diversity, Indian-born postcolonial theorist Homi K. Bhabha poses a question that has long been pertinent to Asian journalists. How can communications establish positive representations of the nation and contribute to the effective functioning of communities when, "despite shared histories of deprivation and discrimination," the populace may have values, understandings, and priorities that "may be profoundly antagonistic, conflictual, and even incommensurable?"[4] The next section explores how theories about *development journalism*, *peace journalism*, and Asian values have been used in attempts to answer this question.

## Development Journalism and Peace Journalism in Asia

The term development journalism was coined in Asia. It has been particularly influential in the postcolonial nations of South and Southeast Asia, although the concept of development journalism has been independently developed or copied by numerous nations worldwide.[5] As the name implies, development journalism simply refers to news, features, analysis, and current affairs that help to support processes of socioeconomic and political development. However, it is far from simple to prescribe how development journalism should work in practice. There are at least five major interpretations of the concept.

The first interpretation of development journalism is relatively nonpolitical and emphasizes that journalists need well-honed skills in agenda setting. In contrast to the focus of most journalism on "spot" and "breaking" news, this form of journalism prioritizes reporting about long-term trends, unfolding issues, processes, and problems occurring in national development. Complex issues need to be explained in simple terms, thus enabling communities to understand the issues and respond effectively. This understanding of development news can be seen in the practices of the global DEPTHnews (Development, Economic and Population Themes News) service that was established and remains centered in Asia.[6]

The second interpretation emphasizes journalists' nation-building role by encouraging positive news stories about community development initiatives, such as attempts to bolster the economy, build stable societies, foster harmony within and between communities, and strengthen consensus between diverse groups. Such journalism would also report on crises and social problems, but in a way that identifies the causes and possible solutions, so that citizens are not overwhelmed by negative news that suggests their societies are being buried by intractable problems. Supporters of this approach are often influenced by

modernization theories, which envisage that journalists are important channels for conveying the insights of government and other elites to the comparatively unsophisticated and unenlightened masses to help build a modern,
rational, urbanized, entrepreneurial culture.

The third interpretation of development journalism positions journalists as
the government's partners in nation building. Journalists promote the development policies of their government leaders, who are seen as the drivers of
development. The common rhetoric of this form of development journalism
talks about the media's "freedom to" support development rather than "freedom from" political or other external influences. Supporting this approach,
former Malaysian prime minister Mahathir Mohamad explained that freedom
of expression may need to be restricted for the sake of prosperity, nationalism,
and unity: "For a society precariously balanced on the razor's edge, where
one false or even true word can lead to calamity, it is criminal irresponsibil-
ity to allow that word to be uttered."[7] The partnership approach to development journalism was adopted across most of Southeast Asia in the 1970s to
1980s, although its influence waned as Singapore achieved a fully developed
economy, and other countries, such as Indonesia, the Philippines, and Thailand, underwent substantial political reform. China and other socialist Asian
nations rarely use the term development journalism, but they adopt very similar language and tenets.

A fourth interpretation of development journalism positions the news
media as a watchdog. In this perspective, journalists must highlight problems
and weaknesses in governance and ensure that governments are responsive
to public concerns and opinions. Support for the watchdog approach surged
after the Asian economic crisis of 1997 because of assumptions that lackluster
financial journalism had contributed to the emergency situation by failing to
shine a light on entrenched corruption and the flawed economic fundamentals of the worst-affected nations.[8] In the wake of the crisis, such organizations as the World Bank, International Monetary Fund, and UN Development
Programme promoted watchdog journalism as a guardian of transparency,
defined as the timely release of reliable information about government activities. In a rejection of the philosophy that freedoms and rights must sometimes
be sacrificed for the sake of development and stability, supporters of the watchdog approach argue that restrictions on free speech, free press, and other civil
liberties undermine good governance, which, in turn, disrupts development.

The various development journalism models are therefore based on fundamentally different assumptions about the best way for governments and
communities to foster development and the correct role for journalists in
mediating the dynamics of governance and democratic life. The propensity
of Asian governments to support the journalism-as-government-partner philosophy has provoked vehement censure from critics who claimed that the

ethic had been co-opted by governments as an apologia for dictatorial leadership and press censorship.[9] The interpretation of development journalism as a government partner has never had much sway with liberals, who have been more influenced by Indian economist and philosopher Amartya Sen's often-quoted claims that famine has never occurred in a democratic country with a relatively free press.[10] The partnership model lost support even among some of Asia's less liberal governments following the 1997 economic crisis.

Despite its tarnished image, the journalism-as-government-partner interpretation is still a powerful force in many Asian countries, even if the old jargon is no longer used much. Although much of the academic research and theorization that backed the journalism-government partnership model is now dated, supporters of the concept still draw strength from more recent theorists such as Indian-born journalist and researcher Fareed Zakaria. Zakaria contends that the path to development and increased sociopolitical freedoms is best paved by helping countries to modernize their economies and to develop the provisions of "constitutional liberalism"—such as rule of law, institutions of governance, property rights, and social contract—that will protect individual freedoms, regardless of majority opinions or decisions. He argues that pressuring countries to introduce elections and other tools of liberal democracy before modernization occurs only leads them to become "illiberal democracies."[11]

Given the many conflicts within and between Asian nations, several aid agencies and nongovernmental organizations (NGOs) have promoted the concept of peace journalism. Peace journalism involves avoiding demonizing language and taking a nonpartisan approach and a multiparty orientation. This contrasts with *war journalism*, which is characterized by a focus on the present problems rather than their causes and solutions, an elite orientation, and a dichotomy of good versus bad actors in the conflict. Despite the development journalism rhetoric of harmony and order, a study of how Asian newspapers covered four regional conflicts—involving India and Pakistan, Sri Lanka, Indonesia, and the Philippines—indicates that war journalism frameworks are dominant.[12] To some degree, a war positioning is inevitable, given that journalists' frameworks for understanding are intensely vulnerable to being shaped by the many threats of censorship and physical risk that they face.

## Asian Values in Journalism

The term *Asian values* has been used since at least the 1970s to differentiate between Asian and Western principles of democracy and human rights, and to investigate whether cultural traditions contributed to the rapid economic development of Japan and the Asian tigers of Hong Kong, China; Singapore;

the Republic of Korea; and Taiwan, China. The concept of Asian values in journalism gained support in the 1980s, as governments and media workers in postcolonial nations of South, East, and Southeast Asia tried to identify and defend what they believed to be unique cultural attributes in the face of the West's perceived economic and cultural dominance.

Asian values relevant to journalism include communitarian principles, willingness to forsake personal freedoms for the prosperity and well-being of the community, support for social consensus and harmony, respect for elders and leaders, and concern for "saving face." Islamic values also encourage communicators to veil the deficiencies of others, and to speak to all people in a "mild manner" and "kindly way."[13] The Asian cultural system, it is argued, "rejects the notion of an uninhibited and robust press that undertakes vehement, caustic and unpleasant attacks on government and public officials."[14]

Purportedly Asian values also underlie the patriarchal leadership style of many Asian countries, whereby government leaders regard themselves as guardians or custodians who control political decision making and public information for the public good. This perspective is reinforced by the stereotypes that exist in most Asian countries about the poorly educated, rural-based subsistence farmers or laborers who make up the majority of Asia's population. The stereotypes imply that the unschooled, unsophisticated masses are prone to becoming inflamed, irrational, or overwhelmed by too much or the wrong kind of information. In such cultures, politicians and bureaucrats are notoriously unresponsive to journalists' requests for information and often consider access to government information as a privilege rather than a right.[15]

Just as development journalism has been criticized as "government say-so" journalism, critics also complain that the Asian values debate has been manipulated by governments that have exaggerated the importance of respect for leaders and harmony in order to muzzle journalists and deny basic rights and civil liberties. Opponents also attack the concept of trying to develop a single set of values to encompass a region as diverse as Asia. A content analysis of posted stories on 10 newspapers' Web sites in East, Southeast, and South Asian countries found that the argument that Asian journalism displays unique values "has some credence, but only marginally." The values of harmony and supportiveness were found to appear in stories about the Asian journalists' home countries, particularly in the Southeast Asian newspapers, where press freedom was lower than in others that were studied. However, Asian and Western news agency reports showed as much conflict and critical reporting as each other in stories about international news.[16] Although there has been little debate about Asian values since the Asian economic crisis, the attempt to divide Asian from Western ideals and practices still strongly influences the understandings, philosophies, and practices of journalism in Asia.[17]

## The Impact of Technologies on Asian Journalism

The reports by Reporters without Borders and other media monitors of press freedom paint a gloomy picture of Asian journalism, since their charter is to spotlight violations and abuses rather than progress and innovation. By contrast, *Journalism Asia*'s editors express the view that Asia's media are "blooming" as the continent finds itself "swept along in the global twin tides of social, political, and economic liberalization and the communication revolution." Although the editors take a cautious view of how well the resultant democracy might actually work, they assert a commonly held view that communications technologies are "pushing nations to ever-increasing degrees of freedom and openness."[18]

From a journalistic perspective, new communication technologies open many possibilities for enhancing democracy. Particularly important is the potential to boost journalism's watchdog and agenda-setting functions by helping both journalists and citizens to bypass censorship or other government controls on gathering and circulating information. Equally important is the prospect of extending the media's gatekeeping capacities. The Internet, for example, has been optimistically described as "a medium for everyone's voice, not just the few who can afford to buy multimillion-dollar printing presses, launch satellites, or win the government's permission to squat on the public's airwaves."[19]

A limiting force on the potential of journalists' use of new technologies to enhance their watchdog and gatekeeping functions is the inequality of access both within and between Asian nations. Figures on Internet access initially seem encouraging, with the number of Internet users in developing countries worldwide quadrupling between 2000 and 2004, and with China and India among those countries recording dramatic increases.[20] However, some Asian countries are conspicuously lagging. The Internet service in Turkmenistan, for example, remains among the most tightly controlled in the world, with only 1 percent of the population able to participate online.[21] Research also shows a vast digital divide in such countries as Bangladesh, Cambodia, India, Nepal, the Philippines, Sri Lanka, and Thailand, where the Internet mainly serves urban elites, the highly educated, and expatriates.[22] Other critical factors that determine whether or not the online media will be widely adopted are levels of education, social capital formation, and political democratization and access to supportive infrastructure, such as telephone lines and reliable electricity supplies.

Even when a thriving online culture exists, the community still may not use the Internet in ways that promote democracy. Countries that encourage widespread Internet use in civil society to promote economic development and in government to assist with administration—such as Singapore and China—often score poorly on other measures of media and democratic activity.[23]

Asian nations usually dominate the list of countries that Reporters without Borders describes as "enemies of the internet."[24] China arguably has the best-honed system for monitoring and censoring the Internet to restrict dissidence and suppress alternative views. Prior to 2003, the Chinese authorities supervised Internet cafés and news sites, censored chat room and bulletin board content, and blocked certain Web sites. Given the impracticality of mass monitoring of the Internet, China began its Golden Shield Project, or so-called Great Firewall of China, in November 2003. The Golden Shield Project uses automated technologies to conduct wide-scale filtering of Internet addresses, blocking of connections to the Internet Protocol addresses of selected Internet hosts, and "poisoning" of the data, in particular the Domain Name System, to prevent citizens from accessing certain types of content. Even following extensive international criticism and complaints from the International Olympic Commission, China reneged on earlier agreements to allow the 30,000 accredited journalists covering the Olympics unfettered Internet access. Although China lifted blocks on such sites as the British Broadcasting Corporation (BBC), it enforced barriers to content relating to the Tibetan uprising and certain other topics with even greater vigor.

Despite the rhetoric of democracy that Western countries espouse, Western business leaders operating in Asia have proved willing to promote censorship and surveillance for commercial gain. Media magnate Rupert Murdoch is well known for his willingness to remove politically sensitive content or publish propagandist material in his Hong Kong, China-based Star TV satellite service, HarperCollins publishing house, and MySpace social networking site in order to expand his media empire into China. AOL, Google Inc., Skype, Windows Live Spaces, and Yahoo are among many other international businesses willing to filter their Chinese services in order to satisfy government conditions for setting up a platform in the country. These international businesses regularly attempt to rationalize their censorship as the lesser of two evils. Typical is a formal statement issued by Google: "While removing search results is inconsistent with Google's mission, providing no information (or a heavily degraded user experience that amounts to no information) is more inconsistent with our mission."

The Internet may also promote what Robert Putnam calls "cyber-balkanization" as much as it does democratization in Asia.[25] Studies of communication about Islamic activism and ethnic and religious massacres in Indonesia, for example, illustrate how the Internet has been misused by some social sectors to inflame violence, conflict between groups, and social breakdown even while other sectors are using it to encourage democracy, community harmony, and social empowerment.[26]

Despite the challenges evident in many nations, multitudinous examples depict how journalists and other social actors have used technologies in almost all Asian countries to evade censorship and advance the boundaries of political discussion. The lengths taken to spread information are often painstaking and involve widespread cooperation. This was the case, for example, during the era of Suharto's presidency in Indonesia, when journalists and activists would send information via well-established networks to organizations in Australia, the Netherlands, and the United States, which would upload the information abroad to reduce the possibility of the Indonesian authorities tracing the source.

Asian journalism can also be celebrated for its progressive uses of technology. The world's three largest newspaper markets in order of size are China, India, and Japan,[27] where media organizations use vast and sophisticated networks of news-gathering, production, and distribution technologies. Journalists in the Republic of Korea have led the innovation of Internet technologies to establish the world's largest, best-known citizen journalism initiative, *OhmyNews*. This online newspaper has captured the public voice through the use of an open-source model in which freelance contributors, mostly ordinary citizens, contribute 80 percent of the content. *OhmyNews* is a politically influential news organization in the Republic of Korea, although it has been unsuccessful in attempts to replicate its model abroad.

East Timorese journalists are among those who also deserve honors not only for their reporting skills, but also for overcoming a dire lack of even the simplest of technologies. After the 1999 independence referendum, anti-separatist militia destroyed most of East Timor's infrastructure, including that critical to gathering and disseminating news. The militia cut all telephone links, razed the offices of the main newspaper, torched all newspaper stocks, and damaged the printing presses and radio relay stations beyond repair. After a four-month period of media silence, intrepid Timorese journalists pooled a small supply of computers and used a hotel photocopier to print a daily newspaper on A4 paper.

## Envelope Culture

Salaries for media workers are poor in many Asian countries, leading journalists to seek supplementary forms of income, with the *envelope culture* being one significant source of funding. The term refers to the envelopes containing money or other valuable gifts that sources of news give to journalists at interviews and press conferences. The countries with the best-documented envelope cultures include Indonesia and the Philippines, although envelope giving has been noted in countries as far afield as China, the Republic of Korea, and Pakistan.

In Indonesia, the envelope culture has arisen since the late 1960s from cultures of gift giving and patron-client relationships that sustain sociopolitical relationships.[28] In this cultural framework, journalists often like to portray themselves as passive recipients who accept envelopes mainly out of deference to the seniority of sociopolitical leaders, who might lose face if their generosity is spurned. Journalists in such countries as Indonesia usually claim that they will reject any envelope that is accompanied by a direct demand to slant coverage.[29] However, whenever the envelope culture exists, a proportion of journalists will exploit it for corrupt purposes. Filipino journalists have even coined the terms "praise release" and AC-DC (attack and collect, defend and collect), to describe journalists who attack or defend reputations based on who is paying them.[30]

Not all journalists rationalize the envelope as being part of a culture of gift giving. In many countries, it results from direct corruption and profiteering. This occurs in nations like Kazakhstan, where government and business figures pay certain journalists to write positive stories about their performance.[31]

Even if the envelope does stem from cultural traditions, it should be recognized that not all forms of gift giving and patron-client relationships are automatically acceptable behaviors for journalists and other democratic actors. Most cultures have notions of public responsibility and define as inappropriate any behavior by public officials that deviates from accepted laws and norms, or involves misuse of public resources and powers (in contrast to use of one's own personal assets) with the aim of serving private ends.[32] In paternalistic political systems, business and political leaders often blur the boundaries between the resources, powers, and interests belonging to the general community and those of the private sphere of individual, family, or clan interests. The news media's ability to sound an alarm over corruption, collusion, and nepotism can be seriously complicated and compromised when journalists themselves straddle or cross these same boundary lines because the envelope usually comes from public or shareholders' funds rather than from the source's own money. A further complication is that the envelope relationship creates a subtle psychological demand on journalists who do not want to injure the feelings or reputation of leaders who have been kind and respectful to them.

Syed Hussein Alatas notes: "Extortion spreads to the professions once it is all-pervasive in government."[33] Unsurprisingly, then, various forms of envelope journalism and journalistic corruption are widespread in those Asian countries that suffer from entrenched corruption in the political-economic spheres and/or large, low-paid bureaucracies. The envelope culture thrived until the 1970s in both Hong Kong, China, and Singapore, but wilted as wages increased alongside a growing economy, strong anticorruption laws, and implementation of regulations. The experience of these two nations demonstrates that widespread envelope cultures can be eliminated, but it requires commitment and resources from newsrooms, ideally with mutually supportive attitudinal changes and reforms in the wider legal, political, and social sphere.[34]

## Watchdogs, Agenda Setters, and Gatekeepers

A short case study of the so-called Saffron Revolution in Myanmar can help to highlight the aforementioned principles about the links between governance and journalism. The Myanmar government attracted intense media attention for its repression of antigovernment demonstrations by students and political activists in August 2007 and by Buddhist monks and their lay supporters in September 2007. In an attempt to control information, Myanmar's military junta relied more on harassing journalists and tightening their grip on old communication technologies than obstructing the use of newer technologies. The regime warned journalists not to cover the demonstrations, tightened official censorship, increased its surveillance of journalists, and blocked telephone lines to the key news sources—the student leaders, opposition politicians, and monasteries. The crackdown rapidly escalated after September 25, with one Japanese journalist being gunned down by a soldier and approximately 15 Myanmar journalists being arrested. Despite high-intensity international media coverage, Myanmar's junta was slow to block newer technologies and did not sever Internet services, most cellular telephone connections, or landline connections out of the country on a widespread scale until September 28. Despite the disruption to these services, the images and stories continued to trickle out to the world, often the result of activists smuggling information across the border into Thailand.

Myanmar rarely jams international radio or satellite television services, and instead relies on counterpropaganda. In what might be regarded as a serious misappropriation of development and Asian values rhetoric, the *New Light of Myanmar* newspaper attempted to smear foreign news services, particularly the BBC and Voice of America. "Saboteurs from inside and outside the nation and some foreign radio stations, who are jealous of national peace and development, have been making instigative acts through lies to cause internal instability and civil commotion," the newspaper reported.[35]

The first and most obvious lesson to be drawn from this example is the way in which the Myanmar junta attempted to crush the important watchdog and agenda-setting activities of journalism. Media reports flagged the serious failures in development processes in Myanmar, where the military powers grow richer while citizens suffer manifest distress as a result of the decline in the long-stagnant economy and the crippling inflation that followed the junta's removal of fuel subsidies in August 2007. Although the junta did restrict the flow of international news, the paramount priority was dampening the Myanmar civil society by censoring local media and targeting news sources, reporters, and editors.

The Internet, mobile telephones, and other new communication technologies greatly assisted in informing, arousing, and mobilizing communities within and outside Myanmar, although the use of new technologies was not essential to this process. The people of Myanmar, in common with citizens of many Asian nations, have proved creative at circumventing censorship by smuggling older technologies—such as videos, tapes, facsimiles, photographs, and printed materials—within and beyond the nation. The real contribution of newer technologies is speedier transmission. Rapid transmission helps to capture public attention as news erupts, and to create a mutually reinforcing cycle in which prompt and continuous updates about civil society activity intensify the already fiery pace of citizens' democratic (and very newsworthy) activity.

The Myanmar case also indicates that journalism's watchdog function of sounding the alarm about problems in government will do little to help nations where civil society and the checks and balances of misappropriation of power are weak. Journalists provided startling coverage of the earlier weeks of the first Myanmar uprising of 1988, with little impact on the final outcome. Although authoritarian regimes would prefer to conduct repressive acts in secrecy, transparency alone will not empower local civil societies or global agencies to prevent their misdeeds. The media coverage could, in fact, have harmed democratic actors. Myanmar's junta is recorded as having used images and stories from the media to help identify and punish participants in demonstrations and other democratic activities.

The Myanmar junta's behavior is an extreme example of the intense repression that some Asian governments will impose when journalists do not follow the government's preferred models of professional practice, particularly when the nation is at flash point. Other Asian governments have similarly punished or harassed development journalists who have employed different models of development journalism than those that the government has officially promoted. For example, the Indonesian government of former president Suharto displayed intolerance to rival models of development journalism. During the mid-1990s, the government increased the number of permits allowed for Western correspondents at an exponential rate, but ironically it also banned journalists from Indonesia who were from the development-focused Inter Press Service. Although the Suharto government espoused development journalism, it insisted on a government-press partnership interpretation. Inter Press Service's emancipatory journalism model was confronting to the regime, and, in fact, more so than the liberal watchdog model of the Western journalists.

In the context of new and transitional Asian societies, blanket attempts by governments to hide their faults or community problems can be destructive. When people cannot obtain news through institutional channels, such as the news media, rumor becomes "the collective transaction through which they try to fill in this gap."[36] Almost all of the Asian nations where journalism is significantly affected by censorship or self-censorship are characterized by a flourishing culture of gossip, rumors, and jokes with double meanings. These are informal means for developing awareness and understanding of events, issues, and trends. East Timorese journalist Virigilio da Silva identified the risk associated with this culture when, in the wake of the 1999 independence referendum, his country was struggling to recover after the destruction of infrastructure essential to journalism and many other facets of life. "There is a news vacuum here and rumours thrive because there are no newspapers," da Silva observed. "Gossip through the grapevine can be damaging to nation-building."[37]

When censorship prevails, Asian journalists have many weapons in their armory for conveying some, if not all, of the facts. Journalists in many Asian countries—such as Malaysia and Indonesia—are masters at using innuendo, allusion, metaphors, satire, and other between-the-lines writing strategies to raise public awareness of issues. Ostensibly nonpolitical stories—such as the "soft" news seen in the social pages and lifestyle, arts, and entertainment stories—are often used to present exposés and explorations of subjects that would be taboo in political or other "hard" news. A "color" story that lauds the panache of the fashions, homes, or leisure pursuits of political leaders and their spouses may seem on the surface to be "fluffy infotainment." The story may also open astute audiences to unstated suggestions that these leaders are self-indulgent, superficial, or profligate to pursue such splendor while the masses struggle to fill their food bowls, or that they are possibly engaging in corruption to attain luxuries with costs beyond their salaries. Word-picture combinations can also invoke subtly subversive meanings. Examples include the television stories that show visuals of plump politicians and bureaucrats dining at lavish luncheons while they break from discussions about the malnutrition and food shortages suffered by their country's poor. The notoriety that former Filipino first lady Imelda Marcos attained for her extensive designer shoe collection typifies the symbolism that the mass media can attach to seemingly nonpolitical activities and attributes.

Such stories should be classed as *elite* communications rather than truly mass communications. Though the educated and middle to upper classes may have the skills, time, and perseverance to read between the lines, the implications may be completely lost on poor and ill-educated people, who form the majority of Asia's population. Such stories also often require insider information before they can be properly understood.

## The Principles in Practice: India and the Democratic People's Republic of Korea

The next section of this chapter involves an in-depth examination of India and the Democratic People's Republic of Korea. The extreme contrasts between these nations are used to illuminate the issues discussed previously, and the ways in which political and economic cultures have shaped and limited the roles and functions of Asia's news media as agents for democracy.

The political structure of the Democratic People's Republic of Korea is commonly described as an extreme model of Stalinist-style political, economic, social, and information control.[38] In a rejection of Western values and in the wake of the Sino-Soviet split, the late president Kim Il-Sung developed a "socialist democracy" based on the theory of juche (translated as "I myself," "independent stand," or "self-reliance"). An estimated 90 percent of the country's economy is centralized, with a small market economy that has arisen mainly in response to the famine of the 1990s.

The Economist Intelligence Unit lists the Democratic People's Republic of Korea as the most authoritarian nation of the 167 countries that it monitors. Freedom to assemble, associate, and receive and impart information—essential for the practice of accurate, comprehensive, and socially inclusive journalism—is almost completely circumscribed. The system of control is so far-reaching that citizens are not permitted to lock their doors at night, in order that security agents may check their activities at any time. Unauthorized assembly or association is defined as a potentially punishable "collective disturbance." Abuses have proliferated in this environment, which allows no media scrutiny of the domineering political and military powers.

Journalists in the Democratic People's Republic of Korea are officially designated the tasks of strengthening political unity, ideological conformity, and the dictatorship of the proletariat. The entire media system is directly controlled by the current leader, Kim Jong-Il, and journalists are carefully trained to extol his virtues. Journalists are also taught to laud the country's socialism and display its superiority over other nations, the majority of which are deemed bourgeois and imperialist. Journalists have an elite status but can face harsh punishments if they offend the authorities, even inadvertently through minor errors. Reporters without Borders reports that at least 40 journalists have been "re-educated" in "revolutionizing camps" since the mid-1990s for mistakes like typographical errors or misspelling of a senior official's name.

The media system replicates the Stalinist model of an inner and outer circle. Korean Central News Agency, which forms part of the Propaganda and Agitation Department of the Korean Workers' Party, issues a number of special bulletins. Bulletin No. 1 is distributed to top leaders. It contains news from local and foreign correspondents, as well as translations of every available report that is published abroad about the Democratic People's Republic of Korea. Less detailed bulletins are distributed to lower ranking officials, local party cadres, and institutions, such as the army, police, and workers' unions, with content being deleted and edited according to the status and type of institution.

By contrast, the general population is permitted to access only the propagandist content of state-owned newspapers, radio, and television services. However, much of the population has little access even to state-owned newspapers, apart from the copies that are posted on public billboards and the stories that are read aloud through loudspeakers in factories and villages. Electricity shortages have often prevented the public from tuning in to radio and television bulletins. There has been a deliberate underinvestment in telecommunications, with relatively few telephones per capita of population and a ban on mobile/cellular telephones since 2004. Only a small number of Internet kiosks exist, with the content heavily filtered.

The system of control includes a self-imposed isolation from most of the outside world. Borders are closed to foreigners, except for a small number of business people and escorted tourists. Imported written material, CDs, DVDs, and videos are banned from the general public, even if the material comes from China, which is the Democratic People's Republic of Korea's closest ally and largest trading partner and aid donor. The authorities also intermittently jam shortwave radio signals, although the energy crisis means that they cannot scramble broadcasts all day on every frequency. The domestic news media are strictly censored, and accessing international publications or broadcasts may result in detention of the whole family in a slave labor camp. Interestingly, some reports claim that Koreans in the north are increasingly defying government authorities by fixing radios and televisions to receive foreign signals, and that a large black market exists for CDs, DVDs, and videos from the Republic of Korea.[39]

The control of the information that flows out of the country is equally tightly maintained. Foreign journalists are treated with suspicion as potential spies, and the Korean Workers' Party has reportedly denounced foreign media for purportedly aiming to destabilize the regime. Most of the news about the Democratic People's Republic of Korea that appears in the foreign media comes from the reports or interviews with aid workers or political figures who have visited the country, but such travel is rare. Even in the face of major catastrophic events, such as the severe floods of August 2007 that affected almost 1 million people, the country retains its secrecy and prevents outsiders from entering the country. United Nations relief workers were eventually granted increased access after the August floods, but only because of the United Nations' World Food Programme's strict "no access-no food" policy.

Not surprisingly, when Reporters without Borders commenced publishing its World Press Freedom Index in 2002, it listed the Democratic People's Republic of Korea as the least free of all countries in which journalists operate. The country retained this least-free position until 2007, when it moved to the second least-free country, after Eritrea.

In stark contrast is India, the world's largest democracy and fourth largest economy in terms of purchasing power parity. Although India followed loosely socialist principles in the decades after it was declared an independent republic, it has implemented a far-reaching economic liberalization since 1991. This has included reduced control over private sector business activity and increased openness to direct foreign investment. Despite ongoing

economic growth, India's development has been unbalanced across socioeconomic groups and various regions. World Bank figures indicate that one-third
(33 percent) of the world's poor live in India, and that 42 percent of Indians
subsist below the international poverty line of US$1.25 per day.[40] Education
and literacy levels vary substantially across regional, class, and gender lines,
with the overall literacy level of 64.8 percent, with 75.3 percent literacy for
men and 53.7 percent literacy for women.[41]

India's thriving media industry includes 1,874 daily newspapers, 312 radio
stations, 562 television stations, and an Internet community of 60 million
users. Newspapers are mainly privately owned by chains and conglomerates,
and 95.7 percent of radio institutions and 98.8 percent of television institutions are held in private hands. Foreign investment is permitted, with caps on
the percentage of foreign equity that is allowed. Community broadcasting is
a very new phenomenon. The government approved a policy in 2002 allowing established education institutions to set up campus radio stations, with
the first being launched in 2004. The Community Radio Policy of 2006 now
allows NGOs, civil society organizations, and nonprofit organizations to apply
for community radio licenses.

Many observers argue that Indian journalists have as much freedom as
their colleagues in the United States and other Western countries, if they wish
to use it. The Constitution of India guarantees freedom of speech and expression, and there is no direct system of censorship. Indian newspapers present
much investigative and analytical journalism that is first-class, particularly
about politics.

There are also complaints that many newspapers slant their coverage in
favor of the narrow party and personal interests of the newspaper owners and
their conglomerates, and that the profit motive leads them to neglect to cover
issues relevant to the wider populace. John Vilanilam is one such critic.

> In the economic system that prevails in India, social communication does not
> serve the bulk of the citizenry, but the dominant, private, selfish interests of
> about 10 percent of the total population. Indian society is stratified along lines
> of caste, class, sex, and ethnicity. The communication system in the country
> seems to be promoting the interests of the rich, the male, and the members of
> the higher ethnic groups, who try to imitate lifestyles in affluent societies with-
> out much regard for the large majority of the population who continue to be
> poor, illiterate, and unaware of their human rights.[42]

Idealistic reporters who attempt to extend the range and repertoire of
issues and sources that appear in the news are limited by the media industry's
circulation wars. Indian journalists are now commonly appointed on a
contract basis for a few years, with the criteria for their reappointment "not
quality of work per se, but their ability to serve the economic interests of the
owners as well."[43]

Private television has honed the technique of using hidden cameras to expose the corrupt or unethical behaviors of politicians, celebrities, sportspeople, and other public figures. Sensational news stories from such sting operations are plentiful and popular, but also controversial. Lawmakers have proposed amending the broadcast act to curb exposure methods that involve entrapment. Critics say that the government aims to protect the powerful, but there has been genuine public concern over the ethics of some stings. One contentious case provoked national outrage in 2007, when a journalist attempted to entrap a schoolteacher, allegedly as part of a vendetta against the woman, by inviting her to procure her students as prostitutes for a fake client. In their hunt for audiences, journalists have descended to other dubious and predatory behaviors. In one example, television journalists in the state of Bihar provoked a huge outcry in 2006 by purchasing gasoline and matches for a desperate man so that he could commit suicide on camera.

Despite being free of censorship, journalists' activities have also long been hampered by a strongly entrenched culture of government secrecy. Scholars and reformists have increasingly argued since the 1990s that a lack of transparency has fueled government and judicial inefficiency, misuse of power, and rampant corruption. It is argued that this has hampered development, and "perpetuated all forms of poverty, including nutritional, health and educational."[44]

Progress in shining a light into the "opaque" halls of government has been slow and uneven. The Indian government passed a Freedom of Information Act in 2002, but this proved weak and inoperable, and it was replaced in 2005 with a Right to Information Act. The newer act relaxes the Official Secrets Act and requires every public authority to computerize its records for widespread distribution and to publish particular categories of information in order to minimize the need for citizens to lodge formal requests for information. Although it is too early for firm measures of the success of the new act, India's information officer points to some positive indicators. These include, as improvements in India's Transparency International rankings, surveys showing that the public perceives a decrease in corruption, low corruption rates among development projects that NGOs have been involved in, and a slowing in the rate of rural-to-urban migration.[45]

The Right to Information Act reflects a new philosophy on development issues and communications, which India's information commissioner describes as "a citizen-centric approach." The key to this citizen-centric approach is involving NGOs and civil society in decision making and the "democratisation of information and knowledge," which are seen as "vital for equalizing opportunity for [national] development."[46] This suggests an increasing commitment to the watchdog and agenda-setting function that the news media and other information sources can serve.

Despite this fresh focus on development projects, the amount of development-related journalism created by Indian journalists has diminished in comparison to previous decades. Previously, most Indian newspapers dedicated a full page to development news. However, in the liberalized economy, media organizations' profit drive has increased, and the development page progressively withered in size to a half page, then to a column, and then to the point where it has almost completely disappeared. Similarly, issues about agriculture, poverty, hunger, drought, education, and health affect hundreds of millions of people, but profit-making imperatives of newspapers have forced the demise of the "rounds" or "beats" in which journalists were dedicated on a full-time basis to these topics.[47] When journalists do cover these development-oriented issues, the stories are likely to have been initiated by the press releases of media-savvy NGOs; the journalists are then likely to simply telephone the NGO spokespeople, gathering story ideas and information from "their air-conditioned offices rather than trudging their way through the fields" to evaluate conditions for themselves.[48]

A content analysis study by the Centre for Youth and Social Development quantifies the problem. A study of five Oriya-language daily newspapers and four leading English-language dailies, conducted over a six-month period, found that the Oriya dailies dedicated less than 4 percent of their space to issues relating to the poor, while the English dailies allocated less than 1.6 percent. The stories that did appear were dull, shallow, and full of stereotypes.[49]

The broadcast media are particularly important in helping developing communities, given India's oral traditions of storytelling and low literacy levels. Radio, in particular, is the main source of news and entertainment. India's public service broadcasters, All India Radio (AIR) and Doordarshan, have been leaders in providing India with development-oriented programs, despite some consumers' complaints about the technical standards and entertainment values of the programs. AIR and Doordarshan operate autonomously from government influence. They are among the world's largest radio and television broadcasters, with many different services operating in various languages and across regions in India.

Despite the commitment of AIR and Doordarshan to reporting on development, India's newly established community radio services, with their use of local languages and creation of locally specific programs, have been able to provide and broker information in a way that has been beyond the capacity of the national broadcasters. Vinod Pavarala and Kanchan Malik's study of the early initiatives of community radio indicates positive outcomes. They describe improved participation, with powerful examples of marginalized groups sharing and discussing issues germane to their health and social well-being. They also present cases of deliberation, with community radio allowing communities to discuss problems and develop solutions that they can enact themselves or pressure the authorities to implement.[50] Community radio cannot solve community needs alone, however, and this is clear from a number of statements from skeptical citizens. "We have nothing to eat or drink," one cynical villager says. "There are no wells or roads. Kids are going hungry. What do we gain from listening to radio? Can a radio drama reduce our hunger?"[51]

The vigor and vitality of India's news media are ironically also the reason that journalistic life is punctuated by many physical threats and risks. The events of 2007 are typical; two journalists were killed for exposing political nepotism and gangsters. Another three media workers died when a newspaper office was firebombed, apparently by supporters of a potential successor to the Tamil Nadu chief minister, when they were angered by an opinion poll that favored the aspirant's younger brother. Despite freedom from censorship and given Indian journalists' constitutional protections of free speech, the ongoing attacks on Indian journalists mean that the nation ranks only 120th out of the 169 countries on the Reporters without Borders World Press Freedom Index.[52]

India also experiences the problems typically seen in conflict regions. In the disputed Indian portion of Kashmir, journalism has been massively disrupted by the violence that has claimed more than 60,000 lives in 20 years. A small example is the month immediately following the mass protests of August 11–12, 2008. A cameraman was killed while covering a demonstration, and at least 32 journalists were beaten. Television broadcasters were ordered to cancel news services on the grounds that news might incite further unrest. Journalists' movements were so badly hampered by curfews and economic blockades that at least half a dozen newspapers were unable to publish.[53]

## Conclusions

Asian journalism is characterized by a remarkable diversity within and between countries and regions. Those who aim to help strengthen the democratic contribution of journalism cannot take a one-size-fits-all approach. There are abundant examples of committed, creative, and courageous journalists who push hard to extend the forums for democratic discussion and to include a variety of frameworks, topics, speakers, and perspectives. However, human rights organizations are correct to identify Asia as a continent of multitudinous dangers for journalists and media organizations. In most Asian countries, journalists find themselves intensely gridlocked by political and economic conditions as well as government and community presumptions about the appropriate relationship between journalists, governments, and societies.

Despite hundreds of millions of international aid dollars dedicated to training Asian journalists, the reports conducted by Reporters without Borders, Freedom House, and other global agencies show little change in the overarching picture of journalistic operations in many Asian nations.[54] Training of journalists may end up equipping them with skill sets that they simply cannot apply, unless there are concurrent efforts to reshape the perspectives, policies, and behaviors of relevant individuals and agencies within government departments and civil society. Little progress will occur in countries with extreme repression of journalism and civil society, such as the Democratic People's Republic of Korea, Myanmar, and Turkmenistan, unless there is substantive change in the political leadership. However, in most countries, training and engagement with officials have the potential to incrementally improve the transparency of opaque bureaucracies and journalists' ability to access and report upon information germane to their societies. Training of journalists and other media workers must be contextualized to take into account the specific cultural, economic, and political factors that shape and limit the media's performance, and how journalists might be best placed to negotiate around them. Such training needs to be sensitive to valid variations in perceptions of what kind of governance and journalism best serves development, without serving politically motivated rhetoric.

The ability of journalists to engage in independent and responsible reporting depends on the financial health of the media organizations that they work for. Consequently, much will also depend on training and support for the media managers, advertising personnel, and other employees to keep media companies operating effectively and profitably. Given the economic state of many Asian countries, assistance with equipment, financial support, or other resources may also be needed. Experience shows that the introduction to equipment and other physical resources must be carefully planned to ensure that they are appropriate for the terrain in which they will be used, and that staff are adequately trained in how to use them.[55] Technologies also need to be appropriate to the resources, storytelling traditions, and technological literacy of local populations. Sometimes support for older technologies, such as radio, may be more important than newer technologies, such as the Internet.

The case of the Indian media, where corporate goals are driven by strong profit motives, suggests that if media organizations are to become more inclusive of the needs of women, children, and marginalized groups, the corporate goals of media organizations must also be considered. Once again, training cannot be effective if it only includes reporters without also reaching the editors, managers, and proprietors who define and interpret the media organization's agendas and mission statements. Because state-funded media often have a very specific charter to provide news and information that assists with development and to serve less profitable rural and remote communities, the government media must not be neglected in this equation.

# Notes

1. This chapter excludes journalism in West Asia, which comprises the Eurasian countries, which are not purely Asian nations, as well as the Arabic states, which are discussed in chapter 13.

2. Cato Institute. 2008. Economic Freedom of the World: 2008 Annual Report. http://blogs.uct.ac.za/blog/amandla/2008/09/16/economic-freedom-of-the-world-2008-annual-report.-cato-institute.

3. Benedict Anderson. 1983. Imagined Communities. London: Verso.

4. Homi K. Bhabha. 2004/1994. The Location of Culture. London: Routledge, 2.

5. The history, philosophies, and practices of development journalism are examined more comprehensively in Angela Romano. 2005. "Journalism and the Tides of Liberalization and Technology." In Journalism and Democracy in Asia, ed. Angela Romano and Michael Bromley, 1–14. London: Routledge Curzon.

6. Floyd J. Mckay. 1993. "Development Journalism in an Asian Setting: A Study of DEPTH-news." International Communication Gazette 51 (3): 237–51.

7. Mahathir Mohamad. 1989. "The Social Responsibility of the Press." In Press Systems in ASEAN States, ed. Achal Mehra, 107–16. Singapore: Asian Media Information and Communication Centre, 114.

8. Leonard R. Sussman. 1998. Press Freedom 1998: Global Warning: Press Controls Fuel the Asian Debacle. Washington: Freedom House.

9. See, for example, Rosemary Righter. 1978. Whose News? Politics, the Press and the Third World, London: André Deutsch.

10. Amartya Sen. 1999. "Democracy as a Universal Value." Journal of Democracy 10 (3): 7–8.

11. Fareed Zakaria. 1998. From Wealth to Power: The Unusual Origins of America's World Role. Princeton, NJ: Princeton University Press; and Fareed Zakaria. 2003. The Future of Freedom: Illiberal Democracy at Home and Abroad. New York: WW Norton.

12. Seow Ting Lee and Crispin C. Maslog. 2005. "War or Peace Journalism? Asian Newspaper Coverage of Conflicts." Journal of Communication 55 (2): 311–28.

13. Imtiaz Hasnain. 1988. "Communication: An Islamic Approach." In Communication Theory: The Asian Perspective, ed. Wimal Dissanayake, 183–89. Singapore: AMIC, 185.

14. Achal Mehra, ed. 1989. "Introduction." In Press Systems in ASEAN States, 1–11. Singapore: Asian Media Information and Communication Centre, 4.

15. See, for example, chapters 9 and 10 in Angela Romano. 2003. Politics and the Press in Indonesia: Understanding an Evolving Political Culture. London: Routledge Curzon.

16. Brian L. Massey and Li-jing Arthur Chang. 2002. "Locating Asian Values in Asian Journalism: A Content Analysis of Web Newspapers." Journal of Communication 52 (4): 987–1003.

17. Cherian George. 2006. "Asian Journalism: Neglected Alternatives." In Issues and Challenges in Asian Journalism, ed. Hao Xiaoming and Sunanda K. Datta-Ray, 79–92. Singapore: Marshall Cavendish; and Xu Xiaoge. 2005. Demysifying Asian Values in Journalism. Singapore: Marshall Cavendish.

18. Center for Media Freedom and Responsibility. 2001. "Press Freedom: A Fragile Reality." Journalism Asia 1 (1): 1.

19. Dan Gillmor. 2004. We the Media: Grassroots Journalism by the People, for the People. Sebastopol, CA: O'Reilly Media, xiii.

20. World Bank. 2004. World Development Indicators. Washington, DC: World Bank.

21. Reporters without Borders. 2008. Turkmenistan: Annual Report 2008. Paris: RSF. http://www.rsf.org/article.php3?id_article=25584.

22. Madanmohan Rao, ed. 2003. *News Media and New Media: The Asia-Pacific Internet Handbook*, Vol. 5. Singapore: Eastern Universities Press.

23. Patrick Bishop and Lori Anderson. 2004. "The Evolution from e-Government to e-Democracy Is Not as Simple as 1,2,3." On Line Opinion. http://www.onlineopinion.com.au/view.asp?article=2109.

24. Internet Enemies. Database. Reporters without Borders. http://www.rsf.org/rubrique.php3?id_rubrique=273.

25. Robert Putnam. 2000. *Bowling Alone: The Collapse and Revival of American Community.* New York: Simon and Schuster, 177.

26. David T. Hill and Krishna Sen. 2005. *The Internet in Indonesia's New Democracy.* London: Routledge; and Merlyna Lim. 2004. "The Polarization of Identity through the Internet and the Struggle for Democracy in Indonesia." *Electronic Journal of Communication* 14 (3–4). http://www.cios.org/www/ejc/v143toc.htm.

27. World Association of Newspapers. 2008. World Press Trends: Newspapers Are a Growth Business. Göteborg, Sweden, June 2. http://www.wan-press.org/article17377.html.

28. See Romano. 2003. *Politics and the Press in Indonesia*, chapter 11.

29. Ibid.

30. Chay Florentino-Hofileña. 2002. "The Ethical Failings of a Democratic Press: The Philippine Case." In *Media Ethics in Asia: Addressing the Dilemmas in the Information Age*, ed. Venkat Iyer, 51–65. Singapore: Asian Media Information and Communication Centre and Nanyang Technological University.

31. Timothy Kenny and Peter Gross. 2008. "Journalism in Central Asia: A Victim of Politics, Economics, and Widespread Self-Censorship." *The International Journal of Press/Politics* 13 (4): 515–25.

32. Syed Hussein Alatas. 1990. *Corruption: Its Nature, Causes and Functions.* Aldershot, England: Avebury, 90–124; and Robin Theobald. 1990. Corruption, Development and Underdevelopment. Houndmills, Hampshire, U.K.: Macmillan, 2, 40–45.

33. Alatas. 1990. *Corruption: Its Nature, Causes and Functions*, 75.

34. Romano. 2003. *Politics and the Press in Indonesia*, chapter 11.

35. The New Light of Myanmar. 2007. "Some Monks and People Enter Homes." Myanmar Information Committee Yangon Information Sheet, September 27. http://www.myanmar-information.net/infosheet/2006/070927.htm.

36. Tamotsu Shibutani. 1966. *Improvised News: A Sociological Study of Rumor.* Indianapolis: Bobbs-Merrill, 62.

37. Sonny Inbaraj. 1999. "East Timor: Journalists Rebuild Media as Well." Inter Press Service. Wire report, November 22.

38. The information about the Democratic People's Republic of Korea is compiled from a large number of sources, including the government's Web site, Amnesty International, Economist Intelligence Unit, Human Rights Watch, Reporters without Borders, and the United Nations. Dated but useful references include Krzysztof Darewicz. 2000. "North Korea: A Black Chapter." In *Losing Control: Freedom of the Press in Asia*, ed. Louise Williams and Roland Rich, 138–46. Canberra: Asia Pacific Press; and Shelton A. Gunaratne and Shin Dong Kim. 2000. "North Korea." In *Handbook of the Media in Asia*, ed. Shelton A. Gunaratne, 586–611. New Delhi: Sage.

39. Sung Jin Lee. 2008. "North Korean People Copy South Korean TV Drama for Trade." Daily NK. February 22. http://www.dailynk.com/english/read.php?cataId=nk01500&num=3290; and Il Geun Yoon. 2007. "South Korean Dramas Are All the Rage among North Korean People." Daily NK. November 2. http://www.dailynk.com/english/read.php?cataId=nk01500&num=2862.

40. Shaohua Chen and Martin Ravallion. 2008. "The Developing World Is Poorer Than We Thought, But No Less Successful in the Fight against Poverty." Policy Research Working Paper 4703, World Bank, Washington, DC.

41. Office of the Registrar General and Census Commission India. Census of India 2001. http://www.censusindia.gov.in/.

42. John V. Vilanilam. 2005. *Mass Communication in India: A Sociological Perspective*. New Delhi and Thousand Oaks, CA: Sage, 35.

43. Arvind Sinha. 2006. "Growing Need of an Alternative Media." In *Making News: Handbook of the Media in Contemporary India*, ed. Uday Sahay. New Delhi: Oxford University Press, 124.

44. M. M. Ansari. 2008. "Impact of Right to Information on Development: A Perspective on India's Recent Experiences." Lecture delivered at UNESCO headquarters, Paris, May 15.

45. Ibid.

46. Ibid.

47. See Uday Sahay, ed. 2006. *Making News: Handbook of the Media in Contemporary India*. New Delhi: Oxford University Press.

48. Navneet Anand. 2006. "What Makes News: Development, No Development, Or None of It." In *Making News: Handbook of the Media in Contemporary India*, ed. Uday Sahay, 96–103. New Delhi: Oxford University Press, 101.

49. Centre for Youth and Social Development (YSD). 2003. *The Vanishing Poor: A Study of the Shrinking Coverage of Pro-Poor Issues in the Print Media*. Bhubaneswar, India: CYSD.

50. Vinod Pavarala and Kanchan K. Malik. 2007. *Other Voices. The Struggle for Community Radio in India*. London: Sage.

51. Ibid., 162.

52. Reporters without Borders. 2008. World Press Freedom Index 2007. Paris: RSF. http://www.rsf.org/article.php3?id_article=24025.

53. This information comes from a number of sources, most particularly Reporters without Borders.

54. Timothy Kenny and Peter Gross (2008) make this observation with specific regard to Central Asian countries, but it is also applicable to most of the region. "Journalism in Central Asia: A Victim of Politics, Economics, and Widespread Self-Censorship." *The International Journal of Press/Politics* 13 (4): 515–25.

55. Krishna Kumar. 2006. "International Assistance to Promote Independent Media in Transition and Post-Conflict Societies." *Democratization* 13 (4): 652–67; and Sam Miller. 2006. "Journalism Training in Sri Lanka: Meeting the Needs of Working Journalists." *Changing English* 13 (2): 173–78.

Part IV

**Conclusions: Summing Up
the Evidence, Identifying
Effective Policy Options**

# 15

# Assessing the Extent to Which the News Media Act as Watchdogs, Agenda Setters, and Gatekeepers

Sina Odugbemi and Pippa Norris

The reform agenda for democratic governance is about how to build states that are effective, responsive to social needs, inclusive, and accountable to citizens.[1] It requires big-picture thinking about the mix of institutions and processes that can contribute to the attainment of these objectives in each country. The fundamental argument of this chapter is that the news media in each country are a vital part of the institutional mix, provided that they are set up in a way that allows them to play the roles of watchdogs, agenda setters, and gatekeepers. The normative framework employed in this book, discussed in the introduction, highlights the ideal roles of the news media as watchdogs, agenda setters, and gatekeepers. If one accepts that these roles strengthen the quality of democratic governance, the question is: Under what conditions do the media perform these roles most effectively? And under what conditions do they fail?

This chapter pulls together the strands of the argument and summarizes the evidence. It highlights the way that a series of barriers—including restrictions on press freedom by the state, market failures, lack of professional journalistic standards, the weakness of civil society organizations, and limited public access and media literacy—cause the news media to often fail to live up to these ideals. The next and final chapter, building on this foundation, sketches the policy agenda that ought to be a central part of the democratic governance reform agenda.

---

We would like to thank Anne-Katrin Arnold, CommGAP research consultant, for her help in researching this chapter.

## The Watchdog Role

The watchdog role requires the news media to provide a check on powerful sectors of society, including leaders within the private and public domains. Journalists are expected to guard the public interest and to protect it from incompetence, corruption, and misinformation. The available empirical evidence suggests that in many countries, the free press does indeed often promote transparency, but journalists often face serious constraints and obstacles in this regard, especially in autocracies.

The most plausible systematic evidence is derived from cross-national comparisons testing whether press freedom and levels of media access function as external control mechanisms on corruption. Brunetti and Weder conclude that an increase by one standard deviation in a country's level of press freedom generally reduces the level of corruption in that country by 0.4 to 0.9 points, on a six-point scale.[2] The reasons, they suggest, are that the press provides a platform for the private sector to voice complaints. In addition, with a free press, journalists have incentives to investigate misconduct by officials. A series of other aggregate-level correlational econometric studies, incorporating the standard controls, generally point to similar conclusions.[3] For example, Lederman, Loayza, and Soares analyzed the effects of democracy, parliamentary systems, and freedom of the press on corruption, and their results confirm the general assumption that a free press inhibits corruption.[4] In addition to press freedom, media access is also found to be important; Bandyopadhyay reported that the degree of media and the level of penetration of information and communication technologies are associated with less corruption, with the strongest effect where newspaper circulation was deepest.[5]

To update the evidence, this chapter compares how freedom of the press (monitored annually by Freedom House) relates to perceived control of corruption (measured by the Kaufmann-Kraay indexes) for different types of regimes. As discussed in chapter 2, the Freedom House measure of freedom of the press is one of the most widely used cross-national indicators. The index is designed to measure the extent to which the free flow of news is influenced by the legal, political, and economic environments. The *legal environment* category encompasses "both an examination of the laws and regulations that could influence media content as well as the government's inclination to use these laws and legal institutions in order to restrict the media's ability to operate." In this category, Freedom House assesses several issues, such as legal and constitutional guarantees of press freedom, penalties for libel and defamation, penal codes, the independence of the judiciary, and other factors. The *political environment* evaluates "the degree of political control over the content of news media." This includes the editorial independence of the media; intimidation and threats to journalists; access to informational sources; and repressive actions, such as arrests, imprisonment, physical violence, and assassinations. Finally, under the *economic environment* category, the characteristics examined are related to "economic considerations that can influence the media's activities." Within this category, Freedom House evaluates the existence of competitive pressures leading to biased press reports and investigations; the extent of sponsoring, subsidies, and advertisement and their effect on press coverage and content; the impact of bribery by self-interested actors on what is published; and the structure and concentration of media ownership.

Both the legal and economic categories vary from 0 (complete freedom) to 30 (lack of freedom), and the political subindex ranges from 0 to 40. A country's overall press freedom score is simply the sum of the scores in each of the subcategories. The assessment of press freedom by Freedom House distinguishes between the broadcast and print media, and the resulting ratings are expressed as a 100-point scale for each country under comparison. The index is based on expert ratings derived from overseas correspondents, staff, and consultant travel; international visitors; the findings of human rights and press freedom organizations; specialists in geographic and geopolitical areas; the reports of governments and multilateral bodies; and a variety of domestic and international news media.[6] For an intuitively clearer interpretation, this chapter reverses the Freedom House index, so that a higher number represents greater press freedom.

The Kaufmann-Kraay indexes of good government have been developed to monitor multiple dimensions, including control of corruption in the public sector, defined as "perceptions of the extent to which public power is exercised for private gain, including both petty and grand forms of corruption, as well as 'capture' of the state by elites and private interests." Their methodology consists of identifying many individual sources of data on governance perceptions, which are then assigned to six broad categories.[7] A statistical methodology known as an "unobserved components" model is used to construct aggregate indicators from these individual measures. These aggregate indicators are weighted averages of the underlying data, with weights reflecting the precision of the individual data sources. For instance, the control of corruption index combines sources, such as data provided by Transparency International, the World Economic Forum Global Competitiveness Survey, and the Political Risk Services International Country Risk Guide.

Figure 15.1 illustrates the simple scattergrams, controlling for three different types of regimes, as classified by the Freedom House measures of political rights and civil liberties into democratic (free), consolidating democracies (partly free), and nondemocratic (not free). The pattern shows the correlation between Freedom House's annual index of press freedom and perceived levels of the control of corruption, as measured by Kaufmann-Kraay. The results show that the regression line provides the best fit for the data in democratic states, generating a strong and significant correlation. Half of the variation in the perceived level of corruption in democratic states is explained by the degree of press freedom ($R^2 = .50***$). Control of corruption sharply accelerates for

### Figure 15.1.  Press Freedom and Corruption under Different Types of Regimes

**(a) Democratic: Free**

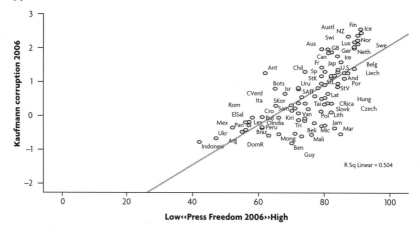

**(b) Consolidating democracy: Partly free**

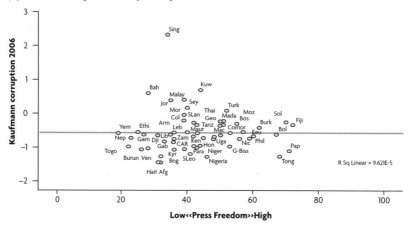

**(c) Nondemocratic: Not free**

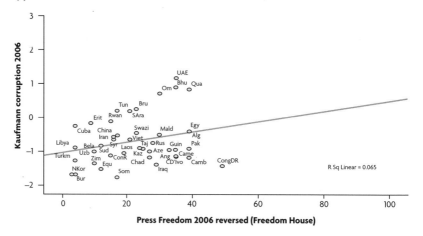

*Sources:* Freedom House. 2006. *Global Press Freedom 2006.* http://www.freedomhouse.org; Daniel Kaufmann, Aart Kraay, and Massimo Mastruzzi. 2008. "Governance Matters VII: Aggregate and Individual Governance Indicators, 1996–2007." Policy Research Working Paper 4654, World Bank, Washington, DC. Available at SSRN: http://ssrn.com/abstract=1148386.

*Note:* The Control of Corruption Index 2006 is measured by the Kaufmann-Kraay Good Governance indicators (Governance Matters VII).

those democracies that are above average for press freedom. Societies such as Canada, Chile, Iceland, and South Africa rank high on both indexes; in these places, a plurality of media outlets and a flourishing independent media sector generate the transparency that encourages clean government. But there is no such correlation in the consolidating democracy (partly free) states, and the figure also highlights important outliers to the general pattern, such as Singapore. The nondemocratic states display only a very modest correlation.

Nevertheless, although the correlation between free press and control of corruption appears quite robust in democratic states, researchers still understand little about how this relationship works in practice, and thus what needs reforming to strengthen good governance.[8] It is commonly assumed that the *availability* of information underlies the relationship, whereby the greater availability of information is expected to generate more efficient political markets. Scandal headlines sell newspapers. A more informed public, aware of the shortcomings of corrupt elected officials, decides to throw the rascal out. But the available measures of media systems at the national level remain extremely abstract. In practice, even in the case of long-established democracies, such as the United States, there are cases of high-ranking officials who have been charged and even convicted of corruption, in some cases attracting widespread headline publicity, yet they are reelected to office by citizens.[9] What is lacking is systematic content analysis data monitoring the extent to which journalists do or do not focus on exposing corrupt officials, investigating financial wrongdoing, or revealing cases of bribery in high office. Researchers also need to dig down to know, in particular cases, what aspects of media systems; what forms of journalism; what types of media outlets, genres, and formats; and what societal conditions, legal contexts, and political environments help to establish the link.

The case of South Africa exemplifies the relationship between a free press and corruption control and the underlying factors in the relationship between a pluralistic media system and government transparency. Following the transitional democratic elections in April 1994, the media landscape was transformed through substantial reforms, including the liberalization and deregulation of state control of broadcasting, the diversification of the print sector, constitutional and legal guarantees of freedom of access to state-held information, and growing use of the Internet. Deregulation, in particular, led to a proliferation of radio stations. Listeners in Johannesburg can tune in to more than 40 radio services, from the national broadcasts of the state-owned South African Broadcasting Corporation (SABC) to community stations targeting local neighborhoods or ethnic groups. SABC operates three national TV networks and two pay-TV channels, while commercial national broadcasters offer free and pay-TV channels, offering the usual mix of news and current affairs, sports and entertainment, movies, reality shows, and soaps, combining locally produced and imported programming. The constitution provides for freedom of the press, and this is generally respected. In 2006, for example, out of 168 nations worldwide, Reporters without Borders ranked South Africa 44th from the top in press freedom, higher than the United States (ranked 53rd) and Japan (51st), and roughly similar to Italy and Spain.[10] Laws, regulation, and political control of media content are considered moderate. Human Rights Watch, an international watchdog body, praises the progress that South Africa has made in freedom of expression, despite remaining critical of the countries' human rights record on other issues, including deep levels of rural poverty, challenges of patriarchy and gender equality, and violations of the rights of asylum seekers and economic migrants.[11] Newspapers and magazines publish reports and comments critical of the government, and the state-owned SABC is far more independent now than during the apartheid era. As a result, although tensions remain in the complex relationship between journalists and the African National Congress (ANC), during the past decade the news media have emerged as an increasingly autonomous actor, less closely aligned with the interests of the government or political parties.[12] In the latest (2008) ranking of perceptions of corruption, South Africa also ranks 54th out of 180 nations worldwide, similar to or marginally higher than Greece, Italy, Poland, and Turkey.[13] In chapter 11, Tettey gives a more detailed account of how this process worked in South Africa, particularly the role of investigative journalism in exposing corrupt campaign finance practices.

By contrast, such countries as Belarus, Syrian Arab Republic, Uzbekistan, and Zimbabwe rank poorly in figure 15.1 in both press freedom and perceived levels of corruption. The case of Syria illustrates the role of the state in severely restricting freedom of expression and independent criticisms of corruption in public life. The Syrian government owns and controls much of the media, including the daily newspapers *Al-Thawra* (the Revolution), *Tishrin,* and the English-language *Syria Times,* and the Baath party publishes *Al-Baath.* There was a brief flowering of press freedom after Bashar al-Assad became president in 2000. The normally staid government newspapers cautiously started to discuss reform and democracy. For the first time in nearly 40 years, private publications were licensed. The new titles included two political party papers, *Sawt al-Shaab* and *Al-Wahdawi,* and a satirical journal. But within a year, under pressure from the old guard, the president cautions against overzealous reform, a subsequent press law imposes a new range of restrictions, and publications can be suspended for violating content rules. Criticism of President Bashar al-Assad and his family is banned, and the domestic and foreign press are censored over material deemed to be threatening or embarrassing. Journalists practice self-censorship, and foreign reporters rarely get accreditation. Reporters without Borders documents common abuses: "Journalists and political activists risk arrest at any time for any reason and are up against a whimsical and vengeful state apparatus that continually adds to the list of things banned or forbidden to be mentioned. Several journalists were arrested in 2006 for interviewing exiled regime opponents, taking part in conferences abroad or for criticizing government policies. They were subjected to lengthy legal proceedings before the Damascus military court that, under a 1963 law, tries anyone considered to have undermined state security."[14]

Critical journalists outside the country write for the Lebanese or pan-Arab press, such as the Beirut daily *Al-Nahar* and the influential London daily *Al-Hayat,* as well as contribute to Al-Jazeera and other regional satellite channels.[15] Syrian TV, operated by the Ministry of Information, operates two terrestrial and one satellite channel. It has cautiously begun carrying political programs and debates featuring formerly taboo issues, as well as occasionally airing interviews with opposition figures. Syria also launched some privately owned radio stations in 2004, but these were restricted from airing any news or political content. Syria had an estimated 1.5 million Internet users as of 2007, and the Web has emerged as a vehicle for dissent. In the view of Reporters without Borders, however, Syria is one of the worst offenders against Internet freedom because the state censors opposition bloggers and independent news Web sites. Human Rights Watch notes that the government of Syria regularly restricts the flow of information on the Internet and arrests individuals who post comments that the government deems too critical.[16] Overall, Syria ranked 154th out of 166 countries in the Reporters without Borders 2007 Worldwide Press Freedom Index. Similarly, in terms of press freedom, Freedom House ranked the country 179th out of 195 states worldwide.[17] In terms of perceptions of corruption, according to Transparency International, Syria ranked 147th out of 180 nations in 2008, about the same level as Bangladesh, Belarus, and the Russian Federation.

These observations are supported by a growing number of case studies, which also illustrate the ways that the news media perform their watchdog role in the fight against corruption. A study of Madagascar's educational system found that the effect of anticorruption campaigns varied by the type of media; in particular, in areas of high illiteracy, radio and television—especially local broadcasts—are more effective at curbing corruption than newspapers and poster campaigns.[18] Ferraz and Finan studied Brazil, where the government published the findings of audits of expenditures of federal funds in selected municipalities.[19] They report that in regions where local radio stations covered the findings of the audit, noncorrupt incumbents experienced a vote bonus. Finally, in the well-known World Bank example, Reinikka and Svensson report that in 1995 only one-fifth of the money allocated to schools in Uganda actually made it to the schools. The government of Uganda initiated a media campaign to enable schools and parents to monitor the handling of school grants by local governments. By 2001, 80 percent of the allocated funds were indeed spent on the schools. The government's newspaper campaign was the major factor in the change.[20]

The research presented in this book describes many additional cases illustrating the way that the news media has the capacity to perform the watchdog role. In the Arab region, for instance, Pintak shows how the arrival of pan-Arab satellite broadcasters like Al-Jazeera led to the advent of more critical, professional watchdog journalism. Similarly, in Asia, Coronel describes the role the media in the Philippines played in bringing down a corrupt president of that country in 2001. The evidence therefore suggests that there is indeed a systematic link between the roles of the press as watchdogs over the powerful and the transparency of government, although certain important exceptions to this rule exist, such as the case of Singapore, which is widely regarded as low on corruption despite restrictions on press freedom, and cases such as Mali, Papua New Guinea, and the Philippines, which continue to be afflicted with corruption despite a relatively flourishing and pluralistic independent media sector.

Yet the conditions limiting investigative journalism are also well known, including those arising from lack of media freedom to criticize the state, commercial pressures from private owners, and also a more deferential culture of journalism that does not recognize this as an important, or even appropriate, role for reporters. There are contrasts in role expectations, even among European journalists.[21] As discussed in chapter 9, in fragile states and those engaged in peace building, such as Ethiopia and Iraq, reporters can see other short-term priorities as more important, with investigative journalism regarded as a destabilizing force for countries seeking to restore public confidence in governing authorities. It is true that "attack-dog" journalism, in which partisan commentators launch fierce and bitter personal assaults on political rivals, can reinforce mistrust within divided communities. Nevertheless, even in these difficult conditions, in the long-run, public trust and confidence in the process of reconstruction is most likely to be established and reinforced where independent investigative journalists can freely highlight cases of misappropriation of public funds, human rights abuses, or examples of corruption among private sector contractors. In the long term, watch-dog journalism can help raise standards in public life, ensuring that development funds are used for the purpose for which they were intended, deterring future misdeeds, and ensuring the conditions of openness and transparency that attract further investment, aid, and confidence in government.

## The Agenda-Setting Role

As agenda setters, the news media ideally should function to raise awareness of social problems by informing elected officials about public concerns and needs. In particular, in terms of the developing world, the press is thought to play an especially important role where it highlights vital issues, such as major disasters, conflicts, or humanitarian crises that require urgent action by national governments or the international community. The concept of the news media's role in agenda setting first entered the study of mass communications in the early 1970s, although the general phenomenon had been discussed well before then.[22] During subsequent decades, an extensive body of literature has examined the factors that determine the salience of issues on the public policy agenda. Many studies have examined the *news media agenda* (gauged by the amount of news media coverage devoted to specific issues) compared with the *public agenda* (measured by public perceptions of the importance of issues in regular opinion polls) and the *political agenda* (typically monitored by the number of the statements, speeches, or press releases emanating from official spokespersons, government officials, think tank and academic experts, and NGO commentators).[23] Yet this is a complex interaction, and considerable care is needed to disentangle the precise timeline involved in the agenda-setting process, to establish who leads and who follows in the dance. In terms of development, most research has focused on whether domestic or international media coverage of specific natural or human-caused disasters, conflicts, and humanitarian crises has influenced either public opinion or the policy response, such as international levels of development aid or foreign policy interventions. The much-debated CNN effect in international affairs is one aspect of this much broader phenomenon.

One of the most often cited studies about the agenda-setting process was conducted by Besley and Burgess.[24] In their analysis of the political economy of government responsiveness, they documented a strong relationship between newspaper circulation and government relief in Indian states. In particular, they reported that a 1 percent increase in newspaper circulation brought a 2.4 percent increase in public food distribution and a 5.5 percent increase in calamity relief expenditures. The authors argued that Indian elected officials are more responsive to problems in their states where newspapers are more active.[25] Along similar lines, in a series of studies, Strömberg made the case for the influence of the news media over public policy in America.[26] Using data from the 1930s in the United States, he showed that the availability of radio significantly determined the extent to which citizens benefitted from government relief spending. Petrova compared the relationship between media freedom and public spending on health and education in democracies and autocracies: in democracies, the study found, media freedom was significantly related to increased spending in these sectors.[27] She concluded that by highlighting social needs, and connecting elected leaders with public concerns, media freedom in democratic states has a real effect on policy outcomes.

This chapter can replicate the Petrova study to describe the correlation between levels of press freedom in each country, as monitored by Freedom House, and domestic patterns of public health spending, measured as a proportion of gross national product (GDP). The latter is only an indirect proxy for the effectiveness of public health; obviously there can be countries, such as the United States, where high costs drive up health expenditure, while in some other cases more efficient health care can be provided with lower spending. Numerous complex factors contribute toward actual health outcomes, beyond government policies, such as patterns of nutrition, overall levels of affluence, and the provision of private hospitals. But the public expenditure devoted to health care (expressed as a proportion of GDP) represents a suitable cross-national proxy for measuring the priority that elected officials give this critical component of social well-being. Figure 15.2 illustrates the correlation, without any prior controls, for contemporary states classified by Freedom House as free, partly free, and not free. The results show that in democratic (free) states, there is a correlation between public health spending and press freedom, but the relationship is far less strong ($R2 = .207$) than that already observed between control of corruption and press freedom. The comparison suggests that the European democracies with the freest press, such as Denmark, Germany, and Iceland, also have relatively high levels of public health expenditure. By contrast, places such as Indonesia, Mexico, and Ukraine rate relatively poorly on both dimensions. But no significant relationships are observable in the consolidating and nondemocracies. Obviously, multiple other factors—including levels of economic development and democratization, the structure and historical legacy of the welfare state, the role of private and public health care, patterns of party competition and the ideology of the governing party, and levels of development aid—may all be contributing toward patterns of health care expenditure, and these may have a stronger impact than the rather limited measures of levels of press freedom. Econometric models seeking to determine the policy impact of the free media are also fairly sensitive to (1) the particular indicators of social welfare expenditure and the choice of lagged measures used in any comparison, (2) any systematic bias arising from problems of missing data, (3) measurement error, and (4) the specific controls that are selected. As observed earlier, what are needed are more systematic and detailed studies of the media's impact on policy making, and more sensitive indicators that can connect the dots in the extended chain of causality between the agenda-setting role of the press, public concerns about an issue, and the response of elected officials to social needs in any democratic state.

As discussed in detail in chapter 4, there is evidence that the news media have an impact on disaster relief spending, but this relationship remains complex; Van Belle reports that the media's impact on U.S. development aid spending has varied during different eras of American foreign policy. In particular, Van Belle notes a strong statistical relationship existed between U.S. media coverage and U.S. humanitarian relief spending during the Cold War years. For instance, during this period, every *New York Times* story on a disaster correlated with a U.S. aid increase of about US$1.7 million. But this

Figure 15.2.  Press Freedom and Public Health Spending under Different
Types of Regimes

(a) Democratic: Free

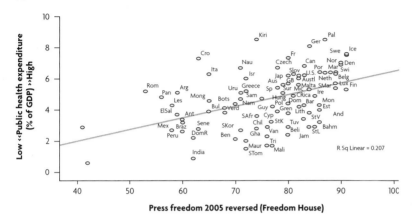

(b) Consolidating democracy: Partly free

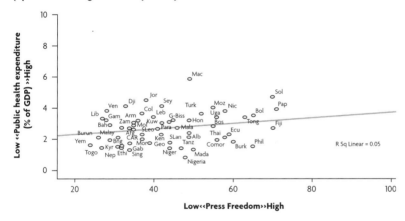

(c) Nondemocratic: Not free

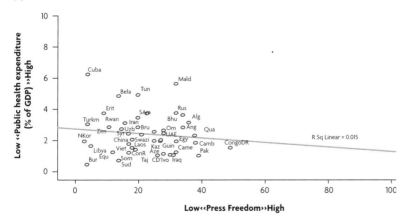

*Sources:* United Nations Development Programme (UNDP). 2008. Human Development Report 2008. New York:
UNDP/Oxford University Press; Freedom House. 2006. Global Press Freedom 2006. http://www.freedomhouse.org.
*Note:* Levels of public health expenditure are measured as a proportion of gross national product (GDP) (UNDP).
Press freedom and the classification of types of states are measured by Freedom House.

relationship broke down during more recent years. Others have also reported similar relationships. For example, Eisensee and Strömberg found a significant effect of news coverage on relief spending: disasters covered in the media were on average 16 percent more likely to receive U.S. disaster relief than similar events not covered by the media.[28] If a marginally newsworthy disaster is covered—at a time when there is little other news available—the probability of disaster relief increases to 70 percent. As Moeller reports in chapter 3 of this book, most of the public will learn about disasters occurring in other countries only when the media choose to report them. At the same time, there are also numerous ongoing challenges of development, often involving extensive casualties and even deaths, that receive minimal attention in the international headlines.

## Gatekeepers and the Public Forum

Finally, as gatekeepers, or indeed, gate openers, it is claimed that the news media should ideally serve as the classical agora by bringing together a plurality of diverse interests, voices, and viewpoints to debate issues of public concern. It is hoped that if the media perform this gatekeeping role well, citizens are more likely to be empowered and informed about their governments, thus keeping political leaders responsive. Gatekeeping also serves to educate citizens and facilitates rational debate and informed public opinion. This gatekeeping role is often regarded as particularly important during election campaigns, when citizens can make an informed choice only if media cover all parties and candidates fairly, accurately, impartially, and without undue favoritism toward those in power.

In chapter 6, Voltmer reports that in many newer democracies, the news media are indeed effective in strengthening political interests and knowledge (less so in affecting people's evaluation of politics). Almost all the media effects she finds in her study are positive for democracy, strengthening citizens' democratic orientation. She concludes that the media are particularly effective in empowering citizens in new democracies. Tettey, also in this book, reports that the news media in Africa, for instance, are "injecting marginalized voices into the public sphere." Microphones are being put before the mouths of those who hitherto had no voice, and they are speaking up. Those being given a voice for the first time include, according to Tettey, the poor and downtrodden, but also gays, lesbians, transsexuals, and, significantly—through the Internet—Africans in the diaspora. The other regional case studies in this volume contain numerous examples of the media playing the public forum role in different political communities.

Yet the lack of balance in the public forum persists—and that matters. The most extreme cases are found in autocracies that use state-controlled media as a mouthpiece. This situation persists, Pintak reports, in much of the Middle East. "In the Arab world, media have traditionally been gatekeepers favoring those in power." Despite this bias, the region has experienced a degree of liberalization and the growth of more critical reporting and independent journalism, following the example set by Al-Jazeera. Moreover, Dragomir emphasizes that even after reform dismantled the traditional state media monopolies in Central and Eastern Europe, old habits die hard, and content analysis of directional balance reveals that broadcasters often continue to favor the party in government, especially in such places as Moldova. This is important for public opinion; Norris and Inglehart compare a wide range of states with restrictive or pluralistic media environments. They find that in restrictive media environments, regular audiences of television and radio news express greater support for the regime. The authors conclude that "state control of the broadcast media and limits on press freedom do achieve their intended effect, by strengthening regime support among the news audiences in these societies." On the other hand, citizens in countries with a high degree of press freedom, which are among the most highly developed democracies, have very little confidence in their governments. These citizens tend to adopt a more critical stance toward their government because they know more about what is really going on.

Overall one can therefore conclude that a substantial gap exists between rhetoric and reality, or between the ideals that are widely articulated in liberal democratic theory and the practices that are commonly found in states around the world. This gap needs to be addressed, and the next chapter identifies a wide range of effective policy interventions and programs that can be implemented by national stakeholders and the international community.

## Notes

1. DFID (U.K. Department for International Development). 2007. *Governance, Development and Democratic Politics. DFID's Work in Building More Effective States.* London: DFID.
2. "A Free Press Is Bad News for Corruption." *Journal of Public Economics* 87 (7-8): 1801–24.
3. Rick Stapenhurst. 2000. "The Media's Role in Curbing Corruption." WBI Working Papers, World Bank Institute, Washington, DC. http://www.worldbank.org/wbi/governance/pdf/media.pdf; Shyamal K. Chowddhury. 2004. "The Effect of Democracy and Press Freedom on Corruption: An Empirical Test." *Economics Letters* 85 (1): 93–101; Sebastian Freille, M. Emranul Haque, and Richard Kneller. 2007. "A Contribution to the Empirics of Press Freedom and Corruption." *European Journal of Political Economy* 23 (4): 838–62; C. Clague, P. Keefer, S. Knack, and M. Olson. 1996. "Property and Contract Rights in Autocracies and Democracies." *Journal of Economic Growth* 1 (2): 243–76; Philip Keefer. 2007. "Clientelism, Credibility, and the Policy Choices of Young Democracies." *American Journal of Political Science* 51 (3): 433–48; A. Adsera, C. Boix,

and M. Payne. 2003. "Are You Being Served? Political Accountability and Quality of Government." *Journal of Law, Economics, & Organization* 19 (2): 445–90; Nicholas Charron. In press. "The Impact of Socio-Political Integration and Press Freedom on Corruption." *Journal of Development Studies.*

4. Daniel Lederman, Norman V. Loayza and Rodrigo R. Soares. 2005. "Accountability and Corruption: Political Institutions Matter." *Economics & Politics* 17 (1): 1–35.

5. Sanghamitra Bandyopadhyay. 2006. "Knowledge-Driven Economic Development." Department of Economics Discussion Paper Series 267, University of Oxford. http://www.economics.ox.ac.uk/Research/wp/pdf/paper267.pdf.

6. For more methodological details and results, see Freedom House 2007. *Global Press Freedom 2007.* http://www.freedomhouse.org. The International Research and Exchanges Board (IREX) Media Sustainability Index provides another set of indicators (http://www.irex.org/resources/index.asp). The IREX index benchmarks the conditions for independent media in a more limited range of countries across Europe, Eurasia, the Middle East, and North Africa.

7. The six broad categories of the Kaufmann-Kraay indexes are (1) voice and accountability, (2) political stability/absence of violence, (3) government effectiveness, (4) regulatory quality, (5) rule of law, and (6) control of corruption. Daniel Kaufmann, Aart Kraay, and Massimo Mastruzzi. 2008. "Governance Matters VII: Aggregate and Individual Governance Indicators, 1996-2007." Policy Research Working Paper 4654, World Bank, Washington, DC. Available at SSRN: http://ssrn.com/abstract=1148386.

8. Samarth Vaidya. 2005. "Corruption in the Media Gaze." *European Journal of Political Economy* 21: 667-87; Henrik Oscarsson. 2008. "Media and Quality of Government: A Research Overview." Quality of Governance Working Paper Series 12, University of Gothenburg, Gothenburg, Sweden. http://www.qog.pol.gu.se/working_papers/2008_12_Oscarsson.pdf.

9. The most recent U.S. case is Alaska's Senator Ted Stevens, returned in the November 2008 elections despite being indicted on seven charges by a federal grand jury.

10. Reporters without Borders. 2006. Worldwide Press Freedom Index 2006. http://www.rsf.org.

11. Human Rights Watch. 2008. *Submission to the Human Rights Council.* April 6, 2008. http://hrw.org/english/docs/2008/04/11/global18513.htm.

12. Sean Jacobs. 2002. "How Good Is the South African Media for Democracy? Mapping the South African Public Sphere after Apartheid." *African and Asian Studies* 1 (4): 279-302; Keyan Tomaselli. 2000. "South African Media 1994-7: Globalizing via Political Economy." In *De-Westernizing Media Studies,* ed. James Curran and Myung Park. London: Routledge; Goran Hyden, Michael Leslie, and Folu F. Ogundimu, eds. 2002. *Media and Democracy in Africa.* Uppsala: Nordiska Afrikainstitutet; Anton Harber. 2004. "Reflections on Journalism in the Transition to Democracy." *Ethics & International Affairs* 18 (3): 79-87.

13. Transparency International. 2008. *Corruption Perceptions Index 2008.* http://www.transparency.org/news_room/in_focus/2008/cpi2008/cpi_2008_table.

14. Reporters without Borders. 2007. *Syria—Annual Report 2007.* http://www.rsf.org/country-43.php3?id_mot=143&Valider=OK.

15. Joel Campagna. 2001. "Press Freedom Reports: Stop Signs." Committee to Protect Journalists. http://www.cpj.org/Briefings/2001/Syria_sept01/Syria_sept01.html.

16. Human Rights Watch. 2007. "Syria: Stop Arrests for Online Comments." http://hrw.org/english/docs/2007/10/08/syria17024.htm.

17. Freedom House. 2008. *Global Press Freedom 2008.* http://www.freedomhouse.org/uploads/fop08/FOTP2008Tables.pdf.

18. Nathalie Franken, Bart Minten, and Johan Swinnen. 2005. "The Impact of Media and Monitoring on Corruption in Decentralized Public Programs: Evidence from Madagascar." LICOS Centre for Institutions and Economic Performance Discussion Paper 155/2005, Katholieke Universiteit, Leuven, Belgium. Available at http://www.econ.kuleuven.be/licos/DP/DP2005/DP155.pdf.

19. Claudio Ferraz and Frederico Finan. 2008. "Exposing Corrupt Politicians: The Effects of Brazil's Publicly Released Audits on Electoral Outcomes." *Quarterly Journal of Economics* 123 (2): 703–45. 20 Ritva Reinikka and Jakob Svensson. 2005. "Fighting Corruption to Improve Schooling: Evidence from a Newspaper Campaign in Uganda." *Journal of the European Economic Association* 3 (2–3): 259–67.

21. Renate Köcher. 1986. "Bloodhounds or Missionaries: Role Definitions of German and British Journalists." *European Journal of Communication* 1 (1): 43–64.

22. Maxwell E. McCombs and Donald L. Shaw. 1972. "The Agenda-Setting Function of the Press." *Public Opinion Quarterly* 36: 176–87; McCombs and Shaw. 1993. "The Evolution of Agenda-Setting Research: 25 Years in the Marketplace of Ideas." *Journal of Communication* 43 (2): 58–67; Maxwell E. McCombs, Donald L. Shaw, David H. Weaver, eds. 1997. *Communication and Democracy: Exploring the Intellectual Frontiers in Agenda-Setting Theory.* Mahwah, NJ: Lawrence Erlbaum.

23. Everett M. Rogers and James W. Dearing. 1988. "Agenda-Setting Research: Where Has It Been? Where Is It Going?" In *Communication Yearbook,* Vol. 11, ed. J. A. Anderson, 555–94. Newbury Park, CA: Sage; Rogers and Dearing. 1996. *Agenda-setting.* Thousand Oaks, CA: Sage; Everett M. Rogers, W.B. Hart, and James W. Dearing. 1997. "A Paradigmatic History of Agenda-Setting Research." In *Do the Media Govern? Politicians, Voters, and Reporters in America,* ed. Shanto Iyengar and R. Reeves. Thousand Oaks, CA: Sage.

24. Timothy Besley and Robin Burgess. 2002. "The Political Economy of Government Responsiveness: Theory and Evidence from India." *Quarterly Journal of Economics* 117 (4): 1415–51.

25. See also Timothy Besley and Robin Burgess. 2001. "Political Agency, Government Responsiveness and the Role of the Media." *European Economic Review* 45 (4–6): 629–40.

26. David Strömberg. 2001. "Mass Media and Public Policy." *European Economic Review* 45 (4–6): 652–63; Strömberg. 2004. "Mass Media Competition, Political Competition, and Public Policy." *Review of Economic Studies* 71 (1): 265–84; Strömberg. 2004. "Radio's Impact on Public Spending." *Quarterly Journal of Economics* 119 (1): 189–221.

27. Maria Petrova. 2008. "Political Economy of Media Capture." In *Information and Public Choice. From Media Markets to Policy Making,* ed. Roumeen Islam. Washington, DC: World Bank.

28. Thomas Eisensee and David Strömberg. 2007. "News Droughts, News Floods, and U.S. Disaster Relief." *Quarterly Journal of Economics* 122 (2): 693–728.

# 16

# Policy Recommendations

Sina Odugbemi and Pippa Norris

Although it is clear that news media have the potential to fulfill the three ideal roles discussed throughout this volume, and thereby to strengthen the democratic public sphere, certain important contextual constraints severely limit their capacity to act as watchdogs, agenda setters, and gatekeepers. Throughout the book, contributors have identified a series of challenges that can be categorized as problems related to the role of the state, problems arising from market failures, limited institutional capacity in the journalistic profession, weakness of civil society organizations, and lack of public access and literacy (see figure 16.1). Each of these, in turn, suggests a series of alternative policy interventions.

Several major donors are active in media development. They include the leading bilateral and multilateral donor organizations as well as private foundations.[1] Despite an upsurge of interest in the field, some common challenges often bedevil media assistance initiatives around the world. What follows sums up the main policy recommendations. It is not a detailed blueprint but rather a menu of alternatives that multilateral agencies, governments, donors, professional journalism bodies, and nongovernmental organizations (NGOs) could consider when designing their policies for media development and reform. The points below provide applicable suggestions to shape efforts to improve democratic governance around the world.

---

We would like to thank Anne-Katrin Arnold, CommGAP research consultant, for her help in researching this chapter.

**Figure 16.1.  Challenges and Opportunities Facing the News Media**

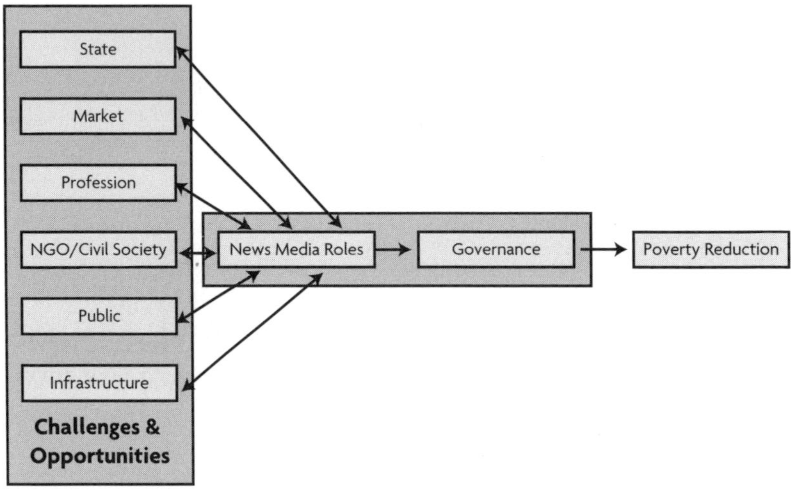

*Source:* Authors.

## Use Needs Diagnostics and Media Performance Indicators

One of the greatest identifiable weaknesses in much of the existing work on media reforms is the lack of a holistic approach by most donors. The primacy of the overall enabling environment is not receiving the attention it deserves.[2] The evidence suggests slow progress in the areas of legal and regulatory reform, yet these areas are the heart of the matter.[3] Above all, economic stability and sustainability of independent media remain major problems.[4] A common theme in most media development projects is journalism training; yet most of the training is episodic and unsustainable and ignores structural constraints on the quality of journalism, such as the rule of law or job security.[5] A severe lack of donor coordination, and conflicting donor ideologies, result in a distorted dispersal of efforts globally. In the field, intermediaries are underdeveloped, and local partners are insufficiently involved. There are few established monitoring and evaluation tools. In addition, research is lacking overall, especially that focusing on developing countries.[6] In light of these challenges, the first recommendation suggests the application of systematic media audits and indicators that are sensitive to each particular context prior to any policy intervention or the implementation of any program.

### Incorporate Media Indicators and Audits into Governance Diagnostics and Needs Analysis

Technical experts who lead work on governance reform need to identify and assess the key governance challenges in any country before appropriate interventions are designed. This diagnostic work can be informed by a set of disaggregated indicators, such as country profiles, or quality of governance assessment frameworks. What is crucial is that indicators for assessing the state of the media system be incorporated prior to any strategic interventions. The United Nations Educational, Scientific, and Cultural Organization (UNESCO) has led a process that has resulted in a comprehensive set of media indicators that, if applied, would highlight where interventions might be most needed. Andrew Puddephatt discusses the UNESCO indicators in chapter 2. He suggests that media indicators should have the following categories: framework for regulation and control; plurality and diversity of media, fair market, and transparent ownership; media as platform for democratic discourse; professional capacity building; and infrastructure. Unless media system indicators are incorporated into governance diagnostics at the country level, an institutional view of the news media will not be integrated into how governance reform work is actually done around the world.

## Reform the Role of the State

In this volume, many chapters illustrate the institutional constraints on the news media arising from the political history of the country. Since political institutions and media institutions are interdependent, a nation's political history influences its contemporary media system. For instance, Marius Dragomir documents in chapter 10 how the communist past of the transitional societies in Central and Eastern Europe has an impact on the media systems there, shaping journalism ethics and the intensity of political interference. In the case of Latin America, Silvio Waisbord shows in chapter 12 that although the media were not nationalized and most are still mainly privately owned, the legacy of military dictatorships continues. Angela Romano, in chapter 14, describes how in Asia the media systems in former one-party dictatorships still continue to be characterized by a high level of state ownership and the overwhelming influence of ruling parties. Finally, in chapter 11, Wisdom J. Tettey demonstrates that in Sub-Saharan Africa, the legacy of one-party dictatorships and military rule means that state ownership of the media remains strong, the private sector is weak, and ethnicity remains a factor.

Several contributions in this volume attest to the impact of the political system, and its past, on the nature of the news media; the former imposes constraints on the latter. Autocracies try to control the media and curb critical reporting, to promote support for the government and its ideology, as Pippa Norris and Ronald Inglehart report in chapter 8. Autocratic states restrict the news media through censorship, state ownership of the media, legal restrictions on freedom of expression and publication, criminal prosecution of journalists, and even violence. Authoritarian regimes also restrict the news media through regulations that require licenses for media outlets and journalists, libel laws, content laws, taxation, official secrets acts, and so on. And as Monroe E. Price, Ibrahim al-Marashi, and Nicole A. Stremlau point out in chapter

9, the news media in postconflict states often face particular difficulties. In such countries, very often the media are in the hands of a few powerful groups intent on using the media to polarize the public. The authors give the example of Iraq, where private media operations reflect political and ethnic divisions and are designed to increase the power of their owners. Finally, the regional surveys in this volume give details, region by region, regarding the constraints imposed on the media by the state. All of these findings give rise to a range of recommendations for reforming the state, in particular by strengthening the framework of civil liberties, by reforming state broadcasting, and by establishing effective and independent broadcasting regulatory agencies.

## Expand the Framework of Civil Liberties and Remove Legal Curbs on the Media

Any overarching constitutional principles, laws, or administrative procedures that inhibit the independence of the press should be reformed in order to strengthen universal human rights, especially fundamental freedoms of expression and publication. Efforts should be directed toward respecting the rights of journalists and revoking punitive legislation against the independent media. Some governments use control of official advertising to muzzle the press; they also use punitive taxation, or licenses for the importation of newsprint. In some countries governments control the printing presses that all newspapers and magazines have to use; if a publication is out of favor with the government, it will simply not get printed. Every effort should be made to make these control devices inoperable.

## Turn State Broadcasters into Public Service Broadcasters

As different authors in the study report again and again, state control of the media, especially broadcasting, inhibits the capacity of the news media to be watchdogs, agenda setters, and gatekeepers. The constant push ought to be to convert state-controlled broadcasters into genuine public service broadcasters. Again, Buckley and colleagues have captured some of the best practice available regarding how to create and secure public service broadcasters.[7] They suggest that public service broadcasting should be editorially independent of government and protected against political and commercial interference. Public service broadcasting should be required to serve the public interest. Public service broadcasting should provide a wide range of programming to educate, inform, and entertain the public, while taking into account ethnic, cultural, religious, and regional diversity. Public service broadcasting should be governed by an independent governing board (with a transparent, fair, and independent process of appointing members of that board, members required to serve the public interest at all times). Finally, public service broadcasting should be financed with public funding through specific mechanisms that protect its independence.

## Ensure the Independence of Broadcasting Regulatory Bodies

Although broadcasting regulation is unavoidable, what is crucial is that bodies overseeing this process be truly independent. A World Bank report has gathered global good practice on how to secure the independence of broadcast regulators.[8] Broadcast regulation should be the responsibility of an independent body whose powers and duties are determined by law and whose principal duty is to further the public interest, not political or economic interests. The process of appointing the members of that regulatory body should be open and transparent. The regulatory body should operate in an open and transparent manner, and should be required to include public participation. The decision-making process of the regulatory body should be transparent. The regulatory body should be subject to judicial oversight and should be formally accountable to the public. And the regulatory body should be required to publish an annual report. While the principles are widely recognized, the challenge in many states remains to make these effective in practice and not merely on paper.

## Address Problems of Market Failure

With the state posing such a huge challenge to the capacity of the news media to fulfill their ideal roles, it is tempting to think that liberalized and competitive media markets would be the perfect solution. As Sheila Coronel shows in chapter 5 of this book, liberal markets and competition can be an asset to watchdog reporting because state influence can be curbed; but they can also be an obstacle because commercial pressures often make the media reluctant to expose the misdeeds of the powerful and hold them to account. Several of the reports in this volume, for example, those by Susan D. Moeller, Marius Dragomir, and Holli A. Semetko, indicate that profit-oriented news outlets tend to lack a public service agenda. In particular, Waisboard's case study on Latin America shows how a strong codependence of state, market, and the press results in severe challenges to the ability of the news media to be watchdogs, agenda setters, and gatekeepers. According to Waisbord, unregulated influence of governments and markets, coupled with the close proximity between official and business interests, have historically undermined the media's role in democracy. As a result, ownership structures limit the spectrum of possible issues that the news media can address. Investigative journalism is not likely to uncover corporate corruption, since the major economic players also own the media. Above all, editorial partisanship is the norm rather than the exception. Finally, on this issue, it is important to note that the market can be a constraint where the advertising industry is not sufficiently developed, as few media outlets can survive financially outside state control. This is often the case in Africa. The reasons can range from the limited size of the domestic economy to the absence of critical advertising infrastructure, like independently audited circulation figures, independently determined audience ratings, and so on.[9] These challenges also suggest a range of interventions that can be designed to counterbalance and address the underlying causes of market failures.

### Ensure That Media Systems Are Pluralistic and Diverse

If there is one overarching object of policy it is this: to make media systems as pluralist and as diverse as possible, and there is a broad consensus that external diversity should be achieved through an appropriate regulatory environment encouraging a wide range of media ownership, outlets, contents, interests, and political perspectives. Nevertheless, there are different philosophies about the most effective way to achieve this goal and, in particular, the most appropriate role of markets and the state in this process. Both excessive state ownership and excessive ownership concentration in the private sector can threaten the news media's plurality and diversity, and these should be the target of legal reform. It is advisable for donors to support small independent media, as outlined in the 2008 Inaugural Report of the Center for International Media Assistance, to offset the potentially negative effects of political and economic pressures on the mainstream media.[10]

The World Bank report Broadcasting, Voice, and Accountability contains good practice suggestions on the regulation of private broadcasting: (1) Introduce positive content obligations (requiring that certain materials be included in broadcasts) to increase the diversity of content and material available to the public. (2) Introduce special content rules during elections (for example, equal time for all parties). Do not introduce restrictions on broadcast content beyond those that apply to all forms of expression. (3) Promote codes of conduct and self-regulation. (4) Introduce sanctions for breaches of content rules that are proportionate to the harm done. (5) Ensure equitable frequency distribution between public service, commercial, and community broadcasters. (6) Introduce "must carry" rules for cable and satellite networks, providing for the inclusion of public service and community broadcasters. (7) Promote public access channels.[11] Again, while commonly recognized, implementing these principles in countries where a few conglomerates own and control a large sector of the media market remains difficult in practice. Yet without them, ideas of gatekeeping, balanced reporting, and independent watchdog scrutiny of corporate governance are not likely to be realized.

### Strengthen Media Markets and Media Industries and Support Media Infrastructure

It is important to realize that the media sector in developing countries has major economic potential. It can be a massive creator of jobs and a generator of wealth. In the European Union, the content production industry accounts for 5 percent of the gross national product (GDP) and employs 4 million people. Film production has a significant economic impact in the Philippines and in India.[12] In 2006, the *Economist* reported that the Nigerian film industry was the second biggest employer in the country.[13] Moreover, the viability, diversity, and independence of the sector are crucial requirements for a free, pluralist, and independent media system. The media sector needs to be regarded as an important development sector. The kind of economic development initiatives directed toward other economic and social development sectors need to be directed to the media sector as well. In that regard, it is important to commission sector studies and develop plans of action for sector development and to support institutions that will strengthen the entire sector, especially audited circulation bureaus for newspapers and magazines, and audience ratings systems for broadcasting.

In addition, the African Media Development Initiative has a number of recommendations that not only are sensible but are generally applicable. The initiative suggests that efforts should be made to do the following: (1) Tailor funds and bridge the finance gap that may exist because the return on investment for media technology or media outlets typically exceeds the usual lending cycle of banks. (2) Improve the utilization of existing finance schemes by increasing awareness of existing funding opportunities among the media sector. (3) Facilitate the funding of equipment. (4) Create mechanisms for media outlets to share technical facilities. (5) Identify opportunities to collectively purchase equipment. (6) Support equipment and skill upgrades.[14]

## Build the Institutional Capacity of the Journalism Profession

The ideal roles of the news media as watchdogs, agenda setters, and gatekeepers have implications for the values, norms, and professional practices of journalists. These roles also have implications for media standards of training, accreditation, organizational routines, and professional associations. For instance, it is implied that the news media have obligations to society and that professional journalists have to be truthful, accurate, fair, and objective.[15] Yet in many countries journalists fall far short of these standards. Most of the chapters in this book describe deviations from the norm. The broader political culture in a country also tends to shape the norms, rules, and professional practices of journalists. The prevalence of political bias is widely reported on these pages, as are sensationalism, a failure to focus on the public interest, the treatment of news as a commodity, bribe taking by journalists, and so on. To build institutional capacity, the following interventions should be considered.

### Make Institutional, Not Individual, Capacity Building a Priority

For the democratic governance agenda, the most appropriate way to view the news media is the institutional perspective.[16] The media system in each country should be regarded as one of the core institutions affecting governance, such as an independent judiciary, free and fair elections, parliaments, and so on. This insight led political philosophers to refer to the free press as the Fourth Estate of the Realm, that is, a coparticipant in governance.[17] Those working on governance reform around the world need to ask: What kind of media systems will help to deliver democratic governance? An institutional view of the media requires a holistic approach to media development, not piecemeal work concentrating mainly on the short-term efforts, such as ad hoc workshops training individual journalists. This is the conclusion of all the leading surveys on the state of media development. Price and his colleagues call for a real focus on the enabling environment of the news media.[18] Buckley and coauthors maintain, rightly, that it is not sufficient for reform efforts to focus on policies to extend access to information without addressing issues of media independence, pluralism, accessibility, and capacity.[19] Finally, the Center for International Media Assistance (CIMA) strongly recommends a holistic approach to media development, saying: "Change will happen faster if all the factors—professional development, economic sustainability, legal-enabling environment, and media literacy—are addressed simultaneously."[20]

### Support Sustainable Professional Development Programs and Expand Institutional Capacity

Journalists need support in at least three areas: professional skills, journalism ethics, and management skills. But what the lessons from actual interventions suggest—and there have been many of those—is that short-term, ad hoc initiatives have not produced desired results. Professional development programs are more effective when they are sustained, especially through existing platforms of learning. More lasting solutions arise from building the institutional capacity of journalism education in each environment; it is also preferable to support professional associations, which are able to promote ethical standards and public interest journalism on a permanent basis. The role of independent press councils, for self-regulation, is also important to set professional standards of accreditation, establish agreed ethical codes, and protect and defend independent journalism from outside pressures.

### Expand Civil Society Organizations

The capacity of the news media to be effective watchdogs, agenda setters, and gatekeepers depends crucially on the vibrancy of associational life in a particular society. Organized groups help to inform and mobilize the news media on specific issues. And when the news media cover an issue or expose official wrongdoing, it is up to NGOs and others to organize the public, unleash a storm of protests, and insist on redress. It is, on many levels, a symbiotic relationship. Coronel illustrates this in her report on the ousting of Philippine president Joseph Estrada. The first coverage of his corruption was initiated by the independent, nonprofit Philippine Center for Investigative Journalism.[21]

After the revelations had been made public, citizens' groups, the Catholic Church, political parties, and other groups organized protests that eventually forced Estrada out of office. In addition, as Coronel and Waisboard both report, NGOs increasingly provide noncommercial alternatives to news media. Above all, there is a growing trend toward NGOs setting up media watchdog groups or observatories. For instance, Media Watch Global was founded in 2002 during the World Social Forum in Porto Alegre to "promote the right of citizens around the world to be properly informed."[22] Media observatories have spread all over Africa. The self-regulatory bodies are committed to uphold press freedom and journalism ethics. Media watch groups have been founded by civil society groups in many more parts of the world, including the Middle East, Iraq, India, the United Kingdom, and the United States.[23] Where there is no vibrant civil society, the news media will not be as effective as they might otherwise be.

### Encourage Links Between News Media and the Rest of Civil Society

Better cooperation between the news media and the rest of civil society is crucial. For one thing, the news media need the active support of groups in civil society in order to strengthen the commitment of each political community to free, diverse, and independent media. Second, NGOs, community-based organizations, and social movements cannot be effective without the active support of free, diverse, and independent news media. In addition, the growing trend whereby NGOs set up media watch groups or observatories deserves support and scaling up. It is a good way of holding the news media themselves accountable; it is also an excellent way of encouraging the news media to focus on the public interest.

### Expand Public Access and Build Media Literacy

Moreover, widespread public access is an essential condition for an effective media. From the point of view of governance, the question of media infrastructure is of crucial importance when one thinks about access to the media or media penetration of a national territory. Public access to media matters in at least two ways. First, the capacity of the government to have the means to communicate with all parts of the territory it governs has always been seen as fundamentally important with regard to both state effectiveness and nation building.[24] Nations are, after all, "imagined communities," and the news media play a crucial role in creating that sense of community.[25] This role becomes obvious in postconflict environments. The United Nations and other agencies often support the development of mass communication systems in peacebuilding efforts in order to restore the sense of one national community able to communicate with itself.[26]

Access to the news media matters in a second way: it is of fundamental importance to citizenship, especially competent citizenship. A segment of the population without access to the news media might as well live in the Dark Ages. As Puddephatt notes in this book, UNESCO considers access to media—to gain information and to be heard—a vital part of human development. Formal media freedoms have little meaning if citizens cannot make use of the media. Not surprisingly, media scholars agree. For instance, Norris and Zinnbauer identify widespread access to mass communication as one of the two conditions under which media can strengthen good governance and development.[27] Norris and Inglehart, in this book, argue that access to alternative media sources can undermine the hold of autocracies because the public is exposed to a wider variety of information and ideas. They note that in some of the poorest countries in the world, between a quarter and a third of the population has no access to the news media.

These days, the problem of access to the media is often discussed in terms of the Internet and new information and communication technologies. Nonetheless, access is a constraint with regard to both new and traditional media. Development assistance projects target both. A good recent example is from Pakistan. In October 2005, an earthquake in Pakistan destroyed newspaper offices and killed journalists, reducing the capacity of local media to respond to the disaster. Pakistanis first learned about the disaster from private television and radio stations—but neither was available in the affected areas. The 3.5 million people affected by the earthquake had no means of finding out what happened or how to get help. To reestablish some degree of media network, the Pakistan Electronic Media Regulatory Authority issued short-term licenses for local radio, disregarding its usually lengthy licensing process and even making military frequencies available to noncommercial broadcasters. Internews, an international media development organization, provided support to build an emergency broadcast sector, providing equipment, content, and training as well as distributing about 10,000 free radio sets among the affected population. The use of radio as a primary source of information rose from 28 percent shortly after the disaster to 70 percent four months later. Television and newspapers remained below 25 percent.

In addition to lack of access, public apathy can be a game-changing constraint. Where the public does not care about what its government is doing, journalists covering corruption, repressive laws, restrictions on freedom of expression, and transparency and openness in government can be overly exposed as isolated crusaders that can be attacked with impunity by the powerful. For instance, polling citizens in about 20 countries, a 2008 World Public Opinion Survey found that majorities in all the nations surveyed support the general principle of press freedom. Yet in some countries, such as Jordan, the Arab Republic of Egypt, and Indonesia, the majority of citizens supported the idea of governments being able to curb news coverage that might be deemed politically destabilizing. The report notes: "In many countries people want more media freedom than they have now, but in many Muslim countries and the Russian Federation, there is substantial support for regulation of news that the government thinks could be politically destabilizing."[28] Tettey, in this book, mentions an incident that illustrates the power of public support for the news media. Because the Kenyan newspaper, the *Standard*, was reporting possible corrupt behavior by officials in government, security forces raided the offices of the newspaper in March 2006. Thousands of citizens and several civil society organizations mobilized in support of the newspaper. Many went to the premises to show support. The public response led to a parliamentary hearing and international press coverage. The government owned up to the raid and subsequently backed off. The point is this: without public support for a free and independent news media, life for brave independent journalists can be lonely and exceedingly dangerous. Addressing these challenges also provides many opportunities for effective policy interventions.

## Expand Public Access to the New Media and Rights to Information

Access gaps that remain need to be closed, not simply the digital divide in information and communication technologies, which has received extensive attention, but also the skills and resources that are necessary to give widespread access to traditional broadcast media. In recent years, important technological innovations have reduced some of the technological hurdles to information access in poorer societies, bypassing some of the obstacles. This includes the availability of wind-up radios, solar-power batteries, wireless connectivity (WiFi, WiMax), US$100 rugged laptops, Internet cafés, community telephone and Internet centers, and cell phones with data services, email, and text messaging.[29] All these developments may help to close access gaps. At the same time, some observers suggest that the core inequalities in information poverty have persisted and may even have deepened.[30] Postindustrial societies and emerging economies that invested heavily in advanced digital technologies have reaped substantial gains in productivity. This may encourage them to build on their success and expand this sector of the economy still further. Moreover, it remains the case that, beyond isolated pockets of innovation, many of the poorest societies in the world continue to lack the basic infrastructure and resources to connect their rural populations to global communication networks and markets.

## Support Media Literacy as Part of Building Citizenship Skills

With regard to the general public, efforts designed to promote media literacy are in their infancy around the world. According to UNESCO, media literacy means "critical knowledge and analytical tools, empowering media consumers to function as autonomous and rational citizens, and enabling them to critically make use of media."[31] These efforts need to be supported and scaled up.

As Price and Krug argue, having citizens that are media literate is part of the enabling environment for a free and independent media.[32] The reasons are obvious. Citizens need to appreciate the value of a media system that is free, diverse, and independent. They also need to be able to assess mediated information.

## Conclusion

In short, the ideals of journalism can be, and often are, challenged, especially in states governed by autocratic regimes and by societies in transition. More often, however, there is broad agreement on what general role the media should play in strengthening democratic governance, but chapters in this volume have documented the many ways that journalistic practices fail to meet these ideals. None of the potential steps identified in this book provide automatic or simple solutions. But certainly broadening the range of interventions beyond the occasional investment in journalism training workshops and similar short-term initiatives would be a step in the right direction, so that media reforms become mainstream to all work on democratic governance. The evidence suggests that, in reality, the performance of media systems often falls far short of lofty aspirations, with important consequences for the workings of the public sphere. This book identifies the most effective strategic interventions designed to overcome these constraints. Interventions include reforms directed at strengthening the journalistic profession, notably institutional capacity building, through bodies such as press councils, press freedom advocacy NGOs, and organizations concerned with journalistic training and accreditation. Other important reforms seek to overcome market failures, including developing a regulatory legal framework for media systems to ensure pluralism of ownership and diversity of contents. Finally, policies also address the role of the state, including deregulation to shift state-run broadcasting to public service broadcasting, overseen by independent broadcasting regulatory bodies, and the protection of constitutional principles of freedom of the press, speech, and expression. Although country contexts vary, efforts of the kind described above not only will strengthen the news media in a durable way, they also will contribute to the overarching objectives of the democratic governance reform agenda: making states that are effective, responsive, inclusive, and accountable.

# Notes

1. Lee B. Becker and Tudor Vlad. 2005. *Non-U.S. Funders of Media Assistance Programs.* Athens, GA: University of Georgia; Monroe Price. 2002. *Mapping Media Assistance.* Oxford: Centre for Socio-Legal Studies.

2. Price. 2002. *Mapping Media Assistance;* CIMA (Center for International Media Assistance). 2008. *Empowering Independent Media. U.S. Efforts to Foster Free and Independent News Around the World.* Washington, DC: National Endowment for Democracy; Steve Buckley, Kreszentia Duer, Toby Mendel, and Seán Ó Siochrú. 2008. *Broadcasting, Voice, and Accountability.* Washington, DC: World Bank Group.

3. Krishna Kumar. 2004. *USAID's Media Assistance. Policy and Programmatic Lessons.* PPC Evaluation Working Paper No. 16. United States Agency for International Development, Washington, DC . http://pdf.dec.org/pdf_docs/Pnadc459.pdf; International Programme for the Development of Communication. 2006. *Evaluation Reports on Selected Projects.* CI-2006/WS/5. Intergovernmental Council, IPDC.

4. Kumar. 2004. *USAID's Media Assistance;* CIMA. 2008. *Empowering Independent Media.*

5. CIMA. 2007. *Global Investigative Journalism: Strategies for Support. A Report to the Center for International Media Assistance.* Washington, DC: National Endowment for Democracy.

6. Price. 2002. *Mapping Media Assistance;* CIMA. 2008. *Empowering Independent Media.*

7. Buckley, Duer, Mendel, and Ó Siochrú. 2008. *Broadcasting, Voice, and Accountability,* 189.

8. Ibid., 156.

9. AMDI (African Media Development Initiative). 2006. *Research Summary Report.* London: BBC World Service Trust.

10. CIMA. 2008. *Empowering Independent Media.*

11. Buckley, Duer, Mendel, and Ó Siochrú. 2008. *Broadcasting, Voice, and Accountability,* 171.

12. Gareth Locksley. 2008. *The Media and Development. What's the Story?* Working paper 158, World Bank, Washington, DC. http://siteresources.worldbank.org/INFOR MATIONANDCOMMUNICATIONANDTECHNOLOGIES/Resources/The_Media _and_Development.pdf.

13. *Economist.* 2006. "Nigeria's Film Industry," July 27.

14. AMDI. 2006. *Research Summary Report.*

15. Denis McQuail. 2005. *McQuail's Mass Communication Theory.* London: Sage, chap. 7.

16. See Bartholomew Sparrow. 1999. *Uncertain Guardians: The News Media as a Political Institution.* Baltimore: Johns Hopkins University Press; Timothy E. Cook. 2005. *Governing with the News: The News Media as a Political Institution.* 2nd ed. Chicago: University of Chicago Press.

17. This statement is attributed to Thomas Carlyle, in *The French Revolution* (1837), building upon the idea of three estates (church, nobility, and commoners) developed by Edmund Burke. Moreover, Jeremy Bentham argued that in a system of representative government, newspaper editors are as important as the prime minister. Jeremy Bentham. 1822/1990. *Securities Against Misrule and Other Constitutional Writings for Tripolis and Greece,* ed. Peter Schofield. Oxford: Clarendon.

18. Price. 2002. *Mapping Media Assistance.*

19. Buckley, Duer, Mendel, and Ó Siochrú. 2008. *Broadcasting, Voice, and Accountability.*

20. CIMA. 2008. *Empowering Independent Media,* 8.

21. The Philippine Center for Investigative Journalism was cofounded by Sheila Coronel.
22. Media Watch. Global. n.d. "Statement of Purpose." http://www.mwglobal.org.
23. Little systematic knowledge can be found regarding media watch groups. This issue warrants further investigation since it raises questions of the watch groups' own bias and accountability.
24. Asa Briggs and Peter Burke. 2002. *A Social History of the Media: From Gutenberg to the Internet.* Cambridge: Polity.
25. Benedict Anderson. 1991. *Imagined Communities.* London: Verso.
26. Shanthi Kalathil. 2008. *Towards a New Model. Media and Communication in Post-Conflict and Fragile States.* Washington, DC: International Bank for Reconstruction and Development/World Bank; Henriette von Kaltenborn-Stachau. 2008. *The Missing Link. Fostering Positive Citizen-State Relations in Post-Conflict Environments.* Washington, DC: International Bank for Reconstruction and Development/World Bank.
27. Pippa Norris and Dieter Zinnbauer. 2002. *Giving Voice to the Voiceless: Good Governance, Human Development, and Mass Communications.* Background paper for HDR 2002, Human Development Report Office, United Nations Development Programme.
28. World Public Opinion. 2008. *World Public Opinion Report 2008.* http://www.WorldPublicOpinion.org.
29. WiMax is important for development because it is a new 802.16 IEEE standard designed for point-to-point and point-to-multipoint wireless broadband access that is cheaper, smaller, simpler, and easier to use than any existing broadband option (such as DSL, cable, fiber, 3G wireless), and it also bypasses the existing wired infrastructure and legacy service providers (that is, the telephone and cable companies).
30. Jeffrey James. 2008. "Digital Divide Complacency: Misconceptions and Dangers." *The Information Society* 24 (1): 54–61.
31. UNESCO. 2008. Media Literacy. Web page. http://portal.unesco.org/ci/en/ev.php-URL_ID=27056&URL_DO=DO_TOPIC&URL_SECTION=201.html.
32. Monroe Price and Peter Krug. 2006. "The Enabling Environment for Free and Independent Media." In *Media Matters: Perspectives on Advancing Governance and Development from the Global Forum for Media Development,* ed. Mark Harvey. Paris: Internews Europe.

# Bibliography and Index

# Bibliography

Ackerman, John M., and Irma E. Sandoval-Ballesteros. 2006. "The Global Explosion of Freedom of Information Laws." *Administrative Law Review* 58 (1): 85–130.

Albrow, Martin, Helmut Anheier, Marlies Glasius, Monroe Price, and Mary Kaldor. 2008. *2007/8 Yearbook of Global Civil Society: Communicative Power and Democracy.* London: Sage.

Amelina, Anna. 2007. "Evolution of the Media and Media Control in Post-Soviet Russia." *Soziale Welt-Zeitschrift für Sozialwissenschaftliche Forschung und Praxis* 58 (2): 163+.

Anable, D. 2006. "The Role of Georgia's Media—and Western Aid— in the Rose Revolution." *Harvard International Journal of Press/Politics* 11 (3): 7–43.

Asante, Clement E. 1996. *The Press in Ghana: Problems and Prospects.* Langham: University Press of America.

———. 1997. *Press Freedom and Development: A Research Guide and Selected Bibliography.* Westport, CT: Greenwood Press.

Ayish, M. I. 2002. "Political Communication on Arab World Television: Evolving Patterns." *Political Communication* 19 (2): 137–54.

Banisar, David. 2006. *Freedom of Information Around the World 2006: A Global Survey of Access to Government Records Laws.* http://www.freedominfo.org.

Bardhan, P. 1997. "Corruption and Development: A Review of Issues." *Journal of Economic Literature* 35 (3): 1320–46.

Bardoel, J. 1996. "Beyond Journalism: A Profession between Information Society and Civil Society." *European Journal of Communication* 11 (3): 283–302.

Baum, Matthew A. 2006, *"Getting the Message: Information Transparency and the Domestic Politics of Militarized Disputes."* Paper presented at the APSA American Political Science Association annual meeting, Philadelphia.

———. 2003. *Soft News Goes to War: Public Opinion and American Foreign Policy in the New Media Age.* Princeton, NJ: University of Princeton Press.

Beck, Rose Marie, and Frank Wittmann, eds. 2004. *African Media Cultures: Transdisciplinary Perspectives.* Köln: Rüdiger Köppe Verlag.

Becker, J. 2004. "Lessons from Russia: A Neo-Authoritarian Media System." *European Journal of Communication* 19 (2): 139–63.

Becker, Lee B., Tudor Vlad, and N. Nusser. 2007. "An Evaluation of Press Freedom Indicators." *International Communication Gazette* 69 (1): 5–28.

Benson, Rodney. 2004. "Bringing the Sociology of Media Back In." *Political Communication* 21 (3): 275–92.

Besley, Timothy, and R. Burgess. 2002. "The Political Economy Of Government Responsiveness: Theory and Evidence from India." *Quarterly Journal of Economics* 117 (4): 1415–51.

Besley, Timothy, and Andrea Prat. 2006. "Handcuffs for the Grabbing Hand? Media Capture and Government Accountability." *American Economic Review* 96 (3): 720–36.

Brunetti, A., and B. Weder. 2003. "A Free Press Is Bad News for Corruption." *Journal of Public Economics* 87 (7–8): 1801–24.

Chowdhury, S. K. 2004. "The Effect of Democracy and Press Freedom on Corruption: An Empirical Test." *Economics Letters* 85 (1): 93–101.

Chu, L. L. 1994. "Continuity and Change in China's Media Reform." *Journal of Communication* 44 (3): 4–21.

Corneo, Giacomo. 2005. "Media Capture in a Democracy: The Role of Wealth Concentration." *European Journal of Political Economy* 21 (3): 37–58.

Cullen, Richard, and Hua Ling Fu. 1998. "Seeking Theory from Experience: Media Regulation in China." *Democratization* 5: 155–78.

Dahl, Robert. 1989. *Democracy and Its Critics.* New Haven, CT: Yale University Press.

de Smaele, H. 2004. "Limited Access To Information As a Means of Censorship in Post-Communist Russia." *Javnost - The Public* 11 (2): 65–81.

Djankov, Simeon, Caralee McLiesh, Tatiana Nenova, and Andrei Shleifer. 2003. "Who Owns the Media?" *Journal of Law and Economics* 46 (2): 341–82.

Donsbach, Wolfgang. 1995. "Lapdogs, Watchdogs and Junkyard Dogs." *Media Studies Journal* 9 (4): 17–30.

Dyczok, M. 2006. "Was Kuchma's Censorship Effective? Mass Media in Ukraine before 2004." *Europe–Asia Studies* 58 (2): 215–38.

Esser, Frank, and Barbara Pfetsch, eds. 2004. *Comparing Political Communication: Theories, Cases, and Challenges.* Cambridge: Cambridge University Press.

Fell, D. 2005. "Political and Media Liberalization and Political Corruption in Taiwan." *China Quarterly* (184): 875–93.

Gunther, A. C., Y. H. Hong, and L. Rodriquez. 1994. "Balancing Trust in Media and Trust in Government during Political Change in Taiwan." *Journalism Quarterly* 71 (3): 628–36.

Gunther, Richard, and Anthony Mughan, eds. 2000. *Democracy and the Media: A Comparative Perspective.* New York: Cambridge University Press.

Haarhuis, C. K., and R. Torenvlied. 2006. "Dimensions and Alignments in the African Anti-Corruption Debate." *Acta Politica* 41 (1): 41–67.

Hallin, Daniel C., and Paolo Mancini. 2004. *Comparing Media Systems: Three Models of Media and Politics.* Cambridge: Cambridge University Press.

Helms, L. 2006. "The Changing Parameters of Political Control in Western Europe." *Parliamentary Affairs* 59 (1): 78–97.

Herman, Edward S., and Noam Chomsky. 1988. *Manufacturing Consent: The Political Economy of the Mass Media.* New York: Pantheon Books.

Hollifield, C. Ann, Lee B. Becker, and Tudor Vlad. 2006. "The Effects of Political, Economic and Organizational Factors on the Performance of Broadcast Media in Developing Countries." Paper presented to the Political Communication Research Section of the International Association for Media and Communication Research, Cairo, Egypt, July 2006.

Holtz-Bacha, Christina. 2007. "Freedom of the Press: Is a Worldwide Comparison Possible?" Paper prepared for the conference "Measuring Press Freedom," Annenberg School of Communication, University of Pennsylvania.

Hyden, Goran , Michael Leslie, and Folu F. Ogundimu, eds. 2002. *Media and Democracy in Africa*. Uppsala, Sweden: Nordiska Afrikainstitutet.

Islam, Roumeen, ed. 2002. *The Right to Tell: The Role of Mass Media in Economic Development*. Washington, DC: World Bank.

———. 2003. *Do More Transparent Governments Govern Better?* Washington, DC: World Bank.

Jakubowicz, K. 2001. "Rude Awakening—Social and Media Change in Central and Eastern Europe." *Javnost - The Public* 8 (4): 59–80.

James, Barry, ed. 2006. *Media Development and Poverty Eradication*. Paris: UN Educational, Scientific, and Cultural Organization (UNESCO).

Janowitz, M. 1975. "Professional Models in Journalism: Gatekeeper and Advocate." *Journalism Quarterly* 52 (4): 618+.

Kalathil, Shanthi, and Taylor C. Boas. 2001. *The Internet and State Control in Authoritarian Regimes: China, Cuba and the Counterrevolution*. Global Policy Program No. 21. Washington DC: Carnegie Endowment for International Peace.

Kelly, Mary, Gianpietro Mazzoleni, and Denis McQuail, eds. 2004. *The Media in Europe*. London: Sage.

Lawson, Chappel. 2002. *Building the Fourth Estate: Democratisation and the Rise of a Free Press in Mexico*. Berkeley: University of California Press.

Maor, M. 2004. "Feeling the Heat? Anticorruption Mechanisms in Comparative Perspective." *Governance* 17 (1): 1–28.

McQuail, Denis. 1992. *Media Performance*. London: Sage.

Mickiewicz, Ellen. 1999. *Changing Channels: Television and the Struggle for Power in Russia*. Durham, NC: Duke University Press.

Mollison, T. A. 1998. "Television Broadcasting Leads Romania's March toward an Open, Democratic Society." *Journal of Broadcasting & Electronic Media* 42 (1): 128–41.

Mullainathan, Sendhil, and Andrei Shleifer. 2005. "The Market for News." *American Economic Review* 95 (4): 1031–53.

Ni, Y. Y. 1995. "State Media Relations under Authoritarian Regimes in South-Korea and Taiwan." *Issues & Studies* 31 (10): 99–118.

Norris, Pippa. 2000. *A Virtuous Circle: Political Communications in Post-Industrial Democracies*. New York: Cambridge University Press.

———. 2001. *Digital Divide: Civic Engagement, Information Poverty and the Internet Worldwide*. New York: Cambridge University Press.

———. 2004. "Global Political Communication." In *Comparing Political Communication: Theories, Cases and Challenges,* ed. Frank Esser and Barbara Pfetsch, 115–50. Cambridge, UK: Cambridge University Press (also published in German as "Globale Politische Kommunikation: Freie Medien, Gutes Regieren und Wohlstandsentwicklung." In *Politische Kommunikation im Internationalen Vergleich*. Hrsg. Frank Esser and Barbara Pfetsch. Germany: Westdeutscher Verlag.

Norris, Pippa, and Ronald Inglehart. 2008. "Silencing Dissent." Paper available from the author: http://www.pippanorris.com.

Norris, Pippa, and Dieter Zinnbauer. 2002. "Giving Voice to the Voiceless: Good Governance, Human Development and Mass Communications." Human Development Report Office Occasional Paper 2002/11, UNDP, New York.

Ognianova, E., and B. Scott. 1997. "Milton's Paradox: The Market-Place of Ideas in Post-Communist Bulgaria." *European Journal of Communication* 12 (3): 369–90.

Pan, Z. D., and J. M. Chan. 2003. "Shifting Journalistic Paradigms: How China's Journalists Assess 'Media Exemplars.'" *Communication Research* 30 (6): 649–82.

Pasti, S. 2005. "Two Generations of Contemporary Russian Journalists." *European Journal of Communication* 20 (1): 89–115.

Peters, Bettina. 2003. "The Media's Role: Covering or Covering Up Corruption?" In *The Global Corruption Report*. Transparency International. http://www.transparency.org/publications/gcr/download_gcr/download_gcr_2003.

Price, Monroe, Beata Rozumilowicz, and Stefaan G. Verhulst, eds. 2001. *Media Reform: Democratizing Media, Democratizing the State*. London: Routledge.

Puddephatt, Andrew. 2007. *Defining Indicators of Media Development: Background Paper*. Paris: UNESCO.

Roberts, Alasdair. 2006. *Blacked Out: Government Secrecy in the Information Age*. New York: Cambridge University Press.

Rozanova, J. 2006. "Behind the Screen: The Role of State-TV Relationships in Russia, 1990–2000." *Canadian Review of Sociology And Anthropology* 43 (2): 185–203.

Sani, M. A. M. 2005. "Media Freedom in Malaysia." *Journal of Contemporary Asia* 35 (3): 341–67.

Schmitt-Beck, Rudig, and Katrin Voltmer. 2007. "The Mass Media in Third-Wave Democracies: Gravediggers or Seedsmen of Democratic Consolidation?" In *Democracy, Intermediation, and Voting in Four Continents*, ed. Richard Gunther, Jose Ramon Montero, and Hans-Jürgen Puhle, 75–134. Oxford, UK: Oxford University Press.

Semetko, Holli A., J. B. Brzinski, David Weaver, and L. Willnat. 1992. "TV-News and United States Public-Opinion about Foreign Countries: The Impact of Exposure and Attention." *International Journal of Public Opinion Research* 4 (1): 18–36.

Servaes, Jan. 2008. *Communication for Development and Social Change*. 2nd ed. London: Sage.

Shah, H. 1996. "Modernization, Marginalization and Emancipation: Towards a Normative Model of Journalism and National Development." *Communication Theory* 6 (2).

Skolkay, A. 1998. "Professionalization of Post-Communist Journalists." *Sociologia* 30 (3): 311–36.

Sparks, Colin, and A. Reading. 1994. "Understanding Media Change in East-Central Europe." *Media Culture & Society* 16 (2): 243–70.

Strömberg, D. 2001. "Mass Media and Public Policy." *European Economic Review* 45 (4–6): 652–63.

Swain, K. A. 2003. "Proximity and Power Factors in Western Coverage of the Sub-Saharan AIDS Crisis." *Journalism & Mass Communication Quarterly* 80 (1): 145–65.

Taylor, Matthew. 2000. "Media Relations in Bosnia: A Role for Public Relations in Building Civil Society." Public Relations Review 26 (1): 1–14.

Tettey, Wisdom. 2001. "The Media and Democratization in Africa: Contributions, Constraints and Concerns of the Private Press." *Media, Culture and Society* 23 (1): 5–31.

———. 2002. *The Media, Accountability and Civic Engagement in Africa. Human Development Report Office Occasional Paper*. New York: UNDP.

———. 2006. "The Politics of Media Accountability in Africa: An Examination of Mechanisms and Institutions." *International Communication Gazette* 68 (3) 229–48.

Vaidya, Samarth. 2005. "Corruption in the Media's Gaze." *European Journal of Political Economy* 21 (3): 667–87.

Van Belle, Douglas. 2000. *Press Freedom and Global Politics*. Westport, CT: Praeger.

Van Belle, Douglas, A. Cooper Drury, and Richard Stuart Olson. 2005. "The Politics of Humanitarian Aid: U.S. Foreign Disaster Assistance, 1964–1995." *Journal of Politics* 67 (2): 454–73.

Van Belle, Douglas, Jean-Sébastien Rioux, and David M. Potter. 2004. *Media, Bureaucracies, and Foreign Aid: A Comparative Analysis of the United States, the United Kingdom, Canada, France and Japan.* New York: Palgrave/St. Martin.

Voltmer, Katrin. 2000. "Constructing Political Reality in Russia—Izvestiya—Between Old and New Journalistic Practices." *European Journal of Communication* 15 (4): 469–500.

Voltmer, Katrin, ed. 2006. *Mass Media and Political Communication in New Democracies.* London: Routledge.

Waisbord, Silvio. 1994. "Knocking on Newsroom Doors: Press and Political Scandals in Argentina." *Political Communication* 11 (1), 19–34.

Waisbord, Silvio. 2000. *Watchdog Journalism in South America: News, Accountability, and Democracy.* New York: Columbia University Press.

Waisbord, Silvio, ed. 2001. *Media and Globalization: Why the State Matters.* New York: Rowan & Littlefield.

Waisbord, Silvio. 2004. "Scandals, Media, and Citizenship in Contemporary Argentina." *American Behavioral Scientist* 47 (8): 1072+.

Wanta, W., G. Golan, and C. Lee. 2004. "Agenda Setting and International News: Media Influence on Public Perceptions of Foreign Nations." *Journalism & Mass Communication Quarterly* 81 (2): 364–77.

Warnock, Kitty, Emrys Schoemaker, and Mark Wilson. 1997. *The Case for Communication in Sustainable Development.* London: Panos.

Wolfsfeld, Gadi. 2004. Media and Paths to Peace. Cambridge, UK: Cambridge University Press.

Woods, Joshua. 2007. "Democracy and the Press: A Comparative Analysis of Pluralism in the International Print Media." *Social Science Journal* 44 (2): 213–230.

# Index

# R

regime support
    limits on media, effect, 193–217
Russian Federation
    election campaigns, news media and,
        165–167, 180–182

# S

social accountability, 139–140
soft news, 275n48
state-run broadcasting
    shift to public service broadcasting, 5,
        398
states
    *see also particular nations; particular
        topics*
    case studies
        Arab states, 329–348
        Asian states, 353–372
        Central, Eastern Europe, 245–272
        Latin America, 305–325
        scope of, 25
        Sub-Saharan Africa, 277–301

constitutional, legal guarantees, 24
limits on media, effect, 193–217
natural disasters, humanitarian crises,
    coverage of, effect, 61–79
role of, reforming, 397–399
role of the state, 5
Sub-Saharan Africa
    case studies, 277–301

# T

third wave democratization, 3, 129,
    137–138, 151
Turkey
    election campaigns, news media and,
        165–167, 183–187

# V

Venezuela, República Bolivariana de, 3,
    311–313, 313*t*.12.2, 315
voting, 155n4, 157n30